THE ROUGH GUIDE TO

The Philippines

This fourth edition updated by

Kiki Deere, Simon Foster and Stephen Keeling

ROUGH
GUIDES

roughguides.com

Contents

Introduction to
The Philippines

Separated from its Southeast Asian neighbours by the South China Sea, the Philippines has always been a little different. As the only Asian nation colonized by the Spanish, this lush archipelago of dazzling beaches, year-round sun and warm, turquoise waters remains predominantly Roman Catholic, and culturally – a blend of Islamic, Malay, Spanish and American influences – it often feels light years away from the mainland, with a string of elegant colonial towns that have more in common with Latin America than the rest of Asia. It's an enticing mix: all over the archipelago you'll discover tantalizing food, friendly people and exuberant festivals. And the variety is astonishing: you can surf, island-hop or dive pristine coral reefs in the morning, and in the same day visit mystical tribal villages, ancient rice terraces and jungle-smothered peaks.

Indeed, the Philippines is often underrated and misunderstood by travellers and its Asian neighbours, casually dismissed as a supplier of maids, tribute bands, mail-order brides and corrupt politicians, epitomized by the gaudy excesses of Imelda Marcos. Don't be put off: while poverty and corruption remain serious problems, the Philippines is far more complex – and culturally rich – than the stereotypes suggest.

The **Filipino people** are variously descended from early Malay settlers, Muslim Sufis from the Middle East, Spanish conquistadors and friars, and later Chinese traders. It's an old cliché, but largely true: Filipinos take pride in making visitors welcome, even in the most rustic barangay home. Equally important is the culture of entertaining, evident in the hundreds of colourful **fiestas** that are held throughout the country, many tied to the Roman Catholic calendar. Never far behind partying is eating: Filipino **food** is heavily influenced by Spanish and native traditions – expect plenty of fresh fish, roasted meats (pork and chicken) and, unlike in the rest of Asia, a plethora of addictive desserts, many utilizing the vast array of tropical fruits on offer.

ABOVE MOUNT MAYON

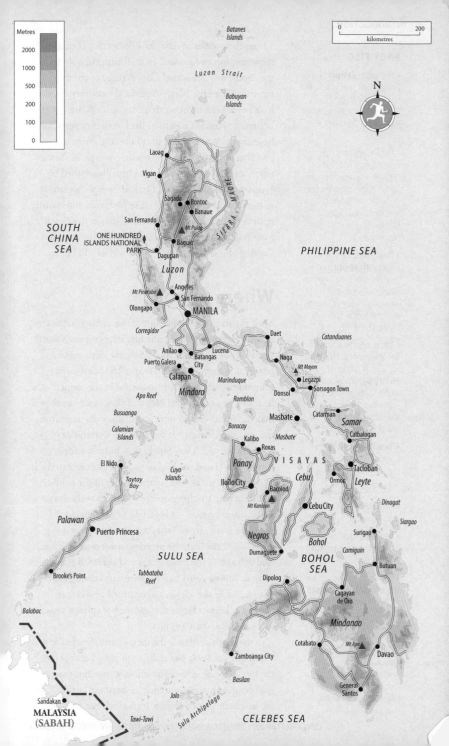

Even the **politics** in Asia's first democracy is rich in showmanship and pizzazz. From Ferdinand Marcos to the "housewife President" Cory Aquino to current paparazzi favourite Ninoy Aquino, the country's leaders have never been short on charisma. But despite impressive economic gains in the last twenty years, all have conspicuously failed to rid the country of its grinding **poverty**, visible everywhere you go in shanty towns and rickety barangay, and brutally exposed by **Typhoon Yolanda** in 2013. Ordinary people somehow remain stoical in the face of these problems, infectiously optimistic and upbeat. This determination to enjoy life is a national characteristic, encapsulated in the common Tagalog phrase *bahala na* – "what will be will be".

Where to go

Most flights to the Philippines arrive in **Manila**, the crazy, chaotic capital which, despite first impressions, is worth at least a day or two of your time. The city's major historical attraction is the old Spanish walled city of **Intramuros**, while the best museums in the country can be found in nearby **Rizal Park** and skyscraper-smothered **Makati**. There are also some worthwhile day-trips from the city; top of the list is the island of **Corregidor** in Manila Bay, which was fought over bitterly during World War II and, with its now-silent guns and ruins, is a poignant place to soak up the history of the conflict.

Within easy striking distance of Manila – about two hours south by road – a highlight of the province of Batangas is the city of **Tagaytay** with its mesmerizing views over **Lake Taal**, the picture-perfect crater lake with **Taal Volcano** in the middle. Around the small coastal town of **Anilao** you'll find the best scuba diving near Manila, while the adjacent agricultural province of **Laguna** is known for its therapeutic hot springs and luscious *buko* (coconut) pies.

To the north of Manila the theme parks, beaches and wreck dives of **Subic Bay** make a tempting break before the long bus ride to the extraordinary attractions and spell-binding mountain scenery of **northern Luzon**. From the mountain city of **Baguio**, it's a rough but memorable

JEEPNEYS

Millions of Filipinos depend on **jeepneys** – a kind of informal minibus service – to get to school and the office, or to transport livestock to market. Jeepneys are able to operate where roads are too narrow for regular buses, and as a result most travellers end up using them at least once. Despite the discomfort, for many it's one of the highlights of their trip – a genuine slice of Filipino life.

The original jeepneys, cannibalized from vehicles left behind by departing Americans at the end of World War II, have evolved over the past six decades into the mass-produced versions that you see on the streets today, decorated with chrome trinkets, blinking fairy lights and images of celebrities. Others sport religious mottos, crucifixes and images of saints, perhaps understandable given the high accident rates they rack up.

trip north along winding roads to tribal communities such as **Sagada**, known for its hanging coffins, and **Banaue**, where you can trek through awe-inspiring rice-terrace countryside. Off Luzon's northern tip are the alluring islands of **Batanes**, one of the country's greatest secrets, while along Luzon's west coast you can surf around **San Fernando** or explore the ravishing colonial town of **Vigan**, a UNESCO World Heritage site.

Head south from Manila through the **Bicol** region and you'll reach perhaps the best-known of Philippine volcanoes, **Mayon**, an almost perfect cone that towers over the city of Legazpi and is a strenuous four- or five-day climb. Around **Donsol** you can swim with whale sharks, and in **Bulusan Volcano National Park** trek through lush rainforest to waterfalls, hot springs and volcanic craters. Even further off the tourist trail, **Catanduanes** offers excellent surfing while **Marinduque** is a pastoral island backwater that only gets touristy for the annual **Moriones festival**, held at Easter.

For most visitors, the myriad islands and islets of the **Visayas**, right at the heart of the archipelago, are top of the agenda – despite large parts of the region being devastated by **Typhoon Yolanda** (Haiyan) in 2013. The captivating little island of **Boracay**, with its pristine beach, is on almost everyone's itinerary. If Boracay's a little too touristy for you, try **Panglao Island** off Bohol, the tantalizing beaches and waters of **Malapascua** off the northern tip of Cebu Island or tiny **Apo Island** near Negros, a marine reserve where the only accommodation is in rustic cottages. For trekking and climbing make for **Mount Kanlaon National Park** on Negros, one of the country's finest wilderness areas. The largest city in the Visayas is **Cebu City**, the arrival point for a limited number of international flights – as well as a major hub for domestic airlines – making it a good alternative base to Manila. It's friendly, affordable and has a buzzing nightlife scene, with great restaurants and live music.

If you're looking for some serious diving, head for **Puerto Galera** on the northern coast of **Mindoro Island**. It also boasts some excellent beaches and trekking through the jungles of the interior to tribal communities. There's more world-class diving off the west coast of Mindoro at **Apo Reef**, although it can be pricey to get here.

To the west of the archipelago, out in the northern Sulu Sea, is the bewitching province of **Palawan**, most of it still wild and unspoiled. Many visitors come for the superb scuba diving, especially on the sunken World War II wrecks around **Coron Town** in the **Calamian Islands** to the north of Palawan proper. Palawan itself is home to the seaside town of **El Nido** and the **Bacuit archipelago**, hundreds of gem-like limestone islands with sugar-white beaches and lagoons. From **Puerto Princesa**, Palawan's likeable capital, strike out for the laidback beach town of **Port Barton** or the **Underground River**, an entrancing cavern system only accessible by boat.

In the far south, the large island of **Mindanao** has long been the Muslim heartland of the Philippines, with enticing destinations ranging from the surf beaches and secret lagoons of **Siargao Island**, to the pristine waters of the **Enchanted River** and tribal homelands of the T'boli people around **Lake Sebu** in the south. Off the island's northern coast, one of the area's major attractions is the wonderfully friendly and scenic island of **Camiguin**. Mindanao's biggest city is durian-capital **Davao**, from where you can head inland to **Mount Apo**, the tallest mountain in the archipelago and a tough ascent even for experienced climbers. Note that much of western Mindanao, including the **Sulu archipelago**, is dangerous to visit because of continuing Muslim separatist unrest.

DIVE PARADISE

The Philippines is blessed by a dazzling richness and diversity of marine life and **diving** is one of the most popular activities in the archipelago. Under the waves lies an underwater wonderland of stupefying **coral gardens** teeming with brilliantly coloured reef fish, turtles, giant clams and starfish, while at depth there are giant rays and prowling sharks. Indeed, this vast tropical archipelago is at the heart of Southeast Asia's "coral triangle", the most biologically diverse marine ecosystem on earth, with over three hundred types of coral and 350 fish species. Diving here is affordable and, thanks to warm waters, can be enjoyed year-round. If you're serious about your diving, booking a trip on a **liveaboard** (see p.39) can be a memorable experience, giving you the opportunity to get away from the more popular dive resorts and explore the wilderness.

When to go

The Philippines has a hot and humid tropical climate with a **wet season** (southwest monsoon, or *habagat*) from May to October and a **dry season** (northeast monsoon, or *amihan*) from November to April. The **best time to visit** is during the dry season, although even during the wet season it doesn't always rain torrentially and days can be hot and sunny, with short, intense downpours at dusk. January and February are the coolest months and good for travelling, while March, April and May are very hot: expect sunshine all day and temperatures to peak at a broiling 36°C. As well as higher humidity, the wet season also brings **typhoons** (see box, p.48), with flights sometimes cancelled and roads impassable. The first typhoon can hit as early as May, although typically it is June or July before the rains really start, with July to September the wettest (and stormiest) months. The southern Visayas and Palawan are less prone to this danger, and Mindanao sees less rain during the wet season and no typhoons.

AVERAGE TEMPERATURES AND RAINFALL

	Jan	Feb	Mar	Apr	May	Jun	Jul	Aug	Sep	Oct	Nov	Dec
MANILA												
°C	25	27	28.5	31.5	31	29	28.5	28	28	28.5	28	27
°F	77	81	83	89	88	84	83	82	82	83	82	81
Rainfall (mm)	0.74	0.46	0.58	1.1	4.2	8.5	13.9	13.6	11.8	6.2	4.8	2.1
BAGUIO (NORTHERN LUZON)												
°C	17	19	20.5	23.5	23	21	20.5	19.5	20	20.5	20	18.5
°F	63	66	69	74	73	70	69	67	68	69	68	65
Rainfall (mm)	0.74	1.2	1.1	1.4	4.8	10.2	14.8	14.2	12.6	8.4	6.6	3.2
SIARGAO (MINDANAO)												
°C	25.5	26	26	27	27	27	27	27	27	27	26	26.5
°F	78	79	79	81	81	81	81	81	81	81	79	80
Rainfall (mm)	17.5	13.4	16.3	8.4	5	4.2	5.7	4.1	5.6	8.8	14.2	20

Author picks

Scaling the forest-smothered heights of its awe-inspiring volcanoes, enduring sweltering jungle heat and traversing some of Asia's most isolated roads, our hard-travelling authors have visited every corner of this vast, magnificent archipelago – from the rice terraces of Luzon to the beaches of Mindanao. Here are their personal favourites:

Best beach hideaway You don't have to travel for days by bangka to find a slice of serenity in the Philippines; *Tuko Beach Resort* in Abra de Ilog, Mindoro (p.259) is just a few hours from Batangas but seems a million miles from anywhere, with dolphins off the beach and monkeys lounging in the trees.

Eat like a Filipino The best fried chicken in the Philippines? For purists, it's still knocked out by *Aristocrat* in Manila (p.89). The *halo-halo* here is amazing also, but *Aling Taleng's* (p.111) in Pagsanjan is sublime. For *buko* pie it's a close call, but *Lety's* (p.110) is hard to beat.

Go wild Tackle the pristine jungle wilderness of Mindoro with an epic climb up Mount Halcon (p.252), or conquer Mount Apo (p.430) in Mindanao; trekking through the UNESCO World Heritage rice terraces in northern Luzon remains an enchanting experience (p.179), while seeing (or even snorkelling with) whale sharks, the world's largest fish, in Donsol (p.224) is truly magical.

Best stash of gold One of many reasons to resist the desire to flee Manila as soon as possible, the Ayala Museum (p.76) is an intriguing introduction to the history and lavish pre-Hispanic culture of the Philippines.

Go paddling Soak up the beauty of southern Luzon by taking a boat through the crystal-clear waters and exploring the awe-inspiring limestone cliffs of the Caramoan Peninsula (p.214).

> Our author recommendations don't end here. We've flagged up our favourite places – a perfectly sited hotel, an atmospheric café, a special restaurant – throughout the guide, highlighted with the ★ symbol.

FROM TOP LETY'S BUKO PIE, LOS BAÑOS; RICE TERRACES, BATAD; GOLD REGALIA, AYALA MUSEUM, MANILA

18

things not to miss

It's not possible to see everything the Philippines has to offer in one trip – and we don't suggest you try. What follows is a selective taste of the country's highlights: idyllic beaches, spectacular hikes, historic sites and fascinating wildlife. All entries have a page reference to take you straight into the Guide, where you can find out more. Coloured numbers refer to chapters in the Guide section.

1

13

1 BORACAY
Page 338
Enchanting White Beach on picture-postcard Boracay Island is one of the country's major tourist draws.

2 SURFING AT SIARGAO
Page 418
Avid surfers will find several locations where they can catch some decent waves, but Siargao, off the tip of Mindanao is one of the best.

3 APO REEF MARINE NATURAL PARK
Page 258
The gin-clear waters of Apo Reef, off the west coast of Mindoro, are a scuba diver's dream.

4 CHOCOLATE HILLS
Page 298
Soak up the bizarre landscape of Bohol's iconic Chocolate Hills, conical brown-green mounds said to be the calcified tears of a broken-hearted giant.

5 VIGAN
Page 142

Wonderfully preserved slice of colonial Spain, with cobblestone streets and gorgeous Baroque architecture.

6 WHALE SHARKS
Page 224

Getting up close to these gentle giants off the coast of Donsol, in southern Luzon, is an unforgettable experience.

7 MOUNT MAYON
Page 219

The almost perfectly symmetrical cone of volcanic Mount Mayon makes for a challenging but thrilling climb.

8 ATI-ATIHAN FESTIVAL
Page 336

At this lively annual festival in Kalibo, on Panay Island, everyone wears indigenous dress and learns tribal dances.

9 BATANES
Page 185

Blissfully remote islands off the northern coast of Luzon, home to rolling hills and wild stretches of coast.

10 MALAPASCUA
Page 285

Gorgeous and isolated island hideaway that survived the ravages of Yolanda, with bone-white Bounty Beach and superb diving.

11 CORON ISLAND BY BANGKA
Page 394

Tour the jagged, gasp-inducing coast of Coron Island by bangka, taking in hidden coves, secret beaches and two pristine mountain lakes fed by springs.

10

11

12 MOUNT PINATUBO
Page 123

The lower slopes of Mount Pinatubo feature canyons formed after the massive 1991 eruption, while the crater is filled by sulphuric mountain lake.

13 UNDERGROUND RIVER
Page 380

One of the longest subterranean rivers in the world, with eerie stalactites, vast caverns and hidden chambers.

14 RICE TERRACES
Page 179

The mind-boggling rice terraces around Banaue stand as one of Asia's greatest sights, and offer superb trekking.

15 TARSIERS
Page 298

Admire these tiny primates with the enormous, sorrowful eyes at their protected sanctuary in Bohol.

16 SAN AGUSTIN CHURCH
Page 62

This elegantly weathered Spanish pile in the heart of old Manila is the archipelago's oldest stone church and the resting place of Miguel López de Legazpi.

17 HALO-HALO
Page 31

Nothing beats a tall glass of this icy Filipino treat on a hot day, a concoction of syrups, beans, fruits and ice cream.

18 EL NIDO
Page 385

The strikingly beautiful limestone islands around El Nido in Palawan offer exceptional exploring and adventure.

12

13

14

Itineraries

The following itineraries span the entire length of this incredibly diverse archipelago, from the historic cities of Luzon to the idyllic islands of the Visayas and the remote jungles of Mindanao. Given the time involved moving from place to place, you may not be able to cover everything, but even picking a few highlights will give you a deeper insight into the natural and cultural wonders of the Philippines.

THE GRAND TOUR

This three- to four-week tour gives a taster of the Philippines' iconic landscapes and islands from the nation's chaotic capital to the pristine sands of Boracay.

❶ Manila The nation's initially chaotic capital is a vast, boiling blend of history, high culture and wild nightlife. **See p.56**

❷ Banaue rice terraces It's worth taking the journey north to see one of the world's great man-made wonders. **See p.179**

❸ Sagada Extend your stay in northern Luzon with a trip to this rambling old town, home of the famed hanging coffins. **See p.172**

❹ Puerto Princesa Backtrack to Manila for the flight to Palawan's sleepy capital and the trip along the Underground River. **See p.370**

❺ El Nido Continue along the Palawan coast to the spectacular limestone scenery of the Bacuit archipelago. **See p.385**

❻ Coron Take the bangka across to Coron, where wreck-diving and dazzling coves await. **See p.394**

❼ Cebu City Fly to the nation's third city, home of Magellan's Cross and a host of historic attractions. **See p.267**

❽ Bohol Take the ferry to this historic island, home of the Chocolate Hills and the loveable tarsier. **See p.292**

❾ Boracay Backtrack to Cebu for the short flight to this famed resort island, where you can end your tour on a sugary white sand beach. **See p.337**

ISLAND-HOPPING: THE VISAYAS LOOP

The physical and historic heart of the nation, the Visayas is perhaps the most alluring region of the Philippines, a sun-bleached concentration of islands littered with beaches, crumbling churches, sugar plantations and untouched reefs. This itinerary needs a minimum of two weeks.

❶ Puerto Galera Begin your tour by taking the short bus-and-ferry trip to this congenial beach and dive resort on the tip of Mindoro. **See p.241**

❷ Romblon Ferries link Mindoro to the more remote Romblon archipelago, three main islands offering untouched beaches and intriguing reef dives. **See p.347**

❸ Boracay It's a short boat ride south to the jewel of Philippine beach resorts, justly renowned for its mesmerizing white sands. **See p.337**

ABOVE LANZONES FESTIVAL, CAMIGUIN ISLAND; ISLAND-HOPPING IN THE BACUIT ARCHIPELAGO; BASILICA DE SANTO NIÑO, CEBU CITY

④ Guimaras Bus across to the south side of Panay, where it's another short boat ride to this island of mangoes, mountain bikes and handsome Spanish chapels. **See p.324**

⑤ Siquijor Traverse Negros and take the ferry to the island of witches, rich in legend, culture and rugged beauty. **See p.301**

⑥ Bohol Cut across the Bohol Sea to absorb the charms of Panglao Island, the Chocolate Hills and those adorable tarsiers. **See p.292**

⑦ Biliran Ferry and bus your way north across Leyte to this little visited gem, home to dizzying falls, coves and even rice terraces. See p.363

⑧ Sohoton Natural Bridge National Park Nip across to the island of Samar to experience this jungle-clad, limestone wilderness, before heading back to Cebu or Manila. **See p.356**

THE GREAT SOUTHERN LOOP

Few travellers make it as far as Mindanao, but there's plenty to see in the exotic deep south of the Philippines – skip Manila altogether and begin and end this tour in Cebu City. This itinerary really needs three weeks to do it justice, but could be obviously extended into a much longer trip.

① Dumaguete and Apo Island Head south to sleepy Dumaguete, where you can arrange dive trips to the stunning reefs off Apo Island. **See p.315 & p.320.**

② North coast, Mindanao Take the ferry to Dapitan and explore the north coast of Mindanao, from the dolphins of Misamis Occidental Aquamarine Park (MOAP) to the falls of Illigan. **See p.400**

③ Lake Lanao If safe, it's worth arranging a trip to the Muslim enclave of Marawi and this tranquil lake, ringed by traditional homes and mosques – make sure you check the current situation, however. **See p.433**

④ Cagayan de Oro This laidback city is a great place to eat, drink and arrange a whitewater rafting excursion **See p.403**

⑤ Camiguin Island Compact, easy to explore island off the Mindanao coast, with gorgeous beaches, hot springs and hikes. **See p.412**

⑥ Siargao Great surfing, empty beaches, cheap lodgings and cool people, a short ferry ride off the coast. **See p.418**

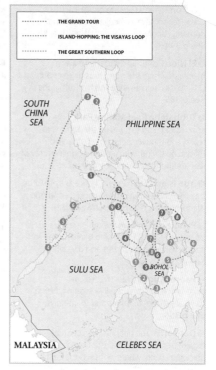

THE GRAND TOUR

ISLAND-HOPPING: THE VISAYAS LOOP

THE GREAT SOUTHERN LOOP

SOUTH CHINA SEA

PHILIPPINE SEA

SULU SEA

BOHOL SEA

MALAYSIA

CELEBES SEA

⑦ Padre Burgos Ferry across to Leyte and the up-and-coming scuba centre of the southern Philippines. **See p.366**

⑧ Camotes Islands Before returning to Cebu, stop off at this tranquil island chain, picture-perfect islets with excellent diving and snorkelling. **See p.287**

THE DIVE MASTER

Millions of visitors come to the Philippines primarily for what's below sea level – the waters surrounding the island chain harbour some of the world's richest marine life. The following tour would ideally take several weeks – and lots of advance planning – to complete.

① Puerto Galera This easy-to-reach resort makes a great introduction to the local dive scene, with plenty of resorts and operators to choose from. **See p.241**

② Apo Reef Take a day or two to explore this protected reef off the west coast of Mindoro, home to sharks, turtles and rays. **See p.258**

③ Coron Try and take the bangka across to Coron for some spectacular wreck diving, primarily Japanese ships from World War II. **See p.394**

④ El Nido Continue on to the Palawan mainland where the numerous dive schools at El Nido can help arrange trips to Tubbataha . **See p.385**

⑤ Tubbataha Reef Marine Park Time-consuming (and expensive) though it is to reach, this is nevertheless the pinnacle of Philippine diving, with a mind-boggling array of reef and pelagic marine life. **See p.376**

⑥ Apo Island From Puerto Princesa fly to Cebu City then head south to Dumaguete and Apo Island, another dive hot spot. **See p.320**

⑦ Panglao Island From Dumaguete it's a short boat ride to languid Panglao Island, home to congenial resorts, beaches and dive sights. **See p.294**

⑧ Padre Burgos Cross over to Leyte to experience this exciting dive location, home to whale sharks, dolphins and manta rays. **See p.366**

⑨ Donsol For the definitive whale shark experience you'll need to continue north across to Luzon, where Donsol is the best place to swim with these gentle giants. **See p.223**

THE BEST OF THE BEACH

The appeal of hiking volcanoes or trudging city streets can wilt (especially in the tropical heat), when compared to the dazzling white beaches on offer in the Philippines. This tour takes in the best of the nation's strips of sand. This itinerary needs a minimum two weeks, but given the focus on beaches, could be obviously extended into a much longer trip.

❶ Marinduque Take the short flight to this lesser visited island and seek out some of the sandy beaches off its eastern coast. **See p.199**

❷ Caramoan Peninsula Back on the Luzon mainland, this rugged promontory harbours blue-water coves and enticing resorts. **See p.214**

❸ Malapascua Island Fly from Legazpi to Cebu City, where it's a four-hour bus and boat ride to this tiny islet ringed by chalky white sands. **See p.285**

④ Siargao Island Double back to Cebu for the short flight to Siargao, best known for surfing but also rich in empty, wild, sandy beaches and offshore islands. **See p.418**

⑤ Camiguin Island From Siargao you can ferry across to Mindanao and take a bus towards Camiguin, another relatively untouched haven, with the gorgeous sands of White Island just offshore. **See p.412**

⑥ Panglao Island Ferry across to Bohol, where another diving hot spot also boasts several enticing stretches of sand. **See p.294**

⑦ Boracay If you love the beach, you can't visit the Philippines without a stop here – it's more developed than most places, but the sand is still spectacular. **See p.337**

THE TIME TRAVELLER

Evidence of the Philippines long and complex history is sprinkled all over the archipelago, but northern Luzon is the most evocative of its tribal and colonial past, with handsome old cities and enigmatic remains.

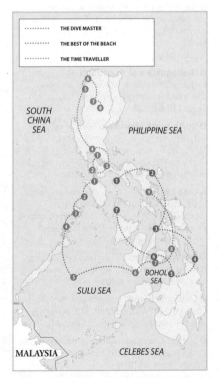

··········	THE DIVE MASTER
··········	THE BEST OF THE BEACH
··········	THE TIME TRAVELLER

SOUTH CHINA SEA

PHILIPPINE SEA

SULU SEA

BOHOL SEA

MALAYSIA

CELEBES SEA

OPPOSITE HANGING COFFINS, ECHO VALLEY, SAGADA

This itinerary could be completed in under a fortnight (ten days minimum), especially if you take some flights, but as with the others, you'll get a lot more out of it if you tackle it more slowly.

❶ Intramuros, Manila The oldest part of Manila drips with history, from Spanish churches and forts to illuminating museums. **See p.62**

❷ Taal Take a tour of this beautiful old town, home to the biggest church in Southeast Asia and *bahay na bato* architecture still redolent of colonial Spain. **See p.116**

❸ Paete The nation's woodcarving capital makes for an intriguing detour, sprinkled with the stores of local craftsmen. **See p.112**

❹ Malolos The oft-overlooked capital of Bulacan province is crammed with colonial remnants, from the elegant Barasoain Church to a smattering of preserved sixteenth-century Spanish homes. **See p.120**

❺ Vigan The best-preserved colonial town in the Philippines is a treasure-trove of tiny museums, chapels and crumbling villas. **See p.142**

❻ Laoag The capital of Ilocos Norte boasts plenty of historic attractions of its own, while the Malacañang of the North, former holiday residence of the Marcoses, is a short ride away. **See p.147**

❼ Sagada Head into the mountainous heart of Luzon, where Sagada is a focus for the Igorots (Cordillera tribes) and the enigmatic hanging coffins. **See p.172**

❽ Banaue and Batad You'd be remiss to travel up here and not spend time among the legendary rice terraces, fantastical ridges in the mountains often shrouded in mist. **See p.179 & p.182**

BANGKA

Basics

Getting there

There are several options for nonstop flights to the Philippines from North America and from Australia; from Europe, the only nonstop flights are from London with Philippine Airlines. Otherwise, reaching the Philippines from outside Asia usually involves a stopover in Hong Kong, Singapore or Dubai. Most major airlines in the region have regular connecting flights to Manila, with a few also flying direct to Cebu.

High season for Philippines travel is November to April, though airfares vary relatively little through the year. This is because the low season for the Philippines (May–Oct) is the peak season in Europe and the US, so flights heading out of these regions to various hub airports are often full.

If the Philippines is only one stop on a longer journey, you might want to consider buying a **Round-the-World** (RTW) ticket. In addition, some agents also offer **Circle Pacific tickets**, which cover Australia, New Zealand, the west coast of North America and destinations in the Pacific. You can include Manila and/or Cebu on some of the itineraries.

From the UK and Ireland

Philippine Airlines (PAL) currently operates nonstop flights between **London** and Manila three times a week, with the outward flight taking 14hr 30min, and the return 15hr 25min. The second fastest option is to route through Hong Kong, from where there are numerous onward flights daily to Manila and Cebu. **From Ireland**, the speediest option is to take a budget airline to London and change there. London–Manila nonstop costs around £800–900, and from around £550 with stops. From the Republic of Ireland, the best fares are around €600–700 via the UK and the Middle East.

From the US and Canada

Philippine Airlines operates nonstop flights to Manila from **Los Angeles**, **San Francisco** and **Vancouver** (and direct flights from Toronto with a stop in Vancouver), charging around US$1000–1500 for the round trip (around Can$2000 from Toronto). **Delta Airlines** flies direct **from Detroit** (an exhausting 18hr 35min via Narita, Japan) for around US$1900. However, you can save around twenty percent on these fares if you travel on another

airline such as **Korean Air** via Seoul. Note that in most cases, the longer you stay in the Philippines the cheaper your flight will be.

From Los Angeles or San Francisco, the flying time to Manila is around eleven hours. From the east coast of North America, flying via the Pacific, the journey will take around twenty hours excluding any layover (allow at least 2hr extra) along the way. If you choose to fly from New York via Paris, say, expect the journey to take around 24 hours altogether.

From Australia, New Zealand and South Africa

Philippine Airlines flies nonstop to Manila from **Melbourne** (8–9hr) three times a week, and from **Sydney** (8–9hr) four times a week; it also flies from **Brisbane** (9–10hr), via **Darwin** (4hr 30min). Return fares online can be as low as Aus$700. **Qantas** also flies Sydney to Manila nonstop four times a week, but fares are usually much higher (from Aus$1500 in high season). If you want to get to **Cebu City**, you can fly via Hong Kong or Kuala Lumpur, although it's probably easiest simply to change in Manila.

From **New Zealand** there are no nonstop flights to the Philippines, so you'll have to go via Australia or a Southeast Asian hub such as Singapore or Hong Kong. A typical fare is NZ$1500 Auckland–Manila via Hong Kong, the journey taking 15 to 20 hours.

From **South Africa** you'll always make at least one stop en route to Manila, and often two. Depending on the length of the stop, the trip will take from 16 to 26 hours. Cathay Pacific is the fastest, with fares from around ZAR9000 return in high season from Johannesburg via Hong Kong.

From elsewhere in Asia

You can fly direct to the Philippines from almost every major city in Asia, with several budget airlines offering cheap fares. Many of these fly to **Clark International Airport** (see p.122), 80km northwest of Manila, so make sure you factor in additional travel time if necessary. Numerous flights make the two-hour trip **from Hong Kong** to Manila, with rates as low as HK$1300 (US$170).

AirAsia Zest zips between Manila and Kota Kinabalu, Kuala Lumpur, Macau and Seoul. **Cebu Pacific** also offers cheap flights from Bangkok, Jakarta, Kota Kinabalu, Kuala Lumpur, Shanghai, Seoul and Taipei to Manila, and several routes direct to Cebu City.

A BETTER KIND OF TRAVEL

At Rough Guides we are passionately committed to travel. We believe it helps us understand the world we live in and the people we share it with – and of course tourism is vital to many developing economies. But the scale of modern tourism has also damaged some places irreparably, and climate change is accelerated by most forms of transport, especially flying. All Rough Guides' flights are carbon-offset, and every year we donate money to a variety of environmental charities.

The **Singapore–Manila** route (3hr 30min) is very competitive, served by Philippine Airlines, Singapore Airlines, Jetstar Asia Airways, Tigerair and Cebu Pacific from S$120 (US$90).

Handy **regional flights** include a Silk Air service (3 weekly; 3hr 50min) linking Singapore with **Davao** (Mindanao), a Malaysia Airlines flight between Kota Kinabalu (Sabah) and **Puerto Princesa** (3 weekly; 1hr 30min) and a China Airlines flight between Taipei (Taiwan) and **Laoag** (northern Luzon). **Kalibo International Airport**, serving Boracay (see p.327), has nonstop flights to Hong Kong, Seoul, Taipei and Singapore.

By boat

Many unlicensed boats ply back and forth between the Malaysian state of Sabah and the southern Philippines, but these are considered unsafe for tourists. At the time of writing the primary licensed (and safer) ferry route linked **Zamboanga City** with **Sandakan**, Sabah (nonstop). Aleson Shipping ferries (☎062 991 2687, Ⓦaleson-shipping.com) depart Zamboanga on Monday at 1.30pm and return on Tuesday (around P3100; 20–24hr), but always check the latest schedule in advance. Cheap bunk-bed accommodation is usually available on deck, as well as a limited number of cabins (from P3500).

There are no regular ferry services to northern **Sulawesi** (**Indonesia**) from the Philippines. Illegal, small boats often make the trip from General Santos; it's far safer and faster to fly via Manila and Jakarta.

AIRLINES

AirAsia Zest Ⓦ airasia.com
Cathay Pacific Ⓦ cathaypacific.com
Cebu Pacific Ⓦ cebupacificair.com
China Airlines Ⓦ china-airlines.com
Delta Airlines Ⓦ delta.com
Jetstar Asia Airways Ⓦ jetstar.com
Korean Air Ⓦ koreanair.com
Malaysia Airlines Ⓦ malaysiaairlines.com
Philippine Airlines Ⓦ philippineairlines.com
Qantas Ⓦ qantas.com.au
Silk Air Ⓦ silkair.com

Singapore Airlines Ⓦ singaporeair.com
Tigerair Ⓦ tigerair.com

AGENTS AND OPERATORS

Absolute Travel US ☎ 1800 736 8187, Ⓦ absoluteasia.com. Luxury tours to the Philippines that can be combined with other destinations in Southeast Asia. The fourteen-day Highlights of the Philippines tour includes Manila, Banaue, Sagada, Baguio, Bohol and Cebu City (US$5255, excluding international flights).

Allways Dive Expeditions Australia ☎ 1800 338 239 or ☎ 03 9885 8863, Ⓦ allwaysdive.com.au. All-inclusive dive packages to prime locations in the Philippines and Southeast Asia from Aus$720 for seven nights (not including flights). Destinations in the Philippines include Coron, Dumaguete, Malapascua, Moalboal, Donsol and Puerto Galera. Also liveaboards to Cebu, Dauin, Tubbataha and Apo reefs, Coron wrecks and Anilao (from Aus$2335).

Bamboo Trails Taiwan ☎ 886 7 7354945, Ⓦ bambootrails.com. Small travel company offering some unique group itineraries in the Philippines, including the "Sugar Trail" through Negros and Siquijor.

Dive Worldwide UK ☎ 0845 130 6980, Ⓦ diveworldwide.com. Specialist dive operator offering trips to a number of destinations in the Philippines, including Tubbataha Reef, Coron, Bohol, Dumaguete and Puerto Galera. A typical fourteen-day trip to Donsol to see the whale sharks including flights, domestic transfers and accommodation starts at £1955.

Grasshopper Adventures UK ☎ 020 8123 8144, US ☎ 818 921 7101; Ⓦ grasshopperadventures.com. Bicycle and guided tour specialists, with a variety of bike tours all over Asia and a seven-day guided tour of Bohol for US$1300.

North South Travel UK ☎ 01245 608291, Ⓦ northsouthtravel.co.uk. Friendly travel agency offering discounted fares worldwide. Profits are used to support projects in the developing world, especially the promotion of sustainable tourism.

Philippine Island Connections UK ☎ 020 7404 8877, Ⓦ www .pic-uk.com. Philippines specialist offering flights to the Philippines, plus hotel bookings, holiday packages and tours. They also offer domestic flight reservations, though it's often cheaper to book once you're in the Philippines.

STA Travel UK ☎ 0871 2300 040, US ☎ 1800 781 4040, Australia ☎ 13 47 82, New Zealand ☎ 0800 474 400, South Africa ☎ 0861 781 781; Ⓦ statravel.co.uk. Worldwide specialists in independent travel; also student IDs, travel insurance, car rental, rail passes and more. Good discounts for students and under-26s.

Trailfinders UK ☎ 0845 058 5858, Ireland ☎ 01 677 7888, Australia ☎ 1300 780 212; Ⓦ trailfinders.com. One of the best-informed and most efficient agents for independent travellers.

Getting around

The large number of budget airlines and ferry services between major destinations makes it easy to cover the Philippine archipelago, even on a tight budget, though the main drawback is that almost everything routes through Manila and Cebu. Long-distance road transport largely comprises buses and jeepneys – the utilitarian passenger vehicles modelled on World War II American jeeps. Throughout the provinces, and in some areas of cities, tricycles – motorbikes with steel sidecars – are commonly used for short journeys.

Airlines and major bus and ferry companies operate to timetables and have published fares, but for smaller **ferries** (typically bangkas or outriggers), **jeepneys** and **tricycles**, it's often a question of asking other passengers how much to pay in order to avoid being surcharged as a tourist.

Note that **holiday weekends** are bad times to travel, with buses full and roads jammed. Cities start to empty on Friday afternoon and the exodus continues into the night, with a mass return on Sunday evening and Monday morning – Metro Manila is especially gridlocked. Travelling is a particular hassle at Christmas, New Year and Easter with buses and ferries full (sometimes illegally overloaded), airports chaotic and resorts charging more than usual. Almost everyone seems to be on the move at these times of year, particularly heading out of big cities to the provinces, and the transport system can become strained. If you have to travel at these times, book tickets in advance or turn up at bus stations and ferry piers early and be prepared to wait.

By plane

Air travel is a godsend for island-hoppers in the Philippines, with a number of airlines linking Manila with most of the country's major destinations; you will usually, however, have to backtrack to a major hub when jumping from one region to another. **Philippine Airlines** (PAL; ⓦ philippineairlines.com) has a comprehensive domestic schedule (along with its budget carrier **PAL Express** ⓦ flypalexpress .com), while **Cebu Pacific** (ⓦ cebupacificair.com) offers even more routes and very cheap fares, particularly if you book some way in advance. There are several other smaller budget airlines – **AirAsia Zest** and **Philippines AirAsia** (both ⓦ airasia.com), **Tigerair Philippines** (ⓦ tigerair.com) and a newer venture, **Fil-Asian Airways** (ⓦ filasianair.com).

Cebu Pacific runs numerous flights out of its hub in **Cebu City**, saving you the effort of backtracking to Manila – you can, for instance, fly straight from Cebu City to Caticlan (for Boracay) and Siargao. **Davao** is a less developed third hub, with connections to Cebu City, Cagayan de Oro, Iloilo and Zamboanga, but even here you'll have to transfer in Manila and Cebu for other destinations.

Airfares

There's not a great deal of variation in **domestic airfares** offered by the main budget carriers, though PAL is usually the most expensive, being the only one offering traditional cabin service (snacks, drinks etc). Cebu Pacific has been known to sell seats for P1, and regularly offers fares of P499 one-way Manila to Coron (Busuanga) and P999 Manila to Zamboanga. But note that the low prices you see quoted on budget airline websites usually don't include taxes and unlike most PAL flights, you can't change bookings once you've paid; there are also charges for bags and seat selection (P180 and P130 respectively on Cebu Pacific).

By ferry

Ferries and **bangkas** – wooden outrigger boats – were once the bread and butter of Philippine travel. Though still important, especially in the **Visayas** (where there's hardly a coastal barangay that doesn't have some sort of ferry service), most of the longer routes have been made redundant by the growth of budget air travel. Not only are flights faster and as cheap (or cheaper) than cabins on longer ferry routes (Manila to Mindanao for example), they are invariably safer. Indeed, despite some improvements in recent years, ferry accidents remain common in the Philippines and even in the dry season the open ocean can get surprisingly rough. The smaller bangkas are often poorly equipped, with little shelter from the elements, while even many of the larger vessels have been bought secondhand from Japan or Europe and are well past their prime. Ferries of all sizes are frequently crowded.

Having said that, for many shorter inter-island trips ferries remain the only form of transport available, and especially in the Visayas, island-hopping by boat can be an enjoyable and rewarding part of your trip.

Ferry companies

There's a hierarchy of vessels, with proper ferries at the top; so-called big bangkas, taking around fifty passengers, in the middle; and ordinary bangkas at the bottom. A number of **ferry lines** operate large ships between major ports in the Philippines, though the sector was substantially reorganized in 2012. Today the major operator is **2GO** (Ⓦtravel .2go.com.ph), with SuperCat (Ⓦsupercat.com.ph) part of the same group; the other key players are **Montenegro Shipping Lines** (Ⓦmontenegrolines .com.ph), **Cokaliong Shipping Lines** (Ⓦcokaliong shipping.com) and **TransAsia Shipping Lines** (Ⓦtransasiashipping.com). These companies have regular sailings on routes between Manila and major cities throughout the Visayas and Mindanao, and on secondary routes within the Visayas. Most post schedules and fares on their websites. On less popular routes you might have to take your chances with smaller companies, which rarely operate to published timetables. In rural areas you may have to ask around at the harbour or wharf as to what boats are leaving, for where and when.

Fares and tickets

Ferry **fares** are very low by Western standards, especially if booked in advance, for example Manila–Cebu (from P480), Manila–Mindanao (P1000); add on around P500–1000 for a private cabin. **Tickets** can be bought at the pier up until departure, though it's often more convenient to avoid the long queues and buy in advance: travel agents sell ferry tickets, and the larger ferry companies have ticket offices in cities and towns. 2GO also offers online ticketing.

Accommodation and facilities

The cheapest **accommodation** is in bunk beds in cavernous dorms either below deck or on a semi-open deck, with shared toilets and showers. Older ships might have just a handful of cramped cabins sharing a tiny shower and toilet. The major operators generally have newer ships with a range of accommodation that includes dorms, straw mats in an air-conditioned area, shared cabins (usually for four) with bathrooms. These ferries usually also have a bar, karaoke lounge and a canteen serving basic meals.

By bus

Bus travel can be relatively uncomfortable and slow, but you'll get a real glimpse of rural Philippines from the window, and meet Filipinos from all walks of life. Buses are also incredibly convenient: hundreds of routes spread out like a web from major cities and even the most isolated barangay will have a service of some sort. You won't go hungry either. At most stops local vendors will jump on and offer you various snacks and drinks,

while on the longer hauls, even express buses stop every three or four hours to give passengers a chance to stretch their legs and buy some food.

There are some downsides. Though the largest bus companies have fleets of reasonably new air-conditioned buses for longer routes, they rarely have toilets. On shorter routes buses can be dilapidated contraptions with no air conditioning and, in some cases, no glass in the windows. You'll also need to develop a high tolerance to loud music or Tagalog movies played at full blast throughout the trip.

Bus fares and frequencies

Fares are low: around P445 from Manila to Baguio and P550 to Naga. Beyond Manila roads can be poor, and even when the distances involved aren't great, the buses will make numerous stops along the way. Some bus companies advertise express services, but in reality a bus that goes from A to B without stopping is unheard of. Buses that have a "derecho" sign (meaning "straight" or "direct") in the window usually make the fewest stops.

Published **timetables** for most bus companies are nonexistent, but departures on popular routes such as Manila to Baguio or Manila to Vigan usually happen every hour or half-hour. The larger operators – such as Victory Liner (Ⓦvictoryliner .com) and Philtranco (Ⓦphiltranco.com.ph) – allow you to book seats in advance on some routes, either online, by telephone (be warned, the lines are often engaged) or at the terminal. A list of bus companies is given in the Manila chapter (see pp.80–83), and details of bus routes, with local contact details, appear throughout the Guide. Note, however, that there are so many bus companies (many of which go in and out of business on a regular basis, or have permits suspended), and so much variation in routes and journey times, that the information we give in the Guide is just a guideline and always subject to change.

By jeepney

The **jeepney** is the ultimate Philippine icon (see box, p.8), and remains an important form of transport, particularly in Manila, Cebu City, Davao and Baguio, where there are frequent services between key locations in each city. In the provinces jeepneys connect isolated barangays to nearby towns and towns to cities, but they might run only two or three times a day, depending on demand, the weather and the mood of the driver. There are absolutely no timetables.

Routes are painted on the side or on a signboard in the window. Even so, using jeepneys takes a little local knowledge because they make numerous stops and deviations to drop off and pick up passengers. There's no such thing as a designated jeepney stop, so people wait in the shade at the side of the road and flag one down. The vehicles are cramped and incredibly uncomfortable, usually holding about twenty passengers inside and any number of extras clinging to the back or sitting precariously on top. It can be a hassle to get luggage on and off – small items might end up on the floor, but larger items will go on the roof. Jeepneys are, however, a great social lubricator; you'll soon find yourself involved in jolly conversations with the rest of the passengers about your nationality, destination and marital status.

Fares are low: in the provinces they start at P7 for a trip of a few kilometres, rising to P50 for two- or three-hour drives. In the cities, a trip of a few hundred metres costs around P7, rising to P25 on longer routes. To pay, hand your money to the passenger next to you and say *bayad po* (pay please). If you're not sitting close to the driver, the fare will be passed down the line of passengers until it reaches him; he will then pass back any change.

By FX taxi and van

Not unlike jeepneys in the way they operate, **FX taxis** are air-conditioned Toyota Tamaraw vehicles (a bit like Range Rovers), with signs in the window indicating their destination. They made their debut in Manila in the late 1990s, and now operate in other cities and on some popular inter-city routes. However, routes are often not set, so it takes a little local knowledge to know where to catch the right vehicle. They can be a little claustrophobic – the driver won't even think about moving until he's got ten people on board, three more than the vehicle is designed for. In Manila most of these taxis charge P2–3 per kilometre.

Elsewhere in the Philippines you may encounter "**vans**" (often labelled "GT Express" meaning "Garage to Terminal"), which are generally cramped Isuzu, Suzuki and Nissan minivans (what would be called small passenger vans in the US) that follow fixed routes. They're usually a little more expensive than buses but they're much faster as, unlike buses, they don't stop off every few hundred metres. In Luzon vans often have their own terminals in major towns, and operate in competition with bus companies and jeepneys over long distances. Destinations are usually clearly marked on the windscreen.

By tricycle and "habal-habal"

The cheapest form of shared transport, **tricycles** are ubiquitous in the provinces. In Manila and Cebu City they are prohibited from using certain roads, but almost everywhere else they go where they like, when they like and at speeds as high as their small engines are capable of. The sidecars are designed for four passengers – two facing forwards and two backwards – but it's not uncommon to see extras clinging on wherever they can, the only limiting factor being whether or not the machine can actually move under the weight of the extra bodies. Tricycles never follow fixed routes, so it's usually a question of flagging one down and telling the driver your destination.

Closely related but even more life-threatening is the motorcycle-for-hire, popularly known as "**habal-habal**" (the nickname is a sexual allusion – ask a Filipino friend). These motorcycles have two wooden platforms attached to each side, sometimes accommodating up to thirteen persons (believe it). Though there have been moves in Congress to change things, at the time of writing the habal-habal was still technically illegal; laughable when you consider how essential they have become in many parts of the country.

Fares typically start at P10 per person for a short trip of a few hundred metres on both forms of transport. Many tricycles charge a set rate per person for trips within town or city boundaries, usually around P10–25 (more in Manila). If you want to use the tricycle as a private taxi you'll have to negotiate a price – P25–30 is reasonable for a trip of up to 2km in the provinces. Anything further than that and the driver will ask for at least P50, though you can always try to bargain him down. Note, however, that tricycle drivers are notorious for ripping off foreigners, and especially in touristy areas you'll need expert bargaining skills to pay anything close to the local rate.

By car

It's possible to **rent** a self-drive car in the Philippines – a standard saloon car costs about P2000 per day – but the question is whether you'd want to. Not only is traffic in Manila and other cities often gridlocked, but most Filipino drivers have a very relaxed attitude towards the rules of the road. Swerving is common, as is changing lanes suddenly and driving with one hand permanently on the horn, particularly if you're a bus or jeepney driver. On the other hand, if you're used to driving in London, LA or New York this might not phase you too much, and in any case, once you reach more rural areas – northern Luzon for example – travelling by car can be incredibly convenient and open up a whole range of otherwise hard-to-reach destinations. Many travellers also rent **motorbikes**, but this is only recommended for experienced riders – the chances of having an accident are statistically fairly high. It's best to avoid driving at night altogether.

If you do drive you'll require your **driving licence** and be prepared to show it if you get stopped (rentals are allowed for up to ninety days – longer stays will require a Philippine licence). Vehicles in the Philippines drive on the right side of the road and distances and car speeds are in kilometres. The highways usually have a nominal speed limit of 100kph, but anywhere else you'll rarely be going faster than 30kph thanks to congestion.

Always **drive defensively** – cars, animals and pedestrians will pull out in front of you without warning (in many rural areas people are still not used to traffic), and always give way to jeepneys, which will happily drive you off the road. When passing anything, sound your horn twice as a warning (horns are rarely used in anger).

Note that **police** and "traffic enforcers" – uniformed men and women employed by local authorities to supplement the police – might try to elicit a bribe from you. If this happens it's best to play the dumb foreigner and hand over the "on-the-spot fine" of a few hundred pesos (make sure you have cash with you). If you take the moral high ground and refuse to play along, you'll probably end up having your licence confiscated or, in the worst case, your car towed away and impounded until you pay a fine to get it back.

CAR AND MOTORCYCLE RENTAL AGENCIES

Avalon Transport Services Ⓦ avalonrentacar.com.
Avis Ⓦ avis.com.ph.
Budget Ⓦ budget.com.ph.
Europcar Ⓦ europcar.com.ph.
Hertz Ⓦ hertzphilippines.com.
JB Rent A Car Ⓦ jbrentacar.com.
Manila Rent a Car Ⓦ manilarentacar.org
National Ⓦ nationalcar.com.
Nissan Rent-A-Car Ⓦ nissanrentacar.com.
Pitstop Bike Adventure Ⓦ pitstopbikeadventure.com.
Rent A Car Manila Ⓦ rentacarmanila.com.
Viajero Rent A Car Ⓦ viajerorentacar.com.
VIP Rent-A-Car Ⓦ viprentacar.com.ph.

Hiring a driver

For about P2000–2500 (plus fuel, driver's food, parking/toll fees) you can hire a small car and driver

from some car rental agencies for up to eight hours, the extra expense more than justified by the peace of mind a local driver brings. Try Manila Rent a Car or the Chauffeur Drive packages at Europcar Philippines.

Beyond Metro Manila, it can be much cheaper to strike a private deal with a car or van owner looking for extra work. A typical rate for their services is P1500 a day (plus fuel and tolls), although you'll need to negotiate. A good way to find someone with a vehicle is to ask at your accommodation; alternatively, locals with cars wait at many airports and ferry ports in the hope of making a bit of money driving arriving passengers into town. You can ask these drivers if they're available to be hired by the day.

By bike

Given the volume of traffic (and driving standards) on most major roads, cycling around the Philippines can be a dangerous proposition, but plenty of locals and travellers do use bikes in rural areas. Outfits such as **Bugoy Bikers** (Ⓦ bugoybikers .com) can help arrange guided or self-guided day-tours or longer excursions by mountain bike.

Accommodation

The Philippines has accommodation to suit everyone, from international five-star hotels and swanky beach resorts to simple rooms – sometimes no more than a bamboo hut on a beach – and budget hotels.

It's generally not necessary to book in advance unless you are visiting at peak times – Easter, Christmas, New Year or during a major local festival (see p.36). As always you'll find the cheapest rates online, but if you do want to book by phone, note that some hotels in out-of-the-way areas won't have a landline telephone on site, in which case they may have a mobile number and/or a booking office in a city (often Manila); details are given in the text as appropriate.

> ### ACCOMMODATION ALTERNATIVES
>
> The following websites are worth checking for useful alternatives to standard hotel and resort accommodation.
> **Airbnb** Ⓦ airbnb.com.
> **CouchSurfing** Ⓦ couchsurfing.org.
> **Vacation Rentals by Owner** Ⓦ vrbo.com.

Hotels and beach resorts

The terms **hotel** and **beach resort** cover a multitude of options in the Philippines. A hotel can mean anything from the most luxurious five-star establishment down to dingy budget pensions or guesthouses with bars on the windows. Beach resorts in turn range from sybaritic affairs on private atolls, with butlers and health spas, to dirt-cheap, rickety one-room cottages on a deserted island. "Resort hotels" are a mid-range or top-range hybrid of the two, sometimes with their own area of private beach.

Many hotels and beach resorts accept credit cards, although there are exceptions, such as in rural areas where electricity supply is not dependable and also in the cheapest budget accommodation, where you must pay cash. It can be worth checking that the air conditioner, where available, isn't noisy. Rooms on lower floors overlooking main roads are best avoided as they can be hellishly noisy; always go for something high up or at the back (or both).

Note that in smaller towns and cities beyond Manila, hotels often use the English term "single" room to mean one double bed, and "double/twin" to mean a room with two double beds; in these cases "single" rooms will obviously be big enough for two people – you will rarely find a true single bed on offer in the Western sense. In the guide, prices quoted are always based on the cheapest room for two people sharing (a "double" in the Western sense), regardless of what the hotel calls it.

Budget

Budget hotels (typically P450–1000) offer little more than a bed, four walls and a fan or small air-conditioning unit, although if you're by the beach, with a pleasant sea breeze blowing and the windows open, air conditioning isn't really necessary. If you do get a private bathroom it will only have cold water, and the "shower" is sometimes little more than a tap sticking out of the wall producing a mere trickle of water. Breakfast is unlikely to be included in the rate, though there may be a canteen or coffee shop on the premises where you can buy food. At the higher end of the budget range, rooms are usually simple but can be reasonably spacious, perhaps – if they are on or near a beach – with a small balcony.

Mid-range

There are plenty of **mid-range hotels** (typically P1500–3000) mostly in towns and cities. The rooms typically have air conditioning and a private bathroom with hot water, and usually TV but no cable. Beach cottages in this bracket are usually quite spacious and will often have a decent-sized veranda too. Most mid-range accommodation will feature a small coffee shop or restaurant with a choice of Filipino and Western breakfasts that may be included in the rate; if it's not expect to pay around P100–150.

Top end

In Manila and Cebu, as well as the most popular beach destinations such as Boracay, you can splash out on **five-star comfort** at hotels and beach resorts owned and operated by international chains (P3500 and up). The cottages at the most expensive resorts are more like chic apartments, often with a separate living area. Many of these establishments include a buffet breakfast in the rate, and sports facilities and outdoor activities are on offer, though you'll have to pay extra to partake.

ACCOMMODATION PRICES

All accommodation prices published in the guide represent the cost of the **cheapest room for two people sharing** – or beach hut sleeping two – **in high season**, namely November to April. Prices during the May–October rainy season are usually about twenty percent lower. Conversely, during Christmas, New Year and Easter, rates in the popular beach resorts such as Boracay can spike by around twenty percent. In some cases hotels will include **breakfast** in the price but it's worth asking about this when you book. You'll also find that as a "walk-in" guest you'll usually be able to get a cheaper rate than the rack rate listed on hotel websites, especially in the off-season and in less touristy areas.

Value Added Tax of twelve percent and an additional service charge is sometimes included in the published rates, but not always. If you see a room advertised at P1000++ (**"plus plus"**) it means you'll pay P1000 plus VAT plus service charge – always ask for clarification if you aren't sure which charge is which. These additional charges have been factored into all our rates.

Where **dormitory accommodation** is available, we've given the price of a dorm bed.

Campsites, hostels and homestays

Campsites are almost unknown in the Philippines. A small number of resorts allow you to pitch tents in their grounds for a negligible charge, but otherwise the only camping you're likely to do is if you go trekking or climbing and need to camp overnight in the wilderness or on a mountain top. Note that rental outlets for equipment are few and far between, so you might need to bring your own gear from home.

There are very few **youth hostels** in the country, most of them in university cities where they may be booked up by students throughout term time. A Hostelling International (HI) card can in theory give you a tiny saving of around P25 a night at the handful of YMCAs and YWCAs in the big cities. The problem is that few staff have any idea what an HI card is.

There's no official **homestay** programme in the Philippines, but in rural areas where there may be no formal accommodation, you'll often find people willing to put you up in their home for a small charge, usually no more than P200 a night, including some food. If you enjoy the stay, it's best to offer some sort of tip when you leave, or a gift of soft drinks and sweets for the children. You can ask around at town halls if you're interested.

Food and drink

The high esteem in which Filipinos hold their food is encapsulated by the common greeting "Let's eat!" Though Filipino food has a reputation for being one of Asia's less adventurous cuisines, there is a lot more to it than adobo (see box opposite), and young, entrepreneurial restaurateurs and chefs have started to give native dishes an increasingly sophisticated touch.

In the Philippines snacks – **merienda** – are eaten in between the three main meals, and not to partake when offered can be considered rude. It's not unusual for breakfast to be eaten early, followed by merienda at 10am, lunch as early as 11am (especially in the provinces where many people are up at sunrise), more merienda at 2pm and 4pm, and dinner at 7pm. Meals are substantial, and even busy office workers prefer to sit down at a table and make the meal last. Never be afraid to ask for a doggy bag – everyone does. The final bill you get in a restaurant usually includes VAT of twelve percent and a service charge of ten percent, adding 22 percent to the price shown on the menu.

Don't be confused by the absence of a knife from most table settings. It's normal to use just a fork and spoon, cutting any meat with the fork and using the spoon to put the food in your mouth. This isn't as eccentric as it first seems. Most meat is served in small chunks, not steak-like slabs, so you usually don't have to cut it at all. Fish can be skewered with your fork and cut with the side of your spoon. And a spoon is so much easier for the local staple, steamed rice, than a knife and fork. That said, in some "native-style" restaurants food is served on banana leaves and you're expected to eat with your hands, combining the rice and food into mouthful-sized balls with your fingers – if you don't feel up to this it's fine to ask for cutlery.

Filipino cuisine

Filipino food is a delicious and exotic blend of Malay, Spanish, Chinese and American traditions. Dishes range from the very simple, like grilled fish and rice, to more complex stews, paellas and artfully barbecued meats, many using local fruits such as calamansi, coconuts and mangoes. **Seafood** is especially rich – expect anything from meaty crabs and milkfish to grouper and stingray on the menu. Most meals are served with San Miguel, the local beer, and are followed by sumptuous tropical fruits and decadent desserts.

The staples

Rice is the key Filipino staple, often accompanied by little more than freshly caught fish with a vinegar sauce. **Lapu-lapu** (grouper) and **bangus** (milkfish) are commonly served, while squid, crab and prawns are especially good and cheap in the Philippines. **Chicken** is another key staple – competition for the best fried or barbecued chicken (*lechon manok*) is fierce. Popular dishes on virtually every menu include **sinigang**, a refreshing tamarind-based sour soup; **kare-kare**, a stew made from delicious peanut sauce with vegetables and usually beef; and sizzling **sisig**, fried pig's head and liver, seasoned with calamansi and chilli peppers. Filipino Chinese dishes such as **pancit** (noodles) and **lumpia** (spring rolls) are common. Probably the most popular meat is **pork**, transformed into dishes such as crispy pata, **adobo** (see box opposite) and **lechon**,

ADOBO HEAVEN

It might seem simple – stewed pork and chicken – but it's hard to resist the justly revered national dish of the Philippines. **Adobo** originally meant "sauce" or "seasoning" in Spanish, but its use has morphed throughout Spain's former colonies – the Filipino version is actually indigenous to the islands, dating back to a dish cooked up here long before Magellan's arrival. Philippine adobo consists of pork, chicken or a combination of both slowly stewed in soy sauce, vinegar, crushed garlic, bay leaf and black peppercorns – it's the latter two ingredients that gives true adobo its distinctive flavour and bite. No two adobos are exactly alike however – you'll discover different versions all over the country.

roasted pig cooked whole on a spit over a charcoal or wood fire. In the Philippines, *lechon* is usually served with vinegar or special sauce (unique to each *lechon* shop but normally made from fruits or liver pâté, garlic and pepper). The meat is deliciously fragrant and juicy, but the real highlight is the crispy smoked skin, a fatty, sumptuous treat sold by the kilo. Pork is also the basis of **Bicol Express**, the best known of very few spicy local dishes, which consists of pork cooked in coconut milk, soy and vinegar, with chillies.

Vegetables are not considered an integral part of Filipino meals, but may well be mixed in with the meat or offered as a side dish. In restaurants serving Filipino food, some of the most common vegetable dishes include *pinakbet*, an Ilocano dish (usually bitter melon, squash, okra, eggplant and string beans cooked in bagoong, a fermented fish sauce), and a version of Bicol Express with leafy vegetables such as *pechay* (aka pak choy) and *camote* tops (sweet potato leaves) in place of pork.

Breakfast

At many hotels and resorts you'll be offered a Filipino breakfast, which typically consists of **longganisa** (garlic sausage), **tocino** (cured pork), fried bangus fish, corned beef or **beef tapa** (beef marinated in vinegar); you'll usually be offered **tapsilog**, a contraction formed from tapa (fried beef), *sinangag* (garlic fried rice) and *itlog* (egg) – which is exactly what you get, a bowl of garlic rice with tapa and a fried egg on top. Other "combo" dishes include tosilog and longsilog (you get the idea).

If this sounds too much for you, there's usually fresh fruit and toast, though note that local **bread**, either of the sliced variety or in rolls known as *pan de sal*, is often slightly sweet (wholegrain or rye breads are unusual in all but a few big hotels). Another option is to ask for a couple of hot *pan de sal* with corned-beef filling, the beef taking away some of the bread's sweetness.

Street food

Though not as common as it is in Thailand or India, **street food** still has a special place in the hearts (and stomachs) of Filipinos as much for its plain weirdness as for its culinary virtues. Hawkers with portable stoves tend to appear towards the end of the working day from 5 to 8pm and at lunchtime in bigger cities. Much of the food is grilled over charcoal and served on sticks kebab-style, or deep fried in a wok with oil that is poured into an old jam jar and re-used day after day. Highlights include deep-fried **fishballs** and squidballs (mashed fish or squid blended with wheat flour), grilled **pig intestines** and adidas – **chicken's feet**, named after the sports-shoe manufacturer. Prices start from a few pesos a stick.

Street vendors also supply the king of Filipino aphrodisiacs, *balut*, a half-formed **duck embryo** eaten with beak, feathers and all; sellers advertise their proximity with a distinctive baying cry.

Carinderias and seafood buffets

Carinderias are usually humble eateries that allow you to choose from a number of dishes placed on a counter in big aluminium pots. Carinderia fare is usually a blend of Filipino and Asian dishes; typical choices might be adobo, pancit, *pinakbet*, chicken curry, grilled pork, sweet and sour fish, fried chicken and hotdogs. The only problem with carinderias is that the food has usually been standing around a while and is often served lukewarm.

In urban areas you'll also find **seafood** restaurants displaying a range of seafood on ice; order by pointing at what you want and telling the waiter how you would like it cooked.

Desserts and snacks

Filipinos adore **sweets** and **desserts**. Sold all over the Philippines, **halo-halo** (from the Tagalog word *halo*, meaning "mix") is a mouthwatering blend of shaved ice, evaporated milk and various toppings such as sweetened beans, fruits and taro, served in

FILIPINO FRUITS

The Philippines is justly celebrated for its variety and quality of fresh fruit, especially its mangoes, which are ubiquitous throughout the islands and always juicy and delicious. The list below is just a selection.

Atis Pine-cone shaped, and about 10cm long with green scaly skin, the ripe flesh of the atis (custard apple or sugar-apple) is gloriously sweet and soft; it might look a bit like custard but it tastes like a combination of banana, papaya and strawberry, or more prosaically, bubble gum. With black pips scattered throughout it can be messy to eat. The main season is late summer to October.

Balimbing (starfruit, aka *carambola*) Crunchy, juicy fruit, with a slightly sweet flavour that tastes a bit like a blend of apple, pear and grape.

Bayabas (guava) Fruit with a tough green skin and distinctive deep-pink pulp that has a sweet flavour, similar to passion fruit mixed with strawberry.

Buko (coconut) Another Philippine staple grown throughout the archipelago year-round, harvested casually by villagers as much as by commercial plantations for its refreshing juice and nutty white flesh. Used to make *buko* pie and a variety of desserts.

Calamansi Little green lime that is squeezed into juices, hot tea, over noodles, fish and *kinilaw* (raw fish salad) and into numerous dipping sauces.

Chico (sapodilla) Roughly the size of an egg, with brown skin and sticky, soft flesh that has a malty, exceedingly sweet flavour.

Durian The "king" of tropical fruit is spiky, heavy and smells like a drain blocked with garbage – but its creamy inner flesh tastes like heaven. Rich in protein, minerals and fat, the durian is one of the more expensive fruits in the Philippines, though in Davao, the centre of production, you can buy whole ones for P50.

Guayabano (soursop) A large, oval fruit with knobbly spines outside and fragrant flesh inside.

Kaimito (star apple) Plum-coloured and round, about the size of a tennis ball, with leathery skin and soft white pulp inside that tastes a bit like grape.

Langka (jackfruit) The largest tree-borne fruit in the world (it can reach 40kg) is also one of the most delicious, with an interior of large, yellow bulbs of sweet flesh that tastes like flowery bananas.

Lanzones Small round fruit grown mostly on southern Luzon, especially in Laguna, and available October to December. It's also grown in northern Mindanao and especially Camiguin, where there is a festival in its honour (see p.412). It tastes a bit like a combination of grape and sweet grapefruit.

Mangga (mango) Eat as much mango as you can in the Philippines – you won't taste any better. Most grown on the islands turn from green to yellow as they ripen and are always very sweet. The main season runs June through August.

Mangosteen Nothing like a mango, this sumptuous fruit the size of a tangerine has a thick, purplish skin and creamy white flesh. The season runs June through August.

Marang If you travel in Mindanao look out for this special fruit. A bit like a breadfruit, it's a cross between jackfruit and *atis* but with a taste all its own.

Pakwan (watermelon)

Papaya You'll see papaya plants growing in gardens and along roadsides all over the Philippines and it's one of the cheapest fruits. Some 98 percent of the annual crop is consumed locally and it's extremely nutritious.

Piña (pineapple) The Spanish introduced the pineapple to the Philippines and thanks to huge plantations run by Del Monte and Dole (both in Mindanao), it's one of the nation's biggest export earners.

Saging (banana) A staple crop in the Philippines, with a remarkable range of size and types grown in Mindanao and the western Visayas throughout the year; the country is one of the largest exporters of bananas in the world.

Santol The *santol* is an apple-sized fruit, with a white juicy pulp often eaten sour with some salt. It's also popular as a jam or a bitter marmalade.

a tall glass or bowl – the "special" version usually has taro ice cream on top. A speciality of Laguna Province (see p.107), **buko pie** is made by layering strips of young coconut and cake mix into a crispy pie crust – the addictive dessert has cult status in the Philippines and an intense rivalry exists between many pie-makers. The most popular traditional Filipino sweet is **polvorón**, a sort of shortbread made with flour, sugar and milk, and often sold in flavours such as cashew nut, chocolate and *pinipig* (crispy rice). Sold on every street corner, **turon** is a crispy deep-fried banana in a spring roll wrapper, while **leche flan** (caramel custard) is a staple on every restaurant menu. Filipinos also eat a huge amount of **ice cream** in an unorthodox range of flavours, including *ube* (purple yam), jackfruit, corn, avocado and even cheese.

For a snack in a packet, try salted dried fish like **dilis**, which can be bought in supermarkets and convenience stores. *Dilis* are a little like anchovies and are eaten whole, sometimes with a vinegar and garlic dip. They're often served along with other savouries (under the collective name *pulutan*) during drinking sessions. Salted dried **pusit** (squid) is also common.

Fast food

You'll find McDonald's in almost every big town, but the Philippines has its own successful **fast-food chains** fashioned after the US giant, with hundreds of branches of Jollibee (chicken, burgers and spaghetti), Chowking (noodle soups, dim sum), Mang Inasal (barbecue and unlimited rice) and Max's (fried chicken) throughout the country – indeed, the corpulent "jolly bee" mascot is more ubiquitous than Ronald McDonald. Western-style sandwich bars are starting to appear too.

Most shopping malls also have **food courts**, indoor marketplaces that bring together dozens of small stalls serving Filipino, Japanese, Chinese, Thai and Korean food. Here you can get a decent lunch for under P250 including a soft drink.

In many provincial cities, look out also for **ihaw-ihaw** (grill) restaurants, usually native-style bamboo structures where meat and fish are cooked over charcoal and served with hot rice and soup.

International cuisine

There are some excellent French, Spanish and Italian restaurants in Manila and Cebu City, and dozens of **European** restaurants in Boracay. Prices depend on where you are. In areas of Manila, you

VEGETARIAN FOOD

Committed **vegetarians and vegans** face a difficult mission to find suitable food in the Philippines. It's a poor country and many Filipinos have grown up on a diet of what's available locally, usually chicken and pork. If you ask for a plate of stir-fried vegetables it might come with slices of pork in it, or be served in a meat gravy. Fried rice always contains egg and meat. Having said that, most Filipinos will be familiar with the concept of vegetarian food and will try to accommodate you where possible.

Chinese and Japanese restaurants offer the best range of vegetable-based dishes, though you'll have to emphasize that you want absolutely no bits of meat added. In Manila, and to some extent in other cities, and in Boracay, pizzas are an option, or you could head to an upmarket restaurant and ask the chef to prepare something special. At least breakfast is straightforward – even in the most rural resorts, you can ask for toast or pancakes and, if you're not vegan, an omelette or scrambled eggs.

can spend P2500 or more for a good three-course meal for two; in Boracay you could have a similar meal for half that. However, European cuisine on the coast tends to be a little less sophisticated, simply because it's hard to guarantee supplies of the necessary ingredients.

There are **Chinese** restaurants in every city and in many provincial towns. Don't expect modish Oriental cuisine though; most Chinese restaurants are inexpensive places offering straightforward, tasty food designed to be ordered in large portions and shared by a group. A good Chinese meal for two often costs no more than P500. Another of the Philippines' favourite cuisines is **Japanese**, ranging from fast-food noodle parlours to expensive restaurants serving sushi and tempura.

Drinks

Bottled **water** is cheap; good local brands such as Nestlé Pure Life, Viva and Hidden Spring cost P20–30 in convenience stores. Fizzy soft drinks such as Coca-Cola and Pepsi are available everywhere.

At resorts and hotels, the "**juice**" which usually comes with breakfast is – irritatingly in a country rich in fresh fruit – often made from powder or concentrate. Good fresh juices, usually available only in the more expensive restaurants, include watermelon, ripe mango, sour mango and papaya. Fresh *buko* (coconut) juice is a refreshing choice, especially on a hot day. In general, sugar is added to fresh juices and shakes unless you specify otherwise, though you might well want sugar with the delightful soda made from calamansi, a small native lime.

Filipinos aren't big **tea** drinkers and, except in the best hotels, the only tea on offer is usually made from Lipton's tea bags. **Coffee** is popular and can be ordered anywhere, but the quality varies widely. It's usually instant, served in "three-in-one" packets, and dominated by Nescafé, though local, Malaysian and Indonesian brands are also available. Where brewed coffee is served, it's often local and very good. Latte-addicts may be tempted by *Starbucks* which has scores of branches across Manila and is popping up in provincial towns such as Bacolod. Fresh milk is rare outside the cities so you'll often find yourself being offered tinned or powdered milk with coffee or tea.

Alcohol

The **beer** of choice in the Philippines is **San Miguel**, the local pilsner established in 1890 and still dominating ninety percent of the domestic market. San Miguel also produces Red Horse Extra Strong lager. The only competition comes from Asia Brewery, which produces the uninspiring Beer na Beer and Colt 45 brands. Only a few foreign beers are available in bars and supermarkets, notably Heineken, Budweiser and Japanese brands. For something stronger there are plenty of Philippine-made **spirits** such as Tanduay rum, San Miguel Ginebra (gin) and Fundador brandy. Wine can be found in liquor stores in the larger cities though the range is usually limited to Australian or New Zealand mass-market brands.

All restaurants, fast-food places excepted, serve alcohol, but **wine** is rarely drunk; a cold beer or fresh fruit juice is much preferred. European restaurants usually have a limited wine list. For an average bottle of Australian Chardonnay or Merlot expect to pay at least P750. For something authentically native, try the strong and pungent **tapuy** (rice wine) or a speciality called **lambanog**, made from almost anything that can be fermented, including fruit. In the provinces both can be difficult to find because they're usually brewed privately for local consumption, though *lambanog* is now being bottled and branded, and can be found on some supermarket shelves in Manila and other cities.

Health

As long as you're careful about what you eat and drink and how long you spend in the sun, you shouldn't have any major health problems in the Philippines. Hospitals in cities and even in small towns are generally of a good standard, although health care is rudimentary in the remotest barangays and anything potentially serious is best dealt with in Manila. Doctors and nurses almost always speak English, and doctors in major cities are likely to have received some training in the US or the UK, where many attend medical school.

We've listed **hospitals** in the accounts of cities and major towns in the Guide; for a full list, plus a searchable database of doctors by location and area and expertise, check Ⓦrxpinoy.com. There are **pharmacies** on almost every street corner where you can buy local and international brand medicines. Branches of Mercury Drug, the country's biggest chain of pharmacies, are listed on Ⓦmercurydrug.com.

If you are hospitalized, you'll have to pay a deposit on your way in and settle the bill – either in person or through your insurance company (see box, p.50).

Stomach upsets

Food- and waterborne diseases are the most likely cause of illness in the Philippines. Travellers' **diarrhoea** can be caused by viruses, bacteria or parasites, which can contaminate food or water. There's also a risk of typhoid or cholera – occasional cases are reported in the Philippines, mostly in poor areas without adequate sanitation. Another potential threat is that of hepatitis A. The authorities in Manila claim **tap water** in many areas is safe for drinking, but it's not worth taking the chance – stick to bottled water (see p.33).

Mosquito-borne diseases

Dengue fever, a debilitating and occasionally fatal viral disease, is on the increase across tropical Asia. Many cases are reported in the Philippines each year, mostly during or just after the wet season when the day-biting mosquito that carries the disease is most active. There is no vaccine against dengue. Initial symptoms – which develop five to eight days after being bitten – include a fever that subsides after a few days, often leaving the patient with a bad rash all over their body, headaches and fierce joint pain. The only treatment is rest, liquids and paracetamol or any other acetaminophen painkiller (not aspirin). Dengue can result in death, usually among the very young or very old, and serious cases call for hospitalization.

In the Philippines **malaria** is found only in isolated areas of southern Palawan and the Sulu archipelago (Basilan, Jolo and Tawi-Tawi), and few travellers bother with anti-malarials if they are sticking to the tourist trail. If you are unsure of your itinerary it's best to err on the safe side and consult your doctor about malaria medication. Anti-malarials must be taken before you enter a malarial zone. As resistance to chloroquin-based drugs increases, mefloquin, which goes under the brand name of Lariam, has become the recom-mended prophylactic for most travellers to the Philippines. This has very strong side effects, and its use is controversial; alternatives are atovaquone-proguanil and doxycycline.

To avoid mosquito bites, wear long-sleeved shirts, long trousers and a hat. Use an insect repellent that contains DEET (diethylmethyltoluamide) and – unless you are staying in air-conditioned or well-screened accommodation – pick up a mosquito net impregnated with the insecticide permethrin or deltamethrin. Mosquito nets are hard to find In the Philippines, so buy one before you go. If you are unable to find a pre-treated mosquito net you can buy one and spray it yourself.

Leeches and rabies

If you're trekking through rainforest, especially in the rainy season, there's a good chance you'll encounter **leeches** (known locally as *limatik*), blood-sucking freshwater worms that attach themselves to your skin and can be tricky to remove (the bite doesn't hurt however). If you find a leech on your skin it's important not to pull it off because the jaw could be left behind and can cause infection. Use an irritant like salt, alcohol or heat from a cigarette or match to make the leech let go, then treat the wound with antiseptic. You can guard against leeches in the first place by securing cuffs and trouser bottoms. Climbers in the Philippines say rubbing detergent soap with a little water on your skin and clothes helps keep leeches at bay. Though leeches might seem unpleasant, they actually present a negligible health risk to healthy hikers, and it's fine to let them drop off of their own accord.

Stray and badly cared for dogs are everywhere in the Philippines and far more dangerous than leeches: **rabies** claims about eight hundred lives a year. The stereotype of rabid animals being deranged and foaming at the mouth is just that; some infected animals become lethargic and sleepy, so don't presume a docile dog is a safe one. If you are bitten or scratched, wash the wound immediately with soap and running water for five minutes and apply alcohol or iodine. Seek treatment immediately – rabies is fatal once symptoms appear.

MEDICAL RESOURCES

Canadian Society for International Health Ⓦ csih.org. Extensive list of travel health centres.

CDC ☎ 1877 394 8747, Ⓦ cdc.gov/travel. Official US government travel health site.

Hospital for Tropical Diseases Travel Clinic ☎ 0845 155 5000 or 020 7387 4411, Ⓦ www.thehtd.org.

International Society for Travel Medicine ☎ 1770 736 7060, Ⓦ istm.org. Has a full list of travel health clinics worldwide.

MASTA (Medical Advisory Service for Travellers Abroad) ☎ 0870 606 2782, Ⓦ masta-travel-health.com. For the nearest clinic in the UK.

South African Society of Travel Medicine ☎ 011 025 3297, Ⓦ sastm.org.za. Offers latest medical advice for travellers and a directory of travel medicine practitioners in South Africa.

Travellers' Medical and Vaccination Centre ☎ 1300 658 844, Ⓦ tmvc.com.au. Lists travel clinics in Australia, New Zealand and South Africa.

Tropical Medical Bureau Republic of Ireland ☎ 1850 487 674, Ⓦ tmb.ie.

The media

Filipinos are inordinately proud of their nation's historic status as the first democracy in Asia, a fact reflected in their love of a free press. Once Marcos was gone and martial law with him, the shackles truly came off and the Philippine media became one of the most vociferous and freewheeling in the world.

There is a dark and apparently contradictory side to this, however – the Philippines is also one of the most dangerous places in the world to be a journalist, with many killed every year. Though press freedoms are enshrined in the Philippine constitution, paramilitary groups, privately owned militias and even politicians (especially in Mindanao) who have been targeted by the press often seek violent retribution. Thanks to corruption, few are brought to justice.

Newspapers

Major English-language daily broadsheet **newspapers** include the *Philippine Daily Inquirer* (W inquirer.net), the *Philippine Star* (W philstar.com), *Manila Bulletin* (W mb.com.ph) and the *Manila Times* (W manilatimes .net). There are dozens of tabloids on the market, all of them lurid and often gruesome. Most of these are in Tagalog, though *People's Tonight* (W journal.com.ph) is largely in English with Filipino thrown in where the vernacular better expresses the drama, such as in quotations from victims of crime and from the police. Foreign news publications are harder to find. The best bet is to visit a five-star hotel, where lobby gift shops sometimes stock the *International New York Times*, *Time* and *The Economist*.

Some of the most trusted reporting on the Philippines comes from the **Philippine Centre for Investigative Journalism** (W pcij.org), founded in 1989 by nine Filipino journalists who wanted to go beyond the day-to-day razzmatazz and inanities of the mainstream press. Journalists working for the PCIJ were responsible for the exposé of former President Joseph Estrada's unexplained wealth, which led eventually to his downfall.

Television and radio

Terrestrial **television** networks include GMA (W gmanetwork.com) and ABS-CBN (W abs-cbn.com), offering a diet of histrionic soaps, chat shows and daytime game shows with sexy dancers. Cable television is now widely available in the Philippines, with the exception of some of the most undeveloped rural areas. Most providers carry BBC World, CNN and Australian ABC. At weekends during the season there's American football, baseball and English Premier League football on Star Sports or ESPN. Movie channels include HBO, Cinemax and Star Movies.

There are over 350 **radio** stations in the Philippines, and between them they present a mind-boggling mix of news, sport, music and chitchat. Radio news channels such as DZBB and RMN News AM tend to broadcast in Filipino, but there are dozens of FM pop stations that use English with a smattering of Filipino. The music they play isn't anything special, mostly mellow jazz and pop ballads by mainstream artists. Among the most popular FM stations are Wow FM (103.5MHz) and Crossover (105.1 MHz). A shortwave radio also gives access to the BBC World Service (W bbc.co.uk /worldservice), Radio Canada (W rcinet.ca), Voice of America (W voa.gov) and Radio Australia (W abc.net .au/ra), among other international broadcasters.

Festivals

Every community in the Philippines – from small barangay to crammed metropolis – has at least a couple of festivals a year in honour of a patron saint, to give thanks for a good harvest, or to pay respects to a biblical character. It's well worth timing your visit to see one of the major events: the beer flows, pigs are roasted, and there's dancing in the streets for days on end.

The main fiesta months are from January to May, with exact dates often varying. Major mardi-gras-style festivals include the **Ati-Atihan** in January in Kalibo (see box, p.336), and the **Sinulog** in January in Cebu (see box, p.271). One of the biggest nationwide festivals is the **Flores de Mayo**, a religious parade held across the country throughout May in honour of the Virgin Mary.

A festival calendar

Listing all Filipino festivals is impossible. Those included here are larger ones that you might consider making a special trip for, at least if you happen to be in the area.

JANUARY AND FEBRUARY

Feast of the Black Nazarene (Jan 9) Quiapo, Manila
W quiapochurch.com. Devotees gather in the plaza outside Quiapo Church to touch a miraculous image of Christ. See p.75.

Ati-Atihan (Variable, usually second week of Jan) Kalibo, Aklan. Street dancing and wild costumes at arguably the biggest festival in the country, held to celebrate an ancient land pact between settlers and indigenous Atis. See box, p.336.

Sinulog (Third Sun in Jan) Cebu City, Cebu W sinulog.ph. The second city's biggest annual event, in honour of the Santo Niño (an image of Jesus as a child). Huge street parade, live music, plenty of food and drink. See box, p.271.

Dinagyang (Fourth week of Jan) Iloilo, Panay Island
W dinagyangsailoilo.com. Relatively modern festival modelled after the Ati-Atihan, which includes a parade on the Iloilo River.

Philippine Hot Air Balloon Fiesta (Feb) Clark, Pampanga
W philballoonfest.net. Balloon rides, microlight flying, skydiving and aerobatics displays.

Pamulinawen (First two weeks in Feb) Laoag City, Ilocos Norte. Citywide fiesta in honour of St William the Hermit. Events include street parties, beauty pageants, concerts and religious parades.

Panagbenga (Baguio Flower Festival) (Third week in Feb) Baguio City, Benguet W panagbengaflowerfestival.com. The summer capital's largest annual event includes parades of floats beautifully decorated with flowers from the Cordillera region. There are also flower-related lectures and exhibitions.

Suman Festival (Third week in Feb) Baler, Aurora. Another mardi-gras-style extravaganza featuring street parades, dancing and floats decorated with the native delicacy *suman* – sticky rice cake rolled in banana leaves.

MARCH AND APRIL

Moriones (Easter weekend) Marinduque. A celebration of the life of the Roman centurion Longinus, who was blind in one eye. Legend says that when he pierced Christ's side with his spear, blood spurted into his eye and cured him. See box, p.201.

Arya! Abra (First or second week of March) Bangued, Abra. Highlights include hair-raising bamboo-raft races along the frisky Abra River and gatherings of northern tribes.

Bangkero Festival (First or second week of March) Pagsanjan, Laguna. Parade along the Pagsanjan River.

Kaamulan (First week of March) Malaybalay City, Bukidnon, Mindanao. Showcase of tribal culture and arts.

Pasayaw (Third week of March) Canlaon City, Negros Oriental. Thanksgiving festival to God and St Joseph, with twelve barangays competing for honours in an outdoor dancing competition. The final "dance-off" is held in the city gym.

Boracay International Dragon Boat Festival (April) Boracay, Aklan. A local version of Hong Kong's dragon-boat races, featuring domestic and international teams competing in long wooden canoes on a course off White Beach.

Allaw Ta Apo Sandawa (Second week of April) Kidapawan City, Cotabato. Gathering of highland tribes to pay respects to the sacred Mount Apo.

Turumba Festival (April & May) Pakil, Laguna. Religious festival commemorating the seven sorrows of the Virgin Mary. The festival consists of seven novenas, one for each sorrow, held at weekends.

MAY

Flores de Mayo (Throughout May) Countrywide. Religious procession celebrating the coming of the rains, with girls dressed as the various "Accolades of our Lady", including Faith, Hope and Charity. Processions are sometimes held after dark and lit by candles – a lovely sight.

Carabao Carroza (May 3–4) Iloilo, Panay Island. Races held to celebrate the humble carabao (water buffalo), beast of burden for many a provincial farmer.

Pahiyas (May 15) Lucban, Quezon ⓦ pahiyasfestival.com; also celebrated in the nearby towns of Candelaria, Tayabas, Sariaya, Tiaong and Lucena. Colourful harvest festival which sees houses gaily decorated with fruits and vegetables. It's held in honour of San Isidro Labrador, the patron saint of farmers.

Obando Fertility Rites (May 17–19) Obando, Bulacan. On the feast day of San Pascual, women gather in the churchyard to chant prayers asking for children, an intriguing combination of traditional dance, Catholicism and far older animist beliefs.

AUGUST AND SEPTEMBER

Kadayawan sa Davao (Third week of Aug) Davao City, Mindanao. Week-long harvest festival with civic and military parades and street dances.

Peñafrancia Fluvial Festival (Third Sat in Sept) Naga, Camarines Sur. A sacred statue of Our Lady of Peñafrancia, the patron saint of Bicol, is paraded through the streets, then sailed down the Bicol River back to its shrine.

OCTOBER

Kansilay (Oct 19 or closest weekend) Silay, Negros Occidental. Modern festival commemorating Silay's charter day. Eating and drinking contests, beauty pageants and an elaborate street parade.

Ibalong (Third week of Oct) Legaspi, Albay and throughout Bicol region. Epic dances and street presentations portraying Bicol's mythical superheroes and gods.

Lanzones Festival (Third week of Oct) Lambajao, Camiguin. Vibrant and good-natured outdoor party giving thanks for the island's crop of lanzones (a tropical fruit). See p.412.

Masskara Festival (Third week of Oct) Bacolod, Negros Occidental ⓦ bacolodmasskarafestival.com. Festivities kick off with food fairs, mask-making contests, brass-band competitions and beauty pageants, followed by the climax – a mardi gras parade where revellers don elaborate mask and costumes and dance to Latin rhythms Rio de Janeiro-style. See p.307.

DECEMBER

Christmas (December 25). The Christmas season officially starts Dec 16 and lasts until Epiphany on Jan 9. Churches are full for Midnight Mass on Christmas Eve, and some towns hold a Panunulúyan pageant in the days

ALL SAINTS' DAY

It's the day for Catholic Filipinos to honour their dead, but **All Saints' Day** on **November 1** is nothing to get maudlin about. Sometimes called All Souls' Day, it's when clans reunite at family graves and memorials, turning cemeteries throughout the country into fairgrounds. You don't pay your respects in the Philippines by being miserable, so All Saints' Day is a chance to show those who have gone before how much those who have been left behind are prospering. Filipinos approach All Saints' Day with the same gusto as Christmas, running from shop to shop at the last minute looking for candles to burn, food and offerings. The grave is painted, flowers are arranged and rosaries fervently prayed over, but once the ceremonial preliminaries are over, the fun begins. Guitars appear, capacious picnic hampers are opened and alcohol flows freely. Many families gather the night before and sleep in the cemetery. With many family graves in the provinces, Manila empties fast the day before All Saints' Day, people leaving the city by anything on wheels. Needless to say, it's a bad time to travel.

leading up to it, commemorating the journey of Joseph and the pregnant Virgin Mary to Bethlehem. Expect garish (and incongruous) decorations and groups of children singing carols all over the archipelago, though Christmas is primarily a family festival, celebrated in the home, without the pageantry on show at other festivals. Christmas Day itself is spent with family and friends – the country largely shuts down for the day.

Outdoor activities

For a sizeable proportion of the tourists who visit every year, the main attraction of the Philippines is the scuba diving. The abundance of exceptional dive sites and the high standard of diving instruction available have made the archipelago one of the world's foremost diving destinations.

It's not all about getting underwater though: there are some superb wilderness areas in the Philippines and dozens of volcanoes and mountains to be **climbed**, from the tallest in the country, Mount Apo (2954m), to more manageable peaks close to Manila in Batangas and Rizal provinces, some of which can be tackled in a day-trip. The country also offers opportunities for **caving**, **whitewater rafting**, **surfing** and **sailing**.

Scuba diving

Diving is possible year-round in the Philippines, with surface water temperatures in the 25–28°C range, the warmest conditions being from February to June. On deeper dives temperatures can drop to 22°C due to the upwelling of deeper, cooler water, so a light (3mm) wet suit is essential. During the typhoon season from June to November, be prepared for your plans to be disrupted if a major storm hits and dive boats are unable to venture out. Visibility depends on water temperature, the strength of the current and wind direction, but generally lies in the 10–30m range, as good as anywhere in the world.

There are currently five **recompression chambers** (aka hyperbaric chambers) in the Philippines to treat recompression sickness (see opposite). All ostensibly offer a 24-hour emergency service, but note that facilities do close for maintenance and/or because there are no staff qualified to use them. You might want to check that your dive operator is aware of the nearest operational facility. If it's not, go somewhere else.

Dive trips

Most dives **cost** around P1800 to P2500, including rental of the boat and equipment such as mask, booties, wet suit, fins, weight belt and air tanks. For night dives and more demanding technical dives, expect to pay around P500 extra. If you've booked a package that includes accommodation at a dive resort, two dives a day will normally be included in the cost.

Courses

All PADI-accredited resorts offer a range of courses run by qualified professional instructors. If you haven't been diving before and aren't sure if you'll

---

TOP 10 DIVE SITES

Anilao Closest dive site to Manila, teeming with soft coral and tropical fish. See box, p.119.
Apo Island Not to be confused with the reef (see below), this island off Negros is swamped with fish and forests of coral. See p.320.
Apo Reef Few divers and lots of big fish, two hours off the coast of Mindoro. See p.258.
Coron The best wreck diving in the country, possibly in the world. There are 24 charted wrecks, Japanese ships sunk in one massive attack by US aircraft in 1944. See p.395.
Puerto Galera Unrivalled all-round destination with something for everyone, from novices to old hands. See p.241.
Padre Burgos Out of the way in undeveloped southern Leyte and a prime spot for discovering new dive sites. See p.366.
Panglao Island The dive sites close to the congenial Alona Beach resorts offer an exceptional range of marine life. See p.294.
Samal Island This sleepy island just off the coast of Davao, Mindanao, harbours numerous dive sites. See p.428.
Subic Bay The former US Navy base is an exceptional location for wreck dives, with the USS *New York* one of the highlights. See box, p.128.
Tubbataha Reef You'll need to book a liveaboard trip but it's worth it, with guaranteed sightings of sharks and a good chance of mantas and whale sharks. See p.376.

MARINE LIFE

The beauty of diving in the Philippines is that you don't have to dive deep to see some incredible marine life. Among the commonest are the exotic and brightly coloured **angelfish**, **damselfish** and eye-catching **humbugs**, striped black-and-white like the sweet. In shallow coral gardens you'll see inquisitive **clownfish** defending their coral nests either singly or in pairs, perhaps with minuscule juveniles at their sides. Also unmissable are the frenetic shoals of **dragonets** and **dottybacks**, with their psychedelic colouring. **Moray eels** take shelter in crevices in the reef and it's not unusual to see one even in the shallows. Even **turtles** can be seen at this depth.

Where the coral plunges away steeply into an inky darkness, at depths of five or six metres, you'll see bright green **parrot fish** and mesmerising **batfish**, who patrol the reef edge in family shoals. These slopes and fore reefs are also home to **snappers**, **goatfish** and **wrasses**, the largest of which – the Napoleon wrasse – can dwarf a person. Deeper still, but usually in the more isolated dive sites such as Tubbataha, it's possible to see sharks, including **white tip reef sharks** and **grey reef sharks**, while if you're lucky an immense but gentle **manta ray** or **whale shark** might drift lazily past.

Poisonous species include the beautifully hypnotic **lionfish** (also called the flamefish), which hunts at night and has spines along its back that can deliver a nasty dose of venom, while shoals of **jellyfish** are common at certain times of year.

take to it, try a gentle twenty-minute "**discovery dive**", guided by an instructor for around P1500, or the longer PADI **Discover Scuba Diving** course for around P3000. The main course for beginners is the PADI **Open Water Diver Course** (from around P20,000) which will allow you to dive at depths up to 18m. You might want to consider doing the pool sessions and written tests before you travel, then doing the checkout dives at a PADI resort in the Philippines. It saves time and means you don't have to slave over homework in the tropical heat. If you choose this option, make sure you bring your PADI referral documents with you.

Once you've passed the course and been given your certification card, you are free to dive not just anywhere in the Philippines, but anywhere in the world. You might also want to take another step up the diving ladder by enrolling in a more advanced course. There are many to choose from, including **Advanced Open Water Diver** (from P16,000), Emergency First Response (from P7000), which is also suitable for non-divers and **Rescue Diver** (from around P20,000).

Liveaboards

There are two great advantages to diving from a liveaboard (a boat that acts as a mobile hotel) – you can get to places that are inaccessible by bangka and once you're there you can linger for a night or two. Liveaboards allow you to explore terrific destinations such as Apo Reef off the coast of Mindoro and Tubbataha in the Sulu Sea, arguably the best dive spot in the country. Packages include all meals and

dives, but vary significantly according to destination; Tubbataha costs at least US$1200–1600 per week, while trips around Coron start at around US$130 per day. Most of the boats used have air-conditioned en-suite cabins for two. Packages often include unlimited diving and are always full board.

LIVEABOARD OPERATORS

Atlantis Dive Resorts ⓦ atlantishotel.com. Operates the 32m-long *Atlantis Azores* with eight luxurious cabins with private bathrooms. Trips to Puerto Galera and Apo Reef (Oct–Dec), Tubbataha (mid-March to early June), Dumaguete (June–Sept) and southern Leyte for the whalesharks (Jan–March). Most trips US$3295–3790 for 7 nights, 6 days.

Expedition Fleet ⓦ expeditionfleet.com. Trips to Tubbataha on the ten-cabin MY *Stella Maris Explorer* (from US$2400; 8 days, 7 nights).

Seadive Resort ⓦ seadiveresort.com. Trips to Apo Reef and the Coron wrecks from P22,500 (2 nights/3 days), including five dives and all entry fees.

Victory Divers ⓦ victorydivers.com. Overnight trips from Boracay to Apo Reef where there are whale sharks, sharks, rays and turtles. P7500/day (minimum of four people).

RECOMPRESSION CHAMBERS

Batangas City St Patrick's Hospital, Lopez Jaena St ☎ 043 723 8388, ⓦ divemed.com.ph.

Cavite City Sangley Recompression Chamber, NSWG, Philippine Fleet Naval Base ☎ 046 524 2061.

Cebu City Cebu Recompression Chamber, Viscom Station Hospital, Military Camp Lapu-Lapu, Lahug ☎ 032 232 2464.

Manila V. Luna Recompression Chamber, AFP Medical Center, V. Luna Rd, Quezon City ☎ 02 920 7183, ⓦ afpmedicalcenter.com.

Sea Dive Resort Barangay 3 Don Pedro St, Coron (Palawan) ☎ 0917 808 6700, ⓦ seadiveresort.com.

DIVING DOS AND DON'TS

Divers can cause damage to reefs, sometimes inadvertently. Be aware of your fins because they can break off coral heads that take years to re-grow. Don't grab coral to steady yourself and always maintain good buoyancy control – colliding with a reef can be destructive. Don't kick up sediment, which can choke and kill corals. For more information about **reef conservation** efforts in the Philippines, check out ⓦoceanheritage.com.ph, the website of the Ocean Heritage Foundation, a local environmentalist group. Below is a list of additional dos and don'ts:

- **Collecting aquatic life** Resist the temptation to take home corals or shells, and never take souvenirs from wreck dives or remove anything dead or alive – except rubbish – from the ocean.
- **Touching and handling aquatic life** For many organisms this is a terrifying and injurious experience. Handling marine life is best left to people who have experience with the creatures concerned.
- **Riding aquatic life** Hard to credit, but some divers still think it's a great lark to hang onto the back of a turtle or manta ray. Simply put, there are no circumstances in which this is right.
- **Spear-fishing** This has been outlawed in the Philippines, and environmental groups are increasingly reporting spear-fishers to the authorities for prosecution.

DIVING RESOURCES

Asia Divers ⓦ asiadivers.com. Thoroughly professional dive outfit with an office in Manila and a dive centre and accommodation in Puerto Galera. Good people to learn with.

Divephil ⓦ divephil.com. Useful guide to scuba diving in the Philippines, plus information about destinations and accommodation.

SeaQuest ⓦ seaquestdivecenter.net. Long-established operator with centres in Bohol and Cebu, offering general diving advice, safaris, courses and accommodation.

Underwater Threesome ⓦ uw3some.com. Online diving portal for several organizations, including *Asian Diver* diving magazine and Scuba Diver AustralAsia.

Trekking and climbing

The Philippines offers plenty of opportunities to explore pristine **wilderness** areas. Luzon, for example, has the Sierra Madre (see p.157), rarely visited by tourists and offering exhilarating trekking through dense rainforest and across dizzying peaks. In Bicol there are some terrific volcano climbs (Mt Mayon and Mt Isarog, for instance; see p.219 & p.213), while Mindoro, Palawan and the Visayas between them have dozens of national parks, heritage areas, wildlife sanctuaries and volcanoes. Mount Kanlaon (see p.313), an active volcano in Negros, is one of the country's more risky climbs, while Mount Halcon (see p.252) on Mindoro offers a raw, mesmerizing landscape of peaks, waterfalls and jungle, typical of wilderness areas throughout the archipelago.

The country actually has more than sixty **national parks** and protected areas, but because funds for their management are scarce, you won't find the kind of infrastructure that exists in national parks in the West. While the most popular climbs – Mount Apo in Mindanao (see p.430) and Mount Pulag in Mountain province (see p.169), for example – have trails that are relatively easy to find and follow, it's important to realize that for the most part trails are generally poorly maintained and hardly marked, if they're marked at all. There are seldom more than a few (badly paid) wardens or rangers responsible for huge tracts of land, and where accommodation exists, it will be extremely basic. Some national parks have administrative buildings where you might be able to get a bed in a dorm for the night, or where you can roll out a mattress or sleeping bag on the floor. They may also have basic cooking facilities, but the closest you'll get to a shower is filling a bucket and washing outside. Deep within park territory, the best you can hope for is a wooden shack to shelter in for the night.

This lack of facilities means you'll need to hire a reliable **guide**. Often, the place to make contact with guides is the municipal hall in the barangay or town closest to the trailhead. **Fees** range from P800–1500 per day depending where you are, plus food and water, which you'll have to bring with you as it's unlikely you'll come across anywhere to buy anything once you're on the trail.

There are some **outdoor shops** in big cities – mainly Manila – where you can buy a basic frame-tent for P3000 and a sleeping bag for P1500. Other essentials such as cooking equipment, lanterns and backpacks are also available, and you may be able to rent some items, though the range of gear on offer is limited even in the best shops.

TREKKING AND CLIMBING RESOURCES

Metropolitan Mountaineering Society Ⓦ metropolitanms.org.
Sociable trekking group running expeditions throughout the year. On the easier treks they may well be willing to take you along at short notice, though you might need to take a basic survival course to be allowed on the more challenging expeditions.

Mountaineering Federation of the Philippines Ⓦ mfpi
.wordpress.com. An umbrella group that can offer general information about routes and practicalities.

Pinoy Mountaineer Ⓦ pinoymountaineer.com. This detailed and well-maintained site is a good place to read up about trekking and climbing, with sample itineraries for major climbs and a long list of climbing clubs in the country.

Caving

It's hardly surprising that **caving** – spelunking – is a growth industry, as there are huge caves to explore throughout the country. The largest cave systems are in northern Luzon – in Sagada (see p.172) and in Cagayan province near Tuguegarao, where the Peñablanca Protected Area (see p.156) has three hundred caves, many deep, dangerous and not yet fully explored. The other exciting caving area is the Sohoton Natural Bridge National Park in Samar (see p.356).

Whitewater rafting and zip-lining

Whitewater rafting is becoming more popular in the Philippines, notably along the Cagayan River and Chico River in northern Luzon (see p.178) and Cagayan de Oro River in Mindanao (see p.406). **Zip lines** have mushroomed all over the islands, but some are much tamer than others – some of the best are near Cagayan de Oro (see p.404) and Davao (see box, p.426).

Surfing

Surfing is now well established in the Philippines, with surfers taking advantage of good waves in eastern Bicol (see box, p.206), Catanduanes (see p.233), eastern Mindanao (especially Siargao Island; see p.418), and around San Fernando in La Union (see p.139). There are also any number of hard-to-reach areas in the archipelago that are visited only by a handful of die-hard surfers, such as Baler in northern Luzon (see p.158), or around Borongan (see p.358) in eastern Samar. For general information visit Ⓦ surfingphilippines
.com, Ⓦ cloudninesurf.com and Ⓦ surfingthe philippines.com.

Spectator sports

When it comes to spectator sports, basketball and boxing are among the biggest passions in the Philippines. Pool – or what Filipinos call "billiards" – is also popular, and football (soccer) has been gaining influence, though mostly via watching international leagues on cable TV. Cockfighting is one of the view popular pastimes that harks back to the pre-Hispanic era.

Basketball

The Filipinos embraced **basketball** as they did everything else American, from pizza to popcorn. Every barangay and town has a basketball court, even if all it consists of are a couple of makeshift baskets nailed to wooden poles in the church plaza. The major league – the equivalent of the NBA – is the **Philippine Basketball Association** (PBA; Ⓦ pba.inquirer.net), founded in 1975. Ten teams compete for honours, all of them sponsored by a major corporation and taking their sponsor's name. You might find yourself watching Meralco Bolts play San Mig Super Coffee Mixers, or Barako Bull Energy take on Talk 'N Text Tropang Texters. PBA games are all played in Manila (see box, p.98).

The San Miguel-Petron franchise (under the name Beermen and now Blaze Boosters) is the most successful, while Barangay Ginebra Kings is the most popular. The players are household names to most Filipinos: Jimmy Alapag (with the Talk 'N Text Tropang Texters), Gary David (Meralco Bolts) and Marc Pingris (San Mig Super Coffee Mixers) command huge attention.

Boxing

Boxing has been big business in the Philippines since the Americans introduced the sport in the early twentieth century. In recent years, one name stands out in particular: **Manny "the Pacman" Pacquiao**, the poor boy from Mindanao who became world champion (see box, p.447). Though you are unlikely to see the great man himself, fights are held almost every week, with major venues in Caloocan (Manila), Cebu City, Mandaluyong (Manila), Tagaytay City, Victoria (Negros) and Taytay in the Luzon province of Rizal. Tickets are cheap and often sell out; whenever there's a bout of any significance Filipinos gather around every available television set. You can check schedules for fights at Ⓦ philboxing.com.

COCKFIGHTING AND THE FILIPINO

Cockfighting has a long history in the Philippines. National hero José Rizal, martyred by the Spanish in 1896, once pointed out that the average Filipino loves his rooster more than he does his children.

Contrary to received wisdom, cockfighting was not introduced to the country by the Spanish. When conquistadors landed in Palawan shortly after the death of Magellan, they discovered native men already breeding domestic roosters to fight, putting them in shared cages and letting them scrap over small amounts of food.

Social scientists say cockfighting is popular in the Philippines because it reflects the national passion for brevity or a quick payoff, the trait of **ningas cogon** (*cogon* being a wild grass that burns ferociously and quickly). Part of the appeal is the **prize money**. For a P200 entrance fee, a struggling farmer from the backwoods could finish the day with P300,000 in his pocket, all thanks to a trusty rooster he has groomed and trained assiduously for months.

In addition to Manny Pacquiao, at the time of writing the Philippines could boast two other world champions: Nonito "The Filipino Flash" Donaire and Donnie "Ahas" Nietes.

Pool

Every town and city in the country has some sort of **billiards hall** (for **pool**, not traditional English billiards), even if it's just a few old tables on the pavement where games are played by kerosene lamps between locals for the price of a few San Miguels. The sport has always been popular – it's cheap and reasonably accessible – but has boomed over the past decade because of the success of Efren Reyes and Francisco Bustamante. Reyes, sometimes called "The Magician", is one of the pool world's great characters; a diminutive fellow with a toothy grin, he picked up the nickname "Bata" ("The Kid") while helping out in his uncle's pool halls in Manila as a child. He was born in Pampanga province, to the north of Manila, and can still occasionally be found on a Friday or Saturday night shooting pool in his hometown bars around Clark, good-naturedly scalping unsuspecting tourists' drinks. In 2006, Reyes and Francisco "Django" Bustamante represented their country as Team Philippines and won the inaugural **World Cup of Pool** by defeating Team USA – a victory of major significance for a country with few global sporting heroes. They repeated the feat in 2009, on home turf. Countrymen Dennis Orcollo and Roberto Gomez were runners up (to China) in 2010.

Cockfighting

Cockfighting is the Filipino passion few Westerners get to see – or understand, for obvious reasons. It's a brutal blood sport where fighting cocks literally peck and jab each other to death as onlookers make bets on the outcome. The fight begins when the two roosters are presented to each other in the pit. Both have a razor-sharp curved blade three inches long strapped to their leg. The fight is over in a burst of feathers in no more than a few minutes, when one rooster is too bloodied and wounded, or simply too dead, to peck back at its opponent when provoked. To make the evening last, most major cockfights feature seven contests. Anyone who likes animals should definitely stay well away.

If you do attend a cockfight (*sabong* in Tagalog), you'll be experiencing Filipino culture at its rawest – at the very least it might make you think again about how much "American influence" dominates the culture. It's best to start at one of the major cockpits in Manila (see box, p.98), or ask your hotel for the nearest place to see one. Entrance fees are minimal, but you'll rarely see women attending – the cockpit is the exclusive preserve of men, who see it as an egalitarian refuge from the world's woes, a place where class differences are temporarily put to one side and everyone wears flip-flops and vests. In Manila foreign females should be OK at the main venues, but in the provinces you'll probably feel more comfortable with a male companion.

Culture and etiquette

For many travellers the Philippines seems less immediately "exotic" than other countries in Asia. English is spoken almost everywhere, people wear Western clothes and visit malls and the main religion is Catholicism. Combined with the approachability and sunny

disposition of your average Filipino, this appears to make for a trouble-free assimilation into the ways and values of the Philippines.

However, this can lead to a false sense of security, which over time – as differences begin to surface – gives way to bewilderment and confusion. There are complex rules of engagement that govern behaviour among Filipinos, and failure to be sensitive to them can cast you unwittingly in the role of the ugly foreigner, ranting and raving with frustration at everyone from the bellboy to the bank clerk.

Filipino etiquette

One of the major controlling elements in Filipino society – undetected by most visitors – is **hiya**, a difficult word to define, though essentially it means a sense of shame. *Hiya* is a factor in almost all social situations. It is a sense of *hiya* that prevents someone asking a question, for fear he may look foolish. It is hiya that sees many Filipinos refuse to disagree openly, for fear they may cause offence. Not to have *hiya* is a grave social sin; to be accused of being *walang-hiya* (to be shameless) is the ultimate insult. *Hiya* goes hand in hand with the preservation of **amor-propio** (the term literally means "love of self"), in other words to avoid losing face. If you ever wonder why a Filipino fails to broach awkward subjects with you, or to point out that your flies are undone, it is because *hiya* and *amor-propio* are at work.

If you are ever in doubt about how to behave in the Philippines, bring to mind the value of **pakikisama**, which in rough translation means "to get along". For example, don't confront the waiter or bark insults if he gets your order wrong. This offends his sense of *amor-propio* and marks you out as being an obnoxious *walang-hiya* foreigner. Talk to him quietly and ask that the order be changed. The same

rules apply with government officials, police, ticket agents, hotel receptionists and cashiers. If there's a problem, sort it out quietly and patiently. A sense of **delicadeza** is also important to Filipinos. This might be translated as "propriety", a simple sense of good behaviour, particularly in the presence of elders or ladies.

Yes, no, maybe…

One of the root causes of frustration during social intercourse is the use of the word yes. In their desire to please, many Filipinos find it difficult to say no. So they say yes instead. Yes (actually *oo* in Tagalog, pronounced oh-oh, though most Filipinos would use the English word when talking to foreigners) can mean one of a multitude of things, from a plain and simple "yes" to "I'm not sure", "perhaps", "if you say so", or "sorry, I don't understand". A casual yes is never taken as binding. The concepts of *hiya* and *amor-propio* also filter through to the language in the form of a multitude of euphemisms for the word no (*hindi* in Tagalog). Instead of replying in the negative, in order not to upset you a Filipino will typically say "maybe" (*siguro nga*), "whatever" (*bahala na*) or "if you say so" (*kung sinabi mo ba e*). These subtleties of language are symptomatic of the unseen ebbs and flows of the tides that govern all social behaviour in the Philippines, few foreigners ever fully coming to terms with the eddies and whirls underneath.

Questions and greetings

Filipinos are outgoing people who don't consider it rude to ask personal questions. Prepare to be pleasantly interrogated by everyone you meet. Filipinos will want to know where you are from, why you are in the Philippines, how old you are, whether you are married, if not why not, and so on and so forth. They pride themselves on their hospitality and are always ready to share a meal or a few drinks. Don't offend them by refusing outright.

STREET KIDS

Despite the very real economic progress made in the last twenty years, millions of Filipinos still live in poverty. **Street children** (many orphaned) are one of the saddest consequences of this – some reports estimate around 1.5 million kids are living rough. In Manila and other large cities you'll see very small children begging for money in the street or dancing in front of cars at dangerous interchanges for tips. You'll also come across kids aggressively begging for change; sometimes they are known as "**rugby boys**" – nothing to do with the sport but a famous brand of glue that they sniff. Many locals refuse to give them money for fear of encouraging dangerous behaviour – others give a few pesos out of pity. If you want to help, a good place to start is Street Kids International (Ⓦ streetkids.org), or the Cavite-based Life Child (Ⓦ lifechild.org).

PROSTITUTION AND SEX TOURISM

The Philippines, like some other Southeast Asian countries, has an unfortunate reputation for **prostitution** and **sex tourism**. It's a huge industry domestically with an estimated 800,000 men, women and, sadly, children working in the trade. The country's international image as a sex destination came about largely as a result of the US military presence here during and after World War II, when "go go" or "girlie" bars flourished around the bases at Clark and Subic Bay.

While it's illegal to sell or procure sex, the trade still operates under the guise of entertainment: sex workers are employed as singers, dancers, waitresses or "guest relations officers" in clubs and bars where they are expected to leave with any client who pays a fee (the "bar fine"). Then there's what are euphemistically dubbed "freelancers", prostitutes that independently cruise bars looking for paying customers. In the Philippines it's common (because it's so cheap) to hire these girls for several days or weeks to have what's called a GFE ("girlfriend experience").

According to the Coalition Against Trafficking in Women (ⓦ catwinternational.org), some 15,000 Australian men a year visit Angeles, north of Manila, on sex tours; plenty of Americans, Brits and Europeans join them, while Koreans, Taiwanese and Chinese have developed their own networks, usually based in karaoke bars and restaurants. Manila, Cebu City, Subic Bay and Pasay City are also major sex destinations.

DATING WEBSITES

Though you will often see older Western men accompanied by young, attractive Filipina women all over the Philippines, don't assume these are prostitutes. The situation is confused by the legal and equally popular phenomenon of **online dating websites** that exclusively pair Filipinas with foreigners – plenty of the men you'll see have been matched with their Filipina "girlfriend" and intend to seriously date or even marry them, however dubious this might seem.

CHILD PROSTITUTION

The Philippine government estimates that almost half the sex workers in the country are **underage**, many of them street children lured from the provinces by the promise of work or simply food and water. In recent years "cyberporn" has become a major problem – in 2014 the British-led Operation Endeavor uncovered a global network of paedophiles streaming live child abuse by video from the Philippines. If you suspect someone of being a paedophile or engaging in any abusive behaviour towards minors, call **hotline** ☏ 1-6-3 or visit ⓦ abs-cbnfoundation.com.

In rural areas it's still common for foreign men to be greeted by passers-by with calls of "Hey Joe!" This harks back to the GI Joes of World War II and American occupation.

Filipino time

Why do you never ask a Filipino to do something by the end of the week? He might think you're being pushy. That's an exaggeration of course, but beyond the cities, the old joke still resonates for longtime residents of the Philippines.

In recent years, perhaps due to the number of young Filipinos returning home after an overseas education, the attitude towards punctuality has begun to change. For medical or work-related appointments you'll need to be on time, but for social gatherings turn up half an hour late: it is considered impolite to be on time for a party, for instance, simply because it makes you look like a glutton who wants to grab the food. The speed of service in restaurants in the Philippines has also improved, but you should still expect your patience to occasionally be tested.

Women travellers

Women travellers rarely experience problems in the Philippines, either travelling alone or as part of a group. The culture, however, is a **macho** one and, especially in the provinces, foreign women may experience being stared at or the occasional catcall or lewd comment in Tagalog. In the barangays, Filipino men hold dear the oft-regurgitated image of themselves in local movies as gifted romancers, able to reduce any lady to jelly with a few choice words and the wink of an eye.

Reacting to this attention is the worst thing you can do. If you smile and remain good-natured

VIDEOKE CRAZY

"Videoke" – **video karaoke** – is a major fad in the Philippines, with cheap videoke bars in almost every town and neighbourhood. While it can be fun to participate in a Filipino singing session, being regaled by drunken wailings wafting through your hotel window in the early hours isn't so amusing. Adding to the mix, most Filipino families own one or more karaoke machines that they use throughout the week, and always on special occasions, birthdays and weddings. Incidentally, a Filipino inventor (Roberto del Rosario) actually holds the patent for the karaoke machine.

but distant, your potential suitors will get the message and leave you alone. To shout back or to poke fun, particularly if Romeo is with his friends, will cause him serious loss of face and lead to resentment and the possibility that they will try to get back at you.

Modesty is essential to the behaviour of young Filipinas, especially in the provinces, and this should also be the case with visitors. Shorts and T-shirts are fine for women anywhere (except for immigration offices), but bikinis are only for the beach, and even then it's considered bad form to wander through a resort's restaurant or souvenir shop without covering up first (a sarong is perfect for this). Topless sunbathing is unheard of among Filipinos, and tourists in popular resorts such as Boracay who remove their clothes are likely to attract an amazed, gossiping crowd of locals. For some Filipino men this reinforces the stereotype that foreign women on holiday are game for anything.

Shopping

The Philippines is a great place to buy indigenous art, woodwork, masks and religious artefacts, mostly at rock-bottom prices. Manila also contains a number of shiny malls with stores offering much the same designer gear you can find in London or New York. The country's two main department-store chains are Rustan's and SM. Both are good for clothes and shoes, at slightly lower prices than in Europe; children's clothes are especially inexpensive.

Souvenirs

Typical souvenirs include **models of jeepneys**, wooden **salad bowls**, cotton **linen** and small items such as **fridge magnets** made of coconut shell or carabao horn. In department stores you can find **cutlery sets** made from carabao horn and bamboo and costing less than P2000. **Woven placemats** and coasters are inexpensive and easy to pack to take home. Filipino **picture frames** are eye-catching and affordable. Made from raw materials such as carabao horn and Manila hemp, they are available in most department stores. All towns have markets that sell cheap local goods such as **sleeping mats** (*banig*) that make colourful wall hangings, and earthenware water jars or **cooking pots** that make attractive additions to a kitchen.

For serious souvenir-hunting, you'll have to rummage around in small **antique shops**. There aren't many of these, and they're often tucked away in low-rent areas. The better shops in big cities are listed in the Guide; elsewhere, ask around at your hotel. Many of the items in these shops are religious artefacts (see below), although you'll also find furniture, decorative vases, lamps, old paintings, mirrors and brassware.

Some souvenir stores and antique shops will ship goods home for you for an extra charge. Otherwise you could send bulky items home by regular post (see p.51). Note that the trade in coral and seashells as souvenirs in beach areas is decidedly unsound environmentally, as is the manufacture of decorative objects and jewellery from seashells.

Tribal and religious artefacts

Not all tribal and religious artefacts are genuine, but even the imitations make good gifts. **Woven baskets and trays** of the kind used by Cordillera tribes are a bargain, starting from only a few hundred pesos. They come in a range of sizes and shapes, including circular trays woven from grass that are still used to sift rice, and baskets worn like a backpack for carrying provisions. The best are the original tribal baskets, which cost a little more than the reproductions, but have an appealing nut-brown tone as a result of the many times they have been oiled. You can find them in antique shops around the country and also in markets in Banaue and Sagada.

Some exceptional home accessories and ornaments are produced by tribes in Mindanao, particularly in less touristy areas such as Marawi City and around Lake Sebu. Beautiful **brass jars**, some of them more than a metre tall, cost around P2000, while exquisite **wooden chests** inlaid with

BARGAINING

Prices are fixed in department stores and most retail outlets in malls, but in many antique shops and in markets, you're expected to **haggle**. Bargaining is always amicable and relaxed, never confrontational. Filipinos see it as something of a polite game, interjecting their offers and counter offers with friendly chitchat about the weather, the state of the nation or, if you're a foreigner, where you come from and what you're doing in the Philippines.

Never play hardball and make a brusque "take it or leave it" offer because that's likely to cause embarrassment and offence. Start by offering **fifty to sixty percent** of the initial asking price and work your way up from there. Foreigners tend to get less of a discount than Filipinos, so if you're travelling with Filipino friends, ask them to do the haggling for you and hover in the background as if you're not interested.

mother-of-pearl cost around P3000, and inlaid serving trays P500.

Rice gods (*bulol*; see p.98), carved wooden deities sometimes with nightmarish facial expressions, are available largely in Manila and the Cordilleras. In Manila, they cost anything from a few hundred pesos for a small reproduction to P20,000 for a genuine figurine of modest size; they're much cheaper if you haggle for them in Banaue or Sagada. At markets in the Cordilleras, look out also for **wooden bowls**, various wooden wall carvings and fabric **wall hangings**.

The best place to look for Catholic **religious art** is in Manila (see p.98), though antique shops in other towns also have a selection. Wooden Catholic statues called santos and large wooden crucifixes are common. Cheaper religious souvenirs such as rosaries and icons of saints are sold by street vendors outside many of the more high-profile pilgrimage cathedrals and churches such as Quiapo in Manila and Santo Niño in Cebu.

Textiles

In market areas such as Divisoria in Manila, Colon in Cebu and the Palitan barter centre in Marawi, Mindanao, you can find colourful raw cloth and finished **batik products**. Don't leave Mindanao without investing a couple of hundred pesos in a **malong**, a versatile tube-like garment of **piña** (pineapple fibre) that can be used as a skirt, housedress, blanket or bedsheet. Ceremonial *malong* are more ornate and expensive, from P4000 to P10,000. Another native textile is **Manila hemp**, which comes from the trunk of a particular type of banana tree. Both *piña* and Manila hemp are used to make attractive home accessories sold in department stores, such as laundry baskets, lampshades and vases. The versatile and pliable native grass, **sikat**, is woven into everything from placemats to rugs.

Department stores everywhere have a good selection of Philippine **linen products** with delicate embroidery and lace flourishes. Some of these are handmade in Taal (see p.116); a good set of pillowcases and bedsheets will cost about P2000 in Taal's market, half the price in Rustan's or SM. In beach areas you'll find a good range of cotton sarongs, cheap (from P200), colourful and versatile – they can be used as tablecloths or throws.

SARI-SARI STORES

A Philippine institution, the humble **sari-sari** store – *sari-sari* means "various" or "a variety" – is often no more than a barangay shack or a hole in the wall selling an eclectic but practical range of goods. If you're short of shampoo, body lotion, cigarettes, rum, beer or you've got a headache and need a painkiller, the local sari-sari store is the answer, especially in areas without supermarkets. All items are sold in the smallest quantities possible: shampoo comes in packets half the size of a credit card, medicine can be bought by the pill and cigarettes are sold individually. Buy a soft drink or beer and you may be perplexed to see the store holder pour it into a plastic bag, from which you're expected to drink it through a straw. This is so they can keep the bottle and return it for the deposit of a few centavos. Most sari-sari stores are fiercely **familial**, their names – the Three Sisters, the Four Brothers or Emily and Jon-Jon's – reflecting their ownership.

The sari-sari store is also held dear by Filipinos as an unofficial community centre. Many sari-sari stores, especially in the provinces, have crude sitting areas outside, encouraging folk to linger in the shade and gossip or talk basketball and cockfighting.

Jewellery

The malls are full of stalls selling cheap jewellery, but you'll also find silver-plated earrings, replica tribal-style jewellery made with tin or brass, and attractive necklaces made from bone or polished coconut shell. In Mindanao – as well as in some malls in Manila, Cebu City and at souvenir stalls in Boracay – **pearl jewellery** is a bargain. Most of the pearls are cultivated on pearl farms in Mindanao and Palawan. White pearls are the most common, but you can also find pink and dove grey. They are made into earrings, necklaces and bracelets; simple earrings cost around P500, while a necklace can range from P1000 for a single string up to P10,000 for something more elaborate.

Musical instruments

In Cebu, and increasingly on the streets of Manila and Davao, you can pick up a locally made handcrafted guitar, *bandurria* (mandolin) or ukelele. Though the acoustic quality is nothing special, the finish may include mother-of-pearl inlays, and prices are low – a steel-string acoustic guitar will set you back P2000. Mindanao's markets – such as Aldevinco in Davao – are a good place to rummage for decorative drums and Muslim gongs.

Travel essentials

Addresses

In the Philippines it is common to give an address as, for example, 122 Legaspi corner Velasco Streets, meaning the junction of Legaspi and Velasco streets (in the Guide this is written "122 Legaspi St at Velasco St"). G/F denotes street level, after which come 2/F, 3/F and so on; "first floor" or 1/F isn't used. Some addresses include the name of a **barangay**, which is officially an electoral division for local elections, but is generally used to mean a village or, when mentioned in connection with a town, a neighbourhood or suburb. The word barangay isn't always written out in the address, although it's sometimes included in official correspondence and signposts, often abbreviated to "Brgy" or "Bgy". The term "**National Highway**" in an address doesn't necessarily refer to a vast motorway – on the smaller islands or in provincial areas, it could mean the coastal road or the main street in town. When it comes to **islands**, Filipinos generally talk loosely in terms of the main island in the vicinity – so, for example, they would talk about visiting Panay when they actually mean offshore Pan de Azucar. We've adopted a similar approach in parts of the Guide, implicitly including small islands in coverage of the nearest large island.

Costs

While upmarket resorts in the Philippines can be as expensive as anywhere else in the world, for anyone with modest spending habits and tastes the country is inexpensive. Outside of Metro Manila you can get by on a frugal **budget** of around P1000 per person (£13.50/US$22/€16) a day, but you might need to avoid the most popular tourist destinations such as Boracay (or visit during the off-season), and you'll be limited to bare-bones cottages and pokey rooms in basic hotels, usually without air conditioning or hot water. On this budget you'd also have to confine your meals to local restaurants and carinderias, with little leeway for slap-up feasts in nice restaurants. You'd also have to plan any flights carefully, only buying the very cheapest tickets online or limiting yourself to buses and ferries.

A budget of P2000 (£27/US$44/€32) a day will take your standard of living up a few notches, allowing you to find reasonable beach cottage and hotel rooms and have enough left for modest eating out, drinking and budget flights. On P3800 (£51/US$84/€62) a day, you can afford to stay in solid, reasonably spacious cottages on the beach, usually with a veranda and air conditioning, and have plenty left over for domestic flights and good meals in local restaurants.

Crime and personal safety

The Philippines has a reputation as a somewhat dangerous place to travel (at least in the US and UK), but if you exercise discretion and common sense this really isn't the case. Politically the Philippines is a volatile place, with secessionist movements present in Mindanao (see box, p.403) and communist guerrillas active in a number of areas. **Insurgency** rarely has an impact on tourists, but you should avoid trouble spots. Updated travel advisories are available on foreign office or state department websites including Ⓦ state.gov in the US and Ⓦ fco.gov.uk in the UK.

There are occasional reports of **thieves** holding up vehicles at traffic lights and removing mobiles and cash from passengers. If you're in a taxi, keep the windows closed and the doors locked, just to be safe. In the Malate area of Manila and Angeles City, the so-called **Ativan Gang** has used the drug Lorazepam (Ativan is one of its proprietary names) to make their victims drowsy or put them to sleep – it's

THE TYPHOON THREAT

Typhoons regularly rip across the Philippines – typically between July and November – and as **Typhoon Yolanda** (known internationally as Haiyan) proved in 2013, the effects can be catastrophic and deadly. Though you should always take typhoon warnings seriously (and check weather reports during typhoon season), there's no need to be unduly paranoid for your own safety: the sad truth is that in the Philippines it's mainly poor neighbourhoods that bear the brunt of storms. Most modern hotels and buildings are built to withstand fierce typhoons, and you'll usually be given plenty of notice if a typhoon is heading your way – if it's a big one, go somewhere else and make sure you're nowhere near a ferry or boat when it hits. Though strong winds can be dangerous, flooding, ocean storm surges and landslides are the main cause of most damage and fatalities – if you are not in areas usually affected by any of these you should be fine. Note also that the aftermath of storms can dramatically affect transportation and the services in smaller villages and towns, though Filipinos are a resilient bunch and tourist services are often up and running remarkably quickly after a storm.

For **weather warnings** visit ⓦpagasa.dost.gov.ph or ⓦweather.com.ph. If you want to volunteer or help in the aftermath of a typhoon, approach official charities such as Care (ⓦcare .org), Save The Children (ⓦsavethechildren.org) and the Philippine Red Cross (ⓦredcross.org.ph).

best to be on your guard in these areas if you're approached by people who seem unusually keen to offer you assistance, especially in bars.

Drug laws in the Philippines are stringent and the police are enthusiastic about catching offenders. No one, foreigner or otherwise, caught in possession of hard or recreational drugs is likely to get much sympathy from the authorities. Carrying 500 grams or more of marijuana is deemed to be trafficking and carries the death penalty, while a lesser amount will usually result in a prison sentence.

The 24-hour **emergency number** throughout the Philippines is ☎0117.

Customs

Visitors are allowed to bring in four hundred cigarettes (or fifty cigars or 250g of pipe tobacco) and two bottles of wine and spirits not exceeding one litre each. If you arrive with more than US$10,000 in cash (unlikely) you are meant to declare it, and you won't be allowed to take out more than this sum in foreign currency on leaving. Note that not more than P10,000 in local currency may be taken out of the country, though this is rarely, if ever, enforced.

Electricity

Wall sockets in the Philippines usually operate at 220 volts (similar to Australia, Europe and most of Asia), although you may come across 110 volts in some rural areas – it's best to ask before plugging in appliances. Most mobile phones, cameras, MP3 players and laptops are dual voltage (older hair-dryers are

the biggest problem for North American travellers). **Plugs** have two flat, rectangular pins, as the US and Canada. **Power cuts** (known locally as "brownouts") are common, especially in the provinces. If you are worried about using valuable electrical equipment in the Philippines – a laptop computer, for instance – you should plug it into an automatic voltage regulator (AVR), a small appliance that ensures the voltage remains constant even if there is a sudden fluctuation or surge in the mains.

Entry requirements

Most foreign nationals do not need a visa to stay in the Philippines for up to **thirty days**, though a passport valid for at least six months and an onward plane or ship ticket to another country are required.

Your thirty days can be extended by 29 days (giving a total stay of **59 days**) at **immigration offices** in Manila or around the country (see relevant chapters). The charge for this is around P3030, and you may be asked if you want to pay a P500 "express fee" that is supposed to guarantee the application is dealt with within 24 hours. If you don't pay the fee, the process can take at least a week. Note that it pays to be presentably dressed at immigration offices, as staff might refuse to serve you if you turn up wearing a vest, shorts or flip-flops.

Many travel agents in tourist areas such as Malate in Manila and Boracay offer a **visa extension service**, saving you the hassle of visiting immigration centres. Whatever you do, don't be tempted to use one of the fixers that hang around immigration offices, particularly in Manila. The "visa" they get you is often a dud and you run the risk of being detained and fined when you try to leave the country.

If you **overstay** your initial thirty days (but have not stayed beyond 59 days) you'll be fined at least P500; overstay longer and you'll be sent to the nearest office of the Bureau of Immigration for a whole lot of trouble.

Temporary Visitor's Visa

If you know you want to spend longer than thirty days in the Philippines, apply for a 59-day **Temporary Visitor's Visa** at a Philippine embassy or consulate before you travel. A single-entry visa (with which you must enter the Philippines within three months of the issue date) costs £22/€27/US$30/Can$34.50/Aus$54/NZ$42/ZAR270, while a multiple-entry visa, valid for one year from the date of issue (but with stays of a maximum 59 days within that year), is £65/€81/US$90/Can$103.50/Aus$162/NZ$126/ZAR810. A six-month multiple-entry visa is £43/€54/US$60/Can$69/Aus$108/NZ$84/ZAR540. Apart from a valid passport and a completed application form (downloadable from some Philippine embassy websites), you will have to present proof that you have enough money for the duration of your stay in the Philippines.

Longer stays

Regardless of how you entered the Philippines, to stay longer than 59 days you must apply for **visa extensions** at immigration bureaus every two months (fees range from P2830 to P4830). At the time of writing the government was considering the introduction of a **Long Stay Visitor Visa Extension** (LSVVE) programme, which would allow visitors to extend stays for six months after their first thirty days in one go; check government websites for the latest.

Note that if you have been in the Philippines continuously for six months, you must have an **Emigration Clearance Certificate** (P710) to pass through immigration at the airport. After six months you must also apply for an **ACR-I card** or "Alien Certificate of Registration" for P2800, and after sixteen months you need approval from the Chief of the Immigration Regulation Division. When you have been in the Philippines for **two years** you really will have to leave.

PHILIPPINE EMBASSIES AND CONSULATES ABROAD

For a full list of the Philippines' embassies and consulates, check the government's Department of Foreign Affairs website at Ⓦ www.dfa.gov.ph.

Australia Canberra ☎ 612 6273 2535, Ⓦ philembassy.org.au; Sydney ☎ 02 9262 7377; Melbourne ☎ 03 9863 7885; Perth ☎ 08 9481 5666. Consulates also in Adelaide, Brisbane, Darwin and Hobart.
Canada Ottawa ☎ 613 233 1121, Ⓦ philippineembassy.ca; Toronto ☎ 416 922 7181, Ⓦ philcongen-toronto.com.
Ireland Dublin ☎ 01 437 6206, Ⓦ philippineconsulate.ie.
New Zealand Wellington ☎ 644 472 9848, Ⓦ philembassy.org.nz.
South Africa Pretoria ☎ 012 346 0451, Ⓦ pretoriape.org.
UK London ☎ 020 7451 1800, Ⓦ philembassy-uk.org.
US Washington DC ☎ 202 467 9300, Ⓦ philippineembassy-usa .org; San Francisco ☎ 415 433 6666, Ⓦ philippinessanfrancisco .org; Los Angeles ☎ 213 639 0980, Ⓦ philippineslosangeles.org; New York ☎ 212 764 1330, Ⓦ philippinesnewyork.org; Chicago ☎ 312 583 0621, Ⓦ philippineschicago.com. Consulates also in Atlanta, Honolulu, Miami and Portland, OR.

Gay and lesbian travellers

Few Filipinos, even the most pious, pay much heed to the Catholic Church regarding homosexuality, and the prevailing attitude is that people can carry on doing what's right for them. **Gay culture** in the Philippines is strong and largely unimpeded by narrow-mindedness, with the possible exceptions within politics and the military, where hetero-sexuality is still considered correct. Gays are respected as arbiters of fashion and art, and beauty parlours are often staffed by transsexuals.

The word **bakla** is used generically by many Filipinos and visitors to the Philippines to refer to gays, but that would be inaccurate. A *bakla* considers himself a male with a female heart – a *pusong babae*. Most are not interested in a sex-change operation and consider themselves a "third sex", cross-dressing and becoming more "female" than many women. Another category of male homosexual is known as **tunay ne lalake**, men who identify themselves publicly as hetero-sexual but have sex with other men. Homosexuals who aren't out permeate every stratum of Philippine society; rumours circulate almost daily of this-or-that tycoon or politician who is *tunay ne lalake*.

Lesbians are much more reticent about outing themselves than gay men, no doubt because there is still societal pressure for young women to become the quintessential Filipina lady – gracious, alluring and fulfilled by motherhood and the home (see p.45). Indeed, some Filipina lesbians complain that the more outspoken **tomboys** – lesbians are often referred to as tomboys – make the fight for women's rights even harder.

The **gay scene** is centred on the bars and clubs of Malate in Manila (see box, p.94), though there are

ROUGH GUIDES TRAVEL INSURANCE

Rough Guides has teamed up with **WorldNomads.com** to offer great travel insurance deals. Policies are available to residents of over 150 countries, with cover for a wide range of adventure sports, 24hr emergency assistance, high levels of medical and evacuation cover and a stream of travel safety information. Roughguides.com users can take advantage of their policies online 24/7, from anywhere in the world – even if you're already travelling. And since plans often change when you're on the road, you can extend your policy and even claim online. Roughguides.com users who buy travel insurance with WorldNomads.com can also leave a positive footprint and donate to a community development project. For more information, go to ⓦroughguides.com/travel-insurance.

also smaller scenes in other major cities such as Cebu, Davao and Cagayan de Oro. The websites ⓦutopia-asia.com and ⓦfridae.asia are useful sources of info on local gay life.

Insurance

A typical travel **insurance** policy usually provides cover for the loss of baggage, tickets and cash, as well as cancellation or curtailment of your journey. When securing baggage cover, make sure that the per-article limit will cover your most valuable possession. Most policies exclude so-called dangerous sports unless an extra premium is paid: in the Philippines this can mean scuba diving, whitewater rafting, windsurfing, trekking and kayaking.

If you need to make a claim, you should keep receipts for medicines and medical treatment, and in the event you have anything stolen, you must obtain an official statement from the police. In the Philippines this is sometimes a slow process that involves the police officer copying, by hand, the details of your loss into what is known as the police "blotter", or file. Once this has been signed by a superior officer you'll get an authorized copy.

Internet

Major cities have dozens of **internet cafés** and even in small towns and isolated resort areas you can usually find somewhere to log on and send email. The cost of getting online at an internet café starts at around P40–60 per hour in the cities, while in the provinces it can be as cheap as P15–20 per hour. **Wi-fi** is more and more common in cafés and hotels throughout the country. Hotels reviewed in the Guide will normally offer free wi-fi unless stated otherwise.

Laundry

There are no coin-operated **launderettes** in the Philippines, but there are laundries all over the place offering serviced washes for about P120–150 for an average load (ranging between P20 and P60/kg). Most of these places will iron clothes for you for an extra charge. It's also possible to get clothes washed at pretty much any guesthouse, resort or hotel.

Living and working in the Philippines

Opportunities to **work** in the Philippines are limited. Most jobs require specialist qualifications or experience and, unlike other parts of Asia, there's no market for teaching English as a foreign language. One possibility is to work for a diving outfit as a dive master or instructor. Rates of pay are low, but board and lodging may be provided if you work for a good operator or resort in a busy area (Boracay or Puerto Galera, for instance). Some international organizations also offer **voluntary placements** in the Philippines.

VOLUNTEERING ORGANIZATIONS

Australian Volunteers International Australia ☎03 9279 1788, ⓦaustralianvolunteers.com. Short- and long-term postings for professionals interested in working in the developing world. Volunteers in the Philippines have helped introduce sustainable fishing and marine conservation programmes and campaigned for the rights of minority groups.

Coral Cay Conservation UK ☎020 8545 7710, ⓦcoralcay.org. Nonprofit organization that trains volunteers to collect scientific data to aid conservation in sensitive environments around the world, particularly coral reefs and tropical forests. At the time of writing marine expeditions were offered in southern Leyte.

Peace Corps US ☎1 800 424 8580, ⓦpeacecorps.gov. Places people with specialist qualifications or skills in two-year postings in many developing countries, including the Philippines.

VSO (Voluntary Service Overseas) UK ☎020 8780 7200, ⓦvso.org.uk. Charity that sends qualified professionals to work on projects beneficial to developing countries. In the Philippines, VSO has a small number of volunteers working within the fields of sustainable agriculture and aquaculture, or with displaced communities in Mindanao.

Mail

Airmail **letters** from the Philippines (W philpost.gov
.ph) take at least five days to reach other countries,
though in many cases it's a lot longer. International
postcards cost P13 while letters up to 20 grams cost
P24–45 depending on the destination. Ordinary
domestic mail costs P9–12 for letters up to 20
grams. **Post offices** are open from 9am to 5pm,
Monday to Friday.

If you have to post anything valuable, use registered
mail or pay extra for a **courier**. DHL (W dhl.com.ph),
Fedex (W fedex.com/ph) and the locally based LBC
(W lbcexpress.com) and 2Go (W 2go.com.ph) have
offices throughout the country (listed on their
websites), and can deliver stuff internationally.
Sending documents overseas this way will cost from
around P1325–1500 (to the US and Australia) to P2400
(to the UK) and takes two to three working days.

Maps

If you want to seek out Philippines maps at home,
you'll probably only find street maps of Manila and
Cebu City, in addition to country maps. **Nelles Verlag**
(W nelles-verlag.de) publishes two good maps – a
country map with a scale of 1:1,500,000 and a Manila
city map. They are sometimes available in Manila
bookshops, but can be hard to track down. The
1:1,750,000 **Hema** map (W hemamaps.com.au) of the
Philippines is another to look out for before you arrive.

Road maps and country maps can be bought
at branches of the National Book Store in all major
cities and towns, although supply is unreliable. Many
bookshops sell the **Accu-map** range of atlases
(W www.accu-map.com), A–Z-like pocketbooks that
cover the whole of Metro Manila and detailed maps
of Baguio, Subic Bay, Cavite, Angeles City, Puerto
Galera, Boracay and other destinations. United Tourist
Promotions publishes a range of decent maps called
EZ Maps (W ezmaps.ph), covering Manila and the
country's regions, with each sheet featuring a combination of area and town maps.

The best map offered by the **Philippine Department of Tourism (DoT)** locally is the free Tourist
Map of the Philippines, which includes a street
map of Manila, contact numbers for all overseas
and domestic DoT offices and listings of hotels,
embassies and bus companies.

For a more varied selection of area maps and sea
charts of the Philippines, try the **National Mapping
and Resources Information Authority** (T 02 810
5466, W namria.gov.ph) in Lawton Avenue, Fort
Bonifacio, ten minutes by taxi from Makati.

EXCHANGE RATES

At the time of writing the **exchange rate**
was around P45 to US$1, P75 to £1 and
P61 to the €1. Rates have remained
relatively stable over the last ten years.

Money

The Philippine currency is the **peso**. One peso is
divided into 100 centavos, with notes in denomina-
tions of P20, 50, 100, 200, 500 and 1000. Coins come
in values of 25 centavos, P1, P5 and P10.

It's best to arrive with some local currency,
though you can easily withdraw cash at **ATMs**.
These are found in cities and tourist destinations
all over the country, but not in less visited areas
such as the interior of Mindanao, the northern
mountains, parts of Palawan (outside Puerto
Princesa and Coron Town), and in remote areas of
the Visayas. It's best to use ATMs at major banks, and
preferably in big cities, because these machines
tend to be more reliable than provincial ones,
which are often "offline" – because there's no cash
in them, the computer has crashed or a power cut
has affected their operation. **Credit cards** are
accepted by most hotels and restaurants in cities
and tourist areas, though the smaller hotels may
levy a surcharge if you pay by card.

Banks are normally open from 9am to 3pm,
Monday to Friday, and all major branches have ATMs
and currency exchange. The best-established local
banks include BPI (Bank of the Philippine Islands),
DBP (Development Bank of the Philippines), Metrobank and BDO (aka Banco de Oro); Citibank and
HSBC also have branches in major cities. Most banks
only change US dollars, and though many hotels will
change other currencies, they offer poor rates. It's
easy to change dollars in Manila, where there are
dozens of small **moneychangers' kiosks** in Malate
and P. Burgos Street, Makati, offering better rates
than the banks; ask around at a few places and
compare. In rural areas there are few moneychangers
and banks don't always change money, so if you're
heading off the beaten track, be sure to take enough
pesos to last the trip.

Opening hours and public
holidays

Most **government offices** are open Monday to
Friday from 8.30am to 5.30pm, but some close
for an hour-long lunch break, usually starting at
noon, so it's best to avoid the middle of the day.

PUBLIC HOLIDAYS

January 1 New Year's Day
February 25 Anniversary of the EDSA Revolution
March/April (variable) Maundy Thursday, Good Friday
April 9 Bataan Day
May 1 Labor Day
June 12 Independence Day
June/July (19 July in 2015, 8 July in 2016 and 27 June in 2017) Eid ul Fitr, the end of Ramadan
August 21 Ninoy Aquino Day
Last Monday in August National Heroes' Day
November 1 All Saints' Day (see box, p.37)
December 25 Christmas Day; the following day is also a holiday
December 30 Rizal Day, in honour of José Rizal (see p.439)

Businesses generally keep the same hours, with some also open on Saturday from 9am until noon. **Banks** are open Monday to Friday from 9am to 3pm and do not close for lunch, except for some of the smallest branches in rural areas. **Shops** in major malls open daily from 10am until 8pm or 9pm, later during the Christmas rush or "Midnight Madness" sales; the latter take place every two weeks on the first Friday after each payday. **Churches** are almost always open most of the day for worshippers and tourists alike. Typically, the first Mass of the day is at around 6am, the last at 6pm or 7pm.

Government offices and private businesses close on **public holidays**, though shops and most restaurants remain open except on Good Friday and Christmas Day. Holidays are often moved to the closest Friday or Monday to their original date (see box opposite), so that people in the cities can use the long weekend to get back to the provinces to spend a few days with their families. This moving of public holidays is done on an ad hoc basis and is announced in the press just a few weeks – sometimes only a few days – beforehand.

Phones

If you want to use a **mobile phone** bought abroad in the Philippines, it will need to be GSM/Triband and to have global roaming activated. For local calls it will probably work out cheaper to buy a local **SIM card**, available at dozens of mobile-phone outlets in malls and convenience stores, for any of the country's four major mobile **networks**: Smart Communications, the best bet for iPhones (Ⓦsmart .com.ph), Globe Telecom (Ⓦglobe.com.ph), Talk 'N Text (Ⓦtalkntext.com.ph) and Sun Cellular (Ⓦsun cellular.com.ph). Local SIMs start at just P40 (Globe and Smart) and you can top up your credit for P100 to P500. Note that your phone must be "unlocked" to use a foreign SIM card (this can usually be done at local electronics shops, for a fee). **Rates** depend on which prepaid package you opt for – most come with unlimited domestic calls and texts to a certain limit. International call charges start at US$0.40 per minute, rising by US$0.04 every six seconds.

Basic mobiles in the Philippines are inexpensive, starting at less than P3000, so it can be worth buying one if you plan to stay for any length of time. Unless you have a permanent address in the country for home billing, you'll be funding your calls with prepaid cards.

USEFUL NUMBERS AND CODES

☎**117** Emergencies
☎**108** International operator
☎**109** Assistance with long-distance domestic calls

☎**114** or ☎**187** Nationwide directory assistance

CALLING ABROAD FROM THE PHILIPPINES

Dial ☎00, then the relevant country code, area or city code and then the number. Note that the initial zero is omitted from the area code when dialling to the UK, Ireland, Australia and New Zealand from abroad.

Australia 61
New Zealand 64
Republic of Ireland 353

South Africa 27
UK 44
USA and Canada 1

CALLING THE PHILIPPINES FROM ABROAD

Dial your international access code, then **63** for the Philippines, then the number.

Time

The Philippines is eight hours ahead of Universal Time (GMT) all year round.

Tipping

Keep your purse or wallet well stocked with P10 coins and P20 notes for tips. In cafés, bars and hotel coffee shops many Filipinos simply leave whatever coins they get in their change. For good service in restaurants you should leave a tip of about ten percent. In more expensive restaurants where the bill could be a couple of thousand pesos, it's okay to leave a somewhat smaller tip in percentage terms – P100 is a reasonable amount. Bellhops and porters get about P20 each and taxi drivers usually expect to keep the loose change.

Tourist information

The **Philippine Department of Tourism** (DoT; Ⓦ wowphilippines.com.ph) has a small number of overseas offices where you can pick up glossy brochures and get answers to general pre-trip questions about destinations, major hotels and domestic travel. These offices are not so helpful, however, when it comes to information about places off the beaten track. The DoT has offices throughout the Philippines, but most of them have small budgets and very little in the way of reliable information or brochures. The best source of up-to-date information on travelling in the Philippines is guesthouses and hotels that cater to travellers, most of which have notice boards where you can swap tips and ideas.

Travelling with children

Filipinos are extravagant in their generosity towards children, but because so much of the country lacks infrastructure, specific attractions for them are often hard to find. Major hotels in big cities such as Manila and Cebu City have playrooms and babysitting services, but even in popular tourist destinations such as Boracay there are few special provisions in all but the most expensive resorts.

This doesn't mean travelling with children in the Philippines is a nightmare – far from it. Filipinos are very tolerant of children so you can take them almost anywhere without restriction, and children help to break the ice with strangers. They'll be fussed over, befriended and looked after every step of the way.

Supermarkets in towns and cities throughout the Philippines have well-stocked children's sections that sell fresh and formula milk, nappies and baby food. **Department stores** such as Rustan's and SM sell baby clothes, bottles, sterilizing equipment and toys. And travelling with children in the Philippines needn't be a burden on your budget. Domestic **airlines** give a discount of around fifty percent for children under twelve and hotels and resorts offer **family rooms**, extra beds for a minimal charge, or don't charge at all for a small child sharing the parents' bed. Most **restaurants** with buffet spreads will let a small child eat for free if he or she is simply taking nibbles from a parent's plate. Try asking for a special portion – the staff are usually happy to oblige.

One potential problem for young ones is the **climate**. You'll need to go to extra lengths to protect them from the sun and to make sure they are hydrated. A hat and good sunblock are essential. As for **medical attention** in the Philippines, there are good paediatricians at most major hospitals, in five-star hotels and many resorts.

Travellers with disabilities

Facilities for the disabled are rare except in the major cities. Taxis are cramped, while bangkas are notoriously tricky even for the able-bodied. For wheelchair users the pavements represent a serious obstacle in themselves. Often dilapidated and potholed, they are frustrating at the best of times and simply impassable at the worst, when pedestrians are forced to pick their way along the gutter in the road, dodging cars and motorcycles.

In Manila, Cebu City, Davao and some other big cities, the most upmarket hotels cater to the disabled and so do malls, cinemas and restaurants. Elsewhere, the good news for disabled travellers is that Filipinos are generous when it comes to offering assistance. Even in the remotest barangay, people will go out of their way to help you board a boat or lift you up the stairs of a rickety pier. Of course once you're on board a ferry, for example, ramps and disabled toilets are likely to be nonexistent.

The government-run **National Council on Disability Affairs** or NCDA (Ⓣ 02 951 6033, Ⓦ ncda .gov.ph) is mandated to formulate policies and coordinate the activities of all agencies concerning disability issues, but it doesn't have much practical advice for disabled travellers. Staff at the group's Quezon City office can give general pointers on transport and where to stay. More useful are **local websites** such as Handi Divers (Ⓦ handidivers.com /en) of Alona Beach (Panglao Island, Bohol), which specializes in scuba diving for disabled travellers.

Manila

MAKATI

1

Manila

If you like big cities you'll love Manila: it's a high-speed, frenetic place, where you can eat, drink and shop 24 hours a day and where the Filipino heritage of native, Spanish, Chinese and American cultures is at its most mixed up. Like many capital cities, Manila bears little resemblance to the rest of the country – something to remember if this is your first taste of the Philippines. With twelve million residents, much of it is chronically overcrowded, polluted and suffers from appalling traffic jams, yet in between the chaos lie tranquil gate-guarded "subdivisions" that resemble affluent parts of the US. There's extreme poverty here, with young children cleaning car windows, dancing or just begging for food at every interchange, while in enormous shopping malls thousands of wealthy, middle-class Manileños are as fashionable and hooked up with iPhones as any of their contemporaries in London or New York.

Technically sixteen cities and one municipality make up what is officially known as **Metro Manila**, covering a vast 636 square kilometres. Travelling around the city takes some effort; its reputation as an intimidating place stems mainly from its size, apparent disorder and dispiriting levels of pollution, exacerbated by the equally fierce heat and humidity. To see the sights you will have to sweat it out in traffic and be prepared for delays, but the good news is that the main attractions are essentially confined to Manila proper, comprising the old walled city of **Intramuros**, **Binondo** – Manila's Chinatown – north of the Pasig River, and the museums and parks grouped along the crescent sweep of **Manila Bay** and Roxas Boulevard. **Makati** and **Ortigas** to the east are glossy business districts best known for their malls and restaurants, though the **Ayala Museum** in Makati should not be missed. **Quezon City** on the city's northern edge is a little out of the way for most visitors, but it does boast some lively nightlife, most of it fuelled by students from the nearby **University of the Philippines**. Indeed, Manila prides itself on the quality of its restaurant, bar and club scene and the ability of its residents to whip up a good time – for many tourists, this will be their enduring memory of the place. The city is also a great place to pick up bargains, from the latest goods cranked out by Chinese factories to intricate native handicrafts.

Brief history
Malay settlements along the Pasig River delta go back at least one thousand years, with the **Kingdom of Tondo** most prominent, benefiting from a profitable trade with Ming-era China. After coming under the sway of the Sultanate of Brunei in the fifteenth century the area was converted to Islam.

FORT SANTIAGO, INTRAMUROS

Highlights

❶ Intramuros The atmospheric old Spanish city, with cobbled streets, the elegant San Agustin Church and poignant Rizal Shrine inside Fort Santiago. **See p.62**

❷ The national museums Two neighbouring museums housing the paintings of Filipino masters, relics from sunken ships and fascinating anthropology displays. **See p.66 & p.67**

❸ Manila Hotel The grand old dame of Philippine hotels. Even if you're not staying here, come to enjoy a drink in the sparkling *Lobby Lounge*. **See p.67, p.86 & p.94**

❹ Ayala Museum One of the best museums in the Philippines, an enlightening and

innovative introduction to the history of the islands. **See p.76**

❺ Barbecue chicken at Aristocrat Manila's most famous restaurant still knocks out the best barbecue, along with a full roster of Filipino favourites. **See p.89**

❻ Night out in Makati From megaclubs to pubs, there's a good night out to suit everyone in Makati. **See p.94**

❼ Manila markets Whether you're looking for native crafts or pearl jewellery, Manila's vibrant and chaotic street markets offer the best bargains. **See p.100**

HIGHLIGHTS ARE MARKED ON THE MAP ON PP.60–61

1

Spanish Manila

The village of **Maynila** fell under **Spanish rule** in 1571 when Miguel López de Legazpi defeated the local ruler Rajah Sulaiman II and established the colony of Manila. Spanish Augustinian and Franciscan **missionaries** subsequently established themselves in villages around the city. The Jesuits arrived in 1581 and set up more missions, forming outlying centres of population – embryonic settlements that became the sixteen cities of today. Manila's central location on the biggest island, Luzon, made it the obvious choice as the **colonial capital**, and it became the hub from which the Spaniards effected the political, cultural and religious transformation of Philippine society. From 1571 until 1815 (when it was ended by the Mexican War of Independence), Manila prospered from the **galleon trade** while the rest of the country remained economically stagnant. At 7pm on June 3, 1863, a catastrophic **earthquake** struck and large areas of the city crumbled, burying hundreds in the ruins. The new

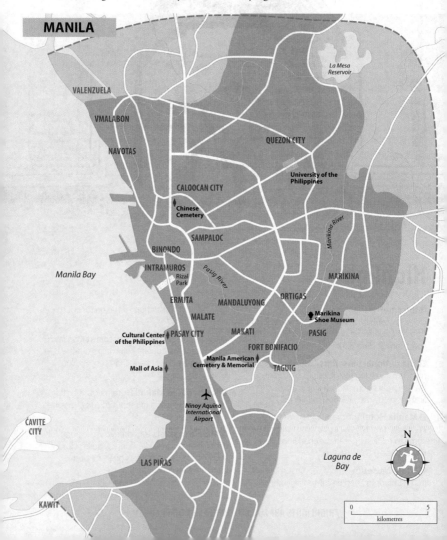

1

MANILA ORIENTATION

The key tourist district is the area fronting **Manila Bay** along **Roxas Boulevard**, taking in the neighbourhoods of **Ermita** and **Malate**, and stretching north to the old walled city of **Intramuros** and over the Pasig River to **Chinatown**, also known as **Binondo**. **Makati**, 8km southeast of Manila Bay, is the city's central business district, built around the main thoroughfare of Ayala Avenue, and home to banks, insurance companies and five-star hotels. Just to the east of Makati (and almost an extension of it), lies the city's newest business and retail hub, **Fort Bonifacio**. The artery of Epifaño de los Santos Avenue, or just **EDSA**, stretches from major transport hub Pasay in the south to Caloocan in the north, curving around the eastern edge of Makati en route. Further along EDSA beyond Makati is the commercial district of **Ortigas**, which is trying to outdo Makati with its hotels, malls and air-conditioned, themed restaurants. Beyond that is **Quezon City**, where many bus routes from the north terminate, though otherwise it's largely off the tourist map.

Manila that grew in its stead was thoroughly modern, with streetcars, steam trains and US-style public architecture, a trend that continued under American rule in the early twentieth century.

World War II

Manila suffered again during World War II. The **Japanese** occupied the city from 1942 until it was liberated by the US at the **Battle of Manila** in 1945. The battle lasted 29 days and claimed 1000 American lives, 16,000 Japanese soldiers and some 100,000 Filipinos, many of them civilians killed deliberately by the Japanese or accidentally by crossfire. Once again, Manila was a city in ruins, having undergone relentless shelling from American howitzers and been set alight by retreating Japanese troops. **Rebuilding** was slow and plagued by corruption and government inertia.

The Marcos era

In 1976, realizing that Manila was growing too rapidly for government to be contained in the old Manila area, **President Marcos** decreed that while the area around Intramuros would remain the capital city, the permanent seat of the national government would be Metro Manila – including new areas such as Makati and Quezon City. It was tacit recognition of the city's expansion and the problems it was bringing. **Imelda Marcos**, meanwhile, had been declared governor of Metro Manila in 1975 and was busy exercising her "edifice complex", building a golden-domed mosque in Quiapo, the Cultural Center of the Philippines on Manila Bay and a number of five-star hotels. Her spending spree was finally ended by the **EDSA Revolution** in 1986 (see p.444).

Manila today

In the 1990s popular police officer **Alfredo Lim** won two terms as Manila mayor – his crime-fighting efforts certainly improved security in the city and he was elected a third time in 2007. He immediately and controversially set about undoing much of the work of his predecessor **Lito Atienza** (mayor 1998–2007), who had spent millions on city beautification projects. Though congestion and pollution remain huge and apparently intractable problems, Lim has presided over a booming economy, managed to remove squatters in Quiapo and has cleaned up the Baywalk area along Roxas Boulevard. Manileños rewarded him with a fourth term as mayor in 2010, just months before the **Manila bus hostage crisis**, when a dismissed police officer hijacked a bus of Hong Kong tourists, eventually killing eight of them; the mayor's handling of the tragedy was highly criticized in the subsequent enquiry. In a remarkable twist, ex-president **Joseph Estrada** (see p.446) was elected mayor in 2013.

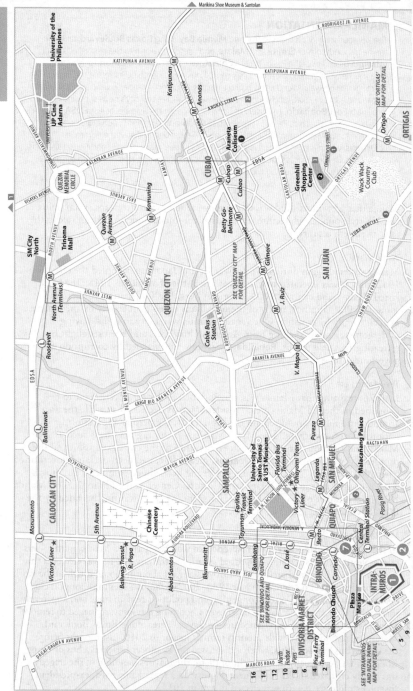

Marikina Shoe Museum & Santolan

University of the Philippines

E. RODRIGUEZ JR. AVENUE

KATIPUNAN AVENUE

UP Cine Adarna

KATIPUNAN AVENUE

Katipunan

Anonas

ANONAS STREET

SEE 'ORTIGAS' MAP FOR DETAIL

Araneta Coliseum

Ortigas

ORTIGAS

CUBAO

EDSA

Cubao

Cubao

CONNECTICUT STREET

ORTIGAS AVENUE

Greenhill Shopping Center

Wack Wack Country Club

QUEZON MEMORIAL CIRCLE

Betty Go-Belmonte

SANTOLAN ROAD

VISAYAS AVENUE

KALAYAAN AVENUE

EAST AVENUE

Kamuning

Gilmore

SAN JUAN

LUNA MENCIAS

NORTH AVENUE

SM City North

Quezon Avenue

Trinoma Mall

QUEZON AVENUE

TIMOG AVENUE

SEE 'QUEZON CITY' MAP FOR DETAIL

J. Ruiz

SHAW BOULEVARD

North Avenue (Terminus)

WEST AVENUE

QUEZON CITY

QUEZON AVENUE

V. Mapa

J. Ruiz

EDSA

Roosevelt

Cable Bus Station

E. RODRIGUEZ SR. BOULEVARD

ARANETA AVENUE

V. MAPA

Balintawak

DEL MONTE AVENUE

GREGO RIO ARANETA AVENUE

V. Mapa

MAGSAYSAY BOULEVARD

Malacañang Palace

NAGTAHAN

CALOOCAN CITY

A. BONIFACIO

MAYON AVENUE

ESPAÑA

Pureza

SAN MIGUEL

JP LAUREL

Pasig River

Monumento

SAMPALOC

University of Santo Tomas & UST Museum

Florida Bus Terminal

Onhayami Trans

Legarda

P. CASAL

5th Avenue

Chinese Cemetery

AURORA BOULEVARD

A.H. LACSON (GOVERNOR)

Victory Liner

MENDIOLA

MALACAÑANG

QUIAPO

Victory Liner

Baliwag Transit

R. Papa

Fariñas Transit Terminal

Tuyumon Transit

RIZAL AVENUE

A. MENDOZA (ANDALUCIA)

Recto

Central Terminal Station

Pasig River

Abad Santos

Blumentritt

Bambang

D. José

C. B. RECTO

BINONDO

Carriedo

Recto

NUEVA

QUEZON BOULEVARD

QUINTA

MARIKINA

JOSE ABAD SANTOS

RIZAL

SEE 'BINONDO AND QUIAPO' MAP FOR DETAIL

Binondo Church

Plaza Mexico

INTRA-MUROS

DAGAT-DAGATAN AVENUE

MARCOS ROAD

DIVISORIA MARKET DISTRICT

BONIFACIO

DRIVE

MIRELLE SAN

16

14

12

10

8

6

4

North Halbot

Piers

Pier 4 Ferry Terminal

2

SEE 'INTRAMUROS AND RIZAL PARK' MAP FOR DETAIL

1

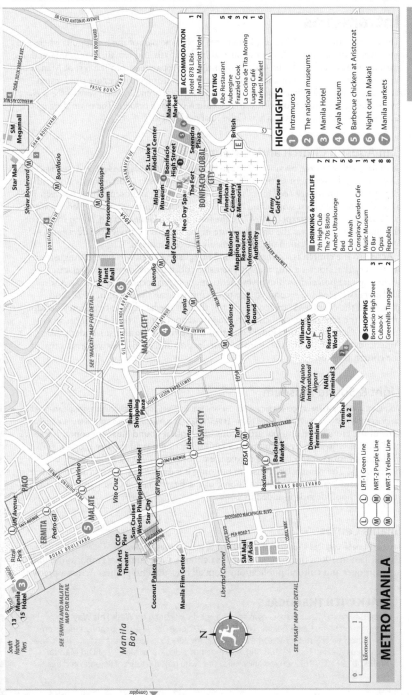

METRO MANILA

■ **ACCOMMODATION**
Hotel B78 Libis — 1
Manila Marriott Hotel — 2

● **EATING**
Abe Restaurant — 5
Aubergine — 4
Frazzled Cook — 3
La Cocina de Tita Moning — 2
Lugang Café — 1
Market! Market! — 6

HIGHLIGHTS
1 Intramuros
2 The national museums
3 Manila Hotel
4 Ayala Museum
5 Barbecue chicken at Aristocrat
6 Night out in Makati
7 Manila markets

■ **DRINKING & NIGHTLIFE**
7th High Club — 7
The 70s Bistro — 7
Amber Ultralounge — 5
Bed — 6
Club Mwah — 1
Conspiracy Garden Cafe — 3
Music Museum — 3
O Bar — 4
Opus — 8
Republiq — 2

● **SHOPPING**
Bonifacio High Street — 3
Cubao-X — 1
Greenhills Tiangge — 2

Ⓛ LRT-1 Green Line
Ⓜ MRT-2 Purple Line
Ⓜ MRT-3 Yellow Line

Ⓛ LRT-1 Green Line
Ⓜ MRT-2 Purple Line
Ⓜ MRT-3 Yellow Line

1

Intramuros

The old Spanish heart of Manila, **Intramuros** is the one part of the metropolis where you get a real sense of history. It was established in the 1570s and remains a monumental, if partially ruined, colonial relic – a city within a city, separated from the rest of Manila by its overgrown walls. It's not a museum; plenty of government offices are still located here, and many of Manila's poorest call the backstreets home. A good way to see it is by arranging a **walking tour** with Carlos Celdran (see box below). The main drag is **General Luna Street**, also known as Calle Real del Palacio.

San Agustin Church and museum

General Luna St • Church & museum daily 9am–noon & 1–6pm • P100 • ☎ 02 527 2746, ⓦ sanagustinchurch.org • LRT to Central Terminal

Dominating the southern section of Intramuros, **San Agustin Church** boasts a magnificent Baroque interior, *trompe l'oeil* murals and a vaulted ceiling and dome. Built between 1586 and 1606, it's the oldest stone church in the Philippines, and contains the modest tomb of **Miguel López de Legazpi** (1502–72), the founder of Manila (see p.438), to the left of the altar. The church was the only structure in Intramuros to survive the devastation of World War II, an indication of just how badly the city suffered.

Access to the church is via the adjacent **San Agustin Museum**, a former Augustinian monastery that houses a surprisingly extensive collection of icons and artefacts, including rare porcelain, church vestments and a special exhibition on Fray Andrés Urdaneta (who led the second voyage to circumnavigate the world in 1528, and pioneered the Manila–Acapulco sea route), though the handsome two-storey building itself and the tranquil central cloisters are just as appealing. The old vestry is where Governor-General Fermín Jáudenes drafted the terms of Spanish surrender to the Americans in 1898, while the oratorio upstairs provides an alternative perspective of the church interior.

Light & Sound Museum

Victoria St at Santa Lucia St • The site opens on demand Tues–Sat 9am–5pm, Sun 10am–6pm for a minimum of ten people; smaller groups can enter but they must pay a total P1500 • P150 per person • ☎ 02 524 2827, ✉ lsm.intramuros@yahoo.com • LRT to Central Terminal

One of the city's more unusual attractions, the **Light & Sound Museum** contains a series of dioramas enlivened by animatronic manikins acting out all the key moments in Philippine history (especially the heroic life of José Rizal) – it's a little cheesy, but fun nonetheless. The church-like museum building is a replica of the structure destroyed during World War II, originally the home of the Beaterio de la Compañía de Jesus, a religious school for girls founded in 1684.

Silahis Center

744 General Luna St • Daily 10am–7pm • Free • ☎ 02 527 2111, ⓦ silahis.com • LRT to Central Terminal

Established in 1966, the intriguing **Silahis Center** is a museum-like emporium selling arts, antiques and cultural publications from all over the Philippines. Across a pretty

---

WALK WITH THE LOCALS

If sightseeing in Manila on your own seems a little intimidating try **Walk This Way**, run by the highly entertaining Carlos Celdran (☎ 0920 909 2021 or ☎ 02 484 4945, ⓦ carlosceldran.com). Carlos takes weekly history-lesson-cum-magical-mystery tours around the old city, the "Classic Intramuros Walking Tour" (P1100; 3hr). Also recommended is Ivan Man Dy of **Old Manila Walks** (☎ 0917 329 1622, ⓦ oldmanilawalks.com), who runs fun tours of Binondo and the Malacañang Palace.

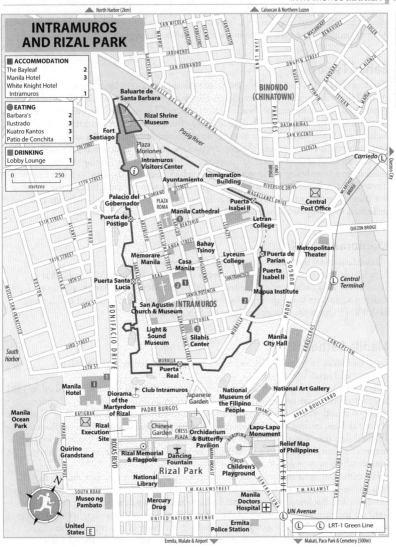

INTRAMUROS AND RIZAL PARK

courtyard reached through the back door are the elegant *Ilustrado* restaurant (see p.89) and the atmospheric *Kuatro Kantos* bar (see p.89).

Casa Manila

Plaza San Luis Complex, General Luna St • Tues–Sun 9am–6pm • P75 • ☎ 02 527 4084 • LRT to Central Terminal

The splendid **Casa Manila**, a sympathetic replica of an 1850s colonial mansion, offers a window into the lives of rich Filipinos in the nineteenth century. Redolent of a grander age, the house contains an impressive *sala* (living room) where *tertulias* (soirees) and *bailes* (dances) were held. The upstairs family latrine is a two-seater, which allowed husband and wife to gossip out of earshot of the servants while simultaneously going

1

about their business. Though it's a faithful reproduction of period Spanish styles, Imelda Marcos commissioned the house in the early 1980s, during her "edifice complex".

Bahay Tsinoy

32 Anda St at Cabildo St • Tues–Sun 1–5pm • P100 • ☎ 02 527 6083, ⓦ bahaytsinoy.org • LRT to Central Terminal

A small but enlightening museum, **Bahay Tsinoy** is a tribute to Manila's influential Chinese population. The name means "house of the Filipino Chinese", and the museum traces the crucial role of the Chinese in Philippine history from their first trade contact with the archipelago in the tenth century to the Spanish colonial period. Besides assorted artefacts and multimedia presentations, the displays include life-sized figures and authentic reproductions of objects related to Tsinoy (or "Chinoy") history. Among the items of interest are a large hologram representing the achievements of the Tsinoys and a charming diorama of the Parian ghetto, the area outside the city walls where Chinese were forced to live during Spanish rule. There's also a gallery of rare photographs and a Martyrs Hall dedicated to Tsinoys who formed guerrilla units against Japanese occupation.

Memorare Manila

Plazuela de Santa Isabel, General Luna and Anda streets • LRT to Central Terminal

Much of Intramuros was reduced to rubble during the Battle of Manila (1945) in World War II, a catastrophe commemorated by the **Memorare Manila**, a series of moving sculptures surrounding a woman weeping as she cradles a dead child. Over 100,000 Filipinos are thought to have died in the fighting.

Manila Cathedral

Plaza de Roma, Cabildo St at Beaterio St • Daily 6.20am–5.30pm, or 7.30pm if special event/mass • Free • ☎ 02 527 1796, ⓦ manilacathedral.org • LRT to Central Terminal

Originally just a nipa and bamboo structure, **Manila Cathedral** was officially raised in 1581 but destroyed numerous times down the centuries by a combination of fire, typhoon, earthquake and war. The seventh version was comprehensively flattened during World War II but the Vatican contributed funds to have it rebuilt. The present Byzantine-Romanesque inspired structure was completed in 1958 from a design by Fernando Ocampo, one of the nation's finest architects, and is similar in style to the cathedral that stood here in the nineteenth century. A major two-year renovation was completed in 2014.

The cathedral lacks the rich historical ambience of San Agustin, but the interior is impressive in its simplicity, with a long aisle flanked by marble pillars, stained-glass rose windows and a soaring central dome. Exhibitions in chapels around the nave throw light on the tumultuous history of the cathedral, and even tackle weighty theological questions such as "what is a cathedral?" and the meaning of the Immaculate Conception (the cathedral was awarded the title of "Basilica of the Immaculate Conception" in 1981). Check out also the faithful reproduction of Michelangelo's *La Pietà* in a special chapel to the left of the entrance.

Fort Santiago

General Luna St at Santa Clara St • Daily 8am–6pm • P75 • ☎ 02 527 2961 • LRT to Central Terminal

The remains of **Fort Santiago** stand at the northwestern end of Intramuros. The first log fortress was built by Spanish conquistador Miguel López de Legazpi in 1571 on the ruins of Rajah Sulaiman's base, but was rebuilt in stone twenty years later. The seat of the colonial power of both Spain and the US, Fort Santiago was also a prison and torture chamber under the Spanish regime and the scene of countless military police atrocities during the Japanese occupation (1942–45).

Just past the entrance to the site, on the left, is the Baluartillo de San Francisco Javier, fortifications built in 1663 which now house the **Intramuros Visitors Center**, a shop and a café. From here you can stroll through the gardens of **Plaza Moriones** to the fort proper, marked by a stone gate, walls and a moat – most of what you see today has been rebuilt in stages since the 1950s, after being virtually destroyed in 1945. Once through the walls, **Plaza de Armas** forms a pleasant green square inside the old fort, with a noble-looking **statue of José Rizal** in the middle.

Rizal Shrine
Tues–Sun 9am–noon & 1–5pm • Entry included with fort ticket

For most visitors the real highlight of Fort Santiago lies on the left side of Plaza de Armas, where the **Rizal Shrine** occupies a reconstruction of the old Spanish barracks (the brick ruins of the original are next door). The site is dedicated to **José Rizal** (see p.439), the writer and national hero who was imprisoned here before being executed in what became Rizal Park in 1896. On the ground floor, the Chamber of Texts preserves some original copies of Rizal's work, while excerpts are artfully displayed on iron girders. You can also peer into a reproduction of the room where he spent the hours before his execution. Upstairs the Reliquary Room displays some of Rizal's clothing and personal effects, while a larger hall houses the original copy of his valedictory poem, *Mi Ultimo Adios*, the greatest, most poignant work of Philippine literature. The poem was secreted in an oil lamp and smuggled out to his family; here it is displayed in various languages around the walls (the original was written in Spanish). While even the best English translations fail to capture the felicity of the original, they do give a sense of the sacrifice Rizal was about to make and of his love of the country:

Farewell, my adored country, region beloved of the sun,
Pearl of the Orient Sea, our Eden lost,
Departing in happiness, to you I give the sad, withered remains of my life;
And had it been a life more brilliant, more fine, more fulfilled
I would have given it, willingly to you.

Rizaliana Furniture Exhibition
Daily 8am–6pm • P10 donation

The eighteenth-century **Baluarte de Santa Barbara** overlooking the Pasig River now houses the mildly interesting **Rizaliana Furniture Exhibition**, showing off Rizal's Spanish colonial writing tables, four-poster bed and the like. More significantly, the exhibit lies above the infamous dungeon where around six hundred American and Filipino POWs were incarcerated and left to drown by the rising tide in 1945. There is a cross and **memorial** outside to mark their final resting place.

Rizal Park and around

The area south of Intramuros is dominated by **Rizal Park**, Manila's primary green space and the city's favourite meeting place since the Spanish era. On the fringes of the park lie two of the most important museums in the country, the **National Art Gallery** and the **National Museum of the Filipino People**, while on the other side of Roxas Boulevard, facing the bay, the **Manila Hotel** harks back to the city's golden age.

Rizal Park
Roxas Blvd • Daily 24hr • Free • **Orchidarium & Butterfly Pavilion** Tues–Sun 8am–5pm • P100 • **Japanese and Chinese gardens** Both daily 6am–10pm • P10 • ⓦ rizalpark.nationalparks.ph • LRT to UN Avenue, then a short stroll north

Still referred to by its old Spanish name of "Luneta", **Rizal Park** is a ten-minute walk south of Intramuros. In a city notoriously short of greenery, the park was where the colonial-era glitterati used to promenade after church every Sunday. These days Rizal Park is an early morning jogging circuit, a weekend playground for children and a refuge for couples and families escaping the clamour of the city. **Hawkers** sell everything from balloons and mangoes to plastic bags full of *chicharon*, deep-fried pigskin served with a little container of vinegar and chilli for dipping. The park is often busy, with many distractions and activities, but few visitors report any problems with hustlers, pickpockets or what Filipinos generally refer to as "snatchers". The whole park is gradually being renovated under an ambitious plan that will take years to complete.

At the far eastern end of the park is an impressive Marcos-era giant **Relief Map of the Philippines**, though in dire need of renovation – in contrast, at the centre lies the lagoon, where the flashy "dancing fountain"' entertains crowds every evening. The park's other sundry attractions include the **Orchidarium & Butterfly Pavilion**, a tranquil haven from the hustle outside; the fairly bare **Japanese Garden**; the **Chess Plaza**, where amiable seniors challenge each other to board games; and the traditional **Chinese Garden**.

Rizal memorials

Diorama of the Martyrdom of Rizal Wed–Sun 8am–5pm • P10 • Light show in English Wed–Sun 8–8.30pm (min 15 people) P50 per person • LRT to UN Avenue

The western end of Rizal Park is most associated with its namesake, **José Rizal**. The main focus is the stolid looking **Rizal Memorial**, raised in 1912, where Rizal is entombed, and the 31-metre flagpole where Manuel Roxas, first President of the Republic, was sworn in on July 4, 1946. Just to the north is the site of **Rizal's execution** in 1896, marked by a memorial that also commemorates the execution of three priests garrotted by the Spanish for alleged complicity in the uprising in Cavite in 1872 – despite the carnival-like atmosphere around it, this is a very poignant site for most Filipinos.

Nearby is the **Diorama of the Martyrdom of Rizal**, containing a series of eight life-size sculptures dramatizing the hero's final days. If the gatekeeper is around you should be able to wander around, but to run the light-and-sound presentation they need at least fifteen people.

National Art Gallery

Taft Ave at Padre Burgos Ave • Tues–Sun 10am–5pm • P150 (free on Sun), includes entry to National Museum of the Filipino People • ☏ 02 527 1215, ⓦ nationalmuseum.gov.ph • LRT to UN Avenue

Just to the north of Rizal Park, the **National Art Gallery** is the foremost art museum in the Philippines, housed in the grand old Legislative Building (completed in 1926 and home of the Senate till 1996) on the northern edge of Rizal Park. Galleries are laid out thematically in rather desultory fashion over two floors, but each one is relatively small and easy to digest. The highlights are paintings by Filipino masters including **Juan Luna** (1859–99), **Félix Hidalgo** (1855–1913), **José Joya** (1931–95) and **Fernando Amorsolo** (1892–1972), with the most famous works displayed in the Hall of the Masters near the entrance; Luna's vast and magnificent *Spolarium* (1884) is here, a thinly veiled attack in oils on the atrocities of the Spanish regime, portraying fallen gladiators being dragged onto a pile of corpses.

Other galleries are dedicated to National Artist award winners (Amorsolo was the first in 1972), showcasing Joya's *Origins* and Amorsolo's *Portrait of President Manuel Roxas*. There's also a section on architect **Juan Arellano** (1888–1960), who designed the building, and a special gallery dedicated to the large Juan Luna collection; look out for his haunting *Mother in Bed* and the simple naturalism of *Study for Rice Harvesting*. The second floor contains mostly minor works from modern Filipino artists, and also a **Bones Gallery** where a huge sperm whale skeleton takes pride of place.

National Museum of the Filipino People

Finance Rd at Padre Burgos Ave • Tues–Sun 10am–5pm • P150 (free on Sun), includes entry to National Art Gallery • ☎ 02 527 1215, Ⓦ nationalmuseum.gov.ph • LRT to UN Avenue

The absorbing **National Museum of the Filipino People** occupies what used to be the Department of Finance Building, a stately Greek Revival edifice completed in 1940. Much of the priceless collection of artefacts on display has been retrieved from shipwrecks, most notably the *San Diego*, a Spanish galleon that sank off Fortune Island in Batangas after a battle with the Dutch in 1600. Recovered in 1992, the ship yielded over five thousand objects, not all intrinsically valuable: you'll see chicken bones and hazelnuts from the ship's store, as well as tons of Chinese porcelain, storage jars, rosaries and silver goblets. Other rooms contain objects from wrecked Chinese junks going back to the early eleventh century – compelling evidence of trade links that existed long before the Spanish arrived.

The well-labelled anthropology section on the third floor is equally engrossing, with displays from almost every region and tribal group in the Philippines, including the enigmatic anthropomorphic jars discovered in Ayub Cave (Mindanao) that date back to 5 BC. These jars were used to hold the bones of ancestors.

Manila Hotel

1 Rizal Park • ☎ 02 527 0011, Ⓦ www.manila-hotel.com.ph • Take a taxi or walk from Manila Ocean Park

The **Manila Hotel**, just northwest of Rizal Park, is the most historic of the city's luxury hotels, though now a little careworn. It's still the best place to get a sense of early twentieth-century Manila, those halcyon days when the city was at its cultural and social zenith; you can even stay (see p.86) in the **General Douglas MacArthur Suite**, residence from 1936 to 1941 of the man Filipinos called the Caesar of America. If even the standard rooms are beyond your means, you can at least sip a martini in the lobby while listening to a string quartet and watching the capital's elite strut by.

When the hotel opened in 1912 it represented the epitome of colonial class and luxury. Lavish dances known as rigodon balls were held every month in the **Grand Ballroom**, with high-society guests dancing the quadrille in traditional *ternos* (formal evening dresses) and dinner jackets. Today staff glide around in similarly elegant attire.

The hotel has its own historical **archive**, containing signed photographs of illustrious guests, from Marlon Brando, looking young and slender in a native *barong* (formal shirt), to Ricky Martin and Jon Bon Jovi. The archive is available to guests only, but if you eat or drink at the hotel, one of the guest relations officers should be able to show it to you. South of the hotel is the **Quirino Grandstand** where various official functions take place, including a military parade on Independence Day.

Manila Ocean Park

Parade Ave, off Roxas Blvd (behind Quirino Grandstand) • Mon–Fri 10am–9pm, Sat & Sun 9am–9pm • Entry P400; packages to see all shows P550–900 • ☎ 02 567 7777, Ⓦ manilaoceanpark.com • Shuttle buses (P30) run between the entrance and UN Avenue LRT station

At the far western end of Rizal Park, along the bayfront, lies **Manila Ocean Park**, one of the city's most popular attractions. The undoubted highlight is the **Oceanarium**, a huge saltwater tank viewed via a 25m-long walkway, packed with some twenty thousand sea creatures. There are also spectacular light shows, musical fountains, sea lion shows, a birds of prey exhibit, a trippy jellyfish installation and a penguin park (all incurring extra charges). It's also the home of the *Liquid Pool & Lounge* bar (see p.94).

1

Museo ng Pambata

Roxas Blvd at South Drive • March–Aug Tues–Sat 9am–noon & 1–5pm, Sun 1–5pm; Sept–Feb Tues–Sat 8am–5pm, Sun 1–5pm • Adults & children P150 • ☎ 02 523 1797, ⓦ museopambata.org • LRT to UN Avenue

The entertaining **Museo ng Pambata** (Children's Museum) has several hands-on exhibitions designed to excite young children; at the Maynila Noon exhibit they can get a feel for history using interactive displays – replicas of ships, churches and native Filipino homes – and there's also a simulated rainforest and seabed. On the first Saturday of every month shadow puppetry is put on; on the third Saturday you can see music and dance (both start at 10am).

Ermita and Malate

Two of the city's oldest neighbourhoods, **Ermita** and **Malate** nestle behind Roxas Boulevard, facing Manila Bay. Ermita was infamous for its go-go bars and massage parlours up until the late 1980s, when tough-guy mayor Alfredo Lim closed most of them, alleging that they were fronts for **prostitution**. Sadly, the massages and KTV hostess bars have gradually slipped back, this time to serve busloads of Japanese and Korean high-spenders, and there has been a resurgence of prostitution in Ermita; it is now the Philippines second largest centre for paid sex after Angeles City.

Ermita and Malate otherwise remain in most part a ragbag of budget hotels, choked streets, fast-food outlets and bars, with street children all too prevalent on every corner, though the area does look to be changing; several high-end residential developments and hotels have already jazzed up some streets. Most of the sights in this area lie along Manila Bay in the form of the **Metropolitan Museum** and the **Cultural Center of the Philippines**, though **Paco Park**, to the east, is also worth a look if you have time.

Metropolitan Museum

Bangko Sentral ng Pilipinas Complex, Roxas Blvd • Mon–Sat 10am–5.30pm (Gold & Pottery Galleries Mon–Fri 10am–4.30pm) • P100 • ☎ 02 521 1517, ⓦ metmuseum.ph • LRT to Vito Cruz, then a CCP orange-coloured jeepney from Taft Ave and Pablo Ocampo St

The **Metropolitan Museum** is best known for the Central Bank's astounding collection of **pre-colonial gold and pottery**, which lies in the basement. Most of this stunning ensemble of magnificent jewellery, amulets, necklaces and intricate gold work dates from between 200 BC and 900 AD, long before the Spanish Conquest. Look out for the extraordinary Kamagi Necklaces (long threads of gold), Islamic art from Lake Maranao, ancestral death masks and items from the Surigao Treasure (see p.438). The pottery section is dull by comparison, though some of the pots here are very ancient. Note though that this whole section is closed on Saturdays. The museum also houses a fine permanent collection of contemporary and historic artworks from Asia, America, Europe and Africa (including Egypt), plus temporary displays from high-profile contemporary Filipino artists.

MANILA BAY BY BOAT

Sun Cruises (☎ 02 527 5555, ⓦ corregidorphilippines.com), CCP Terminal A, Pedro Bukaneg St, near the Cultural Center, runs daily jaunts around the **Manila Bay**, which can be fun despite the often distressing amounts of rubbish floating around – the views of the city at sunset, surrounded by the volcanoes of Bataan and Batangas, are magical. Most cruises (1hr 30min) include a meal on board and run daily at 4.15pm, 6.15pm and 8.15pm. Boats depart from the wharf next to Jumbo Palace at the end of Pedro Bukaneg. Tickets are P550 per person (Fri–Sun P650).

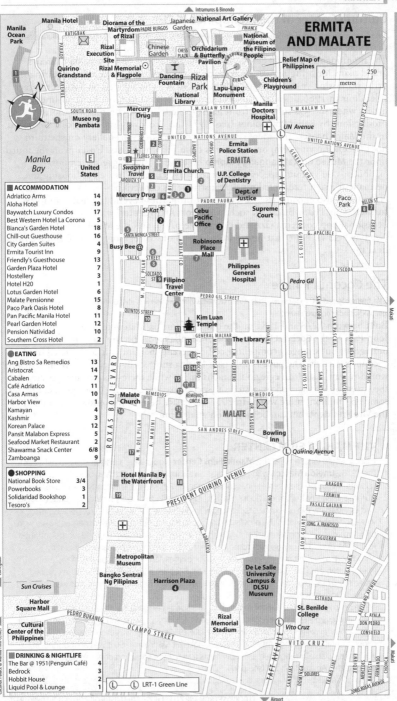

ERMITA AND MALATE

0 — 250
metres

Intramuros & Binondo

Manila Bay

United States

ACCOMMODATION

Adriatico Arms	14
Aloha Hotel	19
Baywatch Luxury Condos	17
Best Western Hotel La Corona	5
Bianca's Garden Hotel	18
Chill-out Guesthouse	16
City Garden Suites	4
Ermita Tourist Inn	9
Friendly's Guesthouse	13
Garden Plaza Hotel	7
Hostellery	3
Hotel H2O	1
Lotus Garden Hotel	6
Malate Pensionne	15
Paco Park Oasis Hotel	8
Pan Pacific Manila Hotel	11
Pearl Garden Hotel	12
Pension Natividad	10
Southern Cross Hotel	2

EATING

Ang Bistro Sa Remedios	13
Aristocrat	14
Cabalen	7
Café Adriatico	11
Casa Armas	10
Harbor View	1
Kamayan	4
Kashmir	3
Korean Palace	5
Pansit Malabon Express	12
Seafood Market Restaurant	9
Shawarma Snack Center	6/8
Zamboanga	9

SHOPPING

National Book Store	3/4
Powerbooks	3
Solidaridad Bookshop	1
Tesoro's	2

DRINKING & NIGHTLIFE

The Bar @ 1951(Penguin Café)	4
Bedrock	3
Hobbit House	2
Liquid Pool & Lounge	1

L — L LRT-1 Green Line

Airport

1

Cultural Center of the Philippines (CCP)

Pedro Bukaneg (off Roxas Blvd) • Tues–Sun 10am–6pm • Free; Museo ng Kalinangang Pilipino P40 • ☎ 02 833 2125, ⓦ culturalcenter.gov.ph • LRT to Vito Cruz, then a CCP orange-coloured jeepney from Taft Ave and Pablo Ocampo St

The monumental **Cultural Center of the Philippines** was one of Imelda Marcos's grand plans for bringing world-class arts to the Philippines. Conceived during the early, promising years of her husband's presidency and opened on a night of great splendour in 1966, it's a slab-like construction typical of those built on Imelda's orders when she was suffering from her so-called "edifice complex". Various productions by **Ballet Philippines** (see p.97) and Broadway-style **musicals** are staged in the **Main Theater**, and there is a decent **contemporary art gallery** on the third floor (free), showing temporary exhibits from Filipino artists. Upstairs on the fourth floor the **Museo ng Kalinangang Pilipino** holds small but engaging temporary exhibitions on various aspects of Filipino native cultures, as well as housing the permanent Asian traditional musical instruments collection.

The CCP also encompasses several other properties beyond the main complex, further along Pedro Bukaneg, such as the **Folk Arts Theater**, which is the venue for occasional pop concerts, jazz and drama (see p.97), and the **Manila Film Center** (see box below). Note that ferries to the island of Corregidor (see p.104) leave from near the CCP.

The Coconut Palace

F. Ma. Guerrero St, next to CCP • Tours Tues–Thurs at 9am, 10.30am & 2pm; free; reserve in advance at ☎ 02 832 6791 or ⓔ drcomia@ovp .gov.ph • No sandals or shorts allowed

Built between 1978 and 1981 on the orders of Imelda Marcos for the visit of Pope John Paul II, the **Coconut Palace** is one of Manila's more bizarre monuments, an outrageous but strangely compelling edifice, seventy percent of it constructed from coconut materials. The pope rightly gave Imelda short shrift when he arrived, saying he wouldn't stay in such an egregious establishment while there was so much poverty on the streets of Manila, and suggested she spend taxpayers' money (the equivalent of some P37 million) more wisely. In 2011 the palace became the residence and office of the **Vice President**, but can be viewed on guided tours.

THE MANILA FILM CENTER

If bricks could talk, those at the **Manila Film Center** would have a sinister story to tell. Back in the 1970s, **Imelda Marcos** wanted to stage an annual film festival that would rival Cannes and put Manila on the international cultural map. But the centre she commissioned for the purpose was jerry-built and a floor collapsed in 1981, allegedly burying workers under rubble and killing many. No one knows exactly how many (some claim around 170) because most were poor labourers from the provinces and records were not kept of their names. Police were told to throw a cordon round the building so the press couldn't get to it, and work continued round the clock. The centre was completed in 1982, some say with dead workers still entombed inside, in time for the opening night of the Manila International Film Festival. Imelda celebrated by walking onto the stage to greet the audience in a black and emerald green *terno* (a formal gown) thick with layer upon layer of peacock feathers that were shipped specially from India.

The centre staged just one more film festival – some say it was haunted and Imelda herself had it exorcized – and it soon had to make ends meet by showing soft-porn (*bomba*) films for the masses. It was briefly rehabilitated in the late 1980s when it was used as a centre for experimental filmmaking, but after an earthquake hit Manila in 1990 it was abandoned. In 2001 it was partially renovated and now hosts transvestite song and dance extravaganzas dubbed the "Amazing Show" (see p.97).

CLOCKWISE FROM TOP KALESA (P.72); SAN AGUSTIN CHURCH (P.62); BINONDO (P.72) >

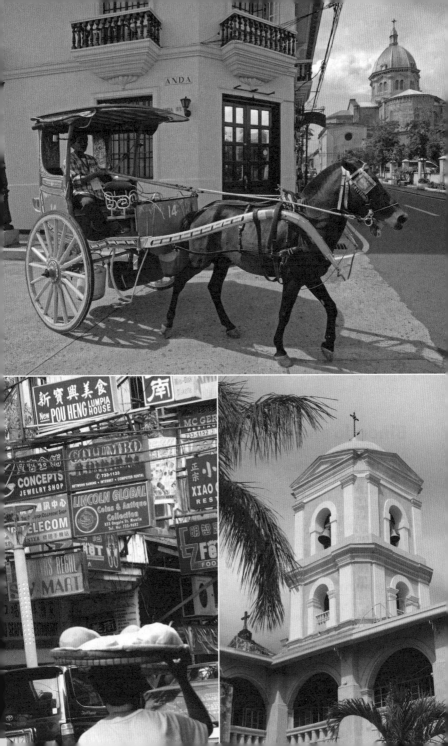

1

Paco Park and Cemetery

General Luna St at Padre Faura St • Tues–Sun 8am–5pm • P10 • Free open-air concerts Fri 6pm • ☎ 02 480 7062 • LRT to Pedro Gil or UN Avenue

A circular walled cemetery with an aged and beautiful garden dominated by a classical rotunda, **Paco Park and Cemetery** was built in 1820 just in time for victims of a cholera epidemic. After his execution in 1896 **José Rizal** (see p.439) was buried here in an unmarked grave. The story goes that his sister, Narcisa Rizal-Lopez, saw a group of guards standing beside a mound of freshly turned earth the length of a man; guessing this must be her brother's grave, she convinced the cemetery guardian to mark the site. Two years later Rizal's remains were exhumed and left in the custody of his family until 1912, when they were deposited beneath the Rizal Memorial (see p.66). A monument marks the location of the original grave.

The park's serenity has made it a favourite setting every Friday for "Paco Park Presents", free **open-air concerts**, usually classical recitals by Filipino artists or students. It's worth timing your visit to take in one of these performances – they're rarely packed, and it's pleasant to sit amid the greenery at sundown listening to Chopin sonatas or a Monteverdi madrigal.

The Museum at De La Salle University

2401 Taft Ave • Mon–Fri 8am–6pm, Sat 9am–noon • P50 • ☎ 02 524 4611, ⊛ themuseum.dlsu.edu.ph • LRT to Vito Cruz

Established in 1911, **De La Salle University**, at the southern end of Malate, remains one of the most prestigious private Catholic colleges in the Philippines. The **DLSU Museum** hosts rotating exhibitions showing work from its substantial collection of modern Filipino artists such as Diosdado Lorenzo and Araceli Dans. It's really just a small gallery but even if you're not an art fan, it's worth a quick look just to get a pass to wander the elegant neoclassical DLSU campus, far more redolent of classical Spain than the city outside. Register at the main entrance first (bring photo ID), then pay at accounting before heading to the gallery in Yuchengco Hall.

Binondo and Quiapo

Manila's Chinatown, **Binondo** exercises a curious, magnetic pull. This is city life *in extremis*, a rambunctious ghetto of people on the make, the streets full of merchants and middlemen flogging fake watches and herbs, sandalwood incense and gaudy jewellery. You can lose yourself for an afternoon wandering through its mercantile centre, snacking on dim sum at one of its many fan-cooled teahouses, and exploring the busiest thoroughfare, **Ongpin Street**. A visit to the sepulchral **Binondo Church** will give you some idea of the area's historical significance. Southeast of Binondo lies **Quiapo**, a labyrinth of crowded streets and cheap market stalls a universe away from the city's plush megamalls. The **Quiapo Church** here is said to be the most visited in the Philippines.

ARRIVAL AND DEPARTURE	BINONDO AND QUIAPO
By foot From Magellanes Drive on the northern edge of Intramuros you can walk to Binondo in 15min across Jones Bridge. **By LRT** The best LRT station for Quiapo and Binondo is Carriedo at Plaza Santa Cruz, only a short walk from the eastern end of Ongpin St.	**By jeepney** There are plenty of jeepneys to Binondo from M. Adriatico in Malate and Ermita, and also from Taft Ave marked for Divisoria. From Plaza Miranda, behind Quiapo Church, there are buses to Makati, and jeepneys and FX taxis to Quezon City, Ermita and Malate.

GETTING AROUND

By kalesa Once in Binondo, you can also hire a kalesa (horse-drawn carriage) – still used by some Binondo residents instead of taxis – to take you from one place to the next. These days, however, they generally serve tourists

1

BINONDO AND QUIAPO

Ⓛ — Ⓛ LRT-1 Green Line
Ⓜ — Ⓜ MRT-2 Purple Line

MORIONES

0   400
metres

Caloocan & Chinese Cemetery

Bambang Ⓛ

N

Tutuban Mall

MAYHALIGUE

REINE REGENTE STREET

DAGUPAN

P. ALGUE

JUAN LUNA STREET

YLAYA

C. M. RECTO AVENUE

CARMEN

C. M. PEÑAS

TABORA

YLAYA

168 Shopping Mall

SOLER STREET

FELIPE II STREET

DIVISORIA MARKET DISTRICT

SANTA ELENA

M. DE SANTOS

Divisoria Mall

SANTO CRISTO

ELCANO

REINE REGENTE STREET

Estero de Magdalena

JUAN LUNA STREET

ALVARADO

BENAVIDEZ

MASANGKAY

GANDARA STREET

LACINOS STREET

Estero San Lazaro

QUIAPO

THOMAS MAPUA

RIZAL AVENUE

OROQUIETA

D. José

Ⓛ

Manila City Jail

Bataan Transit

Philippine Rabbit

SOLER STREET

TETUAN

TORRES

SALES

G. PUYAT

EVANGELISTA

QUEZON BLVD

Recto

Ⓜ

University of Santo Tomas & Quezon City

ONGPIN STREET

Binondo Church

PLAZA SAN LORENZO RUIZ

HSBC

Citibank

ABOCEROS

SAN FERNANDO

Muelle de Binondo

NUMANCIA

CARVAJAL ST.

BINONDO

T. PINPIN STREET

ESPELETA

Santa Cruz Church

First United Building

Regina Building

Escolta Museum

MUELLE DE LA INDUSTRIA

DASMARIÑAS

ESCOLTA

PAREDES

QUINTIN ST.

Pasig River

JONES BRIDGE

RIVERSIDE DRIVE

MAGALLANES DRIVE

MCARTHUR BRIDGE

QUEZON BRIDGE

CARRIEDO

Ⓛ Carriedo

Buses, Jeepways & FX taxis to Makati, Ermita and Malate

PLAZA MIRANDA

Quiapo Church

CARLOS PALANCA SR.

Ilalim ng Tulay

Fort Santiago

Intramuros

● EATING
Eng Bee Tin 3
Ho-Land Hopia
 & Bakery 5
The Original Savory 7
President Grand
 Palace Restaurant 2
Quick Snack 6
Salazar Bakery 1
Tasty Dumplings 4

● SHOPPING
168 Shopping Mall 1
Divisoria Market District ... 2
Ilalim ng Tulay 3

and rates will depend on how hard you bargain. Fares for short journeys should only cost P50, while a 30min tour of the whole Binondo area (or Intramuros) should cost no more than P350.

Binondo Church

Plaza San Lorenzo Ruiz at the western end of Ongpin St • Daily 5am–6.30pm • ☎ 02 242 4041 • LRT to Carriedo; Divisoria jeepneys take you right past the church

The always-buzzing Minor Basilica of San Lorenzo Ruiz is more commonly known as **Binondo Church**. It stands on the spot where Dominican priests established their church when they first came to Binondo in the late sixteenth century, though the original building was destroyed by shelling in 1762 when the British invaded Manila and the Chinese were expelled. The Dominicans left with the Chinese but returned in 1842 and completed the church you see today, a solid granite structure with an octagonal bell tower and elaborate retablo (altarpiece), in 1854.

The church was badly damaged by bombing during World War II and new features include the canopy at the entrance and the strikingly colourful murals on the ceilings. Depicting the life of Christ and the Assumption of the Virgin, these murals were not actually painted on the ceiling but were executed at ground level, then hoisted up.

The church is well known in the Philippines because it was where **Saint Lorenzo Ruiz**, the Philippines' first saint, served as a sacristan. Of Filipino and Chinese parentage,

1

Ruiz was falsely accused of killing a Spaniard in 1636. It was probably because of this that he was encouraged to go to Japan, where he was arrested in Nagasaki in 1637 for spreading Christianity, and was executed for refusing to renounce his faith. The Vatican canonized him in 1987.

Ongpin Street

LRT to Carriedo

Ongpin Street, Binondo's principal thoroughfare, is about 2km long and runs eastwards through the heart of Chinatown to Santa Cruz Church. It was originally called Calle Sacristia but was renamed in 1915 after Roman Ongpin, a fervent nationalist who was said to be the first Chinese-Filipino to wear the *barong tagalog*, the formal shirt that became the national dress for men. Ongpin Street is now chock-full of restaurants, noodle parlours, apothecaries and shops selling goods imported from China, though it tends to shut down early these days; you'll find the nearby **Benavidez Street** more lively at night.

Santa Cruz Church

Plaza Santa Cruz • Daily 6am–10pm • LRT to Carriedo

An immense white Baroque structure, **Santa Cruz Church** was originally completed in the seventeenth century for the swelling ranks of Chinese in the area, but was most recently rebuilt in 1957 after damage from earthquakes and war. The most revered image inside is a 250-year-old replica of the **Nuestra Señora del Pilar**, an apparition of Mary (the original of which is in Zaragoza, Spain), but the interior is otherwise unexceptional.

Escolta

LRT to Carriedo

The shopping street **Calle Escolta**, which leads southwest off Plaza Santa Cruz, was named after the horse-mounted military escorts of the British commander-in-chief during the British occupation of 1762. In the nineteenth century this was where Manila's elite promenaded and shopped, but its dizzy days as a Champs-Élysées of the Orient are long gone. Only a few examples of the street's former glory remain; just across the river on the right is the **First United Building**, a pink and white Art Deco gem designed in 1928 by Andres Luna de San Pedro, the son of painter Juan Luna. Opposite is another of his buildings, the all-white **Regina Building** of 1934, at 400–402 Escolta, with its Art Nouveau cupolas. Both buildings are occupied by shops and small businesses today.

Escolta Museum

2/F, Calvo Building, 266 Escolta St • Tues–Sun 9am–noon & 1–5pm • P100 • ☎ 02 241 4538

The beaux-arts Calvo Building, completed in 1933, contains the quirky **Escolta Museum** (ask the guard at the building entrance to let you in). The main attraction is an extensive collection of multicoloured vintage bottles, but there are also scale models of Escolta's handsome buildings, old photos and paper advertisements from the 1930s.

Quiapo Church

910 Plaza Miranda, a short walk along Carriedo St from Plaza Santa Cruz • Daily 5am–7pm • ☎ 02 733 4434 ext 100, ✪ quiapochurch.com • LRT to Carriedo

Officially called the Minor Basilica of St John the Baptist, **Quiapo Church** – as everyone in Manila calls it – is the home of the **Black Nazarene**, a supposedly miraculous wooden icon that came to the country on board a galleon from Spain in 1606 (it was enshrined here in 1787). The venerated life-size image carries a cross and is on display under glass at the back of the church (behind the altar to the left). On the edge of the nave, hunched old women will, for a fee, tell your fortune, pray the rosary for you or light candles for lost loved ones. The church burnt down in 1928 and was expanded in the 1980s to accommodate the crowds that gather every year on January 9 for the **Feast of the Black Nazarene**, when 200,000 barefoot Catholic faithful from all over the Philippines come together to worship the image.

Ilalim ng Tulay

LRT to Carriedo

The area around Quiapo Church is a good area for bargain-hunters (see p.100). Several stores that sell **handicrafts** at local prices are squeezed beneath the underpass leading to Quezon Bridge (aka Quiapo Bridge) on Quezon Boulevard, a place known as **Ilalim ng Tulay** ("under the bridge" or just Quiapo Ilalim).

University of Santo Tomas Museum

2/F, Main Building, University of Santo Tomas (UST), España Blvd • Tues–Sat 8.30am–4.30pm (closed university hols) • P50 • ☎ 02 781 1815, ⊛ ustmuseum.ust.edu.ph • 20min walk (or a short ride on any jeepney marked UST) from Recto LRT station, via Lerma and España Blvd

The **University of Santo Tomas Museum** is a marvellous throwback to the nineteenth century, an old-fashioned but fascinating private collection of historic documents, rare books and dusty displays on ethnology, natural history, archeology and arts. Indeed, the collection dates back to 1871 and includes a stuffed orang-utan, a chair used by Pope John Paul II and a macabre two-headed calf. There's also some medieval coins, an assemblage of religious statues, a rather incongruous collection of Chinese porcelain, and some decent art, including *Pounding Rice* (1940) by Vicente Manansala, who also created the stunning, Cubist-influenced *History of Medicine* murals adorning the lobby of UST's medicine faculty in 1958.

UST itself has an interesting history. It was founded in Intramuros in 1611, making it the oldest university in Asia, with the current campus established in the 1920s; it served as an internment camp during World War II, while the old campus was virtually destroyed in 1944. Today the university is much larger than it seems from the entrance, with the **Main Building** an impressive Spanish Revival pile completed in 1927, and the elegant **Arch of the Centuries** above the main entrance on España Boulevard combining the ruins of the original arch of 1611 and its 1950s replica.

The Chinese Cemetery

South Gate entrance off Aurora Blvd, 4km north of Binondo • Daily 7.30am–7pm • Free • LRT to Abad Santos

The monumental **Chinese Cemetery** was established by affluent Chinese merchants in the 1850s because the Spanish would not allow foreigners to be buried in Spanish cemeteries. Entire streets are laid out to honour the dead and to underline the status of their surviving relatives. Many of the tombs resemble houses, with fountains, balconies and, in at least one case, a small swimming pool. Many even have air conditioning for the relatives who visit on All Saints' Day, when lavish feasts are laid on around the graves with empty chairs for the departed. It has become a sobering joke in the Philippines that this "accommodation" is among the best in the city.

1 Malacañang Palace and Museum

1000 J.P. Laurel St, San Miguel • Mon–Fri 9am–noon & 1–3pm (closed public hols) • P50 • ☎ 02 784 4286, ⓦ malacanang.gov.ph • Reservation forms plus passport photocopy must be emailed to the palace at least 7 days in advance (see website); no shorts, sleeveless tops or flip-flops • The palace is a short taxi ride east of Intramuros and Quiapo

Home of the governor-generals and presidents of the Philippines since the 1860s, the **Malacañang Palace** (also "Malacañan" Palace) is a fittingly grand and intriguing edifice, well worth the minor hassle involved in arranging a visit (you can also join a tour; see box, p.62). Much of the palace is permanently off-limits to the public, but you can visit the wing that houses the **Malacañang Museum**. Housed in the beautifully restored Kalayaan Hall, completed in 1921, the museum traces the history of the palace and of the presidency from Emilio Aguinaldo to the present day. The origins of the Malacañang go back to a smaller stone house dating from 1750, which was bought in 1825 by the Spanish government and, in 1849, made into the summer residence of the governor-general of the Philippines. After the governors' palace in Intramuros was destroyed in the earthquake of 1863, the move to Malacañang was made permanent and the property was extended several times over the years. President Aquino actually resides in Bahay Pangarap, another property within Malacañang Park, and maintains his office in Bonifacio Hall of the palace.

Makati

Some 5km east of Manila Bay, **Makati** was a vast expanse of malarial swampland until the Ayala family, one of the country's most influential business dynasties, started developing it in the 1950s. It is now Manila's premier business and financial district, chock-full of plush hotels, international restaurant chains, expensive condominiums and monolithic air-conditioned malls.

Opposite the station, the biggest mall is **Glorietta**, which has a central section and side halls numbered 1–5, and heaves with people seeking refuge from the traffic and heat. A short walk from Glorietta to the other side of Makati Avenue is **Greenbelt Park**, a landscaped garden with the pleasant, modern, white-domed **Santo Niño de Paz Chapel** in the centre. The park forms part of Makati's other main mall, **Greenbelt**, which, like Glorietta, is divided into various numbered halls; on the north side is the excellent Ayala Museum (see below).

Just to the north is the pleasant green swathe of **Ayala Triangle**, bordered by Ayala Avenue, Paseo de Roxas and Makati Avenue. Further along Ayala Avenue, at the junction with Paseo de Roxas, is the **Ninoy Aquino Monument**, built in honour of the senator who was assassinated in 1983, while a block further on, the shimmering **PBCom Tower** (259m) at 6795 Ayala Avenue is the tallest building in the Philippines (closed to the public).

Ayala Museum

Makati Ave at De La Rosa St • Tues–Sun 9am–6pm • P425 • ☎ 02 759 8288, ⓦ www.ayalamuseum.org • MRT to Ayala

Makati's one must-see attraction is the **Ayala Museum**, by far the best place in the Philippines to get to grips with the nation's complex history. The mighty Ayala family donated much of the initial collection in 1967, and this modern building was completed in 2004. There are no dreary exhibits here, or ponderous chronological approach – the permanent exhibitions just highlight the key aspects of Philippine history beginning on the **fourth floor** with an extraordinary collection of pre-Hispanic goldware, created by the islands' often overlooked indigenous cultures between the tenth and thirteenth centuries. Over one thousand gold objects are on display, much of it from the Butuan area in Mindanao, including the "**Surigao Treasure**" (see p.438). Don't miss the astonishing Gold Regalia, a huge 4kg chain of pure gold thought to have been worn by a *datu* (chief). Other displays emphasize pre-Hispanic trade links with Asia, especially Song dynasty China, with a huge collection of porcelain and ceramics. On the **third floor** the "Pioneers of Philippine Art" showcases the museum's particularly strong collections of Juan Luna Realism, Fernando Amorsolo Impressionism and Fernando Zobel's more abstract work. On the **second floor** an extensive display of sixty dioramas dramatizes all the key events in Philippine history from prehistory to independence, while three audiovisual presentations tackle the postwar period, the Marcos years and People Power in 1986.

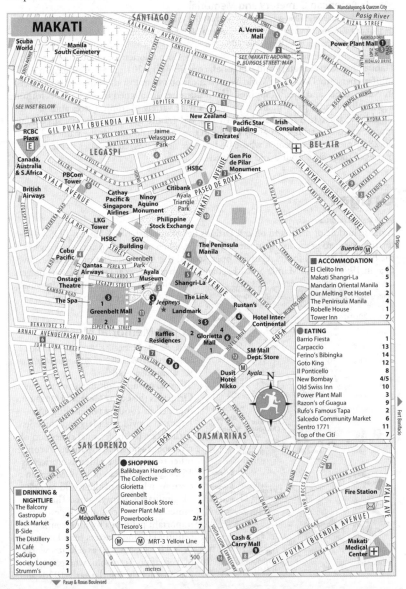

ACCOMMODATION

El Cielito Inn	6
Makati Shangri-La	5
Mandarin Oriental Manila	3
Our Melting Pot Hostel	2
The Peninsula Manila	4
Robelle House	1
Tower Inn	7

EATING

Barrio Fiesta	1
Carpaccio	13
Ferino's Bibingka	14
Goto King	12
Il Ponticello	8
New Bombay	4/5
Old Swiss Inn	10
Power Plant Mall	3
Razon's of Guagua	9
Rufo's Famous Tapa	2
Salcedo Community Market	6
Sentro 1771	11
Top of the Citi	7

SHOPPING

Balikbayan Handicrafts	8
The Collective	9
Glorietta	6
Greenbelt	3
National Book Store	4
Power Plant Mall	1
Powerbooks	2/5
Tesoro's	7

DRINKING & NIGHTLIFE

The Balcony Gastropub	4
Black Market	6
B-Side	8
The Distillery	3
M Café	5
SaGuijo	7
Society Lounge	2
Strumm's	1

M — M MRT-3 Yellow Line

0 — 500 metres

1

Bonifacio Global City (Fort Bonifacio)

Bonifacio Global City (or **Fort Bonifacio**, after the army camp around which it is located) sits on the eastern fringes of Makati but is rapidly developing a separate identity of its own, with skyscrapers, posh condos and shopping malls developed by Ayala Corp. Other than the **Manila American Cemetery and Memorial**, there's little in the way of traditional sights, though the shops, bars and restaurants of Market! Market! (see box, p.90) show off Manila's ambitious, affluent side.

Manila American Cemetery and Memorial

Global City, Taguig, McKinley Rd • Daily 9am–5pm • Free • ☎ 02 844 0212, ⓦ www.abmc.gov • MRT to Ayala; walk across EDSA near its junction with Ayala Ave and then along McKinley Rd, passing Manila Polo Club on your right; cemetery entrance is at the roundabout 1km beyond the polo club; taxi from central Makati around P100

On the southeastern edge of Makati, 3km away from Glorietta mall, lies the serene **Manila American Cemetery and Memorial**, containing 17,201 graves of American military personnel killed in World War II, most of whom lost their lives in operations in New Guinea and the Philippines. The headstones are aligned in eleven plots forming a generally circular pattern, and set among a wide variety of tropical trees and shrubbery. There is also a chapel and two curved granite walkways whose walls contain mosaic maps depicting the battles fought in the Pacific, along with the names of the 36,285 American servicemen whose bodies were not recovered (rosettes mark the names of those since found and identified).

Ortigas

MRT to Shaw Blvd or Ortigas

A dense huddle of malls and offices, **Ortigas** lies 5km north of Makati on EDSA. The district began to come to life in the early 1980s, when a number of corporations left the bustle of Makati for its relatively open spaces; the Asian Development Bank moved here in 1991 and the Manila Stock Exchange followed one year later. Today its biggest draw for Manileños is the **SM Megamall**, one of Asia's largest shopping malls.

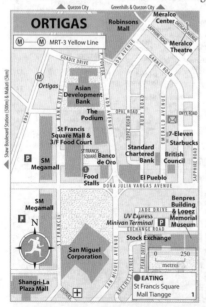

Lopez Memorial Museum

G/F Benpres Bldg, Exchange Rd at Meralco Ave • Mon–Sat 8am–5pm • P100 • ☎ 02 635 9545, ⓦ lopezseum.blogspot.com • MRT to Ortigas (15min walk)

The one genuine cultural attraction in Ortigas is the **Lopez Memorial Museum**, founded in 1960 by tycoon Eugenio Lopez to provide scholars and students with access to his personal collection of rare books and since expanded to contain other treasures. The oldest is a priceless 1524 copy of the account of Magellan's circumnavigation of the world by one Maximilianus Transylvanus. The museum's art collection includes important paintings by nineteenth-century Filipino masters Juan Luna and Félix Hidalgo, as well as selected works by Fernando Amorsolo, who gained prominence during the early 1930s and

1940s for popularizing images of Philippine landscapes and beautiful rural Filipinas. The museum's Rizaliana includes some ninety letters written by José Rizal to his mother and sisters in the 1890s, along with the national hero's wallet and paintbrushes, his flute and personal papers. Exhibits rotate every six months, as there's not enough space to display everything at once, but the library section always contains some of the best rare books, artwork and letters. Note that the museum is expected to move into new digs at **The Proscenium**, a development on Dr Jose P. Rizal Avenue in Makati, sometime before 2016.

Marikina Shoe Museum

J.P. Rizal St, Marikina, 16km east of Rizal Park • Mon–Sat 9am–noon & 1–5pm • P50 • ☎ 02 646 2368 • LRT to Katipunan, then taxi

Nothing symbolizes the vanity of **Imelda Marcos** more than her collection of shoes, which numbered in the thousands on the eve of the EDSA revolution in 1986 (it's not known how many she owns today). This ghastly but admittedly stylish legacy is preserved at the **Marikina Shoe Museum** way out in the eastern suburbs, where 749 pairs belonging to the former first lady are displayed under her giant portrait, along with pairs owned by each president of the Philippines (the worn-out-looking shoes owned by Ferdinand Marcos make quite a contrast) and several other local celebrities. The history of shoemaking is explained upstairs. The reason the museum is in Marikina is that the area was dubbed the "**shoe capital of the Philippines**" back in 1956, and though there are still many factories in the neighbourhood, the industry's heyday was the 1970s and 1980s.

ARRIVAL AND DEPARTURE   MANILA

BY PLANE

NINOY AQUINO INTERNATIONAL AIRPORT

Almost everyone visiting the Philippines arrives at Ninoy Aquino International Airport (☎ 02 833 1180, ⊛ miaa.gov .ph) or NAIA, on the southern fringes of Manila, named after the anti-Marcos politician who was assassinated here in 1983.

Terminals The airport has four separate and unconnected terminals, making it seem, confusingly, as if there are several different airports (you may hear locals refer to them this way). Most international flights arrive at Terminal 1; Terminal 2, relatively nearby, serves only Philippine Airlines (international and domestic); the tiny Domestic Passenger Airport Terminal (aka Terminal 4) is 3km away on the other side of the airport and serves AirAsia Zest, Fil-Asian Airways, SkyJet and Tigerair Philippines flights; further around is Terminal 3, serving Cebu Pacific and PAL Express (international and domestic). Note that there is a long-standing plan to transfer all international flights to Terminal 3 – this started happening in 2011 with ANA, while Cathay Pacific, Delta and Emirates were scheduled to move in 2014. A free shuttle bus connects all the terminals, running frequently throughout the day, but traffic congestion means transfers can take over an hour in some cases – leave plenty of time.

Tourist information Terminal 1 has a small Department of Tourism reception desk (☎ 02 832 2964), open to meet all flights, where you can pick up maps and current

information. Terminals 2 and 3 only have general airport information desks that sometimes carry city maps.

Services There are banks and ATMs at all terminals (BPI is just outside the domestic terminal). There are no left luggage facilities at any of the terminals. Free wi-fi is available inside the terminals.

AIRPORT TRANSPORTATION

The roads around the airport quickly become gridlocked in heavy rain or at rush hour; it can take anything from 20min to 1hr to travel the 7km to the main tourist and budget accommodation area of Manila Bay.

Airport taxis To head into the centre, the best thing to do is to take an official yellow airport taxi; these charge higher rates than normal white taxis (see p.84), but they are safer and use the meter (insist that they use it). The meter starts at P70 (for the first 500m) and adds P4.50 per 300m; reckon on P180–250 to Malate or Makati and P250–300 for Ermita, depending on traffic. Beware of scam artists – if the meter looks like it's going to hit P1000 anywhere inside the city you are being ripped off. Take the taxi number and threaten to report the driver.

Fixed-rate taxis The alternative is to take a fixed-rate or "coupon" taxi (you get tickets for these at desks outside the terminal), but these are very expensive unless you have a large group (the "taxis" are big Toyota vans). The fixed-rate fare is P450 to Malate, P540 to Ermita, P340–450 to Makati and P670–1100 to Quezon City.

1

Jeepneys It is possible to flag down a jeepney from the main roads near any of the terminals, but if you have any luggage it will be hard (or impossible) to drag it on board.

DOMESTIC FLIGHTS

Domestic carriers are covered in Basics (see p.25).

Northern Luzon Batanes (up to 2 daily; 1hr 45min); Laoag (up to 3 daily; 50min); Tuguegarao (1 daily; 1hr 15min).

Southern Luzon Legazpi (up to 4 daily; 1hr 10min); Naga (1 daily; 55min); Virac (1 daily; 1hr 10min).

Mindoro San José (1 daily; 50min).

The Visayas Bacolod (up to 8 daily; 1hr 10min); Caticlan (up to 8 daily; 1hr); Cebu City (up to 16 daily; 1hr 10min); Dumaguete (up to 5 daily; 1hr 15min); Iloilo (up to 11 daily; 1hr); Kalibo (up to 6 daily; 50min); Tablas Island (2 daily; 40min); Tacloban (5 daily; 1hr 10min); Tagbilaran (4 daily; 2hr).

Palawan Busuanga Island (up to 3 daily; 1hr); Puerto Princesa (up to 5 daily; 1hr 10min).

Mindanao Butuan (1 daily; 1hr 25min); Cagayan de Oro (up to 10 daily; 1hr 25min); Cotabato (1 daily; 1hr 35min); Davao (up to 5 daily; 1hr 50min); Dipolog (1 daily; 1hr 30min); General Santos (up to 3 daily; 1hr 50min); Ozamiz (1 daily; 1hr 25min); Surigao (2 daily; 1hr 40min); Zamboanga (up to 4 daily; 1hr 40min).

BY FERRY

Most 2GO Travel ferries (the former Negros Navigation, SuperFerry, Cebu Ferries and SuperCat brands;

ⓦ travel.2go.com.ph) use the new terminal at Pier 4, North Harbor (along Marcos Rd, a few kilometres north of Intramuros), from where a taxi to Ermita costs about P150.

Departures Bacolod (4 weekly; 7hr–9hr 30min); Butuan (1 weekly; 34hr 30min); Cagayan de Oro (4 weekly; 34hr); Cebu City (4 weekly; 11hr); Coron (1 weekly; 14hr); Dipolog (1 weekly; 28hr 30min); Iligan (1 weekly; 42hr 30min); Iloilo (2 weekly; 20hr); Ozamiz (1 weekly; 35hr 30min); Puerto Princesa (1 weekly; 17hr).

BY BUS

Dozens of buses link Manila with the provinces. As a general rule, if you're arriving from the south, you'll end up in the Pasay area of EDSA, in the south of the city near Taft Ave, while if you're arriving from the north you'll find yourself at the northern end of EDSA in Cubao (Quezon City). From Pasay you can take the LRT (see p.83) north to the Malate area (get off at Pedro Gil station) or the MRT (see p.83) northeast to Makati and beyond. Alternatively, a taxi from the Pasay area to Malate costs less than P100. From most bus stations in Cubao it's a short walk to the Cubao MRT station; a taxi from Cubao to Makati costs around P150. Leaving Manila by bus can be confusing, however, as there's no central bus terminal – each company has its own station, albeit clumped together in Cubao and Pasay (a third cluster lies on Rizal Ave, known as "Avenida", in Quiapo). Usually, if you tell your taxi driver your destination, they will bring you to the right station. The list below includes some of the more popular operators.

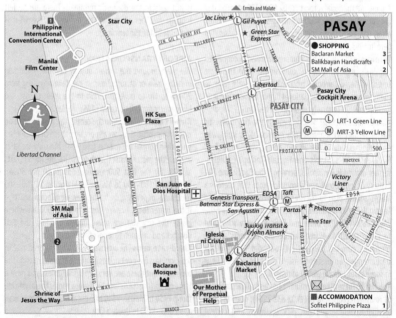

AROUND MANILA

Balanga (2–3hr). Bataan Transit ☎ 02 352 4727, ⊛ bataan transit.com: Five Star Terminal, Cubao (every 15min 1am–11pm); Avenida Terminal, 1612 Doroteo Jose St, Santa Cruz (every 20min 2am–9.30pm). Genesis Transport, 101 A Giselle, Park Plaza, EDSA at Rotonda, Pasay ☎ 02 853 3115, ⊛ genesistransport.com.ph (every 20min 4am–9pm).

Batangas (express 1hr 30min; regular 2–3hr). ALPS ☎ 923 716 0472, ⊛ alpsthebus.com: from Araneta Center Bus Terminal, Cubao (every 30min). JAM ⊛ jam.com.ph: 2124 Taft Ave, Pasay ☎ 02 831 8264; 831 EDSA at Timog Ave, Cubao ☎ 02 990 1289 (hourly 12.40am–11pm).

Clark/Angeles City/Dau (bus terminal) (1hr 30min–2hr). Five Star, 2240 Aurora Blvd, Pasay Terminal ☎ 02 851 6614, ⊛ 5starbus.co (frequent departures). Philippine Rabbit, Rizal Ave at Recto (Avenida) ☎ 02 734 9836 (every 30min 7am–9pm); Philtranco, EDSA at Apelo Cruz St, Pasay ☎ 02 851 8078, ⊛ philtranco.com.ph (to Clark Airport daily 6.30am, 11.30am & 8.30pm). Swagman Travel, *Swagman Hotel*, 411 A. Flores St, Ermita ☎ 02 523 8541, ⊛ swaggy.com (small buses to Angeles City daily 11.30am, 3.30pm and 8.30pm).

Laguna Green Star Express, Taft Ave at Sen Gil Puyat (Buendia Ave), Pasay ☎ 02 831 3178. Frequent buses to Santa Cruz (for Pagsanjan; 2hr 30min) via Calamba (1hr 30min) and Los Baños (2hr).

Lemery/Tanauan (for Lake Taal; 2hr 30min). JAM ⊛ jam .com.ph: 2124 Taft Ave, Pasay ☎ 02 831 8264; 831 EDSA at Timog Ave, Cubao ☎ 02 990 1289 (hourly 4am–8pm).

Lipa (for Taal; 2hr 30min). ALPS, Araneta Center Bus Terminal, Cubao ☎ 923 716 0472, ⊛ alpsthebus.com (every 30min).

Mariveles (3–4hr). Bataan Transit ☎ 02 352 4727, ⊛ bataantransit.com: Five Star Terminal, Cubao (every 20min midnight–9.30pm); Avenida Terminal, 1612 Doroteo Jose St, Santa Cruz (every 30min 3.30am–8pm). Genesis Transport, 101 A Giselle, Park Plaza, EDSA at Rotonda, Pasay ☎ 02 853 3115, ⊛ genesistransport.com.ph (every 20min 1am–7.30pm).

Malalos (1hr). First North Luzon Transit, Five Star terminal, 674 EDSA at Monte de Piedad St, Cubao ☎ 02 851 6614, ⊛ 5starbus.co (hourly departures).

Nasugbu (3hr). Batman Star Express (BSC), Genesis Transport terminal, 101 A Giselle, Park Plaza, EDSA at Rotonda, Pasay (hourly departures).

Subic Bay/Olongapo (2hr 30min–3hr 30min). Saulog Transit/Genesis Transport, 704 EDSA at New York St, Cubao ☎ 02 709 0803, ⊛ genesistransport.com.ph (hourly 4am–6.30pm. Victory Liner ⊛ victoryliner.com: Cubao Terminal, 683 EDSA ☎ 02 727 4534 (every 30min 3am–9pm); Pasay Terminal, 651 EDSA ☎ 02 833 5019 (every 30min 1.30am–9pm); Caloocan Terminal, 713 Rizal Ave Ext ☎ 02 361 1506 (hourly 5.30am–9pm); Sampaloc Terminal, 551 Earnshaw St, a short walk from Legarda LRT station (hourly 5am–8pm).

Tagaytay (1hr 30min). Erjohn & Almark, MRT-Taft (Pasay) on EDSA ☎ 02 529 6148 (every 30min). San Agustin, MRT-Taft (Pasay) on EDSA ☎ 02 872 8497 (every 30min).

NORTHERN LUZON

Alaminos (6–8hr). Five Star, 674 EDSA at Monte de Piedad St, Cubao ☎ 02 851 6614, ⊛ 5starbus.co (every 30min); Victory Liner, 683 EDSA, Cubao Terminal ☎ 02 727 4534, ⊛ victoryliner.com (every 40min–1hr).

Baguio (6–8hr). Dagupan Bus, EDSA at New York St, Cubao ☎ 02 911 7359 (hourly). Genesis Transport, 704 EDSA at New York St, Cubao ☎ 02 709 0803, ⊛ genesis transport.com.ph (hourly 3am–7pm). Partas ⊛ partas .com.ph: 816 Aurora Blvd at EDSA, Cubao Terminal ☎ 02 851 4025; Aurora Blvd (Tramo) at Edang St, Pasay Terminal ☎ 02 852 8194 (daily 24hr service). Philippine Rabbit, Rizal Ave at Recto (Avenida) ☎ 02 734 9836 (every 1–2hr 4am–2am). Victory Liner ⊛ victoryliner.com: 683 EDSA, Cubao Terminal ☎ 02 727 4534 and 651 EDSA, Pasay Terminal ☎ 02 833 5019 (hourly 24hr); 713 Rizal Ave Ext, Caloocan Terminal ☎ 02 361 1506 (7 daily 7am–11.30pm); 551 Earnshaw St, Sampaloc Terminal, a short walk from Legarda LRT station (6 daily 4.30am–11pm).

Baler (5–6hr). Genesis Transport (daily 5am & 6am) and Joy Bus (daily midnight) both leave from the Genesis Transport Terminal, 704 EDSA at New York St, Cubao ☎ 02 709 0803, ⊛ genesistransport.com.ph.

Banaue (8–9hr). Ohayami Trans, J. Fajardo St at Lacson Ave, Sampaloc ☎ 02 516 0501, ⊛ ohayamitrans.com (daily 10pm, plus Fri & Oct–June only 9pm).

Bontoc (12hr). Cable Bus, 269 Rodriguez Ave, Quezon City ☎ 02 257 3582 (nightly buses).

Dagupan (4–5hr). Victory Liner ⊛ victoryliner.com: 683 EDSA, Cubao Terminal (☎ 02 727 4534; every 40min–1hr); 651 EDSA, Pasay Terminal (☎ 02 833 5019; every 40min–1hr 3.20am–9.45pm); 713 Rizal Ave Ext, Caloocan Terminal (☎ 02 361 1506; every 40min–1hr 5am–9pm).

Kiangan/Lagawe (8hr). Ohayami Trans, J. Fajardo St at Lacson Ave, Sampaloc ☎ 02 516 0501, ⊛ ohayamitrans .com (daily 9.30pm).

Laoag (12–14hr). Fariñas Transit, Laon Laan St at M. de la Fuente St, Sampaloc ☎ 02 731 4507 (hourly 6am–4am). Partas ⊛ partas.com.ph: 816 Aurora Blvd at EDSA, Cubao Terminal ☎ 02 851 4025; Aurora Blvd (Tramo) at Edang St, Pasay Terminal ☎ 02 852 8194 (daily 24hr service).

Lingayen (4–5hr). Five Star, 674 EDSA at Monte de Piedad St, Cubao ☎ 02 851 6614, ⊛ 5starbus.co (hourly). Victory Liner, 683 EDSA, Cubao Terminal ☎ 02 727 4534, ⊛ victoryliner.com (every 40min–1hr).

San Fernando (La Union; 6–8hr). Dominion Bus Lines, EDSA at East Ave, Cubao ☎ 02 741 4146 (hourly). Genesis Transport, 101 A Giselle, Park Plaza, EDSA at Rotonda, Pasay ☎ 02 853 3115, ⊛ genesistransport.com.ph (hourly 2am–6.30pm). Partas ⊛ partas.com.ph: 816 Aurora Blvd at EDSA, Cubao Terminal ☎02 851 4025; Aurora Blvd (Tramo) at Edang St, Pasay Terminal ☎02 852 8194 (daily 24hr service).

Tuguegarao (10–12hr). Baliwag Transit, EDSA, corner New York St, Cubao ☎02 912 3343; Caloocan (Grace Park) Terminal, 2nd Ave ☎02 364 0778 (frequent departures). Partas ⓦpartas.com.ph: 816 Aurora Blvd at EDSA, Cubao Terminal ☎02 851 4025; Aurora Blvd (Tramo) at Edang St, Pasay Terminal ☎02 852 8194 (daily 24hr service). Victory

Liner ⓦvictoryliner.com: 651 EDSA, Pasay Terminal ☎02 833 5019 (every 1–2hr 5am–11.30pm); 713 Rizal Ave Ext, Caloocan Terminal ☎02 361 1506 (6 daily 4am–7.30pm).

Vigan (8–10hr). Dominion Bus Lines, EDSA at East Ave, Cubao ☎02 741 4146 (hourly). Fariñas Transit, Laon Laan St at M. de la Fuente St, Sampaloc ☎02 731 4507 (daily). Partas ⓦpartas.com.ph: 816 Aurora Blvd at EDSA, Cubao Terminal ☎02 851 4025; Aurora Blvd (Tramo) at Edang St, Pasay Terminal ☎02 852 8194 (daily 24hr service).

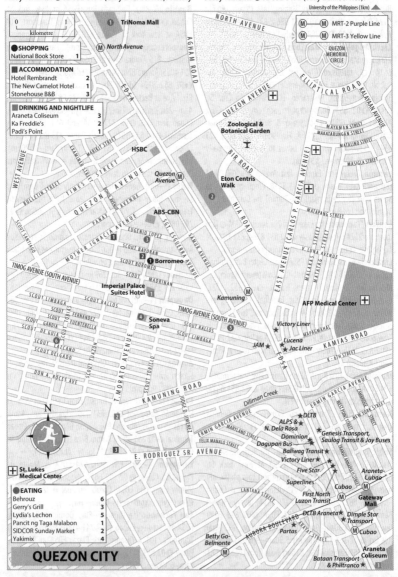

QUEZON CITY

TO SOUTHERN LUZON

Daet (7–8hr). ALPS, Araneta Center Bus Terminal, Cubao ☎923 716 0472, ⓦalpsthebus.com (every 30min 4–9pm only). DLTB, EDSA Cubao, in front of NEPA Q-Mart ☎02 466 1914, ⓦdltbbus.com.ph (8 daily). Philtranco, EDSA at Apelo Cruz St, Pasay ☎02 851 8078, ⓦphiltranco.com.ph (6 daily). Superlines, EDSA Cubao, between New York St and Monte de Piedad St ☎02 414 3319.

Legazpi (8–10hr). ALPS, Araneta Center Bus Terminal, Cubao ☎923 716 0472, ⓦalpsthebus.com (every 30min 4–9pm only). Philtranco, EDSA at Apelo Cruz St, Pasay ☎02 851 8078, ⓦphiltranco.com.ph (2 daily).

Lucena (3hr 30min). Jac Liner ⓦjacliner.com: Donada St at Gil Puyat (Buendia), Pasay ☎02 404 2073; Araneta Center Terminal, Cubao ☎0922 852 2904 (every 30min 2am–10pm Mon–Thurs, 24hr Fri–Sun). JAM ⓦjam.com .ph: 2124 Taft Ave, Pasay ☎02 831 8264; 831 EDSA at Timog Ave, Cubao ☎02 990 1289 (hourly 12.40am–11pm). Lucena Lines, 713 EDSA, Cubao ☎02 416 4668 (every 30–40min). N. Dela Rosa, EDSA, Cubao, between Ermin Garcia St and New York St (every 30–40min).

Naga (8–10hr). ALPS, Araneta Center Bus Terminal, Cubao ☎923 716 0472, ⓦalpsthebus.com (every 30min 4–9pm only). DLTB, Araneta Center, beside Ali-Mall, Cubao ☎02 921 3462, ⓦdltbbus.com.ph; Taft Ave at Gil Puyat (Buendia) Ave, Pasay (beside Buendia LRT Station) ☎02 419 9971 (6 daily). Philtranco, EDSA at Apelo Cruz St, Pasay ☎02 851 8078, ⓦphiltranco.com.ph (7 daily).

Sorsogon City (10–12hr). Philtranco, EDSA at Apelo

Cruz St, Pasay ☎02 851 8078, ⓦphiltranco.com.ph (1 daily); a number of local bus companies also operate this route.

TO MINDORO

Sabang & Muelle pier (Puerto Galera; 4hr). Si-Kat, City State Tower, 1315 Mabini St, Ermita ☎02 708 9628, ⓦsikatferrybus.com (daily 8.30am).

San José (10–12hr). Dimple Star Transport, Ali Mall, Cubao Terminal ☎02 517 9677: via Batangas, Abra de Ilog & Sablayan (2 daily; 10hr), via Batangas, Calapan and Roxas (1 daily; 12hr). JAM ⓦjam.com.ph: 2124 Taft Ave, Pasay ☎02 831 8264; 831 EDSA at Timog Ave, Cubao ☎02 990 1289: via Calapan and Batangas ferry (every 2hr 2am–9pm).

TO THE VISAYAS

Panay Philtranco, EDSA at Apelo Cruz St, Pasay ☎02 851 8078, ⓦphiltranco.com.ph. To Iloilo (2 daily; 17hr), via Mindoro.

Samar/Leyte Philtranco, EDSA at Apelo Cruz St, Pasay ☎02 851 8078, ⓦphiltranco.com.ph. To Ormoc (2 daily; 28hr) via Tacloban (26hr).

TO MINDANAO

Cagayan de Oro (2 days). Philtranco, EDSA at Apelo Cruz St, Pasay ☎02 851 8078, ⓦphiltranco.com.ph (via Surigao, 1 daily).

Davao (2–3 days). Philtranco, EDSA at Apelo Cruz St, Pasay ☎02 851 8078, ⓦphiltranco.com.ph (via Surigao, 4 daily).

GETTING AROUND

There are so many vehicles fighting for every inch of road space in Manila that at peak times it can be a sweaty battle of nerves just to move a few hundred metres. **Walking** is usually out of the question, except for short distances, because **buses** and **jeepneys** belch smoke with impunity, turning the air around major thoroughfares into a poisonous miasma. Fortunately, Manila's **taxis** are not expensive and are mostly air-conditioned – many visitors use them all the time. Manila's two light railway lines, the **LRT** and the MetroStar Express (**MRT**) are cheap and reliable, but they use mutually exclusive ticketing and the interchanges are poorly designed. Often very cramped and uncomfortable during the day, try to avoid them completely during rush hour (Mon–Fri 7–9.30am & 5–8pm) when you'll have to line up just to get into the stations, let alone the jam-packed trains.

METROSTAR EXPRESS (MRT)

The MetroStar Express (daily 5.30am–11pm; every 3–6min; ⓦdotcmrt3.gov.ph) is also known as MRT-3 (or yellow line, formerly the blue line). It runs for 16.95km along EDSA from Taft Ave in Pasay City in the south to North Ave, Quezon City in the north, connecting with the LRT at both ends.

Fares A single-journey ticket costs P10–15 (at the time of writing fares were expected to rise by P5–10), or you can buy a multiple-journey ticket covering P100 worth of travel; if you plan to use the MRT a lot, you'll save a lot of time buying the latter (you'll still have to line up for a bag check before entering the station, but will avoid having to line up again for a ticket).

Safety Security guards patrol stations (and the first carriage is usually reserved for women), but watch out for pickpockets and the more brazen "snatchers", who rip phones, bags and wallets from your hand and make a run for it.

MANILA LIGHT RAIL TRANSIT (LRT)

The LRT (ⓦlrta.gov.ph) is an elevated railway system with two lines: the 17.2km Green Line (LRT-1); and the 13.8km Purple Line, which confusingly is known as MRT-2. The Green Line runs from Baclaran in the south to North Ave in Quezon City in the north, where it connects with MRT-3. The Purple Line runs from Santolan in Pasig City to Recto in Quiapo, close to the Green Line's Doroteo Jose station. Trains on both lines run frequently from 5am to 10pm.

1

Fares Tickets range from P12 to P20 (at the time of writing fares were expected to rise by P5–10). P100 stored value tickets are also available.

JEEPNEYS AND FX TAXIS

Jeepneys are the cheapest way to get around, and they run back and forth all over the city. At the time of writing fares were expected to rise to P10 for the first 4km, and increase by P1.75/km thereafter. Destinations are written on signboards at the front.

FX taxis You'll also see tiny minivans or "FX taxis", usually labelled UV Express, that zip between fixed points, usually without stopping, for around P20–30 per ride. While sometimes useful (linking SM Mall of Asia and Baclaran station, for example), both forms of transport are usually incredibly cramped, and traffic congestion can make even short journeys last hours.

BUSES

Local buses in Manila bump and grind their way along all major thoroughfares, such as Taft, EDSA and Gil Puyat (Buendia) Avenue, but are not allowed on most side streets. The destination is written on a sign in the front window. Most vehicles are ageing contraptions bought secondhand from Japan or Taiwan, and feature no particular colour scheme; it's a matter of luck whether any one bus has air conditioning.

Fares Most fares range P15–20 for the first 5km, and increase P2–2.20/km thereafter. As with jeepneys, traffic congestion will add travel time and even larger buses will often be packed.

TAXIS

Most Manila taxi drivers are honest these days and use the meter, though some may still try and set prices in advance or "forget" to switch it on (insist on the meter). Taxis come in a confusing mix of models, colours and shapes; most metered taxis are white (and often called "white taxis" to differentiate them from the yellow airport taxis that have higher fares).

Fares Fares are good value and you'll save a lot of time using white taxis over any other form of transport. The metered rate is an initial P40 (for the first 500m), plus P3.50 for every 300m thereafter (every 2min waiting adds P1).

INFORMATION

Tourist information The Tourist Information Center is located inside the Department of Tourism Building, 351 Sen Gil Puyat (Buendia) Ave (Mon–Fri 7am–6.30pm, Sat 8am–5pm; ☎02 525 2000 ☜visitmyphilippines.com) in Makati. Plans are in the works for a dedicated tourist information office for Manila, but don't hold your breath.

Maps Many bookshops (see p.98) sell the Accu-map range of atlases (☜www.accu-map.com), A–Z-like pocketbooks that cover the whole of Metro Manila.

Listings Daily newspapers such as the *Philippine Daily Inquirer* (☜inquirer.net) and the *Philippine Star* (☜philstar.com) have entertainment sections with details of movies, concerts and arts events in Manila. Online, ClickTheCity (☜clickthecity.com) has an events calendar, movie and gig guides and listings of restaurants and hotels.

TOURS AND ACTIVITIES

Tours Filipino Travel Center, G/F *Palm Plaza Hotel*, 524 Pedro Gil St at M. Adriatico St, Ermita ☎02 528 4507, ☜filipinotravel.com.ph (Manila day-trips from P1700). Also Walk This Way and Old Manila Walks (see box, p.62).

Dive operators Adventure Bound G/F, GBI Building, 2282 Pasong Tamo Extension, Makati ☎02 813 2067, ☜adventurebound.com.ph; Scuba World, 1181 Pablo Ocampo St ☎02 895 3551, ☜scubaworld.com.ph.

ACCOMMODATION

Most of Manila's budget accommodation is in the Manila Bay area, specifically in the enclaves of **Ermita** and **Malate**, which also have a high density of cheap restaurants, bars and tourist services. In recent years a number of reasonably priced mid-range hotels have sprung up, as well as several five-star places along Manila Bay, joining the historic *Manila Hotel*. In the business district of **Makati**, there's some mid-range accommodation in and around P. Burgos St at the northern end of Makati Ave, beyond the *Mandarin Oriental Manila*. This is close to the red-light district, so if you want somewhere else in Makati try the somewhat anaemic but comfortable chain hotels in Arnaiz Ave (formerly Pasay Rd), behind the Greenbelt mall. The hotels in **Quezon City** are almost all around Timog Ave and Tomas Morato Ave, close to the nightlife; if you're planning to catch an early bus from Cubao it might be worth considering staying here. If you have an early flight and a bit more cash to spend there are some convenient and luxurious options close to the airport.

AIRPORT AREA (PASAY CITY)

Manila Marriott Hotel 10 Newport Blvd, Newport City Complex ☎02 988 9999, ☜marriott.com; map pp.60–61. Fabulous luxury hotel, right across from Terminal 3 (with free shuttle bus to all terminals). Stylish rooms come with flatscreen TVs and funky bathrooms with

CLOCKWISE FROM TOP LEFT JEEPNEYS, MAKATI; STREET FOOD, BACLARAN MARKET (P.100); ILALIM NG TULAY (P.75); SENTRO 1771 (P.92) >

1

glass walls (with shades for the modest) and big tubs. The pool is a great place to chill out during the day. P9800

INTRAMUROS AND RIZAL PARK

The Bayleaf Muralla St at Victoria St ☎02 328 3170, �🅦thebayleaf.com.ph; map p.63. Swish boutique hotel in the historic heart of the city, with spacious, modern rooms (featuring floor-to-ceiling windows), roof deck bar and restaurant with great views and free wi-fi throughout. P4000

Manila Hotel 1 Rizal Park ☎02 527 0011, �🅦www .manila-hotel.com.ph; map p.63. Esteemed establishment that is undoubtedly past its best but nevertheless reeks of history (see p.67), at least in the old wing where General Douglas MacArthur stayed during World War II; if you've got P32,000 to spare you can stay a night in his suite. The lobby is a grand affair with black-and-white-tiled flooring and oxblood velvet sofas. The rooms, many in need of a revamp, remain stubbornly traditional, with dark wood and four-poster beds. P4500

White Knight Hotel Intramuros Cabildo St at Urdaneta St, Plaza San Luis Complex ☎02 526 6539, �🅦whiteknighthotelintramuros.com; map p.63. Nineteenth-century building with heaps of character and 29 simple but spacious rooms tastefully furnished in period style, with bathroom, a/c, flatscreen TV and free wi-fi. Worth considering for the novelty of staying in the most historic part of the city. P1960

ERMITA AND MALATE

ERMITA

Best Western Hotel La Corona 1166 M.H. del Pilar St at Arquiza St ☎02 524 2631, �🅦bestwesternhotel manila.com; map p.69. Solid choice featuring stylish double a/c rooms with a modern Filipino theme, cable TV and free wi-fi. Good location and the rate includes a buffet breakfast for two. P2600

City Garden Suites 1158 A. Mabini St ☎02 536 1451, �🅦citygardensuites.com; map p.69. Standard hotel with sparsely furnished but clean a/c rooms and a reasonable coffee shop in the lobby; Filipino buffet breakfast included. P2350

Ermita Tourist Inn 1549 A. Mabini St at Soldado St ☎02 521 8770; map p.69. Very basic choice on the edge of Ermita close to Malate, with thirty ageing a/c rooms with hot showers and simple breakfast included (no TV or wi-fi). There's a travel agent downstairs for flights and visas. P1050

★**Hostellery** 418 Plaza Nuestra Senyora De Guia, Alhambra St ☎02 521 6545, ✉hostellery@gmail.com; map p.69. Stylish budget option on the bay opened in 2013, with free wi-fi (and computers), cable TV, snacks and beers. Spotless mixed dorms P500, en-suite doubles P2000

★**Hotel H2O** Manila Ocean Park (behind the Quirino Grandstand) ☎02 238 6100, �🅦hotelh2o.com; map p.69. The most original boutique hotel in Manila, with a chic "aqua" theme and fabulous views of the bay or Ocean World pool (for the nightly fountain shows). Rooms sport a trendy minimalist design and LCD TVs; some even have stunning wall-sized in-room aquariums. The only (slight) downside is that the hotel is a bit cut off from the rest of the city. P3200

Lotus Garden Hotel 1227 A. Mabini St at Padre Faura St ☎02 522 1515, �🅦lotusgardenhotelmanila.com; map p.69. Snazzy modern rooms with cable TV and free wi-fi,; an excellent location and decent buffet breakfast make this chain hotel a good deal – book online for the best rates. P2015

Southern Cross Hotel 1125 M.H. del Pilar St ☎02 521 2013, ⓦthesoutherncrosshotelmanila.com; map p.69. Friendly budget hotel with small but comfy rooms equipped with a/c, cable TV, bathroom and fridge. It's owned by an Australian national and there's an Aussie-style bar and food, large-screen TV and billiard table downstairs. Walk-in rates tend to be cheaper than booking online if paying in cash. P1699

MALATE

Adriatico Arms 561 J. Nakpil St ☎02 521 0736; map p.69. A pleasant no-frills hotel in an unbeatable location. The 28 a/c rooms are smallish, but well kept and functional, with TV but no breakfast. Nearby is *Café Adriatico* (see p.90), where you can sit and watch the beautiful people stroll by. P1700

Aloha Hotel 2150 Roxas Blvd ☎02 526 8088, ⓦalohahotel.net.ph; map p.69. A Manila Bay stalwart, the *Aloha* boasts a fine location with views of the bay from the front (5/F or above), though the rooms (all a/c and free wi-fi) have seen better days – ask to see a selection before you hand over any money. There's a small café and a Chinese restaurant. P2500

★**Baywatch Luxury Condos** 2057 M.H. del Pilar St ☎0919 490 1330, ⓦbaywatch1403.com; map p.69. These two studio apartments (identical units 1403 and 1903) are fabulous deals, with handsome interiors, free wi-fi, flatscreen TVs and spectacular views over Manila Bay from the balconies. There's also a small kitchen and use of pool. P3400

★**Bianca's Garden Hotel** 2139 M. Adriatico St ☎02 525 2846, ⓦbiancasgardenhotel.com; map p.69. This idyllic provincial-style retreat on the southern edge of the tourist area is understandably popular with backpackers and divers stopping off in Manila for a few nights on their way to the beach. Rooms are spacious and elegant, decorated with Philippine antiques evoking the building's former incarnation as a wealthy Spanish-style home. There's a small swimming pool in the shady garden. P1000

★**Chill-out Guesthouse** 612 Remedios St at Remedios Circle ☎939 517 7019, ⓦmanila-guesthouse.com; map p.69. This hostel, run by an enthusiastic young French crew, reopened in new digs in 2013, with a choice of fan or a/c en-suite rooms (P1500) and dorms; the back rooms are quieter. There's a common kitchen area for self-caterers, lockers and free wi-fi. A/c dorm P350, fan doubles P700

Friendly's Guesthouse 1750 M. Adriatico St at Nakpil St ☎02 474 0742, ⓦfriendlysguesthouse.com; map p.69. The chilled-out balcony common area, bird's-eye view over Malate and free wi-fi and hot drinks at this backpackers' hostel are plus points, but it's not the cleanest. Self-catering cooking facilities available. Many rooms have shared bathrooms. Fan dorms P450 (a/c P495); fan doubles P695

Malate Pensionne 1771 M. Adriatico St ☎02 523 8304, ⓦmalatepensionne.com; map p.69. Tucked behind *Starbucks* in an unbeatable position, this has been one of the area's most popular guesthouses for years. Rooms are furnished in Spanish-colonial style and book up quickly. Dorm P475 (fan only), doubles P1100

★ **Pan Pacific Manila Hotel** M. Adriatico St at General Malvar St ☎02 318 0788, ⓦpanpacific.com/manila; map p.69. This is the top choice in Malate for superlative service (each room comes with 24hr butler service), luxurious rooms and a buffet breakfast that could feed an army. Passing from the chaos outside to the soothing outdoor swimming pool and jacuzzi is a surreal but pleasant experience. P6500

Pearl Garden Hotel 1700 M. Adriatico St at General Malvar St ☎02 525 1000, ⓦpearlgardenhotel.net; map p.69. One of the best mid-range hotels on the block, with 83 small but clean and elegant boutique-style rooms. The main downside (for non-smokers) is that the whole hotel is smoker friendly, and the free wi-fi is a bit unreliable. P3400

Pension Natividad 1690 M.H. del Pilar St ☎02 521 0524, ⓦpensionnatividad.com; map p.69. Spacious, impeccably clean rooms (some en suite and with a/c) in a quiet old family house that was built before World War II and partially destroyed by bombing. The terrace café is a good place to meet other travellers, and there's free wi-fi. One of the best budget places to stay in the area and handy for the airport. Dorm P400, doubles from P1000

Sofitel Philippine Plaza CCP Complex, off Roxas Blvd ☎02 551 5555, ⓦsofitelmanila.com; map p.80. If you can afford it and want a luxurious room with a balcony and a view of the Manila Bay sunsets, this is the place to stay. The *Sofitel* is big, brash and has a number of pricey bars and restaurants. First choice for many Japanese and Korean tour groups. P5850

PACO PARK

Garden Plaza Hotel 1030 Belen St ☎02 522 4835, ⓦgardenplazamanila.com; map p.69. Congenial and well managed, the *Garden Plaza* is right next to Paco Park and has adequate a/c rooms, a cute little swimming pool on the roof and the excellent *Old Swiss Inn* restaurant. Internet in lobby. P1800

Paco Park Oasis Hotel 1032–1034 Belen St ☎02 521 2371, ⓦoasispark.com; map p.69. Next door to the *Garden Plaza* (see above) outside the walls of Paco Park. Economy, standard, deluxe and superior rooms, some with four-poster bed and whirlpool bath (the "new" rooms have flatscreen TVs and free wi-fi; P3250) – overall a much better deal than its neighbour. Large swimming pool, pleasant terrace area, restaurant and a travel agency in the lobby. P2000

MAKATI

El Cielito Inn 804 Arnaiz Ave (Pasay Rd) ☎02 815 8951, ⓦelcielito-makati.com; map p.77. Small but clean glass-fronted mid-range hotel close to Makati's malls, with modern, carpeted a/c rooms and a coffee shop. P3050

★ **Makati Shangri-La** Ayala Ave at Makati Ave ☎02 813 8888, ⓦshangri-la.com; map p.77. If you fancy a splurge, this is the best choice in town, a top-notch establishment in the heart of Makati with chic rooms, fabulous service, waterfalls on every floor and a host of quality restaurants on site. P9990

Mandarin Oriental Manila Makati Ave at Paseo de Roxas ☎02 750 8888, ⓦmandarinoriental.com /manila; map p.77. Five-star establishment that serves as a good landmark in Makati, opposite Citibank and a short walk from the shops. Rooms are spacious, with all the comforts you'd expect from this luxury chain. Good deals online. P5500

Our Melting Pot Hostel 4/F Mavenue Bldg, 7844 Makati Ave at Guerrero St ☎02 659 5443, ⓦourmelting potmakati.com; map p.77. Friendly hostel with four dorms and private rooms with shared bathroom, all with a/c and free wi-fi. The rooftop is a chilled place for a beer, but the streets outside can be noisy. Dorms P550, doubles P1600

The Peninsula Manila Ayala Ave at Makati Ave ☎02 887 2888, ⓦpeninsula.com/Manila; map p.77. Ostentatious five-star that takes up a city block and has a cheesily opulent lobby where people go to drink coffee and to see and be seen. There are no fewer than seven restaurants, running the gamut from Asian to French. Rooms are as you'd expect at this price, with luxurious furnishings and all mod cons. P10,000

Robelle House 4402 Valdez St ☎02 899 8061, ⓦrobellehouse.net/Robelle_House; map p.77. This rambling family-run pension has been in business since 1977 and is still the most atmospheric Filipino budget accommodation in the business district. The property is old and the location isn't great though: it's a good walk from the Makati shops in a desolate backstreet area. The floors are polished tile and the wooden staircases are authentically creaky, although the rooms are no more than serviceable. Ask for one on the first floor overlooking the small pool. The cheapest have shared bath; en suites cost P1560. P1110

1

Tower Inn 1002 Arnaiz Ave (Pasay Rd) ☎02 888 5170, ⓦtowerinnmakati.com; map p.77. Modern business hotel with 48 rooms with cable TV (but not many channels), free wi-fi (lobby only) and including breakfast. It's within walking distance of Makati's shops and restaurants. **P3100**

AROUND P. BURGOS STREET

Best Western Oxford Suites Makati 518 P. Burgos St at Durban St ☎02 899 7988, ⓦoxfordsuitesmakati .com; map p.88. One of the best hotels on the P. Burgos strip, with 232 spacious rooms and suites, gym, 24hr coffee shop and fourth-floor restaurant. Some rooms have kitchenette, living room and terrace. Buffet breakfast included. **P3600**

City Garden Hotel Makati 7870 Makati Ave at Kalayaan Ave ☎02 899 1111, ⓦcitygardenhotels.com /makati; map p.88. A comfortable, modern boutique hotel with spacious and well-maintained a/c rooms, small rooftop swimming pool and giddy views from the rooftop café. Good location, the staff are efficient and you can negotiate a discount off-season. **P3600**

★**Clipper Hotel** 5766 Ebro St ☎02 890 8577, ⓦtheclipperhotel.com; map p.88. This Art Deco gem is more South Beach than south Manila, an atmospheric budget hotel that opened in 2009. Rooms are simple but spacious, and there's cable TV, free wi-fi and a desktop in the lobby for guests (10min free). The only catch is its relative proximity to girlie bars and clubs, and the street outside can be noisy at night. **P2200**

Jupiter Suites 102 Jupiter St at Makati Ave ☎02 890 5044, ⓦjupitersuites.com.ph; map p.88. Offers spacious a/c singles and doubles, all en suite and with cable TV and LAN internet (you have to pay P100 for a cable if you don't have one). Ask for a room at the back – those at the front overlook the busy street and you'll wake to the sound of jeepneys honking their horns at 5am. **P3980**

St Giles Makati Makati Ave at Kalayaan Ave ☎02 988 9888, ⓦstgilesmanila.com; map p.88. Snazzy hotel that opened in 2010, close to all the action. There's a pool and gym, and the rooms are elegantly furnished in light neutral tones. Free wi-fi. **P3300**

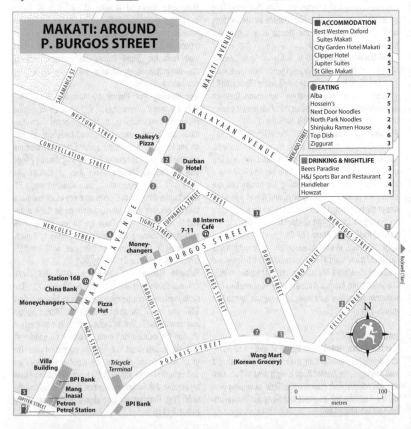

MAKATI: AROUND P. BURGOS STREET

■ ACCOMMODATION
Best Western Oxford Suites Makati	3
City Garden Hotel Makati	2
Clipper Hotel	4
Jupiter Suites	5
St Giles Makati	1

● EATING
Alba	7
Hossein's	5
Next Door Noodles	1
North Park Noodles	2
Shinjuku Ramen House	4
Top Dish	6
Ziggurat	3

■ DRINKING & NIGHTLIFE
Beers Paradise	3
H&J Sports Bar and Restaurant	2
Handlebar	4
Howzat	1

MAKATI AVENUE

SALAMANCA ST

NEPTUNE STREET

CONSTELLATION STREET

KALAYAAN AVENUE

Shakey's Pizza

Durban Hotel

DURBAN STREET

HERCULES STREET

TIGRIS STREET

EUPHRATES STREET

88 Internet Café

7-11

Money-changers

P. BURGOS STREET

MERCADO STREET

MERCEDES STREET

DURBAN STREET

EBRO STREET

Station 168
China Bank

Moneychangers

Pizza Hut

CACERES STREET

BADAJOS STREET

FELIPE STREET

N

ANDA STREET

POLARIS STREET

Wang Mart (Korean Grocery)

Villa Building

Tricycle Terminal

BPI Bank

Mang Inasal

JUPITER STREET

Petron Petrol Station

BPI Bank

Rockwell (1km)

0		100
	metres	

QUEZON CITY

Hotel 878 Libis 878 E. Rodriguez Jr. Ave ☎ 02 709 0154, ⊕ hotel878libis.com; map pp.60–61. Fine mid-range option, with 29 stylish doubles all with verandas, cable TV and free wi-fi. The super-cool lofts (P2550) and suites (P6400) are also worth considering. P1900

Hotel Rembrandt 26 Tomas Morato Ave Extension ☎ 02 373 3333, ⊕ hotelrembrandt.com.ph; map p.82. Medium-sized, modern hotel with a/c rooms, a gymnasium, a cosy piano bar on the top floor with views of the metropolis and a branch of *T.G.I. Friday's* on the ground floor. P2850

The New Camelot Hotel 35 Mother Ignacia Ave ☎ 02 373 2101, ⊕ camelothotel.com.ph; map p.82. You can't miss it: look out for the mock Arthurian spires rising above one of Quezon City's shantytowns. The rooms are like a bad medieval dream with their imitation-silk sheets, plastic-flower arrangements and chairs carved with Gothic quatrefoils. There are suits of armour in the lobby, the coffee shop is called the *Winchester*, and the bar the *Dungeon*. Need a present for someone special? Look no further than Lady Guinevere's Gift Shop. P1390

Stonehouse B&B 1315 E. Rodriguez Snr Ave ☎ 02 724 7551, ⊕ stonehouse.ph; map p.82. Cosy budget option with cable TV, en-suite rooms and a tasty breakfast for two. The nightly live jazz bands provide plenty of on-site entertainment. Free wi-fi in café area only. P1180

EATING

Eating in Manila is a real treat; there's a full range of international and Filipino cuisine on offer, and budget eats available on every street corner and in every mall in the form of vast food courts (see box, p.90). Filipinos are big fans of fast-food franchises, with national chains such as *Jollibee*, *Chowking*, *Mang Inasal* (with unlimited rice) and *Max's* (for fried chicken) dotted all over the city. You should also pay a visit to one of the ubiquitous *Goldilocks* (⊕ padala.goldilocks.com.ph) stores, purveyors of the best *polvoron* (peanut candy) and cakes since 1966.

INTRAMUROS AND RIZAL PARK

The old walled city of Intramuros doesn't have many restaurants, but those it does have are mostly in old colonial buildings and are significantly more atmospheric than anything beyond the walls. For cheap eats, try the stalls (plates from P50) just within the walls on the eastern edge of Intramuros, or in nearby San Francisco St, in an area known as Puerta Isabel II.

Barbara's Plaza San Luis Complex, General Luna St ☎ 02 527 4086, ⊕ barbarasheritagerestaurant.com; map p.63. Elegant dining in a colonial setting, with woody interiors and rich Filipino and Spanish food pioneered by founder Barbara de los Reyes in the 1970s. Best known for its touristy buffets (around P245 for lunch; P710 for dinner) and the Kultura Filipina traditional music and dance show from 7.15pm. A la carte dishes average P250–400. Daily 11am–2pm & 6.30–9pm.

★**Ilustrado** 744 General Luna St at the back of Silahis Center, facing Cabildo St ☎ 02 527 3674, ⊕ ilustradorestaurant.com.ph; map p.63. Nothing compares to *Ilustrado* if you are looking for the ambience of colonial Manila. The floors are polished wood, the tables are set with starched linen, ceiling fans whirr quietly and the cuisine is grand. Signature dishes include paella, creamy *bagnet* (deep-fried pork) and tender *lengua con setas* (ox tongue with brown sauce). Mains P450–850. Mon–Sat 11.30am–3pm & 6–10pm.

★**Kuatro Kantos** 744 General Luna St ☎ 02 527 2345; map p.63. This charming little bar and café in the same old building (with same owners) as *Ilustrado* opens for breakfast – perfect for a good cup of coffee or a bite to eat while you're wandering around Intramuros. The hot *pan de sal* with corned beef or *carabao* cheese makes an excellent and very affordable snack, and their pesto is home-made and organic. Mains P280–450. Daily 8am–7pm.

Patio de Conchita 681 Beaterio St ☎ 02 311 5417; map p.63. This great find is off the beaten path but an excellent place to have lunch. Food is served buffet style, with a range of top-notch Filipino dishes; try the *sinigang na baboy* (sour soup with pork) and freshly barbecued squid from P120. Mon–Sat 9am–3pm & 6–11pm.

ERMITA AND MALATE

Almost everyone who dines out in Ermita and Malate does so either in one of the big hotels or in the area around J. Nakpil Street and Remedios Circle, where most of the restaurants are small, intimate and not owned by big corporations. Bear in mind that J. Nakpil is a fickle, faddish area, and restaurants come and go.

Ang Bistro Sa Remedios 1911 M. Adriatico St, just off Remedios Circle ☎ 02 523 9153; map p.69. Informal and homey little restaurant with pretty Filipiniana interior and charming staff. The food is exclusively Filipino, with cholesterol-filled fried pig's knuckles, beefy stews and hefty chunks of roast pork. There's also good fish and prawns, but not a great deal for vegetarians, although pineapple fried rice is on the menu (average meals P300). Mon–Fri 11am–3pm & 6–11pm, Sat & Sun 11am–3pm & 6pm–midnight.

★**Aristocrat** 432 San Andres St, facing Roxas Blvd ☎ 02 524 7671, ⊕ aristocrat.com.ph; map p.69. Established out of an old van in 1936, *Aristocrat* is an institution among Filipinos for its justly lauded barbecued chicken (P195) and pork (P175), as well as the whole spread of Filipino comfort

1

TOP MANILA FOOD MARKETS

Food markets are scattered throughout the city, from no-frills street stalls to air-conditioned food courts in Manila's poshest malls – cuisine runs the gamut from Filipino snacks to high-end sushi. In general you'll be spending a lot less here than at sit-down restaurants, with small portions meaning plenty of scope of sampling different vendors.

Market! Market! Mabini Ave at McKinley Parkway, Bonifacio Global City ☎02 886 7519; map pp.60–61. This spotless high-end market comes with tempting fresh fruit stalls and a massive covered food court. Daily 10am–10pm.

Power Plant Mall Rockwell Drive at Estrella St, Makati ☎02 898 1702, ⓦpowerplantmall.com; map p.77. For a large and slightly more upmarket selection of restaurants and stalls check out this plush mall on the edge of Makati. There's also a huge Rustan's supermarket (ⓦrustansfresh.com; same hours), a good choice for self-catering. Mon–Thurs 11am–9pm, Fri 11am–10pm, Sat 10am–10pm, Sun 10am–9pm.

St Francis Square Mall Tiangge Julia Vargas Ave at Bank Drive, Ortigas ⓦstfrancissquare.com.ph; map p.78. The alley along the east side of this budget

mall is cheap-eats paradise at lunchtime, with huge pots of delicious Filipino food dolled out for a few pesos. Inside St Francis Mall itself, the 3/F Food Court is another excellent place for local food (with a/c). Mon–Thurs 10am–8pm, Fri & Sat 10am–9pm, Sun 9am–9pm.

★**Salcedo Community Market** Jaime Velasquez Park, Bel-Air, Makati; map p.77. One of Manila's culinary highlights, featuring a dazzling display of gastronomic delights from all corners of the Philippines to take away or enjoy at one of the communal tables. Sat 7am–2pm.

SIDCOR Sunday Market Eton Centris parking lot, EDSA at Quezon Ave, Quezon City; map p.82. Features 450 stalls selling a variety of fresh veg, fruit, meat and seafood. Sun 6am–2pm.

food. The special *halo-halo* (P125) here is an extravagant concoction of taro ice cream, sliced banana, beans, *nata de coco*, ice and evaporated milk. Don't miss the famous *bibingka* stall outside. Daily 24hr.

Cabalen Robinsons Place (G/F, Padre Faura Wing), Pedro Gil St at Adriatico St ☎02 536 7987; map p.69. Hugely popular chain of restaurants famed for their gut-busting buffets (P368, plus P60 for drinks) of traditional dishes from the province of Pampanga, including *camaru* (rice-field crickets), *batute* (fried pig's trotters), *kuhol* (escargots), *sinigang tiyan ng bangus* (milkfish belly) and desserts such as *halayang ube*. Daily 10am–9pm.

Café Adriatico 1790 M. Adriatico St ☎02 738 8220; map p.69. This chic but casual stalwart of the Malate nightlife scene opened a quarter of a century ago and was at the forefront of the area's revival. Light Spanish-Mediterranean themed meals include salads, omelettes and fondues (dishes average P150–300). Try the authentic *chocolate-eh*, a thick chocolatey drink served as an anytime "snack". Mon–Sat 7am–6pm, Sun 7am–4pm.

Casa Armas 573 J. Nakpil St at J. Bocobo St ☎02 536 1839; map p.69. Fashionable tapas bar serving big plates of sautéed shrimps in olive oil and garlic, fried Spanish sausage and Galician octopus, as well as omelettes, soups and salads. Dishes range from P285 for tapas to P350–750 for mains. Mon–Sat 11am–2am, Sun 6pm–2am.

Harbor View South Gate A, Rizal Park ☎02 524 1532, ⓦharborview-manila.com; map p.69. Located right on the harbour, between the US Embassy and *Manila Hotel*, this place is perfect for sunset viewing, with cool breezes,

fresh seafood from the tank and all the classic Filipino dishes (from P250). It's a bit like a posh beach bar. Daily 11am–midnight.

★**Kamayan** 523 Padre Faura St at Adriatico St ☎02 528 1723, ⓦkamayansaisakidads.com; map p.69. Excellent value buffet restaurant with three sections: a traditional selection of Filipino dishes such as grilled fish, spicy crab, roast chicken and local vegetables; a Western section with more conventional roast beef and the like; and a Japanese area with sushi, tempura and noodles. The staff are dressed in elegant Filipino costumes and strolling minstrels work the tables doing requests. Mon–Thurs lunch is P648, dinner P850; Fri–Sun it's P850 all day. Daily 11.30am–2.30pm & 6–10pm (Sat & Sun opens at 11am).

Kashmir 523 Padre Faura St (next to Kamayan) ☎02 524 6851, ⓦkashmirmanila.com; map p.69. Curry, chicken tikka, a mouthwatering selection of breads and wonderfully cheesy ersatz Raj decor. Be warned, the *Kashmir* chefs can be liberal with the spices, so think twice when the waiters ask if you want it very hot. Main dishes range P350–500. Daily 11am–11pm.

Korean Palace 1799 M. Adriatico St at Remedios St ☎02 521 6695; map p.69. One of a number of excellent Korean restaurants in the area, in part serving the growing numbers of Koreans here on a night out. Large menu that includes some good dishes to share, such as fried beef, chicken or fish with piping-hot rice and various side dishes including tangy *kimchi* (pickled cabbage) – mains P200–550. Daily 10am–midnight.

Pansit Malabon Express 103 B. Ermita Center Bldg, 1350 Roxas Blvd ☎02 521 7403, ⓦpansitmalabon .com; map p.69. Branch of famed purveyor of tasty fried noodles (*pansit Malabon*) in servings large enough for four people (from P300), as well as barbecue chicken meals (P125) and *bangus* (milkfish; P160). Daily 9am–9pm.

Seafood Market Restaurant 1190 J. Bocobo St ☎02 521 4351; map p.69. Here the day's catch is laid out on ice and you pick from whatever the boat brought in. The choice typically includes giant prawns, lapu-lapu, lobster, fish lips and sea slug, all cooked as you watch by wok chefs in a glass-fronted kitchen. It's not so cheap, though – a huge meal for two with drinks will cost around P2500. Daily 11am–2pm & 6–11pm.

Shawarma Snack Center 45 Salas St ☎02 525 4541; map p.69. Two branches of the *SSC* face each other across Salas St, so take your choice of plastic tables or a more rarefied atmosphere with tablecloths. The Middle Eastern dishes in both are superb and plentiful, with possibly the best falafels and kebabs in the city, and certainly the hottest chilli sauce. Mains mostly under P175. Located in a small Muslim enclave in Malate, replete with halal food and a small mosque just off the road. Daily 24hr.

Zamboanga 1619 M. Adriatico St ☎02 521 7345, ⓦzamboangarestaurant.com; map p.69. Fresh seafood from the deep south of the Philippines, a trio of crooning guitarists and nightly cultural shows at 8.30pm (mostly folk dance). This is the restaurant that features on many travel agents' night-time city tours, but still lots of fun after a few drinks (mains range P250–475). Daily 11am–11pm.

BINONDO AND QUIAPO

Binondo has no fancy restaurants and no bistros or wine bars; people come here for cheap, nourishing Chinese food in one of the area's countless Chinese restaurants or hole-in-the-wall noodle bars. Binondo and Quiapo also have a number of bakeries that are known in the Philippines for their *hopia*, a sweet cake-like snack with a soft pastry coating and thick yam paste in the middle.

Eng Bee Tin 628 Ongpin St ☎02 288 8888, ⓦengbeetin.com; map p.73. Filipinos often come to Binondo just to make a pilgrimage to this well-known bakery, which has specialized in various kinds of sweet, sticky mooncake and *hopia* since 1912. The bakers here invented *ube hopia*, made with sweet purple yam and now imitated throughout the country, and you can also buy *tikoy*, the sweet rice cake that is traditionally served during Chinese New Year. Daily 7.30am–8.30pm.

Ho-Land Hopia & Bakery 551 Yuchengco St at Carvajal St ☎02 242 9709; map p.73. Classic bakery (and *Eng Bee Tin* rival) serving *hopia* rolls for P40, but also squid balls and savoury treats. Mon–Sat 7.30am–8pm, Sun 7.30am–5pm.

★**La Cocina de Tita Moning** 315 San Rafael St, San Miguel ☎02 734 2146, ⓦlacocinadetitamoning.com; map pp.60–61. Located in an Art Deco home (the 1937 Legarda House) east of Quiapo, near the Malacañang Palace, this is an exceptional dining experience (expect to spend a minimum P1500/head). Guests get a tour of the house before eating in the antique dining room; expect sumptuous home-cooked Spanish-Filipino dishes such as slowly roasted pork with crackling and candied sweet *camote*, or *kare kare de pata* (peanut stew with pig's trotters) with organic brown rice. Reservations required, 24hr in advance (minimum two persons). Open daily by appointment for lunch and dinner.

The Original Savory 201 Escolta St ☎02 243 0336; map p.73. Legendary masters of fried chicken and sensational gravy since 1950 (half chicken P175, whole P340), with branches in SM Mall of Asia. Also do superb *bagoong* (fermented shrimp sauce) rice (P165) and noodles (from P135). Daily 8am–midnight.

President Grand Palace Restaurant 746–750 Ongpin St ☎02 243 4988; map p.73. Plush Cantonese restaurant with an extensive menu that includes bird's nest and shark's fin (from P350). More mundane and less ecologically contentious dishes include excellent crab, lemon chicken, spicy pork with bean curd and a good selection of fresh vegetables. Best experienced with a group (so you can order multiple dishes to share), but they also serve hearty noodle and rice dishes suitable for single diners (from P150). Daily 10am–11pm.

★**Quick Snack** 637–639 Carvajal St ☎02 242 9572; map p.73. Tucked away down a side alley crammed with wet market stalls, it doesn't get better than this for a cheap, home-cooked Hokkien-style meal. It's best known for its *lumpia* (spring rolls; P45–55), *kuchang-an* (a sort of meat pie), *machang* (*zongzi* or rice wrapped in banana leaf) and oyster omelette (*e-a jian*; P180). Daily 8am–6.45pm.

Salazar Bakery 783 Ongpin St ☎02 733 1392; map p.73. This bakery dates from 1947 and does a tasty *hopia* (P45), but is also great for savoury *asado* rolls and small chicken pies – the hefty mooncakes (P125) are also worth a try. Daily 5am–10pm.

Tasty Dumplings 620 Ongpin St ☎02 242 5195; map p.73. No-frills diner with justly popular pork dumplings going for P80; also does great pork chop rice (P105) and fresh soybean milk (P35). Mon–Sat 10am–9pm, Sun 9am–9pm.

MAKATI

Makati is the best place in the city when it comes to quality and variety of restaurants, with most options in or around the Glorietta or Greenbelt malls, or P. Burgos St further north where there are a growing number of Korean and Japanese places. Bonifacio Global City, to the east, is an emerging destination for mostly high-end restaurants.

1

Barrio Fiesta Makati Ave at Valdez St ☎02 899 4020; map p.77. There are various branches of this colourful Filipino chain restaurant dotted around the city, serving favourites such as crispy *pata* (from P490), *kare kare* (from P220), pork *adobo* (P225) and *lechon* (roast pig; P350) with hefty portions of rice and daily buffet options. Daily 9am–midnight.

★**Carpaccio** 7431 Yakal St, San Antonio Village ☎02 843 7286, ⓦcarpaccio.com.ph; map p.77. Popular but never uncomfortably busy, this casual little restaurant tucked away down a side street behind Makati Fire Station serves excellent regional Italian food and has a good, affordable wine list. The speciality is carpaccio – the beef carpaccio (P480) is delicious – but almost everything is tasty (pasta and pizza P450–550), including the home-made ice creams and sorbets. Daily 11am–3pm & 6–11pm.

Ferino's Bibingka Cash & Carry Mall, South Luzon Expressway at Emilia St ☎0916 633 7298, ⓦferinos bibingka.com.ph; map p.77. This *bibingka* franchise hails back to a family business established in 1938. Look out for their small carts in malls, worth trying for the tasty charcoal-cooked rice cakes (P95–115), daubed with coconut and salted egg. Daily 10am–10pm.

Goto King 8 SM Food Court, Lower Ground Floor, SM Makati, EDSA ☎gotoking.com.ph; map p.77. Beloved *congee* (rice porridge) chain established in 1984 with basic *congee* for P42 and other varieties (egg, *chicharon* or fried pig skin) at P50–75. Has expanded in recent years to serve a wider merienda (snack) menu (*baboy*, *lugaw* etc), with branches in just about every SM mall. Daily 10am–8pm.

Il Ponticello 2/F Antel 2000 Bldg, 121 Valero St ☎02 887 7168; map p.77. A bit tricky to find, tucked away in the backstreets of Makati between rows of office blocks, but worth the effort. It's an Italian restaurant with excellent pizzas (from P410) – a refreshing change from the fast-food pizzas that Manila loves so much – and superb risotto from P390. The best tables are by the window, but you'll have to book to get one of those. There's also a fashionable bar inside called *Azzuri*. Mon–Fri 11am–2.30pm & 5pm–3am, Sat 5.30pm–3am.

New Bombay G/F, Sagittarius Bldg III, 312 H.V. Dela Costa St; G/F, Tower I, The Columns Condominium, Ayala Ave at Gil Puyat (Buendia) ☎02 819 2892; map p.77. Speak to Indian residents in Manila and most will tell you this functional little restaurant is peerless for authentic Indian food. The menu is extensive and includes snacks such as mixed pakora, samosas, curries and freshly prepared naan, roti and chapati. Cheap, cheerful and very tasty (most mains range P170–200). Daily 9am–11pm.

Old Swiss Inn 7912 Makati Ave at Olympia Towers ☎02 818 0098, ⓦoldswissinn.com; map p.77. Traditional food (heavenly Gruyère fondue from P715), funky alpine decor and waitresses in milkmaids' costumes – this place is as Swiss as cheese with a 24hr menu that also includes the classic *gnagi* (pork knuckles; P585) and Zurich *geschnetzeltes* (shredded pork; P385). Daily 24hr.

Razon's of Guagua 22 Jupiter St ☎02 899 7841; map p.77. Lauded Pampanga-style *halo-halo* (P92; shaved ice dessert) and *pancit luglug* (P92; fried noodles) chain, with pork *adobo* from P178. Daily 10am–9.30pm.

Rufo's Famous Tapa G/F, A. Venue Mall, Makati Ave ☎02 899 4207, ⓦrufos.com.ph; map p.77. Chain best known for its *tapa* – tender Batangas beef, marinated and served in a rich, sweet sauce with a side order of fried egg and garlic rice (P108) for breakfast (served all day here). Their boneless *bangus* (milkfish; P126) and *tocino* (cured pork; P104) is also excellent. Daily 24hr.

Sentro 1771 Level 2, Greenbelt 3 ☎02 757 3940, ⓦsentro1771.net; map p.77. Modern Filipino restaurant that's packed with office workers at lunchtime and the pre-cinema crowd in the evenings. The menu (most dishes P220–620) includes modern variations of classics such as pork *adobo*, pancit (noodles) and Bicol Express (spicy stew); the speciality is *sinigang na* corned beef (sour stew with corned beef; P595). Daily 11am–11pm.

★**Top of the Citi** 34/F Citibank Tower, 8741 Paseo de Roxas ☎02 750 5810, ⓦchefjessie.com; map p.77. Mingle with Manila's upper class in this temple to fine dining with soaring views of the city. Top chef Jessie Sincioco crafts modern Filipino cuisine such as crunchy pork *sisig* with mayonnaise, Japanese dishes, pasta, steaks and her famous dessert soufflés (the chocolate flavour is hard to beat), while the trendy bar gets all the attention from 5pm with the best cocktails in the city. Mains average P300–450 (though rib-eye steaks are over P1000). Mon–Fri 11am–11pm.

AROUND P. BURGOS STREET

Alba 38-B Polaris St, Bel-Air ☎02 896 6950, ⓦalba .com.ph; map p.88. Cosy Spanish restaurant with faux adobe walls and a wandering guitarist who croons at your table. Dishes include tasty tapas from P180, a large menu of paellas (from P450), and plenty of fish and stuffed squid from P350. Mon–Sat 11am–11pm.

Hossein's 2/F, 7857 LKV Bldg, Makati Ave ☎02 896 6137, ⓦhosseins.com; map p.88. This glitzy take on a kebab house has froufrou decor and prices to match. If you're not in the mood for a brain sandwich, you can choose from dozens of Persian, Arabian and Indian dishes (with a huge range of curry and kebabs). Mezze plates P150–300. Daily 11am–midnight.

Next Door Noodles/North Park Noodles 7876 Makati Ave ☎02 899 1893; map p.88. Cheap-and-cheerful Chinese *Next Door Noodles* sits almost opposite its sister restaurant, *North Park Noodles*, which has a similar menu at the same low prices. Fantastic value – almost everything is under P200 (dim sum P60–110, noodles in soup P150 to P195 and fried rice P200). Daily 24hr.

Shinjuku Ramen House 7853 Makati Ave at Hercules St ☎ 02 890 6107; map p.88. Some of the best Japanese noodles (*ramen*) in the city, with a vast choice ranging from basic *miso ramen* (P295) to more fancy pork and mushroom versions (P380). Daily 10am–1am.

Top Dish 4890 Durban St, near P. Burgos St ☎ 02 758 1122; map p.88. The best hole-in-the-wall Korean restaurant in town, open late and with reasonable prices (P120–150 for noodles), big portions and excellent *kimchi* (pickled cabbage). Daily 3pm–4am.

Ziggurat G/F Sunette Tower Building (entrance at Euphrates at Tigris Streets) ☎ 02 897 5179, ⓦ ziggurat cuisine.com; map p.88. A seemingly endless menu featuring exotic dishes from all over the Middle East, Mediterranean and East Africa (try the mezze combos from P650), with flavoured hookahs to round things off. Count on about P220–380 for main dishes. Open 24hr.

BONIFACIO GLOBAL CITY (FORT BONIFACIO)

Abe Restaurant Serendra Plaza, Bonifacio Global City ☎ 02 856 0526; map pp.60–61. Most taxi drivers will know this much-loved Filipino restaurant (Pampanga-style), with the two highlights Abe's chicken supreme (chicken stuffed with *galapong* rice, chestnuts and raisins; P895 for two) and mutton *adobo* with popped garlic (P410). Other dishes utilize forest ferns, banana plant, tiny crabs and fabulous pork knuckle. Daily 11am–3pm & 5pm–midnight.

★**Aubergine** 32nd & 5th Bldg, 5th Ave at 32nd St ☎ 02 856 9888, ⓦ aubergine.ph; map pp.60–61. The best reason to jump in a taxi and head over to Fort Bonifacio, this top-notch restaurant and patisserie delivers fresh ingredients and crisp flavours; the French-inspired international menu features slow-cooked Norwegian salmon (P1160), honey-glazed French duck breast (P1350) and Australian lamb rack (P1650). Daily 11.30am–2pm & 6–10pm.

ORTIGAS AND GREENHILLS

★**Frazzled Cook** 916 Luna Mencias St (near Shaw Blvd), Addition Hills ☎ 02 725 3354; map pp.60–61. Shabby-chic purveyor of legendary *paella negra* (P400 for two people), a short taxi ride west of Ortigas proper. Serves an otherwise eclectic menu including squash soup (P130), spicy lamb stew (P400) and scampi pizza (P320). Daily 11am–10.30pm.

Lugang Café 115 Connecticut St, Northeast Greenhills, San Juan (Santolan MRT) ☎ 02 542 0196, ⓦ lugangcafe .com.ph; map pp.60–61. Tucked away in Greenhills,

between Ortigas and Quezon City, this is arguably the best Chinese restaurant in the city, part of the Shanghai-based Bellagio group and best known for its magnificent Taiwanese food, pork buns and *xiaolong bao* (pork dumplings; P248). Daily 11am–3pm & 6–11pm.

QUEZON CITY

Quezon City is a burgeoning alternative to Makati and the Manila Bay area for restaurants and nightlife. Most of the restaurants are on Tomas Morato Ave, which runs north and south from the roundabout outside the *Imperial Palace Suites* hotel. To get to Quezon from the south of the city (from Malate and Makati, for example), you can take the MRT and get off either at Kamuning station or Quezon Avenue station, a journey of about 25min.

Behrouz 63 Scout Tobias St, off Timog Ave ☎ 02 374 3242; map p.82. Great late-night hole-in-the-wall snack place, run by a family of Iranians who cook authentic food, though alcohol isn't served. The lamb kebabs, beef *kobideh* (ground-beef kebab) and aubergine-based *moutabal* (a bit like baba ghanoush) are all superb – reckon on P200–300 for a meal. Cash only. Daily 11am–5am.

Gerry's Grill Tomas Morato Ave at Eugenio Lopez Drive ☎ 02 415 9514, ⓦ gerrysgrill.com; map p.82. This is the original outlet of the now popular chain, serving provincial Filipino dishes such as crispy *pata* (pig's knuckle; P465) and *sisig* (fried pig's ear and pig's face; P196). Mon–Thurs 10am–2am, Fri & Sat 10am–3am, Sun 10am–1am.

★**Lydia's Lechon** 126 Timog Ave ☎ 02 921 1221, ⓦ lydias-lechon.com; map p.82. The *lechon* at this local favourite is delicious (especially the boneless variety stuffed with paella), but the secret is the sauce, a sweet, barbecue concoction that will have you hooked. The meat is priced at around P750/Kg; P190 for a quarter kilo. Daily 9am–9pm.

Pancit ng Taga Malabon G/F Food Center, TriNoma Mall, EDSA ☎ 02 703 2229, ⓦ pancitngtagamalabon .com; map p.82. The chain that claims descent from the original "pancit Malabon" stall in the 1890s, when the addictive concoction of oysters, squid, shrimp, smoked fish (*tinapa*), *chicharon*, crab and duck eggs over thick rice noodles and golden sauce (P85) became known as "*pancit bame*" – Malabon was the location of the stall and has since been applied to noodle dishes nationwide. Mon–Thurs 10am–9pm, Fri–Sun 10am–10pm.

Yakimix 270 Tomas Morato Ave at Scout Limbaga St ☎ 02 332 8073; map p.82. This all-you-can-eat Japanese and Korean food buffet is a fabulous deal (P520 lunch and P620 dinner; P660 dinner Sat & Sun). Add P60 to drink as much San Miguel as you like. Daily 11am–2pm & 5.30–10.30pm.

1

DRINKING AND NIGHTLIFE

Few visitors to Manila are disappointed by the buoyant, gregarious nature of its **bars** and **clubs**. This is a city that rarely sleeps and one that offers a full range of fun, from the offbeat watering holes of Malate to the chic wine bars of Makati. Manila also has a thriving **live music** scene, with dozens of bars hosting very popular and accomplished local bands almost every night. Clubs are especially prone to open, close and change names with frequency, so check before you head out – websites such as ⊛ guestlist.ph are good places to get the latest information.

BARS

AIRPORT AREA (PASAY CITY)

Opus 2/F, Newport Mall, Resorts World Manila ☎ 02 856 0128, ⊛ opusmanila.com; map pp.60–61. This jaw-dropping restaurant-lounge bar has to be seen to be believed, with shiny silver sofas and vast Italian Renaissance-like murals on the walls, glass-encased booths, veined marble bar and an array of glamorous cocktails. Daily 5pm–2am.

INTRAMUROS AND RIZAL PARK

Lobby Lounge Manila Hotel, 1 Rizal Park ☎ 02 527 0011, ⊛ manila-hotel.com.ph; map p.63. It's worth grabbing a coffee or artfully constructed cocktail in this elegant lobby bar, even if you're not staying at the *Manila Hotel* – it's one of the few places redolent of the city's golden age, with capiz chandeliers, *narra* wood ceiling and marble floors. Daily 6am–midnight.

ERMITA AND MALATE

Nightlife in Ermita and Malate comprises a somewhat confusing mixture of budget restaurants, genuine pubs and a once-again flourishing girlie bar scene, with as many Asian (mostly Korean) male patrons as Westerners. If none of that appeals, make for the Roxas Blvd end of Remedios St, which is full of cheap-and-cheerful places popular with students for their cover bands and drinks. Don't make the mistake of

arriving early because most places don't even warm up until after 10pm and are still thumping when the sun comes up, with crowds in summer spilling out onto the streets. Friday, as always, is the big night, with many places closed on Sunday.

Hobbit House 1212 M. H. Del Pilar St at Arquiza St, Ermita ☎ 02 521 7604, ⊛ hobbithousemanila.com; map p.69. In 1973 entrepreneur Jim Turner decided to open a bar that would pay homage to his favourite book, *The Lord of the Rings*. He staffed it with twenty midgets and a legend was born. *Hobbit House* has somehow endured, still employing short people, and offers a huge list of bottled beers, Tex-Mex food and nightly appearances at 9pm by a variety of local bands. It has also become a notorious tourist trap, with busloads of visitors brought in every night to have their photographs taken alongside the diminutive staff. Daily 5pm–2am.

Liquid Pool & Lounge Manila Ocean Park, behind Quirino Grandstand, Roxas Blvd ☎ 02 567 4321, ⊛ manilaoceanpark.com; map p.69. Fun pool bar and club, with grottos, outdoor jacuzzi, DJs spinning and indulgent cocktails (though comparing it to Vegas is pushing things a bit). The pool and bar is open daily 11am to 5pm, but it's over-18s only after 6pm. Wed–Sat 6pm–3am.

MAKATI

Makati nightlife has traditionally revolved around office workers spilling out of the nearby banks and skyscrapers,

---

GAY NIGHTLIFE IN MANILA

The **gay scene** in Manila has been vibrant for many years. Even bars and clubs that aren't obviously gay are unreservedly welcoming and the LGBT community mixes easily and boisterously in the same nightclubs and bars. Traditionally, the whole area around Maria Orosa Street and Julio Nakpil Street in Malate has been lined with gay-friendly bars, though there are signs that the scene here is dying off – the most hip places are now spread out across the city, though the shows at *The Library* (see p.97) are still worth checking out. Other gay resources are covered in Basics (see p.49).

Bed Unit 5, The Portal, Greenfield District, Mayflower St at United Ave, 1552 Mandaluyong City ☎ 02 584 9388, ⊛ bed.com.ph; map pp.60–61. Malate's biggest and boldest gay club has been reborn at this cool, industrial venue with DJs, drag performances and male dancers. Tues 6pm–midnight, Wed 6pm–1am, Thurs 6pm–3am, Fri–Sun 6pm–4am.

Club Mwah 652 Bonifacio Ave, Mandaluyong City ☎ 02 532 2826; map pp.60–61. Club, bar and theatre

featuring a burlesque transvestite show dubbed "Folliespiniana", based on traditional dances and "Las Vegas-Moulin Rouge" inspired acts. Thurs–Sat 9.30pm–1am.

O Bar Ortigas Home Depot, Julia Vargas Ave, Ortigas ☎ 919 996 4154; map pp.60–61. Hip club and lounge bar, always crowded – especially on weekends – and there are sometimes drag shows and go-go dancers. Wed–Sun 10pm–6am.

but these days much of middle-class Manila parties in the bars and clubs here, with plenty of expats and travellers thrown in – it's generally smarter, safer and more fashionable than Malate. The area around P. Burgos St is a bit seedier, though the girlie bar scene here is being driven more by Korean and Japanese KTV-style joints these days, and there are several genuine pubs in between offering cheap beers and snacks.

The Balcony Gastropub G/F, Doña Angel Garden Bldg, 110 C. Palanca Jr. St, Legaspi Village ☎02 818 1551, ⓦbalconygastropub.com; map p.77. Fashionable lounge bar, with big-screen TVs for sports, table football, decent bar food (like veggie tempura and baked artichoke dip) and extensive cocktail list. Morphs into laidback club most nights after 9pm. Free wi-fi. Daily 11am–2am.

Beers Paradise 36 Polaris St at Durban St ☎02 895 9272; map p.88. Small, informal place in which to quaff serious Belgian beers (they also claim to have over one hundred brands from around the world), from the sledgehammer-in-a-glass 12 percent Bush Ambrée ale to the comparatively tame Duvel and Chimay brands (P150–300). Daily 2pm–4am.

The Distillery 20 Jupiter St, Bel-Air ☎02 403 5293, ⓦthedistillery.com.ph; map p.77. Friendly bar with a massive choice of vodka, tequila, single malt Scotch and rare foreign beers. Happy hour runs 6–9pm and DJs get people dancing at the weekends, with especially crazy Fri nights. Mon–Thurs 6pm–4am, Fri & Sat 6pm–5am.

H&J Sports Bar and Restaurant Felipe St ☎02 954 1130; map p.88. The old *Heckle & Jeckle* sports bar moved into these new digs in 2013 – it's a bit smarter, but otherwise boasts the same laidback vibe popular with expats, live blues and rock bands (nightly), Indian food, pool tables and TVs showing live English Premier League football. Happy hour Mon–Fri 2–10pm. Mon–Thurs 4pm–6am, Fri–Sun 24hr.

Handlebar 31 Polaris St ☎02 898 2189, ⓦhandlebar .com.ph; map p.88. Hospitable biker bar owned by a group of Harley fanatics. It's primarily for drinkers (with lots of sport on the TVs) but the food also makes it worth a visit. The menu is nothing exotic, just solid, satisfying pizzas, burgers and pasta, or Big John's BBQ (P265–732). Daily 24hr.

Howzat 8471 Kalayaan Ave at Fermina St ☎02 897 3335, ⓦhowzat.ph; map p.88. Popular sports bar showing all major global sports events on wide TV screens via satellite (including Premier League games). Specials include all you can drink San Miguel (daily 5–8pm) for just P310 (local spirits for P345), curry buffets on Fri and Sat (noon–3pm; P425 with beer) and a scrumptious Sunday roast (noon–3pm) for P545 (including beer). Mon–Thurs 10am–2am, Fri–Sun 24hr.

M Café Ayala Museum, Greenbelt 4, Makati Ave ☎02 757 3000; map p.77. *Museum Café*, or *M Café*, as it's

known, is a swish little place serving drinks and snacks all day, with craft beers on draft and snazzy cocktails at night. Light meals P200–400. On Thurs and Fri it's open till 3am with DJs spinning from 10pm. Mon–Wed, Sat & Sun 8am–midnight, Thurs & Fri 8am–3am.

Society Lounge G/F Atrium Bldg, Makati Ave at Paseo de Roxas ☎02 408 1852; map p.77. Plush French-Asian fusion restaurant that morphs into trendy lounge bar every night, with plenty of fine wines and champagnes on offer. DJs spin house music at the weekends when it becomes more like a club. Daily: restaurant 11am–3pm & 6–11pm; lounge bar Mon till 1am, Tues–Thurs till 2am, Fri & Sat till 4am.

QUEZON CITY

Quezon City's entertainment district is focused on Tomas Morato and Timog avenues, which intersect at the round-about in front of *Imperial Palace Suites* hotel. The area has a growing reputation for quality live music (see below), while for more mainstream nightlife there are plenty of chic bars and franchised hangouts at the southern end of Tomas Morato Ave, near the junction with Don A. Roces Ave.

Padi's Point G/F Imperial Palace Suites, Tomas Morato Ave ☎02 920 7864, ⓦpadispoint.com; map p.82. Boisterous beer hall chain that serves very average Filipino food, although most guests are too drunk to care. Thurs and Sat are disco nights, with happy hour (P100 for 3 bottles) Sun–Thurs 6–10pm. There are several branches scattered around the city, listed on the website. Mon–Thurs & Sun 5pm–5am, Fri & Sat 5pm–6am.

LIVE MUSIC BARS AND VENUES

Quezon City in particular has a reputation for live music, especially from up-and-coming bands formed by students from the nearby University of the Philippines, with an eclectic range of music, from pure Western pop to grunge, reggae and indigenous styles. Many of the venues in the area are dark, sweaty places that open late and don't close until the last guest leaves. Note that the venues below are known primarily for live music, but in Makati and Malate you're never far from a bar or club with a live band, especially at weekends.

ERMITA AND MALATE

★**The Bar @ 1951 (Penguin Café)** 1951 M. Adriatico St, Malate ☎917 858 3009, ⓦbar1951.weebly.com; map p.69. Legendary 1980s bohemian bar *Penguin Café* has been reborn as this two-floor artsy and congenial space (with a cosy loft upstairs), though locals still refer to it by the old name. As before, live indie bands play most nights and work from local artists adorns the walls. Tues–Sat 6pm–2am.

Bedrock 1782 M. Adriatico St, Malate ☎02 522 7278, ⓦbedrockmalate.moonfruit.com; map p.69. A vaguely

1

Flintstones-esque interior, lack of a cover charge and better-than-average cover bands have made this an Adriatico St institution. Two bands play live Wed–Sun nights. Mon–Wed & Sun 6pm–4am, Thurs–Sat 6pm–5am.

MAKATI

SaGuijo 7612 Guijo St, San Antonio, Makati ☎02 897 8629, ⓦsaguijo.com; map p.77. This hip, arty bar is the best indie venue in Manila, with both its live music (from 10.30pm nightly) and art gallery supporting up-and-coming talents. Effortlessly cool, but not pretentious with it. Tues–Sat 6pm–1am.

Strumm's 110 Jupiter St, Makati ☎02 895 4636; map p.77. A party-like atmosphere greets nightly bands at this Makati stalwart, which puts on mostly pop and indie but also old-school jazz on Tues. Cover P400. Daily 8pm–2am.

QUEZON CITY

★**The 70s Bistro** 46 Anonas St, Quezon City ☎02 434 3597, ⓦthe70sbistro.com; map pp.60–61. Legendary (in the Philippines) live music venue that plays host to some of the country's best-known bands as well as to impromptu jam sessions with big local names who happen to turn up – a great Manila experience, and a cheap one too, with admission rarely more than P100. The only problem is it's a bit tricky to find: Anonas St is off Aurora Blvd on the eastern side of EDSA, Quezon City. Mon–Sat 6pm–3am.

Araneta Coliseum Gen. Araneta at Gen. McArthur, Quezon City ☎02 911 3101 ⓦaranetacoliseum.com; map p.82. This huge stadium (aka "Big Dome") is the usual venue for large-scale events and concerts, everything from Fall Out Boy and Ke$ha to Disney on Ice. Opens according to shows.

★**Conspiracy Garden Cafe** 59 Visayas Ave, Quezon City ☎02 453 2170; map pp.60–61. This wonderful little performance venue and café is a meeting place for artists, musicians, poets, songwriters and women's groups. *Conspiracy* was set up by the artists who perform there, among them luminaries of the independent Filipino music scene such as Joey Ayala, Cynthia Alexander and Noel Cabangon, who all perform regularly. Well worth the taxi ride out there, but check first to see who's on. Mon–Sat 5pm–1am.

Ka Freddie's 120 Tomas Morato Ave at Kamuning St, Quezon City ☎915 444 0241, ⓦfreddieanakaquilar

.com; map p.82. Music bar and restaurant (with pool tables and free wi-fi) opened by Filipino folk legend Freddie Aguilar, who still does weekly shows. Check out the website for who's playing. Cover P200–300. Daily 6pm–3am.

Music Museum Service Rd, Greenhills, San Juan ☎02 722 4532, ⓦmusicmuseum.com.ph; map pp.60–61. This "leisure-entertainment hub" hosts concerts, comedy shows, ballet, theatre and poetry readings, but the music is still the main attraction; the acts are mostly popular Filipino pop and rock acts. Times vary according to shows.

CLUBS

7th High Club B3, Quadrant 4, The Fort Entertainment Center, Bonifacio Global City ☎02 856 1785; map pp.60–61. Ultra-stylish club where the emphasis is on drinking and mingling (the dancefloor is quite small) and the elegant lounge area and tables come with a hefty price tag. Scarlet Wednesdays is the most happening midweek party in the city. Cover P500. Wed–Sat 10pm–4am.

Amber Ultralounge Unit F, The Fort Entertainment Center, Bonifacio Global City ☎02 887 6838; map pp.60–61. Another über-hip bar and lounge that morphs into a club later on, with spacious interiors, two floors, thumping sound system and a tempting array of cocktails (think pineapple mojitos and Coco Lychee Smash). Cover P500. Mon–Sat 7pm–2.30am.

Black Market Warehouse 5, La Fuerza Compound 2, Sabio St ☎908 813 5622; map p.77. New club venue opened by the folks at *B-Side* in 2013, with talented resident DJs and an eclectic range of guests. Cover usually P300. Wed–Sat 9pm–6am.

★**B-Side** The Collective, 7472 Malugay St, near Gil Puyat (Buendia) Ave ☎0922 998 9512, ⓦbsidemanila .com; map p.77. Bar/club venue for cutting-edge hip-hop, soul and dance DJs from all over the world. Big reggae/ragga sessions on "Irie Sundays". Cover usually P200–300. Wed–Sat 9pm–4am, Sun 7pm–2am.

Republiq Atrium, Newport Mall, Resorts World Manila ☎0917 550 8888, ⓦrepubliqclub.com; map pp.60–61. New generation of megaclub, with a strong claim to be the best club in the nation, and party central for Manila's beautiful people, with giant LCD screens, top-notch DJs, plush lounge area and a whopping great sound system. Cover usually P600 (includes two drinks). Wed, Fri & Sat 9.30pm–5.30am.

ENTERTAINMENT

Daily shows of **traditional performing arts** (see box opposite) are hosted at the Cultural Center of the Philippines and a handful of other venues. As for **films**, every mall seems to have half a dozen screens, and international movies are rarely dubbed. Good resources for checking upcoming events include Ticketworld (☎02 891 9991, ⓦticketworld.com.ph) and TicketNet (☎02 911 5555, ⓦticketnet.com.ph), on both of which you can buy tickets in advance, as well as listings websites such as ⓦclickthecity.com.

1

FILIPINO FOLK ARTS

The Philippines has a rich folk arts heritage, but a scarcity of funds and committed audiences with money to spend on tickets means it's in danger of being forgotten. Folk dances such as **tinikling**, which sees participants hopping at increasing speed between heavy bamboo poles that are struck together at shin-height, are seen in cultural performances for tourists, but are only performed occasionally in theatres. The same goes for **kundiman**, a genre of music that reached its zenith at the beginning of the twentieth century, and combines elements of tribal music with contemporary lovelorn lyrics to produce epic songs of love and loss. To see if anything is on check out websites like ⓦ ticketworld.com.ph. The CCP sometimes puts on shows (see p.70); otherwise your best bet is to join the tourists at restaurants such as *Barbara's* (see p.89) or *Zamboanga* (see p.91).

CABARET AND BURLESQUE

Amazing Show Manila Film Theater, Jose W Diokno Blvd, Pasay ⓣ 02 834 8870. Fun transvestite musical variety show involving singing, dancing and comedy skits, especially popular with Korean tourists. Tickets for foreigners usually around P2000. Tues–Sun 8–9.15pm.

The Library 1739 Maria Orosa St, Malate ⓣ 02 522 2484, ⓦ thelibrary.com.ph. Nightly stand-up comedy/karaoke from veteran Manila drag queens where audience participation is very much part of the show – attracts local straight and gay audience. P100–500 cover charge. Daily 7pm–1am (shows from 9pm).

THEATRE, DANCE AND CLASSICAL MUSIC

Most performances at the following theatres are listed in the Manila English-language daily press, usually the *Philippine Daily Inquirer* and the *Philippine Star*.

Cultural Center of the Philippines Roxas Blvd, Malate ⓣ 02 832 1125, ⓦ culturalcenter.gov.ph. Events here range from art exhibitions to Broadway musicals, pop concerts, classical concerts by the Philippine Philharmonic Orchestra, *tinikling* and *kundiman*. The CCP is also home to the Tanghalang Aurelio Tolentino (CCP Little Theater), where smaller dramatic productions are staged and films shown; Ballet Philippines (ⓣ 02 832 3689, ⓦ ballet.ph); Bayanihan, the National Folk Dance Company (ⓦ bayanihannational danceco.ph); and the CCP's resident theatre group, Tanghalang Pilipino, dedicated to the production of original Filipino plays (July–March; ⓦ tanghalangpilipino.org.ph). Nearby is the Folk Arts Theater, built for the Miss Universe Pageant in 1974 and now staging occasional rock concerts and drama.

Meralco Theater Meralco Ave, Ortigas. Stages everything from ballet and musicals by overseas companies to pantomimes with local celebs. Check websites such as ⓦ ticketworld.com.ph for the latest shows.

OnStage Theater Greenbelt 1, Makati. Small venue mainly staging drama by local theatre groups, including Repertory Philippines (ⓣ 02 571 6926, ⓦ repertory philippines.com), Manila's premier English-speaking theatre group (Jan–April).

Paco Park/Rizal Park "Paco Park Presents" hosts free classical concerts at 6pm on Friday, performed under the stars in the historic cemetery (see p.72); Rizal Park (p.65) stages similar free "Concerts at the Park" every Sun at 6pm.

CINEMAS

Arthouse cinema A venue for arthouse and independent films is the UP Cine Adarna (ⓣ 02 981 8500, ⓦ filminstitute .upd.edu.ph), UPFI Film Center building at Magsaysay and Osmeña avenues to the northeast of Quezon Memorial Circle, but screenings don't take place every day, so call ahead.

Multiplex cinemas Most shopping malls in Manila house multiplex cinemas that show all the Hollywood and Asian blockbusters in the original languages, including The Podium mall (18 ADB Ave, Ortigas; ⓣ 02 633 8976), with late-night screenings on Fri and Sat; Greenbelt 3 in Makati (ⓣ 02 729 7777) and Power Plant Mall, Rockwell Drive, Makati (ⓣ 02 898 1440). Tickets are usually around P150–210. In the Malate area, try Robinsons Place in M. Adriatico St (ⓣ 02 536 7813). Tickets for cinemas in the Greenbelt and Glorietta malls can be reserved online at ⓦ sureseats .com for collection at the venue.

SPORT

When it comes to sports and games in Manila, you'll have quite a bit of choice if **bowling** or **golf** is your thing. A general overview of sport in the Philippines is given in Basics (see p.41).

BOWLING

Bowling Inn 1941 Taft Ave, Malate ⓣ 02 522 3818. P150–200 per person. Daily 10am–1am.

Coronado Lanes 4/F Star Mall, EDSA, Mandaluyong City ⓣ 02 725 3965, ⓦ puyatsports.com. P100–140 per person (plus P35 for shoes). Open daily 10am–1am.

Paeng's Midtown Bowl Level 2, Robinsons Place, M. Adriatico St, Ermita ⓣ 02 525 6442, ⓦ puyatsports .com. P120–150 per person (plus P35 for shoes). Daily 10am–1am.

1

SPECTATOR SPORTS

Because the PBA (Philippine Basketball Association) teams are owned by corporations, and do not play in a home stadium, most **basketball** games are played at the Araneta Coliseum in Cubao (see p.96) and the SM Mall of Asia Arena in Pasay; games usually run Wednesday, Friday and Sunday from October to July. Tickets in the cheap seats, the "bleachers", cost as little as P10, while a ringside seat will set you back P250–600. Tickets are available from Ticketnet (see p.96) or ⓦ pba.inquirer.net.

Major **cockfighting** venues in Manila include the huge air-conditioned Pasay City Cockpit Arena (Arnaiz Ave at Dolores St), where "derbies" take place most Sundays from noon to 5pm (around P20 entry fee). Fights also take place on Monday, Wednesday and Friday 1–5pm.

GOLF

There are three golf courses in Manila where non-members can turn up and pay for a round – it's usually first come, first served (which means waits of 1–2hr at weekends) – and one where you can reserve in advance. You can book ahead at all three courses via the GolfPH website (ⓣ 02 625 4200, ⓦ golfph.com; P650 per reservation).

Army Golf Club (Kagitingan) Bayani Rd, Fort Bonifacio, south of Makati ⓣ 02 812 7521. Boasts some of the lowest green fees in the country (Mon–Fri P1085;

Sat & Sun P1445; includes caddie fee and insurance). Driving range around P220/hr.

Club Intramuros Bonifacio Drive at Soriano St (formerly Aduana St), Intramuros ⓣ 02 527 6612. Basic facilities and a short eighteen-hole course that runs along the walls of the old city. Figure on around P3500 for green fees (P1500 daily), caddie hire and clubs. Offers night golfing also.

Villamor Golf Course Jesus Villamor Air Base, Pasay ⓣ 02 833 8630. Home of the Philippine Masters; green fees are around P1500 (Mon–Fri) and P2300 (Sat & Sun).

SHOPPING

The combination of intense heat and dense traffic means many Manileños forsake the pleasures of the outdoors at weekends for the computer-controlled climate of their local **mall** – there can be few cities that have as many malls per head of population as this one. Note that the developers rarely pay as much attention to the surrounding roads as they do to their precious real estate, which means that traffic is especially gridlocked in these areas. Despite the growth of malls, there are still plenty of earthy outdoor **markets** in Manila where you can buy food, antiques and gifts at rock-bottom prices, as well as some decent bookshops and fashion boutiques. One trendy local brand to look out for is Bench (ⓦ bench .com.ph), which sells Ben Chan's men's and women's lines in stores all over the city.

BOOKS

National Book Store G/F Harrison Plaza, M. Adriatico St ⓣ 02 525 8205, map p.69; Level 1, Robinsons Place, Ermita ⓣ 02 536 7893, map p.69; Glorietta 5, Makati ⓣ 02 757 0525, map p.77; Sct. Borromeo at Quezon Ave, Quezon City ⓣ 02 373 3454, map p.82; ⓦ national bookstore.com.ph. The country's major bookshop chain, but as ever their stock is limited to contemporary thrillers, literary classics and *New York Times* bestsellers, with much of what's on offer stocked specifically for students. Quezon Ave daily 10am–7pm; Glorietta 5 & Harrison Plaza daily 10am–8pm; Robinsons Place daily 9am–9pm.

Powerbooks Branches at Level 4 Manila Midtown, Robinsons Place, Ermita, map p.69; Glorietta 3, Makati, map p.77; Greenbelt 4, Makati, map p.77. The best general bookshop in Manila, with seven branches around the city. Manila Midtown & Glorietta 3 Mon–Thurs & Sun 10am–9pm, Fri & Sat 10am–10pm.; Greenbelt 4 daily 10am–10pm.

Solidaridad Bookshop 531 Padre Faura St, Ermita ⓣ 02 254 1086; map p.69. The bookshop with the best

literary section in town. It's owned by the novelist F. Sionil José and, apart from stocking his own excellent novels, has a small selection of highbrow fiction and lots of material on the Philippines. Mon–Sat 9am–6pm.

HANDICRAFTS AND SOUVENIRS

There are touristy shops all over Manila selling repro-duction tribal art, especially *bulol* (sometimes spelt *bulul*) – depictions of rice gods, worshipped by northern tribespeople because they are said to keep evil spirits from the home and bless farmers with a good harvest. Genuine *bulol* are made from *narra* wood and are dark and stained from the soot of tribal fires and from blood poured over them during sacrifices. Good places to pick up souvenirs are markets (see p.100) and the Silahis Center (see p.62).

Balikbayan Handicrafts Pasay branch, HK Sun Plaza, Macapagal Ave (just south of the CCP) ⓣ 02 831 0044, map p.80; also 1010 Arnaiz Ave (Pasay Rd), Makati ⓣ 02 893 0775, map p.77; ⓦ balikbayanhandicrafts .com. The first stop for tourists looking for indigenous

LIFE BEYOND THE MALL: INDIE RETAILERS

Megamalls haven't completely taken over Manila. **Cubao-X** (Cubao Expo) is a hub of independent retailers on General Romulo Avenue in Quezon City (a short walk from Cubao MRT station; map pp.60–61), with numerous indie clothing stores, creative furniture stores, art galleries and thrift shops. Similarly in Makati, some of Manila's coolest designers have established **The Collective** (7274 Malugay St, San Antonio; map p.77), the hub of several independent shops, including:

Longboards Manila Unit L ☎0917 850 2025, ⓦlongboardsmanila.com. Skateboarder heaven. Tues–Sat 1–9pm.

Ritual Unit A ☎02 400 4326, ⓦwww.ritual.ph. Organic grocery selling pink rice, local salts, sugar, lemongrass and coffee (bring your own containers). Tues–Sat noon–9pm.

Skitzo Unit M ☎0917 529 7548, ⓦskitzomanila .com. Costume shop crammed with garish outfits, glasses and accessories. Tues–Sat noon–9pm.

Vinyl on Vinyl Unit H ☎0922 848 7427, ⓦvinylon vinyl.blogspot.com. Sells old records and collectable vinyl toys (cartoon and anime characters). Tues–Sat 3–11pm.

gifts and handicrafts is this justly popular store selling a mind-boggling array of souvenirs, knick-knacks, home decorations, reproduction native-style carvings and jewellery, plus some larger items such as tribal chairs, drums and musical instruments; staff can arrange to ship your purchases if requested. The biggest of their outlets is the cavernous Pasay branch. Pasay Mon–Sat 9am–9pm, Sun 10am–9pm; Makati Mon–Sat 9am–8pm, Sun 10am–8pm.

Tesoro's 1325 A. Mabini St, Ermita ☎02 522 1580, map p.69; 1016 Arnaiz Ave (Pasay Rd), Makati ☎02 887 6285, map p.77; ⓦtesoros.ph. Another handicraft chain selling woven tablecloths, fabrics, *barongs* and reproduction tribal crafts such as *bulol*. Not as big as Balikbayan, but more convenient from budget hotels in Ermita. Both daily 10am–8pm.

MALLS

Bonifacio High Street Bonifacio Global City ☎02 818 3601, ⓦwww.ayalamalls.com.ph; map pp.60–61. One of Manila's newest and most lavish malls, which links to the Market! Market! development of themed retail zones, fruit and flower markets and a regional food and hawker's area. The Fort Bus (Mon–Sat 6am–10pm; every 30min) connects Ayala MRT station with the shopping centre. Daily 11am–11pm.

Glorietta Ayala Center, Ayala Ave, Makati ☎02 752 7272, ⓦwww.ayalamalls.com.ph; map p.77. A maze of passageways spanning out from a central atrium, Glorietta has five sections, a large branch of Rustan's department store and heaps of clothes and household goods. At the Makati Ave end of the complex is Landmark, a big, functional department store that sells inexpensive clothes and has a whole floor dedicated to children's goods. Most of the restaurants are near the atrium and there's a food court on the third floor. Mon–Thurs & Sun 10am–9pm, Fri & Sat 10am–10pm.

Greenbelt Ayala Center, Paseo de Roxas at Legaspi St, Makati ☎02 757 4853, ⓦwww.ayalamalls.com.ph; map p.77. This whole area has undergone extensive redevelopment, with five sections: Greenbelt 3 and 4 on Makati Ave are the most comfortable for a stroll and a spot of people watching. Most of the stores are well-known chains – Greenbelt 3 has the affordable stuff (including Nike and Adidas) and Greenbelt 4 is full of expensive big names such as Armani and Jimmy Choo. There are some excellent restaurants in Greenbelt 3 for all budgets and more designers in Greenbelt 5 (DKNY, Hilfiger). Daily 11am–9pm.

Power Plant Mall Rockwell Dr at Estrella St, Makati, about 1km west of Guadalupe MRT (from P. Burgos you can walk it in 15min), ☎02 898 1702, ⓦpowerplantmall.com; map p.77. Upscale mall home to Rustan's supermarket, as well as some furniture shops selling imported teak items from Indonesia. Most of the mid-range brand names are also here, along with small shops selling fashion items for teenagers, a couple of good baby clothes shops, and electronics shops selling mobile phones and cameras. Mon–Thurs 11am–9pm, Fri 11am–10pm, Sat 10am–10pm, Sun 10am–9pm.

SM Mall of Asia J.W. Diokno Blvd (facing Manila Bay) ☎02 556 0680, ⓦsmmallofasia.com; map p.80. It's hard to believe that this vast complex is just the third largest in the Philippines (SM Megamall is the biggest) – it contains the first ever IMAX in the city, a seafront promenade, bowling alley, ice rink and hypermarket, as well as numerous restaurants and stores that appeal to a younger crowd. You can get handy minibuses to here from Baclaran market (see p.100). SM also has the Megamall in Ortigas (daily 10am–midnight), and the smaller department store (Mon–Thurs & Sun 10am–9pm, Fri & Sat 10am–10pm) in Makati, among many locations in Metro Manila. Daily 10am–10pm.

1

DE-STRESSING MANILA: SPAS, STEAM AND SHIATSU

After a day sweating it out on Manila's congested streets, a couple of hours in a **spa** can be extremely tempting, especially now there are plenty of reputable ones serving stressed-out locals rather than sex-starved tourists. Note also that most of the five-star hotels listed in "Accommodation" (see pp.84–89) have excellent spas.

Neo Day Spa G/F, Net One Center Building, 26th St at 3rd Ave, Bonifacio Global City ☎02 815 8233, ⓦneospa.net. Serene modern spa inspired by Zen minimalism, with elaborate Japanese-style massages from P1750 (90min), shiatsu (P950/1hr) and P420 head and neck massages (20min). Mon–Thurs & Sun 1–11pm, Fri & Sat noon–11pm.

Soneva Spa 4th Forum Building, Tomas Morato Ave, Quezon City ☎02 926 6249, ⓦsonevaspa.com. Right on the main strip in Quezon City, this offers great value for your peso – come on a weekday afternoon

and it's a dreamy, tranquil place with a huge roster of Xiamen (Chinese)-style massages from P699 (1hr) to P380 (feet) and P599 (back and feet combos). Daily 1pm–midnight.

The Spa G/F, Paseo de Roxas Drop-off Entrance, Greenbelt I, Makati ☎02 840 1325, ⓦthespa.com.ph. One of a popular chain of deluxe spas, with the full range of treatments, from Swedish massage (P820/1hr) to volcanic rock massages (P1500 for 1hr 15min). Daily noon–9pm.

MARKETS

Taking a taxi from one of Manila's opulent malls to a more traditional market district such as Quiapo or Divisoria is like going from New York to Guatemala in thirty minutes – the difference between the two worlds is shocking. Needless to say, prices in Manila's markets are a lot cheaper than the malls.

168 Shopping Mall Santa Elena and Soler sts, Binondo ⓦ168shoppingmall.com; map p.73. Technically a two-section mall but more like a market, with over a thousand stalls flooded with mostly Chinese-made leather handbags, jackets, T-shirts, wallets, caps, toys, shoes and clothes for incredibly low prices. Forms part of the Divisoria market district (see below). Daily 8am–8pm.

Baclaran market Pasay City; map p.80. This labyrinthine street market is spread tentacle-like around the Baclaran LRT station; little stalls huddle under the LRT line as far as the EDSA station, and fill Dr Gabriel St as far west as Roxas Blvd. The focus throughout is cheap clothes and shoes of every hue, size and style, though you'll also come across fake designer watches and pirated CDs and DVDs. The market is a big, noisy, pungent place, and often incredibly crowded, but lots of fun. It's open all week but especially crowded every Wed, the so-called Baclaran Day, when devotees of Our Mother of Perpetual Help crowd into the Redemptorist Church on Dr Gabriel St for the weekly *novena*. Daily 24hr.

Divisoria Market District Claro M. Recto Ave, North Binondo; map p.73. For a range of bargain goods,

from fabric and Christmas decorations to clothes, candles, bags and hair accessories, try fighting your way through the crowds at the immense market district. The pretty lanterns (*parols*) made from *capiz* seashells that you see all over the country at Christmas cost half what you would pay in a mall. The actual Divisoria Mall is at Tabora and Santo Cristo streets, but it's the warren of streets around it that are good for bargains (especially Juan Luna, Ylaya, Tabora, Santo Cristo and Soler). Daily 24hr.

Greenhills Tiangge Greenhills Shopping Center, Ortigas Ave, San Juan ⓦgreenhills.com.ph; map pp.60–61. Sprawling market inside this mall north of Makati which is notorious for its illegal bargains: fake designer goods as well as pirated software and DVDs. There's also attractive costume jewellery on sale, and an area full of stalls selling jewellery made with pearls from China and Mindanao; a good-quality bracelet or necklace made with cultured pearls will cost from P1000, depending on the style and the number of pearls used. Other sections of the mall offer cheap mobile phones (some secondhand), household goods and home decor. Mon–Thurs & Sun 10am–8pm, Fri & Sat 10am–9pm.

Ilalim ng Tulay Quezon Blvd, Quiapo; map p.73. You can hunt down the cheapest woodcarvings, *capiz*-shell items, *buri* bags and embroidery in Manila among the ramshackle stalls beneath the underpass leading to Quezon Bridge in Quiapo (literally "under the bridge"); tell drivers "Quiapo Ilalim". Daily 24hr.

DIRECTORY

Banks and exchange Most major bank branches have 24hr ATMs for Visa and MasterCard cash advances. The moneychangers of Ermita, Malate, P. Burgos St (Makati) and in many malls offer better rates than the banks.

Citibank is at 8741 Paseo de Roxas, Makati (Mon–Fri 9am–3pm) and at the YET Bldg, 500 San Fernando St at Plaza del Conde, Binondo (Mon–Fri 9am–3pm); HSBC has branches at 6766 Ayala Ave, Makati (Mon–Fri 9am–4pm),

Ramada Manila Central, Ongpin St at Paredes St, Binondo (Mon–Fri 9am–4pm) and Nexor Building, 1677 Quezon Ave, Quezon City (Mon–Fri 9am–4pm).

Embassies and consulates Australia, Level 23, Tower 2, RCBC Plaza, 6819 Ayala Ave, Makati ☎02 757 8100, ⓦphilippines.embassy.gov.au; Canada, Levels 6–8, Tower 2, RCBC Plaza, 6819 Ayala Ave, Makati ☎02 857 9000, ⓦphilippines.gc.ca; Ireland, 3/F, 70 Jupiter St, Bel-Air 1, Makati ☎02 896 4668; New Zealand, 23/F, BPI Buendia Center, 360 Gil Puyat (Buendia) Ave, Makati ☎02 891 5358, ⓦnzembassy.com/philippines; UK, 120 Upper McKinley Rd, McKinley Hill, Taguig City ☎02 858 2200; US, 1201 Roxas Blvd ☎02 301 2000, ⓦmanila.usembassy.gov.

Emergencies ☎117.

Hospitals and clinics Makati Medical Center, 2 Amorsolo St, Makati (☎02 888 8999, ⓦmakatimed.net.ph) is the largest and one of the most modern hospitals in Manila. In the Manila Bay area, there's the Manila Doctors Hospital, 667 United Nations Ave, Ermita (☎02 524 3011, ⓦmanila doctors.com.ph), while St Luke's Medical Center, 279 E. Rodriguez Sr Blvd, Quezon City (☎02 723 0101, ⓦstluke .com.ph) is also highly regarded.

Immigration For visa extensions, head to the Immigration Building, Magellanes Drive, Intramuros (Mon–Fri 8am–noon & 1–5pm; ☎02 527 3257 or 3280).

Internet access The entire Robinsons Place mall in Ermita is a free wi-fi zone. Busy Bee, 1417 M.H. del Pilar St, Malate (☎02 256 4776) has a wider-than-average range of services (it doubles as a Western Union office) and is open 24hr. In the P. Burgos area try Station 168, 1 Hercules St at Makati Ave or 88 Internet Café on Burgos St (both 24hr). Rates are usually P40–60/hr.

Laundry Try Faura Laundry at 570 Padre Faura St in Ermita, next to Robinsons Place (☎02 526 7519; daily except Wed 8am–7.30pm), which charges P33/Kg.

Pharmacies You're never far from a Mercury Drug (ⓦmercurydrug.com) outlet in Metro Manila – at the last count there were two hundred of them. In Ermita, there's one at 444 T.M. Kalaw St (daily 7am–10pm) and 24hr branches at 660 San Andres St, Malate; Plaza Miranda in Quiapo; and Ayala Center, Glorietta 4, in Makati.

Post Makati Central Post Office at Sen Gil Puyat (Buendia) Ave Ave near Ayala Ave (Mon–Fri 8am–5pm; ☎02 844 0150); Ermita Post Office at Pilar Hidalgo Lim St, Malate (Mon–Fri 8am–5pm).

Around Manila

PASGANJAN FALLS

Around Manila

Despite the proximity of the big city, the provinces that cluster around Metro Manila contain a surprisingly rich array of natural attractions. To the south lies stunning Lake Taal and its volcano, best approached from the refreshingly breezy city of Tagaytay, while further south, on the coast, Anilao offers outstanding scuba diving. North of Lake Taal, Los Baños is best known for its delicious *buko* pie, hot springs and mountain pools, and sits not far from the churning waters of the Pagsanjan Falls, where you can take a thrilling (and soaking) canoe ride downriver across a series of rapids. North of Manila you can climb the lush slopes of Mount Pinatubo or Mount Arayat, explore remote Bataan province, or enjoy the beaches and activities on offer at Subic Bay, once a major US navy base.

The region was also the scene of some of the nation's most important historical events. The island of **Corregidor**, out in Manila Bay, is littered with thought-provoking monuments to World War II, while **Malolos**, north of Manila, was where the Revolutionary Congress was convened in 1898. National heroes **Emilio Aguinaldo** and **José Rizal** were both born in the region, and their family homes preserved as museums.

Corregidor

The tadpole-shaped island of **CORREGIDOR**, less than 5km long and 3km wide at its broadest point, is a living museum to the horrors of war. Lying 40km southwest of Manila, it was originally used by the Spanish as a customs post. In 1942 it was defended bravely by an ill-equipped US and Filipino contingent under continual bombardment from **Japanese** guns and aircraft. Some 900 Japanese and 800 American and Filipino troops died in the fighting, and when the Americans retook the island in 1945, virtually the entire Japanese garrison of over 6000 men was annihilated: little wonder Corregidor is said to be haunted. The island was abandoned after the war, and was gradually reclaimed by thick jungle vegetation – it wasn't until the late 1980s that the Corregidor Foundation begun to transform it into a national shrine.

If you visit Corregidor on a day-trip you'll be restricted to a **guided tour**; only if you stay the night (see p.107) are you able to wander around on your own. Perhaps understandably, the tours tend to focus on the heroism, bravery and sacrifice of the men who fought here, rather than the grisly nature of the fighting itself, but they are still a moving experience. Japanese tourists also come here in numbers to pay their respects to the dead of both sides.

Away from the reminders of one of the war's most horrific battles, Corregidor is unspoiled, peaceful and a great break from the city: you can walk marked **trails** that meander through the hilly interior (look out for the monkeys and monitor lizards),

HAWKSBILL TURTLE, ANILAO

Highlights

❶ Corregidor Take the fast ferry to this idyllic, jungle-covered island at the mouth of Manila Bay, a poignant monument to World War II. **See opposite**

❷ Pagsanjan Falls Home to rough rapids and a towering cascade, with the best *buko* pie in the Philippines in nearby Los Baños. **See p.111 & p.109**

❸ Tagaytay Clinging to a high volcanic ridge, this town offers mesmerizing views of Lake Taal and some of the tastiest food in Luzon. **See p.112**

❹ Lake Taal Take a bangka across this gorgeous lake and scramble up to the crater at the top of one of the world's smallest volcanoes. **See p.114**

❺ Taal Wonderfully preserved colonial town, with *bahay na bato* houses, ivy-clad churches and vibrant markets. **See p.116**

❻ Anilao A scenic stretch of coast with some choice resorts and excellent scuba diving. **See p.119**

❼ Mount Pinatubo Enticing volcanic peak, accessible by 4WD and on foot, with a beautiful crater lake at the summit. **See p.123**

HIGHLIGHTS ARE MARKED ON THE MAP ON P.106

rent a kayak or circle the island in a bangka and do some fishing, organized through the ferry company or *Corregidor Inn*.

The war memorials

Sound and light show P200

Tours begin near the ferry dock, with the statue of **General Douglas MacArthur**, who was reluctantly spirited away from the island before its capitulation in 1942. His famous words, "I shall return", adorn the statue's base, though he actually made the pronouncement in Darwin, Australia. From here tours take in all the main sights on the island, including the **Filipino Heroes Monument**, commemorating Philippine struggles from the Battle of Mactan in 1521 to the EDSA Revolution of 1986, and

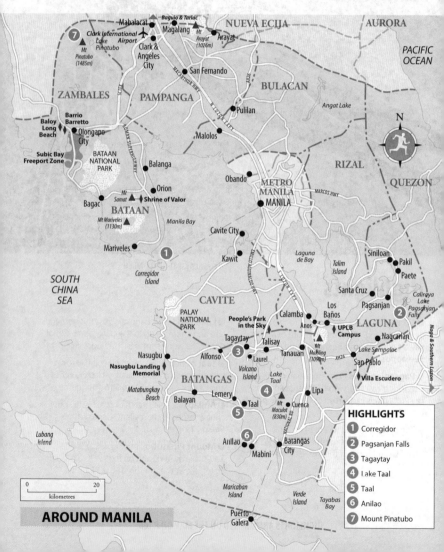

HIGHLIGHTS

1 Corregidor
2 Pagsanjan Falls
3 Tagaytay
4 Lake Taal
5 Taal
6 Anilao
7 Mount Pinatubo

AROUND MANILA

the **Japanese Garden of Peace**, where the Japanese war dead were buried in 1945. Overgrown and lost, it was discovered in the 1980s, when the remains were cremated and brought back to Japan. A statue of the Buddhist bodhisattva Guanyin (or "Kannon" in Japanese) watches over the site. At some point you'll reach the **Malinta Tunnel**, a 253-metre-long chamber and network of damp underground bunkers where MacArthur (and President Manuel Quezon) set up temporary headquarters. You can only see the bunkers in an optional **sound and light show** that dramatizes the events of 1942.

Elsewhere you'll see the ruined concrete shells of the once vast barracks that dotted the island, and the remains of various gun batteries, peppered with bullet and shell holes. You can also visit the **Pacific War Memorial** and its small **museum** containing weapons, old photos and uniforms that were left behind. Finally, clamber the 57 steps to the top of the old **Spanish Lighthouse** at the island's highest point (191m), for stupendous views across to Bataan and Mount Mariveles.

ARRIVAL AND DEPARTURE CORREGIDOR

By boat Sun Cruises (☎02 527 5555, ⌨www.corregidor philippines.com) has a monopoly on transport to the island. It runs day-trips for P2300 (Sat, Sun & hols P2499). If you opt for a walking tour (easy) rather than the bus, the price drops to P1750 (per person, daily). It's best to make reservations in advance, but you can buy same-day tickets (before 7.30am). Check-in takes place at the Sun Cruises office in Manila, CCP Bay Terminal A, Fernando Maria

Guerrero St, at Paseo Palisoc (just beyond Harbour Square mall). Shuttle buses take you to the wharf from here (which is off Pedro Bukaneg St) for the 8am departure and ride to the island (1hr 15 min). Tours usually run on trolley buses that meet the ferries at around 9.30am, returning to the dock in time for the 2.30pm departure – a buffet lunch at the *Corregidor Inn* (see below) is included. You'll be back in Manila at around 3.45pm.

ACCOMMODATION

Corregidor Inn ☎0917 527 6350, ⌨www.corregidor philippines.com. Overnighters stay at the rustic inn, a creaky but atmospheric little place with polished wooden floors, thirty a/c, ageing rooms and a small pool. The ferry

and island tour is extra. The hotel can also arrange camping on the island for just P50 per person, as well as kayaks (P500/hr) and bangkas. **P2000**

South of Manila

The provinces to the south of Manila – **Cavite**, **Laguna** and **Batangas** – are prime day-trip territory, easy to get to and rich in attractions. The star is **Lake Taal**, a mesmerizing volcanic lake with its own mini volcanic island in the centre, but there are plenty of less visited natural wonders that provide a break from the city; you can ride down the river to the **Pagsanjan Falls**, soak in the **Laguna hot springs** or clamber up forested **Mount Makiling** for scintillating views. Divers should check out **Anilao** for the best reef action near the capital.

The region also serves up a healthy dose of history. **Paete** has retained its woodworking heritage and **Taal** itself is one of the most beautiful colonial towns in the Philippines. Lastly, many Manileños come here just to eat; **buko pie** is an especially prized treat made in Laguna.

GETTING AROUND SOUTH OF MANILA

By bus and jeepney Without a car, the easiest places to reach by public transport are the attractions to the south of Laguna de Bay, though Batangas City and Tagaytay are also well served by buses. The lakeside town of Santa Cruz is the main transport hub for the area. All the attractions between Calamba and Santa Cruz are served by buses from the Green Star Express terminal on Taft Ave (in the MRT-Taft

area, Pasay; see p.81). Note that all the Santa Cruz bus terminals line the National Highway outside the town itself, in the barangay of Pagsawitan. Numerous jeepneys also ply the Calamba–Santa Cruz route (around P25–30). Once at Santa Cruz you can catch jeepneys on to San Pablo, Paete and also Pagsanjan.

The Emilio Aguinaldo Shrine and Museum

Tirona Hwy, Kawit • Tues–Sat 8am–noon & 1–4pm• Free • ☎ 046 484 7643 • Take any Cavite-bound jeepney or FX taxi from Baclaran LRT station in Manila

For most Filipinos, the province of Cavite ("ka-vee-tay") will forever be associated with the Philippine Revolution: in 1872 the Cavite Mutiny precipitated the national revolt against the colonial authorities (see p.440), and the province was also the birthplace of independence hero **Emilio Aguinaldo**. That legacy is preserved at the **Emilio Aguinaldo Shrine and Museum** in **KAWIT**, 23km south of Manila. This is the colonial-style house in which Aguinaldo, first President of the Republic, was born in 1869, and also where he is buried, in a simple marble tomb in the back garden on the bank of the river. Philippine independence was proclaimed here and the Philippine flag first raised by Aguinaldo on June 12, 1898, commemorated on this day every year with the president waving the flag from the balcony.

With its secret passages and hidden compartments, the house is testimony to the revolutionary fervour that surrounded Aguinaldo and his men. A number of the original chairs and cabinets have secret compartments that were used to conceal documents and weapons, while the kitchen has a secret passage that he could use to escape if the Spanish came calling. In the general's bedroom, one of the floorboards opens up to reveal a staircase that led to his private one-lane bowling alley under the house and an adjoining hidden swimming pool. Downstairs, the museum displays various Aguinaldo memorabilia including clothes, journals and his sword, while upstairs there is the general's bedroom, a grand hall, a dining room and a conference room.

Calamba

The city of **CALAMBA**, just 54km from the capital, is best known today as the birthplace of national hero and revolutionary **José Rizal**. Once a rural backwater, Calamba is now the largest city in Laguna province and effectively a choked extension of Manila – there's nothing to see in the modern section, but the old barangay of **San Juan** was built in Spanish colonial style around the handsome **St John the Baptist Church** (1859). A marker inside the church indicates that Rizal was baptized here by Fray Rufino Collantes on June 22, 1861.

LAGUNA HOT SPRINGS

Just east of Calamba on the National Highway (accessible by the buses and jeepneys to Santa Cruz), the barangay of **Pansol** touts heavily for tourist custom on the health properties of its **hot springs**, which bubble from the lower slopes of Mount Makiling. There are dozens of resorts of varying quality that use the hot springs to fill their swimming pools, many catering to tour groups, day-trippers, company outings and conferences. It's best to visit on a weekday when the best ones can make for a relaxing few hours.

RESORTS AND SPAS

Makiling Highlands Resort Captain Mamon Rd, Pansol (just off the National Highway) ☎049 545 9703, ⓦmontevista.com.ph. This lush resort has villas and rooms for overnight stays (from P1500) but to use the facilities for the day is just P100–150. Hot pools spread out over many hectares of ground, and – just in case you should start feeling too healthy – 24hr delivery is available from *Max's*, the fried chicken restaurant. You can also rent small wooden *kamaligs* (traditional huts) for P1500–1800 for 12hr.

Monte Vista Hot Springs & Conference Resort National Highway, Pansol ☎049 545 1259, ⓦmonte vista.com.ph. This sister resort to *Makiling Highlands* offers eighteen hot mineral pools, assorted giant slides and enough room for 1500 day visitors, with similar day rates of P100–150.

Rizal Shrine

J.P. Rizal St at F. Mercado St • Tues–Sat 8.30am–noon & 1–4.30pm • Free • ☎ 049 834 1599

The site where José Rizal was born in 1861 is now the **Rizal Shrine**, though the building here is a late 1940s replica of a typical nineteenth-century Philippine *bahay na bato* – it features lower walls of stone and upper walls of wood, *narra*-wood floors and windows made from capiz shell. All the rooms contain period furniture and in the adjacent gallery there are displays of Rizal's belongings, including the clothes he was christened in and a fragment of the suit he was wearing when he was executed. In the garden is a *bahay kubo* (wooden) playhouse, a replica of the one in which Rizal used to spend his days as a child.

2

Los Baños and around

The small lakeside town of **LOS BAÑOS**, around 60km south of Manila, attracts a steady stream of domestic tourists who primarily come to gorge on its delectable **buko pies** (stuffed with young coconut), said to have first been cooked up here in the 1960s by a food technologist from nearby **UPLB**. In and around the campus itself are a couple of enlightening **museums**, the UPLB Museum of Natural History and Riceworld, while the looming volcano cone of **Mount Makiling** makes an enticing target for a day-hike.

UPLB

Jose R Velasco Ave, Los Baños (just off the National Highway) • ☒ uplb.edu.ph • Take Green Star Express bus from Taft Ave at Sen Gil Puyat (Buendia) in Pasay City (destined for Santa Cruz) and ask to get off at "College"; you should be dropped off at the Caltex petrol station, from where jeepneys run to UPLB (P2–3)

Just outside Los Baños is the **University of the Philippines Los Baños** (UPLB) campus at the base of Mount Makiling (see below). This branch of the national public university has a special focus on Asian agriculture and biotechnology, making it one of the foremost research centres in the region.

UPLB Museum of Natural History

UPLB Campus • Mon–Fri 8.30am–4.30pm • P20 • ☎ 049 536 2864

The most absorbing attraction on the campus itself is the **UPLB Museum of Natural History**, which displays thousands of Philippine plants, animals and micro-organisms, including a sperm whale skeleton, giant bamboo, a marijuana exhibit and a controversial (and unsettling) collection of tiny miscarried human foetuses.

Riceworld Museum

Pili Drive • Mon–Fri 8am–5pm • Free • ☎ 049 536 2701 ext 2201, ☒ irri.org

Next door to the campus is the International Rice Research Institute, which is home to the unexpectedly absorbing **Riceworld Museum**, showcasing the importance of the staple that feeds half the world's population. Apart from an overview of the developing world's food shortages, the museum has a number of small but intriguing displays on the history, production and types of rice, including one where visitors can inspect live paddy-field insects such as damselflies, wolf spiders and aggressive fire ants under a microscope.

Mount Makiling

Trail begins at Makiling Center monitoring station, College of Forestry, UPLB campus (☎ 049 536 2577, ☒ mountmakiling.org; P10 registration fee) • From the Los Baños Crossing on the National Highway, take a jeepney to the College of Forestry

The dormant volcano of **Mount Makiling** (1090m) is identifiable by its unusual shape, which is rather like a reclining woman. The mountain is named after Mariang Makiling (aka "Mary of Makiling"), a young woman whose spirit is said to protect the mountain. On quiet nights, so the legend goes, you can hear her playing the harp, although the music is rarely heard any more because Makiling is rumoured to be angry about the scant regard paid to the environment by the authorities. UPLB (see above) now manages the **Mount Makiling Forest Reserve** that blankets the mountain and is hoping to develop its ecotourism potential.

There is a well established but strenuous 8.7km trail up to the summit (4–5hr) starting at the Makiling Center's monitoring station on the UPLB campus. The trail is safe and easy to follow, but be prepared for leeches, sudden downpours and flash floods (the trail was closed for three months after two hikers drowned in 2012). **Guides** are not required. Most climbers start early and complete the hike in one day; you can pitch tents at the Malaboo and Tayabak campsites on the way up, but not near the summit.

2

ARRIVAL AND DEPARTURE   LOS BAÑOS AND AROUND

By bus and jeepney Los Baños is accessible via Green Star Express buses from Manila (p.81) or jeepneys from Calamba. Heading back to Manila from Los Baños, the last bus departs around 8.30pm.

EATING

There are numerous brands and stalls selling *buko* pie along the National Highway outside Los Baños, all priced at around P170 per pie (for the standard 9 inches), or P220 frozen. Note that shops will close early if they run out of pies. As well as those listed here, other specialist snack stores have also set up to cash in on the crowds.

Lety's Buko Pie LBP Building, National Highway, Brgy Anos ☎ 049 536 1332, ⊚ letysbukopie.net. Established by Leticia "Lety" Belarmino in 1976, this is a local favourite (next door to *Orient*). Also sells cassava cake, pineapple pie and banana bread. Daily 4am–8pm.

★ **Net's Cassava Cake** National Highway, Brgy Anos ☎ 049 827 3575. This small stall produces some of the most addictive cassava pudding in the Philippines

(P110–200). Daily 5am–9pm.

★ **Orient – the Original Buko Pie Bakeshop** National Highway, Brgy Anos ☎ 049 536 3783. The best *buko* pies are still baked at this venerable store (note the double-parked cars and buses blocking the road), with young, tender coconut slices in a crispy, well-made crust. From Calamba, the shop is on the left just before you reach the town centre. Daily 5am–8.30pm.

San Pablo and around

Known as the "City of Seven Lakes", **SAN PABLO** was a prosperous Tagalog hamlet named Sampaloc before the Spanish arrived, where *sampalok* (tamarind) trees grew in abundance. It lies southwest of six of the lakes and a five-minute jeepney ride from the seventh and largest of them, **Lake Sampaloc**, which you can circumnavigate on foot in a few hours. There are trails leading through lush jungle and farmland to all of the lakes, and the Lake Sampaloc shore boasts floating restaurants serving native freshwater fish such as tilapia, *bangus*, carp and several species of shrimp. There are plenty of **resorts** in the area to choose from if you feel a day-trip here is too rushed.

Villa Escudero Plantations and Resort

San Pablo City 400 (off the Pan-Philippine Highway) • Museum daily 8am–5pm • Mon–Thurs P1250, Fri–Sun P1400; includes museum, welcome drink, carabao cart ride, use of outdoor recreational facilities, lunch and show (Fri–Sun & hols only, 2–3.15pm) • ☎ 02 523 2944, ⊚ villaescudero.com • Take any bus to Lucena City (see p.83) and ask to get off at Hacienda Escudero (it's a long walk or tricycle ride from the main road)

Half an hour by road south of San Pablo, near Tiaong, the **Villa Escudero Plantations and Resort** is a working coconut plantation founded in the 1880s by Don Placido Escudero and set in a beautiful location surrounded by mountains. Today it's something of an historical theme park, with lunch served beneath a weir followed by the **Philippine Experience Show** of traditional music and dancing, tours in carts pulled by carabao and bamboo rafting; there are overnight cottages (see opposite).

Also on the premises, the **AERA Memorial Museum** is housed in an artful replica of a colonial Intramuros church, with trompe-l'oeil ceilings and a treasure trove of religious art, consisting of silver altars, gilded *carrozas* (ceremonial carriages), ivory-headed santos, oriental ceramics, costumes, dioramas of Philippine wildlife and ethnography, rare coins and antique Philippine furniture.

ACCOMMODATION AND EATING SAN PABLO AND AROUND

Hidden Valley Spring Resort Alaminos (around 14km northwest of San Pablo, off the Pan-Philippine Highway) ☎ 02 818 4034. Resort set amid rainforest in a volcanic crater 100m deep, with, simple but adequate a/c cottages, falls and seven natural spring pools, some deep enough for swimming. The entrance fee for day-trippers is P2200, which includes a welcome drink, buffet lunch, afternoon snacks and use of all the pools. To get to Alaminos catch a local bus or jeepney from San Pablo or Los Baños, or join an organized tour from Manila. P9900

Villa Escudero Plantations and Resort San Pablo City 4000 (13km south of San Pablo, off the Pan-Philippine Highway) ☎ 02 523 2944, ⓦ villaescudero .com. This historic plantation has a range of ageing but pretty rooms, from basic apartments with fans (cheapest) to "aircon units" and executive suites with verandas overlooking a lake. All meals are included. P6490

2

Pagsanjan

Serving as the capital of Laguna province from 1688 to 1858, the town of **PAGSANJAN** lies 100km southeast of Manila and is home to a few old wooden houses, an unusually ornamental stone gate – or **Puerta Real** – and a pretty Romanesque church. The gate sits on the road to Santa Cruz (Rizal Street) and was completed in 1880, while **Our Lady of Guadalupe Church**, dating from 1690 but remodelled in the nineteenth century, is at the other end of Rizal. The town's main claim to fame these days is as the staging point for the dazzling **Pagsanjan Falls**, chosen by Francis Ford Coppola as the location for the final scenes in *Apocalypse Now* in 1975. Most tourists come not for the Hollywood nostalgia value, however, but to take one of the popular "**shooting the rapids**" trips along the Bumbungan River to the falls and back (see box below).

ARRIVAL AND INFORMATION PAGSANJAN

By bus It can take up to 4hr to get to Pagsanjan from Manila if you hit bad traffic (around 2hr normally) – avoid weekends and public holidays. Jeepneys (P10–20) run frequently from Santa Cruz (see p.107) to Pagsanjan.

Tourist information The tourist office is in the municipal building (daily 8am–5pm; ☎ 049 808 3544) in the centre of Pagsanjan, opposite the church.

ACCOMMODATION AND EATING

★**Aling Taleng's** 169 General Luna St (just south of the Balanac Bridge) ☎ 049 501 7861. This popular shop has been serving refreshing seven-ingredient *halo-halo* (P70) since 1933. Also serves all-day Filipino breakfast, home-made burgers and noodles. Free wi-fi. Daily 8.30am–6.30pm.

Calle Arco 57 Rizal St (National Hwy) ☎ 049 501 4584. This old-fashioned restaurant in a whimsical wooden house serves quality Filipino food such as *sinigang na baka sa*

langka (beef tamarind soup with jackfruit, P250). Buy the sweet calamansi and tomatoes in jars (P250) to take away. Cash only. Daily 10am–10pm.

Pagsanjan Falls Lodge Pinagsanjan (Pagsanjan-Cavinti Rd) ☎ 049 501 4251, ⓦ pagsanjanfallslodge .com.ph. This resort has a decent family pool area, restaurant and a good range of very ordinary but clean and spacious rooms including fan rooms, a/c doubles plus

---

SHOOTING THE RAPIDS AT PAGSANJAN

The fourteen **rapids** of the Bumbungan River (bangkas daily 7am–5pm; minimum P1250) are at their most thrilling in the wet season (June–Sept); during the dry season the "shooting the rapids" ride is more sedate. You don't need to be especially daring to do the trip, though you will get wet, so be prepared. All **ticket sales** are supposedly supervised by the local tourism office (see above); ignore touts who try and sell tickets on the street. Most visitors pay P1250–2000 per person for the trip, including the raft ride under the falls (you'll be asked to pay another P200 tip per boatman, though this is not compulsory). Boats leave from the bridge behind the building.

It usually takes around an hour to climb 5.38km up through the dramatic gorge in bangkas; when you get closer to the actual 30m-high **Pagsanjan Falls**, you can float on a bamboo raft (*balsa*) to go directly below the cascade into the cavern known as **Devil's Cave** for a swim, another thirty minutes or so. This is an additional P250 per head if not already negotiated as part of your boat trip.

fifteen rooms for up to three people. To get to the resort, take a jeepney from General Luna St (south of the river) in Pagsanjan. Day-use fee P125. **P1500**

★ **Tio Casio's Bibingka de Macapuno** National Hwy, Sambat, Bubukal (5km west of Pagsanjan) ☎ 049 810 3829. For a real treat make the trip out to this local stall for sumptuous slices of coconut-enriched *bibingka* (rice cake). Daily 7am–6pm.

Paete

Sleepy **PAETE** ("pa-e-te"), is Luzon's **woodcarving capital**, packed with stores selling woodcarvings, oil paintings, wooden clogs (*bakya*) and the gaily painted papier-mâché masks that are used in fiestas. Most of the stores (usually open daily 8am–6pm) are on **Quesada Street** in the centre of town. During the second week of January Paete holds its **Salibanda festival**, the feast of the Santo Niño (Holy Child), which includes a rowdy procession along the main street in which participants and spectators splash water over each other. Paete is also well known for its sweet **lanzones** (harvested Oct–Dec). There is no accommodation, but you can visit the town easily in a day.

Santiago Apostol Parish Church

Quesada St at Roces St • Daily 7am–8pm • ☎ 049 557 0114

The town's crumbling but atmospheric Baroque **Santiago Apostol Parish Church** dates right back to 1646, but in common with many Philippine churches built by the Spaniards, it has been reduced to rubble by earthquakes on a number of occasions and rebuilt. The present structure dates from 1939, and has an ornate carved facade, weathered bell tower and a beautifully sculpted altar finished in gold leaf. Check out also the wonderfully vivid mural paintings near the main entrance, dating from the 1850s.

ARRIVAL AND DEPARTURE PAETE

By jeepney Paete is 10km north of Pagsanjan, just off the main highway that hugs the east coast of Laguna de Bay. It's best approached by jeepney (around P25) from Pagsanjan or Santa Cruz (take any one going to Siniloan).

EATING

★ **Exotik** National Hwy, Longos (around 2km south of Paete) ☎ 049 820 0086. Enchanting restaurant modelled on a native village. The menu features typical Filipino dishes as well as frog, eel and stingray, but ask about seasonal dishes such as snake, wild boar and monitor lizard (which really does taste like chicken). Meats are cooked adobo style, "sizzling" or in coconut milk. Most dishes range P200–300. Daily 7am–9pm.

Kape Kesada Art Gallery & Café Quesada St ☎ 0916 362 4015. Café and gallery (selling paintings and books) that looks like a wooden Japanese house and serves decent sandwiches and brewed coffee (P65). Tues–Sun 9am–6pm.

Tagaytay

The compact and breezy city of **TAGAYTAY**, 55km south of Manila, sits in a magical position on a dramatic 600-metre-high ridge overlooking **Lake Taal** and its volcano, to which it serves as the gateway. The ridge road (known as Aguinaldo Highway west of the central Rotunda) can become very congested, particularly on weekends and holidays when the crowds can be overwhelming, but you still might consider spending the night to enjoy those entrancing vistas. The views make it more expensive to stay here than in one of the barangays by the lake around Talisay (see p.114), where it's quieter and more convenient if you intend to climb the volcano.

Tagaytay Picnic Grove

5km east of the Rotunda • **Grove** Daily 6am–midnight • P50 • **Zipline and Cable Car** Daily 9am–6pm • Mon–Fri P300 one-way, P400 return or combo; add P100 Sat & Sun • ☎ 0906 489 5351, ⊕ tagaytayzipline.com

Most day-trippers enjoy the views from the **Tagaytay Picnic Grove**, a shabby ridge-top park, with huts available to rent. Inside the grove (but separately managed), the **Tagaytay Ridge Zipline & Cable Car** boasts a 250-metre long zip and cable car ride.

People's Park in the Sky

Around 7.5km east of the Rotunda • Daily 6am–6pm • P35

The **People's Park in the Sky** is the highest point in the area (750m) offering magnificent panoramas of the lake, the sea, Laguna de Bay – and the smog that hangs over Manila to the north. It's topped by a collection of abandoned concrete buildings which are a bit of an eyesore; until they are redeveloped, the only other attraction up here is the modest **Shrine of our Lady, Mother of Fair Love**, constructed in 2003.

Sky Fun Amusement Park

Aguinaldo Highway Km 60, beside the *Taal Vista Hotel* • Daily 8am–10pm • P100, plus Sky Eye P150, Super Viking P100, Nessi Coaster P50, Wonder Flight P50

Visitors with kids will enjoy the **Sky Fun Amusement Park**, which contains the "Sky Eye", the tallest Ferris wheel in the Philippines (at 63m), as well as thrill-filled rides such as the "Super Viking" (a giant boat swing), the "Nessi Coaster" mini rollercoaster and "Wonder Flight", a roundabout for young kids.

ARRIVAL AND DEPARTURE   TAGAYTAY

By bus Frequent San Agustin (☎02 872 8497) and Erjohn & Almark (☎02 529 6148) buses run every 30min from MRT-Taft (Pasay) on EDSA (see p.81) to Tagaytay (1hr 30min). Jeepneys run up and down the main road in town for around P8.

ACCOMMODATION

★**Sonya's Garden** Barangay Buck Estate, Alfonso ☎0917 532 9097, ⓦsonyasgarden.com. Romantic cottage accommodation in a blossom-filled garden. Cottages are *bahay na bato*-style, with antique beds, lots of carved wood and shuttered windows. The rate includes a delicious breakfast and wi-fi. *Sonya's* is 12km beyond Tagaytay, so is tricky to reach without private transport: go past Splendido golf course and then look out for the signs on the right. P3000

★**Theodore Hotel** Aguinaldo Hwy Km 54, Silang Crossing ☎046 483 0350, ⓦthetheodorehotel.com. Best of a new generation of boutique hotels on the ridge, this centrally located option offers ten stylish rooms each with its own design theme (from Pop Art to Japan), flatscreen TVs, spa, and a tranquil garden and viewing deck. P6100

EATING AND DRINKING

Adoration Convent of Divine Mercy (Pink Sister's) Off the Aguinaldo Hwy, north of the Rotunda (heading back to Manila – look for the Pink Sister signs). Tranquil religious institution (said to be popular with late President Cory Aquino), that sells home-baked food from a tiny gift shop to the left of the entrance. The nuns' home-made cookies – aka "angel cookies" (tasty oat biscuits that sell for P190 per large jar) – bring in the foodies. Daily 9am–5pm.

★**The Grill by Antonio's** Aguinaldo Hwy Km 54 (at the Rotunda) ☎046 483 4847, ⓦantoniosrestaurant.ph /the-grill. Hands-down the best Filipino food in town, though the views are marred somewhat by the fast-food joints below. Highlights include the huge pots of richly stewed *bulalo* (P700) – a meal for two people – plates of fried *tawalis* (local sardines, P200), a fine adobo (P290) and

the barbecue chicken (P110). Daily 11am–9pm.

Josephine Aguinaldo Hwy Km 58 ☎046 413 1801, ⓦjosephinerestaurant.com. An institution among Filipinos since the 1960s, serving good Filipino dishes such as *sinigang* with mounds of steamed rice to go with those special views. They also do a weekend lunch buffet for P495. Mon–Fri 9am–10pm, Sat & Sun 7am–11pm.

★**Maryridge Good Shepherd Convent** Aguinaldo Hwy Km 59, Barangay Sungay (east of the Rotunda) ☎046 413 1307. This religious institution attracts a steady stream of visitors for its small takeaway food counters run by Bahay Pastulan; the main draw is the pots of addictive *ube* jam (more like frozen ice cream; from P190), but the peanut brittle (P165), mango jam (P125), coconut juice (P40) and *halo-halo* (P75) are also worth

---

THE TASTES OF LAKE TAAL

Lake Taal is famed for its delicious **fresh fish**, especially *tawilis* (a freshwater sardine only found here), tilapia and increasingly rare *maliputo* (a larger fish, also only found in Lake Taal, which is also featured on the back of the P50 note). The other speciality is piping-hot *bulalo*, a rich beef **bone-marrow soup**. You'll find all of these in abundance in Tagaytay's restaurants.

gorging on. It's clearly signposted off the main road. Daily 10am–7pm.

Rowena's 152 Barangay San Francisco (on the Santa Rosa road) ☎ 046 860 2481, ⓦ rowenas-tarts-tagaytay .com. Delicious *buko* pies; stop by for blueberry or strawberry cheese tarts, or the classic *buko* pie (around P170 each), plus excellent coffee. Daily 8am–6pm.

★**Sonya's Garden** Barangay Buck Estate, Alfonso ☎ 0917 532 9097, ⓦ sonyasgarden.com. If you're not staying the night (see p.113), drop by for lunch or dinner: daily set menus cost P683 (breakfast is P500 for non-guests) and include delights such as pasta with sun-dried tomatoes and banana rolls with sesame and jackfruit for dessert. Book ahead.

Lake Taal and Talisay

The country's third largest lake, awe-inspiring **Lake Taal** sits in a caldera below Tagaytay, formed by huge eruptions between 500,000 and 100,000 years ago. The active **Taal Volcano**, which is responsible for the lake's sulphuric content, lies in the centre of the lake, on **Volcano Island**. The volcano last erupted in 1965 without causing major damage, but when it blew its top in 1754, thousands died and the town of Taal was destroyed; it was rebuilt in a new location on safer ground an hour by road from Tagaytay to the southwest of the lake (see p.112). Before 1754 the lake was actually part of Balayan Bay, but the eruption sealed it from the sea, eventually leading to its waters becoming non-saline. Today it's still very active, and the island is occasionally closed – check the **Philippine Institute of Volcanology and Seismology** website (PHIVOLCS; ⓦ phivolcs.dost.gov.ph) for the latest updates.

The departure point for trips across the lake to the volcano (see box below) is the small town of **TALISAY** on the lake's northern shore, some 4km southeast of Tagaytay. This is a much more typical Filipino settlement, with a bustling market, fishermen doubling as tourist guides and nary a fast-food chain in sight.

VOLCANO ISLAND

Visitors to **Volcano Island** often get ripped off by local "guides" but it's easy to avoid making the same mistake; the only price you need to negotiate is the **bangka** to take you out to the island and back (plus the tricycle/taxi fare to the dock). They cost around P2500 (good for 5–6 people) if you arrange one independently, though it's possible to negotiate down to P1500 if it's not busy, and can be arranged at the waterfront market in Talisay, or at any of the resorts (see p.116); *Taal Lake Yacht Club* (see below) is also a dependable choice. **Guides** will charge another P700 or so to take you up to the main crater (and even to cross on the boat with you), though the trail is easy to follow and you do not need one. On the island is a small information office where you must pay an **entry fee** of P50. There's also a basic restaurant, with vendors selling overpriced drinks.

The principal highlight on the island is the walk up to the rim of the 1.9km-diameter **Main Crater Lake**, where you can look down onto tiny Vulcan Point island ("the island on an island"); the lake itself is usually off-limits, depending on current PHIVOLCS warnings (see above). You can ride a **horse** up to the top of the crater for an additional P450 – most tourists do this because of the heat, but the trail is not difficult for anyone in reasonable fitness (and the condition of the horses is pretty appalling). The trail can be dusty, however, so bring a scarf for your mouth or buy a mask on arrival (P20). If you're staying the night by the lake, your hotel can arrange all this for you, with food and refreshments included, typically for P2000–3000 per person. There isn't much shade on the island, so don't go without sunblock, a good hat and plenty of water.

With an early start (boats usually run from 7am), you can climb to the Main Crater Lake and be back in Talisay in time for lunch (the hike takes around 30min depending on fitness level; the trail is around 2.3km with a height gain of 200m). If you want to spend more time on the water, make for the **Taal Lake Yacht Club**, about 1km east of Talisay (☎ 043 773 0192, ⓦ sailing.org.ph/tlyc), where you can rent sailing dinghies (Toppers from P1200/day) and kayaks (P750/day).

2

From Manila you can approach Lake Taal from two directions: from the north via Tagaytay, or via Tanauan, east of the lake. Once in Talisay **tricycles** should take you to nearby hotels or bangka operators for P10 per person, or P25–30 per ride. Some groups take a **taxi** from Manila or the airport all the way to Talisay; reckon on at least P5000.

Via Tagaytay From Tagaytay market, take one of the jeepneys (20–30min; P35) that shuttle back and forth (till around 4pm) to Talisay's lakeshore. Tricycles/taxis will charge at least P200 (but may ask for P350 or more).

Via Tanauan JAM buses from Manila (see p.81) to Lemery stop at Tanauan (around P80). In Tanauan take a tricycle to the Talisay jeepney terminal (P10 per person); frequent jeepneys head to Talisay town from there (30min; P20).

ACCOMMODATION AND EATING

Most of the lakeside **resorts** are between Talisay and the village of Laurel a few kilometres to the south. Hotels are busiest from Sept to Feb (the coolest months) so book ahead if travelling at these times. Weekdays are always much cheaper year-round. Down by the lakeshore in and around Talisay, there are simple **eating** places selling barbecued meat and fish, but quality can be hit and miss; the numerous bakeries in Talisay are a safer bet for a snack.

★**Club Balai Isabel** Brgy Banga, Talisay ☎043 728 0307, ⊕balaiisabel.com. This fashionable lakeside boutique resort is built around a century-old coconut and mango plantation just east of the town. Rates for the cosy hotel rooms and suites include breakfast, while the luxurious lakeshore suites and villas are self-catering (all have kitchens) and can accommodate up to six people. There's a swimming pool, and a variety of watersports and even a lake cruise can be laid on for guests. P5550

Ronnie & Au Talisay–Tanauan Rd, Talisay ☎0918 564 0349. One of the better sit-down options in town, this rustic diner knocks up all the usual favourites and 3-in-1 coffee (breakfast for P50). Staples include adobo, tilapia, *tawilis* and *bulalo* (mains P120–200). Ask what's been freshly caught; they sometimes have *maliputo* (not usually on the menu). Daily 8am–7pm.

Talisay Green Lake Resort Brgy Santa Maria, Talisay ☎043 773 0247, ⊕taal-greenlakeresort.net. This solid budget option lies next to Taal Lake Yacht Club, and offers a range of rooms with bath and TV, set in a large, private compound right on the lakeshore. P1500

Taal

The town of **TAAL**, 130km south of Manila and a further 10km south of its namesake lake, is one of the best preserved colonial enclaves in the Philippines and one of the few places you can get a real sense of its Spanish past. Founded in 1572 by Augustinians, it was moved to this location (and away from the deadly Taal volcano) in 1755 and today boasts a superb collection of endearingly weathered Spanish colonial architecture and *bahay na bato*-style homes, as well as one of the finest basilicas in Luzon. Several of the town's Spanish-era buildings are open to the public.

Basilica de St Martin de Tours
M. Agoncillo St • Daily 7am–8pm • Free; belfry tower P50

On the northern side of Taal's central plaza lies the elegantly weathered bulk of the **Basilica de St Martin de Tours**, said to be the biggest church in Southeast Asia, its facade visibly cracked, peeling and studded with clumps of weeds. The present church, begun in 1856, has a magnificent interior and is often jam-packed for masses throughout the day. The church (and Taal) is a major pilgrimage site thanks to an aged pinewood image of the Virgin Mary known as **Our Lady of Caysasay**, only 20cm high, which is moved to a shrine on the edge of town each week (see opposite). The statue is said to have been fished out of the Pansipit River in 1603; it was lost then found again in a freshwater spring.

Leon Apacible Historic Landmark
M. Agoncillo St • Wed–Sun 8.30am–4.30pm • Free • ☎0999 344 8976

The **Leon Apacible Historic Landmark** is the ancestral home of **Leon Apacible** (1861–1901), lawyer and Filipino revolutionary. Built in the eighteenth century it has the best-preserved interior in Taal: though it was renovated in 1870 and again in 1940, the wide, highly buffed *narra* floorboards, as well as the wide sweeping staircase (with its curved balustrade) are still original. The sliding doors and oriel windows betray American Art Deco influence while the transom filigree, featuring swirling chrysanthemums, is Chinese style.

Marcela Agoncillo Historical Landmark
M. Agoncillo St • Wed–Sun 8.30am–4.30pm • Free • ☎ 0928 227 9126

The **Marcela Agoncillo Historical Landmark** is the most evocative and visibly ageing house in Taal, with creaky wooden floors, a dusty library and old-fashioned *sala* upstairs. The eighteenth-century house is the ancestral home of **Marcela Mariño de Agoncillo** (1860–1946), creator of the first Philippine flag in 1898 (she was in exile in Hong Kong at the time). An exhibit of flags from the days of the Philippine Revolution adorns the lower half of the structure, and her statue (holding the flag) graces the garden.

Felipe Agoncillo Mansion
J.P. Rizal St • Daily 9am–4pm • P50

The pristine all-white **Felipe Agoncillo Mansion** was the birthplace of **Felipe Agoncillo** (1859–1941), a lawyer who helped negotiate the Treaty of Paris, which ended the Spanish–American War in 1898 (his wife was the creator of the Philippine flag; see above). Also known as the Gregorio Agoncillo Mansion (after Felipe's nephew, later owner of the house), it's still privately owned, but ring the bell and the housekeeper will usually give you a short tour of the faithfully preserved interior. Felipe's statue stands in the garden.

Chapel of Caysasay
Calle Vicente Noble • Daily 7am–8pm • Free

The **Chapel of Caysasay**, located on the banks of the Pansipit River on the edge of town, is a beautiful coral-hewn chapel where the Our Lady of Caysasay image is transferred from its shrine in the basilica every Thursday and returned on Saturday afternoon. The ruined **Twin Wishing Wells of Santa Lucia**, a short walk from the chapel, are still reputed to have miraculous healing powers. Locals will point you in the right direction.

ARRIVAL AND INFORMATION — TAAL

By bus and jeepney There is no direct road link between Taal and Talisay/Tagaytay on the northern side of Lake Taal. From Manila the best option is to take an ALPS bus from the LRT-Gil Puyat area (see p.81) bound for Lipa City and get off at the Tambo Exit (1hr 30min). From here, ride a Lipa–Lemery jeepney to Taal (1hr; P50).

Tourist information You can get basic information at the tourist information desk (Mon–Fri 8am–5pm) inside City Hall, on the main town square.

GETTING AROUND

By tricycle Taal's compact centre is easy to explore on foot, but if it's too hot you can easily hire a tricycle to whisk you around (P100–120 depending on how many sights and hours you take).

ACCOMMODATION AND EATING

Casa Cecilia Diversion Rd (just outside the centre) ☎ 043 408 0046, @ casa_cecilia_taal@yahoo.com. Modern, cosy seven-room hotel sporting Spanish-style architecture and a patio overlooking the garden. Rooms are all en-suite doubles or twins with parquet floors, tiled bathrooms, free wi-fi and cable TV, and there's a good restaurant, *La Azotea*, on the ground floor serving typical Batangueño food (such as *bulalo*). Rates include breakfast. **P2500**

★ **Casa Punzalan** C. Ilagan St at P. Gomez St ☎ 043 408 0084. The best budget option in the area, a beautiful and historic property in the town plaza overlooking the basilica. It contains three fan rooms and two a/c rooms, all with four-poster beds and shared bathrooms. **P700**

2

SHOPPING

Taal Public Market Calle Ananias Diokno ☎ 043 408 1504. The market in the centre of Taal is a good place to eat and to look for local embroidery (*burdang Taal*), including cotton sheets, pillowcases, tablemats and *barong tagalog* and *saya*, the national costumes. They're all made by hand in the town's small workshops and are much cheaper here than in Manila, as long as you're prepared to do some haggling. The area is also well known for the manufacture of *balisong*, traditional knives which have a hidden blade that flicks out from the handle (P150–1000), and local food specialities; try Gerry & Lheen Special Tapa & Longganisa (stall 154; ☎ 0916 790 5898), for Filipino-style pork and sausage products. Daily 6.30am–7pm.

Mount Maculot

P10, paid at the Registration Point • Guides can be organized at the trailhead (give at least P500) • From Manila, take a Lemery-bound bus from Taft-Buendia or Cubao LRT stations (2hr 30min; around P150) and get off in Cuenca, from where it's a 2km walk or tricycle ride (P20 per person) to the trailhead

Close to the town of **Cuenca**, on the southeastern side of Lake Taal, some 50km east of Taal itself, **Mount Maculot** (930m) affords mind-bending views across the lake, surrounding jungle and puffy clouds to the horizon from its summit, yet is relatively undeveloped and (weekends excepted) tourist free. If you set out from Manila very early – as most local climbers do – you can climb its lush slopes and be in Taal (or back in the capital) for dinner. One reason for Maculot's popularity is an area of sheer rock near the summit known as the **Rockies** (starting at 706m), which rises vertically up from the jungle and has a platform at the top affording unbroken views across Lake Taal. There's a steep but walkable path around the Rockies that takes you to the platform.

The 2km walk or tricycle ride from Cuenca to the trailhead goes via the **Barangay No. 7 Outpost**, a small hut marked by a barrier across the road. Stop off along the way at the Registration Point near the Cuenca barangay administration hall, where you are supposed to register and pay. Though you can organize guides at the trailhead, they're not necessary – the trail is easy to follow (well marked by white arrows and signs), with steps and handrails most of the way. From the trailhead (behind the little sari-sari store known as the "mountaineer's store") it takes about two hours to reach the summit, depending on your fitness level, via the **Grotto of the Blessed Virgin Mary**, a small shrine.

Nasugbu and around

Some of the finest white-sand beaches near Manila lie along the Batangas coastline around **NASUGBU**, 37km west of Tagaytay. The coast here is pitted with resorts, mostly clearly signposted from the main road and grouped in three areas: to the north of Nasugbu on the chalky sands stretching to Fuego Point; around Nasugbu itself on Nasugbu Beach, which has darker sand and is more crowded; and about 12km south of Nasugbu by road along the similarly darker sands of **Matabungkay Beach**, often marred by the *balsas* (rafts rented by resorts) that line the shore. Other than the beach, the only real sight is the **Nasugbu Landing Memorial**, a steel landing craft and statues of soldiers coming ashore, which commemorates the second landing of American forces in the Philippines in 1945, at the end of World War II.

ARRIVAL AND DEPARTURE

By bus From Manila, there are frequent Batman Star Express (BSC) buses to Nasugbu from the EDSA (MRT-Taft) terminal.

NASUGBU AND MATABUNGKAY BEACH

There are jeepneys every few minutes between Nasugbu and Matabungkay (20min; P25).

ACCOMMODATION

Coral Beach Club Matabungkay Beach ☎ 0917 901 4635, ⌨ coralbeach.ph. A quiet, attractive hotel with restaurant (which is a bit overpriced), bar, pool tables, beachside pool and a/c rooms, all with cable TV and hot showers. Free wi-fi and private transfers to Manila P4000–5000. P2300

Lago de Oro National Highway, Balibago, Calatagan (20km south of Nasugbu) ☎0917 504 2685, ⓦlago-de -oro.com. Modern hacienda-style resort, notable for the cable wakeboard system in its lagoon (daily 9.30am–12.30pm & 1.30–4.30pm; P250/1hr); a cable drags you around the lake rather than a boat. There's also good food in the European-style restaurant and a pool for lounging. Vans to Nasugbu are P600. P3500

The Sanctuary Spa at Maya-Maya Brgy Natipuan (10km north of Nasugbu via Ternate Hwy) ☎0918 909 7170, ⓦmayamaya.com. This spa-cum-upmarket resort offers good-value and reasonably priced thatched cottages with a/c rooms and excellent service, plus boat transfers to and from local beaches and speedboat rentals. The spa offers massages (from P450) and body treatments from P1800. P3000

Twins Beach Club Matabungkay Beach ☎0916 598 9162, ⓦtwinsbc.de. Homely German-managed pension on the seafront, offering en-suite doubles with tiled floors. Small beach, swimming pool and alfresco bar. Some of the best-value accommodation in the area if you're content with the simple life. P2000

Anilao

Some 140km south of Manila, the resort of **ANILAO** (the name refers both to the village and the 13km peninsula beyond it) is primarily a diving destination, popular with city folk at weekends (when the area can get a little busy). During the week it's much more peaceful and you can often negotiate a discount on your accommodation, though there's little point in coming just for the beach.

ARRIVAL AND DEPARTURE   **ANILAO**

To reach Anilao by public transport, take a bus to Batangas City (see p.81) and then a jeepney west to Mabini or the wharf at Anilao village (1hr; P40), and continue by tricycle (P40) along the coastal road to your resort.

ACCOMMODATION

Aquaventure Reef Club Brgy Bagalangit ☎917 5877 848, ⓦaquareefclub.com. Comfortable, unpretentious resort 3km along the coastal road beyond Anilao. Operated by Manila-based dive outfit Aqua One, it's primarily a scuba resort, though it also offers island-hopping and snorkelling trips in rented bangkas. Double rooms come with fan or a/c and bath; buffet-style meals are served in a nice open restaurant overlooking the sea. P3000

★**Casita Ysabel** Brgy San Teodoro ☎917 755 9575, ⓦcasitaysabel.com. Preferred hideaway for non-divers (as well as divers), with its Tree Earth Spa and cosy cottages just off the beach (and local reef). Owner Linda Reyes-Romualdez has used Bali as inspiration for the nicest *casitas*, most of which have ocean views. Meals included. P4000

★**Dive Solana** Brgy San Teodoro ☎02 721 2089, ⓦdivesolana.com. Along the coastal road beyond the *Aquaventure Reef Club*, this is a charming and slightly bohemian little retreat popular with divers and owned by Filipina film-maker Marilou Diaz-Abaya. All rooms (some right on the beach) come with a/c, cable TV and free wi-fi, and the rate includes four buffet meals a day. It's always full at weekends, so book in advance. Quoted rates are per person (P3600). Two people P7200

Planet Dive Brgy San Teodoro ☎0916 704 3718, ⓦplanetdive.com.ph. The last of the resorts along the Anilao strip, these native-style cottages are opposite the Twin Rocks dive site, where the bay is sheltered enough for good snorkelling. You can have candlelit dinners on the shore and there's a viewing deck from which to take in Anilao's wonderful sunsets. Accommodation ranges from the very basic to cottages for six, all of it clean and comfortable. P2500

Vivere Azure Brgy Aguada Km 108, San Teodoro ☎02 771 7777, ⓦvivereazure.com. Elegant boutique resort

---

DIVING AT ANILAO

The **reef** at Anilao is thriving, mainly because this is a protected marine sanctuary, with huge numbers of reef fish, small squid, cuttlefish, colourful nudibranchs (sea slugs) and all sorts of hard and soft coral. There are at least forty dive sites within thirty minutes of most resorts; the best are Twin Rocks, Basura, Mainit Muck (Secret Bay), Kirby's and Bethlehem. It's justly celebrated for Cathedral Rock, a marine park sanctuary at 20–30m; originally barren, the site comprises two large rock formations inside a natural amphitheatre, topped with a man-made cross and seeded with corals. The resorts are the easiest places to arrange dive trips, with basic dives (with equipment) starting at around P1750 from a boat, and P1200 for shore dives. The best time for diving is March through June.

with the best views in Anilao and fourteen luxurious suites, each featuring earthy tones, stone and wood furnishings. Rates include all meals, use of the pool, kayaks and snorkelling gear. Quoted rates are per person (P7250). Two people P15,000

Batangas City

BATANGAS CITY lies on the other side of Batangas Bay from Anilao. The city has one of the fastest growing populations in the Philippines but there's not much to see and its significance for most visitors is as a transit point on the journey to Puerto Galera on Mindoro.

ARRIVAL AND DEPARTURE   BATANGAS CITY

By ferry Batangas Port lies 2km west of the city centre. Ferries to Puerto Galera (around 2hr) depart Batangas Port Terminal 3, where various companies sell tickets to Muelle Pier (P230), Sabang (P230) and White Beach (P270) on large outriggers (daily 6.30am–5pm). A chartered outrigger will cost at least P4000 one-way. Montenegro Lines (Ⓦ montenegrolines.com.ph) operates a car ferry (daily 7am & noon; 2hr; passengers P170) to Balatero, 3km west of Puerto Galera, and hourly ferries to Calapan (P240), 44km southeast of Galera, and Abra de Ilog (3 daily; P260), 30km west. Fast Cat (Ⓦ fastcat.com.ph) also runs between Batangas and Calapan (1am, 6am, 3pm & 8pm; P190) in just 1hr 30min. You need to pay an additional terminal fee

(P30) before boarding; departures for Galera also incur a P50 "Environmental User Fee".
By bus Batangas City is usually 2–3hr bus ride from Manila (1hr 30min via the STAR Tollway), but the roads are often very congested and journey times can vary widely. There is a jeepney station outside Batangas Port Terminal 3, with rides into Batangas City centre costing P10; tricycles will charge at least P50. If you're heading to Nasugbu (2hr), San Pablo (1hr 30min), Santa Cruz (3hr), Taal (1hr 30min) or Tagaytay (1hr 30min), take a jeepney to one of the bus terminals in town. You'll find the JAM, ALPS and Ceres Transport terminals on P. Burgos St, a short ride from the port. Numerous buses wait at Terminal 2 for the frequent trip to Manila.

EATING

★**A&M Village Restaurant** Hilltop Ave, off P. Burgos St ☎ 043 723 1118. This ordinary-looking restaurant, near the University of Batangas, is best known for sumptuous native cuisine such as *bulalo*, *kare-kare* (peanut stew), *buko* juice and *leche* flan (mains P250–350). It's 3km from the port; any taxi or tricycle driver will know it. Daily 8am–9pm.
Hungry Hippo UB Hilltop Arcade ☎ 043 300 2323,

Ⓦ hungryhippo.com.ph. Another store with a cult following, right next to the University of Batangas, this local chain is beloved for its juicy hamburgers (from P85). Daily 8am–10pm.
★**Lety's** 11 P. Dandan St ☎ 043 723 3388. Must-try pancit *tikyano* (red stir-fried noodles; P140) at a no-frills canteen near the basilica and leafy plaza in the centre of the city. Daily 7am–9.30pm.

North of Manila

Most travellers zip through the provinces **north of Manila** – Pampanga, Bulacan and Bataan – to the justly famed attractions of northern Luzon, but there are a few reasons to break the journey. **Malolos** has some historic distractions, while **Mount Pintatubo** and **Mount Arayat** provide energetic hikes and gasp-inducing scenery. **Bataan** is a surprisingly wild province, with some excellent beaches and World War II monuments, while **Subic Bay** is turning into an appealing beach, dive and outdoor activity centre. Buses connect all the main attractions with Manila, though fast ferries are much quicker to Bataan – if they are running (see p.125)

Malolos

The capital of Bulacan province, **MALOLOS** lies some 45km north of Manila, a relatively historic city of 250,000 best known as the location of the **Malolos Convention** of 1898, the meeting of patriots led by Emilio Aguinaldo that led to the establishment of the

SAN PEDRO CUTUD LENTEN RITES

Heading north through Pampanga province, you might be tempted by the rather voyeuristic prospect of watching a dozen or so Catholic devotees being voluntarily **crucified**, a gruesome tradition that started in 1962 and is euphemistically known as the **San Pedro Cutud Lenten Rites**. Every year on Good Friday at San Pedro Cutud, 3km west of **San Fernando**, a dozen or so penitents – mostly men but the occasional woman (and sometimes even the odd foreigner) – are taken to a rice field and nailed to a cross by men dressed as Roman soldiers, using 5cm stainless steel nails that have been soaked in alcohol to disinfect them. The penitents are taken down seconds later. In total some two thousand penitents walk to the site, flagellating themselves using bamboo sticks tied to a rope or shards of glass buried in wooden sticks. The blood – and the cries of pain – are real, but the motivation is questionable to some (one "regular" has been crucified at least 27 times). The Catholic Church does not approve of the crucifixions and does not endorse them, and the media have also turned against the rites, calling them pagan and barbaric – but always managing despite these reservations to allot copious front-page space to photographs of bloodied penitents.

In 2010 the local authorities banned tourists from attending for the first time, but in practice this is virtually impossible to enforce and every year some fifty thousand foreigners and locals attend the spectacle – you'll need to get here early to grab a good view (it's normal and accepted that folks jostle to get close-ups of the nails going in). Victory Liner buses leave every hour for San Fernando from Pasay and Cubao.

First Philippine Republic – the city served as the capital of the short-lived independent nation until 1899. Today, the location of the convention – **Barasoain Church** – is the city's biggest attraction.

Barasoain Church

Paseo del Congreso • Tues–Sun 8.30am–noon & 1–4.30pm • Free • ☎ 044 662 7686, ⓦ barasoainchurch.org

The current incarnation of **Barasoain Church** dates back to 1885, its handsome colonial facade and tower best known as the place where the Revolutionary Congress convened in 1898 (ever the showman, Joseph Estrada chose to be inaugurated president here in 1998). The church also houses the **Ecclesiastical Museum** on the upper floor, which displays religious relics such as antique prayer cards and a bone fragment of San Vicente Ferrer encased in glass, and puts on a light-and-sound presentation depicting events leading to the Philippine Revolution and the Philippine–American War.

Malolos Cathedral

Paseo del Congreso • Daily 7am–8pm • Free

In 1898, Aguinaldo made his headquarters at the grand Malolos Cathedral, aka the **Basilica Minore de la Nuestra Señora de Inmaculada Concepcion**. The cathedral's Spanish origins lie in the sixteenth century, but Aguinaldo ordered its destruction in 1899, part of his "scorched-earth policy" to hamper the Americans. What you see today was primarily rebuilt in the 1930s, though work has continued to the present. Don't miss the venerable tree in front of the cathedral, known as the **Kalayaan Tree** (Tree of Freedom), said to have been planted by Aguinaldo himself.

Casa Real

Paseo del Congreso • Mon–Fri 8.30am–noon & 1–4.30pm • Free • ☎ 044 791 2716

A gorgeous Spanish house with origins in 1580 and serving many functions over the years, the **Casa Real** is primarily a small museum and shrine dedicated to the "**20 women of Malolos**". These pioneers began a daring campaign for a school for women in 1888, and the museum has various displays on other barrier-breaking Filipinas from around the country.

ARRIVAL AND INFORMATION

MALOLOS

By bus First North Luzon Transit buses have hourly departures to Malolos from the Five Star terminal in Cubao in Manila (674 EDSA at Monte de Piedad St).

Tourist information The helpful provincial tourist office is in the Capitol Building (Mon–Fri 8am–5pm; ☎ 044 791 7335, ⌨ bulacan.gov.ph).

EATING

Enlin's Bakeshop 53 A. Mabini St ☎ 044 662 4350. Malolos is famed throughout the Philippines for its *ensaymada*, a sweet, buttery bread treat, often crowned with grated cheese and sliced salted egg. *Enlin's*, opposite

the church, sells boxes of the delicacy for P100 – they also sell *ube* (purple yam) flavour and popular *pastel de leche*. Tues–Sat 8am–7pm.

Clark and Angeles City

Some 80km north of Metro Manila, **CLARK** (or more formally Clark Freeport Zone; ⌨ www.clark.com.ph) is an odd mix of converted barracks, unappealing duty-free malls, IT industrial zones, golf courses and prostitution. Indeed, Clark and adjacent **ANGELES CITY** remain one of the Philippines' most notorious sun and sex destinations, with dozens of "girlie bars" catering to high-spending Western, Korean and Taiwanese males. Clark was the site of an American military base between 1903 and 1991, and like Subic Bay (see p.125) has been transformed into a "freeport zone" (a tax- and duty-free zone) since the departure of the US Air Force. It's been far less successful in shedding its sleazy image, however, though the **airport** has proved popular with budget airlines. If you are travelling to the airport or aiming to climb **Pinatubo** or **Arayat**, you may end up spending some time here, but otherwise there's little reason to linger. If you have to overnight in Clark, keep in mind that the hotels are almost universally geared to prostitution.

The name "Clark" is generally used to refer to the former base and the tourist area of Angeles City around it, particularly **Fields Avenue** on the south side where most of the bars are.

ARRIVAL AND DEPARTURE

CLARK AND ANGELES CITY

By plane Several budget carriers connect Clark International Airport (⌨ crk.clarkairport.com), inside the former base area, with Singapore, Taipei, Seoul, Kuala Lumpur, Macau, Cebu and other regional destinations. Outside the terminal there's a small convenience store and an ATM. Plenty of fixed-rate taxis meet each flight, but these are expensive (and drivers will try and charge more if they can): anywhere within Clark (including Fields Ave) is P350, the Dau bus terminal (see below) is P450 and Angeles City P500. Jeepneys (with a/c) run from the airport when full (minimum eight people) and charge P50 to anywhere in Clark or to the Dau bus terminal. Philtranco (☎ 02 851 8078, ⌨ philtranco.com.ph) runs expensive (P450) but direct buses to Manila from the airport at 12.30am,

12.30pm and 5.30pm. Coming in the other direction, buses depart Manila at 6.30am, 11.30am and 8.30pm.

By bus For most destinations, head to the Dau bus terminal (pronounced "Da-oo") in nearby Mabalacat, served by almost continual buses from the capital and less frequently to and from Baguio, La Union, Aliminos and Vigan. Another option for travelling between Manila and Clark is the Fly-the-Bus service operated by Swagman Travel (☎ 02 523 8541 or 045 322 2890, ⌨ swaggy.com). The bus leaves the *Swagman Hotel*, 411 A. Flores St, Ermita, at 11.30am, 3.30pm and 8.30pm daily and serves a number of hotels in Clark for P600 one-way (it heads back to Manila at 8am, noon and 3pm).

ACCOMMODATION AND EATING

Aling Lucing Sisig G. Valdez St ☎ 045 888 2317. When it comes to eating, Angeles City is known as the "Sisig Capital of the Philippines"; the dish (made from parts of a pig's head and liver, usually seasoned with calamansi and chilli), was first cooked up at this unassuming restaurant in 1974. It's still the best place to sample it but ask how much it'll cost before you order; the restaurant notoriously does not publish prices. Daily 6am–3am.

★ **Gill's Buko Sherbet & Ice Cream** 31-32 Pasillio

Narcisus St, Nepo Mart 1 Complex ☎ 045 323 7832. Much loved local sweet treat supplier, where the signature *buko* sherbet (also served with lychees) comes at P20 per scoop. Daily 10am–6.30pm.

Holiday Inn Clark Mimosa Leisure Estate, Mimosa Drive ☎ 02 845 1888, ⌨ holidayinn.com. Your best bet for accommodation is this decent chain hotel, not far from the airport but slightly isolated from the rest of Angeles City (a good thing). Internet is P500/24hr. P3650

Mount Pinatubo

All visits include a conservation fee (P500) and Aeta passway fee (P150) • Boat rental P350/hr

Nothing has quite been the same around **Mount Pinatubo** (1485m), 25km east of Clark, since 1991, when the volcano exploded in one of the largest eruptions of the twentieth century worldwide (see box below). Today, visits to the resultant moon-like lahar landscape and lake is one of the country's top activities, though independent hikes to the top are not permitted. The local tribe, the **Aetas**, though devastated by the eruption, have legal ownership over the mountain.

At the time of writing, organized trips to the volcano leave from the small town of **Santa Juliana**, about 40km from Clark, where you register. From here, a 4WD takes you for an hour or so across flat lahar beds and over dusty foothills to the start of a gentle hike to **Lake Pinatubo** (around 5.5km, with a height gain of 300m; 2–3hr); some tour companies will take you closer (via the Korean-built "Skyway"), within ten minutes of the crater. The lake itself is stunning, with emerald-green waters and spectacular surrounding views. Bring a picnic; swimming is banned as the lake is now mildly toxic, but you can rent boats.

ARRIVAL AND DEPARTURE
MOUNT PINATUBO

By bus and jeepney The North Luzon and SCTEX expressways make getting to Pinatubo easy enough, and it's feasible to visit as a day-trip from Manila. Coming from Manila or Clark on any Tarlac or Baguio bus, ask to be let off in Capas, where you can catch a jeepney or tricycle to Paitlin (P20), and then a tricycle to the barangay of Santa Juliana for around P60 (or go direct from Capas to Santa Juliana via tricycle; 1hr; at least P500). Once in Santa Juliana the first 4WD trips depart at around 6am from PDC Spa Town (see below).

TOURS

Several companies run Pinatubo trips, though none will volunteer the information that the longer treks are closed, so question them carefully about what's open to trekkers at present. Prices are dependent on group size. **Hiking** all the way is discouraged but possible; since it would take at least 8hr and you'd need to hire a guide – and bearing in mind that camping is not allowed – taking one of the 4WD tours is virtually mandatory.

Mount Pinatubo 4x4 Club Santa Juliana ☎ 0919 608 4313, ⓦ pinatubo.tk. 4WD trips are charged at P3000 for the jeep (for up to five people), plus P500 for the guide, P500 conservation fee (per person) and P150 Aeta passway fee (per person): so P1350 each for a group of five, and P2400 each for a group of two.
PDC Spa Town Santa Juliana ☎ 45 615 0454, ⓔ sales @mtpinatubotour.com or ⓔ pdcspatown@yahoo.com. The Korean-owned PDC Spa Town resort is the main coordinator of trips up the mountain and sells all-inclusive

PINATUBO BLOWS ITS TOP

On April 2, 1991, people from the village of Patal Pinto on the lower slopes of **Mount Pinatubo** witnessed small explosions followed by steaming, and smelt rotten egg fumes escaping from the upper slopes of the supposedly dormant volcano (the last known eruption was six hundred years before). On June 12, the first of several major explosions took place. The eruption was so violent that shockwaves were felt in the Visayas and nearly twenty million tons of sulphur dioxide gas were blasted into the atmosphere, causing red skies to appear for months afterwards. A giant ash cloud rose 35km into the sky and red-hot blasts seared the countryside. Ash paralysed Manila, closing the airport for days and turning the capital's streets into an eerie, grey, post-apocalyptic landscape. By June 16, when the dust had settled, the top of the volcano was gone, replaced by a 2km-wide caldera containing a lake. Lava deposits had filled valleys, buildings had collapsed, and over eight hundred people were dead.

The eruption virtually destroyed the traditional way of life of the **Aeta people**, who had lived on the slopes of the volcano. Over twenty years later, many Aeta have re-established small villages near the mountain. Over seven hundred, however, live in poorly maintained bamboo houses on a special relocation site in Sitio Gala near Subic Bay dubbed the Aeta Resettlement and Rehabilitation Center, where they're almost entirely dependent on charitable organizations for their survival.

packages for P1500 per person, for a minimum four people. If you show up without a reservation, this is likely to be your only option. Groups smaller than four people will have to be paired with others.

Trekking Mt. Pinatubo ☎ 0919 608 4313, ⓦ trekking pinatubo.com. Popular tours from Manila, beginning with a minibus ride to the Crow Valley (2hr 30min), where you transfer to 4WD jeep. Guides are good, but this is a long day-trip (depart 4.30am Mon–Fri, 3.30am Sat, 4am Sun), and you won't get much time on the mountain. Trips from P12,500 for one person down to just P2150 per person in a group of ten or more.

Mount Arayat

Registration should be free, but foreigners are usually asked for P20

Mount Arayat (1026m), a dormant volcano 42km east of Mount Pinatubo, rises from the lowlands of Pampanga in solitary and dramatic fashion, the only mountain for miles around. It is said to be inhabited by Mariang Sinukuan (Maria the Abandoned), a *diwata* (fairy) of Tagalog folklore, and that when Mariang comes down from the mountain and visits the lowlands, her presence can be felt because the air turns fragrant. From the summit all of central Luzon is visible, from the snake-like Pampanga River to the mountains of Zambales, Bataan and beyond.

The entrance to the climb is at **Barangay Ayala**. Here you need to register; you'll need to register again at the small DNER post further up the trail, before trekking to what's known as **North Peak** (via the "new trail"). You can continue on to the **South Peak** from here (a tough hike along the ridgeline), then down to the village of Arayat, or simply return to Ayala. It takes just three to four hours to climb Arayat and get back down, depending on your fitness level; allow ten hours if you intend to complete the traverse between the North and South peaks. Companies can arrange a guide and transport for you, but it is possible to arrange the climb independently.

ARRIVAL AND DEPARTURE
MOUNT ARAYAT

By bus and jeepney The fastest way to Mount Arayat from Manila is to take any bus to San Fernando (2hr; buses are usually bound for Olongapo), and alight at the SM Pampanga mall. From here you'll need to take a jeepney to Magalang (around P40; 30min), from where a tricycle will whisk you to the entrance (P70).

By taxi A taxi from Clark Airport will cost an exorbitant P2000, but hotels should be able to arrange a driver for much less.

Bataan

With 85 percent of it covered in mountainous jungle, the **Bataan** peninsula is one of the most rugged places in the country. The province, forming the western side of Manila Bay, will always be associated with one of the bloodiest episodes of World War II. For four months in 1942, 65,000 Filipinos and 15,000 Americans – "the battling bastards of Bataan" – held out here against the superior arms and equipment of the Japanese. After their surrender in April 1942, the Filipino and American soldiers, weakened by months of deprivation, were forced to walk to detention camps in Tarlac province. About 10,000 men died along the way. **Balanga** is the provincial capital, and there are some picturesque **beaches** on Bataan's southwest coast between **Mariveles**, some 50km south of Balanga, and **Bagac**.

Shrine of Valor

Daily 8am–5pm • P30, lift up crucifix P10 • Cabog-bound jeepneys from Balanga to Bagac stop at the Mount Samat/Diwa intersection (20min); from here tricycles run to the top (30min; P100 one way) or it's a sweaty 7km hike; hiring a van from Balanga should cost around P1500

A poignant memorial to the American and Filipino soldiers that fought and died here in World War II, the "Dambana ng Kagitingan" or **Shrine of Valor** occupies the summit of **Mount Samat** (564m), 16km inland from Balanga. The shrine has a chapel and a small museum of weapons captured from the Japanese, but the centrepiece is a 92-metre **crucifix** with a lift inside (commissioned by Ferdinand Marcos in 1966), that takes you to a gallery at the top with views across the peninsula and, on a clear day, to Manila.

Mount Mariveles

Take a tricycle from Mariveles to the barangay of Alasasin (P100), where you need to register at the barangay hall (P20) and ask for a guide

From Mariveles you can strike out for the ridge of dormant volcano, **Mount Mariveles** (1130m), a tricky overnight climb or a very long day for fit hikers. Apart from food and water, you'll need a good tent or bivouac, a sleeping bag and warm jacket – it can be surprisingly chilly when night falls. The caldera of Mariveles is huge; the ridge runs for 22km and includes several peaks – Tarak Ridge (the most accessible, from Alasasin), Banayan Peak and Mariveles Ridge.

2

ARRIVAL AND DEPARTURE   BATAAN

By bus Bataan Transit (ⓦbataantransit.com) runs frequent a/c services from Manila, originating both at Five Star Terminal, Cubao (to Balanga every 15min 1am–11pm; 2–3hr; to Mariveles every 20min midnight–9.30pm; 3–4hr), and from Avenida Terminal (to Balanga every 20min 2am–9.30pm; to Mariveles every 30min 3.30am–8pm). Genesis Transport (ⓦgenesistransport .com.ph) runs a similar service from Pasay to Balanga (every 20min 4am–9pm) and Mariveles (every 20min 1am–7.30pm), and between Mariveles and Baguio

(every 2hr 2am–1pm). Victory Liner (ⓦvictoryliner.com) connects Balanga with Olongapo for Subic Bay (hourly; 1hr 15min). Cabog-bound jeepneys (6am–8pm; P18) ply the mountain highway between Balanga and Bagac when full. **By boat** From Manila, Baatan is a convenient 1hr zip across the bay – if the ferries are running. Various companies have operated ferries to Mariveles and Orion (near Balanga) in the past, but at the time of writing there was no service. Check with the Manila tourist office (see p.84).

ACCOMMODATION

Montemar Beach Club Brgy Pasinay, Bagac ☎047 888 4719, ⓦmontemar.com.ph. This large, well-established hotel is the best of a number of resorts along Bataan's southwest coast used mostly by Filipinos for weekend

breaks. It's located on a 500m stretch of clean sandy beach, and has watersports facilities and a swimming pool. The rooms have a/c and a private balcony overlooking either the beach or the gardens. **P6100**

Subic Bay

Since the closure of US Naval Base Subic Bay in 1992, **SUBIC BAY** has been reinvented as a gate-guarded playground for the rich, with golf courses, a yacht club, a casino and plush hotels. For most foreign travellers, the main appeal is the wide range of watersports, diving and tranquil beaches on offer.

The Subic Bay area is vast, and is best thought of as several distinct areas. Most of it lies in Zambales province, one hour southwest of Clark via the SCTEX highway, and some 110km northwest of Manila. The old base itself is now the **Subic Bay Freeport Zone** (a tax- and duty-free zone), accessed by "gates" manned by security guards, and comprising two parts: most of the banks, restaurants, shops and hotels are located on a

---

SUBIC BAY BEACHES

All Hands Beach San Bernardino Rd ☎047 250 2270, ⓦallhandsbeach.com. On the north side of the airport and closest to the CBD, this is a tranquil stretch of sand and beach huts shaded by trees. Though it's being developed as a resort, during most weekdays you'll have it to yourself. P150, children under 3ft tall P100; beach package including use of huts P350. Daily 24hr (swimming till midnight).

Camayan Beach Ilanin Rd (off Corregidor Rd) ☎047 252 8000, ⓦcamayanbeachresort .com. South of All Hands, the best beach in

the Freeport Zone is Camayan Beach (formerly Miracle Beach). It's now part of the *Camayan Beach Resort*, offering diving (P1750), snorkelling (P250/2hr), kayaking (P300/1hr) and swimming; day visitors can access the beach for a fee. Day visitors P300 (children under 12, P250). Daily 7.30am–8pm.

Baloy Long Beach After Barrio Barretto's scrappy beach, this is one of the better strips of sand in Luzon; locals charge a nominal entry fee (P30). Daily 24hr.

2

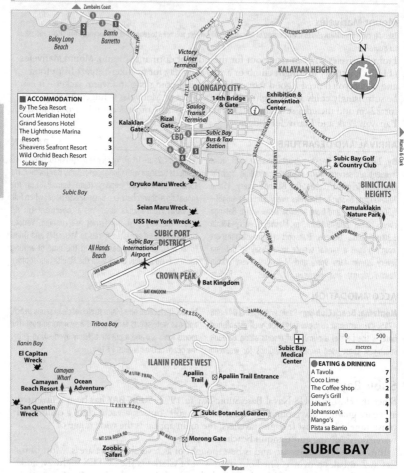

SUBIC BAY

ACCOMMODATION

By The Sea Resort	1
Court Meridian Hotel	6
Grand Seasons Hotel	5
The Lighthouse Marina Resort	4
Sheavens Seafront Resort	3
Wild Orchid Beach Resort Subic Bay	2

EATING & DRINKING

A Tavola	7
Coco Lime	5
The Coffee Shop	2
Gerry's Grill	8
Johan's	4
Johansson's	1
Mango's	3
Pista sa Barrio	6

small island known as the **Central Business District**, while on the **mainland** to the south lie the beaches and most of the outdoor activities, theme parks and attractions; there are several smaller barangays here with tourist attractions, including **Cubi**, on the slopes above the airport.

To the north of the CBD, linked by gates and bridges across the drainage channel (the **Main Gate** is also known as the Magsaysay Gate), **OLONGAPO CITY** lies outside the Freeport Zone but is generally considered part of the Subic Bay area. It is a typical Philippine provincial town, streets crammed with stalls and smoke-belching tricycles. This is where the bus terminals are located, but you won't spend much time here otherwise. Finally, around 5km north of Olongapo along the coast (also outside the Freeport Zone), **Barrio Barretto** is gradually shaking off its go-go bar days, though it still attracts its share of the ageing expat/Filipina "girlfriend" scene. Nearby **Baloy Long Beach** is a better place to crash, a laidback row of bars and hotels right on the sand.

Most travellers come to Subic Bay for the **wreck diving**, which is superb (see box, p.128), but there are plenty of peaceful, clean **beaches** inside the former base if you just want to chill out (see box, p.125).

Ocean Adventure

Camayan Wharf, Ilanin Rd, West Ilanin Forest Area • Daily 9am–6pm • P550; children under 12 P440; swim with dolphins (45min) P3700; beach encounter with dolphins (30min) P2400; dive with dolphins (30min) P4250 • ☎ 047 252 9000, Ⓦ oceanadventure.com.ph • Free shuttle from the CBD 10.45am & 1.15pm (bus & taxi terminal on Aguinaldo St)

Next to Camayan Beach (see box, p.125), **Ocean Adventure** is one of Subic's major tourist draws, comprising a small aquarium and arena for dolphin and sea lion shows. You can also swim, dive (includes dive gear, but bring your certification), or have a brief encounter on the beach with the park's friendly dolphins.

Zoobic Safari

Ilanin Rd, West Ilanin Forest Area • Daily 8am–4pm • P495, children under 1.2m P395 • ☎ 047 252 2272, Ⓦ zoobic.com.ph • Taxis from the CBD are P400

Subic Bay has its own zoo experience, the **Zoobic Safari**, popular with Manileños, but though the animals are well treated if you don't like zoos you really won't like this. Attractions include a tiger safari via jeep (where the guides feed chicken to the "wild" tigers); a serpentarium with iguanas, snakes and lizards; and "croco loco", where crocodiles leap for dangling chickens.

Bat Kingdom

Zambales Hwy, Crown Peak, Cubi • Most hotels can arrange **tours** with guides for around P2000 (including other sights)

Other than a few groups of monkeys, the most visible wildlife in the hills around Subic is a colony of around ten thousand bamboo bats, golden-crowned flying foxes and fruit bats – the so-called **Bat Kingdom**. The colony tends to move around within the Cubi, Crown Peak area, so just ask a local where they are; during the day bats hang from trees asleep (when most of the tours visit), but at dusk thousands of these giant, harmless creatures take to the air to look for food.

ARRIVAL AND DEPARTURE   SUBIC BAY

By bus Most buses (see p.81) arrive in Olongapo City at either the Saulog Transit terminal just across the drainage channel from the main gate, or at the Victory Liner (Ⓦ victoryliner.com) terminal further north at 27 Anonas St at W 18th St (just off Rizal Ave; ☎ 047 222 2241). Destinations Angeles City/Dau (frequent; 1hr, via SCTEX); Baguio (hourly; 8hr); Manila Cubao (every 30min; 3am–9pm; 2hr 30min–3hr 30min).

INFORMATION

Tourist information The Subic Bay Tourism Department (daily 8am–5pm; ☎ 047 252 4194, Ⓦ greatersubic.com or Ⓦ mysubicbay.com.ph) is next to the Subic Bay Exhibition & Convention Center at 18 Efficiency Ave, just off the main highway to Manila at the edge of the Zone. Staff here can help book tours, hotels and provide the latest on what's happening; you'll also need to arrange hikes here (see box, p.129).

Internet access Major hotels in Subic have wi-fi or business centres where you can access the internet, but they charge more than the many hole-in-the-wall internet cafés in Olongapo, most of them along Rizal Ave and Magsaysay Ave. In Barrio Barretto, popular resorts and restaurants such as *Mango's* and *Johansson's* have reliable internet.

GETTING AROUND

SUBIC BAY FREEPORT ZONE

By taxi Jeepneys and tricycles are banned within Subic Bay Freeport Zone, so transport is provided by Megatsai taxis (24hr; ☎ 047 252 8102) and Winstar Transport buses; both have their terminals in the CBD in a car park (known as "park and shop") off the Rizal Highway, close to the Main Gate and a short walk from the Saulog Transit terminal over in Olongapo. Taxis charge fixed rates from here, with most fares P50 within the CBD. Elsewhere it's P200 to Pamulaklakin (see box, p.129) and Cubi, P300 to most beaches, and P400 to Zoobic Safari and Ocean Adventure.

By bus Buses run every 30min but are not that useful; they charge P9 within the CBD, P13 for the Binictican area (Pamulaklakin) and P15 to Cubi.

OLONGAPO

By jeepney In Olongapo all jeepneys are colour-coded; from just outside the Victory Liner bus terminal you can take frequent blue jeepneys (direction "Castillejos") to Barrio Barretto and Baloy (P15).

By taxi and tricycle Taxis will charge at least P500 (tricycles around P150). To travel between Olongapo and

2

DIVE SUBIC BAY

Subic Bay is a popular **diving** site, boasting fifteen shipwrecks in still waters, all no more than fifteen minutes by speedboat from the shore. The **USS New York** is the star attraction of Subic's underwater world, a battle cruiser launched in the US in 1891. When World War II broke out, she was virtually retired, and when the Japanese swept the US Marines out of the Philippines, the Americans had no choice but to scuttle her as they departed from Subic in early 1942. The ship now lies on her port side in 27m of water between Alava Pier in the CBD and the northern end of Cubi Point runway at the airport. For experienced divers, the 120-metre-long hull presents excellent opportunities for what scuba divers call a "swim-through" – an exploration of the inside of the wreck from one end to the other.

The **El Capitan**, a Spanish-era wreck lying 20m down in a pretty inlet on the east coast of Subic Bay is a much easier wreck dive, suitable for novices. The **San Quentin** (16m) is the oldest known wreck in Subic, a wooden gunboat scuttled by the Spanish in 1898 in a futile attempt to block the channel between Grande and Chiquita islands against invading Americans. Other Subic wrecks include the Japanese POW ship *Oryoku Maru* and the *Seian Maru*, a Japanese cargo vessel sunk by the American Navy in 1945.

Two-dive packages with any of the operators start at around P2500.

DIVE OPERATORS

Johan's Adventure Dive Center Right on the shore at Baloy Long Beach ☎ 047 224 8915, ⓦ subicdive.com.

Subic Bay Aqua Sports Building 249, Waterfront Rd ☎ 047 252 6048.

the Freeport, you'll have to walk across the Main Gate to the terminal in the CBD as the two systems are mutually exclusive (see p.127).

By car To rent a car contact Avis (daily 8am–5pm; ☎ 047 250 0357) at Unit 116, Charlie Building, Subic International Hotel Compound.

ACCOMMODATION

SUBIC BAY FREEPORT ZONE

Court Meridian Hotel Lot B, Waterfront Rd at Rojas St ☎ 047 252 2366, ⓦ courtmeridian.com. Modern hotel, very clean with comfortable rooms, free wi-fi, flatscreen cable TV and breakfast included. The location is good, close to restaurants in the Central Business District. P3300

Grand Seasons Hotel Canal Rd ☎ 047 645 0357, ⓦ subicgrandseasonshotel.com. The 84 deluxe rooms here are simple and comfortable, with muted decor and no unnecessary frills (though a/c, TV and wi-fi are standard). There's a casino, various restaurants and an outdoor pool. P3400

★**The Lighthouse Marina Resort** Moonbay Marina Complex, Waterfront Rd ☎ 047 252 5000, ⓦ lighthousesubic.com. Lavish boutique hotel topped with a replica of an actual lighthouse (not working). The room theme is "aqua", with soothing blue and green tones, contemporary furnishings, DVD players, flatscreen TVs and a glass-walled bathroom with an old-fashioned tub. P6000

BARRIO BARRETTO AND BALOY LONG BEACH

By The Sea Resort 99 National Hwy, Barrio Barretto ☎ 047 222 2895, ⓦ bythesea.com.ph. Fifty a/c rooms with cable TV and free wi-fi either right on the beach or set back around a quiet garden. There's a convivial restaurant and bar overlooking the sea, and live music Wed–Sat. P1200

★**Sheavens Seafront Resort** Baloy Beach Rd, Baloy Long Beach ☎ 047 223 9430, ⓦ sheavens.com. Big but peaceful resort-hotel in an unbeatable location right on the water. A wide range of immaculate rooms (including deluxe, P2950), good food (the menu includes European and Thai dishes) and helpful staff who can arrange bangka trips and scuba diving. Fan only P990

★**Wild Orchid Beach Resort Subic Bay** Baloy Beach Rd, Baloy Long Beach ☎ 047 223 1029, ⓦ wildorchidsubic.com. Justly popular choice, with standard "deluxe" rooms equipped with king-size beds, flatscreen TVs, DVD players and free internet. Welcome extras include *Captain Rob's Steakhouse* and *Barefoot Bar* on the beach, and an enormous pool (with jacuzzis and *Scalliwags* swim-up bar). P4000

EATING AND DRINKING

The best places to **eat** and **drink** line the CBD waterfront or beaches to the north and south. The restaurants in Olongapo City are on the main drag, Magsaysay Drive, and tend towards the usual range of fast-food joints. Much of the **nightlife** in Barrio Barretto still revolves around girlie bars, but there are plenty of places in the CBD trying to attract families and a more mixed clientele.

2

HIKING AROUND SUBIC

If you're feeling energetic, there are numerous hiking trails on offer around Subic Bay, though you'll need to contact the tourism department in advance (see p.127) to arrange mandatory guides; there's a standard fee of P50 per hike. The **Apaliin Trail** runs along the banks of the Apaliin River to the coast (2hr), while visits to the rainforest trails within the **Pamulaklakin Nature Park** (daily 9am–4.30pm) can include an optional three-hour tour from members of the **Aeta tribe** ("eye-ta") – for P250 they'll take you deep into the forest. The Aeta are the so-called Negritos, who are thought to have arrived here long before the Austronesian majority; they receive no help or recognition from the government and their situation remains controversial. The Aeta were one of the few groups sad to see the Americans leave – Aeta warriors trained US Marines here for service in Vietnam and were generally well treated. Taxis to Pamulaklakin from the CBD (15min) should cost around P300.

SUBIC BAY FREEPORT ZONE

A Tavola Building 299, Aguinaldo St (behind Venezia Hotel) ☎ 047 252 6556. The undisputed king of Italian restaurants in Subic, this gem is owned by an Italian chef, offering huge plates of home-made pasta (from P300), wood-fired pizza (from P350) and a good selection of affordable wines. Daily noon–3pm & 6–10pm.

Coco Lime Harbor Point Mall, Rizal Hwy, CBD ☎ 047 252 2412. Decent Philippine, Thai and Japanese dishes that taste good if not always totally authentic; great adobo rice and lapu-lapu (P180–220). Daily 11am–2pm & 5–10pm.

Gerry's Grill Waterfront Rd, near Labitan St ☎ 047 252 3021, ⓦ gerrysgrill.com. Big, brash chain restaurant that sells local food in immense portions; think fried chicken (P245), pork *sisig* (P196) and crab rice (P195). Mon–Thurs & Sun 11am–midnight, Fri & Sat 11am–1am.

Pista sa Barrio Building 141, Waterfront Rd at Espiritu St ☎ 047 252 3187. Solid Filipino cuisine – pork adobo for P190, half fried chicken (P210) and a huge range of *sinigang* (Filipino sour tamarind soup) from P170, plus especially good seafood – served inside or on the breezy covered deck. Free wi-fi. Daily 6am–10pm.

BARRIO BARRETTO AND BALOY LONG BEACH

The Coffee Shop 2 Rizal St at the National Hwy, Barrio Barretto ☎ 047 222 4530, ⓦ subicdive.com. Late-night pit stop locally renowned since 1984 for its "jumbo tacos", nine-inch monsters packed with various meats and veggies in a soft taco shell (around P200). Also does decent fried noodles (pancit). Cash only. Daily 24hr.

Johan's Baloy Beach Rd, Baloy Long Beach ☎ 047 224 8915, ⓦ subicdive.com. Friendly pub and diner in Baloy, right on the beach (it also offers rooms from P700), with a range of excellent Belgian beer and plenty of knowledge-able expats dispensing sage advice at the bar. Daily 24hr.

Johansson's 128 National Hwy, Barrio Barretto ☎ 047 223 9293. Popular Swedish-owned hangout, with omelettes for breakfast, and a lunch and dinner menu that includes blue marlin steak (P160), boiled veal with dill sauce (P160), schnitzel, beef stew (P145) and an interesting take on *sinigang* using salmon (P110). Daily 24hr.

Mango's 116A National Hwy, Barrio Barretto ☎ 047 223 4139, ⓦ mangossubic.com. Beach bar, restaurant, cheap inn and local landmark (look out for the neon sign), serving both Filipino and European cuisine. Breakfast from P220, and burgers from P195. Daily 7am–10pm.

Northern Luzon

RICE PADDIES, IFUGAO PROVINCE

Northern Luzon

North of Manila, Northern Luzon harbours some of the archipelago's least-visited wildernesses, and offers thrilling outdoor adventures including whitewater rafting, trekking, surfing, spelunking and mountain biking. With wonderful mountainous areas and volcanic landscapes the region is home to some of the country's best surf breaks, along with wild stretches of coast peppered with virgin beaches and emerald green waters. It is also rich in culture, with a handful of beautifully preserved Spanish colonial towns lining the west coast. Inland are the tribal heartlands of the central Cordilleras mountain range, where spectacular rice terraces lie enveloped in clouds of mist. Further east is the Northern Sierra National Park, the largest protected area in the country, offering exceptional trekking opportunities. More than 100km off the northern coast of Luzon, and closer to Taiwan than the Philippine mainland, lie the remote, scattered islands of Batanes province with their unforgettable hills and wild rugged cliffs.

3

Along the west coast north of Subic, the **Zambales coast** is dotted with laidback resorts, while the Lingayen Gulf is the location of the **Hundred Islands National Park** – a favourite weekend trip from Manila. The neighbouring stretch of coast at **Bolinao** offers wonderful virgin beaches at times flanked by dramatic rock formations. Further along the coast, the province of **La Union** draws visitors particularly for its surfing. North of here is Ilocos Sur, known primarily for the old colonial city of **Vigan**, where horse-drawn carriages bounce down narrow cobblestone streets. The area around the capital of Ilocos Norte province, **Laoag**, features a number of sites related to former dictator Ferdinand Marcos, who was born in the nearby village of Sarrat. On the northwestern edge of Luzon there are excellent beaches around **Pagudpud**. Northern Luzon's east coast offers excellent surfing at **Baler**, while further north **Palanan** is the jump-off point for the barely explored **Northern Sierra Madre Natural Park**.

Despite the obvious appeal of the coast, for many visitors the prime attraction in Northern Luzon is the mountainous inland **Cordillera** region, where highlights include the mountain village of **Sagada** with its caves and hanging coffins, and the stunning rice terraces – designated by UNESCO as a World Heritage site – around **Banaue**. In the village of **Kabayan** in Benguet province, it's possible to hike up to a couple of mountaintop caves to see ancient mummies. Kabayan also provides access to **Mount Pulag**, the highest mountain in Luzon.

VIVA VIGAN BINATBATAN FESTIVAL OF ARTS

Highlights

❶ Surfing in San Juan The sweeping beach in the surf capital of the north has big breakers, magical sunsets and resorts for every budget. See p.139

❷ Vigan Atmospheric old Spanish outpost with cobbled streets, horse-drawn carriages and lively festivals. See p.142

❸ Ilocos Norte The province of Ilocos Norte is full of appeal, from sleepy towns such as Sarrat to a number of important Marcos-related sites. See p.149

❹ Trekking in the Cordillera The Cordillera offers wonderful walks through tribal villages and UNESCO World Heritage rice terrace scenery. See p.160

❺ Kabayan A remote village home to centuries-old human mummies interred in caves and burial niches dug out of solid rock. See p.167

❻ Sagada Celebrated mountain Shangri-La with hanging coffins, caves to explore, whitewater rafting, exceptional trekking and very cheap lodgings. See p.172

❼ Batanes Enchanting group of little-visited rural islands off the northern tip of Luzon, offering unforgettable scenery and terrific trekking. See p.185

HIGHLIGHTS ARE MARKED ON THE MAP ON P.134

The Zambales coast

Zambales is an undeveloped rural province – known for its succulent mangoes – that is still largely undiscovered by foreign tourists. It is, however, worth a stop for its scenic **beaches**, good surfing and relaxing resorts. For a break from beaches you can head inland to **Lake Mapanuepe**, formed after Mount Pinatubo erupted in 1991.

Zambales beaches

The **beaches** along the Zambales coast benefit from wonderful sunsets and views of the South China Sea. One lovely long stretch of white sand lies close to the fishing village of **San Antonio** and its popular barangay of **Pundaquit** (sometimes spelled Pundakit), which is also the access point for **Camara** and **Capones islands** – the latter a great place to camp. If your passion is for surfing, make a beeline for *Crystal Beach Resort* just north of the town of **San Narciso**; the best surf is between September and February. Some 35km further north, **Botolan** offers a couple of sleepy but well-run resorts on a nice wide beach in the barangay of Binoclutan, and there's another attractive (brown sand) beach just 8km north of here in the provincial capital **Iba**; the tourist office can arrange tours focusing on mango production, or activities such as mangrove planting. Another 40km further north, the towns of **Candelaria** and **Santa Cruz** serve as jumping-off points to the **islands** of Potipot, **Hermana Mayor** and **Hermana Menor**.

Potipot Island

You can hire a bangka from Candelaria's northern district of Uacón (5min; P400/boat)

Tiny **Potipot Island** is an idyllic little white sand getaway that you can walk around in just thirty minutes. At times you may have the island to yourself, although it can get busy at weekends and during school summer holidays (mid-March to early June).

The Hermana islands

SeaSun Beach Resort in Santa Cruz (see p.136) can arrange a day-trip to the Hermana islands (45min; P1200/boat)

Close to the border with Pangasinan province, **Santa Cruz** is the main access point for two privately owned islands in Dasol Bay: **Hermana Mayor** and **Hermana Menor**. Neither island has accommodation for visitors, but both have some picturesque coves of fine white sand and good snorkelling.

ARRIVAL AND INFORMATION

ZAMBALES BEACHES

By bus Victory Liner and Saulog have services straight up the coast from Manila, stopping at major towns like Iba and Santa Cruz but able to drop you en route on request, and can often stop right by your resort – make sure to tell the driver where you're going. For Pundaquit, buses stop at San Antonio, a short tricycle ride away (10min), while to get to the Botolan resorts you'll have to catch a tricycle or jeepney (5min) from the spot on the main highway where buses drop you off. Regular local buses also connect all the towns along the coast.

By jeepney A number of jeepneys connect the towns along the coast.

By bangka Bangkas connect the Zambales towns with small islands off the coast – Pundaquit to Capones Island, for example (20min; P1200). Hotels can often help organize bangka hire.

Tourist information Iba has a tourist office on the second floor of the town's Capitol building (Mon–Fri 8am–noon & 1–5pm; ☎ 047 811 7296, ⓦ zambalesnow.com). Tours can be arranged from here.

ACCOMMODATION

SAN ANTONIO-PUNDAQUIT
Nora's Beach Resort ☎ 0918 278 8188. This basic, welcoming place has two little fan-cooled nipa huts on the beach and more comfortable a/c rooms set around a courtyard. The resort rents out bangkas (P1500/day); good

for exploring nearby Camara and Capones islands, as well as Anawangin Cove where there's good snorkelling. **P1000**
Punta de Uian ☎ 0918 800 8426, ⓦ puntadeuian -resort.com. Probably the most upmarket place to stay along the Zambales coast, this large resort offers a selection

of rooms from a/c doubles to family villas (P13,420). Facilities include two pools, basketball and tennis courts, a golf range, playground and stables. **P4160**

SAN NARCISO

Crystal Beach Resort ☎ 02 941 9004, ⓦ crystalbeach .com.ph. Set on a pine tree-lined beach, this surfers' hangout is a large place with a few tiki huts and native houses along the sand, as well as a variety of neat a/c rooms, mostly built with native materials. The vibe is laidback, with hammocks slung between the trees and live acoustic bands playing by the bonfire on weekend nights. Surf lessons (P400/hr) and board rental (P200/hr or P500/half day), too. Budget travellers can opt for a dorm bed, or pitch their own tent (P150/person). Dorms **P300**; doubles **P1000**

BOTOLAN

Kawayan Farm Resort Brgy Santiago ☎ 0921 442 8573, ⓔ georgehill_08@yahoo.com. Run by a friendly British-Filipino couple, this welcoming place has inexpensive bamboo huts (P700) and a handful of chintzy rooms – three are set around a fishpond, each with a balcony from where you can fish directly into the pond (the owners can provide rods). There's an inviting swimming pool, as well as videoke and a pool table. **P1800**

Rama International Beach Resort Km 189, National Road, Brgy Binoclutan ☎ 0918 910 1280, ⓦ ramabeach .com. This Aussie-run resort, with a nice stretch of beach right at the doorstep and a fishpond and chirping birds in the leafy grounds, has a selection of family rooms as well

as doubles a stone's throw away from the sea. They can also arrange trips to limestone caves near Santa Cruz, the old hilltop gold-mining town of Acoe or nearby Mount Binoclutan. **P1695**

IBA

Palmera Garden Beach Resort ☎ 0908 503 1416, ⓦ palmeragarden.com. This shaded beachfront resort, around 2km north of Iba, has a selection of tiled rooms set around a leafy pool with an open-fronted thatched restaurant; all have fridge, a/c and private bath. The free wi-fi, available in the public areas, reaches some of the bedrooms. **P2200**

CANDELARIA

Dawal Brgy Uacón ☎ 0920 665 1577, ⓦ dawal.com.ph. Large concrete-block resort offering clean, good-value poolside accommodation; some of the rooms at the back are a bit dated. There's a barbecue area for guests, and a live band and disco (8pm–2am) on Sat nights. The resort arranges trips to Potipot (P400 for up to six people) but has no snorkelling equipment for rent. **P1800**

SANTA CRUZ

SeaSun Beach Resort ☎ 0921 641 8783, ⓦ seasun .com.ph. Most of the rooms here have pretty blue tiles, private bath and a/c, while the five simple nipa rooms have fan and shared bath. There's a cluster of shaded open-fronted huts to while away the afternoon, an indoor bar with pool table and a coral reef perfect for snorkelling just 50m away. **P600**

The Lingayen Gulf

Much of the western stretch of the **Lingayen Gulf**, between Bolinao and Dagupan, is taken up by working beaches where people fish in the gulf's rich waters and mend their nets. The sand is generally grey and unappealing and the water likewise; much of the coral has been destroyed by dynamite and cyanide fishing. It isn't all bad news though. The gulf's primary attraction, the **Hundred Islands National Park** is home to some lovely beaches, while at the western end of the gulf around Bolinao you'll find wild stretches of coast and good **snorkelling**. At the northeastern end of the gulf the capital of La Union province, **San Fernando**, provides access to more beaches and resorts as well as opportunities for trekking and climbing. There is also excellent **surfing** if you time it right, with surfers congregating in the resorts of **San Juan**.

Hundred Islands National Park

The tiny islands of **Hundred Islands National Park** – there are actually 123, but that doesn't have quite the same ring to it – cover almost twenty square kilometres. Some islands have beaches, but many are no more than coral outcrops crowned by scrub. Sadly, much of the underwater **coral** in the park has been damaged by a devastating combination of cyanide and dynamite fishing, typhoons and the El Niño weather phenomenon. The authorities are, however, going all out to protect what coral is left and help it regenerate, meaning you can only snorkel in approved areas.

Unless you want to camp, or stay at the one guesthouse on the islands, the closest base is the small town of **Lucap**, accessible from Alaminos, where day-trips set off; the town, however, is pretty dull and not recommended as a place to stay. It's far nicer to base yourself at one of the resorts near Bolinao (see p.139).

ARRIVAL AND DEPARTURE

By bus The closest bus station to the Hundred Islands National Park is at Alaminos, 4km south of Lucap, accessible from Lucap by tricycle (see p.138). Victory Liner, Five Star and Dagupan serve Manila (every 40min–1hr; 4–8hr),

HUNDRED ISLANDS NATIONAL PARK

with Victory Liner and Five Star also serving Santa Cruz (every 30min; 2hr). Victory Liner has connections to Bolinao (afternoon services only, leaving when full; 45min), Lingayen (hourly; 45min) and Dagupan (every

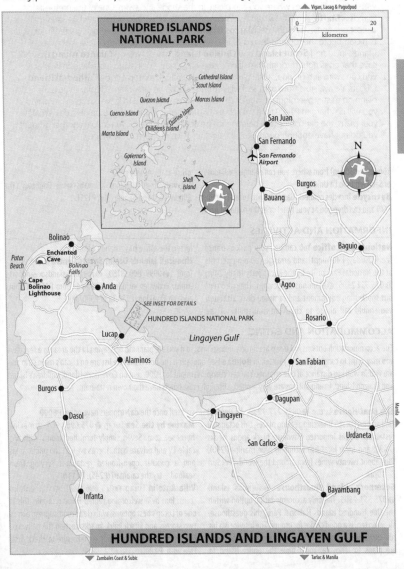

HUNDRED ISLANDS AND LINGAYEN GULF

3

ISLAND-HOPPING IN THE HUNDRED ISLANDS NATIONAL PARK

The best way to visit the pretty cluster of islets that form part of the One Hundred Islands National Park is through an island-hopping trip. The only three islands with any form of development are **Governor's Island**, **Children's Island** and **Quezon Island**. A day-trip to all three from Lucap costs P800 for a small boat for five people (larger boats are also available). You'll need to choose one island on which you will spend most of your time – the boatman will leave you there for a few hours then return, and you'll visit the other two more briefly.

A much more appealing option is to pay P1400 for a "service boat" allowing you to visit the more interesting undeveloped islands. Some of these dots of land are so small and rocky it's impossible to land on them, while others are big enough to allow for some exploring on foot, with tiny, sandy coves where you can picnic in the shade and swim. One of the prettiest islands is **Marta**, actually two tiny islets connected by a thin strip of bright white sand that almost disappears at high tide. **Marcos Island** has a blowhole and a vertical shaft of rock; you can clamber to the top and then dive into a seawater pool about 20m below. A number of islands, including **Scout Island** and **Quirino Island**, have caves; on **Cuenco Island** there's a cave that goes right through the island to the other side. Shell Island has a lagoon in which you can swim at high tide, while birdwatchers should ask to stop beside **Cathedral Island**.

Boats are available from 6am and will return to Lucap no later than 5.30pm; if you are planning to stay overnight on one of the islands then you need to leave Lucap by 5pm, and you will be charged P1400 for a small boat to drop you off and pick you up next day. Whatever your plans, the park office (see below) may be able to arrange for you to join another group if you do not have enough people to fill a boat and want to save some money.

30min; 1hr 30min) from where you can change for Baguio or San Fernando La Union.

By tricycle Tricycles connect Alaminos with Lucap (15min; P60) and can drop you at your hotel or at the national park office at the nearby pier.

By van From Alaminos a/c vans serve Dagupan (1hr 30min; P65) and Baguio (3hr; P175).

INFORMATION AND ACTIVITIES

National park office You can pay your park entrance fee (P20/day, P40/night) and arrange camping permits at the National Park office by the Lucap jetty (daily 24hr; ☎075 551 2505, ⍾alaminoscity.gov.ph). They also rent out snorkelling equipment and camping gear, although you should call ahead to check on availability of the latter. The office has a handy ATM.

Hundred Islands Ocean Sports Centre Lucap waterfront (☎0999 800 8180, ⍾hundredislandsoceansports .com). Activities include parasailing (from P1500/15min) and sea kayaking (P150/hr or P500/day).

ACCOMMODATION AND EATING

The accommodation options in **Lucap** are largely uninspiring, so if you are planning on staying in the area for a few days you may want to consider basing yourself in **Bolinao** (see opposite). The hotels that we list are on Lucap's main strip and are within walking distance of one another. You can **camp** overnight for P200/tent on Governor's Island, Children's Island and Quezon Island. Eating options are very limited, although most hotels have their own restaurant.

The Boat House Lucap ☎0920 227 7239. An unusual find among Lucap's unexciting eating places, this octagonal restaurant serves imported Hawaiian black angus steaks (P490) and fresh local fish including blue marlin (P290). Plus about twenty wines from around the world. Fri–Sun 5–10pm.

Governor's Island Guesthouse Governor's Island ☎075 551 2505. The only accommodation option within the One Hundred Islands National Park, this guesthouse, sleeping ten, is a good choice for groups. The interior is a bit run-down and could do with a lick of paint, although there are plans to renovate. You'll have the entire island to yourself once the day-trippers have gone. **P8000**

Maxine by the Sea Lucap ☎075 696 0964, ⍾maxine bythesea.com. Seven simply furnished rooms with a/c, cable TV and private bath. There's wi-fi in the public areas and a popular open-fronted restaurant serving fresh seafood – try the calamari (P245). **P2110**

Villa Antolin Lucap ☎075 696 9227, ⍾villa-antolin .com. Run by a welcoming retired Filipino couple, this is one of Lucap's best options, with clean rooms spread across two storeys and kitsch knick-knacks dotting the hallways. Not all rooms have hot water – make sure to check first. Free wi-fi. **P1800**

Bolinao and around

The landscape around the town of **BOLINAO** is one of cascading waterfalls, rolling hills and white beaches, including the popular **Patar Beach** and the inviting **Bolinao Falls**. The **Church of St James** in the main square was built by the Augustinians in 1609 and boasts a good collection of wooden santos figures.

Bolinao Museum

Rizal St • Mon–Fri 9am–4pm • P20 • ☎ 075 554 2065, ⓦ nationalmuseum.gov.ph

Under renovation at the time of research, the small **Bolinao Museum** contains natural history objects, ethnographic materials and a selection of archeological finds. Highlights include metal implements, gold trinkets, ornaments and Chinese pottery, dating back to the fourteenth and fifteenth centuries, which were excavated in the towns of Pangasinan province. As the closest point in the Philippines to China, Bolinao was an important trading centre, and Chinese coins – the oldest dating back to 1008 – have also been found. It is believed that traders who came to Luzon exchanged gold coins for gold ornaments; the Filipinos used the coins as charms and jewellery.

Patar Beach

The best-known beach in the Bolinao area is **Patar Beach**, 19km west of town, which has fine white sand and good surf. On the road to Patar a number of pleasant, relaxed beaches and resorts can arrange trips to a large **barrier reef** offshore, near **Santiago Island**, where there is some wonderful solitary snorkelling.

Bolinao Falls

21km south of Bolinao • The falls are not signposted; if driving make sure to ask for directions, or catch a tricycle from Bolinao (P500 return including waiting time; 45min)

The **Bolinao Falls** are two emerald waterfalls perfect for a refreshing dip. Bolinao Falls 1 has a cascading fall with a small pool, while the larger Bolinao Falls 2 has a series of inviting pools where you can easily while away an afternoon. You can rent open-fronted huts here for the day (P100) – there are only two basic stalls selling water and snacks so make sure to bring your own food for a picnic.

Enchanted Cave

Patar Rd • Daily 8am–6pm • P120

A popular attraction in the area is the **Enchanted Cave**, where you can descend a short flight of steep and slippery steps to swim in an underground pool of exceptionally clear water. It can get very busy on weekends; it's best to visit on a weekday.

Cape Bolinao Lighthouse

Close to Patar Beach, some 20km from Bolinao stands the old **Cape Bolinao Lighthouse** (1905), which, sitting on a hill, rises 107m above sea level. There's an easy path to the base of the building; climbing up here from the main road is rewarded by great views across the South China Sea. Though you can't see them, not far offshore lie a number of submerged Spanish galleons and Chinese junks that, according to local lore, still contain treasure.

ARRIVAL AND INFORMATION | BOLINAO AND AROUND

By bus There are regular services from Manila to Bolinao with Victory Liner and Five Star (hourly; 6hr), with stops at Alaminos (45min from Bolinao). Victory Liner buses also connect Baguio to Bolinao (hourly 4–7am; 6hr).

By jeepney Jeepneys connect Bolinao with Alaminos, although they take much longer than the buses (leave when full; 1hr 30min).

By tricycle Tricycles connect Bolinao town to the resorts along the nearby beach (15min; P100) and to Patar Beach (25min; P150).

Tourist information The municipal tourist office is in Bolinao at Rizal St, opposite the High School (Mon–Fri 8am–5pm; ☎ 075 554 4284 or 24hr hotline ☎ 0938 267 6085, ✉ bolinaotourismoffice@yahoo.com).

3

ACCOMMODATION AND EATING

There's only one recommendable **hotel** and no good **restaurants** in Bolinao proper; it's better to stay, and eat, at one of the nearby beach resorts.

BOLINAO

El Pescador Germinal ☎ 075 554 2559, ✉ elpescador _resorthotel@yahoo.com. This large well-kept resort has more than fifty warm and welcoming rooms set in the "new" building, all with a/c and private bath; choose one of these over the "old" ones. There are also seven clean and cosy a/c native huts, all with shared bath, decorated with pretty local materials, as well as a large inviting pool for adults, and a smaller one for children. **P1500**

THE ROAD FROM BOLINAO TO PATAR BEACH

Puerto del Sol Brgy Ilog Malino ☎ 075 710 7371, ⊚ puertodelsol.com.ph. Bolinao's most upmarket resort offers spacious, tastefully decorated a/c rooms in well-tended grounds, with dark wooden furniture, fridges, cable TV, private verandas and tea and coffee amenities. There's a pool, spa, open-air jacuzzi and a restaurant overlooking a pretty stretch of beach with shallow clear water. Free wi-fi. **P8600**

★ **Punta Riviera Resort** Brgy Ilog Malino ☎ 075 696 1350, ⊚ puntarivieraresort.com. The best resort in the area, with well-tended grounds dotted with palm trees, an infinity pool and a colourful dragon-fruit orchard. The tiled a/c rooms (P5000) are clean and spacious, and there's a handful of fan-cooled cabañas. The sauna and open-air jacuzzi are perfect spots to unwind after a kayaking trip through the resort's mangroves. Free wi-fi. **P2000**

Rock View Beach Brgy Patar ☎ 0999 303 4133. The perfect choice for budget travellers, with seven sturdy rustic cabañas, as well as two simple a/c rooms (P2000) in a concrete block, on a spectacular stretch of wild coastline overlooking rock formations. There isn't a restaurant, but guests can cook in the open-fronted kitchen. **P1500**

Villa Carolina y Juan Brgy Ilog Malino ☎ 0921 698 3340, ✉ villacarolinapangasinan@yahoo.com. Just across the street from *Punta Riviera Resort*, the simple rooms at this Belgian/Filipina-owned resort are all in brown, mock-wood concrete buildings, which makes it feel rather dark. There's a pool, kayaks for rent and cooked food upon request. **P3500**

Villa Soledad Brgy Ilog Malino ☎ 075 734 5314, ⊚ villasoledadbeachresort.com. Recently renovated, good-value rooms, although some of the family rooms can be a bit of a squeeze. Accommodation is set around a leafy tropical garden with basketball court and two palm-shaded pools. There's table tennis and billiards, too. **P1500**

PATAR BEACH

Treasures of Bolinao Patar Beach ☎ 075 696 3266, ⊚ treasuresofbolinao.com. Overlooking Patar Beach, this resort has a variety of a/c rooms, most with DVD players and private terraces; the New Villa rooms (P4500) may not have sea views, but are much better value than the Maharlika ones (P8000). There's a pleasant pool area and a deck overlooking the beach. Free wi-fi. **P4000**

San Fernando and around

The capital of La Union province and site of a former US air base, **SAN FERNANDO** has little of interest to tourists. It is, however, the access point for the popular **San Juan** surfing beach, 8km north.

Chinese-Filipino Friendship Pagoda

Take Zigzag Rd or use the steps up Hero's Hill from Quezon Ave

If you have a few hours to spare in San Fernando then take a walk uphill to Freedom Park and the **Chinese-Filipino Friendship Pagoda**. The pagoda boasts great views across the rooftops and out to the South China Sea. There is more evidence of the Chinese influence in the area at the impressive **Ma-Cho temple**, along Quezon Avenue on the northern outskirts of the city.

San Juan

A dramatic crescent with big breakers that roll in from the South China Sea, the coast just north of **SAN JUAN** in the barangay of Urbiztondo is a prime **surfing beach**. Most of its resorts have surfboards to rent (P200/hr) and offer tuition (another P200). For experienced surfers there are two breaks in **Urbiztondo**, one a beach break in front of the main huddle of resorts and the other the **Monaliza** point break at the northern end of the beach. The best spot for beginners is the **Cement Factory** break in the nearby barangay of Bacnotan. The peak season is September to March; at other times there may be no waves but you can get significant discounts on accommodation.

ARRIVAL AND DEPARTURE

By bus The Partas terminal is north of San Fernando's plaza on Quezon Ave, while Dominion's is near *McDonald's* just south of the city centre.

Destinations Baguio (Partas: hourly; 1hr 30min); Laoag (Partas: hourly; 6hr); Manila (Dominion & Partas: hourly; 6–8hr); Vigan (Dominion: every 30min; 3hr 30min; Partas: hourly; 3hr 30min).

SAN FERNANDO AND AROUND

To San Juan Jeepneys (every 30min; 15min; P12) run from the old market in San Fernando to San Juan, while a tricycle will cost P100; alternatively, buses and local buses travelling between San Fernando and Laoag, Vigan or Abra province pass through San Juan – ask the driver to let you off at one of the resorts.

INFORMATION AND ACTIVITIES

Tourist information San Fernando's city tourist office (Mon–Fri 8am–5pm; ☎072 888 6922, ⊛sanfernando .city.gov.ph) is in the city hall, while the provincial tourist office (Mon–Fri 8am–5pm; ☎072 888 2797, ⊛launion .gov.ph) is in the Provincial Capitol building.

Services Quezon Ave, San Fernando's main drag, has a number of banks with ATMs, as well as a police station behind La Union Trade Center.

Scuba diving Ocean Deep Diver Training Centre, on Poro Point just west of the airport (☎072 700 0493, ⊛ocean deep.biz).

ACCOMMODATION AND EATING

Unless you're staying the night in San Fernando before moving on, you're better off heading for the **San Juan resorts**. All the resorts listed are right on the beach and within walking distance of each other, and most of them have **restaurants** (there are no restaurants per se in San Juan).

SAN FERNANDO

Café Esperanza P Gomez St ☎072 242 0659. This pleasant café is a good spot for a quick lunch (sandwiches P80) or a slice of cake (P60), with flavours including carrot and mango. Mains include grilled fish, roast chicken and beef steak (RM110). Daily 7am–7pm.

Halo Halo de Iloko 12 Zandueta St ☎072 700 2030. A restaurant and café with eclectic decor, including zebra-print walls and colourful window panes. The main draw here is the halo-halo (shaved ice with evaporated milk and toppings including fruit and purple yam; P85). Daily 9am–9pm.

Sunset Bay Brgy Canaoay ☎072 607 5907, ⊛sunset bayphilippines.com. Just south of San Fernando, this welcoming resort overlooking the South China Sea has nicely decorated rooms giving onto a well-tended garden with potted plants and local crafts. There's a pool and a coral reef 90m off the shore where you can snorkel. **P2000**

SAN JUAN

Hacienda Peter's Surf Resort ☎072 888 5253. The ten simple rooms here face one another and look onto a tiny fishpond. Each is livened up with colourful polka-dot curtains and a selection of books. **P1500**

Kahuna Beach Resort and Spa ☎072 607 1040, ⊛kahunaresort.com. It may not be entirely in keeping with San Juan's laidback surfer vibe, but this upmarket resort certainly has verve. The rooms are stylish and comfortable, and the infinity pool is a great place to sip cocktails. **P5265**

Little Surfmaid ☎072 888 5528, ⊛littlesurfmaid resort.com. At the northern end of the string of resorts, close to the Mona Liza point break, this Danish-owned place offers spacious a/c rooms with fridge and nice touches including colourful bedspreads from the Cordilleras. The more expensive rooms have little balconies, and there's a restaurant serving good food. Free wi-fi throughout. **P2500**

Monaliza Surf Resort ☎072 888 4892. This friendly family-run resort has been going strong for more than three decades. It isn't the flashiest place around, and there's no food available, but the simple rooms are cheap and decent value. The cheapest have no a/c. There's wi-fi, too. **P1000**

San Juan Surf Resort ☎072 687 9990, ⊛sanjuan surfschool.ph. Squarely aimed at surfers: there's a shop selling kit, and surf conditions are posted by the bar. It has a wide range of rooms; the cheapest have no a/c. Wi-fi around the bar and restaurant. **P1800**

Sebay ☎072 888 4075, ⊛sebeysurfcentral.com. The nicely decorated rooms here give onto a leafy pathway and are set in a thatched building adorned with nipa. There's also a larger wooden structure slightly further back from the beach with more spacious family rooms. Restaurant, and wi-fi. **P1800**

3

Ilocos

Long and narrow, **Ilocos Sur** province is sandwiched by the sea on one side and the Cordillera Mountains on the other. For most tourists the highlight is undoubtedly the once important trading town of **Vigan**, one of the most atmospheric and enjoyable cities in the country. **Ilocos Norte**, meanwhile, is still strongly associated in Filipino minds with former President Ferdinand Marcos, and his family continues to wield considerable political power in the province. Sites related to the Marcos family include Ferdinand's **birthplace** in Sarrat, his **mausoleum** in Batac and the mansion known as the **Malacañang of the North** beside Paoay Lake. On the northern coast, the town of **Pagudpud** draws visitors from across Luzon with some of the best beaches on the island.

Vigan

An unmissable part of any North Luzon itinerary, **VIGAN** is one of the oldest towns in the Philippines. Lying on the western bank of the Mestizo River, it was in Spanish times an important political, military, cultural and religious centre. The **old town** is characterized by its cobbled streets and some of the finest **colonial architecture** in the country, mixing Mexican, Chinese and Filipino features. Many of the old buildings are still lived in, others are used as curio shops, and a few have been converted into museums or hotels. The attractions are within walking distance of one another, with **Plaza Burgos** the most obvious reference point, and, adding to the old-world atmosphere, some streets are open only to pedestrians – unusual in the Philippines – and romantic horse-drawn **kalesas** (from P50 for a short trip).

Brief history

In pre-colonial times, long before Spanish galleons arrived, **Chinese** junks came to Vigan and helped it to become a major trading port. They arrived with silk and porcelain, and left with gold, beeswax and mountain products brought down by inhabitants of the Cordillera. Stories of Vigan's riches spread and before long immigrants from China arrived to settle and trade here, intermarrying with locals and beginning the multicultural bloodline that Biguenos – the people of Vigan – are known for.

Spanish domination

The **Spanish** arrived in 1572. Captain Juan de Salcedo conquered the town and named it Villa Fernandina de Vigan in honour of King Philip's son, Prince Ferdinand, who died at the age of 4. Salcedo then rounded the tip of Luzon and proceeded to pacify Camarines, Albay and Catanduanes. In January 1574 he returned to Vigan, bringing with him **Augustinian missionaries**, and setting about the task of creating a township his king would be proud of, with grand plazas, municipal buildings and mansions.

One of the potentially incendiary results of this Spanish political domination was the rise of a *mestizo* (mixed ethnicity) masterclass, whose wealth and stature began to cause resentment among landless natives. In 1763 things came to a head when revolutionary **Diego Silang** and his men assaulted and captured Vigan, proclaiming it capital of the free province of Ilocos. When Silang was assassinated by two traitors in the pay of the Spanish, his wife, Maria Josefa Gabriela Silang, assumed leadership of the uprising. She was captured and publicly hanged in the town square.

The modern day

Unlike in Manila, many of Vigan's fine **old buildings** managed to survive World War II, though the humidity and their wooden construction makes preservation difficult. Many wealthy inhabitants left town in favour of a new life in Manila, allowing their ancestral homes to fall into partial ruin, though Vigan's 1999 inclusion on the **World Heritage Site** list at least guarantees it some level of protection and funding.

The old town

Most of the beautiful ancestral houses are in Vigan's **old town**. Also known as the Mestizo District or Kasanglayan ("where the Chinese live"), the old town runs roughly from Plaza Burgos in the north to **Liberation Boulevard** in the south. The most

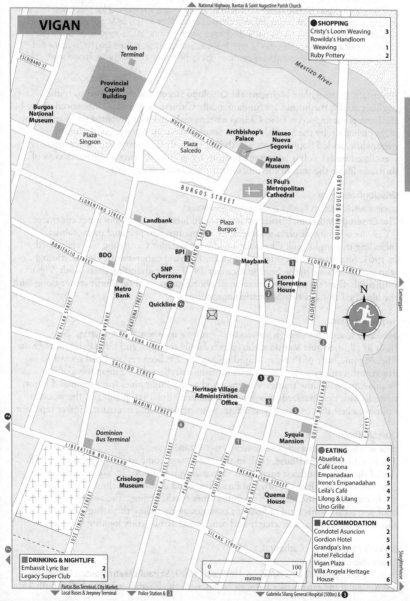

VIGAN

National Highway, Bantay & Saint Augustine Parish Church

SHOPPING
Cristy's Loom Weaving	3
Rowilda's Handloom Weaving	1
Ruby Pottery	2

Van Terminal

Provincial Capitol Building

Burgos National Museum

Plaza Singson

Mestizo River

NUEVA SEGOVIA STREET

Archbishop's Palace

Museo Nueva Segovia

Plaza Salcedo

Ayala Museum

St Paul's Metropolitan Cathedral

BURGOS STREET

FLORENTINO STREET

Landbank

Plaza Burgos

BONIFACIO STREET

BDO

BPI

SNP Cyberzone @

Maybank

FLORENTINO STREET

Metro Bank

Quickline @

Leona Florentina House

SALCEDO STREET

Heritage Village Administration Office

MABINI STREET

Dominion Bus Terminal

LIBERATION BOULEVARD

Crisologo Museum

Syquia Mansion

ENCARNACION STREET

Quema House

SILANG STREET

EATING
Abuelita's	6
Café Leona	2
Empanadaan	1
Irene's Empanadahan	5
Leila's Café	4
Lilong & Lilang	7
Uno Grille	3

ACCOMMODATION
Condotel Asuncion	2
Gordion Hotel	5
Grandpa's Inn	4
Hotel Felicidad	3
Vigan Plaza	1
Villa Angela Heritage House	6

DRINKING & NIGHTLIFE
Embassit Lyric Bar	2
Legacy Super Club	1

0   100
metres

Partas Bus Terminal, City Market,
Local Buses & Jeepney Terminal

Police Station &

Gabriela Silang General Hospital (500m) &

N

VIGAN'S FESTIVALS

The biggest secular festival is the week-long **Vigan Town Fiesta**, involving carnivals, parades, musical extravaganzas, beauty contests and nightly cultural shows. It culminates on January 25 with the celebration of the conversion of St Paul the Apostle, the town's patron saint. Almost straight after that, at the end of January, comes the **Kannawidan Ilocos**, a recent addition to the festival calendar celebrating the culture of Ilocos Sur. It includes a "battle of the bands" and a beauty contest.

The **Viva Vigan Binatbatan Festival of Arts**, held in the first week of May, includes dancing and music; the highlight is the religious celebration on **May 3** (Tres de Mayo), which starts with a Mass at Vigan's cemetery chapel and continues with dancing in Crisologo Street and a kalesa parade. **Holy Week** is also a special time in Vigan, with candlelit processions through the old streets and a *visita iglesia* that sees devotees doing the rounds of churches and cathedrals.

3

important thoroughfare is elegant old **Crisologo Street**, which is closed to traffic. Architecturally, the houses are fundamentally Chinese or Mexican, influenced either by the immigrant architects from China's eastern seaboard who prepared the plans, or by ideas picked up by the Spanish in their South American colony. Local artisans, meanwhile, added flourishes such as sliding capiz-shell windows and *ventanillas* (ventilated walls). A few homes are open to the public, offering an intimate view of ilustrado life at the turn of the nineteenth and twentieth centuries.

Crisologo Museum

Liberation Blvd • Daily 8.30–11.30am & 1.30-4.30pm • Donations welcome

The **Crisologo Museum**, former home of the influential – and sometimes controversial – Crisologo family, displays photographs, mementos and personal memorabilia, including the bright pink Chevrolet in which Governor Carmeling was ambushed in 1961. She survived the attack, unlike her husband congressman Floro Crisologo, who was shot twice in the head in October 1970 while attending mass inside Vigan Cathedral. There's a macabre selection of photographs from the death scene, along with the bloodied trousers he was wearing at the time.

Syquia Mansion

Quirino Blvd at Salcedo St • Mon & Wed–Sun 9am–noon & 1.30–5pm; Tues by appointment only • P30 • ☎ 0915 663 3547

Built in 1830, **Syquia Mansion**, the former family mansion and holiday home of Doña Alicia Syquia, wife of President Elpidio Quirino, has been restored and furnished in nineteenth-century style. The various furnishings reflect the Chinese roots of the Syquia family, wealthy traders who migrated to the Philippines from mainland China to trade with the Spaniards. Look out for the beautiful 1910 piano and the wooden camphor chest that to this day emanates a strong smell that is a natural insect repellent.

Quema House

8 Encarnacion St • By appointment only • Donations welcome • ☎ 075 632 0480

The beautiful **Quema House**, built in the 1820s, was home to Don Mariano Quema, one of the city's wealthiest merchants. The mansion is unique in Vigan in that it contains virtually all of the original furnishings and decor, from the Vienna chairs in the living room to the intricately painted vines on the ceiling. The *volada* on the first floor is typical of this kind of house: a passageway encircling the living area that allowed servants to pass discreetly and functioned as a balcony looking over the street.

St Paul's Metropolitan Cathedral

Burgos St • Daily 6am–6pm

Built by the Augustinians between 1890 and 1900, **St Paul's Metropolitan Cathedral** was designed in "earthquake Baroque" style, with thick ramparts and a belfry built 15m away so that it stood a chance of surviving if the church itself collapsed. Given Vigan's history, it's not surprising that there's some Chinese influence; see, for example, the brass communion handrails.

Museo Nueva Segovia

Nueva Segovia St • Mon–Fri 9am–noon & 1–4pm • P20 • ☎ 077 722 2018

The **Archbishop's Palace** (*Arzobispado*), completed in 1783, is still the official residence of the Archbishop of Nueva Segovia (the old Spanish name for what is now Ilocos Sur). Inside, the **Museo Nueva Segovia** showcases ecclesiastical artefacts, antique portraits of bishops and religious paraphernalia from all over Ilocos Sur.

Burgos National Museum

6 Burgos St • Tues–Sun 8.30am–noon & 1–5pm • P20 • ☎ 0927 263 1481

The **Burgos National Museum** was once home to one of the town's most famous residents, Padre José Burgos, whose martyrdom in 1872 galvanized the revolutionary movement. Between 1972 and 1975, the building became a branch of PNB bank – you can still see the teller windows on the ground floor. The first couple of rooms introduce Ilocano culture and traditions, with displays including farming and fishing tools, wooden coffins and a nose flute. The third room contains the chamber used to execute Burgos and his two companions, as well as an informative miniature model shedding light on the Spanish tobacco monopoly in the early eighteenth century. Furniture and other Burgos family memorabilia is displayed on the first floor.

ARRIVAL AND DEPARTURE
VIGAN

By plane The closest airport is in Laoag (see p.148).

By bus Dominion buses arrive at the terminal at the junction of Quezon and Liberation blvds, while the Partas terminal is by the city market about 300m south of the old town. From Laoag, buses arrive at the local bus terminal to the south of town, also dropping off passengers along the National Highway opposite the Petron petrol station in nearby Bantay, a short tricycle ride from Vigan (5min; P15). If travelling to Vigan from Lingayen, Dagupan or Alaminos in the Lingayen Gulf, head to Urdaneta and catch a northbound bus from there (6hr). Note that buses from Vigan to Manila and Baguio stop off in San Fernando (2hr). Destinations Baguio (Dominion: hourly; 5hr); Laoag (Dominion: hourly; 2hr); Manila (Dominion: hourly; 8–9hr; Partas: hourly, most departures in the afternoon; 10hr).

By van The van terminal is just by the Provincial Capitol Building. There are regular vans to Santa Maria throughout the day (leave when full; 45min; P50).

INFORMATION AND TOURS

Tourist office The provincial tourist office is at Leona Florentino House, 1 Crisologo St (daily 8am–5pm; ☎ 077 722 8520, ⍉ ilocossur.gov.ph).

Tours A nice way to get around town, the kalesas, or horsedrawn carriages, also offer tours (P150/hr). Tell the *kutchero* (driver) where you want to go, or let them suggest a route that will take in the main sights; they normally include a visit to the pretty St Augustine Parish Church in the nearby town of Bantay. The Heritage Village Administration Office (daily 8am–5pm) on Crisologo St runs a free shuttle service to the starting point for the Vigan heritage river cruise, a 45min boat trip with recorded commentary (hourly 8.30–11.30am & 1.30–4.30pm; P100).

ACCOMMODATION

Condotel Asuncion Florentino St at Jacinto St ☎ 077 722 8777, ✉ condotelasuncion@gmail.com. A good self-catering option right in the centre of town, a stone's throw away from Plaza Burgos. The spacious rooms feature a fully equipped kitchenette with microwave, fridge, electric stove and kettle, plus flatscreen cable TV and clean tiled bathrooms. P2000

Gordion Hotel V. De Los Reyes St at Salcedo St ☎ 077 722 2526, ⍉ vigangordionhotel.com. This brightly coloured place offers comfortable, if somewhat musty, rooms. The large chintzy suite has a huge bathroom with a roll-top bath, although the room itself is a bit dark. There are occasional barbecues in the pleasant courtyard. P2600

Grandpa's Inn 1 Bonifacio St ☎ 077 674 0686, ⍉ grandpas-inn.com. This ancestral house with bare brick walls and parquet flooring has been converted into a lovely inn full of old curios. Try room 7, a uniquely furnished twin room where you can sleep in a kalesa (carriage). P1780

★ **Hotel Felicidad** 9 V. de los Reyes St ☎ 077 722 0008, ⍉ hotelfelicidadvigan.com. A charming option in a beautiful colonial mansion offering tastefully decorated rooms with beautiful hardwood floors and high ceilings. The delightful maestro suite (P7150) features a solid ironwood king bed and a lovely antique dresser. Wi-fi throughout. P3135

Vigan Plaza Plaza Burgos ☎077 722 8553, ⓦvigan plazahotel.com. In an excellent location on Plaza Burgos, and just a stone's throw away from the cathedral, this colonial hotel featuring beautiful tiled floors has rooms on three floors. The first- and second-floor options are in a better overall condition than those on the ground floor, most of which give onto a wall and are quite dark. Wi-fi in the lobby. P2800

★**Villa Angela Heritage House** 26 Quirino Blvd ☎077 722 2914, ⓦvillangela.com. The most colonial of all the colonial hotels, this is a beautiful old museum of a place and the top choice if you want to wallow in history. You can ask to be given the room Tom Cruise slept in: he stayed here for a few weeks when *Born on the Fourth of July* was being filmed on the sand dunes near Laoag. P2000

EATING, DRINKING AND NIGHTLIFE

Vigan doesn't offer much in terms of restaurants, although make sure to try some local specialities, including the town's famous crispy **empanada**. Nightlife is generally very low-key, with limited options – things quieten down substantially at 9pm, with the startling exception of *Legacy Super Club* (see below) in the town centre.

CAFÉS AND RESTAURANTS

Abuelita's 39 Governor A. Reyes St ☎077 722 2368. This popular restaurant is dotted with old curios including radios, rusty number plates and an old sewing machine; the speciality is regional Ilocano cuisine. Food is displayed in pots at both lunch and dinner – just take your pick and pay accordingly. A meal will set you back about P100. Mon–Sat 7.30am–8pm.

Café Leona Crisologo St ☎077 722 2212. Travellers are drawn to the outdoor tables that spill out on the street in the evening, although you can also dine in the tavern-style interior. The menu lists Ilocano and Japanese fusion dishes such as *longanisa maki* (P160), as well as pizza (P250) and Vigan specialities – try *daing na bangus*, marinated milkfish (P150). Daily 10am–10pm.

Irene's Empanadahan 13 Salcedo St ☎0922 819 9939. This fourth-generation empanada place has been going strong since the 1930s – locals say it's the best place in town to savour the Vigan speciality, which here comes in five different flavours: pork, beef, chicken, tuna and crab (P35–45). Daily 8am–8pm.

Leila's Café General Luna St ☎077 722 8110. This laidback café with framed pictures and customers' notes pinned to a white mock-brick wall offers sweet and savoury crêpes (P65), sandwiches (P80), pasta dishes (P140) and cupcakes (P45). Daily 10am–10pm.

Lilong & Lilang Brgy Bulala, 2.5km west of Vigan ☎077 722 1450, ⓦhiddengardenvigan.com. This leafy restaurant is located within a pretty plant nursery selling ferns, palms, bonsai and bamboo – a nice spot for a wander. It's a great place to try traditional Ilocano dishes, including *poqui poqui*, mashed grilled eggplant sautéed with onions and tomatoes with egg (P100). For dessert try the colourful halo-halo (P75), beautifully presented in a coconut husk bowl. A tricycle to get here will cost P40 (15min). Daily 6am–8pm.

Uno Grille 1 Bonifacio St ☎077 637 8299, ⓦgrandpas -inn.com. Customers at this courtyard restaurant with an open kitchen are presented with three menus: the first includes grilled foods (P175), the second Asian and Ilocano specialities (P180), and the third has an extensive selection of noodle and pasta dishes (P80). Adventurous types can go for the frog stew (only available in rainy season), or, if you happen to be in town between March and June, the mountain ants. Daily 6–10pm.

BAR AND CLUB

Embassit Lyric Bar Alcantara St ☎077 722 2988. Lively, studenty bar, just under 1km from the centre, with a dark interior featuring octagonal mirrors and glitzy chandeliers. Live bands play weekly: acoustic on Mon, rock bands on Thursday; other nights the DJ plays R&B. Daily 9am–2am.

Legacy Super Club Crisologo St at Mabini St ☎077 722 7396. Owned by an influential local family, this rather incongruous nightclub has somehow been given

---

VIGAN'S CRISPY EMPANADA

Don't leave Vigan without trying the local **empanada** – a crispy deep-fried tortilla of rice-flour dough containing cabbage and green papaya. Some empanadas – sometimes known as "special" – also contain an egg and longganisa (garlic sausage). Either way, eaten with sugar-cane vinegar and chopped shallots they are delicious. The stalls on the western side of Plaza Burgos, known collectively as **empanadaan**, sell empanadas along with *okoy* (egg, prawn, tomato and onion frittata) – again, best eaten dipped in vinegar.

permission to open within the old town. The music is an eclectic mix of R&B, cha-cha, Latin and boogie. P100

entrance fee on Sat (includes one beer). Mon–Thurs 8pm–2am, Fri & Sat 8pm–4am.

SHOPPING

Cristy's Loom Weaving Camangaan, 3km southeast of the city centre ☎0916 491 9320. Here you can watch women weaving at old rickety looms (Mon–Sat 5am–5pm), and buy the finished products, including sheets, pillowcases, tablemats and runners, in the small nearby shop. To get here catch a tricycle from town (15min; P40) Daily 6am–9pm.

Rowilda's Handloom Weaving Crisologo St at General Luna St ☎0927 422 4127. This souvenir shop, with a workshop in nearby Camangaan, offers a selection

of handwoven fabrics including place mats, table runners, napkins and blankets. Daily 8am–7pm.

Ruby Pottery 65 Liberation Blvd ☎077 674 0476. The massive wood-fired kilns here produce *burnay* – huge jars used by northerners for storing everything from vinegar to fish paste. Broken jars, called *gibak*, are used as a bed to dry salt. Carabao pound the wet clay under hoof, although you'll need to arrive between 8 and 11am to see them in action. Daily 8am–6pm.

DIRECTORY

Banks and exchange There are many banks with ATMs on Quezon Ave, including BDO and Metro Bank, a Landbank on Florentino St by Quezon Ave, and a Maybank at the corner of Plaridel and Florentino streets.

Hospital Gabriela Silang General Hospital (☎077 722 2772), south of the centre on Quirino Blvd.

Internet access Quickline, Bonifacio St (daily

8.30am–11pm; P20/hr; ☎077 632 0031); SNP Cyberzone, Bonifacio St (Sun–Fri 9am–7pm; P20/hr; ☎0926 141 1155).

Police station Rivero St, Brgy 8, south of town (24hr; ☎0917 860 7316).

Post office Governor A. Reyes St at Bonifacio St (Mon–Fri 8am–5pm).

3

Santa Maria Church and around

38km south of Vigan • From Vigan, take any Manila-bound bus (1hr), or catch a van to Santa Maria (leave when full; 45min; P50); tricycles to Pinsal Falls leave from Santa Maria town (45min; P160 return)

The UNESCO World Heritage-listed **Santa Maria Church**, dating from 1769, is a solid structure with a brick facade, set on a hill and reached via 83 steps; unsurprisingly it was used as a fortress during the Philippine Revolution. The interior is quite plain with the exception of its geometric floor tiles, and it's inhabited by birds and bats. While in the area it's worth travelling 8km to **Pinsal Falls**, a spectacular set of waterfalls with two large emerald green pools. Make sure to bring snacks and refreshments, as there are no shops.

Badoc

The coastal road north of Vigan to Laoag is sealed all the way and the journey time is only two hours. If you do want to break the journey then you could stop at **BADOC**, the birthplace of the Filipino painter Juan Luna. His reconstructed house, known as the **Juan Luna Shrine** (Tues–Sun 8am–5pm; free; ☎0927 356 9370, ⊛nhcp.gov.ph), stands in a side street close to the seventeenth-century Virgen Milagrosa de Badoc church. About 1km off the coast, **Badoc Island** is gaining a reputation for good surfing (late Oct to early March & late June to early Sept) – get there by renting a bangka from the little wharf in Badoc town.

Laoag

The congested streets of the Ilocos Norte provincial capital, **LAOAG**, can't compete with Vigan's historical core when it comes to aesthetic appeal, but there are a handful of things to do and see, and the city boasts one of the country's best museums. Laoag also makes an excellent base for exploring the beautiful coast at nearby **Suba** or touring sights associated with former dictator **Ferdinand Marcos**.

Museo Ilocos Norte

V. Llanes St at General Luna St • Mon–Sat 9am–noon & 1–5pm, Sun 10am–noon & 1–5pm • P20 • ☎ 077 770 45 87, ⓦ museoilocosnorte.com

Laoag's most interesting attraction, the **Museo Ilocos Norte**, provides an overview of the province's history and culture. Close to the main plaza, it's housed in a restored Spanish-era tobacco warehouse. Exhibits include vintage costumes, farming equipment and tribal artefacts, with a replica of an ilustrado (educated middle-class) ancestral home complete with antiques. The souvenir shop has some appealing books and gifts.

Sinking Bell Tower and around

Bonifacio St • Daily 5am–noon & 1–7pm

It's worth taking a look at the **Sinking Bell Tower**, which was built by Augustinian friars with a door big enough for a man on horseback to pass through. Today, however, the tower has sunk so much that you can only get through by stooping – although sadly the tower remains closed to visitors. Nearby is **St William's Cathedral**, one of the biggest in the Philippines, built in 1880 on older foundations.

Marcos Hall of Justice

V. Llanes St • Mon–Sat 8am–5pm • Free • ☎ 077 771 3768

The **Marcos Hall of Justice**, the square white building on the west side of Aurora Park, was where a young Ferdinand Marcos was detained in 1939 after being accused of the murder of one of his father's political opponents. Marcos wanted to graduate in law and used his time in detention wisely, swotting for the bar examination and successfully preparing his own defence.

ARRIVAL AND INFORMATION

LAOAG

By plane The airport is 7km southwest of town (tricycle P100). PAL and Cebu Pacific serve Manila (1hr).

By bus Partas buses from Manila (hourly; 14hr) and Baguio (hourly; 7–8hr) terminate at the Partas bus station on the western end of Rizal St. Fariñas buses from Manila (hourly; 12–14hr) and Baguio drop passengers off at the corner of Fariñas and Castro streets. GMW buses from Tuguegarao (hourly; 6–7hr) arrive at the terminal at the corner of Gov Agcaoli St and Primo Lazaro Ave. Local buses also connect Pagudpud (every 30min; 1hr 30min) and Vigan (every 30min; 3hr) to Laoag.

By jeepney Jeepneys to Paoay (every 30min; 40min; P34) and Batac (every 30min; 30min; P25) leave from General Hemando Ave, while those travelling to Sarrat leave east of town from J.M. Basa St (every 30min; 10min; P15).

Tourist information The helpful provincial tourist office kiosk is on Llanes St at General Luna St (daily 8am–6pm; ☎ 077 670 0004, ⓦ tourismilocosnorte.com), while the Laoag City tourist office (☎ 077 772 0467, ⓔ dotlaoag @digitelone.com) is in the Pacific Building, Abadilla St.

ACCOMMODATION

Balay da Blas 10 Giron St ☎ 077 770 4389, ⓦ balayda blas-laoag.com. A charming option, with superb-value warm and welcoming rooms decorated with antiques and colourful paintings. The larger family rooms also have a kitchenette, and there's a pleasant leafy seating area in the courtyard as well as an excellent restaurant attached. **P1200**

Fort Ilocandia Brgy 37 Calayab ☎ 077 670 9001, ⓦ fortilocandia.com.ph. Built in 1983 and hastily completed for the wedding reception of Ferdinand and Imelda Marcos's youngest daughter (see below), this expansive resort aims for classic elegance rather than modern chic. It's set in 77 hectares amid sand dunes and pine forests; amenities include a golf course, swimming pool, paintballing, hot-air ballooning and a driving range. **P7000**

Hotel Tiffany General Segundo Ave at M.H. del Pilar St ☎ 077 770 3550, ⓦ hoteltiffany-laoagcity.com. This motel-style place has tried for a 1960s US theme, with mellow polka dot and stripy themed rooms and an attached American-style diner serving cheeseburgers (P65) and milkshakes (P79). The lobby wi-fi reaches some of the rooms. **P1170**

Java Hotel General Segundo Ave, 55-B Salet ☎ 077 770 5996, ⓦ javahotel.com.ph. A pleasant option in a stone building with thatched roof, with tastefully furnished rooms featuring modern amenities. There's a swimming pool, tennis court and gym, and an airy restaurant serving good Filipino dishes. Wi-fi. **P2400**

EATING, DRINKING AND NIGHTLIFE

Cock House F.R. Castro Ave ☎ 077 772 3079. Laoag's only nightlife venue hosts bands from all over the Philippines, playing an eclectic mix from rock to R&B. The atmosphere is generally laidback, with customers enjoying the show as they sip a beer (P60). Daily 8pm–2.30am.

Papa Pau's Diner Rizal St at D.M. Castro Ave ☎ 077 771 5185. There are two dining areas here – an a/c interior and an outdoor area with benches and colourful chequered tablecloths, shaded by a bamboo roof. The speciality is *nanay's binalot*, pork, beef or milkfish served with rice and egg, wrapped in banana leaves (P80). Daily 10.30am–10.30pm.

La Preciosa Rizal St ☎ 077 773 1162, ⓦ lapreciosa -ilocos.com. Considered to be the best restaurant in town, with an emphasis on Ilocano cuisine. Bestsellers include *dinengdeng* (vegetable soup topped with grilled fish; P195) and *crispy dinardaraan* (pork meat cooked in blood sauce; P195). You can dine indoors or on the terrace; there's also a café displaying a selection of cakes (P100). Daily 9am–midnight.

★**Saramsam** 10 General Giron St ☎ 077 670 3219, ⓦ balaydablas-laoag.com. This cosy restaurant features two welcoming dining areas with clusters of lamps, wooden artefacts and shelves lined with beautiful oblong demijohns. The menu offers creative Ilocano dishes with Italian and Mexican influences; the *pinakbet* pizza (P145) is a burst of fresh flavours, while the *mungo* with chipotle sauce (spicy black lentils; P145) and the *poqui poqui* salad (mashed aubergine with onions and tomatoes; P150) are both exquisite. Daily 6.30am–10.30pm.

DIRECTORY

Banks and exchange There are plenty of banks along Rizal, including BDO and BPI.

Hospital Laoag General Hospital, Brgy 46 Nalbo, south of town (☎ 077 772 1108).

Internet access Gym Carry, General Segundo Ave (P10/

hr; Tues–Sun 11am–6pm; ☎ 077 771 3840).

Police Rizal St at Paco Roman St (☎ 077 771 1026).

Post office There's a small post office right by the City Hall (Mon–Fri 8am–5pm).

Sarrat

Some 8km east of Laoag is the sleepy, pretty village of **SARRAT**, where the attractive **Santa Monica Church** hosted the wedding of Marcos's youngest daughter Irene in 1983. Preparations for the wedding – a ceremony that cost US$10.3 million – involved thousands of men remodelling the town and 3500 contracted employees renovating the two-hundred-year-old church. Large parts of Sarrat were reconstructed, with houses torn down and rebuilt in the old Spanish colonial style.

Marcos Birthplace Museum

National Highway • Thurs–Tues 9am–4pm • P30 • Jeepney from Laoag (hourly; 15min; P13)

Ferdinand Marcos was born in Sarrat on September 11, 1917, and his former home has been turned into the **Marcos Birthplace Museum**. The ground floor displays traditional Ilocano weaving instruments, while the first floor showcases Marcos memorabilia, including a set of his clothes worn during infancy, but this place is really for Marcos completists only.

Ferdinand Marcos Mausoleum and Museum

Batac, 15km south of Laoag • **Mausoleum** Daily 9am–noon & 1–4pm • Free **Museum** Wed–Mon 9am–noon & 1–4pm • P50 • ☎ 0917 866 5186 • Buses between Vigan and Laoag pass through Batac – ask the driver to let you off; Batac is also served by regular jeepneys from Laoag (every 30min; 40min; P25)

Marcos spent his childhood in the pretty town of **Batac** before moving to Manila to take up law. The chief attraction here is the **Ferdinand Marcos Mausoleum**, which contains the former dictator's refrigerated corpse – though rumours abound that it's nothing more than a wax model. Imelda wants to bury him in the *Libingan ng mga Bayani* (Heroes' Cemetery) in Manila, a proposal that has failed to find favour with successive governments. The **museum** opposite the mausoleum showcases Marcos memorabilia and traces his political career in glowing terms; there's also a section dedicated to his romance with Imelda, who became his wife after only eleven days of courting.

Paoay

A few kilometres west of Batac, **PAOAY** is the location of a UNESCO-listed **church** as well as the **Malacañang of the North**, the opulent mansion where **Ferdinand Marcos** stayed during presidential holidays.

St Augustine Church

Paoay Church Complex • Daily 6am–6pm • Buses between Vigan and Laoag pass through Paoay – ask the driver to let you off; there are also regular jeepneys (every 30min; 50min; P34) from Laoag via Batac

St Augustine church is perhaps the best-known "earthquake Baroque" church in the Philippines. Begun in 1804, it took ninety years to build and has 26 immense side buttresses designed to keep it standing. Nearby is a bell tower dating from 1793, which you can climb for views of the area.

Malacañang of the North

Suba, Paoay • Tues–Sun 9am–noon & 1–4.30pm • P20 • ☎ 0906 521 1139 • Tricycles from Paoay's St Augustine Church (25min; P120) will then take you on to the Ilocos Norte Sand Dunes (see below) for P150 return

The **Malacañang of the North** is named after the presidential palace in Manila. The mansion, set on a five-hectare estate of gentle lawns giving onto the beautiful Paoay Lake, was the Marcoses' holiday residence between 1977 and the revolution in 1986. The property also comprised a golf course – Marcos was an avid golfer – which is now part of the *Fort Ilocandia* resort (see p.149). In 2012 part of the building was transformed into a **pro-Marcos museum**, with seven galleries highlighting some of the major reforms – but, naturally, none of the corruption or human rights abuses – implemented during his presidency. The Agriculture Room focuses on the building of waterways and dams – aiming for self-sufficiency, Marcos implemented irrigation programmes in order to supply water to the entire archipelago – while the Nation Building Room highlights the President's achievement in uniting his country by connecting the islands via a number of ambitious highways and bridges.

Ilocos Norte sand dunes

The Laoag Eco-Adventure Development (LEAD) Movement Inc (☎ 0919 873 5516, ⊛ leadmovement.wordpress.com) arranges trips combining a 4WD ride and sandboarding (P2500/1hr for 4-6 people), as well as horseback riding on the dunes (P230/hr)

The coastline west of Laoag is a sight to behold. More like desert than beach, it measures almost 1km across at some points and reaches as far as the eye can see, fringed by huge **sand dunes**. The area has become a favourite among Manila film crews; the **Suba** dunes to the south – close to the *Fort Ilocandia* resort (see p.149) – are where Oliver Stone shot segments of *Born on the Fourth of July*.

Pagudpud and around

Seventy kilometres north of Laoag along the coastal road is **PAGUDPUD**, a typical provincial town providing access to several wonderfully picturesque **beaches**. The Pagudpud area is increasingly recognized as having all the beauty of Boracay, but just a fraction of the tourists and none of the nightlife.

Saud Beach

Tricycles from Pagudpud P50 (15min)

Saud Beach ("Sa-ud"), a few kilometres down a narrow road to the north of town, is a beautiful long arch of white sand backed by palm trees. Resorts on the beach rent out snorkelling equipment, and can provide bangkas (P400/hr) so that you can head to the best spots.

Kabigan Falls

Daily 7am–5pm • P10; compulsory guide P100 • Tricycle from Saud Beach P200 (35min), from Blue Lagoon P200 (25min)

About half way between Saud Beach and Blue Lagoon are the **Kabigan Falls**, a beautiful cascade of water flowing down a steep incline of 34m and nestled in a pretty stretch of thick vegetation. There's a refreshing pool at the bottom of the falls, perfect for a swim. At the main road, where tricycles drop off, you'll have to register and hire a compulsory guide who will lead you to the falls – a beautiful 1.5km (30min) walk through picturesque rice paddies and lush mountain scenery.

Blue Lagoon

Tricycles from Pagudpud P300 (40min)

About 18km east of Saud is the glorious **Blue Lagoon** (also known as Maira-ira Beach). The setting is stunning, with dazzling water lapping a sugary crescent of sand; the breaks also attract surfers from July to January. One stretch of the beach has been overdeveloped with a large and incongruous resort, but it's possible to get away from that and still enjoy the sand and sea.

Kingfisher Beach

Tricycles from Saud Beach P150 (20min)

Kingfisher Beach, a gem of a place just 6km north of Saud Beach, is one of the country's best kitesurfing spots, its strong northwest or side shore winds making it an ideal spot for advanced surfers, especially between October and March. The waters are so clear that you're likely to spot flying fish, sea turtles, jackfish and even tuna as you surf. The 250m-wide reef with a flat lagoon is perfect for snorkelling, stand-up paddling and kayaking. You can rent equipment from the well-stocked *Kingfisher Resort* just on the beach.

Cape Bojeador Lighthouse and around

Daily 8am–5pm • Free • To get here from Pagudpud take a jeepney or local bus (both P35) towards Laoag and ask to be let off on the National Highway near the lighthouse; from here you can walk 900m up to the lighthouse (30min) or catch a tricycle (P50; 5min)

Some 36km west of Pagudpud is the **Cape Bojeador Lighthouse**, just outside the town of **Burgos**. Built in 1892, at 19.90m the lighthouse is the tallest in the country, and from the base there are unobstructed views of the coastline and across the South China Sea. It's still in use and its keeper, Vicente Acoba Jr, will be happy to answer any questions you may have.

ARRIVAL AND INFORMATION

By bus Buses arrive on the main road in Pagudpud town. There are services from Manila (12hr), with local buses connecting the town to Laoag (every 15min; 2hr).

Tourist information In the town hall (Mon–Fri 8am–5pm; ☎0939 936 7809, ✉ommpagudpud@yahoo.com).

Services There are no banks, and just one ATM at Aziar I-Mart that only accepts local cards, so make sure to bring enough pesos.

Tricycle tours Tricycles offer tours, taking in the area's major sights for P600/day.

ACCOMMODATION AND EATING

Resorts around Pagudpud are a little pricier than similar establishments elsewhere, and many of them double their prices during high season (April & May, Holy Week & Christmas). It's always worth asking for a discount at other times. Budget travellers should consider a **homestay**. The tourist office has accredited more than thirty, with fixed prices of P250 or P350/person for fan or a/c, and there are at least another forty unofficial homestays in the area. Contact the tourist office for details, or just wander along the road behind the main resorts on Saud Beach.

SAUD BEACH AND AROUND

Apo Idon ☎077 676 0483 or ☎0917 510 0671, ✉apoidon.com. Saud Beach's most upmarket resort offers a selection of comfortable rooms with dark wooden furniture. The more spacious suites (P6000) have private balconies with sea views; there's also a small pool, and a restaurant giving onto a beautiful stretch of beach. The downside is the deafeningly loud hum of the generator around the reception area. **P4800**

★ **BergBlick** Brgy Burayoc ☎0939 458 1642, ✉bergblick-pagudpud.com. Halfway between Saud Beach and Blue Lagoon, this is an unusual find along the highway – a German-owned restaurant with waitresses in traditional Bavarian dress, offering excellent international and local dishes including home-made ravioli (P270) and *pinakbet* lasagne (P295). Try the BergBlick Pan (P460, serving 2–3), a platter with pork chop, pork roast, pan-fried potatoes, cabbage roll and fresh mixed salad, followed by the home-made crème brûlée (P150). Daily 9am–10pm.

★ **Evangeline Beach Resort** Brgy Burayoc ☎077 655 5862 or ☎0927 411 6284, ✉evangelinebeachresort .net. An excellent option comprising six comfortable rooms in a freshly painted thatched building with beautiful wooden interiors; there's also a spacious cottage with two double rooms, lounge area and fully equipped kitchenette. The beachside restaurant offers an extensive menu of Filipino and international dishes. **P2600**

BLUE LAGOON

Agua Seda ☎0920 243 1832, ✉aguaseda.com. Close to the hard-to-miss *Hannah's Beach Resort*, this laidback

family-run place offers nine a/c rooms with private bath. There's a pleasant restaurant in an open-fronted nipa and bamboo hut, and staff are often seen barbecuing fresh fish in the back yard with their guests. **P2000**

★ **Kapuluan Vista** Sitio Banarian, Brgy Balaoi ☎0920 952 2528, ✉kapuluanvistaresortandrestaurant.com. A gem of a place with a pleasant pool area and a great restaurant serving organic produce from the backyard, where free-range chickens also roam. Rooms are tastefully decorated with minimalist decor. Larger deluxe rooms sleeping four (P4750) have a loft and veranda, and there are also excellent-value rooms with shared bathroom sleeping two to six (P650/person). The bar and lounge with cushioned seating and beanbags right on the beach is the perfect spot for a sundowner. **P2700**

Wally's World Homestay Sitio Banarian, Brgy Balaoi ☎0938 615 8791. This friendly place is run by a family of keen surfers who also rent out boards (P200) and offer lessons (P200) at the surf break just outside the front door. There are three colourfully painted tiled a/c rooms, a pleasant cottage with kitchenette sleeping four (P2800) and a wobbly makeshift hut (P800). **P2000**

KINGFISHER BEACH

Kingfisher Resort ☎0927 525 8111, ✉kingfisher beach.com. Popular with kite surfers, this is a very comfortable option with tastefully decorated casitas with modern amenities, some with lofts. Travellers on a budget can sleep in little tiki huts (P2000) with shared bath. The restaurant offers an extensive menu of Filipino and international dishes. **P2500**

The northeast

The **northeast** of Luzon, comprising the provinces of Nueva Vizcaya, Quirino, Aurora, Isabela and Cagayan, is one of the archipelago's least explored regions, with kilometres of beautiful coastline and enormous tracts of tropical rainforest. Following the National Highway from Ilocos as it curves south brings you to the biggest city in the region,

FROM TOP SURFING, SAN JUAN (P.140); VIGAN (P.142) >

Tuguegarao, the starting point for trips to the **Peñablanca Protected Landscape and Seascape**. Turning off the highway and following the north coast road brings you to **Santa Ana**, home to the country's best game-fishing and the departure point for boat trips to the rugged and isolated **Babuyan Islands**.

The coast south of Santa Ana and east of Tuguegarao is cut off from the rest of Luzon by the **Sierra Madre** mountains. One of the only significant settlements is **Palanan**, jump-off point for the barely explored **Northern Sierra Madre Natural Park**. The climbing and trekking possibilities here are exciting, but the area is so wild and remote that it's also potentially hazardous, with poor communications and areas of impenetrable forest. Further south on the coast – but unreachable by road from Palanan – is **Baler**, the best-known tourist destination in the northeast. This coastal town has become a popular surfing destination, but its location six hours from Manila means that it isn't swamped with weekenders.

3 Santa Ana and around

The northern coast of Luzon, part of Cagayan province, is skipped over by many visitors in their haste to head either west to Ilocos Norte or south to Tuguegarao. Yet the untouristy fishing town of **SANTA ANA** – on the northeastern point of Luzon – has much to offer, including some terrific white sand beaches and a number of enticing offshore islands. It is also the departure point for boats to Maconacon and the Northern Sierra Madre Natural Park (see p.157). Boats to the offshore islands leave from the port in **San Vicente**, 6km northeast of Santa Ana town centre.

Anguib Beach
Bangkas from San Vicente (30min) cost P1500 return including waiting time

On the mainland, you can hire a bangka for the day to the lovely and secluded **Anguib Beach** on the eastern part of San Vicente. It is a beautiful 1.8km J-shaped stretch of beach with white sand and crystal clear waters. There is no accommodation, but it's a great place to pitch a tent. Make sure to bring water and food, as there are no shops or restaurants.

Palaui Island
Bangkas from San Vicente to Punta Verde (15min; P750 return) or Cape Engaño (45min; P1800 return); alternatively, the Palaui Environmental Protectors Association (PEPA; ☎ 0927 905 1796) offers a two-day ecotourism itinerary including snorkelling, hiking, planting mangroves and cleaning up the beach

The closest island to Santa Ana is **Palaui**, which has no roads or hotels and only limited electricity. From the main settlement of **Punta Verde** on the east of the island, two trails head north to **Cape Engaño** on the island's northern coast, a beautiful crescent lagoon watched over by an old but still operating Spanish lighthouse – the walk will take about three hours.

The Babuyan islands
MV *Eagle* ferry (☎ 0919 651 5595) from Aparri, 70km west of Santa Ana, to Camiguin (every 2–3 days depending on the weather, at 6am; 2–3hr; P350) and then on to Calayan (4–5hr; P700)– note ferries only run when weather permits; or you can hire a private bangka from San Vicente (6hr; P7500 return)

The MV *Eagle* ferry makes the often rough crossing from Aparri to the isolated and undeveloped **Babuyan islands**, a cluster of 24 volcanic and coralline islands 32km off the coast. Only five of the islands – Camiguin, Calayan, Fuga, Babuyan and Dalupiri – are inhabited and even **Calayan**, the most developed, has limited electricity. There are some beautiful beaches on several of the islands including Fuga and Dalupiri, and hot springs on the volcanic Camiguin.

ARRIVAL AND DEPARTURE

By plane At the time of research a new airport was under construction at Lal-lo, 77km west of Santa Ana.

By boat Weekly bangkas leave from San Vicente pier for Maconacon in the Northern Sierra Madre Natural Park (see p.157).

By bus Guardian Angels (commonly referred to as

SANTA ANA AND AROUND

Everlasting) runs to Santa Ana from Manila (3 daily; 14hr), stopping opposite the main market, Centro Santa Ana, on the main highway. GMW Trans connects Vigan to Santa Ana (2 daily; 12hr).

By van There are regular vans from Santa Ana to Tuguegarao (every 30min 3am–3pm; 3hr; P180).

INFORMATION AND ACTIVITIES

Tourist information In Santa Ana's municipal building (Mon–Fri 8am–5pm; ☎078 858 1004). Can offer advice on island-hopping and arrange homestays.

Game-fishing The seas around Santa Ana offer marvellous

game-fishing (March–July), thanks to the currents that run through the Luzon Strait from the Pacific. Contact the Philippine Game Fishing Foundation (☎0927 320 7261).

ACCOMMODATION AND EATING

SANTA ANA

Jotay Resort ☎078 372 0560, ⓦjotayresort.com. This small resort facing the beach offers a selection of simple rooms with private bath; a few face the little pool area, but the majority are set around the courtyard and parking area at the back. The restaurant specializes in excellent chilli crab – a must, but make sure you give at least a few hours' advance notice. P1000

PALAUI ISLAND

Bayanihan Nature Village Punta Verde ☎0906 845 5472. Run by PEPA, this simple thatched place has just one room sleeping four; you can also pitch a tent in the grounds, just by a honey production centre (Feb–May). The

local community's women's association prepares the food here, and also provides massages in the garden's open-fronted huts. Per person P250

BABUYAN ISLANDS

TPS Homestay Calayan Island ☎0929 837 5737. Run by a chatty woman, this homestay is located in the centre of town near the sea. There are three simple rooms, two of which sleep four and have fan and communal bathroom; the other has a double bed, a/c and private bath (P700). Travellers can also pitch a tent on the grounds, and make use of the kitchen; otherwise, staff can rustle up some food. Per person P250

Tuguegarao

The capital of Cagayan province, **TUGUEGARAO** ("Too-geg-er-rao") is a busy city of choked streets lined with pawnshops and canteens, offering little of interest for travellers. It is, however, convenient to fly to Tuguegarao if you intend to explore the east coast around the Sierra Madre or the northernmost coast near Santa Ana, or head west into Kalinga province and its capital Tabuk. There are also small aircraft flights from Tuguegarao to Batanes.

Don't head off straight away, though, as Tuguegarao is also the best starting point for a visit to a remarkable cave system at **Peñablanca**. In addition, a number of local travel agents offer **whitewater rafting** and **kayaking** trips on the Pinacanauan and Chico rivers, usually from August until February.

Cagayan Provincial Museum

Provincial Capitol Compound, 3km from the city centre • Mon–Fri 8am–5pm • Free • ☎078 846 7337 • Tricycle from Tuguegarao P15 (10min)

The small **Cagayan Provincial Museum** traces the history of Cagayan province; displays include fossilized bones of extinct animals that roamed the area during the Ice Age. The highlight is the replica (the original is on display in Manila's National Museum) of the toe bone of Callao Man, discovered by a team of archeologists in 2007 in nearby Callao Cave. The remains date back 67,000 years and are allegedly the oldest ever found in Southeast Asia. The exhibition then jumps ahead to the age of trade, with displays featuring intricately designed Chinese bowls and porcelain vessels, as well as heirloom pieces from the Spanish and American eras.

ARRIVAL AND DEPARTURE

TUGUEGARAO

By plane Tuguegarao airport lies 2km south of the city centre along the National Highway, easily reached by tricycle (15min; P50). Cebu Pacific flies to Manila (2 weekly; 1hr), as does PAL (1 daily; 1hr). Sky Pasada has flights to Basco (for Batanes Islands; 3 weekly; 1hr; P5225) and Maconacan (for the Northern Sierra Madre National Park; 2 weekly; 30min; P2200). North Sky Air also serves Basco (3 weekly; 1hr; P5100) and Maconacan (2 weekly; 30min; P2100).

By bus Victory Liner buses from Manila stop on the National Highway, while Dangwa and Dalin buses arrive at Don Domingo St.

Destinations Baguio (Dangwa: daily 5pm; 11–12hr; Dalin: daily 3.30pm & 4.30pm; 10–11hr); Manila (Victory Liner: every 1–2hr; 10–12hr).

By van Vans for Santiago (every 30min; 3hr; P160), Santa Ana (every 40min; 3hr; P180) and Tabuk (hourly; 1hr 30min; P80) leave from the Central terminal on the National Highway.

INFORMATION AND ACTIVITIES

Tourist information The regional tourist office (Mon–Fri 8am–5pm; ☎078 844 1621, ⊛dotregion2.com.ph) is in the Regional Government Centre on Pav-Vurulun St, about 500m from the airport. You can ask here about permits and guides for the Peñablanca caves, or book trips in other parts of northeast Luzon including the Northern Sierra Madre Natural Park (see opposite). The provincial tourist office (Mon–Fri 8am–5pm; ☎078 846 7576, ⊕cagayantourism@yahoo.com) is at Capitol Hills by the Cagayan Provincial Museum.

Activities For reliable first-hand information about caving, trekking, abseiling and climbing, contact the Sierra Madre Outdoor Club (☎0917 272 6494). You can also contact Anton Carag at Adventure and Expeditions Philippines (☎0917 532 7480), who heads kayaking and rafting trips locally and in Kalinga province.

ACCOMMODATION AND EATING

AdriNel's 29 Rizal St ☎078 844 1305. One of the city's few non-fast-food restaurants, offering a popular all-you-can-eat Filipino lunch (11am–2pm; P200). Other choices include the large family platter *familia sentenyal* (P750) that includes grilled and barbecued pork, veg, shrimp, crab and grilled fish. Daily 8am–8pm.

Hotel Roma Bonifacio St at Luna St ☎078 844 2222, ⊕info_hotelroma@yahoo.com. The city's largest hotel offers comfortable enough private rooms, although furniture is a bit drab and dated; a number of them give onto the interior patio and are quite dark. Wi-fi throughout, and a popular restaurant. P1600

Mango Suites Rizal St at Balzain St ☎078 304 1302. A good central option with modern, comfortable rooms, wi-fi throughout and free airport transfers. A pleasant café-restaurant serves Filipino food and a smattering of Western dishes. P1200

Peñablanca caves

The major tourist attraction around Tuguegarao is the marvellous **cave system** at Peñablanca, 24km to the east. Peñablanca, officially known as the **Peñablanca Protected Landscape and Seascape**, is riddled with more than three hundred caves, many of them deep and dangerous, and a good number still largely unexplored. Most of the caves are protected, but it's possible to visit three – **Callao**, **Musang** and **Lattu-Lattuc** – without permission; all three can be done in a single day. Several other caves – including Jackpot, Odessa-Tumbali and San Carlos – can be visited with permission from the Sierra Madre Outdoor Club in Tuguegarao (see above). Note that typhoons between August and November can flood the caves and make them impossible to visit.

Callao Cave

P20 (plus compulsory guide; donation P100) • Return boat trips to the bat cave cost P500, including waiting, from the pier close to the cave entrance; kayaks (in season) cost P200/hr

The easiest of the Peñablanca caves to visit is **Callao Cave**, which has seven immense chambers – previously nine but an earthquake in the 1980s cut off the last two. The main chamber has a natural skylight and a chapel inside where Mass is celebrated on special occasions. You'll need a guide – there are plenty at the entrance. Note that there are 184 steps to climb before you reach the entrance of the cave, and inside the rocks can be slippery during the wet season. It's also possible to rent **kayaks** – ask at the cave entrance.

Another attraction here is a short **boat trip** that takes you to the **bat cave**, where at dusk you can see great flocks of the creatures leaving to hunt.

ARRIVAL AND INFORMATION · PEÑABLANCA CAVES

By tricycle A tricycle from Tuguegarao to Callao Cave is P500 including waiting time (30min). You can also hire a van (P2500/day plus petrol), which is particularly worth doing if you want to make a day of it and explore other caves nearby.

Guides Contact the Sierra Madre Outdoor Club (see opposite) for professional guides in caving and other outdoor activities including mountaineering and trekking. Rates for professional guides are P1000/day plus food, and you'll need one guide per five people. Porters charge P200–500/day depending on what they are carrying.

Northern Sierra Madre Natural Park

At almost 3600 square kilometres, the **Northern Sierra Madre Natural Park** remains one of the country's last frontiers and well worth the trouble of getting there. Said by conservationists to be the Philippines' richest protected area in terms of habitat and species, the park is eighty percent land and twenty percent coastal area along a spectacular, cliff-studded seashore.

One of the reasons for the health of the park's ecosystems is its inaccessibility. Though small aircraft connect the towns of **Palanan** and **Maconacon** to the outside world, to the east lies the Pacific, which is too rough for boats during much of the northeast monsoon (Dec–Feb) and typhoon (July–Oct) seasons, while to the west no roads cross the park or lead towards the more populated, rice-growing valleys.

The park has few wardens and no fences, so you can visit any time you want without restriction; it is essential, however, to take a **guide** if you are to visit safely. A guide can take you down the Palanan River to the village of **Sabang**, from where you can walk through farmland and forest to **Disadsad Falls**, a high cascade that crashes through dense forest into a deep pool. For some of the trip there's no trail, so you'll have to wade upriver through the water. Another memorable trip from Palanan takes you northwards along the coast to the sheltered inlets around the towns of Dimalansan and Maconacon. On the isolated beaches here the **Dumagat** people establish their temporary homes (see box below).

ARRIVAL AND DEPARTURE · NORTHERN SIERRA MADRE NATURAL PARK

By plane The small town of Palanan is the main gateway to the park. Sky Pasada has weekly flights from Cauayan (Tues, Fri & Sun 8.30am; 25min; P1900), as does Cyclone Airways (1 daily – check for the latest schedules; 25min; P2100). North Sky Air has flights from Tuguegarao to Maconacon (Tues & Sat 8am; 30min; P2100). Sky Pasada also connects Maconacon to Cauayan (Thurs & Sat 12.30pm; 20min; P2200).

By boat and bus To avoid flying, it's possible to take a long boat journey from San Vicente near Santa Ana (see p.154) to Maconacon (8–10hr; P500), with boats departing about once a week depending on the weather – check at the port for the latest schedules. From Maconacon you can change onto a second boat to Palanan (4hr; P500). Alternatively, take a local bus from Santiago City in Isabela province (itself an 8hr trip from Manila) to Dilasag in

---

THE DUMAGATS

The people known as the **Dumagats** are among the original inhabitants of the Philippines. The word Dumagat translates roughly as "those who moved to the ocean", and the area around **Palanan** is the last stronghold of their vanishing culture and way of life. Some have now settled but others remain nomadic, living in small camps on the beaches around Palanan where they build temporary sloping shelters from bamboo and dried grass. Life for the Dumagats is simple in the extreme: they survive by hunting and gathering, using little modern equipment. The main threats to their existence are through the commercialization and exploitation of their homelands, along with exposure to diseases previously unknown to them. Every March members of the nomadic Dumagat community join with the settled inhabitants of Palanan for the **Sabutan festival**.

Aurora province (daily, 1–2 departures 4am–5am; non-a/c; 10–12hr), from where there are boats to Palanan (no fixed schedules; 6–8hr; P500).

On foot For hardy visitors, the most interesting option is to trek into the park from San Mariano. It's a five- to seven-day trek that requires a guide – contact Albert Gonzales at the Palanan Wilderness Development Cooperative (see below). To get to San Mariano, take a Victory Liner bus from Manila (hourly; 8–10hr).

INFORMATION AND ACTIVITIES

Tourist information The park's tourism officer, Myrose B. Alvarez (☎0906 721 1016), is based at the town hall in Palanan. Along with offering advice and information, she can help with arranging a homestay – there are no guesthouses or hotels in Palanan – and can inform the Department of Environment and Natural Resources (DENR) that you are planning to hike in the area.

Palanan Wilderness Development Cooperative A useful organization based in the town, which can help with guides (☎0928 341 5375, ✉amgpalanan@yahoo.com).

Cagayan Valley Programme on Environment and Development If you are interested in seeing the resident endangered Philippine crocodiles, contact this outfit (☎078 622 8001, ⓦcvped.org).

Baler

The laidback east coast town of **BALER** is known for its excellent, if intermittent, surfing. Surfing scenes in Francis Ford Coppola's *Apocalypse Now* were filmed at a break known as **Charlie's Point** at the mouth of the Aguang River, which is a 45-minute walk north of the main surfing beach of **Sabang**. When the film crew departed they left the surfboards behind, kick-starting local interest in the sport.

Dicasalarin Cove

P300 • Walkable from Digisit (2–3hr) which is 5km beyond Cemento Reef; also accessible from Baler by 4WD, or by renting a boat (40min; P2500–3000/day)

If you're not after some surf, then you could try the white beach at **Dicasalarin Cove**. You can snorkel here too, and there is a spot for shallow diving at the site of a reef rehabilitation programme. There are no shops or restaurants – only picnic cottages, so make sure to bring some drinks and snacks.

Casiguran Sound

D Liner bus (3 daily; 3–4hr) and vans (leave when full; 3–4hr; P220) from Baler

The calm and picturesque inlet of **Casiguran Sound**, north of Baler by either road or sea, is a lovely spot to while away a few hours. Protected from onshore winds and waves by a

---

RIDING BALER'S WAVES

You can **surf** year-round at Baler, although the best waves usually come between September and March, especially early in the morning. The waves, averaging nearly 2m, are ideal for both amateur and experienced surfers. Lessons and kit rental are available at Sabang Beach.

Cemento Reef A strong world-class right-hand reef break, perfect for advanced surfers; competitions are held here.

Charlie's Point The most famous surf spot in Baler, gaining popularity in the late 1970s during the filming of Apocalypse Now.

Dalugan Bay, San Ildefonso This left-hand reef break peninsula offers good surf.

Dianed, Dipaculao North of Baler, this place has typhoon swells holding 1.2–1.8m waves.

Dicasalarin Point Right- and left-hand breaks, with reef breaks for the more experienced surfers and beach breaks

for beginners.

Lobbot's Point, Dipaculao A left- and right-hand beach break holding 0.6–1.8m ground swells that break into the sandy gravel bottom.

Sabang Beach The sandy bottom beach break here is ideal for beginners; there are left and right breaks from September to March. You can rent surfboards for around P200/hr; lessons cost P150/hr.

Secret Point, Castillo This surf spot breaks between two and four times a year and can offer a 140m ride.

finger of hilly land, it's perfect for **swimming** and very undeveloped. There is little here in terms of restaurants and shops, apart from a few sari-sari stores around the fishing village.

ARRIVAL AND INFORMATION   BALER

By bus There are no road links north along the coast to the Northern Sierra Madre Natural Park, but you can catch a D'Liner bus to Dilasag (3 daily; 4hr 30min) where you can get a boat to Palanan (no fixed schedule; 6–8hr; P500).
Destinations Baguio (Lizardo: 3 daily; 6–7hr); Manila

(Genesis: 2 daily; 5–6hr; Joy Bus: daily; 5–6hr).
Tourist information The municipal tourist office is in the Municipal Building (Mon–Fri 8am–5pm; ☎ 0928 983 7668, ⊛ baler.gov.ph), while the provincial tourist office is in the Capitol Compound (☎ 0908 895 3076, ⊛ aurora.gov.ph)

ACCOMMODATION AND EATING

All the best **accommodation** in Baler is on or around the beach at Sabang, which is a short tricycle ride (P15) from town. Apart from during the annual Aurora Cup in February, you won't have any problem finding somewhere to stay. The best eating options are in the hotels; all of the options that we review have decent **restaurants**, some with lovely views.

Bahia de Baler ☎ 0908 982 7064, ⊛ bahiadebaler .com. Set on 2.5 hectares of land right on the beach, this place offers a decent choice of private a/c rooms; guests can use the amenities of the sister resort *Costa Pacifica* nearby, including the swimming pool. There's an attached bar and grill, along with an affiliated surf shop with discounts for customers. **P4278**
Bay-Ler View Hotel ☎ 0927 366 8735, ⊛ baylerview hotel.com. Clean and comfortable accommodation right

on the beachfront with lovely views over the ocean; the restaurant serves local and international dishes, staff are friendly and there's wi-fi in the communal areas. **P1600**
Bay's Inn ☎ 0908 982 3509, ✉ piasb_43@yahoo.com. One of the most popular resorts for budget tourists and out-of-town surfers, boasting panoramic views of Baler Bay, the Pacific Ocean and surrounding cliffs and beaches. It has clean fan or a/c doubles with private showers and a popular restaurant with views. Surfboard rental available. **P1700**

The Cordillera

To Filipino lowlanders brought up on sunshine and beaches, the tribal heartlands of the north and their spiny ridge of inhospitable mountains, the **Cordillera**, are seen almost as another country, inhabited by mysterious people who worship primitive gods. It's true that in some respects life for many tribal people has changed little in hundreds of years, with traditional ways and values still very much in evidence. If anything is likely to erode these traditions, it is the coming of tourists; already an increasing number of tribal people are making much more from the sale of handicrafts than they do from the production of rice.

The **weather** can have a major impact on a trip to the Cordillera, not least because landslides can cause travel delays during the rainy season (particularly May–Nov, but continuing until Jan or Feb). Since the rains come in from the northeast it's the places on the eastern side of the mountains – such as **Banaue** and **Batad** – that are usually worst hit, and fog can roll into those areas any time from October to February. Throughout the region it can get cold at night between December and February. It's worth noting that the rice terrace **planting seasons** vary significantly; the lower-lying areas typically have two plantings a year while the highlands have one. Terraces are at their greenest in the month or so before harvesting, although their barren appearance after a harvest can also look impressive.

Baguio and around

It's fair to say that its heyday as a rural retreat from Manila is far behind **BAGUIO**. The city centre is blighted by a polluted tangle of smoke-belching jeepneys and the large SM shopping mall hardly improves the scenery. Still, its position as a major hub for the Cordillera means that you're likely to pass through, and it does have some interesting sights, plus, as a university city, a number of excellent restaurants and interesting

> ## TREKKING IN THE CORDILLERA
>
> Since the road network is poor in many parts of the Cordillera, and there are so many jungled peaks and hidden valleys, **trekking** is the only way to see some of the region's secrets: burial caves, tribal villages and hidden waterfalls. Gentle **day hikes** are possible, particularly in the main tourist areas of Banaue and Sagada, but there are also plenty of **two- or three-day treks** that take you deep into backwaters. Don't be tempted to wander off into the wilderness without a guide: good maps are almost nonexistent and it's easy to become disoriented and lost. Medical facilities and rescue services are few and far between, so if you get into trouble and no one knows where you are then you'll have a long wait for help to arrive.
>
> Most of the **best trails** are around Sagada, Banaue, Bontoc, Tabuk and Tinglayan. In all of these towns there is a tourist office or town hall where someone will be able to help arrange **guides**. In smaller settlements a good place to look for a guide is at the barangay hall. Many guides won't have official certification, but will know the area exceptionally well. Your guide may also agree to carry equipment and supplies, but don't expect him to have any equipment himself. Most guides happily wander through inhospitable landscapes with only flip-flops on their feet – don't follow suit. Rates start from around P500 a day but they vary; ask in advance if the guide is expecting you to provide food for him. Certainly the guide will expect a tip, even in the form of a few beers and a meal, for getting you home safely.

nightlife. Baguio's municipal centre – the area around **Burnham Park** – was designed by renowned American architect Daniel Burnham in 1904, and based loosely on Washington DC. The main drag, **Session Road**, is lined with restaurants and shops, while the eye-catching **Baguio Cathedral** stands on a hill above.

Brief history

In the sixteenth century, intrepid **Spanish friars** had started to explore the region, finding a land of fertile valleys, pine-clad hills and mountains, lush vegetation and an abundance of minerals such as copper and gold. Soon more friars, soldiers and fortune-hunters were trekking north to convert the natives to Christianity and profit from the rich natural resources. In the nineteenth century, **colonizing Americans** took over and developed Baguio into a modern city, a showcase recreational and administrative centre from which they could preside over their precious tropical colony without working up too much of a sweat. In 1944, when American forces landed in Leyte, the head of the Japanese Imperial Army, **General Yamashita**, moved his headquarters to Baguio and helped establish a puppet Philippine government there under President José Laurel. In 1945 the city was destroyed and thousands lost their homes as liberating forces flushed out Yamashita and his army. The general quickly fled north into the interior.

The city is also etched on the Filipino consciousness as the site of one of the country's worst natural disasters, the earthquake of July 16, 1990, which measured 7.7 on the Richter Scale and killed hundreds, mostly in the city's vulnerable shanty towns, many of which cling precariously to the sides of steep valleys.

Burnham Park

Despite the efforts of the SM mall the city's centrepiece is still **Burnham Park**, a hilltop version of Rizal Park in Manila with a man-made boating lake at the centre. Even if it's a bit past its prime, the park is an interesting place to take a stroll and to watch the people of Baguio at play: there are boats for rent on the lake and tricycles for kids.

Baguio Cathedral

General Luna Rd • Daily 5am–8pm

Standing imperiously above Session Road, **Baguio Cathedral** is a striking example of "wedding cake Gothic" painted rose pink and with twin spires crowned by delicate minarets. Dating from 1936, it became an evacuation centre during World War II and withstood the US carpet-bombing of the city in 1945 – saving the lives of thousands who sheltered inside. There is a steep stairway to the cathedral from Session Road.

City Market

Magsaysay Ave, at the northern end of Session Rd • Daily 5am–8pm

The **City Market** is one of the liveliest and most colourful in the country, acting as a trading post for farmers and tribes not only from Baguio but also from many of the mountain communities to the north. Bargains include strawberries, which thrive in the temperate north, and you can also buy peanut brittle, sweet wine, honey, textiles, handicrafts and jewellery.

St Louis University Museum of Arts and Culture

Bonifacio St • Mon–Sat 7.30am–noon & 1.30–5pm • Free • ☎ 074 444 8246, ⓦ slu.edu.ph

The **St Louis University Museum of Arts and Culture** is a good place to get a general insight into the history of the north, displaying hundreds of artefacts from the Cordillera including tribal costumes, weapons and fascinating black-and-white photographs of sacrifices and other rituals.

Baguio Mountain Provinces Museum

DOT Complex, Governor Pack Rd • Tues–Sun 9am–5pm • P40 • ☎ 074 444 7541, ⓦ baguiomuseum.org

The **Baguio Mountain Provinces Museum** showcases artefacts of indigenous tribes of the Cordilleras. There are separate displays about each of the major groups, including accessories, implements for rice farming, baskets, musical instruments, woodcarving and traditional dress. Upstairs is an exhibition on the history of Baguio. For an idea of how Baguio has changed, take a look at the set of three scale models of the city centre in 1909, 1928 and 2009.

Wright Park

Leonard Wood Rd, 3km east of the centre • Pony rides P200/30min, P300/hr • Taxi from city centre P60, jeepney P8.50

Wright Park is a popular public space where you can hire a sturdy mountain nag – optionally with a dyed-pink mane – for a quick trot around the perimeter beyond. On the other side of Leonard Wood Road, still within the park, is **The Mansion** (not open to the public). Built in 1908 for American governor-generals to the Philippines and damaged in 1945, it was rebuilt in 1947 as a holiday home for Philippine presidents.

Botanical Gardens

Leonard Wood Rd, 4km east of the centre • Daily 6am–6pm • Free • Taxi from city centre P55, jeepney P8.50

Travelling out of the city centre eastwards on Leonard Wood Road for 4km brings you to the **Botanical Gardens**, also known as the Centennial Park. You can wander through thick vegetation along winding concrete pathways, or join the locals relaxing and enjoying barbecued food at weekends.

Mines View Park

6km east of the centre • Taxi from city centre P85, jeepney P10

Mines View Park has a viewing point overlooking an area that used to be the location of mining operations. To get there you have to make your way past countless souvenir stalls and hawkers – if you ever dreamed of having your photo taken with a sunglasses-wearing St Bernard dog then this is the place to do it. A short walk up the hill from the viewpoint is the **Good Shepherd Convent**, with a store inside the main gate where you can buy products made by the nuns, including strawberry, coconut or *ube* (purple yam) jam and cashew or peanut brittle.

Camp John Hay

Loakan Rd, 5km southeast of Baguio • **Historical Core** Daily 8am–5pm • ☎ 074 444 8358 • P60 **Tree Top Adventure** Daily 8am–5pm •
Canopy Ride P350 • ☎ 074 442 0800, ⓦ treetopadventureph.com **Golf Course** ☎ 074 444 2561 • Taxi from city centre P70

Named after US President Theodore Roosevelt's secretary of war, **Camp John Hay** used to
be a rest and recreational facility for employees of the US military and Department of
Defense. During World War II the property was used by the Japanese as a concentration
camp for American and British soldiers. In 1991 the camp was turned over to the

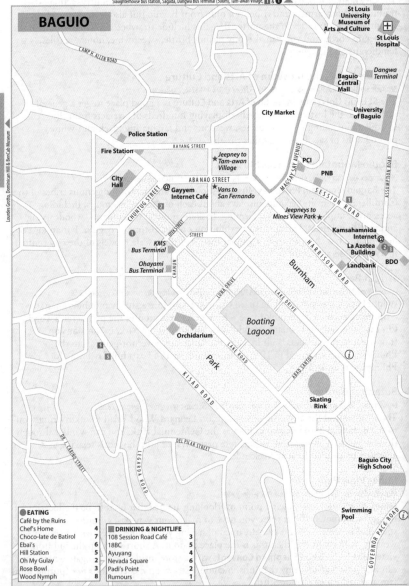

● EATING		■ DRINKING & NIGHTLIFE	
Café by the Ruins	1	108 Session Road Café	3
Chef's Home	4	18BC	5
Choco-late de Batirol	7	Ayuyang	4
Ebai's	6	Nevada Square	6
Hill Station	5	Padi's Point	2
Oh My Gulay	2	Rumours	1
Rose Bowl	3		
Wood Nymph	8		

Philippine government for development into an upmarket country club, with hotels, a **golf course**, private mountain lodges and sundry restaurants and clubhouses.

The expansive, undulating grounds have some nice walks through the pine trees and are also ideal for jogging. Jeepneys can't enter the park itself, so it's best to get a taxi. If you don't have a particular destination in mind then ask to be dropped at the entrance to the **Historical Core**. Here you can buy a ticket to see the Bell House, the holiday residence of the Commanding General of the Philippines, the Bell Amphitheatre and

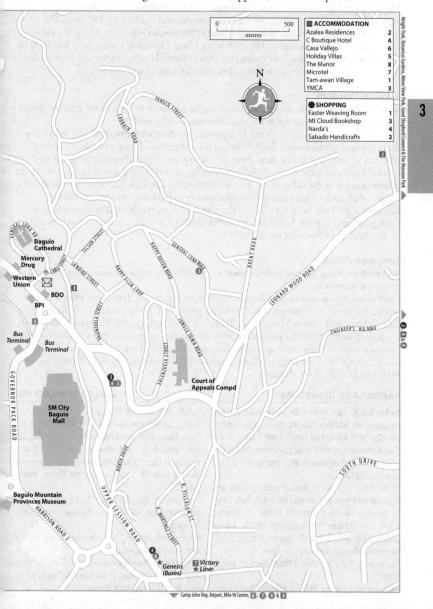

Wright Park, Botanical Gardens, Mines View Park, Good Shepherd Convent & The Mansion Park

0   500
metres

N

■ ACCOMMODATION

Azalea Residences	2
C Boutique Hotel	4
Casa Vallejo	6
Holiday Villas	5
The Manor	8
Microtel	7
Tam-awan Village	1
YMCA	3

● SHOPPING

Easter Weaving Room	1
Mt Cloud Bookshop	3
Narda's	2
Sabado Handicrafts	4

3

YANGCO STREET

LAUBACH ROAD

TECSON STREET

GENERAL LUNA RD

Baguio Cathedral

Mercury Drug

FR. CARLU STREET

SAN DIEGO STREET

HAPPY QUEEN ROAD

HAPPY GLEN LOOP

GENERAL LUNA ROAD

BRENT ROAD

LEONARD WOOD ROAD

Western Union

BDO

BPI

VALENCIA STREET

JUNGLE TOWN ROAD

ENGINEER'S HILL ROAD

Bus Terminal

Bus Terminal

GOVERNOR PACK ROAD

SM City Baguio Mall

Court of Appeals Compd

NOAH DRIVE

Baguio Mountain Provinces Museum

HARRISON ROAD 2

UPPER SESSION ROAD

R. VILLALON ST

Y. MARTINEZ STREET

SOUTH DRIVE

Genesis (Buses)

Victory Liner

the site where General Yamashita formally surrendered to US forces. At weekends, Filipino families congregate close to the entrance to the Historical Core to enjoy picnics. Also close by is the **Tree Top Adventure**, where you can try a canopy ride or join guided walks.

Lourdes Grotto and Dominican Hill

Off Dominican Hill Rd • Taxi from city centre P50, jeepney P8.50

High on a hill in the western part of the city is **Lourdes Grotto**, a Catholic shrine watched over by an image of Our Lady of Lourdes and reached by 252 steps. One kilometre further at the summit of the road is **Dominican Hill**, from where the views across the city are superlative. The crumbling Hotel Diplomat on the peak was built by a Dominican order, then later owned by a controversial entrepreneur and faith healer; it's abandoned and rather eerie today, but you can wander around inside.

BenCab Museum

6km west of the centre, Km 6 Asin Rd, Tadiangan, Tuba, Benguet • Tues–Sun 9am–6pm • P100 • ☎ 074 442 7165, ⓦ bencabmuseum.org • From central Baguio, take a jeepney (P11) in the direction of Asin hot springs or a taxi (around P130)

One of the best art galleries in the Philippines, the **BenCab Museum** is well worth the short trip out of the centre. Built to house the collection of local artist Ben Cabrera, who has a home and studio next door, it's an airy modernist structure with lots of natural light and great views of the surrounding scenery. Two galleries house temporary exhibitions while the other seven contain permanent displays, including anything from Ifugao artefacts and old prints of the Philippines to paintings and sculptures by contemporary Filipino artists. Below the museum is an excellent **café** overlooking a duck pond and organic farm. The beautiful **garden** features cascading waterfalls and an eco-trail to a viewpoint on the hillside.

Tam-awan Village

366C Pinsao Proper • **Village** Daily 7am–6pm **Cultural show** Sat 2–5pm • P50 • ☎ 074 446 2949, ⓦ tam-awanvillage.com • Taxi from city centre P80, jeepney P8.50

On the northwest outskirts of Baguio, 5km from the centre, **Tam-awan Village** is a replica tribal village established in 1996 by a group of Filipino artists, including Ben Cabrera and Jordan Mang-osan. There is a small gallery with changing exhibitions, a gift shop and café, and a cultural show with dancing every Saturday afternoon – you can even stay the night here in a tribal hut (see opposite). Tam–awan means "vantage point" – on a clear evening, you'll see magnificent China Sea sunsets and even the Hundred Islands in the distance.

ARRIVAL AND DEPARTURE

BAGUIO AND AROUND

By bus Though there are a number of terminals, most bus companies use Governor Pack Rd, the Dangwa terminal (off Magsaysay Ave behind Baguio Central mall) or the Slaughterhouse compound on Magsaysay Ave. There is also a Genesis terminal on, and a Victory Liner terminal just off, Upper Session Rd.

Destinations: Chanum St Banaue (KMS: 2 daily; 8hr); Ohayami: daily 9pm; 8hr); Kiangan (KMS: daily 9pm; 7hr).

Destinations: Dangwa terminal Bontoc (JL Lizardo: 6 daily 8am–2.30pm; 5hr); Sagada (JL Lizardo: 7 daily 6.30am–1pm; 7hr); Tabuk (JL Lizardo: 6 daily; 11hr); Tuguegarao (Dangwa Bus: daily 6pm; 12hr).

Destinations: Genesis terminal Manila (Genesis: hourly; 6–8hr).

Destinations: Governor Pack Rd Bolinao (Victory Liner:

5 daily; 5hr); Dagupan (Victory Liner: every 10min; 2hr 30min); Laoag (Partas: hourly; 7–8hr); Manila (Dagupan & Partas: hourly; Philippine Rabbit: every 1–2hr; 6–8hr); San Juan, stopping off in San Fernando (Partas: every 30min; 2hr); Santa Cruz (Victory Liner: hourly; 6hr); Tuguegarao (Dalin & Dalin JD: 3 daily; 12hr); Vigan (Partas: hourly; 5–6hr).

Destinations: Slaughterhouse Bontoc (D'Rising Sun: hourly 6am–4pm; 6hr); Kabayan (Na-Liner: 10am & noon; 3hr 30min).

Destinations: Victory Liner terminal Manila (Victory Liner: every 30min; 6–7hr).

By van A/c vans travel to Kabayan from the Slaughterhouse (hourly; 3hr; P150). Vans to San Fernando (hourly 6am–6pm; 2hr; P100) leave from Abanao St.

INFORMATION

Tourist information The department of tourism is in the Baguio Tourism Complex on Governor Pack Rd (Mon–Fri 7am–6.30pm; ☎074 442 7014, ✉dotregioncar@gmail .com), and there's a smaller city information centre at Burnham Park (Mon–Fri 8am–5pm).

ACCOMMODATION

Hotels in the centre can get quite noisy, so ask for a room away from the road; there are also a number of good choices outside of town in peaceful pine forested areas – a much more pleasant way to experience Baguio than in its traffic-choked centre. You can also stay in traditional huts at the artist-run Tam–awan Village (see below).

Azalea Residences Leonard Wood Loop ☎074 424 8716, ⓦazalea.com.ph. In a quiet location on the northeastern outskirts of the city, these upmarket serviced apartments in a log cabin-inspired hotel include living area, dining room and kitchen facilities. The only downside is that the lower-floor accommodation looks onto a wall – ask for a room on the fourth floor with views across the countryside. P7500

C Boutique Hotel 5 Arellano at Moran, Brgy Gibraltar ☎074 619 0158, ⓦcboutiquehotel.com. A 15min walk from Mines View and Wright Park, this pleasant hotel in a peaceful location has seventeen well-appointed rooms with modern amenities. There are a couple of lounges with wood-burning fireplaces, as well as a restaurant and bar. P3900

★**Casa Vallejo** Upper Session Rd ☎074 424 3397, ⓦcasavallejo-baguio.com. Built in 1909 to house government employees, this Baguio landmark became the city's first hotel in the 1920s. It was one of very few buildings to survive World War II, but by the 1990s it had fallen into disrepair. It reopened in 2010 after extensive renovation with bags of US colonial-era charm; rooms are tasteful, modern and a bargain even in peak season. The windows are not double-glazed, so ask for one away from the road. The *Hill Station* restaurant serves impeccable dishes, and there's also a great bookshop and excellent spa. P2700

Holiday Villas 10 Legarda Rd ☎074 442 6679, ⓦbaguioholidayhotel.com. The apartments here have two bedrooms and a kitchenette, making them a good choice for families. There are also clean doubles that are good value, despite being on the smallish side. P1700

The Manor Camp John Hay ☎074 424 0931, ⓦcamp johnhay.ph. This smart hotel has an enviable location in an alpine setting outside town; surrounded by towering pine trees, it's a great place to relax and enjoy the countryside. Cosy rooms have garden or forest views, and feature modern amenities, wooden furniture and panelled walls. Facilities include a sauna, jacuzzi, gym, piano bar with daily jazz and pop bands, and weekend art activities for children. P5700

Microtel Upper Session Rd ☎074 619 3333, ⓦmicrotel philippines.com. Right behind the Victory Liner terminal, this hotel, with a blue wooden facade, is a good option with neat and tidy rooms set on four floors. The attached restaurant serves Spanish-inspired dishes. P4250

Tam-awan Village 366C Pinsao Proper ☎074 446 2949, ⓦtam–awanvillage.com. An unusual choice featuring accommodation in traditional Ifugao and Kalinga huts that were acquired from the provinces and reassembled at this replica village (see opposite). The huts, all with shared bath, are simple but welcoming, and can sleep up to nine. Note that it can get surprisingly cold. Per person P500

YMCA Post Office Loop ☎074 442 4766. This large, central hostel has spotless twin rooms with flatscreen TVs and single-sex dorms with institutional rows of pine-wood beds crammed in every corner; the maze of echoing corridors gives the place a bit of a soulless feel. There's a large basketball court. Dorms P375; twins P1200

EATING

Baguio has some of the best **restaurants** in the country. There is also a good selection of street food, including a couple of places beside *Casa Vallejo* hotel serving *bulalo* (beef on the bone in a broth), and the usual fast-food outlets in the SM mall.

★**Café by the Ruins** 25 Chuntug St ☎074 442 4010. In a breezy setting with tables dotted around the WWII ruins of the residence of Baguio's first governor, this is one of the city's best restaurants, with excellent organic food prepared with home-grown herbs and served either indoors or in the shady yard. The duck confit with green potatoes (P250) has long been a bestseller; there are home-made breads, pastries, muffins and scones (P50), too. Daily 7am–9pm.

★**Chef's Home** 13 Outlook Drive, Purok 3 ☎0916 444 5756. The Malaysian owner and chef rustles up exceptional Asian fusion dishes embracing Malaysian, Thai and Indian cuisine. Dishes are large enough to share, with most serving two to four; the crispy papaya salad is outstanding (P240). Mon–Sat 11am–2.30pm & 6–8.30pm.

Choco-late de Batirol Gate 2, Igorot Garden, Camp John Hay ☎0915 933 3475. This welcoming open-fronted bamboo café with fairy lights offers nine flavours of hot

3

chocolate (P80) lovingly prepared using recipes based on Spanish traditions. The chocolate is stirred continuously in a jar, a *batirol*, with a wooden stick before being served with a little fanfare. It's best enjoyed with sticky rice wrapped in banana leaf (P64). Daily 8am–9pm.

Ebai's 151 Engineer's Hill, Upper Session Rd ☎ 074 446 9722. The exquisite carrot cake (P68) at this little café was originally baked for the wife of former President Ramos; it's a great little spot to refuel with a slice of cake or a substantial main course of indigenous cuisine (P108). Daily 7am–9pm.

Hill Station Upper Session Rd ☎ 074 424 2734, ⓦ hillstationbaguio.com. Within the *Casa Vallejo* hotel, with a smart but unpretentious dining room and waiting staff in military-style uniforms to reflect Baguio's history as a US hill station. The international menu exclusively features home-made dishes and includes stews from other famous hill stations in countries such as India. There is also a pleasant café/bar with delectable cakes. Daily 7am–11pm.

Oh My Gulay La Azotea Building, Session Rd ☎ 074 446

0108. Hidden upstairs in a shopping mall, this quirky veggie restaurant and art space was designed by renowned Baguio artist Kidlat Tahimik; it's worth coming just to take a peek at the decor – the leafy interior features stone walkways, mismatched furniture, a mock wooden boat and a little pond. Mains P110. Tues–Thurs 11am–8pm, Fri & Sat 11am–9pm, Sun 11am–7pm.

Rose Bowl 88 Upper General Luna Rd ☎ 074 442 4213. This award-winning Cantonese restaurant follows family recipes brought over from China at the beginning of the twentieth century. Dishes are prepared mainly using local products and the fresh fish is transported daily from the beach at San Juan. Dishes serve three to four – try the crispy *pata* (deep fried pork leg; P550). Daily 10am–10pm.

Wood Nymph 36 Military Cut-off Rd ☎ 074 446 0272. One of Baguio's many Korean restaurants, this airy place has been serving the city's Korean community for nearly two decades. The speciality here is seafood – try the seafood soup (P650 for three people). The pork ribs (P250) are great too. Daily 10am–10pm.

DRINKING AND NIGHTLIFE

108 Session Road Café 108 Session Rd. Packed at weekends, this place is a good spot to enjoy a few beers (P60) and live music (daily 5pm–midnight) – anything from country to classical. The American menu features burgers (P55) and buffalo wings (P140). Happy hour 5–7pm. Daily 5pm–1am.

18 BC 16 Legarda Rd. Popular among local and Korean students who flock here at the weekend to socialize en masse. Walls are decorated with wagon wheels and deer-head trophies, but the music is more likely to be acoustic rock than country. Daily 7pm–2am.

Ayuyang Under Baden Powell Inn, 26 Governor Pack Rd. Popular with students and artists, this friendly bar often has live acoustic and reggae music in the evenings, with local bands on Fri nights. Fri 6pm–2am, Sat–Thurs 7pm–midnight.

Nevada Square 2 Loakan Rd. This little square, with a collection of bars and clubs, attracts a student crowd at the weekend, belting out their favourite karaoke and enjoying live bands and DJs. Cover charge P50–100. Daily 7.30pm–3am.

Padi's Point North Rd, Rizal Park ☎ 074 304 5105, ⓦ padispoint.com. Part of a chain with branches across Luzon, this bar has live and loud music until 4am on weekdays and 5am at the weekend. The menu includes a range of local dishes. Happy hour 5–9pm. Daily 5pm–5am.

Rumours 55 Session Rd ☎ 074 619 0152. A straight-forward place to enjoy a drink, without intrusive music or other distractions. There's a better than usual choice of beers (P50) and snacks to enjoy with them. The signature secret-recipe cocktail "Power of Rumours" mixes eight varieties of spirits. Daily 11am–3am.

SHOPPING

Easter Weaving Room 2 Easter Rd, Guisad ☎ 074 442 4972, ⓦ easterweaving.com. Handwoven articles such as rugs, tablemats, wall hangings, textiles, cushion covers and bed linen. You can watch the weavers at work on old hand looms and, if you've got a few weeks to wait, place a personal order. It's on the northwestern outskirts of the city; take a jeepney heading in the direction of Guisad from Kayang St, at the northern end of Burnham Park, or a taxi for around P60. Mon–Sat 8am–5pm.

★**Mt Cloud Bookshop** Casa Vallejo, Upper Session Rd ☎ 074 424 4437, ⓦ mtcloudbookshop.com. This small bookshop has an excellent selection of materials mainly

on the Cordillera region, as well as works by local authors. There are monthly book launches and author talks, too. Daily 10.30am–8pm.

Narda's 151 Upper Session Rd ☎ 074 422 4360, ⓦ nardas.com. The traditional Cordillera Ikat style of weaving has been adapted to contemporary tastes at this shop – choose from a variety of handwoven arts and crafts, including attractive clothes, bags, rugs, linen and tablemats. Daily 8am–7pm.

Sabado Handicrafts 16 Outlook Drive ☎ 074 444 7109. Local artist Greg Sabado displays a wide selection of handicrafts, including beautiful wooden artefacts, as well as furniture. Daily 8am–5pm.

DIRECTORY

Banks and exchange There are plenty of ATMs in the centre and you shouldn't have much trouble finding banks with currency exchange; for emergency cash transfers try the branch of Western Union on Session Rd down from the post office.

Internet access Gayyem Internet Café, Abanao St at Chuntug St (daily 7am–10pm; P15/hr; ☎ 074 424 3772); Kamsahamnida Internet, La Azotea Building, Session Rd (daily 7am–midnight; P15/hr).

Police 24hr police station on Abanao St (☎ 074 300 9230).

Post office At the junction of Session Rd and Governor Pack Rd (Mon–Fri 8am–5pm).

Kabayan and around

An isolated, one-road mountain village 85km north of Baguio, in Benguet province, **KABAYAN** makes a thrilling side trip – although because of the rough road you'll need to spend at least one night. There was no road here until 1960 and no electricity until 1978, and this extended isolation has left the place rural and unspoilt, a good place to experience the culture of the **Ibaloi**. The area around Kabayan is excellent **trekking** country, and climbers are also drawn here for the chance to ascend **Mount Pulag**, the highest peak in Luzon.

Kabayan came to the attention of the outside world in the early twentieth century when a group of **mummies**, possibly dating back as far as 2000 BC, was discovered in the surrounding caves. When the Americans arrived, mummification was discouraged as unhygienic and the practice is thought to have died out. Controversy still surrounds the Kabayan mummies, some of which have disappeared to overseas collectors, sold for a quick buck by unscrupulous middlemen. One was said to have been stolen by a Christian pastor in 1920 and wound up as a sideshow in a Manila circus. Some remain, however, and some have been recovered. Officials know of dozens of mummies in the area, but will not give their locations for fear of desecration. You can, however, see several of them in designated mountaintop **caves**.

Opdas Cave

At the southern end of Kabayan village; follow the signs from the main road • P20 donation

Before heading on to the other burial sites, be sure to visit **Opdas Cave** at the southern end of Kabayan village. It contains around two hundred skulls and bones estimated to be up to a thousand years old, discovered in a pile but now arranged. Nobody knows why they were buried together, but one theory is that they died as a result of an epidemic. Call at the caretaker's house (the green corrugated iron building); a member of the family will open the gate and encourage you to pray to the spirits, asking them to allow you to enter and leave safely.

MAKING A MUMMY

The history of the Kabalan **mummies** is still largely oral. It is even uncertain when the last mummy was created; according to staff at the town's museum, mummification was attempted most recently in 1907 but the wrong combination of herbs was used. It's possible that the last successful mummification was in 1901, of the great-grandmother of former village mayor Florentino Merino.

What is known is the general procedure, which could take up to a year to complete. The body would have been bathed and dressed, then tied upright to a chair with a low fire burning underneath to start the drying process. Unlike in other mummification rituals around the world, the internal organs were not removed. A jar was placed under the corpse to catch the body fluids, which are considered sacred, while elders began the process of peeling off the skin and rubbing juices from native leaves into the muscles to aid preservation. Tobacco smoke was blown through the mouth to dry the internal tissues and drive out worms.

3

National Museum

At the western end of Kabayan beyond the bridge • Mon–Fri 8am–5pm • P50

Kabayan's small branch of the **National Museum** displays the costumes and traditions of the people of Kabayan; exhibits include traditional dress, wild boar skulls, rice wine jars and woven rattan baskets. There is an informative display on centuries-old rituals and beliefs, including burial practices – take a look at the mummy in foetal position inside the coffin.

Tinongchol Burial Rock

3km north of Kabayan • P30; guide P500, including a visit to the National Museum (see above) and Opdas Cave (see p.167) • 4WDs can be arranged at the Pine Cone Lodge (P500)

An hour's hike north of town is the **Tinongchol Burial Rock**, a large rock with deep niches that were carved to inter the mummified dead in coffins. Four of the seven man-made holes contain between five and ten coffins each – to this day it is unclear how the people of Kagayan hollowed these out.

Timbac Cave

1.2km above Kabayan • P30; Ibaloi accredited guide P1000 for up to five people; returning via the Halsema Highway will cost an extra P200 • Outside the wet seasons, 4WDs can be arranged at the Pine Cone Lodge (see opposite) for P2500 (plus an extra P500 if you want to carry on to the Halsema Highway)

It's possible to hike up to see the collection of mummies in **Timbac Cave** and return within the day. It's essential to bring an Ibaloi guide not only to ensure you don't get lost but also to respect local sensibilities: locals believe that unaccompanied outsiders will attract the wrath of the spirits. As one local puts it, "If ever there is a curse, it will not be on you but on us." The tourist office (see below) can arrange an accredited guide.

It's a strenuous four- to five-hour climb to the cave. Take food and drink and aim to set off at around 6am. On the way ask your guide to point out the **Tinongchol Burial Rock**; you'll also see a number of **lakes** and **rice terraces** where farmers grow *kintoman*, an aromatic red rice. Your guide will retrieve the key to Timbac Cave from a caretaker who lives close by, and say the necessary prayers before you enter.

The walk back down to Kabayan takes three hours, or you can walk for an hour or so beyond the cave to the Halsema Highway and flag down a bus (the guide will charge extra for this) directly to Baguio, or head north to Bontoc and Sagada. The last bus will pass around 5pm but don't cut it too fine. It is not recommended that you do this in reverse and approach the cave from the highway, since you risk finding that the caretaker isn't there or offending locals by arriving without a guide.

Bangao Cave

Near Bangao village, 7km north of Kabayan • P30; guide P500 • 4WDs can be arranged at the Pine Cone Lodge (see opposite)

If you don't have time to trek to Timbac Cave, or just want to see as much as possible while in the area, consider visiting the caves around Bangao village. The **Bangao Cave** has a handful of mummies in coffins, although they are in worse condition than those in Timbac. It's a two-hour walk from Kabayan, although you can reduce this to thirty minutes by hiring a 4WD to take you some of the way.

ARRIVAL AND INFORMATION   KABAYAN AND AROUND

By bus NA-Liner buses from Baguio's Slaughterhouse stop along Kabayan's main road, departing Baguio daily at 10am & noon (3–4hr), returning to Baguio daily at 8am & 11.30am.

By van Regular vans connect Kabayan and Baguio, stopping along Kabayan's main road (hourly; 3hr; P150).

Tourist information The tourist information point is at the municipal hall (Mon–Fri 8am–5pm; ☎ 0917 521 5830, ✉ mysticalkabayan@yahoo.com).

Services There is a branch of Rural Bank (Mon–Fri 8am–3pm, Sat 9am–noon) but no ATM at the time of writing, although there are plans to get one. Make sure to bring enough pesos from Baguio. There are no internet cafés.

ACCOMMODATION

Municipal Guesthouse Near the Municipal Hall ☏ 0917 521 5830, ✉ mysticalkabayan@yahoo.com. Small guesthouse with just two single-sex dorms (sleeping six) with pinewood beds and shared bathrooms (no hot water). The walls are dotted with pictures of mummies and the surrounding area. There's a guest kitchen. **P200**

Pine Cone Lodge Main road, Kabayan ☏ 0929 327 7749. As the name suggests, this lodge is decked out in pine; the clean tiled rooms are spacious and all have private bath, and the living area with fireplace gives the place a cosy touch. **P500**

EATING AND DRINKING

There are half a dozen sari-sari stores in Kabayan where you can get snacks, but only a couple of places to eat a meal. Local officials have banned the sale (but not the consumption) of alcohol.

Brookside Café Main road, Kabayan. The friendly owner at this pleasant café with wooden benches rustles up simple dishes including soups, noodles and rice and meat (P80), as well as sugary Benguet coffee that is just the thing on a cold Cordillera morning. Mon–Sat 6am–6pm, Sun 6–8am & noon–6pm.

Torena's Main road, Kabayan. This family-run place makes breakfast to order; otherwise, meals are prepared daily and laid out on the table, with customers picking and choosing what they fancy. They can happily oblige any dietary request – just let them know in advance. Meals P80. Daily 7am–8pm.

Mount Pulag

Standing 2922m above sea level, **Mount Pulag** is the highest mountain in Luzon and even experienced climbers are required to take a guide. The terrain is steep, there are gorges and ravines, and in the heat of the valleys below, it's easy to forget it can be bitterly cold and foggy on top. Despite what villagers may flippantly say, don't underestimate the difficulty of this mountain. It's essential to treat the area with respect: a number of indigenous communities including the Ibaloi, Kalanguya, Kankanay and Karaos live on Pulag's slopes and regard the mountain as a sacred place. They have a rich folklore about ancestral spirits inhabiting trees, lakes and mountains, and while they're friendly towards climbers you should stick to the trails.

The two best **trails** start from **Ambangeg** and **Kabayan**. Less used are the **Mountain Lakes Trail**, an hour's drive north of Kabayan, where you ascend Mount Tabayok and camp at the lakeside, and the **Enchanted Trail** starting in Tawangan, a two-hour drive

---

THE IGOROTS

The tribes of the Cordillera – often collectively known as the **Igorots** ("mountaineers") – resisted assimilation into the Spanish Empire for three centuries. Although the colonizers brought some material improvements, such as to the local diet, they also forced the poor to work to pay off debts, burned houses, cut down crops and introduced smallpox. The saddest long-term result of the attempts to subjugate the Igorots was subtler, however – the creation of a distinction between highland and lowland Filipinos. The peoples of the Cordillera became minorities in their own country, still struggling today for representation and recognition of a lifestyle that the Spanish tried to discredit as unChristian and depraved. The word Igorot was regarded as derogatory in some quarters, although in the twentieth century there were moves to "reclaim" the term and it is still commonly used.

Though some Igorots did convert to Christianity, many are still at least partly animists and pray to a hierarchy of **anitos**. These include deities that possess shamans and speak to them during seances, spirits that inhabit sacred groves or forests, personified forces of nature and generally any supernatural apparition. Offerings are made to benevolent *anitos* for fertility, good health, prosperity, fair weather and success in business (or, in the olden days, tribal war). Evil *anitos* are propitiated to avoid illness, crop failure, storms, accidents and death. Omens are also carefully observed: a particular bird seen upon leaving the house might herald sickness, for example, requiring that appropriate ceremonies are conducted to forestall its portent. If the bird returns, the house may be abandoned.

north of Kabayan. Whichever way you choose to climb Pulag, take a tent and expect to **spend the night** on top.

The Ambangeg trail

Ambangeg is a regular stop on the Baguio to Kabayan bus route; ask the driver to drop you at the visitor centre in the Bokod barangay of Ambangeg. It's a two- to three-hour walk from here to the **ranger station** where the hike officially begins, and where you can hire guides; you can also get a lift to the ranger station on a motorcycle (1hr; around P250). It is best to spend the night at the furthest campsite, about three hours from the ranger station, and ascend to the summit for dawn the next day. If you arrive in Ambangeg too late to ascend, staff at the visitor centre can find you a bed in the state university cottage or a private home.

The Kabayan trail

The trail from **Kabayan**, known as the **Akiki** or **Killer Trail**, starts 2km south of Kabayan on the Baguio–Kabayan road. As the name suggests this is a more difficult route than the Ambangeg trail, taking at least seven hours to reach the saddle camp near the summit. The next morning you will go to the peak, then descend.

INFORMATION   **MOUNT PULAG**

Trail information Before coming to Mount Pulag it's a good idea to contact Emerita Albas, the Protected Area's Superintendent, for up-to-date information on which trails are most accessible at any given time of year (☎ 0919 631 5402, ✉ ambangeg@gmail.com).

Registration and fees You'll need to register and pay an entrance fee (P750), camping fee (P50), green fee (P50) and local government fee (P30). This can be done at the visitor centre in the Bokod barangay of Ambangeg or at

the municipal hall in Kabayan (see p.168).

Guides You can hire a guide for the Ambangeg trail at the ranger station (P500 per group of up to five). The tourist office in Kabayan can arrange guides for the Kabayan trail (P2000 for a group of up to five).

Mountain Lakes and Enchanted trails Contact Kabayan tourism officer Berry Sangao Jr (☎ 0917 521 5830, ✉ berrysangaojr@gmail.com) in advance to arrange either of these routes.

Bontoc and around

BONTOC lies on the banks of the Chico River about an hour east of Sagada. Primarily used by tourists as a transport hub, the town is also a good base for **trekking** and has easy access to the beautiful Maligcong rice terraces. The main road from Baguio to Bontoc is the **Halsema Highway** or "Mountain Trail", a narrow, serpentine gash in the side of the Cordillera that's sometimes no more than a rocky track with vertical cliffs on one side and a sheer drop on the other. Although the surface of the road has been greatly improved in recent years, it can still be an uncomfortable trip by public transport as some of the buses are crowded and not especially well maintained. The views, though, are marvellous, especially as you ascend out of Baguio beyond La Trinidad and pass through deep gorges lined with vegetable terraces.

Bontoc Museum

Next to the post office close to the town plaza • Mon–Sat 8am–noon & 1–5pm, Sun 8am–noon & 1–3.30pm • P60 • ☎ 0918 576 2170

The one sight to see in Bontoc itself is the **Bontoc Museum**, which includes wonderful artefacts and a collection of centuries-old Chinese porcelain and stoneware traded from different parts of the Cordillera region. Take a look at the disturbing photograph of a headhunting victim, whose corpse is being carried away for burial as his head is presented as a trophy around the village. There's a reconstruction of a traditional Bontoc village on the grounds. The shop sells items including handmade jewellery, books and CDs of traditional music.

HIKES AROUND BONTOC

There are a number of **mountain trails** around Bontoc, snaking their way through beautiful rice paddy scenery. Most places are far off the tourist radar, and you probably won't see any Westerners in any of the towns; accommodation is basic, but it's worth heading this way if you want to really get a taster of life in Mountain Province.

MALIGCONG

Nearly 7km north of Bontoc, the stone-walled rice terraces around **Maligcong village** are at their best in June and July immediately before the harvest. From the point where public transport stops, a path descends into a valley and follows the contour of the terraces to Maligcong. There's a friendly homestay (see p.172) and a sari-sari store here, but no café so it's best to bring your own food. Jeepneys to Maligcong from Bontoc (8am, noon, 2.30pm, 4.30pm & 5.30pm; 30min; P20) leave from behind the commercial centre; the last return journey is at around 4pm.

MAINIT

From Maligcong it is a three-hour trek northwest through scenic rice paddies to **Mainit** ("Ma-i-nit"), a village known for its hot sulphurous springs, where you can also overnight (see p.172). You could also get to Mainit on a jeepney from Back Street in Bontoc (daily 1pm & 3pm; 1hr 15min; P35); the return trips are at 7.30am and 8am.

ALAB PETROGLYPH AND GANGA CAVE

A huge rock etched with drawings of humans with bows and arrows, the **Alab Petroglyph** is at the end of a two-hour hike uphill from the barangay of **Alab**, 9km south of Bontoc on the Halsema Highway. Although it was declared a national cultural treasure in 1975, little is known about who created these carvings or why. An hour further along is the **Ganga Cave**, a burial cave containing coffins and jars of bones. You'll need to find a guide in Alab for either destination – ask around for Ofelia Lopez, a reputable tour guide. Regular jeepneys to Alab (hourly; 25min; P25) leave from in front of Bontoc's market.

BARLIG, KADACLAN AND NATONIN

Three villages east of Bontoc are well off the normal tourist route, but their wonderful rice terraces are certainly worth the trip. The closest village to Bontoc is **Barlig**, 40km east, which is also the starting point for a trek up Mount Amuyao (2702m). The trek can be done in a day (guides P1500), or you can continue on to Batad (see p.182), 12km south, making it a two-day trip (guides P3000) – ask about guides at the Barlig town hall. There are two no-frills lodges in town (see p.172). Rarely visited by tourists, **Kadaclan**, 44km east of Bontoc, and **Natonin**, 74km east of Bontoc, are situated among beautiful scenery and are ideal for getting away from it all for a day or two; both have basic accommodation (see p.172). Jeepneys to Barlig (daily 1pm, 2pm & 3pm; 2hr; P80), Kadaclan (daily 1pm & 2pm; 5hr; P140) and Natonin (daily 11am; 6hr; P200) leave from Loc-ong Road beside the Episcopal Church in Bontoc.

ARRIVAL AND INFORMATION

BONTOC AND AROUND

By bus GL Lizardo buses arrive at Circle Station in Bontoc beside the commercial centre, while D'Rising Sun buses stop behind the Municipal Hall and Florida Cable Tours leave passengers halfway up the main drag. Local buses to and from Tabuk and Tinglayan stop at Lower Caluttit opposite Bontoc's Polytechnic College.

Destinations Baguio (GL Lizardo: 8am, 9am, 10am, 11am, 1pm & 2.30pm; 5hr 30min; D'Rising Sun: hourly 6am–4pm; 5hr 30min); Manila (Cable Bus: 1 daily; 12hr); Tabuk (daily 9am; 5hr); Tinglayan (daily 9am; 3hr).

By jeepney Jeepneys for Sagada (hourly 8.30am–5.30pm; 45min; P45) leave from outside the *Walter*

Clapp Inn just off Bontoc's main drag. A daily jeepney to Tabuk (daily 1pm; 5hr; P230) stopping off at Tinglayan (2–3hr; P120) leaves from Lower Caluttit opposite the Polytechnic College.

By van Vans from Bontoc to Banaue (hourly 7.30am–1.30pm; 2hr; P150) leave from beside Cooperative Bank.

Tourist information The municipal tourist office is by the Municipal Hall in Bontoc (Mon–Fri 8am–5pm; ☎0907 489 7663, ⊛bontoctourism.com), while the provincial tourist office is in the Provincial Capitol Building (Mon–Fri 8am–5pm; ☎0930 652 5598, ✉mtprovtourismoffice @yahoo.com).

KILLING ME SOFTLY

One Mountain Province delicacy, served in many restaurants, is **pinikpikan**, a chicken dish that translates as "killing me softly". The preparation involves beating the bird's wings and neck with a stick before it is killed in the belief that the beating brings blood to the surface, making the meat more tender and tasty. Once dead, the chicken is put on an open fire to burn off the feathers and is then mixed with cured pork; the burning of feathers and the blending of two types of meat adds to the flavour of the dish. When performing rituals, mountain tribes traditionally eat the head and the innards for good fortune and good health, the day after the chicken is butchered.

ACCOMMODATION AND EATING

BONTOC

Archog's Hotel Samoki ☏0918 328 6908, ⊕archogs hotel.com. Each named after Bontoc's numerous neighbourhoods, the simple rooms here come with cable TV while the public spaces are brightened up with framed, handwoven textiles. The restaurant offers chicken (P100), beef (P140), seafood (P130) and noodles (P95). Free wi-fi. **P600**

Cable Café Halfway up the main drag ☏0918 521 6790. Bontoc's only nightlife venue, where folk and country bands take centre stage daily at 6pm. Enjoy the mellow tunes with a beer (P50) or a Filipino meal (P100). Daily 8am–10pm.

Ridgebrooke Hotel Samoki ☏0930 795 7117, ⊕ ridgebrooke_hotel@yahoo.com.ph. Beyond the uninspiring concrete facade, this hotel has a pleasant spot of greenery at the back with a few nipa huts where guests can enjoy their dinner – the restaurant itself, decorated with woven fabrics, wickerwork, carabao skulls and a few potted plants, serves probably the best food in town. The tiled rooms are spacious but simple, with a desk, TV and small wardrobe. **P500**

MALIGCONG

Maligcong Homestay ☏0915 546 3557. Small homestay run by a friendly couple with two comfy little rooms with a couple of beds in each. Breakfast (P35) consists of lovely home-made oatmeal bars, and the owner can also rustle up meals (P100) upon request – just let her know a few hours in advance. There are pretty views of the rice terraces from the breakfast table. **P600**

MAINIT

Geston Minerals Spring Resort ☏0907 163 3042, ⊕gestonhotsprings.com. Run by a friendly woman, this green building has brightly painted rooms off a maze of narrow corridors. There are also two thatched cottages, built from stone and dried grass, giving onto four hot pools of varying temperatures – perfect for a soak after a long day's hike. An extra P250 (to cover the costs of gas) gives you access to a rustic kitchen with stove. **P700**

BARLIG

Halfway Inn No phone. The seven tiny rooms at this simple place have wooden floorboards and spindly little desks; there's no hot water in the communal bathrooms but staff will happily boil a pot or two for you. There are pretty views from the terrace, and a restaurant serving very basic grub including hamburgers (P35), pancit (P30) and ice cream sticks (P10). **P400**

KADACLAN

Kadaclan Homestay ☏0948 710 9097. The owner boasts that his town is the "Shangri-La of the edge", and is hugely proud that the country's former President Gloria Macapagal-Arroyo visited this very homestay. Rooms are located in simple cottages, and guests have access to the kitchen. **P400**

NATONIN

Cullalading Lodge Natonin centre. No-frills lodge offering simple rooms, some with bunks. There's no hot water, but staff can provide a heater to warm up just enough water for a quick wash. **P400**

Sagada

The small town of **SAGADA**, 160km north of Baguio, has long attracted curious visitors. Part of the appeal derives from its famous **hanging coffins** and a labyrinth of **caves** used by the ancients as burial sites. But Sagada also has a reputation as a remote and idyllic hideaway where people live a simple life well away from civilization. The landscape here is almost alpine and the inhabitants are mountain people, their faces shaped not by the sun and sea of the lowlands, but by the thin air and sharp glare of altitude. Sagada only began to open up as a destination when it got electricity in the

CLOCKWISE FROM TOP LEFT EAST COAST, BATAN (P.185); IFUGAO WOMEN; SUMAGING CAVE (P.171) >

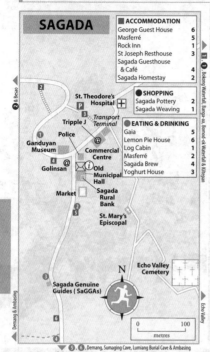

SAGADA

ACCOMMODATION
George Guest House	6
Masferré	5
Rock Inn	1
St Joseph Resthouse	3
Sagada Guesthouse & Café	4
Sagada Homestay	2

SHOPPING
Sagada Pottery	3
Sagada Weaving	1

EATING & DRINKING
Gaia	5
Lemon Pie House	6
Log Cabin	1
Masferré	2
Sagada Brew	4
Yoghurt House	3

St. Theodore's Hospital

Transport Terminal

Tripple J

Police

Ganduyan Museum

Commercial Centre

Golinsan

Old Municipal Hall

Market

Sagada Rural Bank

St. Mary's Episcopal

Echo Valley Cemetery

N

Sagada Genuine Guides (SaGGAs)

0 100 metres

Demang, Sumaging Cave, Lumiang Burial Cave & Ambasing

& Besao

Bokong Waterfall, Banga-an, Bontoc-ok Waterfall & Kiltepan

Echo Valley

Demang & Ambasing

early 1970s, and intellectuals – internal refugees from the Marcos dictatorship – flocked here to write and paint. They didn't produce much of note, perhaps because they spent, it is said, much of their time drinking *tapuy* (the local rice wine). European hippies followed, as did the military, who thought the *turistas* were supplying funds for an insurgency.

There isn't a lot to do in town, although there are plenty of **activities** in the surrounding area. Other than that there's scope for just hanging out, settling down in the evenings by a log fire in one of the wooden cafés or restaurants. With so much fresh fruit and veg grown nearby, the **food** in Sagada is among the best in the country, with lots of veggie choices – something of a rarity in the Philippines. A **curfew** means you can't drink after 9pm, but almost everyone has gone to bed by then anyway.

Ganduyan Museum

Town centre • Opening hours vary • P25; 20min guided tours may be available for a donation • ☎ 0921 273 8097

Set up and run by elderly Christina Aven, the wonderful little **Ganduyan Museum** displays her collection of Igorot artefacts. It's worth asking her for a guided tour, although given her frail health this is not always possible. Among the objects on display are intricate strung-bead necklaces made with snake vertebrae, traditional kitchenware and a collection of spears used for defence.

Demang

If you have time then it's worth wandering down to the village of **Demang**, reached from a turning on the right just beyond the *George Guest House*. The village is older than Sagada and remains practically untouched by tourism. It's a quiet residential area with several *dap-ay* (stone circles where community matters are resolved).

ARRIVAL AND INFORMATION   **SAGADA**

By bus and jeepney The transport terminal is a small market square opposite the commercial centre, close to the main junction. GL Lizardo buses serve Baguio (hourly 5am–1pm; 5–6hr). Jeepneys run to and from Bontoc (hourly 6.30am–1pm; 40min; P45). For Banaue, take a jeepney to Bontoc and change there.

Environmental fee All visitors to Sagada must register and pay an environmental fee (P30), payable at the tourist information centre.

Tourist information There's a small tourist information centre (7am–5pm; ☎ 0905 513 7626) in the old town hall.

Tours The tourist information centre has a list of guided tours with fixed prices, as does the privately owned Sagada Genuine Guides (daily 6am–7pm; ☎ 0912 367 2150, ⓦ saggas.org) close to *Yoghurt House* (see p.176). In addition to adventure activities (see box opposite), North Luzon Outdoor Centre (see box opposite) offers excellent custom-made and off-the-beaten-track tours in the region.

ACCOMMODATION

Most of the village's **guesthouses** – and restaurants – are on the main road, which runs through the town centre past the market, the town hall, the municipal buildings and the police station. Guesthouses are on the whole great value. The town gets packed out at Christmas and Easter, so if you're planning to visit at these times try to book ahead.

ACTIVITIES IN SAGADA

Sagada offers a host of thrilling outdoor **activities**, including **treks** through remote mountain villages and secluded valleys. The most reliable company for adventure sports is the American-run **North Luzon Outdoor Centre** (☎0919 698 8361, ⊕luzonoutdoors.com).

TREKKING

One of the most popular hikes is to see the **hanging coffins** in **Echo Valley**. It's only a 25-minute walk to the coffins, and it can be done alone with a map (souvenir shops sell sketch maps for around P25), but there are numerous paths and it isn't unknown for people to get lost. On the whole, it's better to take a guide (P200/group) who can also fill you in on local history and traditions. The coffins can also be visited as part of the popular three-hour Central Sagada Eco-Tour (P600/group) – ask at the Sagada tourist information centre (see opposite). After the coffins, the path takes you along a short stretch of an underground river at Latang Cave and ends at the **Bokong Waterfall** on the eastern edge of Sagada, where you can swim. The waterfall can also be reached from town without a guide in about half an hour, although it's easy to miss the steps on the left about 500m beyond Sagada Weaving. Other guided hikes offered by the tourist office and Sagada Genuine Guides (see opposite) include a walk to the **Bomod-ok Waterfall**, rice terraces and villages north of Sagada (3hr); a dawn trip to a scenic area of rice terraces known as **Kiltepan** (1hr 30min); and a trek on **Mount Ampacao** (3–4hr).

CAVING

Caving in Sagada's deep network of limestone channels and caverns is exhilarating but potentially dangerous. Many caves are slippery and have deep ravines. A small number of tourists have been killed, so it's essential to hire a reliable, accredited **guide**.

The most commonly visited cave is **Sumaging** (P500 per four visitors, plus P350 for transport), also known as Big Cave, a 45-minute walk south of Sagada. The chambers and rock formations inside are eerie and immense, named after things they resemble – the Cauliflower, the Rice Granary and such like. Guides with lanterns will take you on a descent through a series of tunnels you'll only be able to get through by crawling, ending in a pool of clear water where you can swim. Ideally you should wear trekking sandals, but otherwise shoes can be left at an appropriate point and the final sections negotiated barefoot.

Like many caves in the area, Sumaging was once a burial cave, although there are no coffins or human remains there now. However, a standard caving itinerary will also include a visit to the entrance of **Lumiang Burial Cave**, a short walk south of Sagada and then down a steep trail into the valley. Around a hundred old coffins are stacked in the entrance. Pointing at them is considered the worst kind of bad luck; lizards, on the other hand, are auspicious – you'll see their images carved onto some of the coffins.

Lumiang is also the starting point for the **Cave Connection** trip (P800 for one or two people, P400 for each additional person; transport P400), which heads through passages linking it to Sumaging. It's a three- to four-hour excursion and not for the faint-hearted; it might be best to try Sumaging first. At points you'll need to descend a few metres without ropes, jamming your limbs against the rock walls and edging your way down.

RAFTING

Rafting is possible on the **Chico River** from July until early January, although at the beginning of the season it may only be possible to raft the upper sections. October and November see the most pleasant weather, but the highest water is in December and early January, making it possible to go further downstream. You normally spend 1hr 30min–2hr in the water (P4500/ person for four or fewer, P3000 for five or more). If there are just two of you they might be able to offer a bare-bones trip as a training exercise for their team, at P3500/person. Alternatively, they will try to add you onto a larger group.

MOUNTAIN BIKING

The mountainous landscape around Sagada offers rough terrain and remote trails that are ideal for **mountain biking**. Most tracts are steep and technical, and mainly suited to experienced individuals. Some back roads provide less technical riding, but there are still extended climbs. The cool mountain temperatures, fresh clean air and scenic beauty make this one of the country's best spots to explore on two wheels.

George Guest House ☎0920 948 3133, ✉george _inn05@yahoo.com. A popular choice among travellers, with clean rooms with private showers and hot water; they also have an annexe down the hill with three comfortable cottages sleeping six (P1200) to twelve (P1500), all with kitchen, living area, TV and fireplace. P600

★**Masferré** ☎0918 341 6164, ⊛masferre.ph. One of Sagada's best options right in the centre, offering spotless cosy rooms with pine wood furniture and private bath. There's also a large family option with three connecting rooms, and a good restaurant (see below). Rates include breakfast. Free wi-fi. P1800

★**Rock Inn** Just over 2km east of town ☎0920 909 5899, ⊛rockfarmsagada.com. Set on four verdant hectares with an orange grove, this great place allows guests to pick their own fruit (P50), as well as veggies from the garden. The cosy rooms are in a large building with wooden furnishings, and there's a spacious attic dorm, too. The airy restaurant serves dishes using fresh local produce. Dorm P300; doubles P1500

St Joseph Resthouse ☎0918 559 5934, ⊛stjoseph sagada.com. Converted from a convent and still owned by the Anglican church, this guesthouse has rooms named after the apostles. The cheaper rooms, in a separate block, are very basic, while those in the main building have more character and offer private bath. There are also some cottages (P1700) sprinkled along a grassy slope, the largest of which sleeps eight (P3500). P500

Sagada Guesthouse & Café ☎0921 969 4053. Not to be confused with the much cosier *Sagada Homestay*, this place, a stone's throw away from the bus terminal, has simple economy rooms with spongy beds and shared bathroom, as well as more comfortable doubles. There's a little terrace, though it overlooks the noisy road. P500

★**Sagada Homestay** ☎0919 702 8380, ✉sagada homestay@yahoo.com.ph. This friendly, welcoming homestay offers neat and tidy rooms with or without private bath. There are a couple of lounge areas perfect to meet other travellers, as well as a guest kitchen. There's wi-fi in the main building, and laundry available. P600

EATING AND DRINKING

Gaia ☎0949 137 6777. A few hundred metres from the entrance to Sumaging Cave, this wonderful restaurant offers inventive vegetarian dishes including *miki mi na* – squash noodles sautéed with green beans, carrots and mushrooms (P120). The healthy food here is mainly organic, and is served on a covered patio with terrific views over the rice terraces. Daily 11am–7pm.

Lemon Pie House ☎0907 782 0360. On the southern side of town, this place is renowned for its lemon meringue pie (P30) that customers enjoy at low wooden tables, all designed and assembled by the owner-cum-carpenter. Between March and May they also bake a great blueberry pie using local fresh fruits. Daily 6am–8.30pm.

★**Log Cabin** ☎0920 520 0463. Up the hill beyond the *Sagada Guesthouse*, the *Log Cabin* does some of the best food in town. The welcoming wooden interior is warm and cosy, and the crackling fireplace further adds to the homely atmosphere. Sat evenings see a popular buffet (P390) with fresh ingredients bought from the market, while on other days there's an à la carte menu with a focus on French dishes. Reserve in the morning if you plan to dine in the evening; for the buffet you should reserve a couple of days

in advance. Daily 6–9pm.

Masferré ☎0918 341 6164, ⊛masferre.ph. It's worth coming here to take a look at the wonderful set of black-and-white photographs of Sagada and various indigenous mountain cultures taken by Eduardo Masferré in the late 1930s and early 1950s. The Western menu includes popular super-subs (P170) and sandwiches (P150), as well as burgers and steaks (both P200). Daily 6am–9pm.

★**Sagada Brew** ☎0917 808 7833. This new addition to Sagada's dining scene has really hit the spot; the delectable home-made brownies (P20) are worth every peso, and they even serve proper Italian-style coffee – try the caramel macchiato (P120). The menu includes soups (P80), sandwiches made with freshly baked focaccia (P150) and tasty pasta dishes. Daily 7am–9pm.

Yoghurt House ☎0908 112 8430. A popular place with travellers, this wood cabin offers hearty breakfasts and home-made yoghurt – try the hiker's delight (banana pancake with yoghurt and home-made bread; P180). Main dishes (P200) are pretty good too, which you can enjoy on the narrow balcony as you watch life go by. Daily 7.30am–9pm.

SHOPPING

Sagada Pottery A 15min walk west of the centre. High-quality stoneware. One of the potters will demonstrate their craft for P100, and for another P100 you can have a go yourself. Contact Siegrid Anne Bangyay (☎0919 671 9875) if you wish to visit in the morning. Daily 1–5pm.

Sagada Weaving Nangonogan ☎0919 557 1431. A short walk east of the centre. Here you can buy fabrics

and accessories produced using traditional tribal designs. More than half a dozen people work at sewing machines in the shop itself, while next door you can see the weaving being done on wooden looms. It's a good place to pick up a gift such as a *bahag* (loincloth), an exquisitely hand-loomed piece of long cloth wrapped around a man's middle but increasingly bought by tourists as a throw or table runner. Daily 7am–6pm.

DIRECTORY

Banks and exchange Though there is a branch of the Sagada Rural Bank in town (Tues–Sat 8.30am–5pm), its ATM currently only accepts local cards and there is no currency exchange. Make sure to bring enough pesos.

Hospital For minor ailments you can visit the Municipal Health Office (Mon–Fri 8am–5pm); there's also one small hospital, St Theodore's, on the northeastern edge of the village.

Internet access There are a few small internet cafés in town, such as Tripple J in the commercial centre (daily 8am–7.30pm; P20/hr) and Golinsan on the other side of the road from the tourist office (daily 8am–7pm; P30/hr).

Police Next to the old town hall (24hr; ☎ 0939 918 7127).

Post office In the old town hall (daily 8am–5pm).

Kalinga province

The mountains, rice fields and villages in **Kalinga province** rarely see visitors, never mind foreign tourists. This is real frontier travel, with massive potential for hiking and climbing. Outside the towns of **Tinglayan** and **Tabuk**, the only accommodation is in simple lodges or local homes, the only shops are roadside stores, and electricity is a rarity so make sure you bring a good torch. Note, too, that there are no banks or internet access in Tinglayan.

The Kalinga, once fierce **headhunters**, are remembered for their indomitable spirit and their refusal to be colonized. Most Kalinga communities live on levelled parts of steep mountain slopes, where a small shrine called a *bodaya* guards the entrance to the village. You could also ask your guide (see box below) about visiting a **tattoo artist**, many of whom still work using traditional materials and designs; it may even be possible to have a tattoo yourself (from P500 for a small design).

Tinglayan

The town of **TINGLAYAN**, about 50km from Bontoc and 60km from Tabuk, is well placed if you want to explore Kalinga province. From here you can strike out on **mountain trails** carved by the Spanish when they tried, and failed, to bring the Kalinga people into the Catholic fold. Trails pass through tribal villages and rice terraces at Lubo and Mangali, to the crater of the extinct volcano Mount Sukuok, and to a number of mountain lakes including Bonnong and Padcharao. Rice is planted twice a year around Tinglayan, and the fields are at their greenest from March to April and September to October.

Lubuagan

They don't see many tourists in **LUBUAGAN**, 18km north of Tinglayan on the road to Tabuk, but it makes for a worthwhile stop. The town itself has a makeshift air, lined with grey concrete buildings and with livestock wandering in the street, but it's beautifully located amid rice terraces. Remarkably, it was the capital of the free Philippines for 35 days in 1900, when the revolutionary President Aguinaldo established his headquarters in the town before being forced to flee the US army.

The barangay of Mabilong, east of the centre, is known for its **textiles** and you can arrange to visit one of the women who weave at home, sitting on the floor using

---

HIKING IN KALINGA: GUIDES

Wherever you go hiking in Kalinga you'll need a **guide**; essential not only to avoid getting lost but also to ensure that you respect local sensibilities. Occasionally there are disputes – over water rights, for instance – that result in violence, and a guide will stop you stumbling into any areas where tensions might be high. Law and order in the province still relies very much on tribal pacts (*bodong*) brokered by elders. Staff in Tinglayan's municipal building will usually refer you to Victor Baculi, the former barangay captain of nearby Luplupa. Rates are not fixed and could be anything from P500 to P1000 per day.

> ### RAFTING THROUGH THE RICE TERRACES
>
> The area around Tabuk offers excellent **rafting** opportunities on the Chico River, which snakes its way through spectacular rice terrace scenery. The most reliable company is **Chico River Quest** (☎ 0917 750 2913, ⓦ chicoriverquest.com), which runs trips for all levels – they have seven rafts and use one or two guides per raft. The prime rafting season is July through to October; trips between October and December are dependent on rainfall.
>
> The best run for **beginners** starts at the confluence of the Pasil and Chico rivers, and lasts about two hours (P2000/person for a minimum of five people, including transport and food). More experienced rafters should ask about a longer run which starts upriver in Tinglayan (4–6hr; P6000/person for a minimum of five). This trip also allows you to stop off halfway down for a one-hour canyon hike.

rudimentary hand looms. Ask at the **town hall** to arrange a visit, or for advice about hiking routes and **guides**. You might also ask about the **cultural village**, around thirty minutes from the town, where traditional dance performances occasionally take place.

Tabuk

While it has little to see, the agricultural town and provincial capital of **TABUK**, 50km north of Tinglayan, offers a surprisingly decent choice of accommodation and the only internet and banks in the region. The town serves as a base and jumping-off point for trekking excursions, visits to tribal tattoo artists and **rafting** on the nearby Chico River.

Ryan's Farm

Mapaoay, Ipil, 6km north of Tabuk • P50 • ☎ 0916 755 7078 • A tricycle from Tabuk will cost around P70–100

While in Tabuk, take the time to visit **Ryan's Farm**, owned by Corazon and Jeremy Ryan. They have a prawn hatchery and fishponds, and experiment with vermiculture (worm composting) and organic agriculture, but most of all it's just pleasant to enjoy their conversation – possibly over a glass of home-made *bugnay* (local berry) wine. They can also prepare a meal and possibly even put you up for the night if you call in advance.

ARRIVAL AND INFORMATION   KALINGA PROVINCE

In the **dry season** Tinglayan, Tabuk and Lubuagan can be reached by jeepneys from Bontoc, although services in this area are anything but regular and it's a bumpy road, so the trip can take many hours. In the **rainy season** (particularly July–Oct) it may be impossible to travel between Tinglayan and Tabuk due to the road conditions, in which case Tinglayan is best approached from Bontoc while Tabuk is reached via Tuguegarao.

TINGLAYAN
By bus There's one daily bus from Bontoc to Tabuk that stops off in Tinglayan around 11am (2hr). Heading back the other way from Tabuk to Bontoc, local buses stop in Tinglayan around 11am and noon (2hr).
By jeepney A couple of daily jeepneys run from Bontoc to Tinglayan (2hr; P100) and a handful of jeepneys between Tabuk and Bontoc pass through
Services There are no banks or internet access.

LUBUAGAN
By bus A couple of local buses from Bontoc to Tabuk stop off in Lubuagan between 11am and 1pm (2hr 30min).
By jeepney Jeepneys connect Tabuk and Lubuagan (1hr 30min; P80). There are a couple of morning jeepneys

from Bontoc and Tinglayan that pass through Lubuagan in the mornings.
Services There are no banks or internet access.

TABUK
By bus From Manila, Victory Liner buses run to Tabuk (12hr), while if coming from Baguio (10hr) you can catch a GL Lizardo. There's also one daily bus connecting Bontoc to Tabuk (6am; 4hr). Leaving town, Victory Liner (4.30pm, 5pm & 5.15pm) has regular services to Manila; GL Lizardo buses to Baguio leave daily at 4.30pm.
By jeepney Jeepneys from Bontoc stop off in Tinglayan and Lubuagan before stopping at Tabuk.
Destinations Bontoc (4hr; P220); Lubuagan (1hr 30min; P80); Tinglayan (3hr; P120).

Services All of the accommodation options in Tabuk that we review offer free wi-fi. You can withdraw cash at the PNB and DBP banks in the barangay of Dagupan, and Land Bank and Rural Bank in the barangay of Bulanao.

ACCOMMODATION AND EATING

TINGLAYAN

Luplupa Riverside Inn Luplupa ☎0915 283 7885. Easily the best place to stay in town with rustic parquet floors and simple rooms with wooden shelves, a stool and table. On the first floor there's a little lounge area displaying a lovely collection of local artefacts. No hot water, but staff can boil some for you. **P500**

Sleeping Beauty Poblacion ☎0927 943 2163. Named after the nearby mountain, which is shaped like a female figure, this place has five colourfully painted rooms with cherry-red tiled floors. There's a small communal area and a restaurant upstairs. The owners also rent out a few rooms on the other side of the bridge in Luplupa. **P400**

TABUK

Davidson Hotel Provincial Rd, Bulanao ☎0917 579 7110, ⓦdavidsonhotel.com.ph. One of Tabuk's better-equipped hotels, with a pool, gym and a good restaurant serving local and international dishes. Rooms vary considerably – some are spacious, clean and tidy while others are in disrepair – make sure to take a look at a few before settling in. Wi-fi throughout. **P1050**

Golden Berries San Juan ☎0927 213 5422, ⓦgolden berrieshotel.com. The owners here process, grind and package locally grown coffee beans on the premises – you can buy the finished product at the hotel's little shop. The rooms in the "old" building are a bit tired; those in the "new" block at the back are more comfortable with modern amenities. There's also a restaurant, although the food is less than average. **P1100**

Grand Zion National Highway, Purok 7, Bulanao ☎0916 373 4366, ⓦgrandzionhotel.com. Tabuk's most upmarket hotel features spacious, tastefully decorated rooms in an airy building resembling an alpine lodge. There are pleasant gardens at the back with an inviting swimming pool, and a restaurant serving an array of dishes. **P1950**

Ifugao province

Landlocked Ifugao **province** is characterized by spectacular rugged terrain, lush forests and verdant river valleys dotted with tribal villages. A number of Ifugao communities still wear traditional dress, although you'll have to trek to remote villages to experience authentic tribal life. The Ifugaos are a proud people who have preserved their ancestral past, largely because they managed to sustain resistance during the Spanish colonial regime, which, as in Kalinga, failed in subduing the highlanders. The highlights of the region are the spectacular **rice terraces**, handcarved in the mountainside more than two thousand years ago and now designated by UNESCO as a **World Heritage Site**.

Banaue

It may only be 300km north of Manila, but **BANAUE** might as well be a world away, 1300m above sea level and far removed in spirit and topography from the beaches and

---

BANAUE'S STAIRWAYS TO HEAVEN

The **rice terraces** around Banaue are among the great icons of the Philippines, hewn from the land two thousand years ago by Ifugao tribespeople using primitive tools, an achievement in engineering terms that ranks alongside the building of the pyramids. Called the "Stairway to Heaven" by the Ifugaos, the terraces would stretch 20,000km if laid out end to end. Not only are they an awesome sight, but they are also an object lesson in **sustainability**.

The terraces are on the UNESCO World Heritage list, and they will not last forever if they are not protected. They have always been subject to constant deterioration, due to erosion, imperfect irrigation systems and the actions of earthworms. Following a shortage of young people to help carry out repairs – rice farming held little allure for many of them, understandably tired of the subsistence livelihood their parents eked from the land – strict measures have been taken in recent years to protect and revive the paddies, and young farmers are slowly returning to work in the fields.

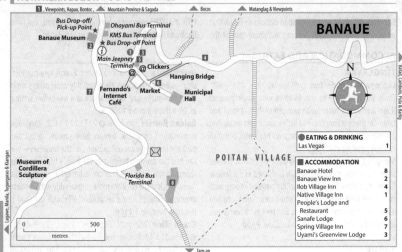

palm trees of the south. The town itself is small and not hugely impressive, centred on a marketplace, with a few guesthouses, some souvenir shops and a couple of good **museums**, but its location is superb. This is the heart of **rice terrace** country: the terraces in Banaue itself are some of the most impressive and well known, and there are hundreds of others in valleys and gorges throughout the area, most of which can be reached on foot. There is rustic accommodation at nearby **Batad** (see p.182), so you could stay overnight and hike back the next morning.

Museum of Cordillera Sculpture

Bissang Tam–an • Daily 8am–5pm • P100 • ☎ 0927 401 1484, ⓦ cordilleranmuseum.weebly.com • P15 tricycle ride from town

The private collection of American expat George Schenk, the wonderful **Museum of Cordillera Sculpture** displays a fine array of Ifugao cultural objects. Highlights include bulol rice deities – guardian figures placed in the rice paddies to protect them from malevolent spirits and bring abundant harvests – and wooden statuettes of pregnant wives, carved by husbands who would devoutly pray to them believing that this would ease their spouse's pregnancy.

Banaue Museum

Poblacion • Daily 8am–5pm • P50 • ☎ 0916 694 4511

The family-run **Banaue Museum** houses part of the collection of American anthropologist Henry Otley Beyer, the grandfather of the current owner. The objects were acquired from Ifugao province and the adjoining areas, and include ceremonial necklaces, black-and-white photographs of tattooed Ifugao ancestors, and wooden gods that were placed in rice granaries, serving as guardians of the harvest and the fields. Don't miss the Ifugao coffin – tradition dictates the dead had to be sealed inside and kept under the house, with the top of the coffin serving as a bench. If the museum is closed during opening hours, ask at the neighbouring *Banaue View Inn* for the key.

Lookout points

Tricycle P200 return

Two kilometres north of town is a series of five **lookout points** for the rice terraces, where Ifugao elders in traditional costume hang out and ask for a small fee if you want to take their photograph. The third lookout point has the view depicted on the P1000 banknote; you'll get the best vista from the fifth lookout.

ARRIVAL AND DEPARTURE

BANAUE

By bus Buses from Manila and Baguio drop passengers off outside the municipal tourist centre, but depart from their respective terminals. Ohayami buses serve Baguio (daily 5pm; 7–8hr) and Manila (2 daily; 8–9hr).

By jeepney Jeepneys coming from Bontoc stop at the market, heading back to Bontoc daily at 9.30am (1hr 40min; P150). Regular jeepneys connect Banaue with the provincial capital, Lagawe (every 30min; 1hr; P37).

By van Vans from Bontoc and Baguio drop passengers off at the market.

Destinations Baguio (hourly 9.30am–5.30pm; 6hr; P360); Bontoc (hourly 8am–3pm; 1hr 30min; P150).

INFORMATION

Environmental fee All visitors must register and pay the environmental fee (P20) at the municipal tourist centre.

Tourist information The municipal tourist centre is on the western end of the main drag, where the buses stop (daily until 8pm; T 0917 552 2501, E elahd_ban@yahoo.com).

Tours You can hire an accredited guide to explore the surrounding area; rates vary depending on where you go – ask at the municipal tourist centre for a list of destinations with fixed rates. Guesthouses can enquire about motorbike rental or call local guide Elvis who rents out his own bike (P1500/day; T 0935 292 2982).

3

ACCOMMODATION

Banaue's accommodation is generally simple but clean and friendly, and many places have restaurants attached. Finding somewhere without a reservation is not a problem, except at Christmas and Easter.

Banaue Hotel Ilogui Tam-an T 0908 400 7596, E pta_banauehotel@yahoo.com. This vast rambling hotel with outmoded furniture and decor hasn't moved on much since opening in the 70s. Rooms are comfortable and spacious nonetheless, and there are deluxe options (P3000) and suites (P7000) with nice views. Plus a pleasant swimming pool and a bar with pool table. Wi-fi in the lobby at P150/day. **P2300**

Banaue View Inn Poblacion T 0916 694 4511, E banaueviewinn_1984@yahoo.com. The tiled rooms here – with shared or private bathroom – are clean, a little boxy but with more character than in some of the other lodges, and there are great views from the shared veranda – or from your private balcony if you choose one of the more expensive rooms. **P1000**

Ilob Village Inn Bocos T 0906 230 5090, E ilobvillage@gmail.com. East of town, this place offers the chance to stay in one of five native huts (P800). The oldest, dating back more than a century, is covered in carabao skulls, butchered during the binogwah ritual, when the Ifugao bring out the skeletons of their forefathers in order to pay respects. The private rooms in the concrete block at the back are spartan and uninspiring. **P400**

★**Native Village Inn** Uhaj, 9km west of Banaue T 0916 405 6743, W nativevillage-inn.com. On the road to Hapao, this wonderful place has stunning rice terrace views – there are two lookout points where guests are encouraged to take their breakfast, and where you can easily while away a few hours just soaking in the scenery. The food is another highlight, including fresh homebaked bread. Accommodation is in seven comfortable native huts dotted around the verdant grounds. Call Elvis (T 0935 292 2982) for a free pick-up from Banaue. **P1900**

People's Lodge and Restaurant Poblacion T 0919 532 5605. This lodge offers simple rooms, some of which share cold showers and toilets, and more expensive, slightly more spacious rooms with private bath and colourful Ifugao blankets. There's a terrace with pleasant views and a little lounge area with rustic wooden benches. **P400**

★**Sanafe Lodge** Banaue Trade Centre, Poblacion T 0939 939 0128, W sanafelodge.com. A great option, with clean rooms with wooden decor; some are more spacious than others so take a look at a few before choosing. The deluxe room (P1600) is worth every peso – clean, spacious and with excellent views over the rice terraces. The place also has one of Banaue's better restaurants, where you can enjoy spectacular scenery from the breakfast table. Free wi-fi. **P800**

Spring Village Inn Poblacion T 0916 927 9623. Run by an affable woman, this pleasant guesthouse with a tiled wooden interior offers clean, comfortable rooms set on two floors, all with private bath and hot shower. The owner's collection of beautiful Chinese vases is on display in the entrance hall. **P1500**

Uyami's Greenview Lodge Poblacion T 0917 591 0981, W ugreenview.wordpress.com. A popular place with a comfortable restaurant offering wi-fi and views over the surrounding terraces. All rooms have wooden floorboards, dressing table and hanging rail and a couple have views over the terraces; the cheaper rooms downstairs are spartan, with common bathrooms and cold showers (hot water is an additional P50). **P500**

EATING AND DRINKING

There are hardly any standalone restaurants of note in town; most of the best food is served in **lodges**. *People's Lodge and Restaurant*, *Uyami's Greenview Lodge* and *Sanafe Lodge* have some good dishes, while *Banaue Hotel* is the most upmarket choice.

Las Vegas Poblacion ☏0915 765 8736. This popular restaurant serving Filipino food has a smattering of American memorabilia sitting alongside the wooden Ifugao statuettes. Once the owner has finished rustling up dinner, he pulls out his guitar and serenades the guests. Daily 6.30am–10pm.

DIRECTORY

Banks and exchange There are no banks in Banaue, but some hotels change money. It's better, though, to bring enough pesos. If you get really stuck, you can head for the provincial capital Lagawe – 25km away – which has branches of PNB and Land Bank with ATMs.

Internet access There are several internet cafés in town – try Clickers (daily 7.30am–8pm; ☏0926 164 6280; P15/hr) or Fernando's (daily 7am–9pm; ☏0918 965 3564; P30/hr).
Post office The post office is to the south of town (Mon–Fri 8am–noon & 1–5pm).

Around Banaue

The area around Banaue offers spectacular **rice terrace** scenery, with five areas designated UNESCO World Heritage Sites. **Trekking** through the stonewalled terraces and overnighting in typical Ifugao huts in rural villages is a major highlight. The most popular trek is to the remote little village of **Batad**, which has become something of a pilgrimage in recent years for visitors looking for rural isolation and unforgettable scenery. Other nearby villages include **Cambulo**, **Pula** and **Banga-an**. While less explored, the barangay of **Hapao** 16km southwest from Banaue, offers stunning terrace scenery that easily rivals that of Batad; 7km farther in the same direction is **Hungduan**, home to spectacular spider web terraces, mainly serving as a base for trekkers climbing Mount Napulawan (2600m).

Batad and around

BATAD nestles in a natural amphitheatre, close to the glorious **Tappia Waterfall**, which is 40m high and has a deep, bracing pool for swimming. There are signs that life here is beginning to change – the village now has electricity and a dozen simple **guesthouses** have sprung up – but it remains peaceful. There are several good hikes, including to **Banga-an**; ask around at the lodges for a guide. One way to head back to Banaue from Batad is to backtrack south for about 16km to the tiny village of **Banga-an**, no more than a few dozen Ifugao homes perched between rice terraces close to the National Highway. You can **stay** here (see below), but it's a good idea to book ahead if you're relying on this after a hike – your guide will probably be able to do this for you.

ARRIVAL AND DEPARTURE   BATAD AND AROUND

On foot It is possible to walk the 16km to Batad from Banaue.
By jeepney Most people cut out the first 14km of the walk from Banaue to Batad by taking a jeepney to Saddle (daily 8.30am; 1hr; P100), from where it is a 45-minute walk downhill to Batad.

ACCOMMODATION AND EATING

BATAD

Batad Pension ☏0918 964 3368, ✉batadpension@yahoo.com. A pleasant pension decorated with wooden furniture made by the owner-cum-sculptor, whose little workshop is in the back yard. The simple rooms are brightened up with a thin layer of paint and colourful blankets – those upstairs have great views. Guests can also sleep in a native hut. **P500**
Hillside Inn ☏0908 601 2888, ✉hillside_inn@yahoo

.com. The basic rooms here are pretty poky, with spindly furniture and thin plywood walls, although the restaurant does have great views over the terraces. The menu offers an eclectic mix of international and local dishes, including Middle Eastern *malawach*, a thick pancake of thin layers of puff pastry (P80). **P500**
Simon's Viewpoint Inn ☏0930 507 7467. This popular guesthouse with walls covered in travellers' notes has a selection of clean simple rooms, some with excellent views

over the terraces. There's a good restaurant serving a variety of international dishes including freshly baked pita bread, Israeli *shakshuka* (P75) and pizza (P100). **P500**

BANGA-AN
Banga-an Family Inn & Canteen ☎ 0909 101 9068. Overlooking the village from the highway, this is where most hikers stop off for the night on the way back to Banaue. Rooms are basic and spartan, with cold showers – you can ask the staff to boil some hot water for you. You can also overnight in traditional huts that sleep four to six people (P600). The restaurant serves simple Filipino dishes (P90). **P400**

Pula and Cambulo

From the Banaue Awan-Igid viewpoint, 9km outside Banaue, you can trek east through fields and terraces to the villages of **PULA** and **CAMBULO**. There are some unforgettable sights along this route, including waterfalls, steep gorges and a hanging bridge near Pula that requires a bit of nerve to cross. The journey from Banaue viewpoint to Pula takes about four hours, and from Pula to Cambulo it's another two hours. You can camp or spend the night at one of the small **inns** or homestays in Cambulo. From here it's two hours to Batad, from where you can walk up to Batad Saddle and hop on a jeepney back to your hotel.

Pula is also the start of a hike up **Mount Amuyao** (2702m), a full day's walk and not something to be attempted without a guide and plenty of stamina. You'll need to sleep at the top and return next day, or you can continue on to Barlig (see p.171) and eventually Bontoc.

ACCOMMODATION	PULA AND CAMBULO

Cambulo Guesthouse Cambulo. This family-run place offers a selection of basic rooms with communal bath (cold showers only). The owners can rustle up a few dishes such as pancakes, omelettes and rice and vegetables. **P500**

Hapao and Hungduan

The rice terraces in the barangay of **HAPAO**, around 16km from Banaue, are spectacular. Hapao has a couple of homestays and is home to the **Hapao hot springs**, where you can take a dip in two natural pools. Further on, the small town of **HUNGDUAN**, less than 10km from Banaue as the crow flies but reached by a protracted looped road, is the location of the **Bacung spider web terraces**, at their best in April and May. The trip is well worth it, and you can overnight in the town itself. Hungduan is also the start of a hike up **Mount Napulawan** (2600m) for which you will need a guide.

ARRIVAL AND INFORMATION	HAPAO AND HUNGDUAN

By jeepney Jeepneys from Banaue run to Hapao (every 30min noon–6pm; 1hr; P25) and Hungduan (every 30min noon–6pm; 1hr 30min; P37).
By tricycle You can travel by tricycle from Banaue to Hapao (1hr; P400) and Hungduan (1hr 30min; P750).

Guides It is possible to organize guides to both Hapao and Hungduan at the tourist information point at Bokikwan on the way to Hapao; this is where all visitors must register and pay an environmental fee of P20.

ACCOMMODATION

Base Camp Hapao ☎ 0935 292 2982, ✉ guitrek_v @hotmail.com. A pleasant place to stay with just two native huts with communal bathrooms. Guests are encouraged to have a go at pounding rice with pestle and mortar before consuming the finished product. You can also plant rice with the locals in harvest season. **P500**

Coop Lodge Hungduan. In a building with a sari-sari store selling snacks and other basic necessities, this simple lodge is popular among climbers heading to Mount Napulawan who overnight here before leaving at sunrise or on their way back to Banaue. Staff can heat up hot water for a quick wash. **P500**

Mayoyao

Home to some beautiful UNESCO rice terraces, **MAYOYAO** is rarely visited due to the poor road condition, although it's well worth taking the time to travel here. The terraces are punctuated by distinctive pyramid-roofed local houses, and by stone burial mounds called Apfo'or. They are at their greenest from April to May and October to November.

There are **buses** to Mayoyao from Banaue (2 daily; 3hr) and Santiago (4 daily; 4–5hr).

ACCOMMODATION

Mayoyao Hostel ☎ 0905 806 4261. Under renovation at the time of research, this hostel is wonderfully located on top of a hill overlooking the rice terraces. There's a stone burial mound at the end of the garden – a pretty spot to sit back and enjoy the views at sunrise. Dorms are comfortable and spacious, and there's a large well-equipped guest kitchen. Per person P200

Kiangan and around

On September 2 1945, General Yamashita of the Japanese Imperial Army surrendered to US and Filipino troops in the town of **KIANGAN**, 10km from the provincial capital Lagawe (which is itself 24km south of Banaue). The surrender is commemorated with a large **shrine** although the actual site of the surrender (marked with a plaque) is now occupied by the library of the nearby Kiangan Elementary School. The hill on the right as you look out from the front of the shrine is where the Japanese holed up for their last stand; it's known as the **Million Dollar Hill** for the supposed cost of the artillery with which the US shelled it. Across from the shrine, the **Ifugao Museum** (Mon–Fri 8am–5pm; P30) displays everyday local artefacts including men's hip bags used to store betel nut, and a mouth harp, considered to be a courtship instrument played to express intimate love.

The **rice terraces** around Kiangan are at their best in April and May. You can take a jeepney to the terraces at either **Nagacadan** (20min; P15) or **Julungan** ("Hul-ungan"; 1hr; P50). Tricycles also make it to Nagacadan (15min; P75 each way). Ask at Kiangan tourist office if you need a guide.

Julia Campbell Agroforest Memorial Park

Brgy Pula, Asipulo • ☎ 0905 732 2942, ⊕ bantaicivetcoffee.com or ⊕ juliacampbellpark.wordpress.com • Volunteers can contact the park direct or make arrangements through Worldwide Opportunities on Organic Farms (⊕ wwoof.ph)

Some 18km west of Kiangan, in the Pula barangay of Asipulo, the **Julia Campbell Agroforest Memorial Park** grows organic coffee made from beans that have been eaten and excreted by civets, a product considered particularly flavourful and sold at a premium price.

By bus The closest bus station to Kiangan is in Lagawe, 14km away, where Ohayami buses from Manila drop off passengers (1 daily; 6–8hr).
By jeepney Jeepneys connect Kiangan and Lagawe (every 30min; 15min; P15), from where there are regular jeepneys to Banaue (every 30min; 1hr; P37).
By tricycle There are tricycles from Lagawe to Kiangan (20min; P100).

INFORMATION

Tourist offices The municipal tourist office is in the town proper (Mon Fri 8am 5pm; ☎ 0920 467 1020, ⊕ kiangan .gov.ph); there is also a provincial tourist office in the barangay of Baguinge, halfway between Lagawe and Kiangan, just by Ibulao, Ibulao guesthouse (Mon–Fri 7.30am–5pm; ☎ 0906 774 8310, ⊕ ifugaotourism.org.ph).

ACCOMMODATION

★Ibulao, Ibulao Ibulao ☎ 0917 553 3299, ⊕ totokalug@yahoo.com.ph. This award-winning eco-lodge and B&B, set in one hectare of land midway between Lagawe and Kiangan, has a selection of creatively presented rooms mostly decorated with Ifugao wood carvings. The family room (P2800) with stone floors is particularly impressive, built around exposed rocks. Owner and doctor Roberto Kalungan also arranges rafting trips.

He is rather selective with his guests, asking them to introduce themselves in detail via email before offering the possibility of overnighting. Bookings are essential; no walk-ins are accepted. P1600

Kiangan Youth Hostel Poblacion ☏ 0915 704 8398. A basic option in the centre of Kiangan with three simple private rooms with private bath (cold showers only) and two single-sex dorms. Dorms P150; doubles P500

Batanes province

Almost 150km off the northern coast of Luzon, **Batanes** is the smallest, most isolated province in the country – the islands are closer to Taiwan than to the northernmost tip of Luzon. This is a memorable place with otherworldly scenery, where doors are rarely locked and welcomes are warm even by Filipino standards. The people are different, the language is different, even the weather is different. The coolest months (Jan–March) can get chilly with temperatures as low as 10°C, while the hottest months (May & June) are searing. For visitors, the islands are at their best from February to June. Just three of the ten islands in the Batanes group are inhabited: **Batan** – the location of the capital **Basco** – **Sabtang** and **Itbayat**.

Batanes can be idyllic, but it would be wrong to portray it as a tropical utopia. Realities of life this far away from the rest of the world can sometimes be harsh. Petrol and provisions are brought in by ship, which means they cost more, and when **typhoons** roar in from the east (July–Sept) it may be impossible for ships or aircraft to reach the islands. Boredom can set in and locals joke that during the typhoon season the cargo ship brings fifty thousand sacks of rice but sixty thousand crates of gin.

The native inhabitants of Batanes, the **Ivatan**, trace their roots to prehistoric Formosan immigrants. Most still make a living by cultivating yams and garlic or raising goats and cows; if you visit a village during the daytime, be prepared to find that almost everyone is out in the fields. Some women still wear rain capes called *vakul*, made from the stripped leaves of the *voyavoy* palm. The main **dialect**, Ivatan, includes some pidgin Spanish: "thank you" is *dios mamajes* and "goodbye" is *dios mavidin* (if you are the person leaving) or *dios machivan* (if you are staying behind).

Batan Island

Batan Island is the biggest in the group and site of the tiny capital, **BASCO**. The town boasts a spectacular location on the lower slopes of **Mount Iraya**, a volcano that hasn't erupted since the fifteenth century but is still officially active. You can walk around the town in half an hour, and there are no specific attractions, but it's a pleasant and friendly place, built

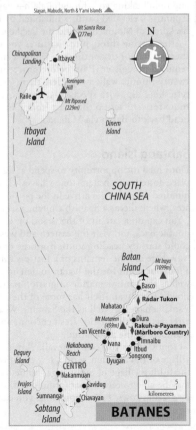

around a rectangular plaza with the municipal buildings and church on the north side and the sea to the south.

Around the island

Most organized tours start by heading south from Basco along the coastal road to the *Batanes Resort* (see p.188), before turning left up a narrow road to an abandoned weather station called **Radar Tukon**. This can also be done on foot as a day hike: it's about an hour from Basco and from here the whole island is spread at your feet. Beyond the weather station is the swanky *Fundacion Pacita* hotel (see p.188), and some tunnels nearby created by the Japanese army during World War II.

After heading back to the coastal road you can return to Basco, or continue south through the pretty old Spanish village of **Mahatao** and on to **Ivana** ("Ih-va-na"), with its eye-catching yellow church, where ferries set off to Sabtang. Just opposite the church is the pier for ferries to Sabtang Island. In Ivana you will also find **Dakay's House**, the oldest stone house in Batanes, built in 1887. Although it is inhabited, you are welcome to poke your head in to take a look at the interior, which has beautiful wooden floors traditionally polished with banana leaves.

The coastal road round the southern end of the island brings you to the village of **Uyugan** before turning north to **Song Song**, where you can see the remains of stone houses that were washed away by a tidal wave. After Itbud there is a turning inland and uphill taking you through **Rakuh-a-Payaman** (known to tourists as "Marlboro Country"), elevated pastures inhabited by Ivatan bulls and horses, grazing against the backdrop of Mount Iraya and the Pacific Ocean.

After passing through the pastures you can either return to Mahatao (and from there to Basco) or continue to **Diura**, a small fishing village where visitors are required to register (P50) before proceeding to the nearby Spring of Youth, a twenty-minute walk away. Here there's a wonderful stone pool perfect for a refreshing dip, with spectacular views over the ocean and Mount Iraya. There's no route for vehicles up the coast from Diura so unless you're hiking you'll need to head back to Basco via Mahatao.

Sabtang Island

Don't miss the opportunity to spend at least a day exploring **Sabtang Island**, a peaceful place dotted with Ivatan stone villages where life seems to have altered little in a hundred years. Ferries arrive in the port on the island's northeast coast, in the **Centro** area, where there's a Spanish church, a school and a few houses.

You can do a circuit of the island on foot, but with a vehicle it's necessary to double back and visit the eastern and western parts of the island separately. You could start by heading south from the port to **Chavayan**, about 10km away. On the way there are the remains of a fortress (*idjang*) that stands high on a hill; it served as a lookout point for the Ivatan to defend themselves from approaching invaders, as well as to monitor marine migration patterns. The path is steep in places, so take it slowly. Chavayan itself has some of the island's best-preserved traditional homes and a small chapel, as well as the Sabtang Weavers' Association, where you can purchase artefacts as well as enjoy fresh coconut and home-made biscuits prepared by members of the association.

From Centro you can also walk 9km to **Sumnanga**, passing through the tiny village of **Nakanmuan**, with a few traditional houses. About 3km further along is the fishing village of Sumnanga, home to the lovely Devuk Bay. From here you may be able to rent a boat (around P500) to visit Ivujos Island – it's inhabited only by grazing cows. From Sumnanga you can hop on a scooter or tricycle (P250) to return to Centro.

Itbayat Island

Of the three inhabited islands in the Batanes group, **Itbayat Island** is the least accessible. There's no public transport, either, so you'll have to get around on foot or by asking one of the residents who owns a motorbike to give you a lift. It's crisscrossed by trails made by farmers and fishermen, making for superb trekking in good weather.

The ferry lands at the west coast harbour of Chinapoliran, from where you can walk or hitch a lift to the pretty little capital, **ITBAYAT**. There are great views of the island, and the others nearby, from the viewpoint of Mount Karaboboan, also known as **Mount Santa Rosa** (277m), on the northern side of the island. Alternatively go looking for the stone boat-shaped burial markers at Torongan Hill, above a cave where the first inhabitants of the island are believed to have lived.

ARRIVAL AND DEPARTURE

By plane The only way to get to the Batanes islands is by air, with all flights landing in Basco. You can fly from Tuguegarao with Sky Pasada (3 weekly; 1hr; P5225) and

BATANES PROVINCE

North Sky Air (3 weekly; 1hr 30min; P5100), while PAL operates daily flights from Manila (1hr 30min; P8500). Basco is also connected to Itbayat (see below).

GETTING AROUND

By ferry Ferries connect Basco, Sabtang and Itbayat. The channel between Basco and Sabtang is known for its strong currents and big waves – avoid the crossing in rough weather. If travelling to Itbayat from Basco, be warned that it can be a very uncomfortable and rough crossing, and that the ferries can be cancelled for several days in a row if sea conditions are particularly poor.

BATAN ISLAND

By plane A tricycle from the airport is P30 to Basco (5min), or P60 to the barangay of Kaychanarianan.
By ferry Ferries to Batan arrive and leave from Ivana, a tricycle ride away from Basco (30min; P200). The 1pm ferry

from Sabtang (30min; P75) arrives around 1.30pm. Ferries for Sabtang leave daily at 6am.

SABTANG ISLAND

By ferry Ferries leave Ivana pier in Batan for Sabtang daily at 6am, returning to Batan around 1pm.

ITBAYAT ISLAND

By plane North Sky has flights from Basco to Itbayat (Mon, Wed & Fri 11.30am; 20min; P1800).
By ferry A daily ferry to Itbayat leaves Basco at 5am (3hr; P450) and returns the same day; you won't have enough time to see much without staying the night.

INFORMATION

Make sure you take **pesos** to Batanes – credit cards are not accepted. You should be able to change US dollars and travellers' cheques at PNB in Basco, but not at a favourable rate; there's also a Land Bank with an ATM in Basco, although it's probably best not to rely solely on this.

BATAN ISLAND

Tourist Information The heritage and tourism section of the governor's office is on National Rd, and there's an information point at arrivals at the airport (both Mon–Fri 8am–5pm; ☎0929 846 8395, ⓦbatanes.gov.ph).
Tours Ivatan Travel & Tours (☎0928 525 0818, ⓦbatanesit our.com) and Batanes Tours and Travel (☎0917 892 2552, ⓦamazingbatanes.com) both organize island tours, as well as biking and trekking. For scuba diving contact Chico at Dive Batanes Lodge (☎0947 817 4977, ⓦdivebatanes.com).

SABTANG ISLAND

Registration fee There is a registration fee of P200 payable on arrival at the tourist centre.
Tourist information The tourist centre (daily 6am–9pm; ☎0918 488 2424) is to the left as you leave the port. They have no maps or brochures but can provide advice on routes, and will collect your registration fee. If you want a tour of the island, call the tourist centre in advance or organize it in Basco.

GETTING AROUND

BATAN ISLAND

By jeepney If you are in a group then the easiest way to get a quick overall picture of the beauty of Batan is to hire a jeepney with driver for the day (P2000) through your

accommodation. It's also possible to travel in public jeepneys that connect settlements along the coastal road, but you'll have to be prepared to wait and probably to do some walking and hitching.

3

By bike Renting a bicycle (P20/hr for regular bikes; try Dive Batanes for mountain bikes for P250/day) or scooter (P150/hr; try your lodging or the Petron petrol station) are good options. The roads are very quiet, but there are a number of blind bends, so take it easy. Make sure to observe the speed limit of 20km/hr in towns.

ACCOMMODATION

BATAN ISLAND

The potential for trekking and camping on Batan is enticing. There are no campsites, but as long as you respect the landscape no one minds if you pitch a tent for the night near a beach. Whatever you do, take food and water, because there are few places to get provisions. All the accommodation listed below is in or around Basco.

Amboy Hometel 3km south of Basco, Brgy Chanarian ☎ 0920 910 3492, ⓦ amboyhometel.com. This recently opened B&B has six comfortable a/c rooms with private bath, each painted in different colours. There's a TV with DVD player in each, wi-fi throughout, and a restaurant by the little garden area serving seasonal dishes (P300). **P2200**

Batanes Resort 2km south of Basco, Brgy Kaychanarianan ☎ 0999 990 7559, ⓔ batanes resort2011@yahoo.com. Tidy little stone duplex cottages, with hot showers, sitting on a breezy hillside with steps leading down to a marvellous black sand cove. The restaurant has good food and a pleasant terrace. **P1800**

Batanes Seaside National Rd, Brgy Kaychanarianan ☎ 0921 229 0120, ⓦ batanesseasidelodge.com. Right on the seafront, this lodge has fifteen decent-sized rooms, although the interiors are a bit dark with drab furniture. There's wi-fi in the lobby, a large restaurant serving Ivatan dishes and a couple of lounge areas with armchairs. **P3200**

★ **Fundacion Pacita** Brgy Chanarian ☎ 0939 901 6353, ⓦ fundacionpacita.ph. The island's most upmarket accommodation option was the former home of artist Pacita Abad until her death in 2004; the common area exhibits Abad's art while the rooms, all with balconies and exceptional views, are tastefully decorated with works of Filipino artists. A portion of the proceeds goes to heritage conservation in Batanes, and provides art scholarships for Ivatan students and supplies for local schools. The restaurant serves wonderful Ivatan cuisine. **P10530**

Octagon Bed & Dine Brgy Kaychanarianan ☎ 0929 597 9380, ⓦ octagonbedanddine.com. The three spacious rooms here are jam-packed with furniture and knick-knacks, including wooden trunks, vases, armchairs and chintzy bedspreads. Accommodation gives onto a balcony from where there are wonderful views of the ocean. **P2500**

Shanedel's Inn & Café Corner 0669 National Rd, Brgy Kaychanarianan ☎ 0920 447 0737, ⓔ shanedels @yahoo.com. One of the best budget options, with practical rooms with kitschy decor. A/c rooms have private bath, while the cheaper fan rooms are slightly smaller with communal facilities. The restaurant overlooking the ocean is a great spot to enjoy sunset views – try the island's speciality coconut crab (P500). **P1400**

SABTANG ISLAND

By jeepney or scooter You should be able to book a jeepney for a group (P1500–2200 depending on distance), or possibly a scooter with driver (around P1000) if you're alone.

Municipal Guesthouse ☎ 0918 488 2424. The municipal tourist office offers simple accommodation in a bright room with five individual beds; there are large windows from where you can watch the waves crash against the shore. There's no door to the bedroom so don't expect much privacy, although if you're here just to lay your head for the night then the place does just the trick. Per person **P300**

ITBAYAT ISLAND

Municipal Guesthouse ☎ 0928 286 2060. The small municipal guesthouse offers two basic rooms with bunk-beds and communal cold-shower bathrooms. There's also a guest kitchen, and a canteen nearby serving simple dishes. You can also pitch a tent in the grounds. Per person **P150**

EATING AND DRINKING

BATAN ISLAND

Several of the lodges in Basco have restaurants or can make food to order, while elsewhere on the island you'll be reliant on the occasional small canteen so it's best to travel with at least a snack and some water.

North Spirit Café National Rd, Ihubok 1, Brgy Kaychanarianan. On the southern fringes of town, Basco's only bar is set in a corrugated tin building with a few wooden benches. The place is mainly frequented by men enjoying a long awaited snifter (cocktails P100, beer P50) – for a small island, things can get quite raucous on weekend nights. Daily 5pm–2am.

Octagon Bed & Dine Brgy Kaychanarianan ☎ 0929 597 9380, ⓦ octagonbedanddine.com. This octagonal restaurant, decorated with colourful paintings, wooden masks and other artefacts, offers what is probably the most extensive menu on the island, with soups (P200), sandwiches (P100), meat and veg dishes (P200) and pasta (P180). Daily 8am–midnight.

Pension Ivatan Brgy Kayvalugan ☎078 373 0587, ⓦpensionivatanbatanes.com. This friendly restaurant is decorated with beautiful glass buoys that were washed up ashore from nearby Taiwan. The menu focuses on traditional Ivatan cuisine – the large Ivatan platter (P1550) will easily feed four to five; it includes coconut crab, lobster, beef ribs, pork, flying fish, taro and *uved*, a Batan delicacy of fish and pork sautéed with coconut. Daily 7am–9pm.

St Dominic College Canteen National Rd. This self-service canteen is popular among students of the attached St Dominic College. There are a variety of inexpensive dishes on offer, including burgers (P40) and cakes (P20). There's also a little shop within the building selling stationery. Mon–Sat 8am–9pm, Sun 8am–8.30pm.

SHOPPING

BATAN ISLAND

Yaru National Rd, Brgy Kaychanarianan ☎0908 920 0289. Run by an association of artists who aim to make the arts a sustainable source of income on the islands, this small gallery and shop sells paintings as well as a few souvenirs, including lovely painted cards of Batanes sights. Mon–Fri 10am–7pm, Sat & Sun 2–7pm.

3

Southern Luzon

MOUNT MAYON

Southern Luzon

Southeast of Manila, the provinces that make up Southern Luzon are home to some of the country's most popular tourist destinations – both active and natural. The area is blessed with some extraordinarily diverse natural phenomena, including the region's top tourist draw, the picturesque Mount Mayon volcano, whose cone is reputedly the most perfectly symmetrical in the world. Southern Luzon is also one of the few places on earth where you can swim with the world's largest fish, the gentle whale shark. It is also blessed with underground rivers, glorious white sand beaches, limestone cliffs, spectacular surfing waves, hot and cold springs and historic buildings dating back to the Spanish colonial era.

The National Highway south from Manila takes you down to **Quezon province**, home to Mount Banahaw, a revered dormant volcano that presents one of the most rewarding climbs in the country. Quezon is linked by ferry to the beautiful island province of **Marinduque**, still largely untouched by mass tourism and best known for its Easter festival, the **Moriones**.

Beyond Quezon is the **Bicol** region, which encompasses the remainder of Southern Luzon and includes the mainland provinces of **Camarines Norte**, **Camarines Sur**, **Albay** and **Sorsogon** and the island provinces of **Catanduanes** and **Masbate**. Known throughout the Philippines as an area of great natural beauty – and for its delicious **cuisine**, characterized by the use of chillies and coconut milk – Bicol is studded with volcanoes including **Mount Bulusan** and **Mount Mayon**, and offers superb coastline with some great beaches and island-hopping opportunities, particularly around **Legazpi** and **Sorsogon City**. Best of all is the **Caramoan Peninsula** where tourism is developing apace but where it's still possible to find deserted hideaways. There are also attractions offshore, and although it can't rival the Visayas for scuba diving, Bicol does have an ace up its sleeve in the form of **Donsol**, home to huge whale sharks. Other water-based activities include surfing in **Daet** and wakeboarding at **CamSur Watersports Complex**. Two island provinces add further variety to Bicol's fabulous mix: **Masbate** is the Philippines' wild east, cattle country where the biggest tourist draw is the annual rodeo in May. **Catanduanes**, meanwhile, is infamous for its exposure to passing typhoons – ironically this extreme weather is, however, what attracts surfers to its beaches.

ARRIVAL AND DEPARTURE

By plane There are commercial airports in Naga, Legazpi, Virac (Catanduanes), Boac (Marinduque) and Masbate City.
By train There is a train line between Manila and Legazpi via Naga, but it was suspended at the time of research. The Philippine National Railway website (⊚ pnr.gov.ph) will have updates.

By bus There are plenty of buses running from Manila down the National Highway via Naga and Legazpi, some going as far as Sorsogon City or beyond.
By boat In addition to ferries between the Luzon mainland and the islands of Catanduanes, Marinduque and Masbate, there are also regular services across

MORIONES FESTIVAL

Highlights

❶ Moriones festival Every Easter the beautiful little island of Marinduque lays on a boisterous religious pageant celebrating the life of Longinus, the Roman soldier who pierced Christ's side at the Crucifixion. **See p.201**

❷ Caramoan Peninsula Limestone cliffs, remote islands and beautiful secluded beaches much beloved by international TV companies – especially since the *Survivor* series was filmed here. **See p.214**

❸ Bicolano cuisine Savour spicy Bicolano cuisine, some of the country's best,

prepared with chillis and plenty of coconut milk. **See box, p.218**

❹ Mount Mayon Even if you don't climb it, you can't miss its almost symmetrical cone standing imperiously above Legazpi. **See p.219**

❺ Whale shark watching in Donsol Snorkel with the gentle giants of the sea, the world's largest fish. **See p.224**

❻ Puraran Beach, Catanduanes This prime surfing beach is not just for surfers; the offshore coral reef is rich with marine life. **See p.234**

HIGHLIGHTS ARE MARKED ON THE MAP ON PP.194–195

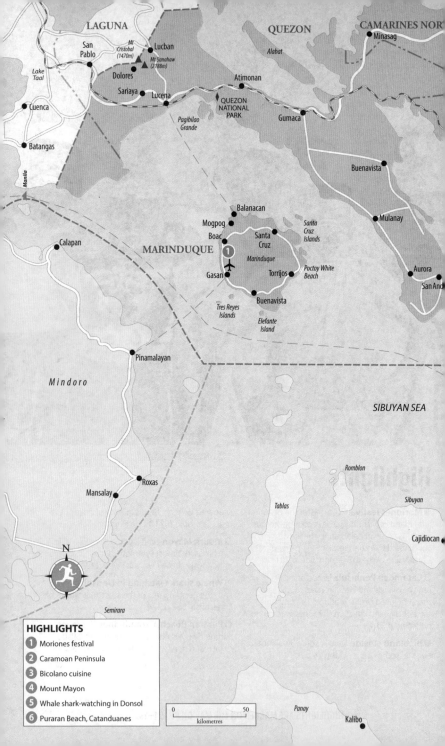

LAGUNA

San Pablo

Mt Cristobal (1470m)

Lucban

Mt Banahaw (2188m)

Dolores

Sariaya

Lucena

Cuenca

Batangas

Lake Taal

Manila

QUEZON

Alabat

Atimonan

QUEZON NATIONAL PARK

Pagibilao Grande

Gumaca

CAMARINES NOR

Minasag

Buenavista

Mulanay

Aurora

San And

Calapan

MARINDUQUE

Balanacan

Mogpog

Boac

Santa Cruz

Santa Cruz Islands

Poctoy White Beach

Gasan

Marinduque

Torrijos

Buenavista

Tres Reyes Islands

Elefante Island

Pinamalayan

Mindoro

SIBUYAN SEA

Roxas

Mansalay

Romblon

Sibuyan

Tablas

Cajidiocan

N

Semirara

Panay

Kalibo

HIGHLIGHTS

1 Moriones festival

2 Caramoan Peninsula

3 Bicolano cuisine

4 Mount Mayon

5 Whale shark-watching in Donsol

6 Puraran Beach, Catanduanes

0   50
kilometres

the Bernardino Strait between Matnog in Sorsogon province and Samar in the Visayas. Masbate has ferry links to several provinces including Romblon, Batangas and Cebu.

Quezon province

Much of the northern part of **Quezon province** is mountainous and hard to reach, although there are isolated communities on the coast. The southern portion of the province serves mainly as a staging post on the road from Manila to the Bicol region, though it does have attractions such as a couple of excellent climbs, **Mount Banahaw** and **Mount Cristobal**. Further east you can explore **Quezon National Park**, which has some fairly easy marked trails. If you happen to be in Quezon in mid-May, check out what is by far the biggest festival in the province, the **Pahiyas**, held in and around **Lucban**, near the very ordinary provincial capital, **Lucena**.

Lucena

The bustling town of **LUCENA** is worth considering for a stop on the route south, as a useful base during the **Pahiyas** festival in nearby Lucban or for those on their way to Marinduque via Dalahican port. The city itself doesn't offer much to visitors, and is home to just one little **museum**.

Gintog Yaman ng Museo Quezon

Provincial Capitol Compound, Belen Drive • Mon–Fri 8am–5pm • By donation • ☎ 042 797 0024

The **Gintong Yaman ng Museo Quezon** displays memorabilia and photographs of illustrious Quezonians, including the late President Manuel Quezon. You can also see household implements and agricultural tools and crafts, along with a reproduction of a former Spanish colonial dining room and bedroom.

ARRIVAL AND INFORMATION   LUCENA

By bus The Grand Central Terminal is on the northern edge of the city on Diversion Rd. It's a 15min jeepney ride (every 15min; 10min; P8) to Quezon Ave, the main thoroughfare.

Destinations Daet (DLTB: hourly; 4–5hr); Legazpi (Raymond Transportation: hourly; 8hr); Manila (JAM, Jac Liner, Lucena Lines & N. Dela Rosa: every 30–40min;

3–4hr); Naga (Raymond Transportation: hourly; 5–6hr); Tabaco (Raymond Transportation: hourly; 9–10hr).
By jeepney Regular jeepneys travel from the Grand Central Terminal to Lucban (every 15min; 45min; P20).
Tourist information The tourist office is on the second floor of the Quezon Convention Centre, Capitol Compound (Mon–Fri 8am–5pm; ☎ 042 373 7510, ⓦ quezon.gov.ph).

ACCOMMODATION

Diamond Resort and Hotel Maharlika Hwy, Brgy Ibabang Dupay ☎ 042 710 7757, ⓦ diamondresortand hotel.com. A/c rooms with private bath, some set around the pool. The main building houses some of the superior rooms (P2900), which all vary considerably in size – make sure to take a look at a few first. The restaurant serves good food, and there's free wi-fi in the lobby and café area. **P2600**
Queen Margarette Hotel 1 People Square, M.L. Tagarao

St at Granja St ☎ 042 797 1881, ⓦ queenmargarettehotel .com. Accommodation set on the fourth and fifth floors of an office block; overall, the rooms are comfortable with modern amenities, although they may have gone a bit overboard with the sumptuously kitsch decor. There's free wi-fi in the lobby, and rates include breakfast at the Chinese restaurant within the same building. There's also a sister hotel just outside town, with a pool. **P2650**

EATING

Giusseppe Lot 2, Block 12, Doña Aurora Blvd, Gulang Gulang ☎ 042 710 5557. This restaurant and café serves home-cooked Filipino meals, most of them cooked with *lambanog*, a local coconut wine. There's also a pretty display of home-made cupcakes (P22) and an assortment

of cheesecakes, including the café's trademark *kamote* cheesecake (P108), made with sweet potatoes. Mains P150. Daily 10am–10pm.
Koffee Klatch 88 Quezon Ave ☎ 042 373 0053, ⓦ dealokoffeeklatch.com. Established in 1958, this

4

café is run by a sprightly septuagenarian baker who has written her own cookbook, on sale for P500, filled with traditional recipes from the "Coconut Province" of Quezon. The many savoury dishes include *hardinera*, pork cooked in tomato sauce (P100), which is traditionally served on special occasions. The real draw here, though, is the selection of excellent home-made biscuits (P60). Daily 7am–8pm.

Lucban

Quezon province's major tourist draw is the **Pahiyas thanksgiving festival**, held every year on May 15 in **LUCBAN**, which sits at the foot of Mount Banahaw, 26km north of Lucena. It's a quaint little town and a pleasant spot to have a stroll, but there's not too much to see; it's worth taking a moment to visit the **St Louis Church**, which dates from the 1730s.

Kamay ni Hesus

Tricycle P8 (10min), jeepney P8 (every 15min; 5min)

You could join the faithful as they climb **Kamay ni Hesus** – a hill on the edge of Lucban peppered with tableaux depicting the stations of the cross and topped with a large, open-armed statue of Christ – in the hope of being cured of various ailments. The route up is exposed, and can be tiring on a hot day, but it's worth it for the wonderful views. Although a church stands at the base of the hill and masses are regularly held, the whole site has something of a theme-park feel, with a children's playground and replica Noah's ark.

ARRIVAL AND DEPARTURE
LUCBAN

By jeepney Regular jeepneys connect Lucban with Lucena (every 15min; 40min; P30).

By van To get to Manila, you'll need to catch a van to Calamba (hourly; 2hr; P120) and change there for an onward bus (every 15min; 40min).

ACCOMMODATION

If you're coming to Lucban during the **Pahiyas festival** you should book well in advance – some places get their first reservations a year ahead. Expect the prices to be inflated. There are surprisingly very few good options in the centre, although staying in the colourful heart of town during festival time makes for a wonderful experience.

Batis Aramin Resort and Hotel Brgy Malupak ☎042 540 4401, ⓦaramin.ph. About 1km from the town proper, this large resort offers a range of rooms connected by a hanging bridge; the fan-cooled attic rooms with shared bath (P1500), with bright interiors and a little desk in each, are much more appealing than the a/c standards (P2000). There's a large pool with an artificial waterfall and slide, a basketball court and a little lake where guests can boat with bamboo rafts. **P1000**

Patio Rizal 77 Quezon Ave ☎042 540 2112, ⓔpatio rizal@yahoo.com. This centrally located hotel is the most comfortable in town, offering decent rooms with carpet; the deluxe (P2600) and premier suite (P3100) are substantially larger and more welcoming. Each floor has a small seating area with wooden chairs and old paintings of the town centre, and there's a good restaurant with wi-fi on the ground floor serving a selection of Filipino dishes. Rates include breakfast. **P1600**

PAHIYAS FESTIVAL

Each May during the **Pahiyas festival** Lucban is transformed into something from a fairy tale, the houses decorated in the most imaginative fashion with fruit, vegetables and brightly coloured *kiping* (rice paper), which is formed into enormous chandeliers that cascade like flames from the eaves. The winner of the best-decorated house wins a cash prize and is blessed for twelve months by San Isidore (the patron saint of farmers). The festival starts with a solemn Mass at dawn and goes on well into the night, with much drinking and dancing in the streets. There is a parade, a beauty contest, a marching band and a carabao parade in which enormous water buffalo, more used to rice fields and mud holes, are led through the streets in outrageous costumes. It's open house for visitors during Pahiyas, and people are especially honoured to have foreigners come in to admire their decorations.

EATING AND DRINKING

Be sure to try the famous garlicky **Lucban longganisa** (sausage) – particularly delicious when served with *achara* (pickled papaya) – and for dessert try *budin* (cassava cake). Cheap food stalls by the church sell **pancit habhab**, a local noodle dish served on a banana leaf and traditionally eaten with your hands.

Buddy's Restaurant Rizal Park ☎042 540 3394. Located on the town's main square, this laidback restaurant has colourful Pahiyas festival *kiping* decorations dangling from the ceiling; seating is on small wooden benches, and the menu includes pancit Lucban (noodles with pork; P160) and longganisa (P115). Daily 9am–10pm.

Café San Luis San Luis St at Regidor St ☎042 540 2122. Located by an ancestral house, this welcoming leafy restaurant has lantern-lit, circular tables set around a pebbly courtyard. Bestsellers include chicken curry (P205) and baby back ribs with rice (P248); make sure to try the frozen margarita made with local *lambanog* wine (P80). Daily 8am–midnight.

Mount Banahaw and around

Northwest of Lucena, the town of **DOLORES** is the starting point for treks up **Mount Banahaw** and **Mount Cristobal**, which stand on either side of the town. Both mountains are protected areas and some trails have been closed for the past few years to reduce human impact on the environment. Other trails, however, are open.

Considered sacred, 2188m Mount Banahaw has spawned a huge number of **legends** and superstitions: one says that every time a foreigner sets foot on the mountain it will rain. Members of various sects still live around the base of the mountain, claiming that it imbues them with supernatural and psychic powers. Its slopes thick with jungle, Banahaw is a challenging but rewarding climb with panoramic views of the surrounding country from the crater rim. Treat this mountain seriously because although the trail looks wide and well-trodden, it soon peters out into inhospitable rainforest – even experienced climbers allow three days to reach the summit and get back down, while a crater descent should only be attempted by experts.

If you haven't time to reach the summit, you might prefer simply to trek to **Kristalino Falls** (Crystalline Falls) and back, which can be done in a day. One and a half hours further on is a second waterfall, whose surroundings make an ideal **campsite**.

Mount Cristobal

Mount Cristobal is seen as the negative counterpart to the positive spiritual energy of Mount Banahaw. It takes up to six hours of serious trekking along an awkward trail to reach Jones Peak, which is 50m lower than the inaccessible summit. The climb isn't recommended for beginners or unaccompanied trekkers.

ARRIVAL AND INFORMATION   MOUNT BANAHAW AND AROUND

By bus, jeepney and tricycle To reach the access town of Dolores, take one of the Jac Liner, JAM, Lucena Lines or N. Dela Rosa buses that runs between Manila (Buendia or Cubao) and Lucena. Get off at San Pablo (hourly; 2hr), from where there are jeepneys to Dolores from the market (hourly; 25min; P18). From Dolores, take a tricycle to the barangay of Kinabuyahan (20min; P250)

Guides The municipal tourist office in Dolores can help

organize guides (from P250 for 6–10 people/day), although you will need to inform the Tourism Officer, Laarni Alilio, a few days in advance (☎042 565 6785, ✉laarni_alilio@yahoo.com).

Permits To reach the summit you need a special permit issued by the Protected Area Management Board; the Municipal Environment and Natural Resources Department can help (☎042 565 6331).

EATING

Kinabuyahan Café 118 Dejarme St ☎0916 221 5791. Owned by artist Jay Herrera, this quirky café and B&B offers accommodation in a rustic tree house and two native

huts. Hearty mains are made to order; the cuisine is mainly international with a Filipino twist. Rates include three daily meals. P2250

Quezon National Park

Quezon National Park, about 25km east of Lucena near the town of **ATIMONAN**, is off the well-beaten trail, far from the picture-postcard beaches of the Visayas and too distant from Manila to make it a viable weekend trip. Though relatively small at just ten square kilometres, the park is so dense with flora and fauna that you have a good chance of seeing anything and everything from giant monitor lizards to monkeys, deer and wild pigs. This is also home to the *kalaw*, a species of hornbill.

It takes about an hour to walk along the paved trail to the highest point, 366m above sea level, which has a viewing deck from where you can see both sides of the Bicol peninsula. The summit is known as **Pinagbanderahan**, meaning "where the flag is hoisted", because both Japanese and American flags were flown there before the Philippine flag was raised in 1946. There are also numerous **caves** in the park that can be explored with guides, experience and the right equipment.

ARRIVAL AND INFORMATION   QUEZON NATIONAL PARK

By bus The turning for the park is on the Maharlika Highway, which runs from Lucena to Atimonan. The winding approach road to the park, known locally as *bituka ng manok* (chicken's intestine), is a challenge for buses: from Lucena's Grand Central station, you can get any bus heading east through Bicol (to Daet, for instance) or an Atimonan-bound bus, as all these vehicles pass the park entrance (every 15min; 1hr).

Guides Enquire at the Atimonan Municipal Tourism Council (☏ 0908 888 7132, ✉ lgu_atimonan@yahoo.com; P300/day for a group of eight).

ACCOMMODATION AND EATING

Doña Rosario Sea Breeze Resort Km176 Maharlika Hwy, Brgy Angeles, Atimonan ☏ 042 778 5373, ⊛ dona rosarioresorts.com/seabreeze.html. This beachside resort offers village-style cottages and recreational fishponds where guests are encouraged to angle fish and crustaceans, including tilapia and crab. Facilities include a swimming pool and bowling alley. P1800

Marinduque

With its numerous caves and pretty beaches, tiny **MARINDUQUE** (pronounced "mar-in-DOO-kay") island, where most of the 230,000 residents lead a life of subsistence coconut farming and fishing, is a great place to get away from it all for a few days. Work your way slowly around the coastal road south of **Boac**, then across the island to **Torrijos** and **Poctoy White Beach**, where you can live cheaply in the shadow of majestic **Mount Malinding**. There's some excellent island-hopping too, with spectacular beaches and coves to explore around the **Tres Reyes Islands** off the southwest coast and the **Santa Cruz Islands** off the northeast coast. The island is known for its **Moriones festival**, an animated Easter tradition featuring masked men dressed like Roman soldiers (see box, p.201). If you plan to visit during Holy Week then you should book ahead.

Marinduque has had its share of problems. When copper mining was begun here in 1969, many thought it was the dawn of a new era. Sadly, the dream ended in disaster and recrimination as waste from disused pits flowed into the island's rivers on two separate occasions, destroying agricultural land, the livelihood of the locals and marine life – which is still trying to recover.

Boac

BOAC ("bow-ak") is an orderly, compact town with neat streets and low-rise buildings laid out around a central plaza. The area around the cathedral has numerous typical Filipino *bahay ng buto* (wooden houses), the windows boasting carved wooden shutters instead of glass and the balconies exploding with bougainvillea and frangipani. Many of these houses were built in the nineteenth century and are now a photogenic, if faded, reminder of a style of architecture that is rapidly disappearing.

The cathedral

High Town • Daily 5am–6pm

Construction of Boac's atmospheric Spanish Gothic **cathedral** started in 1580 in honour of the Blessed Virgin of Immediate Succour, and was used in its early years as a refuge from pirate attacks. Most of the original main structure, including the red-brick facade and the belfry, is well preserved and there's a pleasant garden outside. Look out above the main doors for a stone niche containing a statue of the Blessed Virgin, enshrined here in 1792. Devotees say it is the most miraculous statue in the country and tell of blind people who have regained their sight after praying fervently beneath it day and night.

Marinduque National Museum

Boac Plaza • ☎ 0926 122 3555 • Tues–Sat 8am–noon & 1–5pm • P20

The small **Marinduque National Museum** is located in a lovely Spanish colonial building that previously served as a prison, a boys' school and a courthouse. The museum briefly charts the island's geological history, before introducing more recent history including evidence of pre-Spanish trade with China. Displays include sixteenth-century Chinese storage stoneware jars with dragon designs found on the

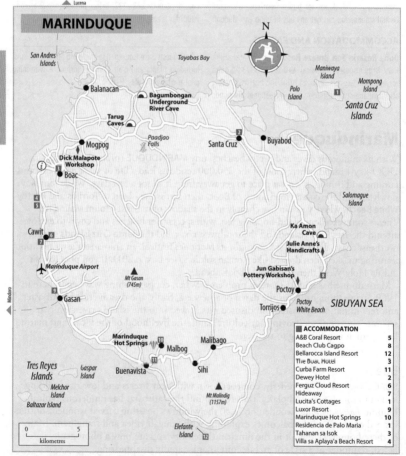

■ ACCOMMODATION	
A&B Coral Resort	5
Beach Club Cagpo	8
Bellarocca Island Resort	12
The Boac Hotel	3
Curba Farm Resort	11
Dewey Hotel	2
Ferguz Cloud Resort	6
Hideaway	7
Lucita's Cottages	1
Luxor Resort	9
Marinduque Hot Springs	10
Residencia de Palo Maria	1
Tahanan sa Isok	3
Villa sa Aplaya'a Beach Resort	4

MORIONES FESTIVAL

The **Moriones festival** celebrates the life of Longinus, the Roman soldier who pierced Christ's side during the Crucifixion. Blood from the wound spattered Longinus's blind eye, which was immediately healed. Converted on the spot, he later attested to the Resurrection and, refusing to recant, was executed. The Marinduqueyo version of this tale is colourful and bizarre, involving fanciful masked figures dressed as centurions chasing Longinus around town and through nearby fields. Several Moriones pageants are staged in Marinduque during **Holy Week**, with extra events added in recent years for the benefit of tourists (see ⓦ marinduque.gov.ph for more information). Although the festival originated in Mogpog, and other towns including Santa Cruz have their own versions, these days the major Moriones celebrations are in **Boac**.

---

seabed by Gaspar Island, as well as early musical instruments used during special events and celebrations. There is also a collection of Moriones masks, along with descriptive captions tracing the festival's roots.

Marinduque's west coast

The **west coast** from Boac south to **Gasan** and a little beyond boasts a number of **resorts**. The beaches are pebbly but they do offer fine views of the sunset and across the sea towards Mindoro in the distance. The resorts are often full for the Moriones festival (see box above) and at Christmas, but at any other time you might find that you are the only guest. South of Gasan lies the sleepy town of **Buenavista**, where jeepneys usually terminate – so you'll have to wait here for onward transport.

Gasan and around

It's much better to stay in the nearby resorts than in **GASAN** itself, though the modern **St Joseph Catholic Church** is worth a look for its views, and the town has a few small souvenir shops selling Moriones-themed products and tasty arrowroot biscuits (which, along with *bibingka* rice cakes, are a Marinduque speciality).

St Joseph Catholic Church

Perched on a hillside, **St Joseph Catholic Church** offers wonderful **bay views** from the leafy back terrace, especially at sunset. Built in the first decade of the new millennium, it features a beautiful thick wooden door carved by a renowned Mogpog sculptor. The intricate ceiling was designed to resemble a palm leaf, while the inner sidewalls are lined with coconut shell dividers. At the back are the remnants of the old church, from 1609.

Tres Reyes Islands

Boat from Sitio Castillo, Gasan P40 (15min); or arrange a private island hopping trip with your resort (P1500)

The beautiful **Tres Reyes Islands** – popularly known as **Baltazar**, **Melchor** and **Gaspar** after the biblical Three Kings – lie a few kilometres off shore. There is some good **scuba diving** here, which can be arranged from various outlets (see p.204) or at one of the resorts. On the far side of Gaspar Island there's a white beach with good coral for **snorkelling**; a small fishing community is located on the eastern tip of the island, but there's no formal accommodation.

Marinduque hot springs

Sitio Mainit, Brgy Malbog, Km3 • Daily 8am–10pm • Day rate P50, night rate (from 5pm) P70 • ☎ 0917 382 9416 • Tricycle from Buenavista P40 (10min)

Located in an eight-hectare lot, the inviting **Marinduque hot spring** pools are a pleasant spot to while away a few hours. There are a couple of large pools, as well as three smaller pools that can be rented out privately (P1000/5hr – call in advance). There are picnic huts, too.

4

Mount Malindig

Enquire at the tourist office in Boac or at the barangay hall in Sihi, Buenavista to organize a compulsory guide (P500/day)

The highest peak of Marinduque is **Mount Malindig**, a 1157m volcano that's considered dormant. It's possible to climb to the summit; the hike can be done in a day starting from the barangay of Sihi in Buenavista, with the ascent taking about three and a half hours and the descent significantly less.

Marinduque's east coast

Marinduque's **east coast** offers a number of wonderful secluded beaches, the nicest of which is **Poctoy White Beach**. There are fewer resorts on this stretch of coast than on the west, and it's well worth spending a couple of days.

Poctoy White Beach

P20 environmental fee • Jeepneys between Santa Cruz and Torrijos stop off at Poctoy (hourly; 1hr 30min; P40)

Just 2km from Torrijos is **Poctoy White Beach**, where the sand is not as pale as the name suggests but is still much better than the pebbles on the west coast. The views across the bay to Mount Malindig can also be spectacular. The stretch of beach is packed with huts which can be rented for the day, and has a small market where you can buy the catch of the day by weight and have it cooked for an extra P25.

Ka Amon Cave

Brgy Bonliw • Compulsory guides (by donation; minimum P50) can be organized at Bonliw Barangay Hall • ☎ 0926 648 7033 • Jeepneys from Torrijos to Brgy Bonliw (hourly; 20min; P18)

Eleven kilometres north of Torrijos is the **Ka Amon Cave**, a series of seven chambers that were once pre-Hispanic funeral grottoes – you can still see skeletal remains and broken potteries as you enter the first chamber. Chambers six and seven are off limits to visitors in order to preserve the cave habitat and fauna, which includes bats and birds. You'll still be able to see about one hundred bats in chamber five, where tours end; there are even more during the rainy season.

Santa Cruz and around

If you're interested in exploring the caves and islands in the northeast of Marinduque, **SANTA CRUZ** is the best base for a day or two. That said, the town is unmemorable – the only sights a whitewashed Spanish-era church and the dilapidated wooden convent next to it – and the narrow streets in the centre are choked with tricycles and jeepneys from dawn to dusk. Be prepared for noise.

MARINDUQUE HANDICRAFTS

On the road from Torrijos to Santa Cruz, there are a couple of worthwhile stops for anyone interested in **handicrafts**. Within the barangay of Poctoy, a short distance from the beach, is the pottery workshop of **Jun Gabisan** (daily 8am–5pm; ☎ 0910 252 5120), who learned the craft from his father and has been making pots since he was 12. He and his father (who speaks better English) offer tuition on the potter's wheel at P300 per hour for a small group. Further along the coastal road in the barangay of Bonliw is **Julie Anne's Handicrafts** (daily 8am–5pm; ☎ 0917 544 6962), a popular stop with the few tour groups who make it to Marinduque. Employing twenty women, the company produces placemats and other textiles on traditional looms, using stalks of the *buntal* palm tree that are threaded, dyed and weaved at the workshop. The weavers are happy to receive visitors and allow photographs, but may not speak much English. Both make for an interesting stop although, as both the pottery and woven products are made to order, there is a limited selection available to buy.

Santa Cruz Islands

Boats leave from Buyabod port, 5km east of Santa Cruz by tricycle P120 (15min); contact Edwin Romasanta to organize a boat (📞 0920 609 9279) for island-hopping (P2000–3500)

The islands of Maniwaya, Mompong and Polo, collectively known as the **Santa Cruz Islands**, make for a wonderful day-trip. The closest to the mainland is **Polo**, rich in wetland forests and transient birds, local macaque monkeys and fruit bats. While the island is dotted with a few pleasant beaches, it's best to head further on to **Maniwaya**, which boasts a long stretch of fine sand lined with a few accommodation options. On the northeastern side of the island is the spectacular **Palad Sandbar**, a stretch of coral sands with crystal clear waters that appears only during low tide. The furthest of the islands is **Mompong**, with its distinctive Ungab sedimentary rock formation that acts as a natural bridge – the waters here are emerald green, and it's a wonderful spot for a swim.

Bagumbongan Underground River Cave

Brgy San Isidro • P300 entry fee including compulsory guide; guides can be arranged at the tourist information centre on the way to the cave • Jeepneys from Santa Cruz (daily 11am & 4pm; 1hr; P28); tricycles from Santa Cruz (45min; P800 including waiting time)

About 24km west of Santa Cruz, the 2km-long **Bagumbongan Underground River Cave** is the longest underground river in the province. There are some fixed ropes and spots where water reaches chest height. Helmets, lights and gloves are provided. Guides will lead you inside the cave for about 1km, ending up at a cascading waterfall of about 10m before turning back; they can also take experienced cavers all the way to the other side. Note that you won't be able to explore the cave during heavy rains.

Mogpog

The little town of **MOGPOG** doesn't offer much for visitors, although it is renowned across the island for being the birthplace of the **Moriones festival** (see box, p.201) and holds its own festivities – smaller in scale than those in Boac – during Holy Week. The word Mogpog comes from the tagalog word *mag-aapog*, which roughly translates as "abundance of lime" and the area around town is indeed rich in limestone, with a number of **caves** to explore.

Dick Malapote workshop

Brgy Janagdong, 1km west of Mogpog • 📞 0939 468 2365 • Tricycle from Mogpog P40 (10min), then ask around – locals know where Dick Malapote lives

One of the most famous Moriones **costume makers**, Dick Malapote has been creating centurion outfits for more than 25 years, selling whole sets of armour for as much as P15,000. He welcomes visitors at his workshop but doesn't speak much English, so the best bet, if you are interested, is to enquire at the provincial tourist office near Boac (see p.204), who can arrange for someone to accompany you.

Tarug Caves

Tarug brgy, Bocboc • By donation to local guides (P50) – ask around at the village you pass through on the way to the cave • Jeepney from Mogpog towards Santa Cruz P20 (every 30min; 30min), followed by a 1.5km (45min) trek; ask the driver where to get off

The **Tarug Caves** are actually one enormous cave with three chambers set inside a 300m-tall limestone spire that's barely 3m wide at the top. You can climb to the top, where the reward is a panoramic view of the Bondoc peninsula to the east and the Tablas Strait to the west.

Paadjao Falls

Brgy Bocboc, 10km from Mogpog • Jeepney from Mogpog P20 (daily 9am & 3pm; 30min), tricycle P400 return including waiting time (30min)

About ten minutes' uphill walk from the main road, nestled within coconut groves, are the gently cascading **Paadjao Falls**. There are a series of pools here, perfect for a little dip – the largest is at the foot of the uppermost fall. Join the locals sitting on the rocks, letting the strong jet stream of water massage your back and shoulders.

ARRIVAL AND DEPARTURE

By plane At the time of writing Marinduque airport was temporarily closed for renovation; flights to Manila (45min) are due to resume as soon as it reopens.

By ferry Montenegro Lines connects Lucena to Balanacan port (4am, noon & 8.30pm; 3hr; P260), while Starhorse have departures at 10.30am, 10.30pm and 6.30pm (the 6.30pm service doesn't run on Sun). Heading back to Lucena, Starhorse ferries depart at 6.30am and 2.30pm, while Montenegro Lines returns at 8am, 4pm and 11.30pm.

There are outrigger services between Gasan on Marinduque and Pinamalayan in Mindoro (daily 8am; 3–4hr; P265). Jeepneys from Boac meet incoming ferries (1hr; P50).

By bangka Daily bangkas connect Buyabod port east of Santa Cruz to Catanauan in Quezon province (daily 11am; 3hr; P200).

By bus Jack Liner travels from Boac to Manila using the roll-on-roll-off ferry (daily 8pm; 8–9hr).

GETTING AROUND

By jeepney No jeepneys loop the entire island; if you're planning on travelling to multiple destinations you'll have to change. On the west and north coasts they run from Boac–Gasan–Buenavista, and Boac–Mogpog–Santa Cruz, while on the east coast there are services from Santa Cruz–Torrijos. To get to Buenavista from Torrijos you'll have to take a jeepney to Malibago and change there. It is possible to travel around the entire island by jeepney in two days, but four or five would be more comfortable, particularly since if you miss the last jeepney (most services stop around 4–5pm) you can easily find yourself stranded.

By van Easier than travelling by jeepney is renting a van for around P3500/day. Most accommodation options can help organize this, or enquire at the provincial tourist office near Boac (see below).

INFORMATION AND ACTIVITIES

Tourist information The helpful provincial tourist office (☎ 042 754 0136, ⊛ marinduque.gov.ph), in the Capitol Building complex on the road between Boac and the airport, has a handful of leaflets, but once on the road be prepared for a lack of reliable information.

Banks and exchange There are banks with ATMs in Boac, including Land Bank, RCBC and PNB, all along Reyes St. RCBC and PNB also have branches in Santa Cruz.

Scuba diving There are no dive shops on the island, but keen scuba divers should contact Freedom Dellosa (☎ 0920 223 0904, ✉ coraldiver@hotmail.com). He can arrange equipment rental, as well as open water courses (P14,000).

ACCOMMODATION

BOAC

The Boac Hotel Deogracias St at Nepomuceno St ☎ 042 332 1121, ✉ theboachotel@yahoo.com. This big yellow building is the oldest hotel in town, and its antiques and wooden furniture lend it an appealing atmosphere. The single rooms with just one single bed allegedly sleep two, although they are tiny, even just for one; you're better off going for a deluxe (P1200) with a double bed. The cheapest rooms are fan-only, while standard rooms and above have a/c. **P500**

Tahanan sa Isok Canovas St ☎ 042 332 1231, ✉ tahanan saisok34@yahoo.com. The entrance of this welcoming hotel has a touch of homely feel, with a glass cabinet with books, a piano and a few religious knick-knacks. The staircase leading up to the accommodation is lined with potted plants, and the rooms are great value, with chocolate-coloured furniture, although some of the single beds are tiny. There's a pleasant pool, and wi-fi in the lobby. **P1000**

THE WEST COAST

★A&B Coral Resort Brgy Balaring ☎ 042 332 0121 or ☎ 0947 556 8986, ✉ paquet.bruno@hotmail.com.

This lovely little place has just three warm and welcoming a/c rooms with private bath in a building overlooking the sea; there are also a couple of pleasant nipa rooms that are an absolute steal. The plant-festooned garden with a large pomelo tree is dotted with knick-knacks, including old carriage wheels, while the lounge area features fibre deck chairs and wicker sofas. There are also two outdoor jacuzzis. **P500**

Ferguz Cloud Resort Cawit ☎ 0928 310 6495, ✉ ferguzcloudresort@gmail.com. An excellent budget option less than 1km from Cawit port, with neat and tidy bamboo cottages set around a pleasant garden area with a swimming pool and a few gnomes. Some rooms have a/c, while others are fan cooled, they're all on the small side, but the grassy grounds and pool make up for it. Massages P450/hr. **P1000**

★Hideaway Cawit ☎ 042 332 1749 or ☎ 0915 285 2643, ✉ marby.montellano@gmail.com. This quirky little place features comfortable a/c rooms, with wooden beds and makeshift lamps, off a shaded pathway. The garden bursts with atmosphere, dotted with masks, statuettes, wooden ladders and buoys, and wind chimes singing in the breeze. There are hammocks and swinging chairs, as well as a little hut with cushioned seating, perfect for kicking back with a book. P1200

Luxor Resort Brgy Pangi, 1.5km north of Gasan ☎ 042 332 0063. This new resort has gone for a Thai Buddha theme, with all seven cottages on the grassy grounds featuring Buddha pictures. All rooms have a/c, flatscreen TV and private bath with rain showers, and there's a pleasant garden with a welcoming shaded area by the sea that is a perfect spot to enjoy a sundowner. P1500

Villa sa Aplaya'a Beach Resort Brgy Ihatub ☎ 042 332 1882, ⓦ villasaaplaya.com. The buildings may be drab and grey, but the great-value rooms are a pleasant surprise; most have a/c, fridge and veranda with loungers. The pebbly garden is dotted with tables and a few concrete deck chairs, and there's a surprisingly large indoor badminton court, too. P1200

BUENAVISTA AND AROUND

Bellarocca Island Resort Elefante Island ☎ 02 310 9931, ⓦ bellaroccaresorts.com. Located just off the coast of southern Marinduque on the small Elefante Island, this upmarket resort attracts well-heeled Filipinos and Korean honeymooners, and features whitewashed houses sprinkled along the island's hillside. It's more for couples than families, with just a small beach but a variety of watersports including jetskiing, kayaking and scuba diving. US$500

Curba Farm Resort Brgy Uno ☎ 0948 714 3488, ⓔ ma.amor_dy@yahoo.com. There's a cowboy theme going on here, with framed guns and Wild West memorabilia decorating the premises. The four rooms are on a grassy slope looking over an inviting pool with an artificial waterfall; there's also a billiards table, and an attached resto-bar with outdoor seating serving local and international dishes, including mixed seafood (P185) and T-bone steaks (P349). Rates include breakfast. P1200

Marinduque Hot Springs Sitio Mainit, Malbog, Km3 ☎ 0917 382 9416. Set on lovely verdant grounds, this resort offers a series of rooms connected by a pebbly pathway dotted with wooden statuettes; the spacious family rooms (P2600) with two double beds are great

value, while the cheaper a/c doubles and twins (P1600) are not as appealing. You can also camp for P300 (plus entrance fee to the springs of P70). P1300

POCTOY

★ **Beach Club Cagpo** Brgy Cagpo ☎ 0921 993 2537, ⓦ beachclubcagpo.com. Located on a lovely stretch of sand, the blue and white rooms take their inspiration from Greece, with rough whitewashed walls and paintings of Greek islands. There's a welcoming a/c cottage (P1350), as well as one standard fan room and a deluxe fan room (P1250). The restaurant serves international dishes prepared with fresh herbs from the garden, including great home-made burgers (P165), vegetable curry (P140) and wood-fired pizzas (P330). There's also an eight-bed dorm with lockers. Dorm P350; double P1100

SANTA CRUZ

Dewey Hotel Brgy Maharlika ☎ 042 660 7904. This new hotel composed of two green and yellow buildings offers clean rooms with mustard-yellow tiles; there are also spacious family rooms (P2200) with two double beds, and a little rooftop pool with a couple of sun loungers. Food can be cooked upon request. P1400

SANTA CRUZ ISLANDS

Lucita's Cottages Maniwaya Island ☎ 0949 854 1229, ⓔ ron_perlada@yahoo.com. This family-run place offers three simple, cosy cottages just a stone's throw from the beach – a great spot if you're on a budget and just want to laze. One of the cottages is larger, with its own well-equipped kitchen (P1500). P1000

Residencia De Palo Maria Maniwaya Island ☎ 0919 237 5633, ⓔ residenciadepalomaria@yahoo.com. The best accommodation option on the island offers comfortable a/c rooms with cable TV (P2000), as well as cheaper native cottages that are equally as welcoming, and even feature their own little outdoor patio with flatscreen TV. There's a breezy restaurant by the swimming pool serving local dishes (P165), and the resort offers all manner of water activities, including banana boating, scuba diving, water skiing and kayaking. P1500

EATING AND DRINKING

BOAC

BFC Restaurant Brgy Malusak ☎ 0921 298 4688. This cosy little restaurant features dark brick walls and wooden tables, and gets particularly busy at lunchtime. The menu includes the usual Filipino staples, including beef steak (P120), chicken dishes (P60) and chop suey (P75). Daily 7am–7pm.

★ **Casa de Don Emilio** Mercader St ☎ 042 332 1699. The best restaurant in town is in a beautiful Spanish

colonial building with polished hardwood floors. The owner, a keen musician, has a fascinating collection of old musical instruments, including an antique double bass, trombone, trumpet and sax – all displayed along the restaurant's walls. The restaurant specializes in coconut dishes – try the native chicken cooked in coconut milk (P225). Daily 10am–9pm.

La Concha Brgy Malusak ☎ 042 332 2854. This no frills self-service joint with menus plastered over the walls offers

4

standard local food for about P75 per dish, as well as pizzas (P70); there's also a Japanese corner featuring vegetable tempura (P60). Daily 6am–9pm.

Kusina sa Plaza Mercader St ☎ 042 332 1699. Popular restaurant on Boac's main square, displaying a range of Filipino dishes that will cost about P75 per meal. The attached coffee shop (with free wi-fi) serves pizzas (P50) and pasta (P44). Daily 7am–7pm.

GASAN

Barbarossa San José St ☎ 0908 377 6656. This German-owned place is where the island's handful of expats regularly meet, gathering over refreshing ice-cold beer in frozen mugs (P88). The menu features a range of inter-national dishes including bockwurst sausage (P250), pizza (P300) and spaghetti bolognaise (P175). There are occasional live bands. Daily 10am–9pm.

Daet and around

The capital of Camarines Norte, **DAET**, 200km southeast of Manila, is overrun with tricycles, but the nearby coastline has more than its fair share of unspoiled beaches and islands; the fickle waves at **Bagasbas Beach** and **San Miguel Bay** are particular attractions for surfers.

Daet's busy little central plaza is a popular meeting place in the evenings. One block north is the 1950s **Provincial Capitol**, in front of which Kalayaan (Freedom) Park features the tallest statue of **José Rizal** outside Manila. Erected in 1899, this was the first monument to Rizal in the country and set the trend for thousands of others in plazas across the archipelago.

Bagasbas Beach

Lovely **Bagasbas Beach**, 4km northeast of Daet, is accessible by tricycle (10min; P40). The waves that crash in from the Pacific are sometimes big enough for **surfing** (see box below), particularly between November and March. In fact, the whole area of coast east of Daet has become something of a surfers' hangout, though the shore can be pretty much deserted by all but stray dogs on weekdays.

ARRIVAL AND INFORMATION

DAET AND AROUND

By bus Buses arriving in Daet stop at the edge of the city on the National Highway, from where it's less than 2km into town; plenty of tricycles travel the route for P30. Philtranco, DLTB and Superlines travel to Manila (roughly hourly; 7–8hr), stopping off in Atimoan (4–5hr) and Lucena (5–6hr).

By van Regular vans connect Naga to Daet (every 30min; 2hr; P180).

Information The municipal and provincial tourist offices

are both in Daet on J. Pimentel St at Magallanes Iraya St (both Mon–Fri 8am–5pm; provincial ☎ 054 721 3087; municipal ☎ 054 441 6163). There's also a tourist information centre on Magalles Iraya St (Mon–Fri 8am–5pm, Sat 8am–noon; no phone). Offering surfing and general information, the Bagasbas United Surfers' Association (see box below) has an information point on Bagasbas Beach, to the left of the public transport drop-off point.

SURFING AND KITE-BOARDING ON BAGASBAS

Several places on **Bagasbas Beach** rent out surfboards and offer tuition. **Experienced surfers** who want to look beyond Bagasbas should ask about the breaks in nearby San Miguel Bay, which often has very good waves close to the town of Mercedes and around the seven islands known as the Siete Pecados.

Bagasbas United Surfers' Association ☎ 0921 251 8747. Tuition for around P200/hr along with board rental (P200/hr). Mon–Fri 8am–5pm.

Hang Loose ☎ 0921 251 8748. Friendly outfit offering surfboard rental for P200/hr and lessons for around P200/hr. Daily 6am–7pm.

Mike's Kites ⊛ mikes-kites.com. Kiteboarding, starting at $65 for a day's equipment rental or $60 for a 2hr intro-ductory session. If the wind and waves are not cooperating, they also rent out sea kayaks and organize island-hopping trips. Daily 5am–2am.

ACCOMMODATION

DAET

Francesco's Suzara St at Dimasalang ☎054 440 0031, ✉francescoinn@yahoo.com. This small new hotel has just four, spacious, modern rooms; all have tea-making facilities, and there's wi-fi throughout. The hotel is set above a Japanese-style restaurant serving, among other things, *shabu-shabu*: beef, chicken or pork submerged in a pot of boiling soup (P220). **P2500**

Hotel Formosa Vinzons Ave, Brgy Lag-On ☎054 571 3566, ✉hotelformosa@yahoo.com. One of the city's best options offers neat and tidy rooms with flat-screen TV and wooden furniture. Some rooms face the interior and as a result may be a bit dark, but the premises are kept spic-and-span and there's wi-fi throughout. **P1600**

BAGASBAS BEACH

Bagasbas Lighthouse Hotel Resort ☎054 731 0355, ⓦbagasbaslighthouse.com. On the seafront, this is by far the area's best option, with stylish accommodation in deluxe rooms (P2750) or cheaper converted trailer rooms. There are also "backpacker rooms" sleeping three (P1650) to eight (P4400) people. The restaurant, with seating beside the swimming pool, serves Filipino favourites and Western fast food, plus Bicol specialities (see box, p.218) including Bicol Express and *laing*. Mains P155. **P1750**

Surfer's Dine-Inn ☎0916 475 9053, ✉surfersdineinn@yahoo.com. This laidback place offers a few simple rooms off a paved walkway; the concrete rooms (P700) are acceptable if you're just here to catch a few waves, although you'll probably have to fend your way through a cobweb or two. There are also a couple of fan-cooled nipa huts. The restaurant serves inexpensive dishes – around P200 for two to three people. **P500**

Zenaida's Palace ☎054 441 6286, ✉shara.1119@gmail.com. This large white and yellow building is an excellent budget option, offering spacious rooms with hot and cold showers. There's a pool at the back and a small lounge area with wi-fi, although it appears to be mostly restricted to the family who run the hotel. **P1000**

EATING

DAET

KFisher 1101 V. Basit St ☎054 571 2211, ⓦkfisherseafooddaet.com. This place specializes in seafood, ranging from *pusit* (squid; P75) to sushi (P298) and sashimi (P175); the decor is a bit drab, but it ranks among the city's best places to eat. There's wi-fi, too. Daily 10am–10pm.

Ksarap Vinzons Ave ☎054 440 5151. Breezy open-fronted restaurant with bamboo walls, a nipa roof and spotlights – and more atmosphere than most places in Daet. The menu offers Bicol delicacies including all manner of pili nut products, from tarts to rolls. Savoury dishes include empanadas (P20), vegetable spring rolls (P100) and fish steak (P80) – most people round things off with the ubiquitous *halo-halo* (P65). Daily 9am–10pm.

BAGASBAS BEACH

Kusina ni Angel ☎0943 682 7870. This no-frills restaurant has a nipa roof and tables clustered together both indoors and out; the menu features the usual Filipino suspects, including meat and poultry (P250) and seafood dishes (P230) to share. Daily 8am–10pm.

Leo's Cuisine ☎0917 315 5531. Right on the beachfront, this is the area's most atmospheric restaurant, with a glass cabinet displaying all manner of knick-knacks, as well as the owner's surfboards and surfing awards. The fish- and seafood-based menu includes sizzling Thai squid (P180) and calamares (P180). Daily 9am–10pm.

Camarines Sur province

Lying at the heart of Bicol, the laidback province of **Camarines Sur**, with a spectacular stretch of rugged coastline to the east, is rich in natural beauty, with secluded beaches and peaceful lakeside spots. The region is fast becoming a prime destination for young adventure sports enthusiasts, many of whom flock here from Manila to wakeboard at the **CamSur Watersports Complex**.

Naga

Centrally located in Camarines Sur, the lively university city of **NAGA** was established in 1578 by Spanish conquistador Pedro de Chavez. Although there are a couple of sights in the city itself, its place on the tourist map is due mainly to the success of the **CamSur Watersports Complex**, or CWC, in nearby Pili (see p.212). Naga offers an alternative base, with a fun nightlife scene thanks in part to its large student population. Things are

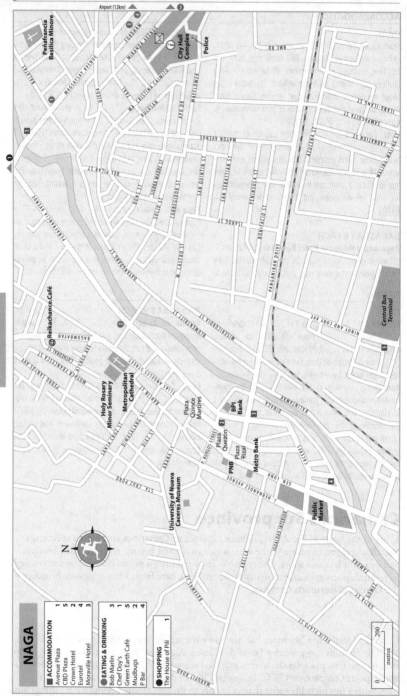

NAGA

■ ACCOMMODATION

Avenue Plaza	1
CBD Plaza	5
Crown Hotel	2
Eurotel	4
Moraville Hotel	3

● EATING & DRINKING

Bob Marlin	3
Chef Doy's	1
Green Earth Café	5
Mudbugs	2
P Bar	4

● SHOPPING

The House of Pili	1

particularly lively during the nine-day **Peñafrancia festival** in September, held in honour of Our Lady of Peñafrancia, when as many as a million devotees and tourists flood the streets.

Naga centre is focused on two main squares, **Plaza Rizal** and **Plaza Quince Martires**, surrounded by fast-food restaurants, banks, convenience stores and pharmacies. The main drag, **Elias Angeles Street**, runs north to south; to the east, along Panganiban Drive, is the Naga River. Vibrant **Magsaysay Avenue**, to the northeast, running from Avenue Square mall to City Hall, has many of Naga's best shops, bars and restaurants, as well as a handful of hotels.

University of Nueva Caceres Museum

J. Hernandez Ave • Mon–Fri 8am–noon & 2–5pm, Sat 8am–noon • Free • ☎ 054 472 6100

Run by an enthusiastic curator who will willingly talk you through the displays, the **University of Nueva Caceres Museum** gives an overview on the city's history from the ancient period to the present day. There is a very concise section on the Arab and Muslim influence in the southern Philippines, and details on Chinese trade. Highlights include Chinese porcelain and earthenware dishes that were bartered for local items, as well as local dresses showing how three hundred years of Spanish rule influenced the attire of Bicolanos.

Holy Rosary Minor Seminary

Elias Angeles Ave • **Archaeological Museum** Mon–Fri 8am–5pm, Sat & Sun by appointment only with the curator (☎ 0919 592 0724) • P20 • ☎ 054 473 8297

One of the country's oldest institutes for higher learning, the beautiful red complex of the **Holy Rosary Minor Seminary** was built in 1785 as a vocation house. It was declared a National Historical Landmark in 1988, and to this day houses the dormitories of priests and seminaries. Inside, the small, privately owned **Archaeological Museum** displays a lovely collection of trade wares from China, Vietnam and Thailand, along with ancient relics – including the country's most extensive collection of primary burial jars from the Bicol region, dating back to 200 AD. By far the most unusual displays are dinosaur eggs from the Mongolian Gobi Desert, dating back 146–165 million years.

Metropolitan Cathedral

Elias Angeles Ave • Daily 7am–5pm

The **Metropolitan Cathedral** is the largest church in Southern Luzon and the seat of the Archdiocese of Caceres. The original structure was built in 1595 near the Naga River; after being destroyed by fire in 1758, it was rebuilt on this site, only to be damaged by a typhoon in 1856, and subsequently an earthquake in 1887. The church was built in Romanesque Baroque style using Spanish Royal funds – note the Spanish royal seal above the door.

At daybreak on the opening day of the **Peñafrancia festival**, an image of the Virgin – known as "Ina" (Bicolano for mother) – is taken from its permanent home at the Peñafrancia Basilica Minore, east of town, and carried to the cathedral by barefoot devotees (*voyadores*); she then spends the nine days of the novena at the cathedral before being returned to her permanent home.

ARRIVAL AND INFORMATION

By plane Naga Airport is 12km east of town, in the provincial capital Pili; taxis connect the city to the airport (15min; P350).

By bus Buses to Naga arrive at the Central Bus Terminal in Central Business District 2 (CB2) on Ninoy and Cory Ave, which is across the river to the south of the town centre, close to the SM mall; you'll have to take a tricycle from here

NAGA

(10min; P8) to the centre. Many companies run the route to Manila, including DLTB (6 daily; 8–10hr), stopping off in Atimonan (for Quezon National Park; 6hr) and Lucena (6hr). Most buses to Manila depart between 6–10pm. There are also local buses to Legazpi (every 30min; 3hr) and Daraga (every 15min; 3hr), although for both these destinations it's quicker to catch a van.

By van Vans arrive and leave from opposite the Central Bus Terminal in Central Business District 2.

Departures Daraga (hourly; 2hr; P130); Legazpi (every 30min; 2hr; P140); San José (for Sabang port on the Caramoan Peninsula; hourly; 1hr 30min; P100); Tabaco (every 30min; 2hr; P180).

Tourist information The Naga City Arts, Culture and Tourism Office is in the DOLE Building, City Hall Complex, J. Miranda Ave (Mon–Fri 8am–5pm; ☎054 478 3987, ⓦnagax.com). Staff can provide city maps and organize traditional Bicolano cooking courses (P1000/day), as well as help organize guides for Mt Isarog (see p.213).

ACCOMMODATION

Many hotels, particularly the budget ones, are fully booked during the **Peñafrancia festival** so make sure to plan ahead if you're coming at this time. For the rest of the year, finding a room shouldn't be a problem.

Avenue Plaza Magsaysay Ave ☎054 473 9999, ⓦtheAveplazahotel.com. In a class of its own in Naga, with rooms of an international standard, along with a swimming pool, gym and sauna, and an excellent restaurant featuring fusion and international cuisine. The hotel is on Naga's entertainment strip, with plenty of restaurants and bars on its doorstep, and there's low-key piano music in the lobby in the evenings. P5400

CBD Plaza Ninoy and Cory Ave, Brgy Triangulo ☎054 472 0318, ⓦcbdplazahotel.com. Just opposite the Central Bus Terminal, this hotel offers good value; the cheaper economy singles (P600) and doubles are located in an annexe and all feature cold showers, while the larger singles (P1000) and doubles (P1300) with a/c, hot shower and cable TV are in the main building. P1000

Crown Hotel P. Burgos St ☎054 473 1845, ⓦcrown hotel-naga.com. A decent option right in the noisy centre of Naga, with a range of rooms. The standard rooms (with a double bed) have slightly shoddy furniture, while the deluxe rooms (P2500) are more spacious and in better shape. Suite A (P6000) is a big jump up with a comfortable living area and king-size bed. There are a couple of 24hr restaurants offering a range of Chinese dishes. P1500

Eurotel Dinaga St ☎054 472 5321, ⓦeurotel-hotel.com. This new hotel features a series of oddly furnished rooms, each featuring a blown-up image of a European landmark – somewhat out of place in central Naga. The rooms are comfortable nonetheless, with hot water, a/c and private bath. Rates are either on a 12- (P1050) or 24hr basis. P1500

Moraville Hotel Caceres St ☎054 473 1247, ⓦmoraville .com.ph. A very reasonable option with appealing rooms at bargain prices. The rock walls and chintz may be a bit too much in some rooms, but overall the a/c accommodation is clean and comfortable – if you're on a budget and only in town for a night you might want to opt for the 12hr rate at P900. P1400

EATING, DRINKING AND NIGHTLIFE

For budget **eats**, visit the small Bora Hut Temple food court, in an alleyway off Peñafrancia Ave, 500m east of San Francisco church. Local specialities include **log-log kinalas** (noodle soup with pork, liver sauce and roasted garlic) often served with toasted **siopao** (a pork bun). The nearby stretch of **Magsaysay Ave** is the centre of the city's nightlife, with scores of restaurants and bars.

Bob Marlin Magsaysay Ave ☎054 473 1339, ⓦbobmarlin.ph. This popular restaurant has an atmospheric outdoor seating area with colourful low lighting and a roof of native reed and reclaimed wooden palates; there's also an indoor area with wall-mounted plates signed by famous visitors, praising the restaurant's award-winning crispy *pata* (deep-fried pork leg; P429 for five people). As the name suggests, the music is laidback, with lots of reggae and ska. Daily 11am–midnight.

Chef Doy's Cereza Compound, Magsaysay Ave ☎054 478 2519. Doy rustles up imaginative Filipino fusion dishes that include sautéed baby squid with garlic, bay leaves and black pepper (P199) and boneless milkfish with vegetables in guava broth (P212). Dishes are large enough to share, and you can either eat alfresco on the patio or in the dark interior with walls plastered with customers' notes and scribbles. Daily 10am–10.30pm.

★**Green Earth Café** 4km east of Naga, 3rd turning on the right off Soriano Ave, Villa Sorabella Subdivision, Concepcion Grande ☎054 475 5018. A truly unusual find in this country of meat-lovers, this excellent vegetarian health-food café serves creative dishes prepared with freshly harvested local ingredients; the bread (P40) is home-made, as is the excellent dairy-free banana mango ice cream (P55). The wide menu includes rice noodle *pad thai* (P185), *pako* salad (P165) and the bestselling club sandwich of home-made tofu, grilled vegetables and veggie burger (P175). To get here catch a jeepney heading for "Centro Concepcion" (every 30min; 20min; P8). Sun–Thurs 10am–9pm.

Mudbugs DMG Compound, Peñafrancia Ave ☎054 472 5432. This well-established, airy sports bar attracts a young clientele for the billiards table, the major sporting events screened on the four TVs, the 3-litre beer towers

(P330), and occasional live music from jazz to reggae. There's also a private soundproof karaoke room (P350/hr) with its own billiards table. Daily 10am–1.30am.

P Bar Magsaysay Ave ☎0949 630 3669. Laidback, inviting and popular bar with low lighting, mellow green walls and a stone-and-pebble walkway. It's a pleasant place to enjoy a beer (P30) or a cocktail (pitchers P150) as you nibble on the signature P-Tatas, fried baby potatoes with garlic mayo dip (P60). There's a pool table and wi-fi, too. Daily 4pm–1am.

DIRECTORY

Banks There are plenty of banks, including Metro Bank, BPI and PNB on Plaza Rizal.

Internet access Reikachance.Café, Lot 215, Lagrimas Dorm, Bagumbayan Sur (Mon–Sat 8am–midnight; P15/hr; ☎054 472 4136).

Police City Hall Complex, Miranda Ave (24hr hotline ☎054 472 3000).

Post City Hall Complex, Miranda Ave (Mon–Fri 8am–5pm).

Shopping The House of Pili, 3km from town at 178 Jacana St, RJ Village, Haring, Canaman (daily 7am–8pm; ☎054 474 5160, ⊛jempastries.com) is a family-run pili production factory where, during working hours (Mon–Fri 8am–5pm), it's possible to watch staff coating, glazing and packaging all manner of pili products – which you can then buy at the attached shop.

CamSur Watersports Complex (CWC)

Provincial Capitol Complex, Brgy Cadlan, Pili • Mon 8am–9pm, Tues–Sun 8.30am–9pm • Prices vary – P370 for half a day on the main course plus P750 for wakeboard rental and P90 for helmet and life-vest rental • ☎054 477 3344, ⊛cwcwake.com

Located just under 10km southeast of Naga, **CamSur Watersports Complex (CWC)** is an international-standard wakeboarding course. There is a beginners' winch park, where you can practise standing up on a straight run, and it's also possible to use a kneeboard on the main course, which involves six turns and an assortment of ramps and rails for those who know what they're doing. The complex includes a swimming lagoon, a swimming pool and a small skatepark.

ARRIVAL AND DEPARTURE   CAMSUR WATERSPORTS COMPLEX (CWC)

By shuttle The easiest way to get to CWC is to take a free shuttle from Naga's SM mall and along Magsaysay Ave – contact CWC for the current timetable. There is also a free airport shuttle service that meets incoming flights at Naga airport.

By bus and jeepney From the bus terminal in Naga you can take a bus towards Legazpi (20min) or a jeepney to Bula or Partido (every 30min; 25min; P12) – ask the driver to let you off by the CWC entrance by the highway. At the entrance you can take a tricycle (10min; P50) or habal-habal (5min; P10) to get into the complex itself.

ACCOMMODATION AND EATING

Villa del Rey Hotel ☎054 477 3349, ⊛cwcwake.com. A huge range of accommodation options, from simple but welcoming tiki huts to cosy wood cabins sleeping two, available in small (P1350), medium (P1750) or large (P1950). There are also private villas (P3500) with small gardens and breezy outdoor bathtubs surrounded by greenery and bamboo shoots. The wi-fi reaches some of the rooms, and there are a couple of restaurants and bars. P1000

Lake Buhi

Mostly enclosed by hills – some of which rise as high as 300m – **Lake Buhi** lies 52km from Naga. From the lakeside market in the surprisingly busy town of **BUHI**, on the south shore, you can charter a **bangka** to take you across the water (20min; P100); once you're across, it's a fifteen-minute walk to the wonderful twin **Itbog Falls** in the barangay of Santa Cruz, 5km from Buhi. The falls crash through thick rainforest into deep pools that are perfect for swimming. You can also trek to the falls from Buhi, a terrific hour-long hike through rice paddies and along rocky trails. You'll have to organize a guide with Mary Grace Oafallas, the Executive Director for Culture and the Arts (☎0947 187 0457, ⊛dj.graceangel20 @yahoo.com).

ARRIVAL AND DEPARTURE   **LAKE BUHI**

Regular **vans** connect Naga to Buhi (hourly; 1hr 30min; P85).

ACCOMMODATION

★**Lake Buhi Resort** Brgy Cabatuan, 4km northwest of Buhi ☎ 0926 616 2131, ✉ lakebuhi_resort@yahoo.com. Owned and run by affable Cyrus Obsuna, this wonderful resort has tastefully furnished accommodation in well-manicured grounds; a spiral staircase leads up to a series of spacious rooms in the main building – the cosy attic rom (P3000) is probably the most inviting, with a living area and terrace. There's also a swimming pool. Rates include breakfast. P2200

Mount Isarog National Park

One of the Philippines' most spectacular and least trampled areas, **Mount Isarog National Park** covers forty square kilometres in the heart of Camarines Sur, about 40km east of Naga. At its centre stands **Mount Isarog** (1966m), the second highest peak in Southern Luzon and part of the Bicol volcanic chain that also includes Mayon. Isarog is considered potentially active, although it is not known when it last erupted.

The jungle is thick and steamy, and the **flora and fauna** are among the most varied in the archipelago. Long-tailed macaques and monitor lizards are a pretty common sight, while with a little luck you may also spot the indigenous shrew rats, reticulated pythons and rare birds such as the bleeding-heart pigeon, red-breasted pitta and blue-nape fantail. Reaching the summit (see box below) takes two days of strenuous climbing. At the top is a large crater with a couple of sulphuric rivers that meet within the crater and stream down the southeastern part of the mountain.

A number of paths on Isarog's lower slopes lead to **waterfalls** – including Mina-Ati, Nabuntulan and Tumaguiti – all of which are surrounded by thick rainforest and have deep, cool pools for swimming. The easiest to reach is beautiful **Malabsay**, a powerful ribbon of water that plunges into a deep pool surrounded by forest greenery. It's a delightful place for a dip. There are also hot springs in the barangay of **Panicuason** (P200), the most popular starting point for climbing the mountain.

4

ARRIVAL AND DEPARTURE   **MOUNT ISAROG NATIONAL PARK**

By jeepney To get to the barangay of Panicuason, starting point for the Panicuason trail (see box below), take a jeepney (hourly; 40min; P30) from close to the market in Naga. There are no jeepneys from Panicuason back to Naga after 3pm (4pm in summer), so keep an eye on the time. If you get stuck you can catch a habal-habal (15min; P100).

ACCOMMODATION

Panicuason Hotspring Resort ☎ 0906 252 7344, ✉ hotspring.resort@yahoo.com. The closest accommodation to the national park, offering simple accommodation in the "old" building along with much more appealing doubles with modern bathrooms in a newer block (P1600). There is no hot water, but the four hot spring pools are just at your feet. Adventure activities include two ziplines (P200–300) and a Waterball (P100/5min), and there's a restaurant. P1300

CLIMBING MOUNT ISAROG

The easiest and most commonly used route to the summit of **Mount Isarog** is the **Panicuason trail**, which starts at the barangay of Panicuason and takes two days. There are two other recognized routes on the mountain – the PLDT trail and the more challenging Patag-Patag trail – both of which also take two days.

You will need a climbing **permit** ($10/day) and a local **guide** (P550/day) to climb Mount Isarog – Kadlagan Outdoor Shop at 16 Damasalang St, Naga (☎ 0919 800 6299, ✉ kadlagan@yahoo.com) can process applications and help with guides; for the latter you can also contact the Naga City Arts, Culture and Tourism Office (see p.210).

The **best time** to trek is between March and May, but it is possible at other times, weather allowing; September to December is particularly wet.

Caramoan Peninsula

The wild and sometimes windswept **Caramoan Peninsula**, 50km east of Naga, is blessed with limestone cliffs and blue-water coves to rival the Visayas or Palawan. Until recently its relative isolation and lack of infrastructure meant that it attracted only a handful of tourists. Then in 2008 the French production of the *Survivor* TV show was filmed here, and other international productions swiftly followed suit. While today the area hardly rivals somewhere like Boracay in terms of development, it is attracting increasing numbers to its rugged, scenic landscape. The **dry season** runs from February to September, while October to December sees the most rain.

Caramoan

There isn't much to delay you in the town of **CARAMOAN** other than a few souvenir shops, a couple of simple restaurants and some decent enough accommodation options. If you have a bit of time to kill, it's worth taking a stroll to the **Michael the Archangel Parish Church**, a pretty redbrick building constructed in the 1600s. The church was originally built with light materials such as bamboo, wood and nipa, but in the 1800s it was renovated using clay, stone and adobe. Opposite is the covered local fresh produce **market**.

Gota Beach

6km northeast of Caramoan town • P300 • Tricycle from Caramoan town P150 (20min)

Part of the **Caramoan National Park**, the government-owned **Gota Beach** became a tourist attraction when accommodation for the filming crew of the *Survivor* series was built here. Reachable from Caramoan town along a surfaced but damaged road, the beach itself is a bit of a let down, although it continues to attract tourists who head to the resort intrigued to see what put this place on the map.

Guinahoan Island

With its grassy terrain and grazing cows, the inhabited **Guinahoan Island** is an unusual sight among the Caramoan Peninsula's jagged limestone cliffs. The island has some lovely **beaches** with white and pink sand; it's a 45-minute trek from the shore to the **Guinahoan Lighthouse**, which still functions as a beacon for fishermen at night and offers wonderful views of the nearby islands.

Lahos Island

Also known as Bichara, the small **Lahos Island** consists of two stunning limestone formations connected by a short stretch of sand. Except during high tide, you can spend some time on the beach that cuts through from one side of the island to the other, which has deep, clear water.

Matukad Island

One of the smallest islands in Caramoan, **Matukad Island** is a pretty spot with some of the whitest sand in the area. Within the island there's a hidden lagoon; you'll have to scramble to the top of rugged limestone cliffs to find it, and you shouldn't attempt to do so without a guide – contact the Caramoan tourist office (see opposite). The lagoon is allegedly inhabited by one milkfish, legend says the little creature protects the island, and brings ill fortune to those who harm it.

Lahuy Island

At 10km long and 3.5km wide, **Lahuy Island** is the largest island in the northern part of the Caramoan Peninsula; it is also known as "Treasure Island" because of its history of gold mining. There is still small-scale gold panning in the barangay of **Gata**, and visitors can try their hand for a small fee. The island is wonderful at low tide when you can see the beautiful white sandbar of **Manlawe** covered in a thin layer of crystal clear water. There are floating cottages (P200) where you can have a snack, although make sure to bring your own food.

Bag'eing and Sabitang Laya beaches

Located on a triangular shaped island of the Lucsuhin group of islands, the lovely **Bag'eing and Sabitang Laya beaches** are among the filming locations of the *Survivor* series. Both have coral-yellow sand dotted with rock formations and shallow emerald green waters that are perfect for swimming and snorkelling.

Paniman Beach

Paniman Beach is one of the jumping-off points for island-hopping tours. The black sand is nothing to write home about, but there are a few accommodation options, so if you don't want to head inland to Caramoan town, you may want to consider overnighting here.

The Shrine of Our Lady The Most Holy Rosary

From the main road in the barangay of Tabgon, 9.5km northwest of Caramoan town, you can climb 524 steps to the top of Caglago Mountain to reach the **Shrine of Our Lady The Most Holy Rosary**, a white concrete statue of the Virgin Mary spreading her arms in benediction; from the 213m summit, you will be rewarded with wonderful views over the peninsula and the surrounding islands. It's a great spot to watch the sun rise over the bay.

ARRIVAL AND DEPARTURE

CARAMOAN PENINSULA

By plane The closest airport is in Virac, Catanduanes (see p.233), from where you can catch a tricycle to Codon port (1hr; P500), and then hire a private bangka to Guijalo ("Gee-ahlo") port (45min; P1500).

By bangka The easiest way to reach the peninsula is by taking a bangka to Guijalo (daily 5.30am, 7am, 8.30am, 11am; 2hr; P120) from the small port of Sabang, east of Naga by van (hourly; 2hr; P100). If you miss the last bangka at 11am, you can hire a boat for P4000 (for six people). From Guijalo it's a 15–20min hop by tricycle (P150) to Caramoan town.

By ferry From Nato port, connected by bus to Naga (leaving Naga daily 4.30am, returning to Naga 1pm; 2hr), there are ferries to Guijalo (daily 6.30am, returning from Guijalo to Nato port 10.30am; 3hr 30min; P150).

By bus Visitors coming direct from Manila can take a Raymond Transport bus from Cubao to Sabang (daily noon, 2pm, 3.30pm & 7pm; 12hr) or to Caramoan town (daily 4pm; 18hr). Both buses pick up passengers in Naga. The road, however, is poor – until it is eventually upgraded, on the whole the sea route is a better option.

INFORMATION AND ACTIVITIES

Tourist information The tourist office is in the Municipal Compound in Caramoan town (Mon–Fri 8am–5pm; ☎0928 407 9960, ✉caramoan.tourism@gmail.com).

Banks and exchange There is a UCPB bank with ATM on Real St in Caramoan town, although it only accepts MasterCard (not Visa), and it's probably unwise to rely upon it – make sure to bring enough pesos.

Internet access Central Dogma on Alvarez St, Brgy Binanuahan (Mon–Sat 9am–9pm, Sun 1–9pm; P15/hr; ☎0919 631 0005).

Activities Island-hopping tours can be arranged through most accommodation or tour operators; Solmairena Travel Services at 28 Valencia St, Brgy Binanuahan, are recommended (☎0908 163 7726, ✉solmairena@gmail.com). Alternatively you can hire a bangka direct from Bikal Wharf or from Paniman Beach, both around 5km north of Caramoan town, at around P1500–2500 for a full day depending on the distance covered. Bicol Adventures (☎0917 642 6147, ⚡bicoladventureatv.com) offers a range of ATV trips starting at P699 for 1hr 30min.

ACCOMMODATION

The two jumping-off points for island-hopping tours, **Paniman Beach** and **Bikal Wharf**, make good bases if you have limited time in the area. It's possible to **camp** on some of the islands, including Matukad, Lahuy and Bag'eing Beach; the inhabited Lahuy Island is probably the most recommendable as, at the time of research, the government was building a water source.

BIKAL WHARF

Rex Tourist Inn Tawog ☎ 0939 204 3692, ⊛ rextourist inn.com. Nearly 1km from Bikal Wharf, this pleasant resort has sixteen rooms in well-tended grounds, all with cable TV and a/c. There's a large room with six queen beds (P4500), a good-sized pool, wall climbing and a rustic bamboo bar looking over the Lubok River, which is a tranquil spot for a few hours' kayaking (P800/day). In busier months, evening bands play at the restaurant. **P1500**

CARAMOAN TOWN

Istaran Teoxon St ☎ 0916 303 4965, ⊛ istaran .wordpress.com. This new addition to town is a reliable budget choice; rooms are neat and tidy, and the premises are overall very clean. There's a small restaurant downstairs with wi-fi, and in-room massage at P350. The hotel offers island-hopping package tours starting at P3000 for two people for two days and one night. **P1000**

La Casa Roa Teoxon St ☎ 0917 596 5881, ⊛ lacasaroa .wordpress.com. The most atmospheric hotel in town, this welcoming place offers comfortable colour-coded private rooms with mock-period furniture. The spacious rooms on the first floor (P1750) have beautiful parquet floors, with room 1 being the best of all. There's also a communal lounge with wicker furniture and a large sunny terrace. The annexe is not as inspiring, with small bare rooms. **P900**

GOTA BEACH

Gota Village Resort ☎ 0920 9650390, ⊛ caramoan islands.com. This resort, built to house the crew of the *Survivor* TV series, has more than 130 cabañas cluttered together on a grassy slope. Between Feb and June the resort is often block-booked for filming, but there's a bit of an eerie feel when the place is empty. The cabañas come in small, medium (P1500) and large (P1875), and are much

more appealing inside than out, with rustic cosy interiors more suited to an alpine lodge than a beach resort. There is also pricier VIP accommodation (P5000) on nearby Hunongan Cove. **P1250**

PANIMAN BEACH

Breeze and Waves ☎ 0918 913 9623, ⊛ caramoan -breezeandwaves.weebly.com. Sea-facing concrete block offering a/c rooms with salmon-pink furnishings; the bare walls could do with a bit of brightening up, but overall the accommodation is clean, and there are hot showers. If you're after something with a bit less concrete, you can try the attached *Daniel's Resort* owned by the same family – where the walls are plastic faux wood. **P1500**

La Playa Puerto Merced ☎ 0920 281 6362, ⊛ eyeon caramoan.com. This resort has a few little fan-cooled bamboo huts with shared bath that are perfect if you're on a budget; there are also a/c rooms (P2500) in a concrete building – some are better than others, and make more use of native materials. There's also a large bungalow sleeping eight (P7000). **P800**

TUGAWE COVE

Tugawe Cove Resort ☎ 0917 501 6711, ⊛ tugawecove resort.com. One of the nicest places to stay on the Caramoan Peninsula – and offering the only way to get to see the private Tugawe Cove – this lovely resort is located on a wonderful stretch of private beach with crystal clear waters. Accommodation is in 27 comfortable cabañas with modern amenities, set around a lake and dotted along the hillside. On the hilltop are the restaurant and an inviting infinity pool with incredible views over the coast and surrounding islands. In the evenings, it's worth heading out on a bioluminescent plankton-watching trip within the cove. **P8000**

Albay province

Thanks to its central location, **Albay province** is considered to be the gateway to the Bicol region. At the heart of Albay is **Mount Mayon**, with its almost perfect cone-shaped bulk rising from paddy fields to the north and majestically looming over the city of **Legazpi**. Legazpi is the jumping-off point for the rest of the region, where highlights in the lovely countryside include quiet beaches around the town of **Santo Domingo**, the eerie remains of a church at **Cagsawa**, buried in the devastating eruption of Mayon in 1814, and the **Hyop-Hoyopan** and **Calabidongan caves**. Northwest of Legazpi is the little port of **Tabaco**, from where there are regular ferries across to Catanduanes.

Legazpi

About 100km south of Naga, the busy port city of **LEGAZPI** (sometimes spelt Legaspi) is the jumping-off point for climbing **Mount Mayon** and makes a convenient base to explore the surrounding area. The city centre is divided into two parts at either end of

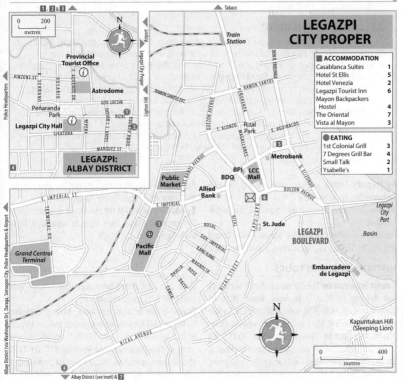

the National Highway. The **old town**, where you'll find the City Hall and most of the top-end hotels, is centred on Peñaranda Park and known as the **Albay district**. A couple of kilometres to the northeast is the new town, or **City Proper**, a muddle of small businesses, banks, cinemas and market stalls where the rest of the hotels are located, along with the waterfront **Embarcadero de Legazpi**, a large mall that also offers go-karting, arcade games, watersports and live music. It's a 25-minute walk between Albay and City Proper, along a busy, polluted road lacking a decent pavement – a tricycle or jeepney is a better option.

Ligñon Hill

Northwest of the city centre • Daily 8am–10pm • P25 • ☎ 0922 883 6722 • Jeepney Loop 1 or 2 (every 20min; 10min; P8), then 2km uphill walk (30min)

Popular with local families, **Ligñon Hill** is not only a great viewpoint for Mayon but also a destination in its own right. Attractions include a zipline, hanging bridge, Japanese war tunnels and quad bikes that can be rented at the base of the hill for tours to see volcanic rock formations. The hill is also the location of the **Philippine Institute of Volcanology and Seismology** (PHIVOLCS) research station (⊕phivolcs.dost.gov.ph).

ARRIVAL AND DEPARTURE   LEGAZPI

By plane The airport is 2km northwest of City Proper; incoming flights are met by tricycles at the airport (5min; P50). PAL and Cebu Pacific serve Manila (3 daily; 1hr 10min).
By bus All buses arrive at the Grand Central Terminal on the western edge of City Proper. Dozens of a/c buses ply the route to Manila, including Philtranco, and there are plenty of local buses.

Destinations Manila (dozens daily; 8–10hr); Naga (every 15min; 2hr); Sorsogon City (every 15min; 1hr 30min); Tabaco (every 20min; 1hr).

4

SPICING IT UP IN BICOL

Bicolano **cuisine** is unusual in the Philippines, noted for its use of coconut and chillis. Most Bicolano dishes are prepared by sautéeing or simmering ingredients in coconut cream – traditionally minced, diced or ground pork, smoked fish (*tinapa*) or small shrimps. Among the most common dishes are **Bicol Express**, named after a famous train service, made with coconut cream, diced pork, small shrimps, chilli and garlic, and sometimes pineapple; **laing**, a spicy dish of delicious taro leaves, coconut cream, ground pork and minced small shrimps; and **pinangat**, which uses the same ingredients as *laing*, although the taro leaves here are tied together and wrapped around the ground pork and small shrimps, before being submerged in coconut cream. To sample some of the best Bicolano cuisine, head for *Small Talk* in Legazpi (see opposite) or *Green Earth Café* near Naga (see p.210).

By jeepney Regular jeepneys make the trip to Santo Domingo (hourly; 30min; P20).

By van Vans arrive at and leave from the Grand Central Terminal.

Destinations Bulan (hourly; 2hr 30min; P180); Donsol (hourly; 1hr 30min; P75); Naga (every 30min; 2hr; P140); Pio Duran (hourly; 2hr; P135); Sorsogon City (every 30min; 1hr 20min; P90); Tabaco (every 30min; 45min; P50).

By boat The wharf is at the eastern end of Quezon Ave in City Proper. Outrigger boats travel to Rapu-Rapu, Albay (daily 7am & noon; 3hr; P150).

INFORMATION AND TOURS

Tourist information The city tourist office is in the City Hall Building on Rizal St in Albay district (Mon–Fri 8am–5pm; ☎052 480 2698, ⓦ legazpicity.gov.ph), while the provincial tourist office is on Captain Aguende Drive, also in Albay district (Mon–Fri 8am–5pm; ☎052 481 0250, ⓦ albaytourism.gov.ph); there is also an info kiosk at the airport that opens when flights arrive. The Department of Tourism Region 5 office is at the Regional Centre Site, Rawis, 2km north of the Albay district (Mon–Fri 8am–5pm; ☎052 482 0712, ⓦ gayonbicol.com).

Tours For private tours, car rental, trekking (including Mt Mayon), ATV rides and other adventure tourism, try Your Brother Travel & Tours (☎052 742 9871, ⓦ mayonatvtour .com) or Bicol Adventures and Tours (☎0917 571 4357, ⓦ bicoladventureatv.com). You can also ask at the tourist offices about arranging a guide for Mt Mayon (see opposite).

ACCOMMODATION

CITY PROPER

★**Hotel St Ellis** Rizal St ☎052 480 8088, ⓦ hotelstellis .com.ph. The only truly high-end option in City Proper, this tastefully decorated hotel offers well-appointed rooms in white and cream, with 32inch flatscreen TVs, work desks, high-speed internet and coffee- and tea-making facilities. There's also a business centre, swimming pool, well-equipped gym, luxurious spa and crèche. P3660

Legazpi Tourist Inn 3rd Floor, V&O Building, Lapu-Lapu St at Quezon Ave ☎052 480 6147, ⓔ legazpi touristinn@yahoo.com.ph. On the second floor of an office block, this simple place offers plain rooms, some with fan, others with a/c and TV (P1200); the deluxe rooms (P1400) with cable TV are worth the extra – they're much larger and in much better condition than the cheaper standards. P700

The Oriental Taysan Hill, Santo Niño Village ☎052 742 8888, ⓦ theorientalhotels.com. This new upmarket hotel, on Taysan Hill overlooking the city, has wonderful views over Mt Mayon and the Gulf of Albay. Comfortable rooms feature modern amenities such as rain showers and high-speed internet; facilities include spa, infinity pool, children's pool, gym and babysitting services. P3300

ALBAY DISTRICT

Casablanca Suites Benny Imperial St ☎052 481 0788, ⓦ casablancasuites.ph. Located in the heart of the business district, this hotel offers nineteen rooms, with carpeted or wood-tile floors, decorated with abstract art; most have views over Mt Mayon. There's wi-fi throughout and a popular Fri buffet (7–10pm). P3300

Hotel Venezia Renaissance Gardens, Washington Drive ☎052 481 0888, ⓦ hotelvenezia.com.ph. Close to the airport, this upmarket hotel oozes minimalist chic, with rooms set on three floors. Standard rooms are tiny, while the much more spacious junior suites (P4270) with king-size beds, sacrifice a little style for a lot more space. There is wi-fi throughout, and a café in the lobby serving delectable cakes. P3050

Mayon Backpackers Hostel Brgy Maoyod ☎052 480 0365 or ☎0905 518 6076, ⓦ mayonbackpackers .wordpress.com. Legazpi's only hostel has a series of tiled four- and six-bed dorms, each with its own bathroom and wooden bunks and lockers. There's one double room with a/c and private bath, a communal guest kitchen, free wi-fi and all-day tea and coffee, and rates include a light breakfast of toast and fruit. Dorm P250; double P1000

Vista al Mayon Washington Drive ☎052 481 0308, ✉ vistaalmayon@yahoo.com. A good choice among the city's inexpensive options, with knick-knacks dotted about the entrance hall and comfortable rooms with little wicker details; there's also a piano, billiards table and a small swimming pool in the courtyard (the pool is used for children's lessons at the weekend, when it can get a bit noisy and crowded). P1450

EATING

1st Colonial Grill Pacific mall, City Proper ☎052 481 1213. This popular restaurant within Pacific mall is renowned for its unique pink chilli ice cream (P79) that gives quite a kick; other flavours include roasted rice and pili nut. The menu features spring rolls (P149), fish and seafood dishes (P210) and meats (P150) that are large enough to share. Daily 9am–8pm.

7 Degrees Grill Bar Rizal St, City Proper ☎052 480 8887. This popular restaurant with laidback seating and wicker chairs features an extensive menu of Filipino dishes. The bestseller is the crispy *pata* (P370) – deep-fried pork – that is large enough for four people to share. Nightly live bands at 7pm. Daily 10am–midnight.

★Small Talk 51 Doña Aurora St, Albay district ☎052 480 1393. The most atmospheric dining experience in the city, located in an ancestral home complete with family pictures and old photographs of Mayon. The menu covers all the Filipino standards, with some twists on Bicolano cuisine (see box opposite) including pasta with Bicol Express (P105) and the fiery Mayon stuffed pizza, with *laing*, longganisa sausage and Bicol Express (P265). Daily 11am–10pm.

Ysabelle's Rizal St, Albay District ☎052 480 0555. This colonial restaurant, with original floorboards, a lovely wooden ceiling and background jazz, offers a range of Filipino dishes; bestsellers include smoked baby back ribs (P300) and authentic Bicol Express (P130); rice is served in cute wooden bowls, and all the juices (P70) and home-made cakes (P80) are freshly prepared. Daily 10am–10pm.

DIRECTORY

Banks There are numerous banks on Rizal Ave as well as ATMs in the shopping malls. In the Albay district, you'll find a Land Bank ATM in the Provincial Capitol Annex.

Internet access There are plenty of internet cafés in City Proper. Try Globalink, 3rd Floor, Pacific mall (daily 9am–8pm; P15/hr; ☎0918 606 9326) or Mocha Bytes Internet

Café, Albay Capitol Annexe (daily 8am–7pm; P15/hr; ☎052 742 0678).

Police The Albay police provincial office is at Camp Gen. Simeon A. Ola (☎052 820 6440), west of the Albay district.

Post office On Lapu-Lapu St at Quezon Ave in City Proper (Mon–Fri 8am–5pm).

4

Mount Mayon

The elegantly smooth cone of **MOUNT MAYON** (2460m) may look benign from a distance, but don't be deceived. The most active volcano in the country, Mayon has **erupted** more than forty times since 1616, the date of its first recorded eruption. The most deadly single eruption was in 1814 when around 1200 people were killed and the church at Cagsawa (see p.220) was destroyed; 77 people, including American volcanologists, were killed in a 1993 eruption. In August 2006, an "extended danger zone" was enforced but the expected eruption did not occur. Three months later, however, Typhoon Durian caused mudslides of volcanic ash and boulders on Mayon that killed hundreds. Further eruptions and ash ejections have occurred since.

The presence of Mayon results in strange **weather conditions** in and around Legazpi, with the volcano and the surrounding area often soaked in rain when the rest of the country is basking in unbroken sunshine.

Climbing Mount Mayon

The traditional window of opportunity for an ascent of Mount Mayon is **February to April**, and even then you'll have to be well prepared for cold nights at altitude and the possibility of showers. At any other time of year you could be hanging around for days waiting for a break in the weather. Though the slopes look smooth, it takes at least two days to reach the highest point of the trail, working your way slowly through forest, grassland and deserts of boulders. Above 1800m there's the possibility of being affected by poisonous gases, although some guides will offer to take you to 2000m.

There are various approaches to Mayon, although the accredited and authorized jump-off point is at **Lidong**, Santo Domingo, where the **Mayon Volcano National Park** is located. You'll have to bring all your food with you from Legazpi; there are sources of water on the volcano, but you'll need purifying tablets.

INFORMATION   MOUNT MAYON

Information and guides Whatever you do, don't attempt the climb without a guide. Guides are mandatory and setting out without one would be foolhardy in the extreme. Local guides at the jump-off point of Lidong, Santo Domingo, can assist tourists, although it's probably wise to arrange one in advance at the tourist offices in Legazpi – where you can also check to see whether conditions are suitable for an ascent. Another good source of information is the Institute Of Volcanology And Seismology (ⓦ phivolcs.dost.gov.ph), in Legazpi on Lignon Hill (see p.217).

Daraga

On the western edge of Legazpi • Jeepney from Legazpi (every 5min; 15min; P8)

Five kilometres west of Legazpi by jeepney, the busy market town of **DARAGA** is home to **Daraga Church**, an imposing eighteenth-century Baroque structure built by Franciscan missionaries from blocks of volcanic lava. The exterior was decorated by skilled stonemasons with statuary, carvings, alcoves and niches, but until recently had been falling into disrepair. It was declared a national cultural treasure in 2008 and a project was undertaken to restore it to its former glory, although in the meantime the work has significantly reduced the appeal of the exterior.

ACCOMMODATION AND EATING   DARAGA

Daraga offers a couple of surprisingly good **dining** options in pleasant surroundings, while **staying** here provides a good alternative to the hustle and bustle of central Legazpi.

Balay Cena Una F. Lotivio at P. Gomez St ☏0917 827 9520, ⓦbalaycenauna.com. Located in a beautifully restored ancestral home with lovely wooden parquet floors, this excellent restaurant serves international dishes – the signature fillet of lapu-lapu (grouper) in gourmet sauce (P265) and the butterflied king prawns in *tilmok* sauce (P302) are great. Meat lovers can treat themselves to Wagyu beef steak (P1512) flown over directly from Japan. There's a Sun buffet (11am–3pm; P350). Mon–Sat 10am–10pm, Sun 11.30am–9pm.

Balay Suanoy 1446 Pag-asa St ☏052 742 0029, ⓦbalaysuanoy.com. This cosy bed and breakfast offers a couple of comfortable doubles with private bath, DVD player and cable TV. The restaurant (daily 10am–2pm & 5–10pm) – cluttered with vintage knick-knacks and WWII newspaper clippings – offers creatively presented Filipino favourites including seafood (P95), beef (P220) and vegetable dishes (P110). P1500

Cagsawa ruins

8km northwest of Legazpi • P10 • Take a jeepney from Legazpi in the direction of Malabog or Polangui; make sure to tell the driver where you want to get off

Eight kilometres northwest of Legazpi, beyond Daraga, the **Cagsawa ruins** are the remains of a Spanish church that was destroyed by the 1814 eruption of Mayon. Around 1200 people were entombed in lava and still remain there. The ruins are small and there's not much to explore, but they are picturesque, standing in gardens close to paddy fields with marvellous views across the plain to Mount Mayon. This is a popular spot, so if you want peace and quiet – or if you want to take photographs before the cumulus roll in to obscure the volcano's tip – take an early jeepney. You can buy drinks and snacks from the souvenir stalls and sari-sari stores outside the ruins. There's a **swimming pool** (daily 6am–10pm; P50) just by the ruins, along with the **Galeria de Cagsawa** (daily 7am–6pm; P20), a small gallery with photos and paintings by local artists depicting Mount Mayon's eruption.

Hoyop-Hoyopan

17km west of Legazpi • Daily 7am–7pm • 1hr guided tour P300/group of six; guides only receive 20 percent of the entrance fee so tips are appreciated • Jeepney from Legazpi to Camalig (every 20min; 45min; P20) and then change to another jeepney towards Cotmon (P10) or catch a habal-habal (15min; P100)

Hoyop-Hoyopan – meaning "Blowing Wind" due to the breeze inside – is the most easily accessible of fourteen limestone **caves** near Legazpi. It's a well-established attraction, privately owned, and guides are available at the entrance, although you could try local guide Bam Nuylan (☏0927 969 9855) if nobody is there. Guides will point out fragments of burial jars dating back two thousand years; incongruously, there is also a concrete dancefloor built in 1972, when parties were held in secret to avoid the curfew of the martial law era. Four local families were evacuated here for one day during Typhoon Yolanda in 2013.

Calabidongan

24km west of Legazpi, 7km from Hoyop-Hoyopan • 3hr tour (compulsory) with guide P550/person

Calabidongan (Cave of the Bats) is a more difficult cave to explore than Hoyop-Hoyopan as it is always partly flooded and at one point requires a very short swim. It is best visited in April and May, as at other times the water level can be too high. Make sure to bring a torch and wear rubber shoes or sandals; don't take a camera unless you have a waterproof bag. Hoyop-Hoyopan is the jumping-off point for Calabidongan; guides there can arrange a habal-habal (15min; P100) if you don't want to walk (7km; 1hr).

4

Santo Domingo and around

About 13km northeast of Legazpi along the coastal road, the small town of **SANTO DOMINGO** is a tidy, friendly little settlement with an atmospheric old Spanish church on the north side of the narrow main street. In the barangay of **Buyuan** is a signposted turning for a nine-hole golf course and stables offering horseriding (P500 to ride to the lowest camp on Mount Mayon).

Calayucay Beach

East of Santo Domingo, a concrete road winds its way up and down through some delightful, pristine countryside, with the main destination being **Calayucay Beach**, 2.5km east of the town. It's pretty but not spectacular, though the views across Albay Gulf are attractive and its resorts are good places to relax.

Sogod Beach

About 10km north of Santo Domingo, near Bacacay, is **Sogod Beach** – a pleasantly rustic stretch of black volcanic sand sometimes known as the Mayon Riviera. In addition to several sets of day-cottages for picnickers, there are a couple of resorts with accommodation.

Cagraray

You can reach Cagraray by boat from Tabaco (3 daily; 1hr 30min; P50), or by taking a bridge from the peninsula east of Santo Domingo – more reliable than a boat during typhoon season, but not used by public transport, so you'll have to rely on a private transfer

The island of **Cagraray**, 26km east of Santo Domingo, connected to the mainland by bridge, has some wonderful white sand beaches in **Sula** and **Misibis** on the southeast coast. There is only one resort here, although you can camp out. Hiring a bangka should cost around P500 for a full day.

ARRIVAL AND DEPARTURE   **SANTO DOMINGO**

By jeepney Jeepneys connect Legazpi to Santo Domingo (hourly; 30min; P20) from where there are services to Calayucay Beach (hourly; 30min; P40). Jeepneys also connect Sogod Beach to Tabaco (every 30min; 30min; P23).

By van From Legazpi there are vans to Bacacay (for Sogod Beach; hourly; 45min; P35).

By tricycle You can get a tricycle from Santo Domingo to

Calayucay Beach (10min; P8) or Sogod Beach (30min; P100). A tricycle from Bacacay to Sogod Beach is P60 (10min).

ACCOMMODATION

Coastal View Beach Resort Calayucay Beach ☎0999 994 1099, ✉coastalviewb@yahoo.com. The first resort you come to on Calayucay Beach is also one of the best on this strip, albeit on slightly overbuilt grounds with a concrete promenade by the sea. The standard rooms are spacious, with poolside or Mt Mayon views, while the executive rooms have more attractive decor. **P2000**

Costa Palmera Calayucay Beach ☎052 822 3550 or ☎0922 874 0287, ⊛costapalmeraresort.com. This is a decent option with great-value a/c economy rooms at bargain prices; the more expensive standards also have fridge. Best of all are probably the two poolside rooms (P3060) – guests who rent out both have exclusive access to the pool. There's wi-fi at reception. **P880**

Misisbis Bay Misisbis Bay ☎02 661 8888, ⊛misisbisbay

.com. This large high-end resort, set in five hectares, offers 37 luxurious villas with prices to match. Facilities include seven swimming pools, three ziplines, a luge run, ball-painting field, dune buggies, mountain bikes, a casino and various watersports. At the time of research, a separate complex nearby was under construction to house "back-packer rooms" (P2000). **$570**

Mullner Beach Resort Sogod Beach ☎0928 450 3185, ✉johnrojero@yahoo.com. Set in pleasant grounds dotted with palm trees, this resort offers simply furnished cottages and more spacious family rooms; the "private room" sleeping three (P2500) is the best value, with a living area and chintzy bedroom. There's cold water only, and no restaurant so you'll have to bring your own food or eat at one of the other resorts. **P1500**

Tabaco

TABACO, 26km northeast of Legazpi, is a busy little port that functions as the gateway to **Catanduanes** (see p.233). The town itself doesn't offer much to visitors, although it has a couple of surprisingly decent hotels if you happen to get stuck here for the night to catch the early ferry to Catanduanes.

ARRIVAL AND DEPARTURE

TABACO

By bus Buses arrive at the bus terminal 1.5km outside the centre; a pedicab to the centre of Tabaco is P10 (10min), while a tricycle costs P25 (5min). A/c PLTB buses travel to Manila (daily 7.30am & 5.30pm; 10–12hr); plenty of local buses also make the journey, with most leaving around 5pm (15 daily; 10–12hr).

By jeepney The jeepney terminal is on the main street just by the Tabaco City mall and market.

Destinations Bacacay (for Sogod Beach; every 30min; 30min; P21); Legazpi (every 15min; 40min; P25); Santo Domingo (every 30min; 30min; P24).

By boat The port is a 10min walk from the jeepney terminal down the road running next to the market. There are ferries to Virac (daily 6.30am) and San Andres (daily 7am & 1pm) on the southwest coast of Catanduanes, which can be a rough crossing particularly from October to December. You can reach the barangay of San Antonio on Cagraray by boat (3 daily; 1hr 30min; P50).

By van Vans to and from Legazpi (every 30min; 40min; P50) and Naga (every 1–2hr; 2hr 30min; P180) use the bus terminal.

ACCOMMODATION

HCG Residence Mansion Hotel Ziga Ave ☎052 487 7333, ⊛residencemansion.webs.com. In the centre of town, opposite the jeepney terminal, this is a good, safe option with clean tiled a/c rooms and wi-fi throughout. The spacious suites (P2690) have fridge, cable TV, DVD player and kettle, and the in-house restaurant serves Chinese, Japanese and Spanish dishes. **P1225**

JJ Midcity Inn Herrera St ☎052 487 4158, ⊛jjmidcity inn.com. Above a small shopping complex, this place is a pleasant surprise – rooms are clean and modern, although the standard single (P800) is a bit of a squeeze. There's a karaoke bar within the hotel, so it can be quite noisy until it closes at midnight. Rates are cheaper for stays of up to 12hr. **P1000**

EATING

Amore Coffee Arellano St ☎0998 978 7986. This little café with wooden stools, a couple of armchairs and a sofa offers eight varieties of coffee beans including

the prized civet coffee (P180); desserts include Belgian waffles (P65) and coffee brownies (P20), and there are savoury snacks too, such as sandwiches (P315) and

nachos (P85). Free wi-fi. Mon–Sat 11am–11pm, Sun 9am–9pm.
Graceland Ziga Ave ☎052 487 7000, ⓦgraceland.ph. Opposite the jeepney terminal, this is one of Tabaco's better

places to eat, offering cheap and cheerful dishes including pork adobo (P65), baby back ribs (P199) and *lechon* Bicol Express (P125); there's also an attached bakery selling cakes (P165). Daily 6am–10pm.

Sorsogon province

A toe of land with a striking volcanic topography and some little-known beaches, lakes, hot springs and waterfalls, **Sorsogon province**, south of Albay, is the easternmost part of mainland Bicol. The province is best known to tourists for the chance to snorkel with whale sharks off the coast near **Donsol**, but it's also a great area for activities such as hiking and caving. **Sorsogon City** makes a good base for exploring the area's many lovely beaches – the nicest stretch of sand being **Rizal Beach**, in the barangay of Gubat to the east of Sorsogon City. There are many pristine coves to explore along the coast around **Bacon**, while south of Sorsogon City **Mount Bulusan** is a climbable, active volcano.

Driving through Sorsogon province you will pass many stalls selling items made from **abacá**, the fibre of a species of banana tree and one of the major products of the province. Sometimes known as Manila hemp, although it also grows in Malaysia and Indonesia, it is processed to make everything from banknotes to teabags.

Donsol

4

The area around the sleepy town of **DONSOL** is best known for one of the greatest concentrations of **whale sharks** in the world. The number of sightings varies: during the **peak months** of January to April there's a very good chance of encountering these gentle creatures, but on some days (particularly early or late in the season, which stretches from December to early June) you might see none. **Swimming** with these colossal creatures as they sedately glide through the clear waters, their enormous mouths opening more than 1m wide to gulp down huge quantities of plankton, is a truly unforgettable experience, but remember that you need to be a good swimmer and a decent snorkeller to get into the water with them.

ARRIVAL AND DEPARTURE
DONSOL

By bus Philtranco has a daily bus from Manila (12hr). Buses travelling between Sorsogon City and Donsol (every 15min; 1hr) arrive at Junction Putiao (see below).
By jeepney Jeepneys and a/c minivans arrive at a terminal on the southern edge of town. For Sorsogon City, catch a jeepney towards Daraga and ask the driver to let you get off at Junction Putiao (every 30min; 1hr; P60), from where the buses leave.

By van There are regular vans to Legazpi (hourly; 1hr 30min; P75).
By ferry Ferries from Masbate arrive at Pilar port, 15km south of Donsol by jeepney (every 30min; P15) or tricycle (30min; P250). There is one daily roll-on-roll-off ferry (departs Pilar 4am–5am depending on the tide; 4hr; P230) and three fast crafts (daily 8am, noon & 4pm; 2hr; P396).

INFORMATION

Tourist information The Visitor Centre (daily 7am–6pm; ☎0927 483 6735, ⓦdonsolwhalesharkecotour.com) is northwest of Donsol among the resorts in the barangay of

Dancalan, P40 away by tricycle from the centre of town. You'll need to check in here if you want to swim with the whale sharks (see box, p.234).

ACCOMMODATION

The **resorts** are about 2km northwest of the town centre and many are closed outside of the whale shark-watching **season** (Dec–June). The town itself is becoming more tourist-oriented as locals aim to capitalize on growing visitor numbers; although there are few hotels, there are numerous **homestays**. Contact the Visitor Centre for an up-to-date list.

WHALE SHARKS IN DONSOL

Known locally as the *butanding*, the **whale shark** is a timid titan resembling a whale more than the shark it is. It can grow up to 20m in length, making it the largest fish in existence. These gentle giants gather around Donsol every year, around the time of the northeastern monsoon, to feed on the rich shrimp and plankton streams that flow from the Donsol River into the sea, sucking their food through their gills via an enormous vacuum of a mouth.

Whale sharks were rarely hunted in the Philippines until the 1990s, when demand for their meat from countries such as Taiwan and Japan escalated. Cooks have dubbed it the "tofu shark" because of the meat's resemblance to soybean curd. Its fins are also coveted as a soup extender. Tragically, this has led to its near extinction in the Visayas and further south in Mindanao. In Donsol, however, where the creatures are protected, attitudes seem to be changing, with locals realizing that whale sharks can be worth more alive than dead, attracting tourists and thus investment and jobs.

WHALE SHARK WATCHING

At the Donsol Visitor Centre (see p.223) you can complete all the formalities for **renting a boat** for a whale shark-watching trip. Boats cost P3500 for up to six people, and there's a registration fee of P300 for foreigners (P100 for Filipinos). In peak season, especially at weekends, queues can start to form before the centre opens, so arrive early.

Before boarding you will need to watch a video briefing in which a **Butanding Interaction Officer** (BIO) explains how to behave in the water near a whale shark. The number of snorkellers around any one shark is limited to six; flash photography is not allowed, nor is scuba gear; and the animal's tail should be avoided as it can do serious damage. Some boatmen flout these rules in order to keep their passengers happy, but this risks distressing the whale sharks and should not be encouraged. Check, too, that your boat has one of the mandatory propeller guards.

Snorkelling equipment can be rented from outside the visitor centre (P150 for mask and snorkel plus P150 for flippers). Each boat has a crew of three, the captain, the BIO and the spotter, each of whom would welcome a token of your appreciation. All this makes it an expensive day out by Philippine standards, but take heart from the fact that your money is helping the conservation effort. Take plenty of protection against the sun and a good book. Once a whale shark has been sighted you'll need to get your mask, snorkel and flippers on and get in the water before it dives too deep to be seen.

DONSOL TOWN

Aguluz San José St ☎0918 942 0897 or ☎0917 514 5905, ⊛donsolaguluzhomestay.com. Run by an affable woman, this welcoming homestay with lovely *narra* wood floors offers impeccably clean rooms with either private or shared bath. Guests can make full use of the well-equipped kitchen, and the owner will rustle up meals upon request. Wi-fi is available. **P1700**

★**Donsoleña** Capobres St ☎0928 508 3415, ⊛donsolena.com. This wonderful homestay in a quiet residential neighbourhood is more of a chic B&B, with polished hardwood floors and tasteful rooms furnished in native materials. There's a spacious terrace overlooking the rice paddies, and a guest kitchen. **P2000**

Giddy's Place 54 Clemente St ☎0917 848 8851, ⊛giddysplace.com. Accommodation in a pink building – standard rooms are at the back by the pool, while the larger deluxe rooms (P3360) are at the front. All have kettle, fridge and TV and there's wi-fi throughout. Attached dive shop and restaurant (see opposite). **P2800**

RESORTS

AGM ☎0919 688 2264 or ☎0906 368 7805, ⊛agmresort.com. The first resort you come to on the strip, with two rows of clean and tidy a/c concrete rooms with hot and cold showers. **P2200**

Elysia ☎0917 547 4466 or ☎0926 475 9762, ⊛elysia-donsol.com. This Korean-owned place is the most upmarket choice along the strip, with minimalist decor, bamboo beds and wooden loungers by the pool. There are a few hammocks slung along the beach and a restaurant serving Filipino and Italian dishes. The resort accepts credit cards, and US dollars and euros can also be exchanged. **P3150**

Vitton ☎0927 912 6313, ⊛whalesharksphilippines.com. One of the area's best resorts, with clean and spacious rooms, most with private veranda. The restaurant serves good international food, and attracts non-guests, too. The *Woodland Beach Resort* next door, owned by the same people, offers "backpacker rooms" sleeping three for P500/person. **P2200**

DONSOL OUTDOOR ACTIVITIES

Although Donsol is famous for its whale shark watching, there are plenty of other activities for nature lovers and outdoor enthusiasts.

SCUBA DIVING

There's scuba diving at the infamous **Manta Bowl**; though it's actually closer to Ticao (see p.232), it is best reached from the dive shops attached to several of the resorts in Donsol. The site is far from shore, and requires divers to descend rapidly and cling onto rocks – try to get a reef hook or gloves. You then use the strong drift to move towards the Manta Bowl, and if you are lucky you will be rewarded with close-up views of mantas or even whale sharks. This is not a dive for beginners, whatever the dive shops may tell you when trying to get your business. Also be on the lookout for shoddy equipment. A reliable outfit is the Brit-run Scubaid (☎0920 403 5596, ⓦscubaid.org) on Dancalan Beach.

FIREFLY WATCHING

Another popular attraction is **firefly watching** (P1250/boat, for up to five people) in the early evening. There are two starting points, one beside the bridge on the main road and the other on the Ugod River. Trips start at 7pm; you can just show up at the starting point in good time, but it's better to enquire at the visitor centre. April and May are said to be the best months, when the air conditions are at their calmest.

OTHER ACTIVITIES

A day **island-hopping** near the island of Ticao in Masbate province (P7000 for up to ten people; plus registration fee P100/person) can be arranged through the visitor centre. *Giddy's Place* (see opposite) can also sort out **kayaking** trips on the Ugod River (P1500/person).

4

EATING AND DRINKING

★**Baracuda** Dancalan Beach ☎0917 624 0163. Sprightly owner Juliet shakes up potent margaritas, daiquiris and piña coladas (P150) at this lovely bamboo restaurant with cushioned seating. Her food is delicious, too, including mouthwatering sashimi (P305), squid salad (P205) and prawns with garlic and olive oil (P180). The laidback *Baracuda Beach Club* next door is the perfect spot to enjoy a post-prandial drink or two. Juliet can serve lunch upon request. Daily 4pm–midnight.

Butanding Bar & Resto 54 Clemente St ☎0917 848 8851, ⓦgiddysplace.com. Part of *Giddy's Place* hotel

(see opposite), this is one of the town centre's better options; the menu is international, with dishes including pork schnitzel (P280), Hungarian sausage (P300) and blue marlin tandoori (P300); they also serve cocktails (P135) and there's wi-fi, too. Daily 6am–midnight.

Shanley's E. Hernandez St ☎0910 933 4760. Right by the bus terminal, this local hangout built in native materials, including bamboo and coconut, hosts live bands on Fri and Sat at 8pm. Expect dancing, drinking (beer P45) and belting out at the karaoke; basic meals are served, too (P150). Daily 8am–11pm.

DIRECTORY

Banks and money There is one ATM, at the Rural Bank of Donsol on Clemente St (Mon–Fri 8am–5pm, Sat 8am–noon), but it only accepts Visa cards (and it's inside the bank so you won't be able to withdraw money when it's closed). It would be unwise to rely on this, so bring enough pesos. Some of the accommodation options,·

including *Giddy's Place* (see opposite), will take credit cards, but the only place offering currency exchange (US dollars and euros) at the time of research was the *Elysia* resort (see opposite).

Internet access Philip-Annie Internet Shop on St Joseph St (Mon–Sat 7am–9pm; P15/hr; ☎0933 166 3680).

Sorsogon City

There are few attractions in **SORSOGON CITY**, although it serves as a base to explore the area's natural sights and has a range of good accommodation. Along the pier, vendors crack open large clams and display them in large buckets. The **boardwalk** on the pier is a good place to watch the sun set, with views of Mount Pulag and Mount Bulusan. Every year, the **Kasanggayahan festival** (roughly Oct 17–23) celebrates the town's history with street parades, traditional dances and beauty pageants.

Museum and Heritage Center

Capitol Compound • Tues–Sat 8am–5pm • Free

The small **Museum and Heritage Center** displays a number of ancient artefacts, including burial jar covers dating back as far as 1000 BC that were found in caves in Bacon. Among the other exhibits are beautiful Chinese porcelain bowls from the Ming dynasty, chairs with Chinese inspired designs and anchors believed to have been used during the Spanish colonial era. Highlights include the skull of a sperm whale, the skeletal system of a dolphin and a 10m long vertebra of a whale shark that was washed ashore in nearby Donsol in 2010.

ARRIVAL AND INFORMATION   SORSOGON CITY

By bus Buses use the Grand Terminal 2km south of the city centre, a P40 tricycle ride away. Local buses make the trip to Legazpi (every 15min; 1hr 30min). Philtranco runs a daily service to and from Manila (10–12hr), as do a number of local companies (13 daily).

By jeepney Jeepneys travel to Gubat (every 10min; 30min; P25), Bacon (every 10min; 30min; P17) and Bulan

(every 30min; 2hr; P75).

By van Regular vans connect the city to Legazpi (every 15min; 1hr; 15min; P85).

Tourist information The provincial tourist office is in the Capitol Compound (Mon–Fri 8am–noon & 1–5pm; ☏ 056 421 5632, ✉ sorsogonprovincial_tourism@yahoo.com).

ACCOMMODATION AND EATING

Fernando's Hotel N. Pareja St ☏ 056 211 1357, ⊛ fernandoshotel.com. This cosy two-storey building offers nicely presented deluxe rooms (P2000) that open up onto a balcony overlooking a leafy breakfast area; they're worth a look for their creative use of natural materials such as coconut and bamboo. The standard rooms on the ground floor are not as inspiring, but they are comfortable enough. Wi-fi throughout. P1600

Fritz Homestay Block 21, Executive Village, Tugos ☏ 056 211 5502, ⊛ fritzhomestay.multiply.com. With nearly twenty rooms, this welcoming homestay 1km north of town is more of a hotel – the rooms are nicely decorated with wrought-iron bed frames, wooden wardrobes and lampshades made with shells. The most expensive rooms are particularly spacious, with knick-knacks dotted about. There are also two little swimming pools in the backyard, and a restaurant (with wi-fi)

serving Filipino dishes. P1100

Siama Hotel Sitio San Lorenzo, Bibincahan ☏ 02 514 2653, ⊛ siamahotel.com. This chic designer hotel offers stylish rooms with creative furniture including oversized armchairs and beanbags. The welcoming rooms with four-poster bamboo beds are set around an inviting 25m pool with deckchairs – a pleasant spot to sip a cocktail at sunset. The hotel organizes pick-up from Legazpi airport. P8500

Una Pizzeria 3257 Pareja St ☏ 056 211 3945. Probably the best restaurant in town, this welcoming pizzeria offers pizzas (P117) and pasta dishes (P122) in a couple of airy rooms with scattered wooden tables, and a few paintings that add colour to the walls; the mellow background music and the two retro sofas add to the inviting atmosphere. Sun–Fri 9am–9pm, Sat 10am–9pm.

DIRECTORY

Banks There are a number of banks (including BPI, PNB and Allied Bank) on Rizal St and Magsaysay St.

Internet access King Evanz Internet on Burgos St (daily 8am–8pm; P15/hr; ☏ 056 255 0858).

Shopping Kasanggayahan Village at the Capital Compound (daily 8am–9pm) has a dozen or so shops selling souvenirs and local products including pili nuts.

Rizal Beach

A short tricycle ride beyond the barangay of **Gubat**, which lies about 12km east of Sorsogon City on the eastern tip of the province, **Rizal Beach** stretches for 2km in a perfect crescent. It's a pleasant spot that can be suitable for **surfing** between October and January; for further information contact Gubat Inc (☏ 0905 242 1693) who rent boards (P150/hr) and organize lessons (P150/hr).

By bus Several companies connect Manila to Gubat (5 daily; 12hr).

By jeepney Jeepneys from Gubat travel to Bulusan (every 15min; 45min; P38) and Sorsogon City (every 10min; 30min; P25).

By tricycle A tricycle from Gubat to Rizal Beach is P50 (10min).

ACCOMMODATION

Lacsa Hilton Beach Resort ☎ 0939 260 1102, ⊚ lacsa hiltonbeachresort.com. By far the best accommodation on this stretch, this resort offers a series of rooms from simple huts built with native materials to larger welcoming suites with fridge and a/c (P1800). There's also a tiled double room with living area and kitchenette (P2500). **P750**

Bacon and around

The small town of **BACON** (pronounced "Backon"), 9km north of Sorsogon City by jeepney, has a grey sand beach with a handful of resorts. Just a ten-minute tricycle ride west is the black sand **Libanon Beach**, where surf hammers dramatically against immense, black rocks that were spewed centuries ago by Mayon. The volcano is visible in the distance.

Paguriran

Bacon is a good base for exploring some of the **islands** in the eastern half of Albay Gulf. The best of these is **Paguriran**, a circle of jagged rock, much like the rim of a volcano, inside which is a seawater lagoon that's wonderful for swimming. The access point from the mainland is **Paguriran Beach**, 20km east of Bacon, from where you can walk across to the island at low tide; make sure to check your timings. Otherwise, you'll have to hire a boatman to paddle you across (P150). Paguriran Beach is a wonderful spot to while away a few hours – the water is crystal clear, and there are lovely views over the neighbouring islands.

By jeepney Regular jeepneys connect Sorsogon City to Bacon (every 10min; 30min; P17) and Paguriran Beach (every 20min; 1hr 30min; P44).

By tricycle A tricycle from Bacon to Paguriran Beach is P500 (45min).

ACCOMMODATION

Fisherman's Hut Brgy Caricaran, 1km east of Bacon ☎ 0909 515 8758. Small, welcoming resort offering a series of comfortable rooms in cute A-frame nipa huts with private bath; four are duplexes that can sleep up to four, while one has a kitchenette with microwave. **P2000**

Paguriran Beach Resort Paguriran Beach ☎ 0919 420 1764. This simple resort on beautiful Paguriran Beach is a nice little place to while away a day or two; there's one cosy a/c A-framed hut with private bath, sleeping five (P3500), as well as two smaller a/c rooms with thatched roof and shared bath. **P1800**

Sirangan Beach Resort Brgy Caricaran, 1km east of Bacon ☎ 0919 582 2732. Under renovation at the time of research, this boutique hotel features spacious, tasteful rooms using natural materials such as granite and rattan throughout. Each has its own character; some have fabulous sea views from their four-poster beds. There's a dive shop and snorkelling out in front of the resort. **P4500**

Bulusan Volcano National Park

Mount Bulusan, in the heart of **Bulusan Volcano National Park**, is one of three active volcanoes in the Bicol region. Trekking has resumed following a series of ash explosions and earthquakes in November 2010, but it remains essential to check the situation before considering an ascent. From **Lake Bulusan** a 6.3km trail (3hr) leads to Aguingay Lake at 940m above sea level. This is where trekkers camp before setting off early to ascend the volcano in time for sunset. At the peak is the Blackbird Crater Lake (1565m), from where there are wonderful 360° views over Mount Mayon to the north, the Philippine Sea and Masbate to the west, the Pacific to the east, and as far afield as the Visayas to the south. Although it is possible to climb the volcano year round, the **best months** are April and May. If you're feeling really energetic, you can join the **Sky Run**, a yearly race to the volcano's peak that starts in **Bulusan town**, 8km from Lake Bulusan – the record holder is a Kenyan who raced to the peak and back in 3hr 47min in June 2013.

ARRIVAL AND INFORMATION

To Lake Bulusan You can take a jeepney to the town of Irosin from Sorsogon City (every 15min; 45min; P45) or Bulan (15min; 30min; P25) and then another towards Bulusan town (hourly; 30min; P20) – you'll need to jump off at the junction to the volcano, so ask the driver where to get off.
Guides and information Hikers will be refused access by rangers if an eruption warning is up; for guides and

BULUSAN VOLCANO NATIONAL PARK

up-to-date details about the state of the volcano, contact the environmental organization AGAP, who can also provide accredited guides (P350 registration fee; guides P1000/ group of five; ☎0919 223 1536, ✉agapbulusan@yahoo .com). You should also consult the Philippine Institute of Volcanology and Seismology website (☺phivolcs.dost .gov.ph).

ACCOMMODATION

Balay Buhay Bee Farm 5km south of Lake Bulusan ☎0912 790 7046, ✉balaybuhaybeefarm@gmail.com. A lovely bee farm offering accommodation in pleasant grounds with one thousand bee colonies, a tilapia pond and a freshwater shrimp hatchery. There's also a pretty

stone swimming pool with fresh water flowing directly from a spring. Simple rooms have bunks and shared bath; at the time of research, more comfortable duplex cottages were under construction. P1200

Masbate province

The province of **Masbate** ("Maz-bah-tee") lies in the centre of the Philippine archipelago. It comprises the **island of Masbate**, site of the small capital of **Masbate City**, plus two secondary islands – **Burias** and **Ticao** – and numerous smaller islands. There are a number of attractions here – exceptional beaches on Masbate island, such as **Bituon**, for example, along with immense caves in thick jungle such as **Kalanay** and **Batongan** – but it's the infrastructure that's lacking. This is slowly changing, however, with an increased emphasis on tourism and an anticipated new ferry route to Manila via Caticlan (and Boracay).

The position of Masbate at the heart of the Philippines leads to some complicated **cultural blending**, with a mix of **languages** including Cebuano, Bicolano, Waray, Ilonggo, Tagalog and Masbateño. The province has long had something of a reputation for violence, with an image throughout the Philippines as a lawless "Wild East" frontier. Like many isolated areas of the archipelago, Masbate does seem a law unto itself and political killings are certainly not unheard of, but its reputation for unfettered goonish violence is mostly unfair. It is highly unlikely that tourists will feel any less **safe** here than in most other parts of the country.

The Wild East moniker is, however, apt for reasons other than lawlessness: Masbate ranks second only to the landlocked province of Bukidnon, Mindanao, in raising **cattle**. There's even an annual **rodeo** in Masbate City in May, where cowpokes do battle for big prize money. If you're on the island on a Thursday, take the time to visit the **Uson Livestock Auction Market**, 42km southwest of Masbate City. It is one of the country's largest, with traders from various islands selling carabao, pigs, horses, chickens and goats.

Masbate City

The provincial capital of **MASBATE CITY** is attractively situated, nestling between the sea and the hills, but spoiled slightly by unstructured development. The best time to come is during the **Rodeo Masbateño**, a four-day orgy of bull-riding and steer-dogging held every May (usually May 6–9).

A number of activities and sights around Masbate City together make a good day-trip by **bangka**. The tourist office should be able to help with arrangements for bangka rental, or you could bargain directly with a fisherman at the pier close to the main transport terminal. Expect to pay around P1000 for a small boat, or P2500 for a medium-sized one.

Pawa boardwalk

4km southwest of the city centre • Jeepney P15; tricycle P75 (15min)

The **Pawa boardwalk** was built primarily to shorten the distance to school for students in the barangay of Pawa. The 1.3km path extends into protected **mangroves** at each side, where migratory birds can be seen, particularly at low tide. The **Pawa Women Mangrove Guardians Association** (☎0910 811 5215), housed in a hut along the boardwalk, organize boat paddling, fishing, shell collecting and mangrove planting. They can also rustle up meals, although make sure to give them at least one day's notice.

Buntod Sandbar

P50 conservation fee • From town, take a tricycle to the barangay of Nursery (P50), where there are bangkas for private hire (for a round trip including waiting you'll pay P500 for up to three people, P800 for larger groups; 10min)

Out in the pass between Masbate and Ticao islands, in a marine protected area, the **Buntod Sandbar** is a popular spot at the weekend but empty during the week. After paying your conservation fee at the large open-fronted hut, you can relax at a picnic table – be sure to bring some supplies – or on one of the four floating platforms. There's decent snorkelling, too – and equipment for rent at the hut (P50/day).

ARRIVAL AND DEPARTURE   MASBATE CITY

By plane The airport is on the outskirts of town; a tricycle to the centre is P50 (5min). Cebu Pacific has weekly flights from Cebu (3 weekly; 55min), while PAL flies to Masbate from Manila (1 daily; 1hr 15min).

By ferry Masbate City's ferry pier is west of the centre There are also boats to Cawayan, on the southern side of Masbate island, from Bogo on Cebu (daily noon; 5hr; P350) and to Mandaon, on the west side, from Roxas (2 weekly; 4hr 30min; P450) and Cajidiocan on Sibuyan (1 weekly; 4hr; P450).

Destinations Batangas (Super Shuttle: roll-on-roll-off; 1 weekly; 12hr; P555); Bulan, Bicol (Kulafo: 1 daily

Mon–Sat; 4hr; P200); Cebu (Super Shuttle: roll-on-roll-off: 1 weekly; 10hr; P555; Trans-Asia: 2 weekly; 12hr; P625); Manila (Montenegro Lines: 1 daily; 11–12hr; P850); Pilar, 15km south of Donsol, Sorsogon province (3 fast crafts daily; 2hr; P394; Denica Lines: 1 roll-on-roll-off daily; 4hr; P230); Pio Duran, Albay (Medallion Transport: 1 daily; 3hr 30min; P200; Isarog: 1 daily; 3hr 30min; P200).

By bangka Bangkas connect Masbate with Lagundi on Ticao Island (every 30min 8am–4pm; 45min; P80).

By bus and jeepney Buses, jeepneys and vans use a terminal on Diversion Rd on the southern edge of town, a little beyond the fishing port.

INFORMATION

Tourist information The provincial tourist office (Mon–Fri 8am–5pm; ☎056 333 2220, ✉gerardopresado@yahoo .com) is in the Capitol Building, while the city tourist office is in the City Hall (Mon–Fri 8am–noon & 1–5pm; ☎056 588 2402, ⊛masbatecity.gov.ph). Both can advise on itineraries, although they have little in terms of printed materials.

ACCOMMODATION

★**7-AR Golden Beach Resort** Nursery Blvd ☎056 582 0175, ⊛7ar.ph. This pleasant resort is by far the best option in town – the a/c rooms with flatscreen TV are clean and comfortable. Doubles have a small lounge area, but the singles are very poky. There's a lovely garden with an inviting pool with loungers, a breezy jacuzzi, a thatched restaurant and a nice café with a few books and magazines. P2500

Backpack 25 Ibingay St ☎056 333 2682. An excellent

budget option, this small friendly hotel with just four rooms has a family feel; rooms have parquet flooring and come in different colours, from peach to olive green. There's a small communal area and wi-fi reaches most of the rooms. The owner can rustle up meals upon request. P1100

Baywalk Garden Blvd Extension, Ibingay St ☎056 333 6648, ✉baywalkghotel@yahoo.com.ph. Pleasant hotel with spacious and well-kept rooms with fresh paint and

polished furniture. There's a garden with a couple of shaded areas for breakfast, and wi-fi at reception. **P1350**
MG Hotel Punta Nursery ☎ 056 333 5614, ✉ MG_hotel 2013@yahoo.com. One of the city's best hotels offers

spacious a/c rooms with very decent-sized beds (for Filipino standards). Pricier rooms also have a fridge, with the most expensive options set around the small pool area. There's wi-fi at the restaurant. Rates include breakfast. **P1200**

EATING

Bialetti Café 33A Quezon St ☎ 056 333 2847. This small welcoming café, decorated with trinkets, offers a selection of sweet and savoury crêpes (P75), hot chocolate (P80), smoothies (P110) and iced coffees (P100). It's a pleasant spot to sit back with a book, and there's wi-fi too. Mon–Sat 8am–10pm.

Binalot at Bulaco Brgy Ibingay ☎ 056 582 9891. This friendly little native-style restaurant with wicker lamps, wooden tables and bamboo walls is famous for its *bulalo* special (P160) – bone marrow broth with cabbage and onion leaves. There are plenty more local dishes on offer, including seafood and fresh fish. Daily 10am–10pm.

Minlan 1 Osmena St ☎ 056 333 6886. Simple restaurant, with low wooden benches, serving the usual Filipino staples – noodles (P120), pork (P140) and chicken (P140). Walls are brightened up with gold and red wallpaper and a splash of red paint, with a few framed miniature bowls and teapots to look at. Daily 9.30am–9pm.

Tio Jose Steak Grills Ibingay St ☎ 056 582 0193. This popular restaurant is a stab at a US-style bar, with sizzlers, steaks and grills (P180) on the menu as well as "Aussie starters" that include *calamares fritos* (P180), onion rings (P95) and buttered chicken (P155). It gets pretty lively in the evenings, when Filipinos belt out karaoke. There's wi-fi, too. Daily 11am–11pm.

DIRECTORY

Banks There are plenty of banks along Quezon St, including DBP and Land Bank.
Internet access Loyola on Ibanez St (daily 8.30am–

9.30pm; P13/hr; ☎ 0907 111 1054).
Police The police station is in the City Hall (☎ 056 582 0875).

4

Bituon Beach

The sand at **Bituon Beach** (aka Bagacay Beach), 14km south of Masbate City and 2km down a dirt road from the barangay of **Bagacay**, is not as blindingly white as some, but that's a minor quibble. Some 2km long, the beach, with palm trees at the edge and beautifully clear shallow water, is nonetheless a pretty crescent bay.

ARRIVAL AND DEPARTURE | BITUON BEACH

By jeepney From Masbate City it's a short jeepney ride to Bagacay (hourly; 20min; P20); they stop on the main road from where you can either walk to Bituon Beach (20min) or

take a tricycle down the track (P40; 5min). A tricycle all the way from Masbate City should cost P300.

ACCOMMODATION

Cocoview Lagoon About 5km north of Bituon. This pleasant resort is set on a beautiful verdant stretch of land; there's a freshwater pool that over the weekends attracts

scores of masbateños from all over the municipalities to cool off. At the time of research, accommodation was under construction. **P1500**

Batongan Cave

20km inland from Mandaon • Local guide P500; ask around where the jeepney drops you off, or organize in advance at the Masbate City tourist office (see opposite) • Jeepneys (hourly; 45min; P80) and buses (hourly; 1hr) run from Masbate City towards Mandaon; ask the driver to let you off at the caves – note there are boats to Mandaon from Roxas, in Panay (2 weekly; 4hr 30min; P450) and Cajidiocan on Sibuyan (1 weekly; 4hr; P450)

The town of **MANDAON** is 64km west of Masbate City on the opposite coast. The trip by jeepney takes you along a scenic road that passes through pastureland, paddy fields and a number of isolated settlements inhabited by subsistence farmers. There's not much in Mandaon itself, but it's a good base for exploring two of the island's most noted natural wonders: **Kalanay Cave** on the northwest coast 40km from Mandaon, and, 20km nearer town, **Batongan Cave**. Both make excellent day-trips, but Batongan is the better of the two, with immense caverns and a large population of bats whose guano is collected and used as fertilizer. About 100m away is an **underground river**, which you can swim in. It's easy to get lost in these parts and if you fall and get injured you might not be found for days, so don't explore the caves or the river without a **local guide**.

Palani Beach

About 5km north of Balud on the island's western coast is **Palani Beach**, a wonderful, 5km-long virgin stretch of sand fringed with palm trees and lapped by crystal-clear waters. There are only a handful of simple resorts here, but if you're happy to stay in basic accommodation then it's a wonderful place to unwind for a few days. During the week you'll have the entire beach to yourself, while on weekends it gets busy with *masbateños* from all over the island. You can also camp here.

ARRIVAL AND DEPARTURE
PALANI BEACH

By jeepney Regular jeepneys make the journey from Masbate City to Balud (hourly; 3hr; P100), from where you can take a tricycle to Palani Beach (15min; P100).

ACCOMMODATION

Bataga Resort Palani Beach ☎ 0920 735 9395. One of the very few resorts along this beautiful stretch of coast, this simple place consists of a handful of basic fan and a/c rooms with cold showers; all are very simple, but it's a great place to get away from it all. **P500**

Placer

On Masbate island's southwest coast, the small town of **PLACER** doesn't offer much to visitors, but it does have a pleasant stretch of beach with a few newish resorts. The waters around here are rich in giant squid, scallops and, in particular, **crabs** – the provincial tourist office in Masbate City (see p.230) can help organize a visit to a crab production plant.

ARRIVAL AND DEPARTURE
PLACER

By jeepney Regular jeepneys make the journey from Masbate City to Placer (hourly; 2hr; P140). There are also boats from Bogo on Cebu (daily noon; 5hr; P350) to Cawayan, which is 60km north of Placer.

ACCOMMODATION

Virginia Beach Resort Pasiagon ☎ 056 986 2663, ✉ virginiadabbeni@ymail.com. One of the best places to stay on the whole of Masbate island, this pretty resort, a short tricycle ride (5min) from Placer, offers four tastefully furnished rooms facing a leafy pool area. All have a wooden four-poster bed, kitchenette with fridge and kettle, and a patio with cushioned rattan seating. There are a couple of slightly smaller rooms too, as well as a great-value *kubo* hut with bunk bed (P800). The resort organizes bangka hire (P2500) to nearby islands. **P1800**

Ticao Island

Ticao Island, across the Masbate Passage from Masbate City, is well worth the one-hour bangka trip. The infrastructure is mostly basic and the roads can be very difficult in the rainy season, but Ticao is home to beautiful scenery and lovely **beaches** with crystal-clear waters. A convenient way to get around is to hire a bangka for around P3000 and explore the coast. Ask the boatman to take you to **Talisay**, the island's finest beach, and then on to **Catandayagan Falls**, the only waterfall in the country – and one of the very few in the world – where fresh water cascades directly into the sea. It's an impressive sight, plunging 60m into the emerald-green waters below. It's a perfect spot to have a swim, too.

ARRIVAL AND DEPARTURE
TICAO ISLAND

By bangka Bangkas connect Masbate pier to Lagundi, on Ticao's southwest coast (every 30min 8am–4pm; 45min; P80); there are also bangkas from Bulan in Sorsogon province to San Jacinto on the northeast of Ticao Island (5 daily; 1hr; P100) and from Pilar to Monreal in the north (2 daily; 1hr 30min; P145).

ACCOMMODATION

Altamar Boutique Resort ☎02 817 7463, ⓦticao altamar.com. Set on 11 hectares of land, this lovely resort consists of a hilltop villa, Yellow House, with a welcoming lounge and four cosy private rooms decorated with ceramic vases, rugs, books and wicker and wood furniture. There are also attractive cottages set around the grounds, with neat and tidy rooms, although they are smaller than in the main building, and not quite as homely. Activities include kayaking, horseriding along the beach and island-hopping trips. Full board only. **P3500**

Ticao Island Resort ☎02 893 8173, ⓦdonsolecotour .com. This friendly resort has nine comfortable a/c cabañas with parquet flooring and spacious bathrooms set on a pretty stretch of beach. There are also four welcoming budget rooms (1700/person full board) at the back. The resort grows its own vegetables, and the restaurant menu includes home-made bread, pizza and pasta. Staff can organize fishing trips, kayaking, firefly river tours and horseriding. **P2600**

Catanduanes

The eastern island province of **Catanduanes** is ripe for exploration, a large, rugged, rural island with endless stretches of majestic coastline. While **surfers** have known about Catanduanes for some time, attracted to the big waves off **Puraran Beach** on the wild east coast, the island has still barely felt the impact of tourism, although with four flights a week from Manila and improvements to the main road around the island, this is slowly changing. There are several good beaches within easy reach of the capital **Boac**, along with the immense caves in **Lictin**, while the undeveloped west coast offers the opportunity to blaze a trail into areas few travellers see. Above all Catanduanes is a friendly, down-to-earth place to hang out for a few days, adjusting to a slower pace of life and travel.

It isn't all good news though. When Filipinos think about Catanduanes they think mostly of **bad weather** – the island lies on the exposed eastern edge of the archipelago, smack in the middle of the "typhoon highway". Unless you are a surfer (surf season is roughly July–Oct), the best time to visit is from March to June, when the chances of rainfall are slight and the wind is less wicked. During the wet season (July–Nov), the island can be hit half a dozen times by **typhoons**, causing extensive damage to crops and homes and sometimes loss of life.

Virac

VIRAC is an anonymous provincial town, busy with mercantile activity and the noise of jeepneys. There is a small central plaza with a cathedral and a busy market, and an interesting local **museum**, but for most visitors Virac will simply be a base for exploring the rest of the island.

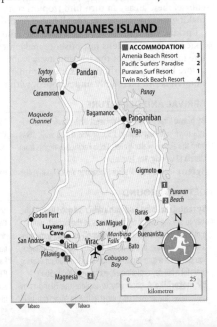

CATANDUANES ISLAND

◼ ACCOMMODATION
Amenia Beach Resort — 3
Pacific Surfers' Paradise — 2
Puraran Surf Resort — 1
Twin Rock Beach Resort — 4

Museo de Catanduanes
Old Capitol Building, Santa Elena St • Mon–Fri 8am–4pm • P50

The **Museo de Catanduanes**, within the same building as the tourist office, is worth a look. Artefacts include fishing implements and trumpet shells used to send out signals to local communities. Objects from the Spanish colonial era include the intricately decorated walking cane of a Spanish congressman, which he allegedly used to accessorize his sharkskin coat and felt hat.

Around Virac

You will find some good, surfable **beaches** west of Virac in the villages of **Magnesia**, **Buenavista** and **Palawig**, although none is as pretty or as popular as Puraran (see below). Inland from Palawig there are enormous limestone **caves** near the village of **Lictin**. To get there you'll have to find a guide in Lictin (there are no established rates, but P500 is a reasonable amount to pay); contact the tourist office in Virac before setting out, or ask at the barangay hall or in any of the village stores. The best known is **Luyang Cave**, whose waters are said to have healing properties. Another good short trip from Virac is to the **Maribina Falls**, between the barangays of Marinawa and Binanwahan – thus the name – fifteen minutes inland by jeepney. The waterfall plunges more than 10m into a crystal-clear pool that's good for swimming.

Puraran Beach

30km from Virac • Surfboard rental P200/hr, lessons P150/hr • One morning jeepney from Virac passes Puraran (1hr; P50) on its way to Gigmoto at around 10.30–11am; there are also jeepneys from Virac to Baras (hourly; 40min; P40) from where it's a P150 tricycle trip (20min) to the beach; when you're ready to leave the resort owners can arrange a tricycle to Baras, or all the way to Virac for P700 if you've missed the last jeepney

The break at beautiful **Puraran Beach** is referred to as **Majestic** by surfers. Majestic is fickle but it's generally thought that the best bet is to come here between **July and October**, when low-pressure areas lurking out in the Pacific help kick up a swell. Of course, these areas can turn into tropical storms and typhoons that batter the coast, making surfing impossible for all but experts and the foolhardy.

Luckily, you don't have to be a surfer to enjoy a few days on a beach as lovely as this. Extensive **coral gardens** just offshore make for wonderful snorkelling, and swimming is safe inside the line of the reef and away from the rocks – ask for advice at your resort before heading out, though, as it is not unknown for swimmers to get into trouble. Puraran is still mercifully undeveloped, with just three basic resorts.

ARRIVAL AND DEPARTURE
CATANDUANES

By plane Virac's airport is 4km west of the town. A tricycle into town will cost around P50, or less if you walk away from the airport waiting area. Cebu Pacific has flights from Manila (4 weekly; 1hr 10min).

By ferry There are ferries from Tabaco to Virac (1 daily; 4hr; P240) and San Andres (2 daily; 3hr; P200).

By bangka From Guijalo port in the Caramoan Peninsula you can hire a private bangka to Codon port on the western coast of Catanduanes island (45min; P1500), from where you can catch a tricycle to Virac (1hr; P500).

GETTING AROUND

By rental car Hiring a car with a driver is a good if expensive way to see the island; try the drivers at the airport, visit the provincial tourist office in Virac or simply ask your accommodation to arrange it. For about P2000–3000, for instance, you can get a return trip to Puraran Beach including waiting time; for a full day exploring expect to pay P4000–5000.

By motorbike A good way to explore the island is by motorbike; the provincial tourist office in Virac can help arrange rental (P500/day).

By bus, van and jeepney Buses, vans and jeepneys to destinations on the west side of the island leave from the barangay of Gogon in Virac. From Gogon buses and vans to Pandan (buses every 2hr; 4hr; vans hourly 1–5pm; 3hr; P150) pass through Caramoran (bus 3hr 30min; vans 2hr 30min; P150); there are also jeepneys to San Andres, with the first departure at 6am, and sporadic departures thereafter

(20min; P30). From Virac pier, vans run to Bagamanoc (every 2hr until 1pm and then hourly thereafter; 1hr 30min; P80)

and Viga (hourly; 1hr 15min; P80); there are also local buses to Bagamanoc (noon & 2pm; 2hr).

INFORMATION

Tourist information The provincial tourist office (Mon–Fri 8am–5pm; ☎0929 399 8437, ⓦcatanduanes.gov.ph) is on the second floor of the Old Capitol Building on Santa Elena St in Virac.

Services All the services are in Virac. There are a few banks, including PNB and BDO on the main plaza and a

branch of DBP on the ground floor of the Old Capitol Building, just below the tourist office. The post office (Mon–Fri 8am–5pm) is at the back of the municipal building. For internet, try WorldNet.com on Salvacion St (Mon–Sat 8am–8pm; P20/hr; ☎0919 773 5578).

ACCOMMODATION

If you're keen to stay out of town, but within reach of Virac's amenities, try the *Twin Rock* or *Amenia Beach* resorts. The resorts at Puraran Beach are very laidback and it is not unusual to end up staying for longer than you had planned. Electricity is often limited to a few hours a day and the nearest internet access is in Virac.

VIRAC

ARDCI Corporate Inn 4th Floor, ARDCI Corporate Building, San Roque ⓦardciinnvirac.weebly.com. On two floors of an office block with floor-to-ceiling windows, this is a good option; rooms are comfortable and the bathrooms have rain showers. There's a wi-fi-equipped café with views over the rice paddies and Virac. Breakfast included. **P1000**

Midtown Inn San José St ☎0947 563 8165, ⓦcatmidinn.com. The pick of the Virac bunch, just off the main roundabout, with a little communal lounge on the first floor. Most rooms are a/c and have cable TV and private bathrooms with hot showers. Wi-fi throughout. **P1344**

Rakdell Hotel San Pedro St ☎052 811 0881, ⓔjosh pampanga@yahoo.com. Budget option with acceptable a/c rooms with private bath and hot shower – but its location opposite the town's only nightspot means it can be noisy. On the plus side, there's a restaurant and a roof deck where guests can enjoy their meals. Wi-fi in the lobby. **P1000**

AROUND VIRAC

Amenia Beach Resort Palawig Beach, San Andres, 12km southwest of Virac ☎0915 353 0020. The real draw here is the lovely beach outside; it's popular with day-trippers

but also a pleasant spot to stay – the nine rooms, named after local trees, are appealing enough, with decent-sized beds, and there are a couple of swimming pools. **P2000**

Twin Rock Beach Resort Brgy Igang, 10km south of Virac ☎0928 836 2648, ⓦtwinrock.com.ph. One of the island's most developed resorts, with leafy grounds on a lovely stretch of beach in front of two jagged rock formations. Boxy rooms, and a couple of claustrophobic rock cottages with a single bed (P1000). There's a zipline over the sea, climbing wall, kayaks and pool with two slides. The noisy karaoke is a drawback. **P1500**

PURARAN BEACH

Pacific Surfers' Paradise Middle of the beach ☎0917 738 2941. Under construction at the time of research, this place looks promising – the eight small cottages are mostly decorated with native materials and there's a nipa restaurant serving Filipino dishes. **P750**

Puraran Surf Resort Northern end of the beach ☎0915 764 9133, ⓦpuraransurf.com. The six simple, welcoming bamboo and palm-leaf cottages (P600) with wooden beds are far better than the rooms in the concrete block at the back. There's also a four-bed room (P1500). **P500**

EATING AND DRINKING

VIRAC

Blossoms Salvacion St ☎0932 710 0576. The most atmospheric restaurant in town, serving pasta (P60) and pizza (P125), as well as seafood (P195), noodles (P40) and cakes (P55). Mon–Sat 7am–10pm.

Café de Au Salvacion St ☎0939 158 1749. This tiny, welcoming café makes great coffee, using a proper coffee machine (P50). Plus snacks and substantial meals including American breakfasts (P65) and pasta (P35). Mon–Sat 8am–10pm, Sun 3–10pm.

Elit Kape Constantino St ☎0929 189 5879. Authentic Thai food including curry (P229), *tom yam* (P189) and *pad thai* (P120). At lunchtime there is a selection of

dishes laid out in pots, or you can order Filipino and international dishes à la carte. Free wi-fi. Mon–Sat 9am–10pm.

Sea Breeze Pier Side, PPA Building, Brgy Salvacion ☎0906 494 6597. By the pier, with shaded wooden huts by the beach, this is a pleasant spot for a beer (P50) and a sea breeze; the food, however, is less than average. Free wi-fi. Daily 7am–1am.

SOG Santa Elena St. Apparently it's an acronym for "Squid on Go". The town's only nightspot is a simple little bar hosting acoustic bands on Thurs, Fri and Sat; other nights you can sip beer (P60) as the locals belt out videoke. Daily 9.30pm–2.30am.

4

Mindoro

BANGKA, SABANG

5

Mindoro

Within a few hours of Manila, yet worlds away, Mindoro remains undeveloped even by Philippine provincial standards. Much of the island is wild and rugged, with some near-impenetrable hinterlands and an often desolate coastline of wide bays and isolated fishing villages. The island, seventh largest in the archipelago, is divided lengthways into two provinces, Mindoro Occidental and Mindoro Oriental; the latter is the more developed and visited. Most travellers head this way only for the beaches, scuba diving and nightlife around the picturesque town of Puerto Galera on Mindoro Oriental's northern coast, a short ferry trip across the Isla Verde Passage from Batangas, but there is much more to Mindoro than this. Few people, Filipinos included, realize that the island is home to several areas of outstanding natural beauty, all protected to some degree by local or international decree.

ARRIVAL AND DEPARTURE

MINDORO

BY PLANE

San José airport, in the south of Mindoro Occidental, is served by 1 daily flight (55min) from Manila with Cebu Pacific. There is no airport serving Puerto Galera.

BY BOAT

Manila to Puerto Galera A good way to reach Puerto Galera and Sabang from Manila is to buy a combined bus-boat ticket with Si-Kat (daily 8.30am; arrive Sabang 12.15pm and Muelle pier 1pm; ☎ 02 708 9628, ⊛ sikatferrybus.com; P700); the bus departs from their office at City State Tower, 1315 Mabini St, Ermita.

Batangas City to Puerto Galera and Balatero The main ferry port for departures to Puerto Galera's Muelle pier is Batangas City (see p.120). There are frequent departures (daily 6.30am–5pm) from Batangas to Muelle pier (P230), Sabang (P230) and White Beach (P270) on large outriggers, easy to find on arrival at Batangas Port Terminal 3; companies running them include Father and Son Shipping Line (FSL; ☎ 043 287 3047, ⊛ puertogalera ferry.net). A chartered outrigger will cost at least P4000 one way. All passengers must also pay the terminal fee (P30), and those disembarking at Puerto Galera an Environmental User Fee (P50), before boarding. In addition, Montenegro Lines (⊛ montenegrolines.com.ph) operates a car ferry from Batangas City to Balatero, 3km west of Puerto Galera (daily 7am & noon; 2hr; passengers P170).

Batangas City to Calapan and Abra de Ilog Montenegro Lines (⊛ montenegrolines.com.ph) runs hourly ferries to Calapan (P240), 44km southeast of Galera, and Abra de Ilog (3 daily; P260), 30km west. Fast Cat (⊛ fastcat .com.ph) also runs between Batangas and Calapan (1am, 6am, 3pm & 8pm; P190) in just 1hr 30min.

Batangas City to San José Montenegro Lines also operates ferries to San José (Mon, Wed & Fri 6pm; P726).

Roxas to Caticlan (for Boracay) Roxas is a key link on the Strong Nautical Highway route to Boracay, and there are regular ferries departing for Caticlan (4hr). Starlite Ferries runs twice daily (☎ 043 723 9965; 9pm & 11pm, returning noon & 4pm; P420), while Montenegro Lines (⊛ montenegrolines.com.ph) has five daily boats (usually 4am, 10am, 4pm, 8pm & midnight; P460).

San José to Taytay and Cuyo Montenegro also links San José with Taytay in Palawan (P1065) and the tiny island of Cuyo (P498) – call to confirm times.

BY BUS

Manila to San José Dimple Star Transport (☎ 02 517 9677) runs two direct bus routes to Mindoro from Manila (3 daily) from Ali Mall in Cubao and Pasay to San José, both via Batangas port (10hr). From here some buses take the ferry between Batangas and Abra de Ilog before continuing on to San José via Sablayan, while other buses take the ferry between Batangas and Calapan and then continue on to

WHITE FAN CORAL, MINDORO

Highlights

❶ Puerto Galera The area around this picturesque coastal resort has some fine beaches, challenging treks and scuba diving for every level. **See p.241**

❷ Tribal visits Get an intriguing insight into a marginalized culture by meeting the island's original inhabitants, the Mangyan. **See p.245**

❸ Mount Halcon Mindoro's highest peak is a serious hiking challenge through mist-shrouded jungle to jaw-dropping vistas of the whole island. **See p.252**

❹ Mounts Iglit-Baco National Park See the rare tamaraw, a type of water buffalo, as you trek

through some of the most enchanting countryside on Mindoro. **See p.256**

❺ North Pandan Island Idyllic island hideaway just off the west coast, a tranquil resort offering scuba diving, snorkelling or the chance to just laze on the bone-white sands. **See p.257**

❻ Apo Reef Superlative diving in one of the most pristine marine environments in the world, where sharks, rays and other pelagics are common sightings and you can spend the night on a remote islet. **See p.258**

HIGHLIGHTS ARE MARKED ON THE MAP ON P.240

5

San José via Roxas. Tickets will be at least P1100 one way. JAM Transit (☎ 02 831 8264, ⓦ jam.com.ph) runs a similar service from its Manila terminals (p.83) to San José via Calapan and Roxas (every 2hr; 2am–9pm).

Mindoro Oriental

More accessible and developed than its poorer neighbour across the mountains, most visitors head to **Mindoro Oriental** to dive in the marine reserve at **Puerto Galera**, in the north of the province. Nearby **Mount Malasimbo** is also protected because of the

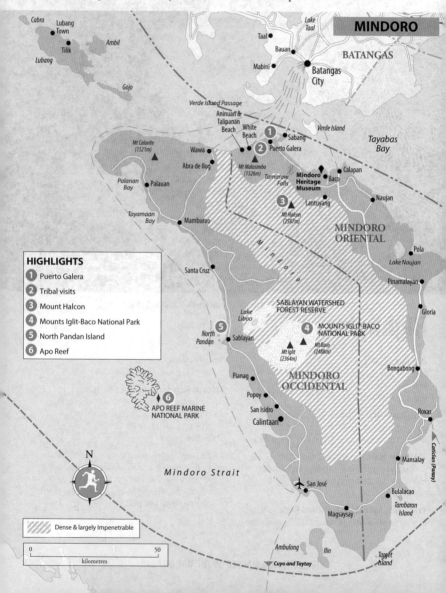

MINDORO

HIGHLIGHTS

1. Puerto Galera
2. Tribal visits
3. Mount Halcon
4. Mounts Iglit-Baco National Park
5. North Pandan Island
6. Apo Reef

Dense & largely Impenetrable

0 — 50
kilometres

N

biodiversity of its thickly jungled slopes. To the east of Puerto Galera, near the port of **Calapan**, is **Mount Halcon** – at 2587m, Mindoro's tallest peak and a difficult climb even for experienced mountaineers. The south of the island is less populated than the north, with few tourists making it as far as **Roxas** on the southeast coast unless they're taking a ferry to Caticlan (for Boracay).

Puerto Galera

One of the country's most popular resorts, **PUERTO GALERA** (meaning "Port of the Galleons") boasts some of the most diverse coral reef diving in Asia and gorgeous, bone-white beaches, as a result of which the whole area is often mobbed during national holidays. Arriving by ferry is a memorable experience, the boat slipping gently through aquamarine waters past a series of headlands fringed with haloes of sand and coconut trees. Brilliant white yachts lie at anchor in the innermost bay and in the background looms the brooding hulk of Mount Malasimbo, invariably crowned with a ring of cumulus cloud.

Founded by the Spanish in 1574, the town was once an important port and served as Mindoro's capital until 1837, when Calapan assumed the role. Today it's a natural choice for escaping Manileños, so book ahead if you're planning to visit during Easter and summer weekends. There's also plenty on offer in addition to diving, including excellent snorkelling, trekking into the mountains and beach- and island-hopping by bangka.

Poblacion (Puerto Galera town)

Poblacion, Puerto Galera town itself, occupies a marvellous location, overlooking Muelle Bay on one side and with green hills behind it, and you could sit for hours over a cool drink at one of the sleepy little cafés right on the waterfront at Muelle Pier watching the bangkas phut-phut back and forth. The town has various souvenir shops, general stores and a handful of modest places to stay, but despite its beautiful views and appealingly sleepy tropical ambience, there are no compelling reasons to base yourself here and most tourists move straight on to the beaches and dive resorts.

Excavation Museum

Nautical Hwy at P Concepcion St • Daily 8-11.30am & 1.30-5pm • Free (donation suggested)

Located near the town hall and within the grounds of the Immaculate Concepcion Church, the **Excavation Museum** contains a small but intriguing collection of items excavated from gravesites and underwater wrecks in the region – some items date back to 200 BC. Highlights include fragments of ancient Chinese porcelain and Siamese pottery, as well as Ming dynasty burial jars.

5

PUERTO GALERA ORIENTATION

Though Puerto Galera does have a commercial centre (aka **Poblacion**), the name is generally used to refer to the whole area between **Sabang**, 5km to the east, and **White Beach**, 8km to the west. Most visitors head straight for Sabang and the nearby beaches of **Small La Laguna** and **Big La Laguna**, home to a diverse range of accommodation, diving, restaurants and nightlife. There are also a number of family-friendly resorts near the village of **Palangán**, about halfway along the road from Puerto Galera to Sabang. Northeast of Palangán there's a small isolated cove at **Sinandigan** with a handful of very peaceful options. In the other direction, picturesque White Beach has plenty of accommodation and is popular with partying Mileños at the weekends. For more of a remote experience, walk – or take a tricycle – round to beautiful **Aninuan Beach** and **Talipanan Beach**, both of which have comfortable, affordable places to stay.

Nearby, near the pier, the canon-flanked marble **Cross at Muelle** was erected by the Spanish to commemorate the sinking of the battleship *Canonero Mariveles* in 1879 during a storm.

Sabang and around

Set in a pretty cove, **Sabang** is jam-packed with hotels, restaurants and dive schools, popular primarily with foreign tourists. However, the beach itself is nothing special, and not great for swimming, while the very visible girlie bar scene comes as a shock to many visitors. If you arrive here by bangka from Batangas City, you'll be dropped in front of *At-Cans*, a little east of the main road. From here it's just a short walk to several more enticing beaches.

Small La Laguna

Just a few minutes' walk northwest along the coast from Sabang beach, **Small La Laguna** is the ideal choice if you're looking for a range of friendly accommodation in a quiet location – most of it right on the water – with good dive operators and a handful of informal bars and restaurants.

Big La Laguna

Just around the corner from Small La Laguna, the sheltered cove of **Big La Laguna** has dive shops and a good choice of accommodation, some with convivial beach-style bars and restaurants attached. With largely clean sands, this is the best spot in the Sabang area for swimming, and there's safe snorkelling over the offshore coral reef (boats are prohibited). Further west lies pretty **Coco Beach**, dominated by the plush *Coco Beach Island Resort* (see p.247).

Palangán and Sinandigan Cove

There are some quiet and comfortable places to stay around the small barangay of **Palangán**, a few kilometres east of Sabang. Some are on the ridge above the road, with marvellous views across Puerto's bays and islets and just a short walk from the beach. Not all of these resorts have dive centres, but they can all help arrange diving through operators in Sabang. Quiet **Sinandigan Cove**, also known as Coral Cove, is twenty minutes northeast of Palangán by jeepney

White Beach

A once quiet crescent of sand, spectacular **White Beach** has in recent years been populated by small resort hotels and cottage rooms popular with Filipino families. Unlike Sabang, there are no girlie bars and fewer scuba divers too, but it does have a number of lively discos and bars that can get a bit noisy. White Beach gets especially busy at peak times, notably New Year and Easter, when backpackers and students from

Manila hold all-night rave parties on the sand. There are still some quieter spots on the beach, but those looking for an isolated and quiet beach experience should head around the corner to Aninuan and Talipanan (see below).

Aninuan and Talipanan

With White Beach becoming increasingly busy, travellers looking for something more pristine are slowly moving further west along the coast. Both **Aninuan** and **Talipanan** are easy to reach: at low tide you can walk to Talipanan along the shoreline (20min from White Beach), and when the tide is in there's a pathway that leads up over the headland. Aninuan is more popular, while Talipanan is for those seeking real solitude. There's no nightlife and no karaoke – just you, the fishermen and the fireflies.

ARRIVAL AND INFORMATION
PUERTO GALERA

By boat Most travellers arrive at Puerto Galera via boat from Batangas at Muelle pier in Poblacion, or direct to Sabang and White Beach (see opposite). Though no boats travel direct to Aninuan or Talipanan, Minolo Shipping Lines (☎043 287 3614) offers a free shuttle to both beaches from Muelle pier. For Abra de Ilog further west in Mindoro Occidental (the road to Abra is impassable except on foot or trail bike), there are daily bangkas from Balatero at around 10.30am (around P250; 1hr), providing the seas

aren't too rough (check with your hotel), although a safer way to get there is to head back to Batangas and then take a ferry from there.

By jeepney Jeepneys to Calapan (1hr 30min; P100) leave when full from the Petron petrol station on the edge of Poblacion from early morning until mid-afternoon; a/c mini-vans also make the trip from a depot 2km further out of town, but are usually double the price (the road is now fully paved).

5

DIVING IN PUERTO GALERA

The beauty of scuba diving around Puerto Galera is the number and variety of dive sites that can be reached by boat in a matter of minutes. These offer something for everyone, from exhilarating dives in raging currents to gentle drifts along sheltered coral reefs.

A good dive for novices is **Shark's Cave**, a drift dive along a reef that takes you past a cave where you might get a close-up of sleeping whitetip sharks. **Fish Bowl**, a blue-water descent to the top of a reef where sweetlips and rainbow runners are common, is another popular spot. **Sabang Point**, just off Sabang Beach, makes a good night dive, while **Monkey Wreck**, only five minutes from Sabang, is a local cargo boat that sank in 18m of water in 1993, and now plays host to large schools of batfish and snappers. Finally, don't miss the **St Christopher**, a retired diving boat that was deliberately sunk and is a refuge for the extraordinary frogfish, an ugly character with large fins and a flabby, drooping face.

More challenging dives include **Canyons**, which has a healthy reef split into three slab-like sections (hence the name) and some fierce currents that mean it's usually for advanced divers only. What makes it special is that it's the best place in the area to encounter large pelagics such as sharks and barracuda. Occasionally manta rays, eagle rays and hammerheads pass through. For a real thrill there's not much to beat the **Washing Machine**, a notorious dive near Verde Island, where currents are so strong and the topography so tricky that divers report being thrown around underwater and disoriented.

DIVE OPERATORS

There are dozens of dive operators in Sabang, Small La Laguna and Big La Laguna, and a smattering in White Beach and the beaches nearby. Rates are around P1700–1800 for a dive with full equipment, or P1250 if you bring your own wet suit and buoyancy control device, but the more dives you do, the cheaper it gets. Reckon on around P14,000 for a 1–2 day PADI course. Established firms include:

Action Divers Next to *Deep Blue Sea Inn* on Small La Laguna ☎ 043 287 3320, ⓦ actiondivers.com.
Asia Divers Next door to *El Galleon*, Small La Laguna ☎ 043 287 3205, ⓦ asiadivers.com.
Badladz Adventure Divers In the hotel of the same name at Muelle pier ☎ 0927 268 9095, ⓦ badladz.com/diving.
Frontier Scuba Near *Angelyn Beach Resort* in Sabang ☎ 043 287 3077, ⓦ frontierscuba.com.

By bus One Calapan-bound jeepney also leaves from Sabang each morning.

Tourist information There's a small tourist office (daily 7.30am–5pm; ☎ 043 287 3051) at Muelle pier.

TOURS

The following operators can arrange trips (see box opposite), though most hotels can also organize these for you. Expect to pay between P1000 and P2000 depending on the destination.

GPLP Tours Sabang, on the main road to Poblacion ☎ 0927 326 0535, ⓔ adventures172001@yahoo.com. Runs island-hopping day-trips, with lunch (daily 10am–4pm; P1000, minimum 8 people), plus inland trips (P1200) to the Tamaraw Falls, the Hanging Bridge and Mangyan villages, with optional jungle river kayaking (an additional P800).
Islands Destination Travel & Tours Poblacion ☎ 043 287 3145, ⓦ islandsdestinationtravelandtours.weebly.com. Arranges dive and snorkelling trips, Mangyan cultural tours and beach-hopping.

GETTING AROUND

By tricycle Tricycles are always available and the most convenient way to zip between the various beaches in Galera, though they are notorious for ripping off tourists. Locals pay around P30/person (P50 at night) between Muelle pier/Poblacion and Sabang for example, but as a foreigner you'll be asked for at least P200/tricycle (getting them down to P100 is quite an achievement). To White Beach, Aninuan and Talipanan reckon on at least P160 (or P40/person if you can share with four people).
By bangka Bangkas regularly ply between Sabang and White Beach (40min); for around P1500 the boat will wait for you (one way will cost P1000-plus). You can arrange bangkas between just about any beach; rates will depend on how long you need the boat for and your haggling skills. Small pumpboats travel between Sabang and Big/Small La Laguna beaches for around P200 (P400 at night).

DAY-TRIPS AROUND PUERTO GALERA

MANGYAN VILLAGES AND MUSEUM

Two Mangyan tribal villages (see box, p.250) are easily accessible from Puerto Galera, while others require a bit more effort in the form of some stiff uphill hiking, but are rewarded with a more genuine experience. To get the most out of your visit it's worth organizing through one of the travel agents in Poblacion or Sabang (see opposite), who can provide an interpreter and cultural etiquette tips. The **Baclaran Mangyan** village is just a thirty-minute walk from Poblacion, while **Barangay Dulangan** is a short jeepney ride from Baco, 34km southeast of Galera. Some 12km beyond the town of Baco itself (and not far from the Mangyan village), the small **Mindoro Heritage Museum** (daily 9am–5pm; P50; ☎ 043 743 0038) at the *Dolce Vita Di Jo Resort* contains a rare collection of artefacts from each of Mindoro's Mangyan tribes.

TAMARAW FALLS

Off the main road to Calapan lie a number of caves and thundering waterfalls, and thirty minutes from Puerto Galera, in the barangay of Villaflor, the **Tamaraw Falls** (P30) is the mother of all cascades. Here cool mountain water plummets over a 132-metre precipice and into a natural pool and man-made swimming pool. The falls have become a popular sight (hence the entrance fee), so avoid going at the weekend, when they are overrun. Lots of travellers hire scooters or motorbikes (P800/day) in town to save the cost of a guided tour (and to spend more time at the falls). The cheapest option is to take the Calapan-bound jeepney at Poblacion and ask to get off at the falls, which are right beside the road (30min; around P40).

MOUNT MALASIMBO

One of the best day-treks is from White Beach into the foothills of **Mount Malasimbo** (1168m), where there are a number of tribal communities, as well as waterfalls with cold, clear pools big enough for swimming. To tackle the summit itself, pick up the trail at Talipanan Beach (take a tricycle) and through the Iraya Mangyan village just inland. Total trek time is around 5hr for a reasonably experienced hiker (no permits necessary).

PYTHON CAVE AND HOT SPRINGS

This popular day-trek takes you 3km out of town along the Calapan road, from where a narrow, unsigned 2km trail leads up to the immense **Python Cave** through thick vegetation and piping-hot springs deep enough for a swim. Tricycles will ask for at least P400 for the return trip (including the wait).

By jeepney Jeepneys shuttle back and forth between Sabang and Poblacion (they depart up the hill from Muelle pier, on Concepcion St; 6am–6pm; 15min), although these won't leave until they are overflowing. Jeepneys also run along the west coast to White Beach and Aninuan. Most routes are P20–25, but note that most stop running after 5pm, when you'll be at the mercy of the tricycle drivers.
By scooter/motorbike You can rent scooters and motorbikes in Poblacion and Sabang for around P800/day; try Aldy's Motorbikes (☎ 0927 437 9724, ⓦ aldysbikes.9f.com).

ACCOMMODATION

With direct boats from Batangas to Sabang and White Beach, there's really little need to stay in **Poblacion (Puerto Galera town)**; that said, if you want to escape the beach scene, there are a few decent hotels here. Power failures are a regular occurrence in Puerto Galera, so it's worth asking resorts if they have a backup generator before committing yourself to staying. Accommodation choices in **Sabang** range from cheaper cottages in small hotels to more expensive dive resort options. Generally speaking the accommodation to the west of the main road, which is closer to the nightlife, is pricier than that to the quieter east. **White Beach** is now very popular, and room prices have rocketed. For those on a budget it can be hard to find a decent room, particularly at weekends and holidays; it's definitely worth booking in advance.

POBLACION (PUERTO GALERA TOWN)

Badladz Dive Resort Muelle pier ☎ 043 287 3693, ⓦ badladz.com; map p.243. Geared to divers rather than beach-lovers, with great bay views and spacious rooms with hot water, a/c and cable TV. There's also a dive shop

(see box opposite) and free wi-fi. P1738

Bahay Pilipino Hotel P. Concepcion St ☎ 043 442 0266; map p.243. A friendly place run by Bavarian native Dr Fritz and his Filipina wife Jasmin. The fan rooms are small and well kept, but have shared bathrooms. The

5

attached restaurant serves German and Swiss sausages (see p.248). **P550**

★**The Manor** Yacht Club Rd, Barangay Santo Nino (500m west of the Immaculate Concepcion Church) ☎ 0926 937 7908, ⓦ themanorpuertogalera.com; map p.243. The only luxury offering in the town is this modern mansion, on a ridge above the Yacht Club with spectacular views in all directions. Each room is individually decorated and features high-quality furnishings and modern art – the "Presidential Suite" and "Indonesian Room" are particularly impressive. There are also a couple of houses for rent, which are great for families. In the grounds you'll find tennis courts and an infinity pool, and there's a free boat shuttle from the Yacht Club. **P5500**

SABANG

Angelyn's Dive Resort Far western end of the beach ☎ 0915 266 1564, ⓦ angelynsdiveresort.com; map pp.246–247. Good location right on the beach and only a short walk from dive operators, bars and restaurants, with a choice of accommodation ranging from basic lodge rooms to en-suite cabins, some with balconies and all with a/c and cable TV. There's also a small open-air restaurant with free wi-fi (public areas only). **P1600**

Big Apple Dive Resort ☎ 043 287 3134, ⓦ dive bigapple.com; map pp.246–247. Set back from the shore on the main footpath, this is one of Sabang's best-known resorts, with its own dive centre and rooms in a quiet garden surrounding a swimming pool. There's a choice of fan, a/c deluxe and a/c superior rooms, the latter of which are worth the extra outlay (P1100). Free wi-fi throughout. **P500**

Capt'n Gregg's Turn left at the end of the road in Sabang, then 2min walk along the beach ☎ 0917 540 4570, ⓦ captngreggs.com; map pp.246–247. A popular, well-established resort catering mainly to divers, with acceptable rooms (the cheapest come with fans only, but all have free wi-fi and flatscreen TVs), decent food and useful advice from the resident divers in the dive shop, many of whom have lived in Sabang for years. **P800**

★**Steps Garden** Almost at the far western end of the beach, 60m inland ☎ 043 287 3046, ⓦ stepsgarden .com; map pp.246–247. Discreetly tucked into the western end of the cove, Swedish-owned *Steps* has a wide variety of comfortable a/c huts spread through the lovely hillside gardens (inspired by the Greek island of Santorini), many of which have great balcony views. There's also an attractive pool, a good restaurant and friendly staff. Free wi-fi throughout. **P1600**

Tropicana Castle Dive Resort Sabang Rd (the main road coming into Sabang from Poblacion) ☎ 043 287 3075, ⓦ tropicanacastleresort.com; map pp.246–247. An extraordinary faux German *schloss* owned and operated by the Maierhofer family, *Tropicana* has medieval-themed rooms with four-poster beds and all mod cons (including wi-fi in public areas only). There's a swimming pool, a small spa and a restaurant. Many guests are on all-in packages from Europe that include diving. **P1750**

SMALL LA LAGUNA

El Galleon Beach Resort ☎ 043 287 3205, ⓦ asiadivers .com; map pp.246–247. Professionally run, tropical-style hotel with airy bamboo a/c rooms, many with balconies, ranging from no-frills budget to spacious seaview cottages. The pleasant seaside restaurant serves breakfast and a good range of lunch and dinner dishes including pasta, chicken, salads and seafood, produced by the resident French chef. **P2360**

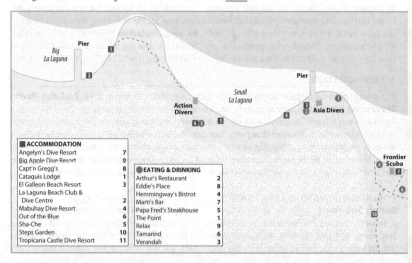

■ ACCOMMODATION	
Angelyn's Dive Resort	7
Big Apple Dive Resort	9
Capt'n Gregg's	8
Cataquis Lodge	1
El Galleon Beach Resort	3
La Laguna Beach Club & Dive Centre	2
Mabuhay Dive Resort	4
Out of the Blue	6
Sha-Che	5
Steps Garden	10
Tropicana Castle Dive Resort	11

● EATING & DRINKING	
Arthur's Restaurant	2
Eddie's Place	8
Hemmingway's Bistrot	4
Marti's Bar	7
Papa Fred's Steakhouse	5
The Point	1
Relax	9
Tamarind	6
Verandah	3

Mabuhay Dive Resort ☎043 287 3232, ⓦmabuhay -dive-resort.com; map pp.246–247. Not to be confused with its near namesake (*Dive Resort Club Mabuhay*) over in Sabang, this is a substantial resort set in expansive tropical gardens and finished to a high standard. All rooms are a/c with cable TV and have balconies overlooking the central swimming pool. Their stylish *Mabuhay Beach Restaurant* is right on the shore and there's a silent 24hr generator should the power fail. P2900

★**Out of the Blue** 30m back from the beach ☎043 287 3357, ⓦoutoftheblue.com.ph; map pp.246–247. Sophisticated apartments set on the hillside above the beach, most of which feature huge windows and balconies looking out to sea. There's also two pools, and a great restaurant, *Verandah* (see p.249). P3560

Sha-Che Roughly midway along the beach ☎0928 411 3748; map pp.246–247. Small but friendly place with a choice of clean a/c and fan rooms, with cable TV, fridge and wi-fi. P1200

BIG LA LAGUNA

Cataquis Lodge ☎0916 31 9877; map pp.246–247. Brightly coloured, no-frills concrete huts with a/c, cable TV and hot water, in an exceptional location, just paces from the sea. There are cheaper wooden cottages with fans at the back (P700). P1500

La Laguna Beach Club & Dive Centre ☎043 287 3181, ⓦllbc.com.ph; map pp.246–247. Substantial resort with various palm-roofed rooms and cottages surrounding a beautiful swimming pool. All rooms have a/c, hot water, cable TV and DVD player. On site are a reputable diving school, a first-class restaurant serving Asian and European food and the relaxing upstairs *Gecko Bar* with a large balcony for sunset-watching. P2900

COCO BEACH

Coco Beach Island Resort ☎0917 883 9334, ⓦcoco beach.com; map p.241. Reachable only by private bangka (they'll collect you in Batangas or at Muelle pier), this is secluded and idyllic, with airy rooms built of indigenous materials and a full range of activities on offer, including day-trips, diving and tennis. There's also a large outdoor swimming pool in the well-kept grounds. The only problem is that you'll have to depend on the resort's bangkas to take you anywhere, even out for dinner at night. The resort does, however, have several restaurants of its own. P3025

PALANGÁN

Blue Crystal Beach Resort ☎043 287 3144, ⓦblue crystalbeachresort.com; map p.241. For those seeking a remote escape without foregoing everyday luxuries, this imposing colonnaded building right on the seashore may be the answer. Rooms have a/c, cable TV and are grandly decorated with heavy furnishings, and some have kitchenettes. There's also a decent pool and beautiful coastal vistas. In fact the only downside is that the beach here isn't that great. P2700

★**Kalaw Place** ☎043 422 0209, ⓦkalawplace.com .ph; map p.241. This is something special, a gracious and relaxed family-run resort on a promontory to the north of the road just before you reach Palangán. Options range from rooms in the main house to whole wooden houses (P3300), good for up to six people. All rooms are beautifully furnished in native style and many boast expansive bamboo balconies with fabulous views. The owners prepare the food served in the restaurant, including vegetarian dishes. P1700

▲ Bangkas to Batangas City

SABANG TO BIG LAGUNA

0   50
metres

Floating Bars

Sabang Beach

Ferry Terminal

General stores

N

GPLP Tours
▼ Maxbank & Puerto Galera

5

WHITE BEACH

Coco Aroma ☎0916 616 7337, ⓦcocoaromawhite beach.com; map p.241. At the quieter western end of the beach this is one of the few remaining simple beachside places and has basic fan nipa huts, a couple of nicely styled a/c cottages, a laidback café and lots of ambience. **P1650**

Lenly's Cottages ☎0921 584 7570; map p.241. Set behind the first row of stalls back from the beach, *Lenly's* is one of the few bargains left at White Beach. There's a range of spacious a/c (P1500) and fan cottages, some of which have kitchenette and fridge, behind a popular beach bar. **P1000**

Marco Vincent Dive Resort ☎043 287 3590, ⓦmarco vincent.com; map p.241. Set a few hundred metres back from the beach, with plush a/c rooms set around a central courtyard with pool, this hacienda-style development is as grand as it gets in White Beach. The resort has wi-fi throughout, and also has a dive centre. **P5385**

Summer Connection ☎043 287 3688, ⓦwww .summerconnection.net; map p.241. Located at the attractive western end of the beach, *Summer Connection* has managed to retain much of its original charm in spite of having added a modern concrete block. Standard rooms are clean and functional with a/c, cable TV, fridge and shower (only deluxe rooms have hot water), and there are a few simpler nipa huts at the back (P800). **P2200**

ANINUAN

Sunset at Aninuan Beach Resort Halfway along the beach ☎0920 931 8946, ⓦaninuanbeach.com; map p.241. This marble-floor complex right on the sand has tastefully styled, a/c rooms which look out over the sea. The reef right in front of the resort is perfect for snorkelling, and there's a relaxing pool, open-air bar and a good restaurant with wi-fi. **P3000**

Tamaraw Beach Resort At the White Beach end of Aninuan ☎0921 279 5161, ⓦtamarawbeachresort .com; map p.241. *Tamaraw* has an unbeatable location on the beach and pleasant rooms with balconies overlooking the sea, perfect for watching the sunset. The main building is an ugly motel-style box (rooms P800), so go for a separate cottage. They do good, reasonably priced food – mostly grills and salads with rice. Cottage **P2000**

TALIPANAN

Luca's At the far end of the beach ☎0916 417 5125, ⓦlucaphilippines.com; map p.241. *Luca's* has well-designed rooms with a/c, cable TV, fridge and hot water, plus genuine Italian food at the beautifully situated restaurant. **P1500**

Mountain Beach Resort In the middle of the beach ☎0906 362 5406, ⓦmountainbeachresort.com; map p.241. A good choice of rooms, from basic doubles with fans to nipa huts with kitchens and cable TV, and a/c bungalows on the beach. Free wi-fi in the restaurant. **P1000**

EATING AND DRINKING

Most of the dive resorts in **Sabang** have their own restaurants and bars where divers tend to congregate – *Big Apple Sports Bar* at the eponymous dive resort (see p.246) and *Capt'n Gregg's* (see p.246) are popular spots. If you're feeling more adventurous, swim out to one of the floating bars on the main Sabang beach. Outside of the resorts and listings below, Sabang's night scene is dominated by the go-go bars, and gets seedier as the night progresses. Most of the resorts at **White Beach** have their own simple restaurants, usually offering basic dishes such as grilled fish and adobo. The beach is also lined with small-scale cafés and restaurants which serve simple, relatively overpriced food and Puerto Galera's trademark cocktail, the "**Mindoro Sling**" (basically a combo of rum, Sprite and various fruit juices).

POBLACION (PUERTO GALERA TOWN)

Bahay Pilipino Hotel P. Concepcion St ☎043 442 0266; map p.243. This restaurant serves simple German dishes, including authentic German and Swiss sausages and mushroom schnitzel (P285), in addition to all the Filipino staples (adobo, *sisig*, *sinigang*). Daily 8am–8pm.

Hangout Bar & Restaurant Muelle pier; map p.243. Popular spot for a drink or light meal as you watch the boats come and go in the beautiful natural harbour. The menu includes tasty pizzas, pancakes and toasted sandwiches (from P150). Daily 7am–7pm.

SABANG

Eddie's Place Right on the seashore near the pier; map pp.246–247. *Eddie's* is a breezy spot for a sunset beer or mango shake, and a good place to wait for the ferry.

Two pool tables in the back. Daily 24hr.

Hemingway's Bistrot On the front towards the western end of the beach ☎043 287 3560, ⓦhemingways -bistrot.com; map pp.246–247. Renowned for offering the finest Western cuisine on the strip, German-owned *Hemingway's* has a top-class chef, imported ingredients (including Angus beef from the US and German Paulaner beer), and the highest prices in Puerto Galera – traditional *Nürnberger Rostbratwürste* sausage starts at P475, with the finest "Cowboy" rib-eye steak (21oz or 600g) running to P2695. Daily 10.30am–10.30pm.

Marti's Bar ☎0921 723 3006; map pp.246–247. Owned by an affable Antipodean, *Marti's* is popular with locals for a quiet drink and a chat, as well as Mon "joker jackpot", regular drink specials and organized pub crawls dubbed the "blood run". Cash only. Daily 4pm–2am.

★**Papa Fred's Steakhouse** ☎043 287 3361, ⓦsteak house-sabang.com; map pp.246–247. Justly popular meat specialist (Fred is a German expat), serving hefty, perfectly grilled steaks (from P695) but also a decent selection of Filipino favourites and superb seafood (P345–595). The lunch menu is a bit cheaper (P300). Also has a great wine list. Daily 11.30am–11.30pm.

Relax Off the main alley through town ☎0920 708 4471; map pp.246–247. A friendly little restaurant serving mainly excellent Thai and Filipino dishes like chicken curry and adobo, plus a few Western offerings (P200–250). Daily 6am–3.30am.

★**Tamarind** On the front at the western end of the beach ☎043 287 3085; map pp.246–247. Offering tropical charm, wonderful ocean vistas and tasty Thai and international dishes, *Tamarind* is one of Sabang's most popular restaurants. Highlights include spicy Thai salads, *tom kha gai*, spare ribs marinated in honey and its seasoned Filipino beef steak (mains from P300). Daily 8am–11pm.

SMALL LA LAGUNA

Arthur's Restaurant El Galleon Beach Resort ☎043 287 3205, ⓦasiadivers.com; map pp.246–247. Great views and excellent European and Filipino cuisine (mains P200–300) continue to make this one of the most popular restaurants in Small La Laguna. Don't leave without trying the sumptuous banana and mango shakes. Daily 7am–10pm.

The Point El Galleon Beach Resort ☎043 287 3205, ⓦasiadivers.com; map pp.246–247. Though it's located on the headland between Sabang and Small La Laguna, this popular sunset drinks spot with amazing views is part of the *El Galleon* resort, with a huge cocktail list (drinks from P120) and food available from the hotel menu. Daily 10am–midnight.

★**Verandah** Out of the Blue ☎043 287 3357, ⓦoutof theblue.com.ph; map pp.246–247. Perched high above the beach, this is the best restaurant in Small La Laguna and serves salads, excellent Australian wagyu beef steaks and pizzas (from P220), either in the tasteful wood-furnished interior or out on a breezy terrace overlooking the ocean. There's also a decent wine list (from P750). Daily noon–3pm & 6–10pm.

WHITE BEACH

Coco Aroma ☎0916 616 7337, ⓦcocoaromawhite beach.com; map p.241. A pleasant exception to the uniformity of most of White Beach's restaurants, *Coco Aroma*, with its low tables looking out to sea, has good Western, veggie and Filipino dishes (P170–470) and its own, souped-up version of the Mindoro sling – the Coco Aroma Sling. Daily 6am–2am.

DIRECTORY

PUERTO GALERA

Banks and exchange Allied Savings Bank (Mon–Fri 9am–3pm; ☎042 442 0203) near the turn-off for Muelle pier in Poblacion exchanges foreign currencies and has an ATM, but is not always online, so bring enough pesos, or dollars, for your time here. The well-stocked Candava Supermarket at 62 P. Concepcion St also changes dollars. Otherwise the nearest banks with international Cirrus/Maestro links are in Calapan or Batangas (there are also ATMs at Batangas port).

Clinics and pharmacies The Puerto Galera Medical Clinic is in Axalan St in town, a short walk up the hill from Muelle pier, opposite the church. There are a number of other rudimentary clinics in the town; if in doubt you can always ask the dive operators, who know where the best doctors are. There are also a few small pharmacies in town.

Immigration The immigration office is inside the munici-pal compound, a short walk from Muelle pier, and can provide on-the-spot visa extensions (Mon–Wed 9am–noon only). You can photocopy your passport entry stamp page in shops nearby.

Internet access Internet access is widely available from P25/hr. The *Hangout Bar* (see opposite) has free internet.

Police station The police station (☎043 281 4043) is inside the municipal compound.

SABANG

Banks Maxbank (on the road heading back to Poblacion) has an ATM that usually accepts international cards.

Internet access There are a few small internet cafés dotted along the main alley through Sabang, and most hotels and resorts have wi-fi.

Calapan

About 45km along an often unpaved road east of Puerto Galera, the busy port city of **CALAPAN** is the capital of Mindoro Oriental. It's not a tourist destination, depending for most of its livelihood on trade, but it has good transport connections and is the base for a trek up **Mount Halcon**, the fourth highest mountain in the country and supposedly the toughest to climb. Calapan's main street is **J.P. Rizal Street**, which is only 500m long and runs past Calapan Cathedral south to Juan Luna Street.

5

THE MANGYAN

It's estimated that there are around one hundred thousand of Mindoro's original inhabitants, the **Mangyan**, left on the island, who have a way of life not much changed since they fought against the invading Spanish in the sixteenth century. With little role in the mainstream Philippine economy, the tribespeople, who divide into eight tribal groups, subsist through slash-and-burn farming of taro and yams, a practice the elders insist on retaining as part of their culture despite the destruction it causes to forests.

You may well see Mangyan as you travel around the island, often wearing only a loincloth and machete and carrying produce for market, but if you want to actually visit them in their villages, it's best to go with a guide who can act as an interpreter. You can break the ice with a few treats such as cigarettes, sweets and matches, but if you want to take photographs make sure you have their permission. Treks to Mangyan villages are possible in several parts of the island (see boxes, p.245 & p.256). Visit the Mangyan Heritage Center in Calapan (see below) for a more in-depth introduction to the culture.

Mangyan Heritage Center

Bishop Finnemann Compound, Quezon Drive, Brgy Calero • Mon–Fri 8.30am–noon & 1.30–4.30pm • Free • ☎ 43 288 5318, ⓦ mangyan.org • Take a tricycle from Calapan port (P20)

Library, archive and research and education centre, the **Mangyan Heritage Center** is the place to go for an in-depth introduction to the culture of Mindoro's oft-misunderstood Mangyan peoples (see box above). There's usually a small exhibition of photos, books and handicrafts on display.

ARRIVAL AND INFORMATION
CALAPAN

By boat Arriving in Calapan by ferry from Batangas City (see p.120), the city centre is a 15min ride away by tricycle (P35).

By bus and jeepney If you're heading for Puerto Galera, many resorts will send transport to meet you if you book and pay in advance. Otherwise you can take a jeepney (every 45min 6am–5pm; 1hr 30min; P100) from the petrol station out beyond the Provincial Capitol building on J.P. Rizal St (trikes charge P10 to the depot). Many of these jeepneys don't go as far as Sabang or White Beach, so you'll need to change to tricycle or taxi at Poblacion (Puerto

Galera town). For Roxas (3–4hr), jeepneys head out from the market, small buses leave from a terminal on the corner of Roxas and Magsaysay streets and there are also minivans from the Angel Star terminal on Mabini St (every 15min daily 5am–5pm; P200; ☎ 02 783 0886), while larger Dimple Star buses leave from the ferry pier (2 daily), destined for San José via Roxas.

Tourist information The main tourist office for Mindoro Oriental is in the Provincial Capitol building on J.P. Rizal St (daily 9am–4pm; ☎ 043 288 5622).

ACCOMMODATION AND EATING

Accommodation options in Calapan don't set the pulse racing, but there are some decent budget hotels. As for **eating**, a walk along the traffic-clogged length of J.P. Rizal St in town will take you past the usual Philippine fast-food outlets, including *Jollibee*, *Chowking* and *Mister Donut*.

Calapan Bay Hotel Nautical Hwy (Quezon Drive), Salong ☎ 0920 477 6169. Bright and clean a/c rooms with cable TV and hot water, and free wi-fi in the lobby. There's also an atmospheric restaurant with a patio overlooking the ocean. P1200

Parang Beach Resort 15min southeast of town in Brgy Parang ☎ 043 288 6120, ⓦ parangbeachresort .com. A number of plain but comfortable and well-kept

rooms in tin-roofed cottages right on the shore, plus a beachside restaurant. P1350

Riceland II Inn M.H. Del Pilar St ☎ 043 288 5590, ⓦ ricelandinn.com. This hotel has a range of motel-style standard rooms in the main building, and more comfortable rooms in the annexe at the back (P750). Choice of fan or a/c, and with or without cable TV determine the rate. There's also free wi-fi. P450

DIRECTORY

Banks There are numerous banks with ATMs along J.P. Rizal St, including Metrobank (Mon–Fri 9am–5pm; ☎ 043 288 1985).

Immigration The immigration office (Thurs & Fri only;

☎ 043 288 2245), where you can extend visas, is at J Luna St.

Internet access There are plenty of internet cafés on J.P. Rizal St, near the junction with Bonifacio St.

FROM TOP JEEPNEY, MINDORO; MANGYAN HOUSE >

5

Mount Halcon

Check ⑩ pinoymountaineer.com for up-to-date information • Expect to pay P2000 per person (in a group), including permit, guide fees but excluding food and water, plus P50 for entry to the trail

Rugged **Mount Halcon** rears up dramatically from the coastal plain of Mindoro Oriental, 28km southwest of Calapan. At an altitude of 2586m, it's Mindoro's highest peak, and surrounded by some of the most extensive tracts of rainforest on the island. Conquering the summit is a major target of mountaineers from all over the globe, though since 2006 the trails have been officially closed. In 2013 hikes unofficially resumed, with the blessing of the local Mangyan community, though the situation remains confusing, and don't even think about climbing Mount Halcon on your own – hire a Mangyan guide at Bayanan.

Unusually for the Philippines, Halcon is not of volcanic origin, created instead by a massive geological uplifting millions of years ago. The total climb – **Dulangan** and Halcon combined – is longer than that to the summit of Mount Everest from Base Camp; allow four to five days for the ascent and descent. There are many obstacles, not the least of which is the sheer volume of **rain** that falls on the mountain. There is no distinct dry season here and heavy rain is virtually a daily occurrence, resulting in an enormous fecundity of life – massive trees, dense layers of dripping moss, orchids, ferns and pitcher plants – but also making the environment treacherous and potentially miserable for climbers. Another irritation is the *limatik*, a kind of small leech that quietly clings to your boots and skin. You'll be sleeping on the mountain for at least three nights, so will need to bring a tent and other equipment. Make sure you have good waterproof clothing and a waterproof cover for your backpack.

ARRIVAL AND DEPARTURE   MOUNT HALCON

By jeepney and tricycle The lower slopes of Mt Halcon are about 1hr from Calapan; take a jeepney to Baco (around P30), where you are supposed to register at the town hall. From Baco you'll take a tricycle (P35/person) up an unsealed track to barangay Bayanan, where you pay P50 to the barangay head and organize guides. You can also approach the mountain from Puerto Galera, taking a jeepney for Calapan and getting off at the Baco turn-off.

By minibus Chartering a van at Baco market will cost at least P1000.

Roxas

Unless you just have a penchant for rough road driving and are planning to head across the mountains to San José and beyond, the main reason for heading down the east coast to **ROXAS** is to take the ferry to Caticlan (for Boracay) or Romblon. Roxas is a busy town, where there's a lively market (Wed & Sun) and a few hotels and beach resorts with long, hot stretches of grey sand 5km out by the port at **Dangay** – and not much else.

ARRIVAL AND DEPARTURE   ROXAS

Ferries to Caticlan leave around the clock, so there's really little reason to stay in Roxas unless you're too late to get onwards transport to San José or Calapan.

By bus Buses and jeepneys run north and south from Roxas, leaving from near the market on Administration St, and Dangay pier which is on the eastern edge of town. Heading north to Calapan is simple enough and there are a series of minivan depots on Magsaysay St which operate cramped but speedy trips (3–4hr). A couple of jeepneys journey west over the mountains to San José (2hr) every morning, while comfy a/c Dimple Star (see p.238) buses run to San José and north to Calapan (for Manila) twice a day.

By ferry Roxas is a key link on the Strong Nautical Highway route to Boracay, and there are regular ferries departing for Caticlan (4hr) from Dangay pier (P20 by tricycle from the market). Starlite Ferries runs twice daily (☎ 043 723 9965; 9pm & 11pm, returning noon & 4pm; P420) and Montenegro Lines (⑩ montenegrolines.com.ph) has five daily boats (usually 4am, 10am, 4pm, 8pm & midnight; P460).

INFORMATION

Tourist information There's a tourist office (Mon–Fri 8am–5pm; ☎ 043 289 2824) at the entrance to Dangay pier.
Services The Allied Savings Bank on Administration St has an ATM (Mon–Fri 9am–3pm; ☎ 043 289 2749). There's a Mercury Drug pharmacy next to Roxas Villas, and a doctor's surgery at the *RL Ganan Hotel*.

ACCOMMODATION AND EATING

If you find yourself with a few hours to wait for a ferry, the best thing to do is to stay on **Dalahican Beach**, just along the coast from Dangay pier, although most of these places get very busy on weekends. For something to **eat**, try *LYF Hotel*.

Cruzsmart Beach Resort Dalahican ☎ 043 289 2421. Simple resort with a pool (P75 for non-residents) and a/c rooms which are rentable in 4-, 12- and 24hr segments. It also has pergolas for rent (P250/half-day), but the bad news is there is also karaoke. **P900**

LYF Hotel Roxas market, Bagumbayan ☎ 043 289 2819. Painted brilliant orange, this place has small, lean fan and a/c rooms with cable TV, although some have no windows, and the walls are very thin. The canteen serves up some good food. **P350**

South of Roxas

The coastal road south from Roxas trundles through **Mansalay** and on to the small town of **Bulalacao**, the jumping-off point for a bangka ride to some beautiful and remote islets, including Target, Aslom, Buyayao and **Tambaron Island**.

ARRIVAL AND DEPARTURE   SOUTH OF ROXAS

By bus The road between Bulalacao and San José is now surfaced all the way, making the journey to the airport just 45min. Vans and jeepneys ply the coast north to Roxas (1hr) and Calapan (4–5hr), and across to San José, but you can also catch the twice daily service north and south on Dimple Star buses (p.238).
By bangka From Bulalacao you can hire bangkas to the islands for P1000–1500.

ACCOMMODATION

Tambaron Green Beach Resort Tambaron Island ☎ 0929 893 7871, ⓦ tambaron.com. This charmingly isolated resort has dorm beds and large, simple family cabins set amid trees on a beach frequented by green sea turtles. There's night-time electricity and a communal kitchen. Meals are usually P175/person, and the bangka to the island is P600 one way. Closed June–Oct. Dorm **P200**, cabin (for two people) **P700**

Mindoro Occidental

Aside from a few intrepid wildlife enthusiasts and divers around Sablayan, **Mindoro Occidental** remains wonderfully undiscovered, and travellers with flexible travel plans and a penchant for bumpy jeepney rides will have their efforts rewarded with wild jungle-covered mountains, remote beaches, and maybe meetings with a few local Mangyan people along the way.

San José on the southwest coast has the only functioning airport on Mindoro and makes a logical gateway for trips north to the fishing town of **Sablayan**, itself the jumping-off point for a sight no scuba diver should miss, the **Apo Reef Marine Natural Park**, a vast reef complex offering some of the best diving in the world. As well as organizing a trip from Sablayan, you can also do so in advance at a dive shop in Manila (see p.84) or Busuanga (see box, p.395). Sablayan is also a base for a visit to the **Mounts Iglit-Baco National Park**, home to the tamaraw – a dwarf buffalo endemic to Mindoro and in acute danger of extinction – and to **Sablayan Watershed Forest Reserve**, a lowland forest with beautiful Lake Libuao at its centre. The northwest of the island is little visited, though there are some unspoilt beaches around the town of **Mamburao**, the low-key capital of Mindoro Occidental.

5

San José

On Mindoro's southwest coast, the intensely sun-bleached and noisy port town of **SAN JOSÉ** is a quintessential Philippine provincial metropolis, with traffic-dense streets lined with drugstores, cheap canteens and fast-food outlets. Travellers usually only see San José as they pass through on their way from the airport to Sablayan or the Mounts Iglit-Baco National Park (see p.256), for which permits can be obtained here. Though Apo Reef is close by, there are no major dive operators in town and it's best to organize a trip there through the *Pandan Island Resort* or in Sablayan (see p.257).

ARRIVAL AND DEPARTURE
SAN JOSÉ

San José is bounded on its northern edge by the Pandururan River, beyond which are the pier and the airport. Arriving by jeepney from Roxas, or bus from Sablayan, you'll find yourself in C. Liboro St in the west of town. From here it's a short walk (or tricycle ride; P10) to the main thoroughfare, Rizal St, which runs across town and turns into the National Highway in the east, where it runs inland to Magsaysay.

By plane San José Airport is a 20min (P20) tricycle ride from town, or you could take one of the private cars that act as airport taxis, for which you'll pay at least P100 (fix the price before you get in). The airport is served by one daily flight from Manila (45min) with Cebu Pacific, whose office is at the airport.

By boat Cheap flights have superseded boats to San José, and there's little benefit from taking a ferry here. If you are yearning for a sea voyage, Montenegro Lines (ⓦ montenegrolines.com.ph) does operate ferries to Batangas (Sun, Tues & Thurs 6pm; P726), and less regular

services to Cuyo Island and Taytay in Palawan (check in advance). One route worth checking out is the "Bunso boat" to Coron (see p.394), an informal bangka service that usually departs Tues & Fri 9am (P1200; buy tickets from any agent in town). The boat returns from Coron Mon, Wed & Fri. The trip is supposed to take 6hr but can take much longer. You must embark via a smaller boat from the beach in front of central San José (another P20).

By bus Buses leave from the Dimple Star depot (ⓣ 0921 568 6449) on Bonifacio St at 6am, 11am, 3pm, 5pm, 7pm, 8pm and 11pm for Sablayan (3hr), Mamburao (5–7hr)

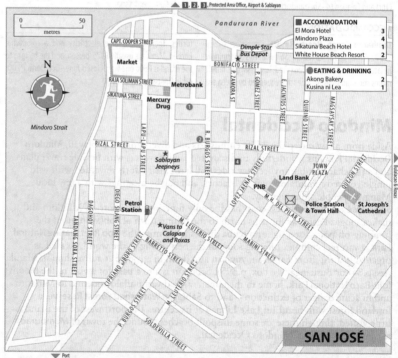

▲ **1**, **2**, **3**. Protected Area Office, Airport & Sablayan

ACCOMMODATION

El Mora Hotel	3
Mindoro Plaza	4
Sikatuna Beach Hotel	1
White House Beach Resort	2

EATING & DRINKING

Akong Bakery	2
Kusina ni Lea	1

SAN JOSÉ

and Abra de Ilog (7hr), while vans for Calapan via Roxas leave at 3.30am and 2pm (check the latest times in advance). All of these services continue on to Batangas by ferry, and then Manila by bus, but if you're not planning to stop anywhere along the way, it's almost as cheap, and much quicker to fly. If you want to reach Puerto Galera, you'll need to take a bus to Abra de Ilog, then a jeepney to Wawa on the north coast, and finally take (or charter) a bangka the rest of the way.

By jeepney Two or three jeepneys depart every morning (check in advance) from just south of Rizal St on C. Liboro for Sablayan (3–4hr) and Roxas (2hr).

INFORMATION

Permits and guides You can apply for a permit (free) and organize a local guide for Mounts Iglit-Baco (you'll meet the guide at the park entry station; see p.256) at the Protected Area Office (Mon–Fri 8am–4pm; ☏ 043 491 4200) in the LIUCP Building on Airport Rd.
Services There are a number of banks, including PNB on

M.H. Del Pilar St, and Metrobank on Sikatuna St (at Liboro St), both of which have ATMs. Close to PNB are the police station, town hall and post office. There are a handful of small internet cafés along Rizal and Liboro streets, though places frequently open and close.

ACCOMMODATION

Unless you arrive too late to move on, there's little reason to stay in San José, but if you find yourself with a night here, the choices are between one of the budget options in town, or spending a little more out at the beach on the edge of town.

El Mora Hotel Brgy San Roque 1 ☏ 043 491 4869, ⓦ elmorahotel.com. Hip boutique hotel with a choice of five themed rooms (Japanese, Filipino, etc) all with a/c and cable TV, and there's also a swish pool. Free shuttle to airport. **P2500**
Mindoro Plaza Zamora St ☏ 043 491 4661. Friendly central option with shabby but clean and tiled double rooms with fans (pricier rooms have a/c) and old TVs, cheap drinks and an on-site canteen. There are also larger family rooms. **P550**
Sikatuna Beach Hotel Airport Rd, Brgy San Roque

☏ 043 491 4108, ⓦ sikatunabeachhotel.com. Pleasant beachside spot with friendly staff and simple, ageing rooms with cable TV (some with a/c look out to the ocean). It could do with renovation, and it's worth haggling for a lower rate and checking your room before paying. There's also a decent open-sided restaurant with wi-fi. **P1500**
White House Beach Resort Airport Rd, Brgy San Roque (next to El Mora) ☏ 0919 616 7160. This marble-floored house boasts five spacious a/c rooms plus cable TV, ocean-view balconies and free wi-fi in the dining room – the owning family still lives on the second floor. **P2500**

EATING

Sit-down dining options in San José principally revolve around the hotels, and of these the restaurants at *Sikatuna Beach Hotel*, *El Mora Hotel's Pilot's Lounge* and the canteen at the *Mindoro Plaza*, are your best options.

Akong Bakery Rizal St. The best bakery in town is a 24hr haven of tempting aromas – fresh-from-the-oven *pandesal* and other pastries are knocked out throughout the day for a handful of pesos. **Daily 24hr.**

Kusina ni Lea Sikatuna St. Cheap soups, sandwiches and Filipino dishes in a traditional Filipino-style wooden dining hall (mains P130–200). Also has a/c. Daily 6.30am–11pm.

Sablayan

A very bumpy 40km north of San José, the unhurried fishing town of **SABLAYAN** is the perfect jumping-off point for several nearby attractions including Mounts Iglit-Baco National Park, the Sablayan Watershed Forest Reserve and Apo Reef. The town, small enough to cover on foot, has a central plaza (with free wi-fi) with a town hall and a stretch of scrappy black-sand beach lined by bangkas.

ARRIVAL AND INFORMATION
SABLAYAN

By bus There are buses and jeepneys north to Mamburao (3hr) and Abra de Ilog (4hr), and south to San José (3–4hr) from the bus station, which is at the southern edge of town on the National Highway, while slightly faster Dimple Star services (with onwards boat-bus connections for Batangas

and Manila; 4 daily; 8–10hr) leave from their terminal, also on the National Highway. The pier is a 5min walk south of the bus station.
Tours, permits and guides To arrange permits for Mount Iglit-Baco (free), guides and boats to North Pandan

5

Island and the Apo Reef Marine Natural Park, head to the friendly Sablayan Eco-Tourism Office (Mon–Sat 8am–noon & 1–5pm; ☎ 0928 465 9585, ⊛ sablayan.net) in the town plaza.

ACCOMMODATION

La Sofia Apartelle 483 P. Urieta St, Brgy Buenavista ☎ 043 743 0209. The simple but clean and modern rooms in the new wing of *La Sofia Apartelle* have a/c, free wi-fi and cable TV (P750). Fan-cooled rooms with shared bathroom in the older main building are basic but clean. **P450**
Landmanz Hotel 8914 Arellano St, Brgy Buenavista ☎ 043 458 0182. Barebones but clean rooms and cheaper than *La Sofia Apartelle*, though the plumbing can be sketchy. Has a mediocre restaurant attached. **P400**

Sablayan Adventure Camp Punta, Poblacion ☎ 0917 850 0410, ⊛ sablayanadventurecamp.com. Out by the pier, this cheery establishment has spacious a/c rooms set in cottages looking out to the beach, although the walls dividing the rooms don't stretch to the ceiling, meaning you'll hear everything that your neighbours do. They also have a fairly basic restaurant and can arrange boats to Pandan. **P800**

EATING

Camalig Restaurant National Hwy. Excellent seafood (P100–300) served in big portions designed to share – try the exceptional *adobong pugita* (spicy octopus). They also serve fresh seasonal fruit juices. The restaurant is a 5min tricycle ride (P10) from the main plaza. Daily 11am–9pm.
GVD Restaurant (on the main plaza). Another seafood

specialist, not quite as good as *Camalig*, though conveniently located in the centre of town. Serves various sushi/sashimi, as well as Filipino favourites such as adobo and *bulalo*. Kids get to amuse themselves on toy bikes in the playground. Mains P140–200, and merienda P25–40/person. Daily 6am–10pm.

Mounts Iglit-Baco National Park

The isolated and wonderfully raw jungles of **Mounts Iglit-Baco National Park** are dominated by the twin peaks of **Mount Baco** (2488m) and **Mount Iglit** (2364m). It can take up to two days of tough hiking to reach the peak of Mount Iglit, while the vegetation is so dense there have been no officially recorded ascents of Mount Baco.

There are also a number of more leisurely treks through the foothills to areas in which you are most likely to see the endangered **tamaraw** (*Bubalus mindorensis*), a dwarf buffalo endemic to the island (the 2013 annual headcount identified just 374 individual animals in the wild, but the total is now rising every year). The tamaraw, whose horns grow straight upwards in a distinctive "V" formation, has fallen victim to hunting, disease and deforestation in the past, and to create more awareness of its plight there is talk of designating it the country's national animal. The Sablayan Eco-Tourism Office (see above) can advise on visits to the **Tamaraw Conservation Program**, known as the "Gene Pool Farm", a small laboratory where scientists are trying to breed the tamaraw in captivity. Apart from tamaraw, the park is also prime habitat for the Philippine deer, wild pigs and other endemic species such as the Mindoro scops owl and the Mindoro imperial pigeon. It's also home to two **Mangyan** groups – the Tau-Buid and Buhid – some of whom you are likely to meet on guided hikes.

ARRIVAL AND INFORMATION   MOUNTS IGLIT-BACO NATIONAL PARK

By bus/jeepney Reaching the park by public transport from Sablayan means taking one of the regular buses or jeepneys south along the coastal road to the barangay of Popoy, then a jeepney up the bumpy and rutted track to the park itself.
Guided hikes To visit the park, you'll first have to secure a permit (free) and arrange a guide (P1500–2000 for up to three days), either in San José at the Protected Area Office

(see p.255) or the Sablayan Eco-Tourism Office (see above). Both of these offices can help put together all of the logistics for your trip, including camping options. Guided hikes usually include a 3hr stroll to the park bunkhouse (aka station 2) where you can stay the night, before the steep hike up to Mt Magawang (just above station 3; 2hr) where you should see the famed buffalo (and can also spend the night).

Sablayan Watershed Forest Reserve

Hire a vehicle and driver in Sablayan (P2500 for a day-trip), or take a bus along the coastal road and ask to be dropped at the turn-off for the penal colony, near the town of Pianag; buses and jeepneys run from Pianag for the return trip

The **Sablayan Watershed Forest Reserve** is unusual among protected wilderness areas because it contains the **Sablayan Prison and Penal Farm**, a huge open prison for low-risk inmates established in the 1950s, surrounded by agricultural lands worked by the prisoners. The inmates also produce handicrafts, and are distinguishable from the guards only by their orange T-shirts and the fact that they are not armed. Nearby are a number of villages where staff and prisoners' families live; beyond the last of these villages is a motorable track that ends on the edge of the dense Siburan Forest, close to Lake Libuao.

Lake Libuao

P50

Shallow, roughly circular **Lake Libuao** is covered in lotuses and alive with birds, including kingfishers, bitterns, egrets and purple herons. An undulating footpath around the lake makes for some wonderful walking, taking you through the edge of the forest and through glades from where there are views across the water; you'll see locals balanced precariously on small wooden bangkas fishing for tilapia. If you're reasonably fit you can walk round the lake in three hours, starting and finishing at the penal colony, though allow an hour to get between the colony and the main road.

North Pandan Island

Idyllic **North Pandan Island**, ringed by a halo of fine white sand, coral reefs and coconut palms, lies 2km off the west coast of Mindoro. In 1994 a sanctuary was established around the eastern half of the island so the **marine life** is exceptional; with a mask and snorkel you can see big grouper, all sorts of coral fishes, even the occasional turtle (sharks are very rare, however).

The island is the site of the well-run *Pandan Island Resort* (see below). On most days the resort's scuba-diving centre organizes day-trips to **Apo Reef** (see p.258), and longer overnight safaris both to Apo and to Busuanga, off northern Palawan (see p.390), if there are enough passengers. Even if you don't dive, there's plenty to keep you occupied on and around the island itself, including kayaking, jungle treks, windsurfing and sailing.

ARRIVAL AND DEPARTURE   NORTH PANDAN ISLAND

By boat If you want to just visit the island for the day (open to day guests 8am–6pm only), it's easy to arrange a boat to Pandan (those staying at the resort can take a bangka; see below) from the Sablayan Eco-Tourism Office (see opposite). You'll need to pay a P100 fee to set foot on the island. Once there, the *Pandan Island Resort*'s dive shop will kit you out for snorkelling or scuba diving (from P1650 with equipment). There's also an additional "environmental fee" of P275 for divers and P55 for non-divers; guests at the resort also pay these fees.

ACCOMMODATION AND EATING

★ **Pandan Island Resort** ☎ 0919 305 7821, ⊛ pandan .com. This well-run, back-to-nature private hideaway was developed by the French adventurer who "discovered" the island in 1986. There are four types of accommodation: budget rooms, standard double bungalows (P1600), larger bungalows for four (P2400) and family houses for up to six (P3450). During the diving season (Nov–May) the island is so popular that all rooms are often taken, so it's important to book in advance. Guests are required to take at least one buffet meal (P470) at the resort restaurant every day, and this is no bad thing: the chef dishes up excellent European and Filipino cuisine (try the tangy fish salad in vinegar) and the beach bar serves some unforgettable tropical cocktails. There is an internet point set up in the diveshop (P150/hr). To get there, take a tricycle to "Punta" where the resort bangka charges P200 for one person and P50 for each additional person (plus P50 for night crossings). Budget rooms P800

5

Apo Reef Marine Natural Park

Lying about 30km off the west coast of Mindoro, magnificent **Apo Reef** stretches 26km from north to south and 20km east to west, making it a significant marine environment and one of the world's great dive destinations. There are two main atolls, separated by deep channels, and a number of shallow lagoons with beautiful white sandy bottoms. Only in three places does the coral rise above the sea's surface, creating the islands of Cayos de Bajo, Binangaan and **Apo**, the largest.

Apo Island is home to a ranger station and a lighthouse, and you can spend a magical night here in tents (turtles often lay eggs on the beach), though the experience comes at a price. The diving is really something special, with sightings of manta rays, sharks (even hammerheads), barracuda, tuna and turtles fairly common. Most of the Philippines' 450 species of coral are here, from tiny bubble corals to huge gorgonian sea fans and brain corals, along with hundreds of species of smaller reef fishes such as angelfish, batfish, surgeonfish and jacks.

ARRIVAL AND INFORMATION   APO REEF MARINE NATURAL PARK

Experiencing Apo Reef isn't cheap. For starters, everyone who visits needs to pay an "environmental fee": P1750 to dive and P450 for everyone else (including snorkellers). Transport by boat (1hr 30min from *Pandan Resort*) is extra, and you'll pay additional fees if you want to dive (as opposed to just snorkel).

Tours from Pandan Island Resort *Pandan Resort* rates for Apo Reef depend on the boat and the number of people on it, per person prices ranging from P6820 (two people) to P1590 (eleven). Overnights cost considerably more: P11,390 (for two people), to P3655 (for eleven)/person. These rates do not include the marine park fee, or even diving fees, which will cost at least another P1650 (snorkelling is included, plus the park fee).

Tours from Sablayan If you're not staying at *Pandan Resort* you can visit the reef on one of the liveaboard trips offered by many dive operators in Coron Town (in Busuanga; see box, p.395) or Manila, or organize a trip with the Sablayan Eco-Tourism Office in Sablayan (see p.256); a ten-person boat out to the reef is P7500 (snorkelling only), while a six-person boat for divers is P8000 (maximum of four dives, which cost extra). The Sablayan office will arrange overnight tent rentals for just P300/person, but you must bring your own food (and the toilets are very basic).

The northwest

It's hard to believe that the quiet, relatively isolated west coast town of **MAMBURAO**, 80km north along the coastal road from Sablayan, is the capital of Mindoro Occidental. With a population of around forty thousand, Mamburao is significant only as a trading and fishing town, although the coastal road is undeniably scenic, with blue ocean on one side and jungled mountains on the other. North of town there are some alluring stretches of white-sand **beach**, which are slowly being developed for tourism. The best of these is **Tayamaan Bay**, 4km north of Mamburao (day-visitors pay P30).

North of Mamburao the road forks. From here, jeepneys and some buses head northwest along the coast to Palauan or northeast to **Abra de Ilog**, near the north coast; the journey to Abra de Ilog takes you past dazzling green paddy fields and farmland planted with corn. The easily motorable road ends at the pier at **Wawa**, 1km past Abra de Ilog, although the track to Puerto Galera is a popular route with bike riders, and hikers have also made the trip.

ARRIVAL AND DEPARTURE   THE NORTHWEST

By bus The most comfortable way to traverse the west coast is via the 4–5 daily services on Dimple Transport, which shuttle between Mamburao and San José (5–7hr), Sablayan (2–3hr) and Abra de Ilog (2hr), with connections to Batangas and Manila.

By boat From Wawa, the easiest way to get to Puerto Galera is to take a bangka. Sometimes there are morning passenger bangka services, but don't be surprised if you end up having to charter your own (about 2hr; P1500–2000).

ACCOMMODATION

MAMBURAO

La Gensol Plaza Hotel National Hwy ☎ 043 711 1072. No frills hotel where the cheapest rooms are fan singles with tiny cold showers, though they also have larger, more comfortable doubles with a/c and cable TV. Doubles P900

ABRA DE ILOG

★**Tuko Beach Resort** Munting Buhangin Beach ☎ 0918 528 2173, ⊛ tukobeachresort.com. Though this is a 20min bangka ride from Abra pier (P800), it's by far the most enticing and comfortable lodgings in the region, a tranquil, plush German-owned beach hotel with spacious a/c or fan cottages and breakfast and dinner provided (add P350 for full board), monkeys in the trees and dolphins frolicking offshore. Rates are per person; two people P3300

5

The Visayas

CHOCOLATE HILLS, BOHOL

The Visayas

The Visayas, a collection of islands large and small in the central Philippines, are considered to be the cradle of the country. It was here that Ferdinand Magellan laid a sovereign hand on the archipelago for Spain and began the process of colonization and Catholicization that shaped so much of the nation's history. The islands were also the scene of some of the bloodiest battles fought against the Japanese during World War II, and where General Douglas MacArthur waded ashore to liberate the country after his famous promise, "I shall return".

6

The Visayas comprises thousands of islands and everywhere you turn there seems to be another patch of tropical sand or coral reef awaiting your attention, usually with a ferry or bangka to take you there. There are nine major island groups – **Cebu, Bohol, Siquijor, Negros, Guimaras, Panay, Romblon, Samar,** and **Leyte** – but it's the hundreds in between that make this part of the archipelago so irresistible. Of the smaller islands, some are famous for their beach life (especially **Boracay**, off the northern tip of Panay), some for their fiestas and some for their folklore.

No one can accuse the Visayas, or the Visayans who live here, of being a uniform lot. Visayan is the umbrella **language**, the most widely spoken form of which is Cebuano (see box, p.266), but in some areas they speak Ilongo or Waray Waray, in others Aklan; all three languages are closely related Malayo-Polynesian tongues. The diversity of languages is a symptom of the region's fractured topography, with many islands culturally and economically isolated from those around them, part of the Philippine archipelago in little more than name.

2013 was a very tough year for the Visayas, with a substantial quake in Bohol in October, and then in November **Typhoon Yolanda** tore through the region, leaving a broad band of destruction along its path (see box, p.359). Numerous destinations of interest to travellers were affected, including southeastern Samar, Tacloban, Ormoc, the Camotes, Bantayan and Malapascua. While we have removed the worst affected areas from this edition, wherever possible we have included practical detail so that visitors can still travel to these areas and help bolster local economies. Although we have provided the most up-to-date information possible, note that some places may not manage to reopen, while others might use the rebuild as an opportunity to improve or renovate – call or check online for the latest information.

TARSIERS

Highlights

❶ Malapascua A little gem off Cebu, boasting the dazzling Bounty Beach, islets to explore and scuba diving with thresher sharks. **See p.285**

❷ Pescador Island Marine Reserve Tiny Pescador is only 100m long, but has a glorious reef attracting divers from around the world. **See p.289**

❸ Bohol Everything good about the Philippines in one compact island package: superb diving, fine beaches, old Gothic churches, the iconic Chocolate Hills and, uniquely, the world's smallest primate (above). **See p.292**

❹ Mount Kanlaon National Park Active volcano at the centre of dense forest offering some extreme trekking and climbing. **See p.313**

❺ Apo Island Robinson Crusoe-esque hideaway off Negros, with excellent diving. **See p.320**

❻ Ati-Atihan Festival, Kalibo The biggest bash in the Philippines: wild costumes, outdoor partying and copious food and drink. **See p.336**

❼ Boracay Though verging on overdeveloped, Boracay's White Beach is still one of the best anywhere, with great dining and nightlife, and there's so much to do you'll never be bored. **See p.337**

❽ Sibuyan Island One of the country's most intact natural environments, with dramatic forest-cloaked Mount Guiting Guiting at its heart. **See p.351**

HIGHLIGHTS ARE MARKED ON THE MAP ON PP.264–265

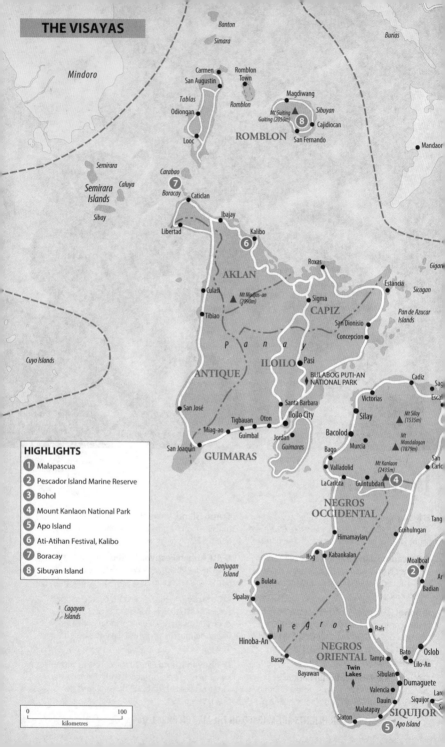

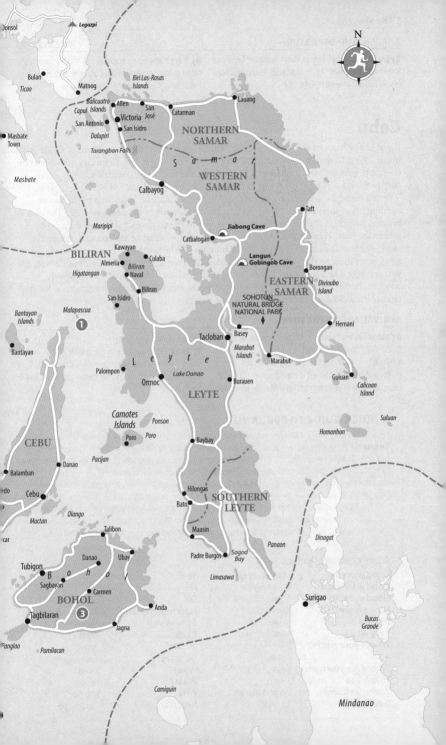

ARRIVAL AND DEPARTURE

By plane Cebu, Bohol, Negros, Panay, Romblon, Leyte and Samar are all accessible by air, most with daily flights from Manila and, in some cases, Cebu City.

By ferry Major ferry companies still also ply some routes between Manila and the Visayas, although with increasingly low airfares, these services are dwindling.

Cebu

6

Right in the heart of the Visayas, nearly 600km south of Manila, the island of **CEBU** is the ninth largest in the Philippines and site of the second largest city, **Cebu City**, an important transport hub with ferry and air connections to the rest of the country. Cebu is a long, narrow island – 300km from top to bottom and only 40km wide at its thickest point – with a mountainous and rugged spine. Most tourists spend little time in the towns, heading off as soon as possible to the beaches and islands of the north or west. The closest beaches to Cebu City are on **Mactan Island** just to the southeast, although they are by no means the best. Head north instead to the marvellous island of **Malapascua**, where the sand is as fine as Boracay's; to tranquil **Bantayan** off the northwest coast; or to really get away from it all, to the isolated **Camotes Islands**. Alternatively, to the south of Cebu City, you can take a bus across the island to the diving haven of **Moalboal** and its nearby beaches. Finally, right down in the south of the island, **Oslob** has become famous for the chance for a close-up encounter with whale sharks.

ARRIVAL AND DEPARTURE

By plane Getting to Cebu is simple. There are dozens of flights daily from Manila and less frequent flights from a number of other key destinations within the Visayas (Kalibo and Tacloban), the rest of the Philippines (Camiguin, Coron, Davao and Puerto Princesa) as well as the rest of Asia (Hong Kong and Singapore).

By ferry Cebu's position in the middle of the country makes it an excellent place to journey onwards by ferry, with sailings to Luzon and Mindanao and elsewhere in the Visayas.

A QUICK GUIDE TO CEBUANO

Filipino (Tagalog) might be the official language and English the medium of instruction, but **Cebuano**, the native language of Cebu, is the most widely spoken vernacular in the archipelago, not only used in Cebu but also throughout most of the central and southern Philippines. Cebuano and Tagalog have elements in common, but also have significant differences of construction and phraseology – it's quite possible for a native Manileño to bump into a native Cebuano and not be able to understand much of what he or she says.

Cebuano is evolving as it assimilates slang and colloquialisms from other Visayan dialects, as well as from Tagalog and English. Confused? You will be. Most Cebuano conversations veer apparently at random between all three languages, leaving even Filipino visitors unable to grasp the meaning.

SOME CEBUANO BASICS

Good morning	Maayong buntag	**Yes**	O-o
Good afternoon	Maayong hapon	**No**	Dili
Good evening	Maayong gabi	**OK**	Sigi
How are you?	Kumusta?	**How much is this?**	Tag-pila ni?
I'm fine	Maayo man	**Expensive**	Mahal
Very well	Maayo ka'ayo	**Cheap**	Barat
What's your name?	Umsay pangalan ni mu?	**Idiot!**	Amaw!
		Go away!	Layas!
Where are you from?	Taga din ka?	**Who?**	Kinsa?
Thank you	Salamat	**What?**	Unsa?
You're welcome	Walay sapayan	**Why?**	Ngano?
Goodbye	Ari na ko	**Near/Far**	Duol/Layo

Cebu City

Gateway to the Visayas, **CEBU CITY** is the Philippines' second largest city, home to nearly a million people. Nicknamed the "Queen of the South", it's peppered with historic attractions, and worthy of a day or two's exploration before moving on to the beaches and islands beyond. While an easier introduction to urban life in the Philippines than Manila, Cebu is not without its problems: streets are often clogged with smoke-belching jeepneys, and "rugby boys" (see box, p.43) are a common sight.

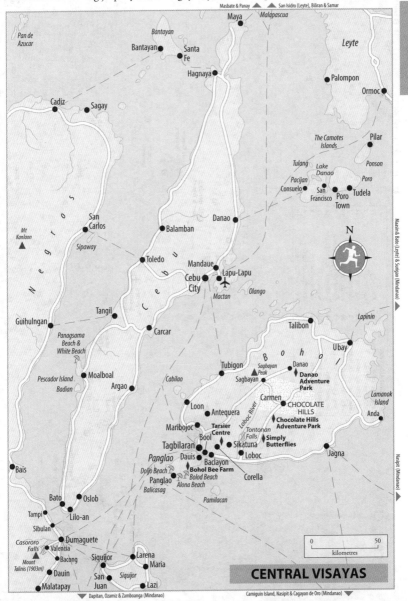

CENTRAL VISAYAS

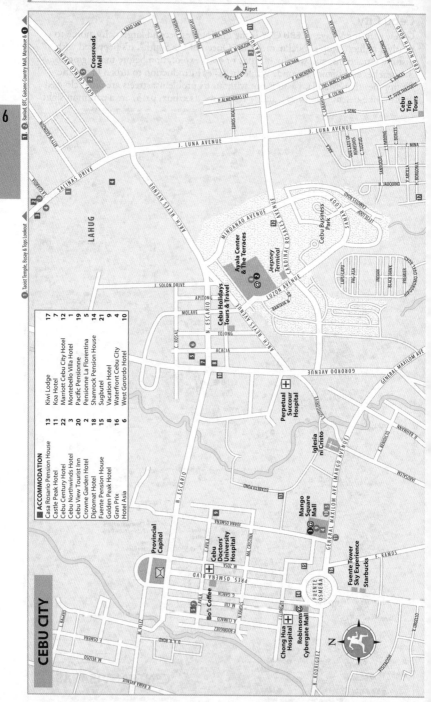

CEBU CITY

■ ACCOMMODATION

Casa Rosario Pension House	13	Kiwi Lodge	17
Castle Peak Hotel	11	Koa Hotel	7
Cebu Century Hotel	22	Marriott Cebu City Hotel	12
Cebu Northwinds Hotel	3	Montebello Villa Hotel	1
Cebu View Tourist Inn	20	Pacific Pensionne	19
Crowne Garden Hotel	2	Pensione La Florentina	5
Diplomat Hotel	18	Shamrock Pension House	14
Fuente Pension House	15	Sugbutel	21
Golden Peak Hotel	8	Vacation Hotel	9
Gran Prix	16	Waterfront Cebu City	4
Hotel Asia	6	West Gorordo Hotel	10

Airport

Crossroads Mall

Cebu Trip Tours

LAHUG

Ayala Center & The Terraces

Cebu Business Park

Jeepney Terminal

Cebu Holidays Tours & Travel

Perpetual Succour Hospital

Iglesia ni Cristo

Mango Square Mall

Provincial Capitol

Cebu Doctors' University Hospital

Bo's Coffee

Chong Hua Hospital

Robinsons@ Cybergate Mall

Fuente Tower Sky Experience Starbucks

Taoist Temple, Busay & Tops Lookout

Banilad, BTC, Gaisano Country Mall, Mandaue &

N

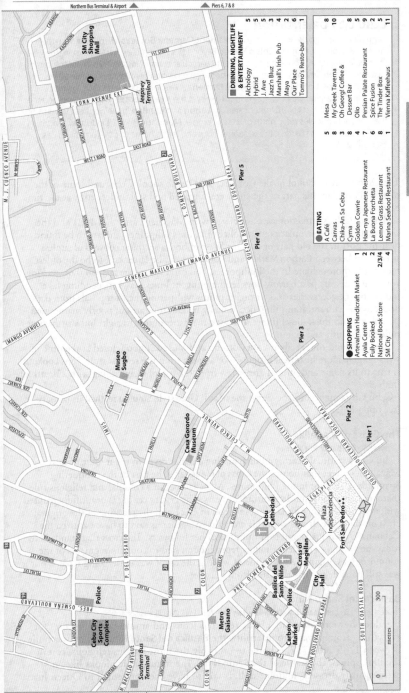

Northern Bus Terminal & Airport ▲   ▲ Piers 6, 7 & 8

Jumalon Museum & Butterfly Sanctuary ▲

6

● EATING
A Café	5
Canvas	8
Chika-An Sa Cebu	3
Cyma	4
Golden Cowrie	7
Han-nya Japanese Restaurant	6
La Buona Forchetta	8
Lemon Grass Restaurant	2/3/4
Marina Seafood Restaurant	4

Mesa	5
My Greek Taverna	8
Oh Georg! Coffee & Dessert Bar	3
Olio	8
Persian Palate Restaurant	9
Spice Fusion	2
The Tinder Box	5
Vienna Kaffeehaus	1

■ DRINKING, NIGHTLIFE & ENTERTAINMENT
Alchology	5
Hybrid	5
J. Ave	5
Jazz'n Bluz	3
Marshall's Irish Pub	4
Maya	2
Our Place	6
Tommo's Resto-bar	1

● SHOPPING
Artevalman Handicraft Market	1
Ayala Center	2
Fully Booked	2
National Book Store	2/3/4
SM City	4

SM City Shopping Mall

Jeepney Terminal

Museo Sugbo

Casa Gorordo Museum

Cebu Cathedral

Cross of Magellan

Basílica del Santo Niño

City Hall

Police

Fort San Pedro

Plaza Independencia

Metro Gaisano

Carbon Market

Cebu City Sports Complex

Southern Bus Terminal

Police

GENERAL MAXILOM AVE (MANGO AVENUE)

PRES. OSMEÑA BOULEVARD

QUEZON BOULEVARD (DOCK AREA)

S. OSMEÑA BOULEVARD

SOUTH COASTAL ROAD

M. J. CUENCO AVENUE

COLON

Pier 1
Pier 2
Pier 3
Pier 4
Pier 5

0   300
metres

6

CEBU CITY ORIENTATION

Cebu City's main north–south artery is **President Osmeña Boulevard**, running from the Provincial Capitol Building to **Colon Street**. Beyond this is a jumble of streets that in true Philippine urban tradition appears to have no particular centre. Nostalgics may cite the earthy, careworn charms of Colon Street and the **port** as the beating heart of Cebu, while others focus on the hotel and bar hub of **Fuente Osmeña**, 1km north, but these days the best dining and shopping are to be found in the malls at the **Ayala Center**, **The Terraces** and the trendy residential and entertainment areas of **Lahug** and **Banilad** in the northern suburbs of the city. Thirty minutes' drive north of the city proper, **Mandaue** is a light industrial suburb that functions as one of the city's economic hubs and is also home to government offices and consulates.

The October 2013 Bohol quake (see box, p.292) also shook Cebu, and some of the older buildings in this part of the city were damaged and still under repair at the time of writing.

Many of Cebu's attractions are associated with Magellan's arrival in 1521 and the city's status as the birthplace of Catholicism in the Philippines, and are to be found near the **port** in the old part of the city. West of here a seething cobweb of sunless streets run between **Carbon Market** and **Colon Street**, the latter said to be the oldest mercantile thoroughfare in the Philippines. You can explore the area on foot, picking your way carefully past barrow boys selling pungent limes, hawkers peddling fake mobile phone accessories and, at night, pimps whispering their proposals from dark doorways. A vibrant, humming, occasionally malodorous area of poorly maintained pavements and thick diesel fumes, it's not a mainstream tourist sight but worth some time for its spirit and vigour.

Further inland the excellent **Casa Gorordo** and **Museo Sugbo** (closed at the time of writing) give more historical insights. For a break from the serious stuff, **Tops Lookout** is true to its name and offers a great view from the top of Cebu, along with a breath of fresh air.

Cebu City's main tourist event is the Mardi Gras-style **Sinulog festival** in January (see opposite).

The Cross of Magellan

Magallanes St · Closed at the time of writing

Cebu City's spiritual heart is an unassuming circular crypt in the middle of busy Magallanes Street that houses the **Cross of Magellan**. The first of the conquering Spaniards to set foot in the Philippines, Magellan began a colonial and religious rule that would last four hundred turbulent years. The crypt's ceiling is beautifully painted with a scene depicting his landing in Cebu in 1521 and the planting of the original cross on the shore. It was with this cross that Magellan is said to have baptized the Cebuana Queen Juana and four hundred of her followers. The cross that stands here today, however, is a modern, hollow reproduction said to contain fragments of the conquistador's original. At the time of writing the crypt was undergoing repairs, but it was still possible to view the cross from outside.

Basilica del Santo Niño

President Osmeña Blvd, next to the Cross of Magellan · Daily 9am–7pm · Free · ⓦ basilicasantonino.org.ph

Heralded by vendors selling plastic religious icons and amulets offering cures for everything from poverty to infertility, the **Basilica del Santo Niño**, which was built between 1735 and 1737, is home to probably the most famous religious icon in the Philippines, the statue of the **Santo Niño**. The statue, which looks like an extravagantly dressed children's doll, is said to have been presented to Queen Juana of Cebu by Magellan after her baptism, considered the first in Asia, in 1521. Another tale has it that 44 years later, after laying siege to a pagan village, one of conquistador Miguel López de Legazpi's foot soldiers found a wooden box that had survived the bombardment inside a burning hut. Inside this box was the Santo Niño, lying next to a number of native idols. If you want to see the statue, let alone touch it, you'll have to join a queue of devotees that often stretches through the church doors and outside. The church's bell tower was damaged during the October 2013 quake, however, and at the time of writing masses were being held in the courtyard outside until repairs were complete.

6

Cebu Cathedral

Legazpi.St • Closed at the time of writing (usually daily 9am–7pm; free)

An imposing sixteenth-century Baroque structure, **Cebu Cathedral** has felt the force of nature and conflict several times in its four hundred-year history. An early version was completely destroyed by a typhoon before construction was even completed, and the cathedral was almost completely destroyed during World War II. It was quickly rebuilt, and renovated in 2009, but was damaged once again by the October 2013 quake.

Carbon Market

MC Briones St • Daily 6am–6pm • Free

No longer the coal unloading depot from which its name is derived, **Carbon Market** is now an area of covered stalls where the range of goods on offer, edible and otherwise, will leave you reeling – shining fat tuna, crabs, lobsters, coconuts, guavas, avocados, mangoes and more. The market is alive from well before dawn and doesn't slow down until after dark.

Fort San Pedro

Near the port area at the end of Sergio Osmeña Blvd • Daily 8am–8pm • P30

When he arrived in 1565, conquistador Miguel López de Legazpi set about building **Fort San Pedro** to guard against marauding Moros from the south. It was here, on December 24, 1898, that three centuries of Spanish rule in Cebu came to an end when their flag was lowered and they withdrew in a convoy of boats bound for Zamboanga, their way station for the voyage to Spain. The fort has been used down the centuries as a garrison, prison and zoo, but today is little more than a series of walls and ramparts with gardens in between. On Sundays, the park opposite, **Plaza Independencia**, seethes with locals playing ghetto-blasters and families enjoying picnics.

SINULOG

Almost as popular as Kalibo's Ati-Atihan (see box, p.336), the big, boisterous **Sinulog festival**, which culminates on the third Sunday of January with a wild street parade and an outdoor concert at Fuente Osmeña circle, is held in honour of Cebu's patron saint, the Santo Niño. The Santo Niño statue itself (see opposite) is brought on a boat from Mandaue to the city proper, festooned with candles and garlands, and is then paraded through the streets. Sinulog is actually the name given to a swaying **dance** said to resemble the current (*sulog*) of a river and is said to have evolved from tribal elders' rhythmic movements. Today, it's a memorable, deafening spectacle, with hundreds of intricately dressed Cebuanos dancing through the streets to the beat of noisy drums. Most of the action happens on President Osmeña Boulevard, but to escape the crowds, grab a spot on one of the smaller roads, such as N. Escario Street, where security is less zealous and you can slip underneath the velvet ropes and join the dancers. For information about Sinulog and details of the exact route, which varies every year as the festival grows, visit Ⓦsinulog.ph. If you plan to visit Cebu during Sinulog, make sure you book accommodation well ahead of time.

Casa Gorordo Museum

35 Lopez Jaena St, off the eastern end of Colon St • Tues–Sun 10am–6pm • P70 • ☎ 032 255 5630

Built in the middle of the nineteenth century by wealthy merchant Alejandro Reynes, the marvellous **Casa Gorordo** is one of the few structures of its time in Cebu that survived World War II. Owned by a succession of luminaries, including the first Filipino Bishop of Cebu, Juan Isidro de Gorordo, it was acquired in 1980 from the bishop's heirs and opened as a museum three years later.

The house is a striking marriage of late Spanish-era architecture and native building techniques, with lower walls of Mactan coral cemented using tree sap, and upper-storey living quarters built entirely from Philippine hardwood held together with wooden pegs. The interior offers an intriguing glimpse into the way Cebu's rich once lived, elegantly furnished with original pieces from America and the Old World – a Viennese dining set, a German piano, American linen and Catholic icons from Spain and Mexico. In the ground-floor library are photographs of Cebu during the American regime.

Museo Sugbo

MJ Cuenco Ave

Housed in the former Carcer del Cebu (provincial jail), and damaged by the October 2013 quake, the excellent **Museo Sugbo** was closed for repairs at the time of writing but was set to reopen by the end of 2014. Exhibits are well laid out and labelled in English, tracing the island's history from early Chinese and Siamese trading to the arrival of the Spanish, and the modern era. The highlights are the World War II exhibits, including banned "guerilla money" issued after the Japanese had instituted their own currency, and possession of which was punishable by death. There are also wartime notices detailing the types of foods Filipinos weren't allowed to eat: one of the few local staples not on the list was sweet potato, meaning that during the occupation, many people survived on these alone. Towards the rear of the complex, a separate room houses finds excavated from Plaza Independencia including a spooky fifteenth-century death mask made of gold leaf.

Fuente Tower Sky Experience

President Osmeña Blvd • Mon–Fri 2pm–midnight, Sat 10am–2am, Sun 10am–midnight • Entry P250, Sky Walk Extreme P300, roller coaster P300, climbing wall P600 (includes entry fee and 3 attempts); package including entry fee, 4D movie screening, either of the two "sky experiences", plus lunch, a short massage and use of the swimming pool P888 • ☎ 032 418 8888, ⓦ skyexperienceadventure.com

For an exhilarating view out over the city, make for the **Fuente Tower**, where the **Sky Walk Extreme** offers the chance to walk the glass-bottomed rim of the 37th floor. There's also a rooftop **roller coaster** which tilts up to 55 degrees, a **climbing wall**, or for a break from adrenaline-fuelled activities, a black-light mini-golf course.

Taoist Temple

Beverly Hills • Free • Return taxi P400–500 including waiting time; Lahug jeepneys (P8) run to Gaisano Bridge, from where it is a 1.5km walk

The tranquil **Taoist Temple** is set in the exclusive Beverly Hills subdivision 3km north of the city bustle. The temple is dedicated to the Taoist founder, Lao Tze, but also stands testament to the wealth of Cebu's Tsinoy community. It's a little tricky to get to unless you take a taxi.

Tops Lookout

Busay • P100 • Return taxi P1000 including waiting time; Busay jeepneys (P8) from SM City and Ayala Center stop 1km from Tops from where there are habal-habals (P300 round trip, or it's a steep walk)

The road that winds northwards out of Cebu City eventually finds its way to **Busay**, the high mountain ridge that rises immediately behind the city. At the top there's a wide concrete lookout area known to locals as **Tops**, where you pay an entrance fee – buy a stick of barbecued chicken from one of the vendors, and sit and watch the sunset. Tops is popular at dusk, so don't expect romantic solitude, but the view is great and the air cooler and cleaner than in the concrete jungle below.

Jumalon Museum and Butterfly Sanctuary

Jumalon St, Basak • 9am–5pm • P50 • ☎ 032 261 6884 • Taxis cost P150 (20min); alternatively, take any jeepney heading along the Cebu South Rd to Friendship Village or Basak, get off at the Holy Cross Parish Church and look out for Jumalon St near Basak Elementary School

Four kilometres west of the centre in the largely residential suburb of Basak, the **Jumalon Museum and Butterfly Sanctuary** is lepidopteran heaven, with rooms full of glass display cases and a large garden at the back with live butterflies fluttering around. As well as everyday species such as monarchs and viceroys, there are also rare examples such as albinos, melanics, dwarfs and conjoined twins.

6

ARRIVAL AND DEPARTURE   CEBU CITY

BY PLANE

Mactan Cebu International Airport Cebu flights land at Mactan Cebu International Airport (☎ 032 340 2486, ⓦ mciaa.gov.ph) on Mactan Island. There is a tourist information counter in the arrivals hall (5am–9pm) where you can pick up the Department of Tourism's city and island map. The arrivals hall also has car rental booths for Avis, FastTransit and Friends, all reputable and offering a car with driver from P2000 per day. The departure tax from Cebu is P550 for international flights; this is now included in domestic fares.

Getting into town To get into Cebu City, 8km across the suspension bridge, yellow airport metered cabs (P250–350) are cheaper than white fixed-rate taxis, but the latter are reasonable for destinations further afield (P2300 for Hagnaya for example). State your destination at the kiosk and you'll be escorted to your car.

Airlines Air Asia, Cebu Pacific (both ☎ 032 236 9328), SEAir and Tiger Airways (both ☎ 032 342 8062) all have representatives at the airport, as well as offices in town; other airlines include Asiana Airlines (☎ 032 342 8062); Cathay Pacific (☎ 032 340 3254); Cebu Pacific (☎ 032 230 8888); Korean Air (☎ 032 340 5431); Philippine Airlines (☎ 032 340 0181); PAL Express (☎ 032 415 9901); Silk Air (☎ 032 340 0042); and Zest Air (☎ 032 341 0226). You can also book tickets at most travel agents.

Routes Cebu Pacific operates flights to all of the destinations below, whilst PAL serve all but Camiguin, Caticlan and Clark. Air Asia has flights to Cagayan de Oro, Kalibo, Manila and Puerto Princesa.

Destinations Bacolod (3 daily; 45min); Cagayan de Oro (5 daily; 50min); Camiguin (4 weekly; 50min); Caticlan (3–5 daily; 1hr); Clark (3 weekly; 1hr 20min); Davao (6 daily; 1hr); Iloilo City (4–6 daily; 50min); Kalibo (daily; 50min); Manila (36 daily; 1hr 10min); Puerto Princesa (2–3 daily; 1hr 15min); Tacloban (2 daily; 50min); Zamboanga (1-2 daily; 1hr 5min).

BY BOAT

ESSENTIALS

Piers The arrival point for ferries is one of eight large piers stretching along the harbour area beyond Fort San Pedro. Pier 1 is closest to Fort San Pedro, just a few minutes on foot, while Pier 8 lies several kilometres to the northeast.

Jeepneys and buses line up along nearby Sergio Osmeña Blvd for the short journey into the city. Taxis wait to meet arriving ferries and should agree to use the meter.

Bookings and information As well as ticket offices at the piers, travel agents and hotels throughout the city can book ferry tickets (see p.275). A good place to get up-to-date ferry information is from the shipping pages of local newspapers. There's also a shipping schedules channel on the local Sky Cable TV network, available in some hotels.

SHIPPING LINES AND FERRIES

The three main fast boat companies are Oceanjet, Weesam and 2Go. 2Go is a conglomerate of ferry companies (Cebu Ferries, Negros Navigation, SuperCat and SuperFerry) acquired by the Chinese government a few years ago, which operate both fast and slow boats and generally offer the most comfortable and professional service. Confusingly, routes operated by SuperCat still go under this name, and you may also see reference to the other old company names in outdated print material and signage.

2Go Pier 4 ☎ 032 233 7000, ⓦ travel.2go.com.ph. Includes SuperCat.

Aznar Shipping Pier 4 ☎ 032 234 4624.

Cokaliong Pier 1 ☎ 032 232 7211, ⓦ cokaliongshipping .com.

F. J. Palacio Lines Pier 1 ☎ 032 253 7700.

George & Peter Lines Pier 3 ☎ 032 254 5154.

Gothong Lines Pier 7 ☎ 032 231 7100.

Gothong Lines Pier 4 ☎ 032 232 9998, ⓦ gothong.com.

Island Shipping Lines ☎ 032 416 6884.

Kinswell Pier 2 ☎ 032 255 7572, ⓦ kinswellshipping .webs.com.

Lite Shipping ☎ 032 416 8562, ⓦ liteferries.com.

Oceanjet Pier 1 ☎ 032 255 7560, ⓦ oceanjet.net.

Roble Shipping Pier 7 ☎ 032 255 5904.

Supershuttle Ferry Pier 8 ☎ 032 345 5581, ⓦ super shuttleferry.com.

Trans-Asia Shipping Lines Pier 5 ☎ 032 254 6491, ⓦ transasiashipping.com.

Weesam Pier 4 ☎ 032 231 7737, ⓦ weesam.ph.

DESTINATIONS

Cebu is connected by boat to almost every major port in the Philippines and a number of minor ones. Fast boat and catamaran services link Cebu with Bohol and Leyte all within 3hr, but these services are significantly more expensive than regular ferries (for example, Cebu–Tagbiliran costs P525 compared with P210 for the slower Cokaliong service). As well as ferries to Dumaguete, another way to Negros is to ride the bus down to Bato or Lilo-an, or over to Toledo, and take a ferry or big bangka across (see p.317).

Biliran Naval (Roble Shipping 5 weekly; 9hr 30min).

Bohol Tagbilaran (slow ferries: Cokaliong 1 weekly, F.J. Palacio Lines 3 weekly, Trans-Asia Shipping Lines 1 weekly; 5hr; fast ferries: Oceanjet 6 daily, SuperCat 2 daily, Weesam 3 daily; 2hr); Tubigon (Island Shipping Lines; 4 daily; 1hr 20min).

Leyte Hilongos (Kinswell 1 daily; Roble Shipping 1 daily; 3hr 15min); Maasin (Cokaliong and Trans-Asia 3 weekly; 6hr); Ormoc (slow ferries: Lite Shipping 6 weekly, Roble Shipping 1 weekly; 6hr; fast ferries: Supershuttle Ferry 3 weekly; Weesam 2 daily; SuperCat 3 daily; 3hr).

Manila (Gothong Lines 4 weekly; 2Go 5 weekly; 23hr).

Masbate (Trans-Asia Shipping Lines 6 weekly; 13hr 30min).

Mindanao Cagayan de Oro (2Go 3 weekly; Gothong Lines 2 weekly; Trans-Asia Shipping Lines 1 daily; 8–10hr); Dapitan (Cokaliong 4 weekly; George & Peter Lines 3 weekly; 9hr); Iligan (2Go 2 weekly; Cokaliong 5 weekly, via Ozamiz; 13hr); Nasipit (2Go 1 weekly; 9hr); Ozamiz (2Go 2 weekly; 7hr; Cokaliong 5 weekly; 10hr); Surigao (Cokaliong 4 weekly; 9hr 30min); Zamboanga (George & Peter Lines 1 weekly; 16hr).

Negros Dumaguete (Cokaliong 4 weekly; George & Peter Lines 6 weekly; Oceanjet, via Tagbilaran 1 daily; 4–6hr).

Panay Iloilo City (Cokaliong 1 weekly; Trans-Asia Shipping Lines 4 weekly; 12–14hr).

Samar Calbayog (F.J. Palacio Lines 3 weekly; 12hr); Catbalogan (Roble Shipping 1 weekly; 3hr 30min).

Siquijor (Oceanjet, via Tagbilaran and Dumaguete 1 daily; 4hr 50min).

BY BUS

Bus terminals Ceres Liner (☎ 032 345 8650) is the main bus company in Cebu and operates out of two terminals. The Northern bus terminal, served by jeepneys marked "Mandaue" (P8), is on the coastal road, 4km east of the city centre, and is used by buses and jeepneys for destinations north of the city (all every 20–30min). The Southern bus terminal, for buses south, is on Bacalso Ave, west of President Osmeña Blvd and is accessible by jeepneys marked "Basak" (P8).

Destinations from the Southern terminal Badian (4hr); Bato (4hr); Lilo-an (3hr); Moalboal (3hr); Oslob (3–4hr); Toledo (for San Carlos; 2hr 30min).

Destinations from the Northern terminal Danao (for Camotes; frequent; 1hr); Hagnaya (for Bantayan; 7 daily; 3hr 30min); Maya (for Malapascua; every 20min; 3–4hr).

BY CAR

Car and driver You may prefer to charter a car with driver to get around the island; many tourists simply flag down a taxi and negotiate a flat rate with the driver, usually P2000–2500 for the day or a one-way trip to, say, Moalboal or Maya. Many of the bigger hotels have their own cars with drivers, but you'll pay significantly more.

Rental companies Many firms, including Alamo and Avis, have kiosks at the airport. In town, Alamo is at the *Waterfront Cebu City*, Salinas Drive (☎ 032 232 6888) and Hertz is at the *Marriott*, Cardinal Rosales Ave (☎ 032 232 6100).

GETTING AROUND

By bus Cebu City's Bus Rapid Transit System is still on the drawing board, meaning jeepney and vans are the principal public transport.

By taxi Taxis are plentiful and it's not hard to find a driver who's willing to use the meter. The tariff is P2.50 per 200m plus a flagfall of P40; a typical cross-city trip costs P100–150 outside rush hour.

By jeepney and van Jeepneys and open-sided Isuzu vans painted in outrageous colours ply dozens of cross-city routes. From Colon St, they run almost everywhere: east to the piers and the SM City Mall, north to Fuente Osmeña, northeast to Ayala Center and south to Carbon Market. There are also jeepneys along N. Escario St, north of Ayala Center, heading east to Mandaue and west and southwest to the Provincial Capitol Building, Fuente Osmeña and the Colon St area. The standard fare for each leg, or part thereof, is P8.

INFORMATION

Tourist information The main tourist office is the Department of Tourism's Cebu regional office (Mon–Fri 8am–5pm; ☎ 032 254 2811) in the LDM Building on Legazpi St, near the junction with Lapu-Lapu (close to Fort San Pedro). There's also a branch at the airport (daily 6am–9pm). As well as information about the festival, The Sinulog Foundation website (☯ sinulog.ph) also has a wealth of information about the city.

Maps Of the city maps available, the best is *EZ Map* (P99), which is available at National Book Store and some hotels, but the free one given out at the tourist offices and kiosks isn't bad.

Newspapers There are a number of English-language local newspapers, including the *Cebu Daily News* (☯ cdn.ph), and the *Sun Star Cebu* (☯ sunstar.com.ph), both of which have ferry timetables, local events listings and restaurant reviews.

TOURS

Travel agents Travel agents can be found in most malls and many hotels and can arrange tours of the city, ferry tickets, flights and vehicle hire (with driver). A few to try include: Cebu Holiday Tours & Travel, 4 AD Building, Tojong St ☏ 032 231 5391, ⓦ cebuholidaytours.com; Cebu Trip Tours, M.J. Cuenco Ave ☏ 032 268 5470, ⓦ cebutriptours.com; Grand Hope Ventures Travel, 4/F Ayala Center ☏ 032 268 9008; Land and Sky Travel, Rivergate Complex, General Maxilom Ave ☏ 032 253 9022, ⓦ landskytravel.com; Rajah Travel, *Waterfront Cebu City*, Salinas Drive ☏ 032 232 2113, ⓦ rajahtravel.com.

ACCOMMODATION

Some of the cheapest accommodation in Cebu City is in the old **Colon Street** area, though the streets in this neighbourhood can be a little scary at night, with roaming pimps and a number of shabby massage parlours and girlie bars. Hotels around **Fuente Osmeña** are better, and further out, options near the **Ayala Center** and in **Lahug and Banilad** are close to the big malls and many of the city's more fashionable restaurants.

COLON STREET AND AROUND

Cebu Century Hotel Colon St at Pelaez St ☏ 032 255 1341, ⓦ cebucenturyhotel.com. This hotel has seen better days, but is redeemed by its low prices. Deluxe rooms have fridge, cable TV and have been more recently renovated. **P820**

Cebu View Tourist Inn 200 Sanciangko St ☏ 032 254 8333, ⓦ cebuviewtouristinn.com. Reasonably comfortable and secure, offering a/c rooms with cable TV, although it can be noisy. There are cut-price 9pm–7am rates. **P1000**

FUENTE OSMEÑA AND AROUND

★ **Casa Rosario Pension House** 101 E Ramon Aboitiz St ☏ 032 253 5134, ⓦ casarosario.net. Stylish mid-sized hotel in a quiet part of town but just minutes away from Fuente Osmeña. All of the boldly painted a/c rooms have cable TV and attractive furnishings. There's free wi-fi throughout and a nice breakfast bar in the lobby. **P1200**

Diplomat Hotel 90 F. Ramos St ☏ 032 253 0099, ⓦ diplomathotelcebu.com. Substantial and popular hotel in a good location set back from F. Ramos St. Standard rooms are perfectly adequate, but often booked out long-term by Koreans, while superior rooms are bigger, brighter, and some have decent views. All rooms are a/c, and have hot water, cable TV, fridge, safe and (pay) wi-fi connection. **P1040**

★ **Fuente Pension House** 0175 Don Julio Llorente St ☏ 032 412 4989, ⓦ fuentepensionhouse.com. The newly renovated lobby makes the *Fuente* seem like a trendy boutique hotel at first glance, but the rooms are simple, clean and good value. All have hot water and cable TV, and the rooftop restaurant offers free wi-fi. 24hr rates regardless of when you check in and single rates available too (P945). **P1145**

Gran Prix Pacific Coast Building, General Maxilom Ave ☏ 032 254 9169, ⓦ granprixhotels.com/cebu. Economy hotel in a great location near Fuente Osmeña with small, modern rooms (many without windows though), free wi-fi and *Jollibee* vouchers for breakfast. **P1399**

Hotel Asia 11 J. Avila St ☏ 032 255 8536, ⓦ hotelasia cebu.com. In a good location north of Fuente Osmeña, this neat, medium-sized and well-run hotel has an airy white-tiled lobby and small, well-appointed rooms, each with a high-tech Japanese toilet. Larger, deluxe rooms boast stone bathtubs. The Japanese restaurant is open 24hr and there's a rooftop bar. **P1950**

Pacific Pensionne 313-A President Osmeña Blvd ☏ 032 253 5271, ⓦ pacificpensionne.com. Just off Osmeña Blvd, this is a welcoming, quiet little hotel with a bright café in the lobby and a range of rooms from very affordable singles to four-bed family options. Staff are charming and can help with travel arrangements. There's also a coffee shop with free wi-fi. **P1040**

Shamrock Pension House Fuente Osmeña ☏ 032 255 2900, ⓦ shamrockotap.com/pension-house. Budget a/c accommodation in the hubbub of Fuente Osmeña. Rooms range from standard and deluxe doubles to studios for two. **P900**

Vacation Hotel 35 Juana Osmeña St ☏ 032 253 2766. The best rooms at this charming little place, north of Fuente Osmeña, are on the second floor, with balconies overlooking the small pool, although the beds are very soft. Downstairs some of the rooms at the front have little verandas, but others are darker and less enticing – ask to see a few. **P1600**

AYALA CENTER AND AROUND

Golden Peak Hotel Gorordo Ave ☏ 032 233 8111, ⓦ goldenpeakhotel.com. Good-value, mid-range hotel with efficient staff and rooms with views if you ask to be on one of the higher floors. The more expensive deluxe rooms aren't worth the extra outlay. Decent buffet breakfast included in the price. **P1500**

Kiwi Lodge 1060 G. Tudtud St, Mabolo ☏ 032 232 9550, ⓦ kiwilodge.org. Friendly, well-run small hotel in a residential area south of Ayala Center and Cebu Business Park, with a range of comfortable a/c rooms at reasonable prices. Rooms in the new wing (P1690) have flatscreen TVs and safes. The popular restaurant serves hearty Western cuisine (including meat pies and fish and chips), while the bar is a great place to pick up travel advice from the long-term expat clientele. **P1298**

6

Koa Hotel 157 Gorordo Ave ☎032 520 5455. Legendary boho hangout *Kukuk's* is reborn as *Koa*, and the new owners have breathed some new life into the spacious but previously tatty rooms. Daily rates are on the high side for what you get, but for long-termers the weekly (P9000) and monthly (P15,000 excluding electricity and water) rates are great value. Each of the four wooden-floored rooms has a small kitchen, bathroom with hot and cold water, wi-fi, a/c and terrestrial TV. There's also a popular resto-bar with live music on site, and pizzas are available from the *La Bella Napoli* kiosk. **P1500**

★**Marriott Cebu City Hotel** Cardinal Rosales Ave, Cebu Business Park ☎032 411 5800, ⓦmarriott.com. The *Marriott* is housed in a twelve-storey building just a short walk through parkland from the Ayala Center and fine dining at The Terraces. There are over three hundred rooms, all remodelled in sleek, modern style, plus three restaurants, a poolside café and a health club. For trips downtown there are taxis on the doorstep. **P5300**

Pensionne La Florentina 18 Acacia St ☎032 231 3118. Friendly, family establishment in an attractive old building set back from Gorordo Ave. Rooms have a/c and cable TV, and the coffee shop offers simple native dishes plus wi-fi. The shops and restaurants of Ayala are a short walk away. **P850**

West Gorordo Hotel 110 Gorordo Ave ☎032 231 4347, ⓦwestgorordo.com. Bright, clean and comfy rooms with a/c and cable TV in a decent location not too far from Ayala. Deluxe rooms (P2380) have a fridge and balcony **P1980**

LAHUG AND BANILAD

Cebu Northwinds Hotel Salinas Drive ☎032 233 0311, ⓦcebunorthwinds.com. Close to Lahug's bars and restaurants, this modern hotel has a/c, hot water, cable TV, wi-fi and a coffee shop, restaurant and bar. The more expensive superior rooms on the front side of the hotel are bigger but noisier. There's cabled in-room internet but you need to pay P25 for a cable. **P1288**

Crowne Garden Hotel Salinas Drive ☎032 412 7157,

ⓦcrownegardenhotel.com. Formerly the *La Guardia*, this hotel has a good location close to the action on Salinas Drive. Rooms are bright, clean and comfortable and have a/c, hot water, cable TV, fridge and there's room service. Many rooms also have bathtubs. Free wi-fi in the lobby. **P1250**

Montebello Villa Hotel Banilad ☎032 231 3681, ⓦmontebellovillahotel.com. Rambling establishment set in its own neat gardens behind the popular Gaisano Country Mall, with an expansive garden area and two swimming pools. The renovated deluxe rooms (P4550) are substantially nicer than the superior rooms (P3700). There are good dining and nightlife options in Banilad, but for downtown sightseeing you'll need to take a cab (or jeepney). **P3100**

Waterfront Cebu City Salinas Drive ☎032 232 6888, ⓦwaterfronthotels.com.ph. A city landmark, the *Waterfront* is a world unto itself with a casino, several upscale restaurants, bars, gym and a large pool. The grandeur of the maritime themed lobby doesn't extend to the standard rooms, but the deluxe rooms are far more tastefully styled and have bathtubs. All rooms have free wi-fi, cable TV, fridge and hot water. **P4000**

ELSEWHERE IN THE CITY

Castle Peak Hotel F. Cabahug St at President Quezon St, Mabolo ☎032 233 1811, ⓦcastlepeakhotel.net. Clean and affordable hotel in a quiet area east of Ayala. Although starting to show signs of age, the rooms are spacious and the bathrooms are well maintained. Handily, there's a taxi rank right next to the hotel. Internet facilities are available and there's a decent restaurant. Free wi-fi in the lobby. **P1588**

Sugbutel S. Osmeña Blvd ☎032 232 8888, ⓦsugbutel .com. The economy version of Japan's capsule hotels, this bizarre budget business stopover has the best dorms in the city. Large rooms have been subdivided into train-like compartments which house 2–6 bunk beds, each of which has an overhead light, small safety box, plug socket, shoe ledge and wi-fi. Double rooms have bathrooms plus cable TV. Dorm **P250–300**, double **P1200**

EATING

Cebu's well-regarded dining scene offers everything from excellent local snack joints to top-quality international restaurants. Though there are places to eat all over Cebu, many of the best options are to be found in the city's malls, notably **The Terraces** at the Ayala Center, a tastefully designed food court overlooking atmospheric gardens which offers everything from Greek to Vietnamese cuisine. North of the centre, **Banilad Town Center** (BTC) and **Gaisano Country Mall** also offer good mall restaurants. Fast-food joints and coffee shops can be found all over the city and in the malls.

FUENTE OSMEÑA AND AROUND

Han-nya Japanese Restaurant Hotel Asia, 11 J. Avila St ☎032 255 8536, ⓦhotelasiacebu.com. Authentic Japanese cuisine served around the clock in a lattice-screened restaurant with raised seating areas. Sushi starts at P120 and there's *ube* ice cream (P70) for dessert to remind you that you're in the Philippines. Daily 24hr.

My Greek Taverna Mango Square Mall. This tiny kiosk turns out tasty and authentic hummus (P85), gyros, doner kebabs (P85–185) and salads to the hungry Mango Square crowd. Daily 5pm–5am.

Persian Palate Restaurant Mango Square Mall ☎032 236 0448, ⓦpersianpalaterestaurant. Very spicy Indian and Middle Eastern dishes, including chicken biryani (P195), samosas (P75), baba ganoush (P110) and naan bread which you can wash down with a mango lassi (P85). There's another branch on the second floor of Ayala. Daily 10am–8pm.

Vienna Kaffeehaus General Maxilom Ave ☎ 032 688 8922, ⊕ viennakaffeehaus.com. Founded more than twenty years ago by an expat Austrian, the *Kaffeehaus* – now a franchise with numerous branches – is a little corner of imperial Europe in the tropics. There are nine types of coffee including Viennese iced coffee and excellent espresso. The lunch and dinner menu is also Austrian, with wholesome goulash, schnitzel (P280) and delicious home-made sauerkraut and sausage. Daily 9am–midnight.

AYALA CENTER, THE TERRACES AND AROUND

Canvas Level 2, The Terraces ☎ 032 417 1978. Australian-owned art café serving a wonderfully eclectic selection of fusion and single cuisine dishes. Appetizers include wasabi- and *dalandan*- (a local sweet citrus fruit) battered garlic prawns (P340), while mains run the gauntlet from Japanese to traditional Aussie pub grub – the beef and onion pie with mash and peas (P260) is a surefire winner. Daily 11am–11pm.

★**Cyma** Garden Level, The Terraces ☎ 032 417 1351, ⊕ cymarestaurants.com. Delicious Greek salads, *dolmadakia* (stuffed vine leaves; P230), tzatziki (P275) and souvlaki in an attractive Greek-themed restaurant. They also have branches in Manila and Boracay. Daily 11am–10.30pm.

La Buona Forchetta 139 Acacia St ☎ 032 231 3398. Finding this place is half the fun, but once you're here the staff are welcoming, the dining room is cosy and the food is superb. Fresh pasta is the house speciality, but the pizzas are also excellent (both P450–500). Daily 11am–2pm & 6–11pm.

Lemon Grass Restaurant Level 1, The Terraces ☎ 032 233 8601. Bright restaurant with garden views. Thai and Vietnamese dishes are as close to authentic as they can be, with lots of well-seasoned and spicy coconut curries. The *banh xeo* (sizzling Vietnamese crêpes; P245) are also delicious, and to refresh your palate there's citrus and herb lemonade (P85) or Singha beer for P120. Daily 11am–11pm.

Mesa Level 1, The Terraces ☎ 032 505 6372. This busy restaurant serves traditional Filipino dishes with a modern twist. Try *salpicao* ostrich (cooked with soy and garlic; P345), pomelo salad with *latik* (coconut cream; P265) or sea bass steamed in *dayap* (key lime) and chilli (P95 per 100g). Daily 9am–10.30pm.

Oh Georg! Coffee & Dessert Bar Level 1, Ayala Center ☎ 032 233 4735. In a mall chock-full of fast-food restaurants and coffee shops, this one deserves special mention. The menu includes a usually delicious soup of the day, Greek salads (P190) and a Mexican salad (P225) that's big enough to share. There's another branch, called

Café Georg, on the ground floor of the MLD Building in Banilad. Daily 10am–9pm.

LAHUG AND BANILAD

A Café Crossroads Mall, Banilad ☎ 032 505 5692, ⊕ theabacagroup.com/a-cafe. Tucked away at the back of the Crossroads Mall, this small but sophisticated café-restaurant has a wide-ranging menu offering everything from battered fish burgers (P375) to classic mac and cheese, all served up by sleek staff clad in black. Daily 7am–10pm.

Chika-An Sa Cebu Salinas Drive ☎ 032 233 0350, ⊕ creativecuisinegourmetgroup.com/chikaan. A Cebu institution that serves popular rustic food such as chicken or pork barbecue sticks (P36), *lechon kawali* (crispy pork; P159), sizzling *bangus* (P149) and *bulalo*. There's another branch in SM City Mall. Daily 11.30am–2pm & 6–10pm.

Golden Cowrie Salinas Drive ☎ 032 233 4670, ⊕ golden cowrienativerestaurant.com. The interior is Philippine Zen with cream walls and dark-wood furniture and there's a pleasant outdoor dining area. Favourite dishes include green mango salad (P65), blue marlin (P167) and pork Bicol (P129). There are less atmospheric branches at Robinsons Cybergate Fuente Osmeña and as *Hukad*, at The Terraces. Daily 11am–2pm & 6–10pm.

Marina Seafood Restaurant Nivel Hills, Lahug ☎ 032 233 9454. Laidback native-style alfresco restaurant on a hill above the city (a taxi from the centre will cost P100). Two people can feast on tuna belly, grilled marlin and shrimps with chilli and coconut for about P300 a head. Daily 11am–8pm.

Olio Crossroads Mall, Banilad ☎ 032 238 2391. High-end fusion restaurant specializing in seafood and steaks, with a tempting but expensive (P1100–4700) wine list. The 400g New York steak (P1400) is a carnivorous treat. Other good meals include herb-crusted rack of lamb with crispy potatoes (P1400), or for a light lunch there's mozzarella and tomato salad (P550). Daily 11am–2pm & 6–11pm.

★**Spice Fusion** Banilad Town Center (BTC) ☎ 032 344 2923. A small, stylish and very popular fusion restaurant with appealing dishes such as mango curry chicken (P288), ginger clams and coffee curry pork ribs. Daily 11am–2pm & 6–10pm.

The Tinder Box Next to Crossroads Mall ☎ 032 234 1681. Classy restaurant with informal dining at the downstairs deli or more refined service in the main dining room. Hearty breakfasts include smoked farmer's ham and Cheddar cheese omelette (P245), and imported US steaks (P1225–1395) are dinner favourites with the upscale clientele, which includes politicians and local celebs. The deli has a great range of tasty goodies, while the comfy leather sofas in the bar are the perfect place for a pre-dinner cocktail (P222). There's a less-well stocked branch at the airport. Daily 7am–midnight.

DRINKING, NIGHTLIFE AND ENTERTAINMENT

Cebu, like its big brother Manila, is a city that never – or rarely – sleeps. You don't have to walk far in the centre to pass a pub, karaoke lounge or a music bar, although you'll want to choose your venue carefully – while many of the biggest clubs are to be found in **Mango Square** on General Maxilom Avenue, further along the street almost all of the establishments near the Iglesia ni Cristo are girlie bars. Generally speaking, door policies are relaxed compared to Manila, but some of the places at Mango Square have a "no shorts, trainers or flip flops" dress code. Many of the nicest places for a drink are at the **malls**, and in the suburbs of **Banilad**.

BARS

★**Jazz'n Bluz** 27 F. Cabahug St ☎032 232 2698, ⍟jazznbluzcebu.com. Opposite the *Castle Peak Hotel*, Cebu's best jazz bar is low-lit and sophisticated and has nightly jazz and blues from 8.45pm, after which time there's a cover charge (P100–150). Drinks and snacks are served to the lounge and bar tables while you enjoy the show. Mon & Sun 6pm–1am, Tues–Sat 6pm–2am.

Marshall's Irish Pub General Maxilom Ave ☎032 412 6418, ⍟marshallsirishpub.com. A little less brash than the bars along the street at Mango Square, *Marshall's* has a cosy interior, great happy hour deals (P40 beers with appetizers 4–7pm) and live acoustic music every night. Daily 11am–1am.

Maya Crossroads Mall, Banilad ☎032 238 9522, ⍟theabacagroup.com/maya-mexican-restaurant-cebu. The place to whet your sombrero with an exhaustive tequila list (from P210) which includes an eleven-year aged Asombroso which goes for P8955 a shot (apparently a couple of people have actually tried it). There are also tasty Mexican treats including burritos and fajitas to soak up the alcohol. Mon–Thurs & Sun 5pm–midnight, Fri & Sat 5pm–2am.

Our Place Pelaez St at Sanciangko St ☎032 416 8243, ⍟ourplacecebu.com. Under new management, *Our Place*

remains a Cebu stalwart, straight from the pages of Graham Greene. A small upstairs bar is cooled by inefficient ceiling fans, where expat men swill San Miguel (P40) into the early hours and complain about the hardships of life in the tropics. Daily 6pm–2am.

Tommo's Resto-bar The Hangar, Salinas Drive. Big, busy, open-sided drinking and dining hall with cheap drinks (San Mig or Tanduay both P40) and *pulutan* (bar snacks, such as grilled pork belly for P80). There's a big TV screen for sports and live music from 9pm. Daily 24hr.

CLUBS

Alchology Mango Square ☎0922 238 8977. The current place to be, with the best light show in the city and group VIP tables for a minimum of P3000 consumable. Daily 9pm–6am.

Hybrid Mango Square. A hot spot for young Cebuanos, this place doesn't really get going until midnight. Daily 9pm–3am.

J. Ave Mango Square ☎032 505 6332, ⍟j-avesuperclub .com. Lively newcomer popular with locals and tourists alike, and with a capacity of over a thousand clubbers. Tues–Thurs 9pm–3am, Fri & Sat until 6am.

SHOPPING

BOOKSHOPS

Fully Booked Level 2, The Terraces, Ayala Center ☎032 417 1400. The country's best bookstore has a broad range of titles and also sells magazines and stationery. Daily 10am–10pm.

National Book Store Branches in SM City Mall ☎032 231 5496, Ayala Center ☎032 231 4006, Mango Plaza on the edge of Mango Square Mall ☎032 268 3055; ⍟nationalbookstore.com.ph. The choice of literature isn't vast, but you will find a good selection of paperback bestsellers, along with classics such as Dickens, plus stationery galore. Daily 9am–7pm.

MALLS

Aside from the big two below, Crossroads, Gaisano Country Mall and Banilad Town Center (BTC) are all worth checking out for their dining scenes.

Ayala Center Cebu Business Park ☎032 516 3025. Opened in 1994, the Ayala Center was reinvigorated by the

opening of The Terraces dining complex in 2008. Now it plays host to some of the city's best restaurants as well as a huge selection of local and international stores, along with coffee shops, cinemas, dentists, internet cafés and travel agents. Daily 10am–9pm (later for restaurants at The Terraces).

SM City J. Luna Ave ☎032 231 3446. The city's other megamall has all the usual shops, movie theatres and services (plus a bowling alley) spread between the old Southern Wing and the newer Northern Wing, but definitely loses out on its dining scene against the Ayala. Daily 10am–9pm.

SOUVENIRS

If you don't get time to seek out the stores below then there are also a half-dozen souvenir stalls inside the airport departure lounge. As well as Alegre on Mactan (see p.282), for handmade guitars and ukuleles you could also try Borremeo St, a 10min walk south of Colon St.

CLOCKWISE FROM TOP LEFT CROSS OF MAGELLAN (P.270); FORT SAN PEDRO (P.271); CEBU GUITARIST; CARBON MARKET (P.271) >

Artevalman Handicraft Market Mandaue ☎ 032 346 0644. A short taxi ride from the centre of town (P150), this emporium has a large collection of crafts from around the Visayas. Daily 9am–6pm.

DIRECTORY

Banks and exchange There is no shortage of places to change currency, particularly along the main drag of President Osmeña Blvd, on Fuente Osmeña and in all shopping malls. Beware the 24hr exchanges in the bar districts unless you really have to – rates are often substantially lower than elsewhere. Also try to use guarded indoor ATMs if you need to withdraw cash late at night – ATM muggings are not unheard of. There are plenty of banks on President Osmeña Blvd including BDO, PNB and Allied, all north of Fuente Osmeña, a Metrobank just south, and a BPI opposite the *Gran Prix Hotel* on General Maxilom (Mango Ave). There are also ATMs in all of the malls.

Cinemas Ayala Malls 360 in the Ayala Center (☎ ayalamalls .com.ph/movies) has the most comfortable movie theatre in Cebu, and shows the latest movies in English daily.

Consulates A number of countries have consular offices in Cebu, among them the UK, at Villa Terrace, Greenhills Rd, Mandaue City (☎ 032 346 0525) and the US, *Waterfront Cebu City*, Salinas Drive (☎ 032 231 1261), though these are open only part-time and don't offer a full consular service.

Emergencies ☎ 161.

Hospitals Among the best equipped are Cebu Doctors' University Hospital, President Osmeña Blvd (☎ 032 253 7511); Chong Hua Hospital, J. Llorente St, just north of Fuente Osmeña (☎ 032 254 1461, ☎ chonghua.com.ph); and Perpetual Succour Hospital on Gorordo Ave (☎ 032 233 8620).

Immigration The Cebu Immigration District Office is in P. Burgos St, Mandaue (☎ 032 345 6442). You can extend your 30-day visa to 59 days here in a few hours. A new sub-office has also opened on the ground floor of the Gaisano Mactan Island Mall Annex Building on Quezon Ave in Lapu-Lapu, Mactan Island (Mon–Sat 7am–5pm).

Internet access Most malls have internet cafés, often on higher floors; Netopia is on level 4 of the Ayala Center. There are also net cafés in Mango Square on General Maxilom Ave. Many hotels, restaurants and coffee shops have free wi-fi; the latter include *Starbucks* on President Osmeña Blvd and at The Terraces, plus *Bo's Coffee* on F. Ramos St and at Robinsons Cybergate on Fuente Osmeña.

Pharmacies There are large pharmacies in all malls and you'll also find 24hr pharmacies that are often little more than holes in the wall, but carry a good stock of essentials. There's a big branch of Mercury drugstore at Fuente Osmeña, and a Watson's just round the corner on President Osmeña Blvd.

Police The main Cebu City Police Office is south of Fuenta Osmeña (☎ 032 231 5802 or ☎ 032 253 5636), close to Cebu State College. There's a branch of the tourist police opposite Cebu City Hall near Fort San Pedro.

Post The main post office (Mon–Fri 8am–noon & 1–5pm) on Quezon Blvd close to the port area (at the back of Fort San Pedro) has a packing service. There's also a branch in the Capitol complex.

Mactan Island

The closest beaches to Cebu City are on **MACTAN ISLAND**, linked to the main island of Cebu by the Mandaue–Mactan Bridge and the New Mandaue–Mactan Bridge. Off the southern coast of Mactan and linked by two short bridges is **Cordova Island**, a relatively undeveloped slab of land with a couple of secluded, upmarket resorts on the beach. While the beaches and scuba diving on these islands don't compare with Malapascua, for instance, they are easier to reach and the many resorts here offer plenty of other watersports.

Lapu-Lapu

On the island's northern shore, close to the Mandaue–Mactan Bridge, the small capital of **LAPU-LAPU** has a heaving central market, a mall, a post office and some small hotels, but not much for tourists. For many, an obligatory souvenir purchase is a handmade **guitar** from one of Mactan's diminishing number of small guitar factories (see p.282).

The east coast

The beach on Mactan's **east coast** is not especially attractive and in some cases has been expensively groomed and landscaped to try to make it look like a tropical beach should – with the predictable result that it looks fake. Most of the clientele at the resorts are rich Filipinos, and package tourists from Hong Kong, Japan and South Korea.

6

THE BATTLE OF MACTAN AND THE DEATH OF MAGELLAN

Everything seemed to be going well for Portuguese explorer **Ferdinand Magellan** when he made landfall in Samar early in 1521 and claimed the pagan Philippines for his adopted country, Spain, and the true religion, Catholicism. He stocked up on spices and sailed on, landing in Cebu. It was here that he befriended a native king, Raja Humabon and, flush with his conquest of the isles, promised to help him subdue an unruly vassal named **Lapu-Lapu**. Early on the morning of April 27, 1521, Magellan landed at Mactan and tried to coerce Lapu-Lapu into accepting Christianity. Lapu-Lapu declined and when Magellan continued to hector he angrily ordered an attack. As his men fled quickly to their ships, Magellan, resplendent in polished body armour, backed away towards safety, but was felled by a spear aimed at his unprotected foot. Lapu-Lapu's men quickly moved in for the kill. **Magellan's Marker** and **Lapu-Lapu's Monument**, in the north of Mactan island, are both memorials to the battle. Seventeen months later, on September 8, 1522, the last remaining ship in Magellan's original fleet sailed into Seville with eighteen survivors on board. After three years and the loss of four ships and 219 lives, the first circumnavigation of the globe was complete.

ARRIVAL AND DEPARTURE MACTAN ISLAND

By jeepney Mactan is a P14 jeepney ride from the jeepney terminal by Cebu City's SM City Mall in J. Luna Ave Extension, close to the *Sheraton Cebu Hotel*. In Lapu-Lapu, jeepneys stop near the small market square, where you can catch another jeepney onwards towards the beaches of Mactan's east coast.

By taxi From the airport to anywhere on Mactan is a short journey that costs no more than P150 by taxi. Getting to Cordova takes a little longer and will cost up to P200.

INFORMATION AND ACTIVITIES

Scuba diving Simon Timmins (☎ 032 345 0071, ⓦ sidive .com) is an experienced dive instructor who offers very competitive rates for dives and PADI packages – Open Water costs P13,500–14,500 depending upon how many people are taking the course. He can also help to organize trips to swim with the whale sharks in Oslob (see box, p.291). Scotty's Dive Center at Punta Engano Rd, Lapu-Lapu (☎ 032 231 0288, ⓦ divescotty.com) is also reliable for dive trips from Mactan.

Services In Lapu-Lapu, the police station (☎ 032 341 1311) is on B.M. Dimataga St facing Upon Channel, the thin stretch of water that separates Mactan from the Cebu mainland, and there's a Philippine National Bank on Quezon National Highway. The best hospital is the Mactan Doctor's Hospital (☎ 032 341 0000, ⓦ cebudocgroup.com /mactandoctors.html), near the airport in Basak.

ACCOMMODATION AND EATING

Lapu-Lapu has a handful of functional, affordable hotels with a/c and restaurants. On Mactan's **eastern shore** there are about twenty beachfront resorts, mostly overpriced mid-range resorts or top-of-the-line international affairs, but there are a couple of cheaper options; while there's some good dining here, it's expensive. If you're travelling independently you'll save some money by booking in advance with a travel agent or online.

LAPU-LAPU

Bellavista Hotel Quezon Hwy, Lapu-Lapu City ☎ 032 340 7821, ⓦ thebellavista-hotel.com. The bright blue box of the *Bellavista* has had a makeover, and rooms are sleek and modern, with good amenities. There's a pool and travel desk, and room rates include breakfast and round-trip airport transfers. **P2684**

Hotel Cesario Quezon Hwy, Lapu-Lapu City ☎ 032 340 7480. Modern mid-range hotel with a/c rooms, use of the pool at the *Bellavista* next door, and a buffet breakfast included in the rate. Helpful staff can handle travel reservations. **P1400**

EAST COAST

Costabella Tropical Beach Hotel Buyong ☎ 032 238 2700, ⓦ costabellaresort.com. Expansive tropical-style resort with palm trees, swimming pool and a/c rooms on the shore. Friendly, less showy and a little cheaper than many other Mactan resorts, and there's the usual range of activities, including jet-skiing and scuba diving. **P5000**

Kontiki Beach Resort Maribago ☎ 032 340 9934, ⓦ kontikidivers.com. By far the best bet on Mactan's east coast if you're looking for somewhere with genuine charm and without the frills and fuss of the five-stars. *Kontiki* is

6

mainly geared to divers, with good simple a/c rooms in a pretty building on the shore. The beach is rocky but has flat areas for sunbathing and the "house reef" is one of the best in the area. **P1320**

Mövenpick Hotel Punta Engaño ☎ 032 492 7777, ⓦ moevenpick-hotels.com. Rising from the ashes of the old *Hilton Resort*, the newest player on Mactan's upmarket resort scene has already made a stir with its contemporary styling and lively *Ibiza Beach Club*, complete with ironwood decking and jacuzzi looking out to sea. Rooms are modern, stylish and feature full-length windows to make the most

of the views. Guests can be picked up from the airport by Porsche Cayenne. **P8000**

Shangri-La's Mactan Island Resort Punta Engaño ☎ 032 231 0288, ⓦ shangri-la.com. Not as tasteful as its Boracay cousin, the Mactan *Shangri-La* is still super-comfortable and has every amenity imaginable. There are five hundred rooms, eight restaurants and bars and, if the traffic is getting you down, a helicopter to meet you at the airport. Also plenty of activities, some of which you pay extra for, including scuba diving, windsurfing, banana-boat rides and, for relaxation, the renowned Chi Spa. **P10500**

SHOPPING

Alegre Guitar Factory Pajac–Maribago Road, Lapu-Lapu ☎ 032 340 4492. A visit to this famous guitar factory offers the chance to see instruments being made as well as doing a little souvenir shopping. The cheapest steel-stringed acoustic guitars (from P2000) are not so well constructed that you'd want to stake a musical career

on one, but for serious enthusiasts with more to spend there are top-quality models. If a guitar is too much to carry around, smaller ukuleles and mandolins (starting from P1000) make novel gifts. The factory is a P250-300 taxi ride from central Cebu. Daily 8am–6pm.

Olango Island

Five kilometres east of Mactan Island, **Olango Island** supports the largest concentration of **migratory birds** in the country. About 77 species, including egrets, sandpipers, terns and black-bellied plovers, use the island as a rest stop on their annual migration from breeding grounds in Siberia, northern China and Japan to Australia and New Zealand. Declared a **wildlife reserve** in 1998, the island is also home to about sixteen thousand resident native birds which live mostly in the northern half; the southern half of the island is made up of a wide, shallow bay and expanses of mud flats and mangrove. The reserve is at its best during peak migration months: September to November for the southward migration and February to April northbound.

ARRIVAL AND TOURS   OLANGO ISLAND

Day-trips Most resorts on Mactan can organize a day-trip to Olango, though you could visit independently; there are hourly bangkas (P40) to Santa Rosa on Olango Island from the wharf near the *Mövenpick* on Mactan Island, or you can hire your own bangka from Maribago Beach to the island and back for around P2000. From the small Santa Rosa

wharf it's only a short tricycle ride (P100) to the sanctuary.

Tours If you want a knowledgeable guide, make arrangements with the Coastal Resource Management Project of the Department of Environment and Natural Resources (☎ 032 518 5430) in Mandaue, which runs an Olango Birds and Seascape tour.

ACCOMMODATION

Nalusuan Island Resort & Marine Sanctuary ☎ 032 361 1093, ⓦ nalusuan-island.com. One of the few places to stay close to the island, *Nalusuan* is set on an islet rising out of Olango's western coastal reef and has a choice of fan rooms or a/c cottages on stilts in the water. The open-air

restaurant specializes in seafood caught on the doorstep and there are nightly campfire cookouts where you can barbecue food as you like it. The resort can collect you in Mactan, if requested in advance, and there are kayaks available to explore the area. **P2440**

Toledo and Balamban

On the west coast of Cebu, less than two hours from Cebu City by road, **TOLEDO** has several daily ferries for **San Carlos** in Negros (see p.307) – make sure you get there before mid-afternoon as Toledo isn't a place you'd choose to stay. You're better off heading twenty minutes north to the town of **BALAMBAN**, which has slightly more to offer in its clutch of deserted black-sand **beaches**.

ARRIVAL AND DEPARTURE

By bus Buses leave Cebu City's Southern bus terminal for Toledo from 5am daily (P60). If you're heading from Cebu City to Negros, catch an early bus to Toledo to make sure you don't miss the last ferry.

TOLEDO AND BALAMBAN

By ferry Several ferries including Montenegro Shipping Lines (☎ 0922 774 8199, ⓦ montenegrolines.com.ph) run daily to San Carlos in Negros (40min; P40).

ACCOMMODATION AND EATING

Aleu's Lodge Polyapoy St, Toledo ☎ 032 322 5672. If you do get stuck in Toledo there is one rudimentary hotel, on the southern edge of town. **P750**

Sailor's Cabin Abucayan, Balamban (look out for the big white and blue entrance) ☎ 032 465 2816, ⓦ sailors -cabin.com. Accommodation in this German-owned place

comprises three types of apartments, with cable TV and private bathrooms. The menu at the restaurant includes German sausage, smoked ham with sauerkraut and Hungarian goulash. The proprietor can organize trips to some undiscovered areas of the rural west coast. **P950**

Bantayan Island

Just off the northwest coast of Cebu, quiet, bucolic and low-lying **BANTAYAN ISLAND** was badly hit by Typhoon Yolanda (see box, p.284). The lack of coral and diving opportunities (and therefore diving clientele) means that it may take Bantayan longer to get back on its feet than Malapascua, but it certainly shouldn't be written off. For now the beaches may not be quite as picture-perfect as previously, but – with fewer visitors – the island's pleasant, low-key resorts will welcome you with open arms. Most of the island's resorts and beaches are around the attractive little town of **SANTA FE** on the southeast coast, which is where ferries from mainland Cebu arrive.

Bantayan Town

Along the west coast, the port town of **BANTAYAN** has no decent accommodation but it's worth a quick visit. There's an elegant Spanish-style plaza on the south side of which stands the **SS Peter and Paul Church**. The original structure was torched by marauding Moros in 1640, with eight hundred local folk taken captive and sold as slaves to Muslim chieftains in Mindanao. Every Easter Bantayan holds solemn processions of decorated religious *carozzas* (carriages), each containing a life-sized statue representing the Passion and death of Jesus Christ. Thousands of locals and tourists turn out to join in the processions, many setting up camp on the beaches because resorts are full.

ARRIVAL AND DEPARTURE   BANTAYAN

By bus To reach Bantayan from Cebu City you can take a bus (7 daily; 3hr 30min) from the Northern bus terminal to the port town of Hagnaya, where you pay a P10 pier fee and P170 for the ferry crossing to Santa Fe (6–7 daily; 1hr).

By taxi Taxis from Cebu to Hagnaya can be negotiated for around P2000, or as little as P700 on the way back.

By bangka There are big bangkas to Bantayan from Cadiz on Negros. Coming from Malapascua, bangkas can be chartered for around P2500, but only take this route in good weather. If you intend to stay in Santa Fe, you can get a pedicab from the pier to your accommodation, though some resorts can send a representative to collect you at the pier.

GETTING AROUND

The only local transport is a habal-habal, or the trusty tricycle, known on Bantayan as a *tricikad*. It's fun to hire a motorbike or moped (P300) or bicycle and tour the island yourself by the coastal road, though inspect the bike thoroughly beforehand.

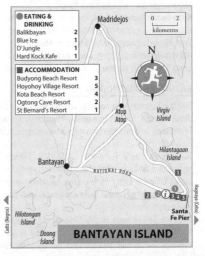

EATING & DRINKING
Balikbayan	2
Blue Ice	1
D'Jungle	1
Hard Kock Kafe	1

ACCOMMODATION
Budyong Beach Resort	3
Hoyohoy Village Resort	5
Kota Beach Resort	4
Ogtong Cave Resort	2
St Bernard's Resort	1

0 — 2 kilometres

N

Madridejos

Atop Atop

Virgiv Island

Hilantagaan Island

Bantayan

NATIONAL ROAD

Hilotongan Island

Doong Island

Santa Fe Pier

Cadiz (Negros)

Hagnaya (Cebu)

BANTAYAN ISLAND

6

BANTAYAN AND YOLANDA

Few buildings on Bantayan escaped damage during Yolanda, and egg production, one of the mainstays of the local economy, came to a complete standstill. At the time of writing boat services to the island were limited and many hotels were still closed or only partially open. Partial electricity returned to the island in February 2014, but check ⓦfacebook.com /choosebantayan for the latest situation. **The Back to Sea Project** (ⓦbacktoseaproject.com) is a great initiative offering visitors the chance to help out financially and physically with the reparation projects, including helping to build boats and to make fishing implements (P3500 per project).

INFORMATION

Tourist information Though closed at the time of writing, the small tourist office in Santa Fe should be up and running by the time you read this, and has simple photocopied island maps (P5) and a few hotel brochures. For information about Bantayan before your trip ⓦwow bantayan.com is a good resource.

Services Next to the tourist office in Santa Fe there's a health centre and a police station. The Marque Internet Café in Santa Fe market has web access for P20/hr. There's a post office and an Allied Bank with ATM in Bantayan Town, but it's best to bring enough cash to last your stay. Currency can be changed at some of the resorts and at an exchange office next to Palawan Pawnshop in Santa Fe.

ACCOMMODATION

★**Budyong Beach Resort** A short ride west of Santa Fe by pedicab ☎0921 314 5275. A good selection of fan and a/c (P1560) cottages set in a coconut grove on one of the island's nicest stretches of beach within easy walking distance of the town centre. There's a simple restaurant here too. **P800**

Hoyohoy Village Resort Just west of Santa Fe pier ☎032 438 9223, ⓦhoyohoy-villas.com. Set in pleasant gardens with a small central pool, *Hoyohoy*'s spacious and solid villas-on-stilts contain some of Bantayan's best rooms, all of which have a/c, cable TV and fridge. The rooms and grounds are sprinkled with antiques, and there's free wi-fi. The only downside to this place is that this stretch of beach is very close to the ferry pier. **P3500**

Kota Beach Resort A short ride west of Santa Fe by tricycle ☎032 438 9042, ⓦkotabeach-bantayan.com. Next door to *Budyong*, Kota has a range of different rooms and cottages set in attractive gardens on a lovely stretch of beach. The superior cottages (P1300) are right on the sand,

and for those on a budget, the economy and fan rooms at the back offer decent value. **P770**

Ogtong Cave Resort About 15min west of the Santa Fe pier by tricycle ☎032 438 9129, ⓦogtongcave.com. On a headland looking out over Sugar Beach, and set in pleasant gardens with a spring-fed swimming cave and pool, this is Bantayan's best hotel. The vast range of rooms on offer includes a budget option with fan, regular a/c rooms (P3200), deluxe (P3500), sea-view villas (also P3500) and exclusive suites with access to a separate private pool (P16,000). A short walk takes you down to the beach, where you can arrange fishing expeditions with the locals and bring your catch back to the *Ogtong* chef to be cooked. Free wi-fi. **P1600**

St Bernard's Resort North of Santa Fe Beach Club on Alice Beach, and 5min by tricycle from the pier ☎0917 963 6162, ⓦbantayan.dk. Quaint little circular cottages set in narrow gardens leading down to a very local patch of beach. There's a small restaurant where you can get a good meal for P150–200. **P950**

EATING AND DRINKING

Dining in Bantayan has a way to go before it becomes a culinary destination, but there are a few places to try after a hard day at the beach. A great cheap breakfast option is just to buy banana bread from the bakery by the main junction in Santa Fe and some fresh mangoes from the market across the road.

Balikbayan Santa Fe ☎0921 505 5189. Friendly restaurant in the backstreets of Santa Fe with cosy pergolas dotted around a pretty garden. Great breakfasts, good pasta and the house coconut shake is as good as you'll find anywhere. Daily 7.30am–11pm.

Blue Ice On the main strip in Santa Fe. This popular Swedish-owned place has music and dancing in the evenings. Sides include "Nick the Greek" salad, and there's

an extensive selection of mains including steaks, seafood and pizza (P200). Daily 8am–late.

D'Jungle Santa Fe. On the main strip, foreign-owned *D'Jungle* offers excellent buffets and Mongolian barbecue, plus there's good old shepherd's pie (P95) and fish and chips (P165), as well as delicious chilli crab. Backpacker rooms are available to rent for a bargain P200–250. Daily 7am–midnight.

Hard Kock Kafe On the main strip in Santa Fe ☎ 032 438 9013. This café has a terrible name but a good atmosphere and decent curries, and is usually the liveliest place for a drink in the evening (San Mig P45). Daily 8am–midnight.

Malapascua Island

Eight kilometres off the northern tip of Cebu, the tiny island of **MALAPASCUA** is often touted as the next Boracay, largely because of **Bounty Beach**, a blindingly white stretch of sand on the island's south coast. The island also has great **diving**, and is renowned for the chance to see thresher sharks (see box below). The nearest airport is Cebu, meaning that so far the island has escaped overdevelopment, but Malapascua was just hitting the big time when **Typhoon Yolanda** struck. Almost every roof on the island was destroyed, and most of the local population was left without shelter. Substantial private reparations contributions have helped the island to begin to find its feet. Although at the time of writing only the bigger, more established resorts were operational, by the time you read this the vital tourist economy should be up and running and will hopefully facilitate the community's recovery. In spite of recent challenges, the inhabitants of Malapascua remain some of the warmest, most welcoming people you'll ever meet, and are renowned for their love of a party. No matter when you visit, chances are there'll be some kind of fiesta or pageant.

Around the island

It's worth taking a stroll in the cool of the late afternoon to the **lighthouse tower** on Malapascua's northwest coast for tremendous views across the Visayan Sea. Or for more of an adventure, you can **walk** the entire circumference of the island in a few hours, a journey which will take you through sleepy fishing villages lined with mangroves, to remote white sand beaches where you'll feel as if you have the whole island to yourself. Take water, sunscreen and don't be afraid to ask directions – there are a bewildering array of trails for an island just 1km wide.

Calangaman and Carnassa islands

Day-trip bangka hire costs from P3000 to either island

Whether you're diving or not, don't miss the opportunity for a day-trip to **Calangaman**, a beautiful, remote islet that consists of no more than a strip of sand just a few metres wide with a few trees at one end. Another gem in the area – two hours to the northeast by bangka – is the Robinson Cruso-esque **Carnassa Island**, where you land at a picturesque bay fringed by palm trees.

ARRIVAL AND DEPARTURE | **MALAPASCUA ISLAND**

From Cebu Most visitors head from Cebu City's Northern bus terminal to Maya by Ceres Liner bus (3–4hr) or private taxi (P2500), and then take a bangka (hourly; P80) across to the island. The last boat to Maya is usually at 4pm,

---

DIVING AT MALAPASCUA

Although some shallower dive sites were damaged by Yolanda, the major drawcard – **thresher sharks** – remain in residence and anyone staying more than a few days is almost guaranteed a sighting. There are also plenty of wrecks in the vicinity, including the passenger ferry **Dona Marilyn**, which went down in a 1984 typhoon and is now home to scorpionfish, flamefish and stingrays.

DIVE OPERATORS

Divelink ☎ 032 231 4633, ⓦ divelinkcebu.com.
Evolution ☎ 0917 628 7333, ⓦ evolution.com.ph.
Malapascua Exotic Island Dive and Beach Resort (see p.286).

Sea Explorers Cebu ☎ 0917 320 4158, ⓦ sea-explorers .com.
Thresher Shark Divers ☎ 0927 612 3359, ⓦ malapascua-diving.com.

6

although boatmen may try and tell you it's earlier to get you to charter a bangka (P500–1000 depending on the boat and your bargaining). At either end you may need to transfer to a small boat to the shoreline (P10).

From Bantayan You'll need to charter a bangka from Malapascua (2–3hr; P2500); only undertake this trip if the weather is set fair.

From Leyte there is a daily boat at 7am from San Isidro to Maya (P180), returning at 10am.

INFORMATION

Services There are no banks on Malapascua, and while you can change money at some of the resorts it's best to bring enough pesos with you. For internet there used to be connected computers and wi-fi at *Maldito's Bar*, which should be operational by the time you read this. There's also a tiny internet café at the bangka terminal on Logon village beach (2km west of Bounty Beach), although it didn't have connection at the time of writing.

ACCOMMODATION

There are about a dozen **resorts** on Bounty Beach and a number of others dotted around the island. Places book up fast (especially budget rooms) in peak season when it's worth securing a reservation in advance. Most of the places listed below were at least partially open for business at the time of writing, and it is hoped that by the time you read this all of Malapascua's hotels will be fully up and running.

BOUNTY BEACH

Blue Corals Beach Resort Western end of Bounty Beach ☎032 437 1021, ⓦmalapascuaisland.com.ph. This blue concrete box doesn't exactly blend into the scenery, but its location at the end of the beach gives fantastic views in both directions. Large a/c rooms are nicely painted and have good balconies. Fan rooms are similar without the balcony. The hotel was damaged by Yolanda and undergoing renovations at the time of writing. P1500

Blue Water Beach Resort Middle of the beach ☎0917 627 2951, ⓦmalapascuabeachresort.com. Badly damaged by Yolanda, *Blue Water* was closed at the time of writing but should now have reopened, with the same clean nipa chalets around a pleasant garden area. Rates include breakfast and there's also free wi-fi. P1000

Daño Beach Resort Close to Malapascua Exotic Island Resort ☎0915 666 1584, ⓦdanobeachresort.com. Previously *Daño* had some of the simplest huts on the beach, nicely spread through extensive coconut grove grounds, but almost all were badly affected by Yolanda and the resort remained closed at the time of writing. P1300

Malapascua Exotic Island Dive and Beach Resort Far eastern end of Bounty Beach ☎032 437 0983, ⓦmalapascua.net. One of the best established resorts on the island, *Exotic* escaped lightly from Yolanda, with only two rooms suffering damage, and it was business as usual at the time of writing. There's a huge range of rooms on offer ranging from basic beds in the Diver's Lodge (P500; in-house divers only), and budget rooms in the Go Pro Lodge, through to standard a/c rooms (P3900) and pricey super deluxe rooms (P5500). There's also a decent restaurant and 24hr electricity. P1600

Mike & Diose's Close to Malapascua Exotic Island Resort ☎0917 523 4105, ⓦaabana.de. A couple of very simple beach huts plus two newer fully kitted out cottages with a/c, cable TV, DVD player, fridge and wi-fi. Both room types are in an excellent location tucked in a garden at the east end of Bounty Beach. P1000

★**Ocean Vida Beach and Dive Resort** Bounty Beach ☎0917 303 8064, ⓦocean-vida.com. Lovely rooms right on the beach make Swiss-German owned *Ocean Vida* a popular choice for both divers and sunseekers. Prices are high (P4700 for beachfront), but then so is the quality of service and rooms, and the bar is one of the liveliest on the strip. P2900

AROUND THE ISLAND

Bantigue Cove ☎032 437 0322. On a peninsula between two bays at the far northern end of the island, *Bantigue* is wonderfully remote and many of its ridge-top cottages have great views, although the resort suffered badly at the hands of Yolanda and remained closed at the time of writing. There's a choice of fan or a/c rooms and also a small restaurant. To get here either charter a bangka or take a habal-habal. P1500

★**Mangrove Oriental Resort** Logon ☎0926 418 6264, ⓦmangroveoriental.com. A couple of kilometres along the west coast from Bounty Beach (P30 by habal-habal), this wonderfully romantic and secluded exotic hideaway nestled around a small cove was badly damaged by Yolanda, but was already partially open at the time of writing. Many of the cottages (P3700–5600) are uniquely styled, and the Kasbah, which is perched on top of the hill, features inlaid furniture from Mindanao. The budget cottages, right on the sand, have brightly painted exteriors and simple but comfortable furnishings. P800

Tepanee Beach Resort Logon Beach ☎0917 302 2495, ⓦtepanee.com. On a headland just west of Bounty Beach, *Tepanee's* Italian owners have re-invented and glamorized good old *Logon Beach Resort*. Most cottages are now a/c (P2500–3500), but for now at least, there are still four of the fan originals which look straight out to the ocean. P1500

White Sand Bungalows Logon Beach ☎ 0927 318 7471, ⓦ whitesand.dk. Karl's three simple huts have had

an upgrade and now feature a simple upper mezzanine level with a double mattress (P100 per extra person) as well as the main downstairs room. Many of the palms in the garden were damaged by Yolanda, but *White Sand* is open for business, and the beachside location is as appealing as ever. P1000

EATING AND DRINKING

★**Angelina's** Logon Beach ☎ 0915 340 4906, ⓦ angelina beach.com. Easily the best (and most expensive) place to eat on the island, *Angelina's* serves top-quality Italian fare looking out over pretty Logon village beach. Top dishes include beef carpaccio (P320) and *tartar di tonno* (P345), but the pizza (from P350) and pasta dishes are also excellent. Good coffee (P80–120) and *crema catalana* (P165) rounds the meal off nicely. Daily 8am–10pm.

Ging Ging's In the maze of lanes which run behind Bounty Beach. Obliterated by Yolanda, old backpacker

favourite *Ging Ging's* was serving food again in a makeshift dining room at the time of writing and planned to rebuild fully. The menu still holds a host of mains for less than P100, plus outstanding chocolate-and-banana pancakes (P75). Daily 6.30am–10pm.

Maldito's Logon Village Beach. Set a little back from the beach, *Maldito's* bar-restaurant was also seriously damaged by Yolanda, and was being re-roofed at the time of writing. When it reopens, plans are for the same large-scale dining and drinking establishment. Daily 8am–midnight.

The Camotes Islands

About 30km northeast of Cebu City, the friendly, peaceful **CAMOTES ISLANDS** are named after the sweet potatoes which thrive on the islands' rocky topsoil cover. The island group, which once sheltered Magellan's fleet, are gradually opening up to tourism, and were nowhere near as badly affected by Typhoon Yolanda as Bantayan and Malapascua. The two principal islands, **Poro** and **Pacijan**, are linked by a causeway, which makes exploring by motorbike an appealing prospect.

Pacijan

The main town on Pacijan is **SAN FRANCISCO**, on the eastern edge of the island, where the causeway runs across to Poro. "San Fran" has a pretty 150 year-old church, but little else to detain you; most of the resorts are on the beaches of the northwest and south coasts.

Beaches

A ten-minute habal-habal ride from Consuelo, on Pacijan's west coast (where boats arrive), **Heminsulan Beach** is a short, attractive stretch of beach with two resorts to choose from. Pacijan's widest stretch of sand is **Santiago Beach**, another ten minutes round the toe of the island, which has a selection of resorts to choose from. In the northwest of the island, lower-key options include **Bakhaw Beach**.

Lake Danao and around

Greenlake Park entry P15; swimming pool P100/person; boat rides P50/person

To get the lay of the land head up to **Arquis Viewing Deck** in the north of the island. From here you can see **Lake Danao**, an extensive body of water, and the site of **Greenlake Park** where you can take *sakanaw* (local boat) trips out to the mangroves, have some lunch in the simple restaurant or take a swim in the large, attractive pool.

Tulang Island

Bangka P10/person, or P100 for the whole boat

In the north beyond Lake Danao, **Tulang** is a picturesque islet lapped by turquoise waters, which has good snorkelling and diving and is accessible by a short bangka ride from Tulang Daka Beach.

6

Poro

Just across the causeway on rugged Poro, **Buho Rock Resort** (P20) is stretching the use of the word resort (there are no rooms or places to eat), but it does have a lovely swimming spot. At the eastern edge of the island you swim in a series of small underground caves in **Bukilat** (p10), while easier swimming awaits at **Busay Falls** just a short walk from Tudela on the south coast.

6

Ponson

Take a ferry from Tudela on Poro's south coast (2hr), or a bangka from Puerto Bello on Poro's northeastern coast (45min; P50)

To really get away from it all, make for the easternmost (and smallest) Camotes island, **Ponson**, There are some quiet, attractive white sand beaches here, but currently there's nowhere to stay. Bangkas arrive at the main settlement of Kawit.

ARRIVAL AND DEPARTURE — THE CAMOTES ISLANDS

By boat Previously the Camotes were accessible by fast ferry from Cebu City, but at the time of writing the easiest way to get here was using the regular Jomalia (T 032 346 0421) boats from Danao to Consuelo (5.30am, 8.30am, 11am, 2pm, 5.30pm and sometimes 9pm; 2hr; P180). Danao is 1hr from Cebu's northern terminal by bus (or P700–900 by taxi). There's a P5 terminal fee.

GETTING AROUND

By motorbike Hiring a motorbike (P300/day from *Mangodlong Paradise Beach Resort*) is the easiest way to get around.

By habal-habal Short trips by habal-habal cost P50.

INFORMATION

Tourist information San Francisco has a friendly tourist information kiosk (daily 8am–5pm; T 0948 133 7577).

Services In Poro, there's a post office at the town hall and DBP Bank with an ATM, but this doesn't accept foreign cards or exchange, so bring enough cash to last. For internet access head to NJ Internet in San Francisco (8am–midnight; P15/hr). Several of the resorts also have wi-fi.

ACCOMMODATION AND EATING

DANAO

Sunshine Shin Beach Resort Brgy Taytay, a short tricycle ride north of the port T 032 200 4170, W tomesunshine.com. If you're stuck in Danao, this Japanese-owned resort has a nice pool and isn't a bad place to spend the night. Fan rooms P850

PACIJAN

Bellavista Mare Santiago Beach T 032 318 0806 or T 0917 792 5583, E bvmarecamotes@gmail.com. This small, Italian-owned budget choice enjoys a good location looking out over the broad expanse of Santiago Beach. There's a choice of fan or a/c doubles (P1150) or family rooms, plus snorkelling gear (P250/day) and wi-fi (P60/day). P750

Borromeo Beach Resort Bakhaw Beach T 0908 626 1585, W borromeobeachcamotes.com. Borromeo is a comparatively upmarket option on beautiful Bakhaw Beach, featuring four oversized rooms with high ceilings and grandiose furniture, although it somehow all feels a little out of place. There's a decent kitchen for guest use but no restaurant. This part of the island had been without power since Typhoon Yolanda, but hopefully it will have been restored by now. P2500

Keshe Beach Resort Bakhaw Beach, next to Borromeo Beach Resort T 0929 892 5792. For those seeking real isolation, *Keshe* has just three simple nipa huts on the beach. There's a "café" which can turn out basic dishes, or guests are free to cook for themselves. Like *Borromeo*, *Keshe* had no power at the time of writing. P1500

Mangodlong Paradise Beach Resort Heminsulan Beach T 032 328 0500, W mangodlongparadiseresort.com. The most upmarket choice on the Camotes, *Mangodlong Paradise* has a range of clean, comfortable rooms with cable TV set around a large oceanfront garden and pool. There's also a dive centre, and a decent café which serves plenty of fish dishes, plus pasta and sandwiches. P3000

Pito's Sutokil Santiago Beach. Laidback and popular little beach café serving breakfasts (P65–95), simple meals (P90–110) and whole native chicken (P300) right on the sand. *Nena's Bar & Grill* next door serves similar fare. Daily 5am–10pm.

Santiago Bay Garden and Beach Resort Santiago Beach T 032 345 8599 W camotesislandph.com. A huge choice of room types, all set on a hillside overlooking pretty Santiago Beach. The villas (P2500) and bungalows (P3000) are the nicest places to stay, but the fan rooms offer decent value and full use of the resort's facilities which include two pools. Free wi-fi in the restaurant. P1000

PORO

Heritage Inn Poro Town ☎ 0928 751 8004. If you don't mind being away from the beach you'll find some of the nicest and best value rooms on the island at this brand new hotel owned by the mayor of Poro's brother. Rooms are clean and pleasant and have wi-fi, parquet flooring and some also have small balconies. P1500

Moalboal

Three hours by road and 89km from Cebu City, on the southwestern flank of Cebu Island, lies the sleepy town of **MOALBOAL**, jumping-off point for the resorts of **Panagsama Beach**, a boozy hangout for travellers and scuba divers (see box below), 3km away on the coast. Sun-worshippers looking for a Boracay-style sandy beach will be disappointed – the shoreline is a little rocky in places and not generally suitable for recreational swimming. Nonetheless, Panagsama's village makes up for this in other ways, with a great range of cheap accommodation, a marvellous view of the sunset over distant Negros and some good discounts on diving and rooms. Sunbathing by resort pools, diving and drinking take centre stage, and there's little else to do in town. If being on the beach is top of your list, head 8km north along the coast to **White Beach**, an attractive strip of sand with several mid-range resorts. Note that – confusingly – the whole area around Panagsama, including White Beach, is often referred to as Moalboal.

Away from the coast, the jagged limestone peaks and lush river valleys of Cebu's central mountains offer canyoning, hiking, kayaking, mountain biking and horseriding all within easy reach of Panagsama.

Naomi's Bottle Museum and Library

Panagsama, 300m inland • No fixed hours • Free

For a break from the beach, bars and diving, it's just a short walk to the quirky **Naomi's Bottle Museum and Library**, where recycled bottles from the resorts adorn every available surface. Each bottle is filled with a message of goodwill, and visitors are given miniature versions as gifts. There are also bottles and other trinkets for sale.

DIVING AT MOALBOAL

Pescador Island, thirty minutes by bangka from Panagsama, is one of the best dive sites in the country, surrounded by a terrific reef that teems with marine life, and renowned for its swirling sardine shoals. Barely 100m long, the island is the pinnacle of a submarine mountain reaching just 6m above sea level and ending in a flat surface, making it look from a distance like a floating disc. The most impressive of the underwater formations is the **Cathedral**, a funnel of rock that is open at the top end and can be penetrated by divers. Pelagic fish are sometimes seen in the area, including reef sharks and hammerheads, while at lesser depths on the reef there are Moorish idols, sweetlips, fire gobies and batfish. There are at least ten other dive sites around Panagsama, including the gentle Balay Reef, Ronda Bay Marine Park, Airplane Wreck (which was sunk by Savedra) and Sunken Island (an advanced site).

Arranging diving trips is easy, with a dozen **operators** at Panagsama Beach. Dives typically cost P1300 for a shore dive and P1600 for a boat dive, including equipment.

DIVE OPERATORS

Blue Abyss Dive Shop ☎ 032 474 3036, ⓦ blueabyss diving.com.

Savedra Dive Center ☎ 032 474 3132, ⓦ savedra .com.

SeaQuest Dive Center ☎ 032 232 6010, ⓦ seaquest divecenter.ph.

Visayas Divers ☎ 032 474 0018, ⓦ visayadivers .com/wpvd.

Wolfgang Dafert ☎ 0928 263 4646, ⓦ freediving -philippines.com. For something a little different, Wolfgang Dafert, who is based up at White Beach, arranges free-diving courses which aim to assist guests in holding their breath longer and diving deeper unassisted. Prices start at US$125/day.

ARRIVAL AND DEPARTURE

MOALBOAL

By bus A number of bus companies, including Ceres Liner (☎ 032 345 8650), run regular services to Moalboal town from Cebu City's Southern bus terminal (3hr), but make sure the driver knows where you want to get off, as most buses continue beyond Moalboal. Moalboal proper is on the road that follows the coast; Panagsama Beach is a P100 tricycle ride from the point on the main road where buses drop passengers. Heading south for Lilo-an and Negros, there are regular Ceres Liner buses, or you can arrange a van through one of the resorts (P1500).

By taxi A quicker option than the public buses is to negotiate a rate with a Cebu taxi – P2000–2500 is a reasonable price to Moalboal.

INFORMATION AND ACTIVITIES

Services Moalboal now has an ATM which accepts foreign cards in the 360 Pharmacy, though it's still best to bring enough cash with you. There's a moneychanger by the police station.

Activities To get away from the dive scene and explore the wild hinterlands of western Cebu, head for Planet Action Adventure (☎ 032 474 3016, ⓦ action-philippines.com) at the *Tipolo Beach Resort* (see below). Jochen and Jinky can organize caving, trekking, canyoning and mountain-biking trips, and rent out mountain bikes (P300–700/day). Adventure day-trips start from P2200.

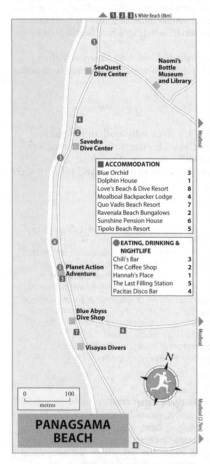

▲ **1**. **2**. **3** & White Beach (8km)

SeaQuest Dive Center

Naomi's Bottle Museum and Library

4

2 Savedra Dive Center

3

■ ACCOMMODATION	
Blue Orchid	3
Dolphin House	1
Love's Beach & Dive Resort	8
Moalboal Backpacker Lodge	4
Quo Vadis Beach Resort	7
Ravenala Beach Bungalows	2
Sunshine Pension House	6
Tipolo Beach Resort	5

4

5 Planet Action Adventure

5

● EATING, DRINKING & NIGHTLIFE	
Chili's Bar	3
The Coffee Shop	2
Hannah's Place	1
The Last Filling Station	5
Pacitas Disco Bar	4

Blue Abyss Dive Shop

7

6

Visayas Divers

N

0	100
metres	

PANAGSAMA BEACH

8

ACCOMMODATION

PANAGSAMA BEACH

★ **Love's Beach & Dive Resort** Right at the southern end of the beach, a 5min walk from Quo Vadis ☎ 032 474 0140, ⓦ lovesbeachresort.com. Attractive and well-cared-for resort on a quiet section of coast. There's a wide variety of fan and a/c rooms (from P1600) to choose from, a nice pool, free wi-fi in the public areas, and a lovely restaurant looking out to sea. **P1300**

Moalboal Backpacker Lodge Towards the north end of the beach ☎ 0917 751 8902, ⓦ moalboal-backpackerlodge.com. The cheapest place to stay in Moalboal, with very simple dorms and a few private rooms, some of which have their own bathroom (P650). Free wi-fi. Dorms **P275**, double **P480**

Quo Vadis Beach Resort Towards the southern end of the beach ☎ 032 474 3068, ⓦ quovadisresort.com. Attractive place set in coastal gardens with a good choice of rooms. Economy rooms are in a block at the back, while a/c huts and cottages (from P1625) are closer to the front. There's also a pool and a bar-restaurant looking straight out to sea. Free wi-fi. Visaya Divers is also located here. **P1340**

Sunshine Pension House 50m inland from Blue Abyss Dive Shop, opposite Marcosas Cottages ☎ 0921 689 1865, ⓦ sunshinepension.webs.com. Budget favourite, set in a pleasant garden with a pool. The simple rooms come with fan and private bathroom, but walls are very thin. **P850**

★ **Tipolo Beach Resort** Just south of the centre of the beach ☎ 0917 583 0062, ⓦ tipoloresort.com. Lovely little resort owned by the friendly folk behind Planet Action Adventure and *The Last Filling Station*. Rooms are tastefully furnished in bamboo, and look out onto an attractive garden, with the sea beyond. Free wi-fi throughout. If *Tipolo* is fully booked ask about their new budget property, *Bamboo Inn* (from P750), a 10min walk back towards Moalboal. **P1800**

WHITE BEACH

Blue Orchid On a coral promontory at the far end of the beach ☎0929 273 1128, ⓦblueorchidresort.com. Beautifully isolated property with a pool, dive school, well-designed rooms and a small animal shelter for rescued endemic species. P3000

Dolphin House Southern end of the beach ☎032 474 0073, ⓦmoalboal.net. The most sophisticated place to stay on White Beach has a lovely pool and free wi-fi, but the shoreline is rocky here. P5250

Ravenala Beach Bungalows Roughly in the middle of the beach ☎032 254 9563, ⓦravenala-resort -moalboal.com. Laidback resort right on a lovely stretch of beach, with comfortable wooden cottages set around a small garden. P3000

FURTHER AFIELD

Badian Island Resort & Spa Badian Island ☎032 475 1102, ⓦbadianhotel.com. Luxurious resort on Badian Island, 10km south of Panagsama. There's a huge list of facilities – as well as diving, tennis and glass-bottomed boat rides you can get a four-hand massage for $95. Round-trip transfers from Cebu City or the airport cost $60/person; alternatively make your own way to Badian Town from where the resort can pick you up by private bangka. P9650

EATING, DRINKING AND NIGHTLIFE

PANAGSAMA BEACH

Chili's Bar Midway along the beach path. Popular with divers ("get out of that wet suit and into a dry martini"), this place has great sea views, two pool tables and serves Jaeger beer for just P99. Snacks and meals are also on offer. Daily 9am–1.30am.

★**The Coffee Shop** North end of the beach path ☎0906 353 4315. A fantastic new café, *The Coffee Shop* offers great breakfasts (try the Parisienne, P180), French crêpes (P220), good coffee (P60–80) and daily specials. The owner, Sebastien, is as friendly as the vibe, right down to the sand on the floor. Free wi-fi. Daily 7am–10pm.

Hannah's Place Northern end of the beach. In spite of Hannah's passing, good seafood (P350), tranquil ocean views and laidback service continue to be the hallmarks of this small restaurant-bar. Daily 8am–10pm.

★**The Last Filling Station** Tipolo Beach Resort ☎0917 583 0062, ⓦtipoloresort.com. Friendly, laidback place rustling up tasty international dishes and great wood-oven pizzas (P245), as well as freshly baked bread and home-made yoghurt (P125) for breakfast. Free wi-fi. Daily 6.30am–10pm.

SWIMMING WITH WHALE SHARKS AT OSLOB

In recent years the previously sleepy little town of **Oslob**, towards the southern tip of Cebu, has become famous for the near guaranteed chance to get close to – and even swim with – **whale sharks** off the nearby barangay of Tan-awan. Marine biologists raise **ethical questions** about the nature of human–whale shark interaction and doubt whether the Oslob population can even be considered as wild anymore, but while the opportunity to swim with the animals remains, tourists flock here on a daily basis. Visitors are given a mandatory orientation, and those who plan to swim with the gentle giants are required not to wear sunscreen, not to use flash photography, and not to get closer than 5m to the whale sharks.

The most painless way to arrange a visit is to book through **Oslob Whale Sharks** (ⓦoslobwhalesharks.com; from P2500/person for a group of four), or a dive shop in Cebu, Moalboal or Dauin (on Negros). Tours from Cebu leave early morning and head first for the whale sharks, then stop for lunch before heading back to the city. It's far cheaper to arrive independently by Ceres Liner bus from Cebu (3–4hr) and then organize the trip at Tan-awan. A thirty-minute boat ride (the maximum duration) costs P500 per person (P300 for Filipinos), or P1000 for snorkelling (P500 for Filipinos). Given the large number of visitors a morning visit is recommended. The piers at Lilo-an and Bato are only a short hop away and travellers visiting both Cebu and Negros can make Oslob a stop on the journey between the two.

ACCOMMODATION

Alcoy Resort A 30min drive north of Oslob ☎032 483 8059, ⓦdivepoint-alcoy.net. A selection of garden bungalows, or singles (P2000) and sea-view doubles (P4000) in the attractive whitewashed beach house. There's also a dive centre and a pool. P3400

Ester's Place Book via Oslob Whale Sharks ☎032 515 4010, ⓦoslobwhalesharks.com. Simple a/c rooms with shared bathrooms conveniently located within walking distance of Tan-awan pier. Guests also have use of the communal living room and kitchen. P1200

Pacitas Disco Bar Just north of Tipolo Beach Resort. An empty space six days a week, *Pacitas* comes alive on Sat nights, when it functions as the biggest disco in the area, attracting a healthy crowd of locals plus a fair few travellers. An a/c disco hall has replaced the old outdoor scene, but the music is as loud as ever and there's plenty of fun to be had. P30 cover charge. Sat only 9pm–3am.

Bohol

BOHOL, a two-hour hop south of Cebu, is an attractive little island where life today is pastoral and quiet. The only sign of heavy tourist activity is on the beautiful beaches of **Panglao**, a magnet for scuba divers and sun worshippers, close to the utilitarian port capital of **Tagbilaran**. Most visitors only leave the beach for a day tour taking in Bohol's most famous attractions: the much-touted **Chocolate Hills**, a glimpse of the endangered **tarsier**, lunch on the **Loboc River** and a visit to the **Blood Compact** site, memorial to Bohol's violent past. Those with more time can be rewarded by trips to other parts of the province, including the adventure centre at **Danao**, the attractive island of **Cabilao** and the pretty beaches of **Anda**.

Bohol is also renowned for its wonderful old Spanish churches, many of them built with coral, which can be found all over the island, notably at **Baclayon** – though several were destroyed during the October 2013 quake (see box below). May is **fiesta** month on Bohol with island-wide celebrations including barangay festivals, beauty pageants, street dancing and solemn religious processions.

ARRIVAL AND DEPARTURE   BOHOL

BY PLANE
Air Asia, Cebu Pacific and PAL have daily flights to Tagbilaran from Manila (1hr 15min).

BY BOAT
Tagbilaran is Bohol's principal port, though there are also services from Tubigon, Ubay and Jagna.

Tagbilaran The Cebu–Tagbilaran route is operated by several fast ferry companies (2hr; P500–800) including Oceanjet (6 daily), SuperCat (2 daily) and Weesam (3 daily). Other operators such as Cokaliong (1 weekly), F.J. Palacio Lines (3 weekly) and Trans-Asia Shipping Lines (1 weekly) also have cheaper slower services (4–5hr; P195) on this route.

Destinations Cagayan de Oro (6 weekly; 9hr), Cebu City (hourly; 2–5hr); Larena (3 weekly; 3hr); Siquijor (2 daily; 3hr 30min), via Dumaguete (2 daily; 2hr).

Tubigon Island Shipping operates fast ferries between Cebu City and Tubigon (4 daily; 1hr 20min).

Ubay A number of ferries and pumpboats depart from Ubay, including to Maasin (3 weekly; 3hr 30min) and Bato (daily; 6hr) on Leyte.

Jagna Oceanjet and Supershuttle ferries run one daily service each to Camiguin Island (2hr). Oceanjet also have a daily service to Cagayan de Oro (4hr 30min) on Mindanao.

Tagbilaran

There are plenty of hotels and lodges in **TAGBILARAN**, the hectic port capital of Bohol, but with so many beaches and sights nearby, there's no real reason to stay here. From Tagbilaran you can be on Panglao Island in less than twenty minutes and even the Chocolate Hills, hidden in the hinterlands, are less than an hour away by road.

Aside from the museum (see opposite), the only sight in Tagbilaran itself is the **Cathedral**, opposite the plaza in Sarmiento Street, a nineteenth-century hulk standing

---

OCTOBER 15, 2013 QUAKE
The whole of Bohol was shaken up by a magnitude 7.2 **earthquake** which struck the island on October 15, 2013. The quake did damage as far away as Cebu City, and on Bohol over two hundred people died and thousands of homes and buildings were destroyed (including the Chocolate Hills Complex and some of the island's beloved Spanish-era churches). While houses and modern buildings are being reconstructed, many of the Spanish churches remain in ruins and for now their future remains unknown.

on the site of an original that was destroyed by fire in 1789. On the edge of town, **Island City Mall** is packed full of shops, cafés and restaurants. The **Tagbilaran City Fiesta** takes place on May 1.

Bohol Museum

Carlos P. Garcia Ave (known as CPG) • Mon–Fri 10am–4.30pm • P10

Set in the former home of Carlos Garcia (the fourth President of the Philippine Republic), the **Bohol Museum** isn't worth a special trip, but if you have some time to kill, the presidential memorabilia and collection of shells are worthy of half an hour's exploration.

6

ARRIVAL AND DEPARTURE   TAGBILARAN

By plane The airport lies less than 2km outside Tagbilaran; tricycles into town cost P50, and taxis are only a little more on the meter.

By boat The ferry pier in Tagbilaran is off Gallares St, a 1km tricycle ride from the city centre. Taxis and vans for hire also wait to meet passengers arriving on ferries.

By bus All bus journeys around the island start at Dao Integrated Terminal, near Island City Mall and the Central Market, 10min outside Tagbilaran by jeepney or tricycle. Buses leave here (every 30min–1hr) for all destinations both clockwise and counter-clockwise around the main coastal road, as well as along the cross-island road via Carmen and the Chocolate Hills.

Destinations Anda (2hr 30min); Baclayon (20min); Bool (10min); Carmen (90min); Jagna (90min); Tubigon (90min); Ubay (4hr).

By taxi, van and tricycle Travel agents and most hotels in Tagbilaran and Panglao can arrange car or van hire, but the cheapest way is to negotiate directly with a taxi which should cost P2000–4000/day, dependent on your destinations. Heading for Panglao, it's not hard to find a taxi, van or tricycle at the airport or pier in Tagbilaran to whisk you across the bridge and out to Panglao. If you negotiate a little you won't pay more than P500 for a taxi to Alona, or P250 for a tricycle.

By jeepney Jeepneys leave from Dao, making trips clockwise and anticlockwise around the coast, but they stop often and become uncomfortably overloaded, so are best used only for short trips (P8 to Baclayon for example).

By motorbike The whole island is accessible by motorbike – a cheap, fun and flexible way to see Bohol. Rentals are easily available in Tagbilaran and Panglao (around P400/day).

INFORMATION AND ACTIVITIES

Tourist information As well as tourist information kiosks at the airport and ferry pier, there is a branch of the Bohol tourism office (Mon–Fri 8am–noon and 1–5pm; ☎038 501 9186, ⓦtourism.bohol.gov.ph) just off Plaza Rizal, on J.S. Torralba St.

Tours and activities For trips into the interior there are a few good travel agencies in Tagbilaran which specialize in adventure and eco-tours. Barkada Tours (☎0920 901 2792, ⓦbarkadatours.blogspot.com) operates from Island Buzz Outdoor Shop on Gallares St and offers mountain bike and hiking trips around Bohol from P1800 per person per day. They can also organize night kayaking trips to see fireflies.

ACCOMMODATION

Dao Diamond Dao, north of Island City Mall ☎038 411 5568, ⓦdaodiamond.com. Away from the hustle of downtown, _Dao Diamond_ has good-value fan and a/c rooms (P1400) with cable TV, fridge and microwave. The hotel is run by the Bohol Deaf Academy and it's easy to learn a little sign language during your stay. There's also a small pool in the grounds. **P975**

Metrocentre Hotel & Convention Centre CPG Ave ☎038 411 2599, ⓦmetrocentrehotel.com. The marbled lobby has a coffee shop with wi-fi, and there's a gym and

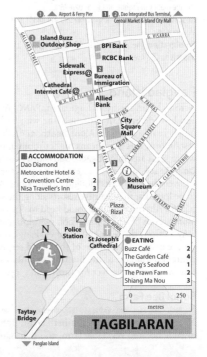

TAGBILARAN

a small pool on the top floor. Rooms are tasteful and comfortable (P1590), all with cable TV and fridge, although the cheapest standard rooms are windowless. The hotel has a well-stocked 24hr convenience store which also sells local handicrafts and *pasalubong*. **P1400**

Nisa Traveller's Inn 14 CPG Ave ☎ 038 412 3731, Ⓦ nisatravellersinn.com. One of the better budget places in town, featuring good doubles with fan and clean bathroom, as well as more expensive a/c rooms (P1000). Rooms at the front are noisy. **P500**

EATING

Buzz Café Island City Mall ☎ 038 510 1822, Ⓦ bohol beefarm.com. Owned by Bohol Bee Farm (see below) and featuring the same exquisite range of fresh dishes as the hotel restaurant, including organic garden salads (P120) and honey-glazed chicken (P160). They also have delicious ginger lemonade (P50) and sell packaged local delicacies. Free wi-fi. Daily 8am–9pm.

★**The Garden Café** Plaza Rizal ☎ 038 411 3701. Established by the Bohol Deaf Academy and providing training for deaf students, this café has a menu mixing Mexican and Filipino dishes (P150–300). You can communicate with the staff in writing, or with sign language (a few basic signs are listed in the menu). Downstairs, tasty mango pies are on sale in the cake shop, and upstairs is a fun-filled Wild West-themed restaurant with moose heads on the wall, wooden booths and cowboy-booted staff. Daily 7am–10pm.

Joving's Seafood By the pier. Immense menu that includes grilled tuna, marlin and lapu-lapu, chilli crab and king prawns. All dishes are served with a hefty mound of steaming hot rice; two people can fill up here for around P500. Next door *MR Seafood* offers similar fare. Daily 10am–10pm.

The Prawn Farm Island City Mall. Surprisingly chic for small-town mall dining, *The Prawn Farm* serves excellent tilapia in lemon butter sauce (P155), and equally tasty prawns in garlic and chilli (P215). Daily 8am–9pm.

Shiang Ma Nou Gallares St ☎ 038 501 0076. Popular and friendly Cantonese restaurant serving dim sum, noodles (P75) and *siomai* (dumplings; P45). As well as the menu items you can also choose from the live seafood display. Meals can be enjoyed in the cool of the a/c interior, or in the outdoor dining area. Daily 10am–10pm.

DIRECTORY

Banks There are plenty of banks with ATMs (including BPI and Metrobank) to be found on CPG Ave. You can also change money in Tagbilaran City Square Mall.

Hospitals The Provincial Hospital (☎ 038 411 4831) is on M. Parras St.

Immigration The Bureau of Immigration (☎ 038 235 6084) is on CPG Ave.

Internet access To get online, try Cathedral Internet Café on M.H. Del Pilar St, or Sidewalk Express around the corner on CPG Ave. Many coffee shops have free wi-fi connection, including Bo's Coffee and Buzz Café in Island City Mall.

Police The police station is near City Hall, behind St Joseph's Cathedral.

Post The post office is on CPG Ave.

Panglao Island

Across the bridge from Tagbilaran, **PANGLAO** boasts beautiful beaches, first-rate diving and historic Spanish churches. The whole island is enjoying increasing popularity, nowhere more so than **Alona Beach**, and while there is now a great choice of hotels and restaurants, this also means higher room and food prices. The best quieter stretches of white sand are **Bolod Beach**, **San Isidro Beach**, **Bikini Beach**, all on the south coast, and **Doljo Beach**, near the westernmost tip of the island.

Given the dive boats filling the coast along Alona, the best sea **swimming** on the island is to be found at the exclusive resorts along the south coast, such as *Bohol Beach Club* (see p.296). Alternatively you could head to one of the quieter north coast beaches at Doljo or **Momo**, both of which have good swimming at certain times of year.

Away from the reefs and beaches, Panglao has two main towns, **Dauis** and **Panglao**, on the east and west sides of the island respectively, both of which hold pretty Spanish churches. The rest of the interior presents a verdant rural pastiche of nipa huts and towering palms, perfect for short walks, cycle rides or touring by motorbike.

Bohol Bee Farm

Dao, Dauis • Daily 8am–5pm • ☎ 038 510 1822, Ⓦ boholbeefarm.com

Near Dao on the island's southern coast, **Bohol Bee Farm** offers the chance to tour an organic bee and vegetable farm, and then sample the delicious produce at the restaurant

DIVING AT PANGLAO

The **reef** at the western end of Panglao, a few minutes by bangka from Alona Beach, has healthy corals, a multitude of reef fish and perpendicular underwater cliffs that drop to a depth of 50m. This is where most of the island's dive sites are, though you can go further afield to **Doljo Point** and **Cervira Shoal**, or use Alona Beach as a base for diving at Cabilao (see p.299). Dives typically cost around P1500 per time, plus equipment, but as always, the more dives you do the cheaper it gets. Dolphins, and sometimes whales, can also be seen off the coast of Panglao. Day-trips also run to the **Balicasag**, a beautiful halo of coral with steep drop-offs to the southwest and **Pamilacan**, a further 22km east, where mantas and whale sharks can be seen between January and April.

DIVE OPERATOR

Sea Explorers ⓦ sea-explorers.com. Sea Explorers are one of the best dive outfits in Alona and have a base at *Alona Vida* resort (see below).

or buy some of the goodies to take home. You can also watch local handicrafts being made here, and even stay the night (see p.296).

ARRIVAL AND DEPARTURE

PANGLAO ISLAND

From Tagbilaran Almost everyone arrives at Alona by van (P500–600) or tricycle (P250) from Tagbilaran port or airport, in which case you'll be dropped as close to your accommodation as possible (you'll need to walk to get to some of the beach cottages).

From elsewhere in Bohol Coming from elsewhere in Bohol you might arrive via Dao Integrated Terminal, from where there are jeepneys and buses to Panglao. These services will drop you on the main road from where it's a 5min walk down to the beach.

INFORMATION AND TOURS

Tourist information The tourist centre in Alona (daily 9am–9pm), really just a glorified shop, is near the beach opposite the *Alona Kew* restaurant. In case of any trouble, head for the tourist assistance centre, near Graziella.

Tours Seashine Tours (☎ 038 502 9038, ⓔ seashinetravel @yahoo.com), next to the tourist information centre, can book all ferry tickets, as well as arrange day-trips around Bohol, van hire and boat trips (P1500–2500 for a boat for the day).

ACCOMMODATION

Hotel prices have gone skywards in **Alona**, and there are hardly any budget options actually on the beach, but if you don't mind a short walk to the sea, there are still a few cheapies out there. For those who prefer to be away from the Alona buzz, there are some fantastic resorts dotted **around Panglao**, although most are in the mid-range to high price bracket.

ALONA BEACH

Alona Grove Tourist Inn Set back from the western end of the beach ☎ 038 502 4200. One of a number of small budget resorts at the western end of the beach, *Alona Grove* has simple huts, some with a/c, fridge and cable TV. P700

Alona Tropical Beach Resort Eastern end of the beach ☎ 038 502 9024, ⓦ alonatropicalbeachresort .com. One of the better big resorts, with a wide selection of rooms spread along a quiet section of beach and up the hillside behind. Beachfront fan bungalows (P5000) are way overpriced, but the budget fan rooms still have sea views and are far better value. There are also a/c rooms (P2980) with cable TV and hot water, plus a decent pool up the hill, and free wi-fi at reception and the beach bar. Wildlife lovers won't enjoy the sight of caged birds in the tropical gardens though. P1320

Alona Vida Beach Resort Halfway between the main access road and the eastern end of the beach ☎ 038 502 9180, ⓦ alonavida.com. Excellent rooms decorated in

earthy tones just a few metres back from the beach. Deluxe and superior rooms come with fridges, mini-bars, kettles, safety deposit boxes and room service, plus there's one budget room but it's a little too close for comfort to the lively *Coco Vida* bar. There's also the Sea Explorers dive centre on site (see box above), plus a nice pool and free wi-fi throughout. P3000

★ **Charts Resort** By the turn-off for Ester Lim St ☎ 038 502 9095, ⓦ charts-alona.com. A beautifully designed boutique resort, *Charts* is intimate, well managed, and has some of the most tasteful rooms on the island, set around a compact garden with a dolphin-shaped pool. Standard rooms come with a double bed, while the luxurious suite has an expansive roof terrace, and there's also one budget "Flashpacker" room (P1500) by the chill-out bar. The upstairs arts café showcases works by local artists and there's also a small handicrafts store near the reception. The only downsides are that it's not on the beach, and there can be a little road noise. Free wi-fi. P3500

▲ Tagbilaran

ALONA BEACH

■ ACCOMMODATION

Alona Grove Tourist Inn	8
Alona Tropical Beach Resort	5
Alona Vida Beach Resort	7
Charts Resort	1
Citadel Alona Inn	2
Flower Garden Resort	3
Paragayo Resort	4
Peter's House	6

● EATING & DRINKING

Buzz Café	7
Charts	1
Graziella	5
Hayahay	6
Helmut's Place	2
Jugali's Bistro	4
Le Rendez-Vous	3

ESTERLIM STREET

Jad-ski

BPI ATM

Tourist
Assistance Center

Alona
Kew

Oops
Bar

Seashine
Tours

Panglao Bay

N

0   200
metres

Citadel Alona Inn On the main road ☎ 038 502 9424, ⓦ citadelalona.com. An interesting budget option with simple but stylish, brightly painted rooms spread through a large house. There are various sizes of standard rooms, plus family rooms, but none of them have en-suite bathrooms. The shared facilities are clean, and there's also a communal kitchen, wi-fi and a small café with local artwork on display. **P750**

★ **Flower Garden Resort** Ester Lim St ☎ 038 502 9012, ⓦ flowergarden-resort.com. Efficiently managed by a resident Swiss, this wonderful little resort has pretty chalet-style houses and spacious bungalows, plus a pool, all set in tropical gardens a short stroll inland from the beach. All rooms have a/c, cable TV, fridge and kitchen facilities, plus wi-fi access on balconies. Excellent value. **P1700**

Paragayo Resort On the main road through town, next to Jad-ski ☎ 038 502 4043, ⓦ paragayoresort.com. A new budget option with clean, comfortable rooms set around pretty gardens just off the main road, but not too noisy. There's free wi-fi in the lobby, plenty of good restaurants nearby, and the beach is a 5min walk away. **P1200**

Peter's House Eastern end of the beach ☎ 038 502 9056, ⓦ genesisdivers.com. One of the last genuine budget options right on the beach, Peter's has simple and cosy nipa rooms above the bar. Owned by Genesis Divers, the hotel has an in-house divers-only policy during peak season. **P500**

BOLOD BEACH

Amarela Brgy Libaong, western part of Bolod Beach ☎ 038 502 9497, ⓦ amarelaresort.com. Perched on top of a hill looking out to the inviting sea, *Amarela* is an intimate, sophisticated hideaway with stylish rooms and good amenities. Heavy wood furnishings define the rooms, all of which have a/c, balconies, hot showers, cable TV and DVD players. The popular restaurant has wi-fi and enjoys wonderful views, and from here steps lead down to a pretty stretch of white beach, plus there's a pool. **P6000**

Bohol Beach Club Bolod Beach ☎ 038 502 9222, ⓦ boholbeachclub.com.ph. Large resort split into two wings named after the Philippines' two monsoons, "Habagat" with recently renovated native-style cottage blocks, some with sea views, and the plusher "Amihan" boasting more elegant rooms surrounding two swimming pools, with a few grand suites fronting the beach. There's free wi-fi in the business centre, but you need to pay to use it in your room. Watersports are also on offer, along with a range of other facilities and services. Day visitors can use the beach and pool for P500 (all but P150 of which is consumable). **P8000**

Bohol Bee Farm Dao, Dauis ☎ 038 502 2288, ⓦ bohol beefarm.com. As the name suggests this place offers the unique opportunity to stay on a local bee farm. As well as getting to enjoy the farm's organic produce in the excellent restaurant, overnight guests are given a complimentary tour. Comfortable cottages with a/c, cable TV and hot water are dotted throughout the property and there's also a pool and oceanside swimming platform. Free wi-fi in the lobby, and the store sells organic goodies and handicrafts produced here. **P3000**

ELSEWHERE ON THE ISLAND
The Bellevue Resort Doljo Beach ☎038 422 2222, ⓦthebellevue.com. Panglao's newest big player, *The Bellevue* has firmly planted sleepy Doljo Beach on the map. The hotel features a huge beachfront pool and super comfortable rooms, with breathtaking sea views from the balcony, and is less than 50m from a beautiful stretch of white sand that's nowhere near as busy as Alona Beach. **P5800**

Panglao Island Nature Resort Near Dauis, on the island's north coast ☎038 501 7288, ⓦpanglaoisland.com. Upmarket resort that can be reached by taxi from Tagbilaran in 20min. Spacious villas are either on the beach or in a quiet garden, all with large *lanai* (veranda). A good restaurant, large swimming pool, gym and massage are also available. Breakfast, dinner and Tagbilaran transfers are included in the price. **P10,175**

6

EATING AND DRINKING

In Alona itself, there is a good selection of **restaurants**, both on the beach and along the road into town. Many of the beachside places set up tables and chairs on the sand which make the perfect spot for a sunset beer, whether or not you choose to dine there. **Nightlife** mainly revolves around resort and dive-shop bars (*Coco Vida* – at *Alona Vida* – and *Oops*, next door, are both popular), but there are a few independent places by the beach turn-off.

ALONA BEACH
Buzz Café 100m west of Alona Kew Resort ☎038 510 1822, ⓦboholbeefarm.com. Owned by Bohol Bee Farm (see p.294), this is a great addition to Alona's café line-up and serves excellent mango pancakes with bacon and eggs, along with regulars from the farm menu. The second-floor restaurant looks out over the beach and they sell packaged local delicacies downstairs. Free wi-fi. Daily 8am–9pm.

Charts By the turn-off for Ester Lim St ☎038 502 9095, ⓦcharts-alona.com. Lovely daytime café where you can get a decent cup of coffee while looking at local artwork. Daily 7am–6pm.

★Graziella On the main road to the beach ☎0920 561 6169. Previously known as *Kamalig*, this Italian-owned restaurant continues to turn out the best pasta on the island with a delicious carbonara (P235). Beef carpaccio (P215), *caffè carretto* (with amaretto) and Italian house wine are also on the menu. Tues–Sun 6–10pm.

Hayahay Eastern part of the beach ☎038 502 9288, ⓦhayahay.net/restaurant.html. *Hayahay* serves a mean

pizza (try the Balicasag with salmon and tuna, P240) right on the beach. Daily 7am–midnight.

Helmut's Place On the corner of the main road turn-off to Alona Beach. Owned by a German biker, this enduringly popular bar has friendly service, live sports, a pool table, plus decent European food. Daily 10am–2am.

Jugali's Bistro On the main road to the beach ☎0929 410 3189, ⓦjugalis-bohol.com. Owned by a German chef and named for his sons, *Jugali's* is a modest-looking place which serves fantastic food using super-fresh ingredients. Top choices include lapu-lapu in potato crust with buttered vegetables (P390) and mango chicken (P300). In the morning the heavy-duty breakfast (P330) packs enough Brazilian beef strip, potatoes, onion and egg to see you through until dinner. There's also free wi-fi for customers. Daily 7am–11pm.

Le Rendez-Vous On the main road by the turn-off to the beach ☎038 503 8328. One of a new breed of trendy places to eat in Alona, French-owned *Rendez-Vous* serves healthy breakfasts (P40–200), panini, salads, aged cheeses and has a decent wine list. Daily 7am–10.45pm.

DIRECTORY

Banks There's a BPI ATM next to *Jugali's* in Alona, but don't count on it having cash. There are also plenty of places to change money in Alona – Jad-ski, a small shop on the main road, offers competitive rates.

Internet There's internet available at Alona's tourist

centre for P60/hr. Many beach resorts and restaurants also have wi-fi for customers.

Laundry Laundry can be done at Dada's, next to the tourist centre in Alona.

The interior

Apart from the famous Chocolate Hills, Bohol's **interior** hosts a range of sights worth exploring. Take your pick from historic churches (some of which were damaged by the 2013 quake), markets, waterfalls, tiny tarsiers and a jungle adventure camp.

Antequera Market

Sun 7am–noon • Bus, jeepney or taxi from Tagbilaran, or visit as part of a day-trip (from P2000 for a vehicle)

A number of resorts offer half-day trips to the town of **ANTEQUERA**, 15km north of Tagbilaran, to see the lively Sunday **market**. Craftsmen and traders from around the island congregate to sell locally made handicrafts such as baskets, hats and various home decor items like linen tablecloths, mirrors and attractive bowls made from stone or coconut shells. Prices are significantly cheaper than in the cities and it's a fun place to haggle and pick up a few inexpensive souvenirs.

The Tarsier Visitors Center

Tues–Sat 9am–4pm • P50 • Hiking guides P500 per group of two for 4hr • ☎ 0927 541 2290, ⓦ tarsierfoundation.org • No flash photography • Bus or jeepney (P25) from Tagbilaran to Corella and then a tricycle for the last 4km, or stay on the bus towards Sikatuna and ask to be dropped at the entrance from where it's a 500m walk to the sanctuary; alternatively you can visit as part of a day-trip

Ten kilometres northeast of Tagbilaran, the **Tarsier Visitors Center** is dedicated to protecting what is left of the native population of tarsiers, cuddly saucer-eyed creatures you will see on posters throughout the country. Often mistakenly referred to as the world's smallest monkey, the **tarsier** – all 10–15cm of it – is more closely related to the lemur, loris and bushbaby and has been around for a staggering 45 million years.

It is also possible to do **jungle hikes** from the centre. Knowledgeable **guides** at the centre can usually lead visitors to their favourite haunts, though spotting them among the thick foliage is difficult during the day when these nocturnal creatures rarely move. When they are awake they study visitors with wide-eyed curiosity, sometimes swivelling their heads a disconcerting 180 degrees to get a better look. Night hikes (6–8pm) offer the chance to see more wildlife, but need to be scheduled two to three days in advance.

The Loboc River

Private boats cost P600 for the return trip (1hr); all-you-can-eat floating barge buffet P350 per person • Loboc Riverwatch (☎ 038 537 9460) is one of the most professional outfits

Eleven kilometres east of Corella, the town of **Loboc** is the starting point for **boat trips** along the jungly **Loboc River** to **Tontonan Falls**. Whichever way you choose to cruise, it's a pretty journey past idyllic villages, green paddies, twisted roots and towering palms. After rounding a bend you approach the falls themselves, which are attractive, but not breathtaking. Some boat operators offer photo opportunities with captive tarsiers – note that this is illegal (visit the Tarsier Visitors Center instead).

Simply Butterflies

Bilar • Daily 8am–4.30pm • P40 • ☎ 038 535 9400, ⓦ simplybutterfliesproject.com

Halfway between Loboc and Carmen, **Simply Butterflies** is a well-run butterfly sanctuary with over 150 different types of lepidopterans. The ticket price includes a guided tour, and night safaris to spot nocturnal wildlife can be organized, including of course, the tarsier. It's also possible to stay and eat here (see opposite).

The Chocolate Hills

Chocolate Hills Adventure Park P60 • ☎ 0932 667 7098 • To get to the Chocolate Hills Adventure Park or Complex independently take a bus to Carmen (hourly; 90min; P60) from the Dao terminal in Tagbilaran, and then hop on a habal-habal (around P50) • **Sagbayan Peak** P20 • Bus from Tagbilaran to Sagbayan town, then rent a motorbike or walk to the peak complex

Renowned throughout the Philippines, the surreal **Chocolate Hills** are one of the country's biggest tourist attractions. Some geologists believe that these unique 40m mounds – there are said to be 1268 of them if you care to count – were formed from deposits of coral and limestone sculpted by centuries of erosion. Most locals, however, will tell you that the hills are the calcified tears of a broken-hearted giant; others prefer the idea that they were left by a giant carabao with distressed bowels. What you think of the hills will depend largely on the time you visit. During the glare of the day the light casts harsh shadows and the hills lose their definition. But at **dawn or dusk** they look splendid, especially during the dry season (Dec–May) when the scrub vegetation that covers the hills is roasted brown, and they really do resemble endless rows of chocolate drops.

Previously most visitors headed for the **Chocolate Hills Complex**, but this was badly damaged by the October 2013 quake and remained closed at the time of writing. In the meanwhile the **Chocolate Hills Adventure Park** offers vistas, plus a host of attractions and activities, including a canopy walkway, a high-rope challenge course and even a bike zip-line.

For a different view of the Chocolate Hills, exploring the backroads by motorbike, bike or on foot is definitely worthwhile; contact Barkada Tours (see p.293) for hiking or biking trips. Alternatively you could head to **Sagbayan Peak**, northwest of Carmen, where there's another tourist complex which offers closer-up, quieter views.

6

Danao Adventure Park

Entry P25, river tubing P200, "plunge" P700, climbing P400–600, caving P350, kayaking P200, quad biking P1800/hr • ☎ 0921 759 4403, ⓦ eatdanao.com • The easiest and quickest way to get here is to arrange a car and driver through your resort (around P3000 return); alternatively, take a bus from Tagbilaran to Danao (or Sagbayan, where you'll need to change buses), where you can charter a tricycle (P100)

A few kilometres from the small town of Danao, north of the Chocolate Hills, **Danao Adventure Park** occupies an area of rugged jungle-covered massif cut by deep valleys. Established in 2006, the park has become the centre for outdoors pursuits in Bohol, offering everything from river tubing to the white-knuckle inducing "plunge", which involves being lowered down a cliff on a rope and pendulum swung across the canyon. You can also try climbing, caving, kayaking and quad biking.

ACCOMMODATION AND EATING   THE INTERIOR

Danao Adventure Park 2km from Danao ☎ 0921 759 4403, ⓦ eatdanao.com. There's a canteen and four simple but spacious fan rooms, plus four smaller a/c rooms (P1000) at the centre, or you can camp if arranged in advance. **P600**

Nuts Huts 2km north of Loboc ☎ 0920 846 1559, ⓦ nutshuts.org. Run by two friendly Belgians, this resort's cottages are basic but charming and have balconies with river views. There are also simple dorms with mosquito nets. The outdoor restaurant is perched on a hill with views down the valley across a dense green canopy of rainforest. Activities on offer include rafting, trekking or mountain biking. The easiest way to get here is to charter a boat from the Sarimanok Boat Company (P100/person) in Loboc for the 10min trip to the resort. Dorm **300–400**, double **P600**

Simply Butterflies Bilar ☎ 038 535 9400, ⓦ simply butterfliesproject.com. The butterfly sanctuary has dorm beds and a few native-style cottages set in the pretty gardens, plus delicious local snacks and meals (including home-made ice cream). **P250**, double **P850**

The west and north coasts

Bohol's pretty northwest coast is lined with mangroves and dotted with Spanish-era ruins, and is also the access point for the dive sites of **Cabilao Island**. Further north, **Tubigon** has fast craft to Cebu (see p.292), while on the opposite side of Bohol to Tagbilaran, the dull agricultural town of **Ubay** has transport connections to Leyte (see p.292).

Maribojoc

Take a bus or jeepney from Tagbilaran

The pretty coastal town of **MARIBOJOC** lies just 14km from Tagbilaran. The town is the site of the old Spanish **Punta Cruz watchtower**, one of a number of old watchtowers of note on Bohol. Once a lookout for marauding pirates, Punta Cruz is now a viewing deck from where you can gaze across to Cebu and Siquijor. The town's Santa Cruz church was completely destroyed by the 2013 quake.

Cabilao Island

Bus to Loon and then change to a jeepney (P10) for Mocpoc pier on Sandingan Island; bangkas from Mocpoc to Cabilao cost P20 (20min)

The pretty little island of **Cabilao** has a handful of modest but very comfortable resorts aimed largely at divers. These resorts can arrange trips to local dive sites such as the **Wall at Cambaquiz**, where there are turtles and baby sharks, and **Shark View Point**, where one of the attractions – apart from sharks – is pygmy sea horses.

Lapinig

Just offshore from Ubay, the undeveloped island of **Lapinig** offers some good diving, some of it extreme in subterranean caves. To explore you can rent a bangka for the day at the small pier in Ubay, but the easiest way to dive here is to arrange a trip through one of the dive operators in Panglao.

ACCOMMODATION **THE WEST AND NORTH COASTS**

CABILAO ISLAND

Polaris Dive Centre On the main beach on the island's northwest coast ☏ 0918 903 7187, ⓦ polaris-dive.com. A choice of cottages ranging from simple wooden tree-houses to more substantial a/c doubles, bungalows and family houses. P1800

Vida Amorosa Cambaquiz, on the island's northeast coast ☏ 032 234 0245, ⓦ sea-explorers.com. Formerly the *Cabilao Beach Club*, *Vida Amorosa* offers quality lodgings at a range of budgets. The economy rooms are out the back, while deluxe a/c rooms (P4700) sit atop a small cliff looking out over the ocean. There's also a popular beach bar. P2900

The south coast

Aside from the beautiful beaches and diving at **Anda**, and a few Spanish ruins, the south coast has little to offer travellers aside from transport options from the typically busy little port town of **Jagna** to Camiguin Island and Mindanao (see p.292). Buses run along the coastal road to all of the destinations below.

Bool

Some 5km east of Tagbilaran, the coastal fishing town of **BOOL** is said to be the oldest settlement on the island. It's also the location of the **Blood Compact Site**, marked by an attractive bronze sculpture on the seafront. This is the spot where local chieftain Rajah Sikatuna and Miguel López de Legazpi concluded an early round of Philippine–Spanish hostilities in 1565 by signing a compact in blood. Every year for one week in July, Boholanos gather in Bool for the **Sandugo** (One Blood) **festival** which, apart from the usual beauty pageants and roast pig, includes a passionate re-enactment of the blood ceremony.

Baclayon Church

About 2km east of Bool, **BACLAYON** is the site of **Baclayon Church**, the oldest stone church in the Philippines, which was badly damaged by the 2013 quake. Much of the newer Augustinian facade collapsed, along with the upper half of the bell tower. The rest dates back to 1595 and was declared a national historical landmark in 1995. Until the quake the church's convent functioned as an intriguing **ecclesiastical museum** housing a number of priceless religious icons, although this remained closed at the time of writing.

Anda and around

Buses run from Tagbilaran (3hr)

Around 100km east of Tagbilaran, the countless white sand coves near the town of **ANDA**, in beautiful Guindulman Bay, are an emerging choice for those looking to escape Panglao's commercialized beach and dive scene. Most of the resorts which have popped up in recent years are mid-range to high end, although there are also a few budget options. Offshore, **Lamanok Island**'s hematite cave paintings add credence to Anda's claim as the "cradle of Boholano culture", while on land there are several caves offering clear-water swimming – **Kabagno Cave** has a 6m-deep pool, but you'll need to hire a ladder (P10) from the neighbouring house to get out.

ACCOMMODATION **THE SOUTH COAST**

ANDA

Anda White Beach Resort Northern end of the beach ☏ 0917 700 0507, ⓦ andabeachresort.com. For pure beach lovers, this place can't be beaten, with attractive rooms, the best of which front onto a bright white strip of sand. There's also a pool, billiards and wi-fi (P100/hr). P4400

Blue Star Dive and Resort 1km north of the market ☎0949 733 4583, ⓦbluestardive.com. British-owned *Blue Star* stands out for divers and has a good dive centre, pool, wi-fi, a tiny beach at low tide and good snorkelling on the house reef. Both a/c and fan rooms are spacious and tastefully designed and the latter have lovely views out over the bay. **P4900**

La Petra Beach Resort A 2min walk from Anda's White Beach ☎038 331 1316, ⓦlapetraresort.com.

One of the few more moderately priced options in Anda. Standard rooms are in a nondescript concrete block (P3300), but the cheaper nipa fan huts look right over the beach. There's a minimum two-nights advance booking, but once you've seen the beach, had a swim in the pool and enjoyed a meal at the restaurant, it's not a difficult feat to do the same again the following day. Travellers holding a copy of this guide get a fity percent discount on their fourth night and beyond. **P2950**

6

Siquijor

Small, laidback **SIQUIJOR** lies between the islands of Cebu, Negros and Bohol and makes a worthwhile stop on a southern itinerary. Very little is known about the island and its inhabitants before the arrival of the Spanish in the sixteenth century, who named it the Isla del Fuego ("Island of Fire") because of the eerie luminescence generated by swarms of fireflies. This sense of mystery still persists today, with many Filipinos believing Siquijor to be a centre of **witchcraft** (see box, p.302). Shamans aside, the island is peaceful, picturesque and a pleasure to tour, whether by bike, tricycle, motorbike or jeepney – the entire 72km coastal road is paved (a rare delight in the Philippines) and traffic is light. The **beaches** alone make it worth a visit, but there are also **mountain trails**, waterfalls and old churches to explore as well as decent scuba diving. The island was shaken by the October 2013 quake (see box, p.292), but while many roads and buildings were damaged, only one life was lost.

Most places to stay are within half an hour of the port towns of **Siquijor** and **Larena**, notably around **San Juan**, south of Siquijor, and at **Sandugan**, north of Larena. A

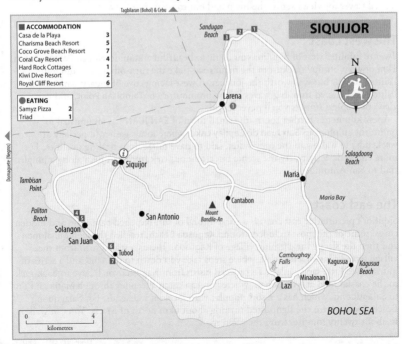

Tagbilaran (Bohol) & Cebu

SIQUIJOR

N

■ ACCOMMODATION
Casa de la Playa	3
Charisma Beach Resort	5
Coco Grove Beach Resort	7
Coral Cay Resort	4
Hard Rock Cottages	1
Kiwi Dive Resort	2
Royal Cliff Resort	6

● EATING
| Samyz Pizza | 2 |
| Triad | 1 |

Dumaguete (Negros)

Sandugan Beach

Larena

Siquijor

Tambisan Point

Paliton Beach

Solangon
San Juan

Tubod

San Antonio

Mount Bandila-An

Cantabon

Maria

Salagdoong Beach

Maria Bay

Cambughay Falls

Lazi

Minalonan

Kagusua

Kagusua Beach

BOHOL SEA

0   4
kilometres

6

SORCERORS ON SIQUIJOR

Every Good Friday herbalists from around Siquijor and from the rest of the Visayas and Mindanao gather in **San Antonio**, in Siquijor's pea-green hinterlands, to prepare potions made from tree bark, roots, herbs and insects. The culmination of this annual Conference of Sorcerers and Healers – now rebranded the **Folk Healing Festival** because it sounds less menacing – is the mixing of a mother-of-all potions in a large cauldron. As the mixture is stirred, participants gather in a circle and mumble incantations said to imbue it with extraordinary healing powers (the ceremony takes place on Good Friday in the belief that on Christ's day of death, supernatural forces are free to wander the earth). It's evidently a strong brew, with wide-ranging powers that include provoking a good harvest, securing a spouse or getting rid of that troublesome zit. The festival attracts spiritualists and tourists from across the Philippines and beyond – be sure to book your accommodation long in advance if you plan to visit.

---

number of resorts have certified **dive operators** who will take you on trips to places such as Sandugan Point and Tambisan Point, both known for their coral and abundant marine life. At Paliton Beach there are three submarine caves where you can see sleeping reef sharks and at Salag-Doong Beach, on the eastern side of the island, divers have occasionally reported seeing manta rays and shoals of barracuda. Further afield but still within easy reach, Apo Island (see p.320) is another dive favourite, and is worth a visit even if you stay above water.

Siquijor Town

SIQUIJOR TOWN is a likeable enough place though without anything to keep you there for long. There is an atmospheric eighteenth-century church on the seafront, the **Church of St Francis of Assisi**, which was built in 1783 partly from coral. You can climb its bell tower for views across the town and out to sea.

The west coast

Twenty minutes west of Siquijor you come to beautiful and undeveloped **Paliton Beach**, 1km down a bumpy track from the main road (take the turn-off at the church in Paliton Town), but well worth the journey. A west-facing cove of sugary-white sand, Paliton is sheltered from big waves by the promontory of **Tambisan Point**, and has views of tropical sunsets you'll never forget.

A few kilometres further south, the small town of **SAN JUAN** has an unusual focal point: the sulphurous **San Juan de Capilay Lake**, where locals gather (especially at weekends) to wallow in the eggy water, said to have miraculous healing qualities. For more energetic activity, try the scenic but strenuous trek from San Juan along a jungled trail to San Antonio.

The east coast

Siquijor's picturesque east coast is a rural littoral of sun-bleached barangays and hidden coves, some of the most secluded around **Kagusua Beach**, reached through **Minalonan** and then the sleepy little fishing village of **Kagusua**. There's a sealed road from the village to the edge of a low cliff, where steps take you down to the sand and a series of immaculate little sandy inlets. To proceed north from Kagusua you'll have to backtrack to the coastal road at Minalonan, where you can catch a jeepney through **Maria** and on to **Salagdoong**, which has a resort popular with locals at weekends. For Salagdoong Beach, look out for the signposted turning about 6km north of Maria. You can walk it in about twenty minutes from the main road.

CAMBUGHAY FALLS (P.304) >

Heading to Minalonan from the west you'll pass through **Lazi**, with its delightful nineteenth-century church built of coral and stone and right opposite it, the oldest convent in the Philippines, a low-rise wooden building now sagging with age but still beautiful. A few kilometres inland from Lazi, **Cambughay Falls** are the island's most accessible and popular waterfalls. Steep steps lead down to the pretty falls which are a pleasant spot for a picnic or a swim.

Larena and around

Some slower ferries arrive at the port of **LARENA**, from where the beaches of Sandugan are only a brief jeepney or tricycle ride to the north. From the pier it's just a short walk to the town centre, which has a town hall, plaza and church, but not much else. There are a couple of basic lodges in Larena, but with plentiful jeepneys and tricycles to nearby Sandugan, there's really no need to stay.

Sandugan

Six kilometres northeast of Larena is the village of **SANDUGAN**, where there's a beach and a number of resorts, one with professional **scuba-diving** facilities. To reach the beach, take a tricycle or jeepney from Larena to Sandugan and then negotiate the rutted path that leads to the shore. All the tricycle drivers know it, so you won't get lost.

Mount Bandila-an

You can enquire about guides at the tourism assistance centre in Siquijor Town, although many resorts can also offer advice and arrange for a local to show you the way • Access is via either the village of Cantabon (take a tricycle or jeepney from Larena), or Cangmonag in the south

At 628m, **Mount Bandila-an** is Siquijor's highest point and accessible to anyone reasonably fit. It lies at the centre of the island in an area still recovering from damage inflicted during World War II, when acres of forest were razed by retreating Japanese troops. Now the entire area is part of the Siquijor Reforestation Project and while rehabilitation is not yet complete, wildlife such as the leopard cat and long-tailed macaque survive.

Mount Bandila-an can be climbed in a day, and you'll need a guide. On the way to the peak you'll pass the **Stations of the Cross**, where a solemn religious procession re-enacting the Passion of Christ is held every Easter, and there are a number of springs and caves. Ask the guide to point out the huge old **balete tree** at the side of the trail, said to be home to spirits, imps and guardians of the forest. To ask their permission to pass, the polite thing to say is *tabi tabi lang-po*, which means "excuse me, please step aside".

ARRIVAL AND DEPARTURE
SIQUIJOR

By boat Siquijor is not accessible by plane, but between Delta (☎035 225 3128), GL Shipping Lines (☎035 480 5534) and Oceanjet (☎032 255 7560 in Cebu, ⓦoceanjet .net) there are up to six fast ferry connections from Dumaguete to Siquijor Town (daily 6am–3pm; 45min). Oceanjet also has a combined service from Cebu to Tagbilaran, then Dumaguete and finally on to Siquijor Town (4hr 50min). A few slower Montenegro Lines (☎032 238 5820 in Cebu, ⓦmontenegrolines.com.ph) and F.J. Palacio Lines (☎032 253 7700 in Cebu) ferries run from Dumaguete and Tagbilaran to Larena (3hr). Onwards boat tickets can be arranged through most resorts or directly at Siquijor Town and Larena piers.

INFORMATION

SIQUIJOR TOWN
Tourist information There's a tourism assistance centre (Mon–Fri 8am–noon & 1–5pm) at the pier in Siquijor Town which has a few maps and brochures and can also help arrange transport and guides.
Services There are a few small internet cafés, including the intriguingly named Melbon Rub.

LARENA AND AROUND
Services Larena has a post office and an Allied Bank with an ATM. You can get online in Larena at Mykel's Internet, next to the pension of the same name.

GETTING AROUND

If you've booked accommodation in advance, you may get a free pick-up from your port of arrival; otherwise there are tricycles from the main port of Siquijor, and jeepneys from Larena. You could also arrange a tour through your resort.

By motorbike Renting a motorbike (or bicycle) is the cheapest and best way to get around the island. Motorbikes can be rented for around P400/day from many resorts, or at Scandinavian Rent-A-Motorbike

(☎0939 640 5132) on the National Highway in Siquijor Town.

By bangka To take you along the coast by sea, bangkas can be chartered in Larena, Siquijor Town and Lazi.

ACCOMMODATION AND EATING

SIQUIJOR TOWN

The main drag in Siquijor Town, Rizal St, is chock-a-block with cheap canteens and bakeries selling fresh *pan de sal*.

Samyz Pizza Mabini St. This is a pleasant enough place to while away time if you find yourself waiting for a ferry, and does okay pizza. Daily 11am–8pm.

THE WEST COAST

Charisma Beach Resort Solangon, 3km west of San Juan ☎0929 807 0515, ⓦcharismabeachresort.com. British-owned place with dorm beds, simple rooms right on the beach and spick-and-span, white, motel-style rooms arranged around a swimming pool (P1750–2500). Dorm P350, double P1400

★**Coco Grove Beach Resort** Tubod, 3km east of San Juan ☎035 481 5008, ⓦcocogroveresort.com. By far the island's most luxurious resort, Australian-owned *Coco Grove* occupies a prime stretch of palm-fringed beach. Rooms range from modest but tasteful standards to newer executive suites and luxury villas, all of which have a/c. There are two restaurants, two pools, a swim-up bar, dive centre, kayaks, massage and wi-fi, among other amenities. The resort also runs daily dive trips to Apo Island (where *Apo Island Beach Resort* is under the same ownership; see box, p.320). P2700

Coral Cay Resort Solangon Beach, 3km to the west of San Juan ☎0919 269 1269, ⓦcoralcayresort.com. This resort is owned by an expat and his Filipina wife. Accommodation ranges from clean, simple rooms with fan and cold shower to spacious a/c cottages with a small living area and separate bedroom (P3450). The restaurant menu is surprisingly urbane for such an isolated place, featuring coq au vin and Australian Chardonnay. Jeepney tours, trekking, scuba diving, mountain bikes and anything else you care to ask for can all be arranged. P1000

Royal Cliff Resort Close to Coco Grove, Tubod ☎035 481 5038, ⓦroyal-cliff-resort.de.tf. As its name

THE WEST COAST

suggests, this laidback resort sits on coral cliffs overlooking a tiny stretch of beach lapped by glass-clear water. Simple rooms are spread through a lovely garden and the restaurant looks out over the sea. P980

LARENA AND AROUND

Casa de la Playa Sandugan ☎035 377 2291, ⓦsiquijor casa.com. Owners Terry and Emily have established a New Age tropical spa that offers yoga sessions, food made with organic vegetables from the resort's own garden and even massages from a local shaman. Accommodation is in a range of lovingly built fan and a/c huts and houses (P1100–2400); some are set back from the shore in a pretty garden bursting with frangipani and white *sampaguita* blossom, while others are on the beach and have sea views. P1100

Hard Rock Cottages 2km east of Sandugan ☎0926 278 6070, ⓦhardrockcottages.com. Four very simple cottages in a lovely, quiet spot overlooking the ocean. Two of the cottages are on the clifftop, while the other two are down by the sea. There's a small bar and restaurant here. P1200

Kiwi Dive Resort At the eastern end of Sandugan Beach (turn right at the end of the path) ☎035 424 0534, ⓦkiwidiveresort.com. Pleasant, small-scale resort with attractive stone cottages on a low hill overlooking a private cove, all with bathrooms and the better ones with solar hot water (P1090). Omelettes, nourishing stews, curry, fish, spaghetti and vegetarian dishes are some of the tasty options available at the restaurant. One of the owners is a dive instructor and can organize trips to nearby sites. They also have wi-fi and rent out mountain bikes (P275/day) and motorbikes (P590/day). P450

Triad Restaurant Larena ☎0917 321 2124. Perched atop a hill a short ride from Larena, *Triad* offers tasty food and expansive views over the coast. Dishes on offer include buttered shrimp (P270), *lechon kawali* (P90) and pancit (P95). Daily 10am–9pm.

Negros

The island of **NEGROS**, fourth largest in the country and home to 3.5 million people, lies at the heart of the Visayas, between Panay to the west and Cebu to the east. Shaped like a boot, it's split diagonally into the northwestern province of Negros Occidental and the southeastern province of Negros Oriental. The demarcation came when early missionaries decided the thickly jungled central mountain range was too formidable to cross, and is still felt today with each side of the island speaking different languages – Cebuano to the east and Ilonggo to the west.

Today Negros is known as "Sugarlandia", its rich lowlands growing two-thirds of the nation's sugar cane, and you'll see evidence of this in the vast silver-green expanse of sugar-cane plantations stretching from the Gulf of Panay across to the gentle foothills off the volcanic mountains of the interior and beyond. The mountains rise to a giddy 2465m at the peak of **Mount Kanlaon**, the highest mountain in the Visayas. For the intrepid this means there's some extreme trekking and climbing on Negros, from Mount Kanlaon itself to **Mount Silay** in the north.

From **Bacolod**, the capital of Negros Occidental, you can follow the coastal road clockwise to **Silay**, a beautifully preserved sugar town with grand antique homes and old sugar locomotives. Much of the north coast is given over to the port towns through which sugar is shipped to Manila, but at the southern end of the island around **Dumaguete** there are good beaches and scuba diving, with a range of excellent budget accommodation. The **southwest coast** – the heel of the boot – is home to the island's

THE BITTER HISTORY OF SUGAR IN NEGROS

Land reform – or the lack of it – has been at the root of simmering discontent on Negros that began in the 1970s under Ferdinand Marcos and continues to this day. All of Negros's sugar-producing land is held by two percent of the people and half the arable land by five percent. Negros's gentry see the land as a way of life, while the Church, the New People's Army (NPA; see p.445) and various peasant organizations see it as a source of food. The NPA has been screaming about land reform for years, intimidating *hacienderos* and seizing land. The *hacienderos* have responded with private armies and acts of repression, turning Negros into a battleground for the struggle between rich and poor, in which the rich have all the guns.

In the 1970s and 1980s this struggle was played out against the background of Ferdinand Marcos's thieving dictatorship. Marcos monopolized sugar trading, placing it in the hands of crony **Roberto Benedicto**, who ended up controlling 106 sugar farms, 85 corporations, 17 radio stations, 16 television stations, a Manila casino, a *Holiday Inn* and a major piece of the national oil company. Known as the Sugar Czar, he effectively controlled the supply chain, allowing him to steal tens of millions of dollars from his neighbours on Negros by paying them a quarter of the price he received when he resold their sugar. For good measure Marcos gave him control of the bank that was the planters' principal lending agency.

In 1974, as prices of sugar on the world market rose steadily, Benedicto began hoarding, speculating that the price would continue to rise. When sugar prices plummeted in 1984, Benedicto responded by paying planters less for their sugar than it cost to grow. The planters took their land out of cultivation and as a result, production in 1985 was half that of ten years earlier. Thousands were thrown out of work and hunger and malnutrition set in on a massive scale. Benedicto got out of the sugar business and was promptly appointed Philippine ambassador to Japan.

In 1981 the **Pope** visited Negros and thrust the island into the international limelight with his words of condemnation ("injustice reigns"), in stark contrast to Imelda Marcos's message that "Negros is not an island of fear, but an island of love". Five years later Marcos was overthrown, and **Cory Aquino** gave the impression during her election campaign that she was willing to give up her family's hacienda north of Manila in the name of nationwide land reform. But once elected she produced a watered-down land bill which she dumped in the lap of a newly elected Congress dominated by landed oligarchs. "She might as well have appointed a crack addict to run her drug treatment programme," said an opposition senator.

As for Benedicto, under a deal struck with Aquino's Presidential Commission on Good Government, established to recover the ill-gotten wealth of Marcos and his cronies, he was allowed to keep US$15 million of the fortune he amassed. He lived quietly in Negros until his death in 2000.

best beaches, and remains charmingly rural and undeveloped, with carabao in the fields and chocolate-coloured roads winding lazily into the farming barangays of the foothills.

Brief history

Among Negros's earliest inhabitants were dark-skinned natives belonging to the **Negrito** ethnic group – hence the name Negros, imposed by the Spanish when they set foot here in April 1565. After appointing bureaucrats to run the island, Miguel López de Legazpi placed it under the jurisdiction of its first Spanish governor. Religious orders wasted no time in moving in to evangelize the natives, ripe for conversion to the true faith. The latter half of the eighteenth century was a period of rapid economic expansion for Negros, with its **sugar industry** flourishing and Visayan ports such as Cebu and Iloilo open for the first time to foreign ships. In the last century the rapacious growth of the sugar industry and its increasing politicization were to have disastrous consequences that are still being felt today (see box opposite).

6

ARRIVAL AND DEPARTURE   NEGROS

By plane The main airports on Negros are Bacolod and Dumaguete, both with flights from Manila and Cebu City.

By boat The biggest and busiest ports on the island are Bacolod and Dumaguete, which are connected by regular ferries with Manila and Mindanao. Bacolod also has ferry connections with Iloilo on Panay, and Dumaguete also has services to Cebu, Tagbilaran (Bohol) and Siquijor. Many other coastal towns have smaller ferries and bangkas going to neighbouring islands as well as to other destinations on Negros itself. Boats from San Carlos, on the east coast, head to Toledo (7 daily; 2hr) on Cebu, while Cadiz has three weekly boats for Bantayan Island (3–4hr). There are also regular ferries on the useful crossing from the southerly tip of Cebu to the east coast of Negros. These ferries sail between Bato (Cebu) and Tampi (north of Dumaguete) and Lilo-an (Cebu) and Sibulan, also north of Dumaguete.

Bacolod

On the northern coast of Negros, **BACOLOD** is a half-million-strong provincial metropolis, known as the "City of Smiles" and famed for its flamboyant **Masskara Festival** (third week of October). Its tourist attractions aren't significant enough to make you linger for more than a day or two, but it's a major transit point and a good base from which to visit nearby historic towns such as Silay and Victorias, or to arrange more adventurous excursions to Mount Kanlaon.

The old **city centre**, chaotic and choked with traffic, is best defined as the area around the **City Plaza** at the northern end of Araneta Street. North of here, Bacolod's main thoroughfare, and the city's social hub, is **Lacson Street**, which runs past the Provincial Capitol building and has good restaurants, shops and bars. There are more places to stay, eat and party 3km south of the town centre at the **Goldenfields Commercial Complex**.

Negros Museum

Gatuslao St • Tues–Sun 9am–noon & 1–6pm • P10 • ☎ 034 433 4764

Housed in an elegant Neoclassical building dating from the 1930s (though badly damaged by a storm in 2012), the **Negros Museum** details five thousand years of island history. It's only really worth a look though for its "iron dinosaur" steam engine, once used to haul sugar cane, and exhibited outside. The 1930s Provincial Capitol building next door is another of the city's few architectural highlights.

Negros Forest and Ecological Foundation

South Capitol Rd, just south of the Provincial Capitol • Mon–Sat 9am–noon & 1.30–4pm • Suggested donation P20 • ☎ 034 433 9234

The rescue centre at the **Negros Forest and Ecological Foundation** is an unexpected reprieve from the streets. It's not a huge site, but conservationists do what they can to care for endangered animals endemic to Negros, including leopard cats, the Visayan spotted deer and the bleeding-heart pigeon.

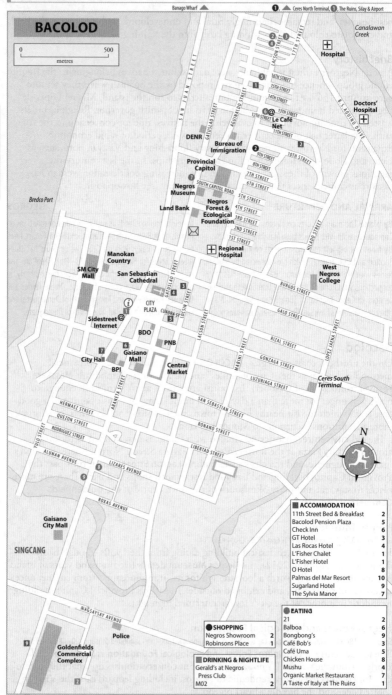

BACOLOD

0 ——————— 500
metres

6

Banago Wharf ▲

❶, ▲ Ceres North Terminal, ❶, The Ruins, Silay & Airport

Canalawan Creek

SAN JUAN STREET

GATUSLAO STREET

AGUINALDO STREET

LACSON STREET

17TH STREET

16TH STREET
15TH STREET
14TH STREET
13TH STREET
12TH STREET Le Café Net
11TH STREET
10TH STREET
9TH STREET
8TH STREET
7TH STREET
6TH STREET
5TH STREET
4TH STREET
3RD STREET
2ND STREET
1ST STREET

B.S. AQUINO DRIVE

✚ Hospital

✚ Doctors' Hospital

DENR

Bureau of Immigration

Provincial Capitol

SOUTH CAPITOL ROAD

Negros Museum

Land Bank

Negros Forest & Ecological Foundation

✚ Regional Hospital

HILADO STREET

Bredco Port

Manokan Country

SM City Mall

San Sebastian Cathedral

GATUSLAO STREET

CITY PLAZA

CUADRA ST.

LACSON STREET

West Negros College

BURGOS STREET

GALO STREET

RIZAL STREET

MABINI STREET

GONZAGA STREET

LOPEZ JAENA STREET

Sidestreet Internet

BDO

BPI

City Hall

Gaisano Mall

PNB

Central Market

LUZURIAGA STREET

Ceres South Terminal

SAN SEBASTIAN STREET

ARANETA STREET

HERMAEZ STREET

QUEZON STREET

RODRIGUEZ STREET

YULO STREET

ALUNAN AVENUE

RONANO STREET

LIBERTAD STREET

LIZARES AVENUE

ROXAS AVENUE

N

Gaisano City Mall

SINGCANG

NAGSAYSAY AVENUE

Police

Goldenfields Commercial Complex

▼ ⑩

◼ ACCOMMODATION
11th Street Bed & Breakfast	2
Bacolod Pension Plaza	5
Check Inn	6
GT Hotel	3
Las Rocas Hotel	4
L'Fisher Chalet	1
L'Fisher Hotel	1
O Hotel	8
Palmas del Mar Resort	10
Sugarland Hotel	9
The Sylvia Manor	7

● EATING
21	2
Balboa	6
Bongbong's	9
Café Bob's	3
Café Uma	5
Chicken House	8
Mushu	4
Organic Market Restaurant	7
A Taste of Italy at The Ruins	1

● SHOPPING
Negros Showroom	2
Robinsons Place	1

◼ DRINKING & NIGHTLIFE
Gerald's at Negros Press Club	1
M02	2

The Ruins

Talisay • Daily 10am–8pm • P60 • ☎034 476 4334, ⓦ theruins.com.ph • Round-trip taxis cost P250–300, depending on how long you stay

Seven kilometres north of the Capitol, on the edge of town, **The Ruins** makes a great short excursion from the city. Officially the "Don Mariano Ledesma Lacson Mansion", the building is the Philippines' answer to the Taj Mahal, hauntingly beautiful and complete with a sad story of love lost. The Lacsons were one of the island's pre-eminent sugar families in the nineteenth century. When Maria Lacson died during pregnancy with the couple's eleventh child, Don Mariano was inconsolable and set about building a memorial mansion. During the outbreak of World War II, the building was razed to prevent it being used as a headquarters by the Japanese. The fire left behind the building's complete superstructure, including the double-M motif used throughout. Mariano died in 1948, and the building was forgotten about until his great-grandson decided to open it to the public. There is also an atmospheric restaurant (see p.311).

6

ARRIVAL AND DEPARTURE

BACOLOD

By plane Bacolod-Silay Airport is located 15km northeast and is linked to Bacolod by taxi (P500), shuttle buses from SM City Mall (P150) or, cheapest but least convenient, by jeepney from the North bus terminal to Silay (P13), from where it's a short tricycle ride (P15/person or P60 for private hire). Philippine Airlines has offices at the airport (☎034 435 2011), as do Cebu Pacific (☎034 435 2156), who also have an office in Victoria Arcade in Rizal St (☎034 434 2052).
Destinations Cebu City (3 daily; 50min); Davao (3 weekly; 1hr 10min); Manila (11 daily; 1hr 15min).

By boat Most ferries are coming from Iloilo and dock at Bredco port, a short tricycle ride (P10–20) west of City Plaza. Oceanjet (☎032 255 7560 in Cebu, ⓦ oceanjet.net), 2Go (☎034 435 4965, ⓦ travel.2go.com.ph) and Weesam Express (☎034 709 0830, ⓦ weesam.ph) services have ticket offices and depart from here. Long-distance ferries to Manila and Mindanao leave less often and use the old Banago wharf, 8km north of Bacolod. Jeepneys from Banago into town cost P25/person.
Destinations Cagayan de Oro (1 weekly; 21hr); Iligan (1 weekly; 14hr); Iloilo (frequent; 1hr); Manila (4 weekly; 24hr); Ozamiz (1 weekly; 18hr).

By bus Ceres Liner buses (☎034 434 2387) drop passengers at one of two main terminals. The South terminal, for destinations south, is on Lopez Jaena St, just east of the old city, while the North terminal is several kilometres north of town on the National Highway (continuation of Lacson St). Buses from the North terminal head along the coastal road to Cadiz, from where there are boats to Bantayan Island; some continue on to San Carlos and round to Dumaguete, 313km away, though the quickest way to Dumaguete is down the west coast and then via the inland road which runs from Kabankalan across the mountains. A few services cover this route directly, but most of the time you'll need to change in Kabankalan. There's also a Ceres Liner bus from Bacolod that travels (clockwise) to San Carlos, where it boards a ferry for Toledo on the western coast of Cebu and continues on to Cebu City. Buses heading south along the coast road for Sipalay leave from the Ceres Liner South terminal.
Destinations Cadiz (frequent; 1hr 30min); Cebu City (8 daily; 8–10hr); Dumaguete (every 30min; 6hr); San Carlos (hourly; 3hr); Silay (frequent; 30min); Sipalay (hourly; 4–5hr); Victorias (frequent; 1hr).

By jeepney Jeepneys, FX vans and tricycles congregate in the City Plaza and run to most locations across town for P7. For Silay (P13) you'll need to change at the North bus terminal.

INFORMATION AND TOURS

Tourist information The tourist office (Mon–Fri 9am–5pm; ☎034 432 2881) is in the administrative building of the provincial government complex in City Plaza, San Juan St.
Tours To arrange hiking or biking trips in the foothills of Mount Kanlaon contact the tourist office, the DENR on Gatuslao St (☎034 434 7411, ⓦ denr.gov.ph), or local guide, Angelo Bibar (☎0917 301 1410, ⓔ angelobibar @gmail.com; see p.313).

ACCOMMODATION

Hotels are spread throughout the city, but short-term visitors are really faced with three areas to choose from: foodies will relish the uptown choices along the northern section of **Lacson St**; bargain-hunters are best off in the shabbier **town centre**; and nightlife fiends will find surprisingly quiet accommodation around **Goldenfields**, a modern complex 3km south of town and also the city's red-light district.

6

CITY CENTRE

Bacolod Pension Plaza Cuadra St, opposite City Plaza ☎034 433 4547. Not to be confused with the *Bacolod Pension*, this place is bigger and more central, with old but well-maintained rooms. P800

Check Inn Luzuriaga St ☎034 432 3755. Decent-value option near the old town centre with clean and comfortable rooms, the best of which are on the wi-fi-enabled business floor (P950) set around the roof garden. P850

GT Hotel Locsin St at Galo St ☎034 432 1888. Brand-new hotel with friendly staff and attractive, modern rooms styled in muted tones. Mod cons include low lighting, flatscreen TV and fridges. P1020

Las Rocas Hotel Gatuslao St ☎034 433 3190. Dark, small fan or a/c (P550) rooms with no views, but they're among the cheapest in Bacolod and you're right in the middle of the action, opposite City Plaza and the cathedral, a stone's throw from shops and restaurants. P300

O Hotel 52 San Sebastian St ☎034 433 7401, ⓦohotel .com.ph. Large, modern motel-style hotel with attractively styled rooms with cable TV, fridge and mini-bar, although those facing the front are noisy. There's also wi-fi and an ATM in the lobby. P1400

The Sylvia Manor San Juan St ☎034 434 9801, ⓦsylviamanor.com. Quality hotel in a central location one block south of City Plaza. Wide range of comfortable, high-ceilinged a/c rooms and suites (from P5000), all tastefully decorated and with cable TV and, in some cases, a kitchenette. There's a laidback café-bar in the lobby. Free in-room wi-fi. P1990

LACSON STREET

★**11th Street Bed & Breakfast** 14 11th St ☎034 433 9191, ⓦbb11st.webeden.co.uk. A great-value little pension in a quiet location within walking distance of the plentiful restaurants on Lacson St. Rooms are clean and simple with cable TV and bathrooms, and a/c rooms (P850) have hot water. There's free wi-fi throughout. P550

L'Fisher Chalet Lacson St ☎034 433 3730, ⓦlfisher hotelbacolod.com. The budget wing of *L'Fisher* offers the best-value rooms in the city, plus access to all of the hotel's excellent facilities. All rooms are a/c and feature modern furnishings, cable TV, fridge, safe, and free wi-fi, but budget and economy rooms are windowless, and it's worth paying more for the standard rooms (P1795) which have balconies looking out over the city. P1195

★**L'Fisher Hotel** Lacson St ☎034 433 3730, ⓦlfisher hotelbacolod.com. One of Bacolod's best top-end hotels, this glass-fronted estalishment has a great location amid the dining options on Lacson St. Deluxe rooms are comfortable and well maintained, but the newly renovated super-deluxe rooms (P4400), tastefully decorated in understated style, are worth the extra. All rooms are a/c and have cable TV, fridge, safe and free wi-fi. There's also a 24hr poolside café that offers buffet lunches and dinners. P3500

ELSEWHERE IN THE CITY

Palmas del Mar Resort J.R. Torres Ave, 2km southwest of Goldenfields ☎034 434 8987, ⓦpalmasdelmarresort .net. Family resort in a residential area close to the sea, with a good range of accommodation, including regular a/c rooms, family rooms and cottages. There's a decent-sized pool and the restaurant serves local specialities and European dishes. Pleasantly quiet during the week, when you might have the pool to yourself, but weekends can get busy. P1500

Sugarland Hotel Araneta St ☎034 435 2691, ⓦsugarlandhotel.com. Good-value modern hotel with stylish and well-kept a/c rooms with free wi-fi. There's also a small pool and a couple of good restaurants in the hotel. P1900

EATING

Bacolod's dining scene has moved uptown and upscale of late, and there's a cosmopolitan range of trendy cafés and restaurants along northern **Lacson St**, while time-tested favourites still hold their own in the **old city**. As well as the listings below it's worth checking out the row of identikit chicken restaurants at **Manokan Country**.

SNACKS

Bongbong's Araneta St ☎034 704 2530, ⓦbongbongs piaya.com. For a real taste of Sugarlandia, *Bongbong's* sells everything from banana-honey chips to *piyaya* (a hardened pancake with sugar melted inside) and delicious *bay ibayi* (sugar and coconut bar). They also have an outlet at the ferry terminal. Daily 9am-7pm.

CAFÉS AND RESTAURANTS

★**21** 21st St at Lacson St ☎034 435 3852, ⓦ21restaurant.com. Popular with Bacolod's elite and families alike, this institution dishes out amazing *batchoy* (noodle soup with crispy pork; P75–90) and excellent

seafood from blue marlin with herb butter (P285) to good old-fashioned fish and chips (P265). White tablecloths and attentive service complete the picture. Daily 10am–11pm.

Balboa 13th St at Lacson St ☎034 435 8642. A welcome addition to Bacolod's restaurant scene, *Balboa* is a clean, bright diner with a Negrense twist. Along with diner staples including pizza (P219–289) and spareribs (P139), local offerings include *kare kare* (P199) and *lechon kawali* (P149). Daily 11am–10pm.

Café Bob's 21st St at Lacson St ☎034 709 1091. Super-popular diner which efficiently turns out coffees (P55–135), sandwiches (P95–169) and burgers (P85–195), plus has a huge range of imported goods for sale in the deli (which closes at 9pm). Daily 8am–midnight.

Café Uma 15th St at Lacson St ☎034 709 9966, ⓦcafeuma.com. Like *Trattoria Uma* just around the corner on Lacson St, this super-trendy little café is owned by the Gaston family. The café serves delicious but expensive drinks, snacks and meals including eggs Benedict (P450), fish and chips (P450) and lemon-herb-roasted chicken (P450). There's free wi-fi for customers. Daily 10.30am–9.30pm.

★ **Chicken House** Araneta St ☎034 842 3096. An oldie but a goodie, *Chicken House* has been serving up sumptuous roast chicken (P75) for three decades and continues to draw in the local crowds with its distinctive flavours and low prices. Daily 10am–10.30pm.

Mushu 20th St ☎034 435 0972. Funky and friendly place just off Lacson which features lively pictures by local artist Charlie Co. Good pan-Asian menu ranges from Korean beef skewers (P200) to grilled pork belly with coconut and lemongrass (P155), and banana and choco spring rolls (P130) for dessert. After 10pm groups fill the large booths, the lights are dimmed and the music is cranked up as *Mushu* morphs into a lounge bar. Sat nights feature DJs. Daily 11am–2pm & 5pm–midnight (Sat till 2am).

Organic Market Restaurant Behind the Provincial Capitol Building, Gatuslao St. A great organic restaurant in the fruit and veg market, serving all sorts of health foods from organic rice dishes (P40) to shakes (P35) and coffee. Meals for less than P100. Daily 6am–6pm.

A Taste of Italy at The Ruins Talisay ☎034 476 4334, ⓦtheruins.com.ph. The Italian food here is authentic and tasty, but it's the atmosphere that will really captivate your senses, surrounded by the enchanting ruins of the Ledesma sugar hacienda (see p.309). As well as the obligatory pizza and pasta dishes (P220–400), there's *osso buco* and *salsiccia in padella* (Italian sausages in a tomato-based sauce; both P350), and the dessert line-up includes delicious *zuppa inglese* (P150). It's easiest to get here and back by taxi (P250–300 including waiting time). Daily 11am–8pm.

DRINKING AND NIGHTLIFE

Goldenfields Commercial Complex in Singcang is cited as the city's nightlife district, but while there are a few regular bars and clubs, in truth many of the places here are girlie bars catering to an exclusively male crowd. In addition to the places below it's also worth checking *Mushu* (see above).

Gerald's at Negros Press Club San Juan St ☎034 704 3655. This small friendly venue in the press building is pleasantly located overlooking City Plaza. Drinks are cheap (San Mig P47), there's live music from 8.30pm and snacks to stave off hunger. Daily 5pm–midnight.

MO2 Goldenfields ☎034 433 6026. Chain bar-club serving reasonably priced drinks (San Mig P50) and featuring nightly live music from 9pm. Also has a quieter punkah-cooled outdoors sitting area. Next door, *Annex* has pool tables and is equally salubrious. Daily 8pm–2am.

SHOPPING

Negros Showroom Lacson St at 9th St ☎034 433 8833. For handicrafts, this extensive showroom has top-quality products from all over the island. Daily 9.30am–7pm.

Robinsons Place Lacson St, 1km north of B.S. Aquino Drive ⓦrobinsonsmalls.com. Everyday needs plus clothes stores and fast-food outlets on northern section of Lacson St. Daily 10am–9pm.

DIRECTORY

Banks There are plenty of banks with ATMs in Bacolod, many of which can be found on Araneta St, including BDO, PNB and BPI. There's also a BDO ATM out at Goldenfields.

Cinema There's a Cineplex cinema at Robinsons Place on the northern section of Lacson St (☎034 441 0453, ⓦrobinsonsmovieworld.com).

Hospitals Bacolod Doctors' Hospital (☎034 433 2741, ⓦthedoctorshospital.com) is on B.S. Aquino Drive, northeast of the centre.

Immigration The Bureau of Immigration is at the back of the National Bureau of Investigation office on

Aguinaldo St (☎034 433 8581).

Internet access The trendy Le Café Net on Lacson St at 12th St (Mon–Sat 8.30am–1am, Sun noon–midnight; P25/hr) is the most comfortable place to get online in Bacolod, but other places include Sidestreet Internet (8am–1am; P20/hr) on San Juan St, in the malls. Many hotels and cafés have free wi-fi access.

Police Police headquarters is at Magsaysay Ave in Singcang (☎034 434 1152).

Post The post office is on Gatuslao St, near the junction with Burgos St (Mon–Fri 9am–5pm).

Silay

The elegant town of **SILAY**, about 20km north of Bacolod, is an atmospheric relic of a grander age, when Negros was rich from its cultivation of sugar cane. In the late eighteenth century it was talked about as the "Paris of Negros", with music performers from Europe arriving by steamship to take part in operettas and *zarzuelas*. This passion for music and the arts gave Silay – and the Philippines – its first international star, **Conchita Gaston**, a mezzo-soprano who performed in major opera houses in Europe in the postwar years. Japanese forces occupied the city in World War II, after which the sugar industry declined and Silay lost its lustre – many of its European residents departing for home. Today, Silay's major tourist draw is its **ancestral homes**, most of them built between 1880 and 1930 and some of the best are open to the public, giving a glimpse of what life was like for the sugar barons.

The main road runs through Silay as **Rizal Street**, passing the central public plaza halfway along its kilometre strip of shops, hotels and restaurants. The major annual festival in town, the **Kansilay**, lasts one week and ends every November 13 with a re-enactment of a folk tale showing the bravery of a beautiful princess who offered her life for justice and freedom.

The Balay Negrense Museum

Cinco de Noviembre St, a 5min walk west of the central plaza • Tues–Sun 10am–5pm • P50 • ☎ 034 714 7676

The **Balay Negrense Museum** was once the home of Don Victor Gaston, eldest son of Yves Leopold Germaine Gaston, a Frenchman who settled in Silay in the mid-nineteenth century. After World War II the house was left deserted and by 1980 was a sad ruin, known only by locals for the ghosts that were said to roam its corridors. Now restored by the Negros Foundation, the house is a glorious monument to Silay's golden age, with rooms of polished mahogany furnished with antiques donated by locals.

Don Bernardino-Ysabel Jalandoni House Museum

Rizal St • Tues–Sun 9am–5pm • P50 • ☎ 034 495 5093

Hard to miss at the northernmost end of Rizal Street is the pink **Don Bernardino-Ysabel Jalandoni House Museum**, known throughout town as the Pink House. Built in 1908 it gives some idea of the luxury of the time and features displays of antique law books and Japanese occupation currency. The price includes a guided tour – ask them to show you the huge metal vat in the garden, which was used to make muscovado sugar.

Manuel and Hilda Hofileña ancestral house

Cinco de Noviembre St • Open by appointment; call ☎ 034 495 4561 or the tourist office

The first ancestral home in Silay to open its doors to the public, the **Manuel and Hilda Hofileña ancestral house** is one of the last vestiges of the city's artistic history. The house holds a gallery of works collected by Manuel and Hilda's son, Ramon, which includes contemporary Filipino painters and masters such as Juan Luna and Amorsolo. Also on display are countless fascinating antiques and curiosities which include part of a meteorite fragment, one of Negros's oldest pieces of pottery and (allegedly) the world's smallest dolls, visible through a magnifying glass.

Church of San Diego

Zamora St, on the north side of the public plaza

Built in 1925, the **Church of San Diego** is a dramatic sight, with a great illuminated crucifix on top of the dome that is so bright at night it was once used by ships as a navigational aid. Behind the church are the ruins of the original sixteenth-century Spanish church, now converted into a grotto and prayer garden.

Guinhalaran

About 10min by tricycle or jeepney from town (P15)

Silay is known for **pottery** made from the red clay endemic to the area. In the barangay of **Guinhalaran** on the National Highway you can visit the potters and watch them making high quality jars and vases, which are for sale at bargain prices.

Hawaiian Philippines Sugar Company

About 15min by tricycle from town • Mon–Fri 8am–5pm • ☎ 034 495 2085

Just a short drive from Silay, this historic **Hawaiian Philippines Sugar Company** mill offers the chance to take a ride on one of the famed "iron dinosaurs" and see the workings of a genuine sugar mill. North along the rugged coast, the Victorias Milling Company is the largest integrated mill and sugar refinery in Asia, although it wasn't open for visits at the time of writing; enquire at the tourist office in Silay or Bacolod for up-to-date information.

6

ARRIVAL AND INFORMATION   SILAY

By bus and jeepney Buses and jeepneys from Bacolod arrive at the southern end of Rizal St, from where it's a short walk or tricycle ride to most of the accommodation. Tricycles to the airport cost P15/person, or P60 for the whole vehicle.

Tourist information The Silay tourist office (Mon–Fri 8am–5pm; ☎ 034 495 5553) is in the central plaza. The helpful staff can arrange informal guided tours of some ancestral houses that aren't usually open to the public, and there's also a small museum tracing Silay's history opposite the office (same hours).

Services The police station is opposite the tourist office. For long-distance calls there's a PLDT office in Rizal St; the Silay Internet Café is next door.

ACCOMMODATION AND EATING

Baldevia Pension House Rizal St, near the busy junction with Burgos St ☎ 034 495 0272. Fan rooms at this atmospheric former ancestral home are low on modern amenities, but high on faded old-world charm. A/c rooms (P600) and suites (P1000–1400) are bigger and brighter. **P450**

Café 1925 4 J. Ledesma St ☎ 034 714 7414. This pretty little place dishes up Italian classics, sandwiches (P55–90), rosti (P130) and excellent coffee. Daily 9.30am–9.30pm.

El Ideal Bakery & Refreshment 118 Rizal St ☎ 034 495 4430. Established in 1920, this bright and airy café-deli does a range of specialities that include coconut pie (P300), cassava cake (P160), meringue (P45) and halo-halo (P70). Daily 6.30am–6pm.

Mount Kanlaon National Park

Thirty kilometres southeast of Bacolod, **Mount Kanlaon** (2435m) is the tallest peak in the central Philippines and one of the thirteen most active volcanoes in the country. Climbing it offers a potentially dangerous challenge, with the real possibility of violent eruptions – climbers have died scaling it – and the crater's rim a forbidding knife-edge overhanging an apparently bottomless chasm. The dense surrounding **forest** contains all manner of wonderful fauna, including pythons and tube-nosed bats, and locals believe the mountain is home to many spirits. It also features in Philippine history, being where President Manuel Quezon hid from invading Japanese forces during World War II.

There are three main routes up the volcano itself. The **Guintubdan trail** is the easiest and most common ascent, but even this should not be underestimated. From here, although it's only 8km to the top, the trail is best broken with an overnight stop (see p.314). The 14km-long **Mananawin trail** works best over three days and offers the chance to really get to know the region, while the short, steep **Wesey trail** is very exposed and only for experienced tropical mountaineers. It goes without saying that for whichever route you choose, you'll need a guide.

ARRIVAL AND INFORMATION   MOUNT KANLAON

By jeepney Guintubdan is 2hr by jeepney from Bacolod, with a change at La Carlota.

Guides Whichever way you choose to ascend, a permit (P500) and guide (P700/day) are mandatory, and a porter (P500) might come in handy. The easiest way to make all of these arrangements is through the DENR (☎ 034 434 7411, ⊛ denr.gov.ph), or directly with Angelo Bibar

(☎ 0917 301 1410; ✉ angelobibar@gmail.com). Contact Angelo as far in advance as possible (ideally a month) and he can arrange everything from permits, guides and porters to tents and meals. Coming from further afield you can also arrange to climb Kanlaon through Dumaguete Outdoors in Dumaguete (see p.317).

6

ACCOMMODATION

Neither of the options below has canteens so come prepared with enough food to last your stay.

The Pavilion Guintubdan ☎ 034 460 2582. Clean and simple accommodation (with cold showers) in an attractive lodge nestled in the forest. Dorm P̄100, twin P̄800
Rafael Salas Nature Camp Guintubdan ☎ 034 461 0540. Just up the road from *The Pavilion*, this nature camp is the headquarters of the 300-hectare Rafael Salas Nature Park, named after the late statesman who was a native of Bago City. It's not quite as pretty as *The Pavilion* but still feels like the ultimate in luxury after a night on the mountain. Dorm P̄100, double P̄400

Sagay and around

SAGAY is a hectic industrial and fishing city 15km east along the coast from the sugar port of **Cadiz**, at the mouth of the Bulanon River. Head for the city plaza and take a look at the **Legendary Siete**, or Train Number Seven, an "iron dinosaur" that once hauled lumber for the Insular Lumber Company and now stands in the middle of the plaza, restored and sparkling in all her 75-tonne liveried glory. Both Sagay and Cadiz were hit by Typhoon Yolanda and remained largely without power at the time of writing.

Sagay Marine Reserve

Free • Bangkas leave from Sagay wharf (30min; P70/person)

Sagay is the jumping-off point for one of the Philippines' least-visited natural wonders, the beautiful **Sagay Marine Reserve**. The sanctuary boasts some marvellous beaches and with its maximum of seventy visitors per day its reef remains a picture of health; with a mask and snorkel you can see giant clams, puffer fish, immense brain corals and the occasional inquisitive batfish.

ARRIVAL AND DEPARTURE   SAGAY AND AROUND

By bus Regular buses from Bacolod stop in Cadiz (1hr 30min) and Sagay (2hr) on their way along the coastal road.

By boat There are three services each week from Cadiz (usually early morning) for Bantayan Island (3–4hr).

Bais and around

The town of **BAIS**, about 40km to the north of Dumaguete, is a good place to see **dolphins and whales** in Bais Bay as they migrate through the Tanon Strait separating Negros from Cebu. Tours run between March and October (see box below).

Twin Lakes

Daily 8am–5pm • Entry foreigners P100, Filipinos P10; kayak rental P100/hr • From Bais either take a jeepney to Amlan (P15) and then a motorcycle up to the lakes (P300 round-trip) or hire a van from Bais or Dumaguete (around P2500) • Day-trips and hikes from Dumaguete can be booked through Dumaguete Outdoors or *Harold's* (from P500/person including transport and lunch); see p.317

Nestled in a jungled crater 15km west from the main coastal road, the **Twin Lakes** of Balinsasayao and Danao make for an excellent day out. Getting there is part of the adventure and is best done by motorbike as the last part of the track is often inaccessible to larger vehicles. Alternatively you can make the strenuous 15km **hike** in

WHALE-WATCHING AROUND BAIS

The city government operates the cruise vessels *Dolphin I & II*, *Vania I & II* and *Horizon* out to view the **whales and dolphins** in Bais Bay, which each accommodate 15–20 people (P3000–4000). Tours operate all the way through to October, and bookings are recommended at least a month in advance, especially during the peak whale-watching season (March–Sept) – call the tourist office or ☎ 035 402 8174. It is also possible to just turn up at Bais pier and negotiate with local boatmen, or more easily, to take a day-trip from Dumaguete.

from the little town of **San José**, nearly midway between Dumaguete and Bais. The hike takes you past a couple of waterfalls where you can swim and through settlements of the indigenous Bukidnon people who inhabit the area. Once at the lakes it's possible to rent a kayak and head out onto the water, and to hire a pair of binoculars to check out the wildlife, which includes tarictic hornbills, monkeys and eagles; there's also a café.

ARRIVAL AND INFORMATION

BAIS AND AROUND

By bus and jeepney Bais lies on the main coastal road and is well served by buses and jeepneys from Dumaguete (1hr).

Tourist information The tourist office (Mon–Fri 8am–5pm; ☎ 035 402 8338) is in the public plaza in the centre of town.

ACCOMMODATION AND EATING

Campuyo Aroma Beach Resort Manjuyod ☎ 0928 407 2999. A few kilometres north of Bais and right on the beach, *Aroma* has clean, a/c rooms with cable TV. They also have a restaurant and free wi-fi and can arrange dolphin-watching trips. P850

La Planta Hotel Mabini St ☎ 035 402 8321, ⓦ laplanta .com.ph. Clean and comfortable twin rooms in a quaint and cosy place that used to be the city's power plant. Also has a pool and restaurant. P1540

Dumaguete

DUMAGUETE ("dum-a-get-eh"), known in the Philippines as the City of Gentle People, is capital of Negros Oriental and lies on the southeast coast of Negros, within sight of the southernmost tip of Cebu Island. With its attractive architecture, laidback university town ambience and lovely **seafront promenade**, shaded by acacia trees and coconut palms and lined with lively bars and restaurants, it's easy to see why the town is increasingly becoming a mainstream tourist destination.

While Dumaguete doesn't possess major sights, it is a great base from which to explore the region. Day-trips include the Twin Lakes of Balinsasayao and Danao (see opposite) and dolphin- and whale-watching at Bais (see box opposite), while scuba diving can be arranged from the affordable resort accommodation around Dauin (see p.319).

St Catherine of Alexandria Cathedral
Governor Perdices St, Quezon Park

Dumaguete is centred on the grand **St Catherine of Alexandria Cathedral**, which dominates Quezon Park. The cathedral was originally built in 1754, although the current version dates from 1957. Standing next to the cathedral, the **belfry** was completed in 1867, and its statue of the Lady of Lourdes is a popular site of worship in its own right.

Silliman University
Anthropological Museum Assembly Hall (go through the university gate on Hibbard Ave and past the fountain) • Mon–Fri 9am–4pm • Free

The oldest Protestant university in the Philippines, **Silliman University**'s strong reputation has largely been built on the work of its marine laboratory which has spearheaded efforts to protect the island's mangroves and stop illegal fishing. The university also has an interesting **Anthropological Museum** housing some Song and Ming dynasty porcelain and relics from minority tribes in the Philippines.

Centrop
Near the Silliman Medical Centre • Daily 9am–5pm • P10

On the far side of Silliman University campus, close to the hospital, the **Centre for Tropical Studies (Centrop)** offers a rare glimpse of Negros wildlife, including a reticulated python, long-tailed macaques and warty pigs, and is worth a quick visit.

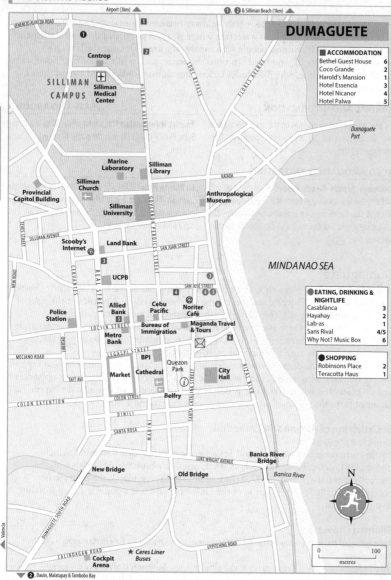

DUMAGUETE

Airport (3km)

1 2 & Silliman Beach (1km)

VENENCIO ALDECOA ROAD

Centrop

SILLIMAN CAMPUS

Silliman Medical Center

HUBBARD AVENUE

LOOC BYPASS

FLORES AVENUE

Dumaguete Port

Marine Laboratory

Silliman Library

KATADA

Silliman Church

Provincial Capitol Building

Silliman University

Anthropological Museum

GOVERNOR PERDICES STREET

REYES STREET

SILLIMAN AVENUE

Scooby's Internet @

Land Bank

SAN JUAN STREET

MINDANAO SEA

NEW ROAD

CERVANTES

REAL STREET

UCPB

SAN JOSE STREET

Police Station

Allied Bank

Cebu Pacific

@ Noriter Café

EATING, DRINKING & NIGHTLIFE
Casablanca	3
Hayahay	2
Lab-as	1
Sans Rival	4/5
Why Not? Music Box	6

Bureau of Immigration

Maganda Travel & Tours

LOCSIN STREET

LIBERTAD

Metro Bank

MECIANO ROAD

LEGASPI STREET

BPI

Quezon Park

City Hall

RIZAL BLVD

SHOPPING
Robinsons Place	2
Teracotta Haus	1

TAFT AVE

Market

Cathedral

Belfry

SANTA CATALINA STREET

COLON EXTENTION

COLON STREET

DINILI

SANTA ROSA

MABINI

LUKE WRIGHT AVENUE

Banica River Bridge

New Bridge

Old Bridge

Banica River

N

Valencia

CALINDAGAN ROAD

★ **Ceres Liner Buses**

Cockpit Arena

UYPITCHING ROAD

0   100
metres

2, Dauin, Malatapay & Tambobo Bay

ACCOMMODATION
Bethel Guest House	6
Coco Grande	2
Harold's Mansion	1
Hotel Essencia	3
Hotel Nicanor	4
Hotel Palwa	5

ARRIVAL AND DEPARTURE

By plane Dumaguete's small airport is in Sibulan, a few kilometres north of the city centre on the far bank of the Bona River. PAL has offices at the airport, as does Cebu Pacific who also have an office on Governor Perdices St, just north of Quezon Park. Tricycles make the trip to the city for P100; there are also jeepneys waiting for city-bound passengers outside the airport perimeter fence, or you can haggle with one of the private car and van drivers who

greet incoming flights. P200–300 is reasonable into town, or P500–700 to Dauin.

Destinations Cebu (1 daily; 30min); Manila (5 daily; 1hr 15min).

By boat The ferry pier is near the northern end of Rizal Blvd, within easy walking distance of the centre. A tricycle costs P20. Oceanjet (☎0923 725 3734, ⓦoceanjet.net) run (unreliable) daily services to Tagbilaran and Cebu,

Cokaliong (☎ 035 255 3599, ⓦ cokaliongshipping.com) and George & Peter Lines (☎ 035 225 2345) have slower boats serving Cebu (6 weekly; 6hr) and Dapitan (6 weekly; 4hr), while Supershuttle Ferry (☎ 0922 880 2517, ⓦ supershuttleferry.com) have a faster daily Dapitan service (3hr). Heading to Siquijor, Delta (☎ 032 422 1335 in Cebu), GL Shipping Lines (☎ 035 480 5534) and Oceanjet (☎ 032 255 7560 in Cebu, ⓦ oceanjet.net) have several daily boats. For southern Cebu the quickest way is to head up to Sibulan, or further to Tampi, and then take a ferry across to Lilo-An or Bato respectively (see p.366).

Destinations Cagayan de Oro (weekly; 7hr); Cebu City (1–2 daily; 4hr); Dapitan (on Mindanao; daily; 3hr); Manila (weekly; 19hr); Siquijor (6 daily; 45min); Tagbilaran (1–2 daily; 2hr).

By bus and jeepney The Ceres Liner terminal (☎ 035 225 9030) is on Governor Perdices St, 1km south of Quezon Park. A tricycle costs P20, but if you haven't got much luggage you can walk it almost as fast. For departures to the north of the island, it's worth making sure that you get on an express bus, shaving a few painful hours from journey times. There are hourly buses to Sipalay (4–5hr) via Kabankalan or Hinoba-an, and Bacolod (6hr). For the short hop to Dauin, there are plenty of jeepneys and buses going back and forth most hours of the day and night.

To Cebu For Cebu island, take a van (P11) or tricycle (P120) north to Sibulan from where there are boats (every 30min; 30min; P35–70) to Lilo-An; from Lilo-An buses run up the east coast to Cebu City. Alternatively, continue beyond Sibulan to Tampi, from which boats go to Bato on Cebu (every 90min; 30min; P70). From Bato buses go north to Moalboal, and then on to Cebu City. You can buy bus tickets for the Cebu leg of the journey at the Sibulan pier ticket office.

INFORMATION AND TOURS

Tourist information In town, there's a tourism office kiosk in Quezon Park (Mon–Fri 8am–4pm; ☎ 035 225 2500).

Tours There are a number of decent travel agencies and tour operators in town who can arrange trips to nearby attractions. *Harold's Mansion* (see below) runs good budget trips to Casororo Falls, Bais and dive trips to Apo Island. Maganda Travel & Tours offers an extensive line up of tours and has offices on Locsin St (☎ 035 422 6023, ⓦ magandatravel.com) and also at Level 2 of Robinsons Place (☎ 035 421 2173). For more adventurous trips, including Mt Kanlaon ascents, Dumaguete Outdoors (☎ 0919 747 7470, ⓦ dumagueteoutdoors.com) is based out in Amlan, halfway to Bais.

ACCOMMODATION

Dumaguete has plenty of inexpensive accommodation in the city centre or within walking distance of it, but rooms can get booked up fast in high season. Another option is to base yourself in Dauin (see p.319) and see Dumaguete on a day-trip.

Bethel Guest House Rizal Blvd ☎ 035 225 2000, ⓦ bethelguesthouse.com. In an excellent location on the seafront, this modern four-storey building has clean studio rooms and doubles, some with a sea view (for which you'll pay extra). Rooms at the front are big and bright, with picture windows. Efficient and friendly staff, and there's a reasonable restaurant. Strictly no alcohol or smoking, but free in-room wi-fi. P1100

Coco Grande Hibbard Ave, a short walk north from Silliman University ☎ 035 422 0746, ⓦ cocogrande hotel.com. Under the same ownership as *Coco Grove* on Siquijor and *Apo Island Resort* on Apo, this remains one of the best places in town. The spacious rooms are attractively styled and come with a/c, cable TV and fridge, but are in need of some TLC. Free wi-fi in the lobby. P1350

★**Harold's Mansion** 205 Hibbard Ave, a short walk north from Silliman University ☎ 035 225 8000, ⓦ haroldsmansion.com. Owned by affable adventurer Harold Biglete, this rambling hostel offers great-value rooms plus a roof-deck coffee shop perfect for meeting other travellers. A/c rooms (P600) have cable TV, shower with hot and cold water, free wi-fi and included breakfast. Fan rooms are cheaper, but may be preferable as the a/c units can be noisy. Harold is a great source of travel information and can make arrangements to visit the Twin Lakes, climb Mt Talinis, dive Apo Island or pretty much anything else you can think of. If you want to enjoy some fresh air without going too far from the city ask about their (very simple) eco-lodge up in Valencia (see p.318). Dorm P250, double P500

Hotel Essencia 39 Real St ☎ 035 422 1137, ⓦ hotel -essencia.com. Opened by Filipino Chinese in late 2013, this is Dumaguete's newest big player and offers clean, comfortable and stylish rooms in a central location. Staff are friendly and promo rates make for a good deal. P1200

Hotel Nicanor San José St ☎ 035 226 3330, ⓦ hotel nicanor.com. Modern, comfortable rooms with a/c, cable TV, hot showers and free wi-fi. Standard rooms are windowless, making it worth the extra P400 to upgrade to a bigger superior room. P1000

Hotel Palwa Locsin St ☎ 035 422 8995, ⓦ hotelpalwa .com. Excellent budget option with small but nicely styled a/c rooms with flatscreen TV. There's a pleasant café with free wi-fi in the lobby. P969

6

EATING, DRINKING AND NIGHTLIFE

Dumaguete has an expanding **food** scene which features everything from fresh seafood stalls to quality international cuisine. **Nightlife** is mostly focused on Rizal Blvd, although, like many Philippine port towns, the scene gets a little sleazy here as the night wears on.

Casablanca Rizal Blvd ☎ 0929 231 4088, ⓦ dumaguete -restaurants.com. Movie-themed, Austrian-owned restaurant which offers fine European cuisine to a mainly expat clientele. Maybe not a place for the environmentally conscious as all of the meat is imported, though the signature (Brazilian) steak Casablanca with wasabi mash (P485) is undeniably excellent. The restaurant also has its own bakery and deli, a decent wine list and a changing daily menu. Daily 8am–midnight.

Hayahay 201 Flores Ave, a few hundred metres north of the ferry port ☎ 035 225 1651. Lively pizza restaurant right next to *Lab-as* (see below) which has nightly live music and stays open late. The extensive menu features some interesting options including fruit pizza (banana, mango and mozzarella; P235). Daily 10am–midnight (Wed, Fri & Sat until 2am).

Lab-as 201 Flores Ave, a few hundred metres north of the ferry port ☎ 035 225 1651. Deservedly Dumaguete's most popular seafood restaurant, *Lab-as* serves super-fresh fish, shrimps, squid and crab which can either be enjoyed in the cosy wooden interior, or outside looking over the road to the ocean. Daily 10am–10pm.

Sans Rival San Jose St & Rizal Blvd ☎ 035 421 0338. The original little cake shop on San Jose St still turns out delicious cakes and coffee, while its larger sister round the corner on Rizal serves a host of tasty but inexpensive meals (P120–250) including lasagne, salads, burgers and sandwiches. Daily 9am–9pm.

Why Not? Music Box 70 Rizal Blvd ☎ 035 225 7725. The most popular nightlife venue in town *Why Not?* has a selection of different bars to choose from, plus a disco, often overrun with ladyboys. There's also a games room, internet café and even a deli. Daily 10am–2am.

ENTERTAINMENT

Dumaguete Cockpit Arena Calindagan Rd. Cockfights are held at 2pm on weekends (P100 general entry, P300 ringside), usually on Sun after church, and sometimes on weekday evenings. From the seafront, walk south along Rizal Blvd and across the Banica River Bridge, past the Ceres Liner bus terminal.

SHOPPING

Robinsons Place On the southern edge of town. Decent sized mall with supermarket, National Book Store, plenty of clothes and electronics stores, cafés and restaurants, plus a bouncy castle for kids. Daily 10am–8pm.

Terracotta Haus Sililiman University Co-operative. For Negros souvenirs including basketware and bags, seek out the tiny souvenir kiosk in the Sililiman University Co-operative. Daily 9am–5.30pm.

DIRECTORY

Banks There are a number of banks with ATMs, including BPI on Governor Perdices St opposite Quezon Park and an Allied Bank and a Metrobank opposite one another on Locsin St.

Hospitals Dumaguete's best hospital is the Silliman Medical Center (☎ 035 420 2000) on Venencio Aldecoa Rd.

Immigration Dumaguete's bustling immigration office is at Lu Dega Building, 38 Dr V. Locsin St, at the end of a narrow shopping arcade signed off Locsin St (Mon–Fri 8am–5pm; ☎ 035 225 4401).

Internet access As you'd expect of a university town, there's no shortage of net cafés. One of the nicest places to get online is Noriter Café on Santa Catalina St, but there are also plenty of places around the university, including Scooby's Internet on Real St, and World Beat Net on the airport road. Many hotels offer free wi-fi.

Police The main police station is at the west end of Locsin St near the Central Bank.

Post The post office is on Santa Catalina St.

Valencia and around

An 8km drive inland and uphill from the coast, the town of **VALENCIA** offers fresh air, thundering waterfalls and adventurous trekking nearby, and a fascinating museum. While there are a few places to stay here, Valencia can easily be visited as a day-trip (or half-day-trip) from Dumaguete or Dauin. The town itself has an attractive main square and a few cafés, but the reason to come out here is to experience the beauty of the mountain scenery.

Casororo Falls

Apolong • P10 • Habal-habal from Valencia to drop-off point of Casaroro Falls, P100/person round-trip or you can take one of the day-trips with Harold Biglete in Dumaguete (see p.317; P300/person).

It's a steep and progressively more slippery 5km drive up from Valencia to the starting point of the steps down to **Casororo Falls**, best accomplished in a 4WD, but habal-habals can also make the journey. Once you've descended the steps it's a 500m scramble up the valley with a couple of river crossings before you round a bend to view the towering 30m falls, surrounded by lush tropical greenery. Locals (or your habal-habal driver) might offer to show you the way, in which case it's a good idea to tip them a small amount.

Mount Talinis

It's advisable to arrange a private jeepney (P1500 for ten people), guide (P500–700/day) and porters (P500/day) for the trip – contact Harold Biglete in Dumaguete (see p.317) who can arrange day hikes (P1500), overnight treks (P2500) and full mountain assaults

The challenging trail up **Mount Talinis** (1903m) begins at Apolong near the entrance to Casororo Falls and *Harold's Eco Lodge*. There are several different routes up the mountain, all of which require two to three days of steep jungle-trekking through dense foliage, but are rewarded by steaming fumeroles, tranquil lakes and spectacular views. You're definitely best with a guide for this trek, and will need to bring tents, sleeping bags and food with you.

Cata-al WWII Museum

Jose Romero Rd at Legarda St • Daily 8am–5pm • Donations welcome

The slopes of Mount Talinis were a hotbed of activity during World War II and were bombarded by US ships trying to force out the entrenched Japanese forces. Local resident Felix Constantina V. Cata-al (aka "Tantin") has been hunting out war memorabilia from the surrounding forests since he was a boy, and his huge and captivating collection is now on display at the **Cata-al WWII Museum**. Samurai swords, dog tags and old uniforms are just a few of the items on show, and Cata-al's collection now has so many missile shells that he's ingeniously constructed a stair balustrade from them. Ask to see the pair of recently found US radios.

ARRIVAL AND DEPARTURE — VALENCIA AND AROUND

By bus, van and jeepney Regular jeepneys leave Dumaguete for Valencia (P13), or you can take a tricycle (P30/person). Vans and jeepneys can be chartered for around P1500 (or a tricycle for P250 although this won't make it all the way to Casororo). Alternatively, you could hire a tricycle at Bacong, halfway between Dumaguete and Dauin, for the steep ride up to Valencia for P100.

ACCOMMODATION

The Forest Camp On the road up to Casororo ☎0917 312 0853. This family-run camp has grown over the years and now has a few attractive cabins where you can overnight as well as day-use cottages (P300–500). There's also a network of trails, some lovely pools and a simple restaurant. P80 entrance fee if you're not staying. **P1000**

Harold's Eco Lodge Casororo Trailhead, Apolong ☎0915 290 9931, ⓦharoldsmansion.com. Ultra-simple huts without toilets at the start of the trail to Casororo Falls. Pool table and 24hr electricity though. **P500**

Dauin and around

South of Dumaguete is beach-and-dive-resort country, with a decent range of accommodation. However, beaches are brown sand and the sea can be choppy from November to May, which makes the nearby island of Siquijor (see p.301) a more appealing prospect for pure beach enthusiasts. This said, divers will find the quality of nearby dive sites is more than adequate compensation.

DAUIN is a popular port of call 15km south of Dumaguete. The beach has a dramatic backdrop of palm trees and ruined watchtowers built in the nineteenth century as protection against raiding Moro pirates.

Malatapay market

Malatapay, Zamboanguita • About 20min southwest of Dauin by road, or 20km from Dumaguete • Wed dawn–noon • Most of the resorts in Dauin arrange trips to the market or you can flag down a jeepney, or charter a tricycle (P150–200 round-trip from Dauin including waiting time)

One of the most unusual markets in the Philippines is held every Wednesday in the seaside barangay of **MALATAPAY**. Buyers and sellers at **Malatapay market**, also known as **Zamboanguita market**, still use the traditional native barter system, with farmers from the surrounding villages and Bukidnon tribespeople from the interior meeting with fishermen and housewives to swap everything for anything – livestock, fish, exotic fruit, strange vegetables and household items. You'll have to be up bright and early to visit the market: the bartering begins at first light and is usually more or less finished by noon. Malatapay is also the departure point for boats to Apo Island (see box below), so a visit to the market and island can easily be combined.

Tambobo Bay

Most resorts can arrange trips or hop on any bus or jeepney (P60) from Dumaguete or Dauin heading south along the coast; get off at Siaton and then take a tricycle for the last few kilometres (P50/person) to the beach; if you have your own vehicle it's far simpler to leave the main road at Mayabong Crossing (Km39) from which it's a beautiful but very bumpy 10km to Tambobo

Forty kilometres south of Dumaguete, at the very southern tip of Negros near the small town of Siaton, **Tambobo Bay** is a beautiful, serpentine bay, popular with foreign yachties for the protection it affords from storms, but also for its laidback lifestyle and

---

APO ISLAND AND OTHER DIVE SITES

Tiny, volcanic **Apo Island**, 7km off the south coast of Negros, has become a prime destination for divers, most of whom head out for the day from Dumaguete, Dauin or Siquijor. Site of one of the Philippines' first and most successful marine reserves, Apo has a series of reefs teeming with marine life, from the smallest nudibranch to the largest deepwater fish. The sanctuary area is on the island's southeast coast, while much of the flat land to the north is occupied by the only village, home to four hundred fisherfolk and farmers. Non-divers needn't be bored; Apo has some fantastic snorkelling and it's a great little island to explore on foot.

Organized trips from Dumaguete or Dauin cost P1000–3000 per person depending on the level of comfort and number of people in your group, or you can travel independently on one of the regular bangkas from Malatapay. The trip takes about 45 minutes and the price is fixed at P2000 for a small bangka (good for four), P3000 for a large bangka (up to ten people), or alternatively you can arrange a place on one of the four daily *Liberty Lodge* shuttles (P300/person; see below). General **admission** to the marine sanctuary is P100.

Among other dive sites, **Calong-Calong Point** off the southern tip of Negros is known for its dazzling number of smaller reef fish. Nearby is **Tacot**, a tricky deep dive where sharks are common. From the coastal towns to the south of Dumaguete you can take a bangka to Siquijor (see p.301), where sites such as **Sandugan Point** and **San Juan** go as deep as 65m, and where you can expect to see tuna, barracuda and sharks plus, from March to August, manta rays.

Sightseeing trips to Apo can be arranged through most hotels in Dumaguete, but for dive trips you're best to proceed through dive resorts in Dauin (or Siquijor if you're staying there) – *Atmosphere*, *Liquid* and *Mike's Dauin Beach Resort* are all recommended. In Dumaguete *Harold's Mansion* runs day-trips (1–3 dives P2000–3300), or you can just snorkel (P1000).

ACCOMMODATION

Apo Island Beach Resort Apo Island ☎ 0939 915 5122, ⓦ apoislandresort.com. Under the same ownership as *Coco Grove* (Siquijor) and *Coco Grande* (Dauin). this lovely little place sits at the back of a tiny isolated sandy cove hemmed in by rocks. It's expensive, and the beach and restaurant can get overrun with day visitors, but when they've left for the day the true magic of this location reveals itself. Dorm P800, double P2700

Liberty's Lodge Apo Island ☎ 0920 2385 704, ⓦ apoisland.com. Set above the main beach, *Liberty's* offers good views and reasonable rates for the sweet little rooms, which are also inclusive of all meals. Wi-fi for P50/day (if there is electricity). Shuttle boat to Malatapay four times per day. P1950

pretty mangrove- and palm-fringed beaches. It's a great place to spend a lazy afternoon swimming and snorkelling, and there are also a few decent places to stay.

ARRIVAL AND DEPARTURE

By bus and jeepney Buses and jeepneys leave Dumaguete for Dauin (20–30min), Malatapay (40min), Zamboanguita (45min) and Siaton (1hr) from either the Ceres Liner terminal or the area around the market. An

DAUIN AND AROUND

alternate route to Valencia leaves the main highway at Bacong, halfway between Dumaguete and Dauin; tricycles can be chartered from here for the steep ride up to Valencia for P100.

ACCOMMODATION AND EATING

DAUIN

Atlantis Dauin ✆035 425 2327, ⊛atlantishotel.com. A/c cottages with TV, mini-bar and private bathrooms set amid lovely gardens, and for a little more, you can get sea views. *Atlantis* is primarily a dive resort, though it offers non-divers a large pool, loungers on the sand and day-trips to Dumaguete, Bais (for dolphin- and whale-watching) and Apo Island. P2700

★**Atmosphere** Maayong Tubig, 5km south of Dauin ✆035 400 6940, ⊛atmosphereresorts.com. British-owned *Atmosphere* is easily the most upmarket place in this part of the world. Beautiful suites, apartments and penthouses, with state-of-the-art facilities and wonderful outdoor bathrooms, are spread through well-manicured gardens. There's also a quality dive shop, the excellent Sanctuary spa, a top-class restaurant and a lovely infinity pool. The Kids Cove day care centre also makes *Atmosphere* a good choice for families. P9500

Giuseppe's Inn Brgy Lapayo, Dauin ✆0928 559 5611. Surprisingly smart Italian restaurant and deli on the main road south towards Dauin, serving an excellent antipasti platter (P650) and pizzas (P360–650), and even has a small swimming pool. Daily 11am–10pm.

★**Liquid** Brgy Bulak, Dauin ✆0917 314 1778, ⊛liquid dumaguete.com. Run by a friendly British–Canadian couple, this low-key dive resort has eight attractively decked-out beach huts, all with sea views. There's wi-fi and a pool, and the rooftop café serves tasty meals, good cocktails and has a small bakery. Also has a few super-cheap rooms (P350) at

the back, although these are exclusively for the use of dive instructors and students. P1450

Mike's Dauin Beach Resort Poblacion Dauin ✆0916 754 8823, ⊛mikes-beachresort.com. Attractive, small-scale and homely resort on a pretty stretch of beach. Rooms are spread over two floors in one large block, and there's a lovely pool down by the beach. Also has a popular dive centre. P2800

Pura Vida Brgy Lipayon, Dauin ✆035 425 2274, ⊛pura-vida.ph. Stylish option with a range of tasteful native fan and a/c huts, a lovely beachside pool and free wi-fi in reception and at the restaurant. P3300

MALATAPAY

Dream Resort Just along from the Apo Island bangka station ✆0915 629 9606. Opened in 2013 by a British-Filipina couple, this lovely little café right on the seashore makes a great stop after a visit to to Malatapay market or Apo Island. They serve decent omelettes (P70), pancakes (P50), coffee and juices, plus home-made mango ice cream (P25). There's also a couple of basic rooms for rent (P1200). Daily 7am–late.

TAMBOBO BAY

Kookoo's Nest ✆0919 695 8085 or ✆0926 708 1188, ⊛kookoosnest.com.ph. Wonderfully remote little British-run place with simple cottages on stilts overlooking a pretty cove at the entrance to Tambobo Bay. There are kayaks for rent and the restaurant turns out tasty meals and snacks. P1000

Sipalay and around

Nearly 200km south of Bacolod, on the heel of Negros, **SIPALAY** is the access point for the lovely resorts of **Sugar Beach** and **Punto Ballo**, a few kilometres north and south of town respectively. There are a couple of hotels in town, but given the proximity of the beaches there's no need to stay unless you arrive late. Sipalay's historical focal point is the plaza and the church, but these days most activity centres around its pier and the main drag, **Alvarez Street**, where there are numerous canteens, bakeries and convenience stores.

Punta Ballo and Campomanes Bay

Punta Ballo can be reached by tricycle from Sipalay (P150 direct with a driver, or P300 through a resort); it's a walk from Punta Ballo to Campomanes Bay

Just 6km south of Sipalay, **Punto Ballo** has a pretty stretch of beach and offers great snorkelling and diving from the shoreline. A couple of kilometres south, **Campomanes**

6

Bay, also known as Maricalum Bay, is a natural harbour that's said to be deep enough to hide a submarine. Shaped like a horseshoe and 2km wide and backed by steep cliffs, it's a fantastic day-trip with some good snorkelling and scuba diving, though there's no accommodation here.

Sugar Beach

Resorts can arrange boat transfer, picking you up from Poblacion Beach in Sipalay (P300/boat for 4–6 people). A cheaper, less direct alternative is to take a tricycle to Nauhang (P150), then a small paddle boat across the creek (P20), and walk around the headland; if you decide to take this route, ask to be let off the bus in Montilla rather than Sipalay, which is closer to Nauhang

Although it's just 5km as the crow flies from Sipalay, the absence of road access to beautiful **Sugar Beach** makes it feel more like an island. While it may not have the white sand and azure waters of Boracay, it offers a relaxed vibe, plus a good selection of small resorts ranging from ultra-budget to mid-range.

ARRIVAL AND INFORMATION

By bus Coming from Dumaguete the quickest bus route follows the coast south around the toe of the island and then north through Hinoba-an, but an equally scenic option is to head north and then across the mountains to Kabanklan before travelling south for Sipalay. Buses from Bacolod or Dumaguete will drop you at Poblacion Beach in Sipalay Town. Moving on there are hourly buses from Sipalay for Bacolod (5–6hr), but only one direct service for

SIPALAY AND AROUND

Dumaguete (5am; 4–5hr), so you're best hopping on the first southbound bus and then changing in Hinoba-an.

Tourist information There's a small tourist office at the beach end of Alvarez St (Mon-Fri 8am–noon & 1–5pm) where you can enquire about transport and accommodation.

Services Internet can be found at Lance's on G.P. Avarez St, which branches off Alvarez St. Jamont Supermarket in *Sipalay Suites* hotel has surprisingly well-stocked shelves.

ACCOMMODATION AND EATING

SIPALAY

Driftwood City On the town beach ☎ 0920 900 3663. Simple beach café (under the same ownership as *Driftwood Village* on Sugar Beach) serving pizza and pasta dishes (P100–150). They can also arrange bangkas to Sugar Beach (P300). Daily 7am–7pm.

Sipalay Suites Mercedes Blvd ☎ 034 473 0350, ⓦ sipalaysuites.com.ph. The most comfortable place to stay in town has clean, characterless rooms close to the beach. They also have a nice pool and their restaurant, *La Verandah*, has good beach views. **P1800**

PUNTA BALLO

Artistic Diving Beach Resort ☎ 034 453 2710, ⓦ artisticdiving.com. Beachfront accommodation in fan or a/c (P1770) rooms, or a/c villas with cable TV (P2170). There's also a decent bar and restaurant with wi-fi (P20 per device for three days), plus a pool and dive centre. **P1370**

Easy Diving ☎ 0917 300 0381, ⓦ sipalay.com. Simple fan rooms and pleasant a/c stone cottages (P1900–2700), with attractive rattan and wooden furnishings and spacious verandas, set in hillside gardens looking down to the white sand beach. Wi-fi P200/5hr. **P1600**

SUGAR BEACH

Except for *Fiesta Cove*, all of the resorts below have their own restaurants, and these are the only places to eat.

Bermuda Next to Takutuka Lodge ☎ 0920 529 2582,

ⓦ bermuda-beach-resort.com. *Bermuda* offers spacious and tastefully decorated fan-cooled beachfront bungalows (P1550) and smaller a/c rooms (P950–1450) at the rear of the property. The restaurant serves Italian and Thai cuisine, but the Filipino dishes are recommended. Wi-fi costs P100/hr. **P950**

Driftwood Village Halfway along the beach ☎ 0920 900 3663, ⓦ driftwood-village.com. A backpacker favourite, Swiss-owned *Driftwood* has a wide range of budget huts set in palms behind the beach. There's also a basic dorm and a café. Dorm **P250**, double **P450**

Fiesta Cove At the far northern end of the beach ☎ 0927 350 9358. One of the few locally owned places on Sugar Beach, *Fiesta* has modern, clean and comfortable second-floor rooms. Each has a/c, TV and hot water, plus a balcony with beach views, but there's no restaurant. **P1500**

Sugar Rocks Music Bar Northern end of the beach ☎ 0908 429 8413. It's worth the clamber up the hill to get to this cosy nook of a bar overlooking the beach. Drinks are reasonably priced and rooms will also be available soon. Daily 2pm–2am.

Sulu Sunset Beach Resort Towards the northern end of the beach ☎ 0919 716 7182, ⓦ sulusunset.com. German-owned *Sulu* has simple but attractive fan-cooled cottages which look straight out onto the beach. The restaurant serves Filipino food, a few European dishes including schnitzel, and cold beer. Free transfer from Sipalay if you stay three nights or more. **P550**

CLOCKWISE FROM TOP LEFT DIVING AT APO ISLAND (P.320); ALONA BEACH, PANGLAO ISLAND (P.294); MIAG-AO CHURCH, PANAY (P.332) >

★**Takatuka Lodge** The furthest south of the resorts 📞0920 230 9174, 🌐takatuka-lodge.com. This wonderfully wacky *Takutuka* is the result of the unhinged creativity of its Swiss-German owners. Each room features one-of-a-kind furnishings, from the pink Cadillac bed in the Superstar room, to the microphone light fittings in Rockadelic. All rooms have verandas, and given the quality and originality, rates are very reasonable. For a/c or hot showers you simply add P200–300/night. The restaurant serves the best food on the beach and the *salamizza* (salami rosti) is particularly recommended. Wi-fi costs P600 for unlimited use during your stay. *Takutuka* also has one of the few dive centres on Sugar Beach. P1050

6

Danjugan Island and Punta Bulata

Lying 3km off the southwest coast of Negros and accessible through the small town of **Bulata**, about 10km north of Sipalay, **Danjugan** (pronounced "Danhoogan") **Island** is a little gem. Managed as a nature reserve by the Philippine Reef and Rainforest Foundation (PRRCFI) NGO, it's fringed completely by vibrant coral reefs and so well forested that it's home to such rarities as the white-bellied sea eagle and the barebacked fruit bat. There are also a number of small **islets**, including Manta Island and Manta Rock, and three offshore **reefs** that are home to about 270 species of fish. Most people visit Danjugan as a day-trip from the mainland but staying overnight is a magical experience, as you're lulled to sleep by the sound of lapping waves on the beach (see below).

ARRIVAL AND DEPARTURE

DANJUGAN ISLAND AND PUNTA BULATA

By bus and tricycle Buses driving the coastal road pass through Cartagena, where you should alight and look for a tricycle to take you the last few kilometres to Punta Bulata. Alternatively the resort can arrange for a tricycle pick-up if you contact them in advance, or you could hire a tricycle from Sipalay.

Tours Day-trips from the *Punta Bulata White Beach Resort* (see below) cost P1750, including transfers, lunch, a trekking guide and kayaking.

ACCOMMODATION

Danjugan Island 📞034 441 6010, 🌐prrcf.org. PRRCFI's accommodation is available in dorms or in one of two mud-brick "eco-cabanas" (each of which can sleep four). Facilities are basic but include a communal shower block and solar-powered electricity. Meals and drinks as well as scuba diving can be arranged in advance. Rates include return transfers, all meals, a boat tour, trekking guide and kayak use. Dorm P2750

Punta Bulata White Beach Resort & Spa Accessed along a 2km dirt road from Bulata Town 📞034 433 5160, 🌐puntabulata.com. The resort has a good range of comfortable huts, rooms and family cabins for six, all a/c. There's also a pleasant bar and a hillside native-style restaurant with ocean views. P3900

Guimaras

Separated from the Panay mainland by the narrowest slither of ocean, the small island of **GUIMARAS** is best known for producing the tastiest mangoes in the Philippines. The bounteous fruit is celebrated on the third weekend of April at the **Manggahan Guimaras festival** in San Miguel, the island's capital, which includes an eating contest that sees competitors consuming as many of the super-sweet mangoes as they can in thirty minutes.

The island has some good, affordable **resorts**, exceptional **beaches** – especially around **Nueva Valencia** on the southwest coast – and a few enticing **islands** offshore. Its undulating **interior** makes it a beautiful place to explore by mountain bike and main roads are reasonably signed, though there are a bewildering array of secondary roads, trails and tracks. There's also a smattering of history, with defiant old Spanish churches and the country's only **Trappist monastery**. During the Filipino–American War, General Douglas MacArthur, then a first lieutenant, built the wharf near Buenavista, which is still being used by ferries today.

Guimaras was badly affected by an oil spill from the tanker, *Solar 1*, which sank off the northern coast of the island in 2006. Although today there is little evidence of the spill to the casual observer, and beaches look back to their pristine best, it will take decades for the island's mangrove ecosystems (and fish stocks) to fully recover. The north was once again threatened by a smaller-scale spill in January 2014.

Jordan and San Miguel

Tourists only visit **JORDAN**, in the north of the island, because most bangkas from Iloilo arrive at Hoskyn port 2km to the west. Nearby **SAN MIGUEL**, the capital, is rarely visited at all but is the handiest place hereabouts if you need cash or to make a phone call. There's no accommodation in either town and not much in the way of food – numerous no-nonsense carinderias offer little more than adobo and rice.

Macopo Falls

P5 • A tricycle will take 15min from Jordan and 10min from San Miguel (P150–200 round-trip including waiting)

Guimaras has some pretty waterfalls in its hinterland, the best of which is **Macopo Falls**, between Jordan and San Miguel. Steps lead to a steep and sometimes slippery track through the undergrowth down to the falls, where you can swim in a beautifully chilly mountain pool formed by water gushing through a rocky gorge from high above.

Our Lady of the Philippines Trappist Monastery

2km south of San Miguel

Founded in 1972 by Americans, **Our Lady of the Philippines Trappist Monastery** lies on the main road southwest from San Miguel. The monks seem to do very nicely, with orchards that grow assorted tropical fruit and an interesting souvenir shop where banana fries, cashews, guava jelly, mango jam and even holy water are sold under the Trappist Monastic Products brand name.

Navalas and the north

The barangay of **NAVALAS** on the island's northern coast has two interesting sights, one religious, the other an imperious temple to Mammon. The seventeenth-century **Navalas Church**, an atmospherically decrepit relic of the Spanish regime, is a good starting point for exploring this coast. A short walk away on a promontory overlooking Iloilo Strait stands a villa known as **Roca Encantada** (Enchanted Rock) or, more sneeringly, Lopezville, vacation house of the wealthy Lopez clan who hail from Iloilo.

Siete Pecados

30min by bangka from Navalas • Small boats (fitting 4–6 people) charge P400 for the first hour, then P150 for succeeding hours; alternatively you can arrange to visit as part of an island day-trip through your resort

Opposite the Roca Encantada's promontory is a picturesque group of coral islets called **Siete Pecados** (Isles of the Seven Sins). The largest of the islets has an impressive house perched on top, but the others are bare. There are no beaches but it's worth the trip for the snorkelling.

The mango plantations

Kokomojo Farms ☏ 033 337 7620 or ☏ 02 759 2302 · **National Mango Research and Development Center** ☏ 033 237 0912

You could hardly leave Guimaras without a visit to one of the **mango plantations**. All have just the right soil, elevation and exposure to the elements to produce succulent fruit ready for the main harvest season in April and May. The most visitor-friendly plantation on the island is **Kokomojo Farms**, near Millan, roughly in the centre of Guimaras, where the owners will show you around personally if you call ahead.

If your interest in mangoes runs deep, you can also visit the **National Mango Research and Development Center**, just west of San Miguel on the road to Lawi.

Offshore islands

Bangkas can be arranged at Hoskyn port or through any of the resorts for around P300/hr

Exploring the beautiful islands and islets in the south of Guimaras makes a good day-trip. Off the southeast coast there's **Sereray Island** and **Nao-wai Island**, both with tiny sandy coves where you can picnic and swim. Off the southwest coast is **Taklong Island**, a marine reserve whose mangroves and beds of sea grass are breeding grounds for hundreds of marine species.

ARRIVAL AND INFORMATION   GUIMARAS

To/from Panay Frequent bangkas (P15) leave Ortiz wharf in Iloilo City for Hoskyn port on the west coast of Guimaras (20min). Some resorts can send a bangka to collect you at Iloilo, which usually adds about P1500 to your accommodation bill.

To/from Negros There is a daily bangka (P70) from Valladolid, south of Bacolod, to Cabalagnan on Guimaras' south coast, and more frequent services from Pulupandan, north of Valladolid, to Suclaran (P60) on the east coast.

Tourist Information On arrival at Hoskyn port look for the Guimaras Tourism Assistance kiosk (daily 7.30am–4.30pm; ☏ 033 238 1500).

GETTING AROUND

By jeepney Open-sided minivans and jeepneys make regular circuits of the island's major towns and ports and can be useful for touring the island if you're not laden down with luggage. Jeepneys charge P12 per section; the journey from Jordan to Nueva Valencia (90min) costs P45.

By tricycle and habal-habal Since many of the resorts lie off the main jeepney and minivan routes, hiring a tricycle or habal-habal is the most convenient option for getting to your accommodation. They can be hired for short journeys, and if you like the driver, for day-trips – expect to pay P700–1000

for a full day's tricycle hire, depending on where you go.

By motorbike and bicycle To get the most out of exploring the island by two wheels it's worth enquiring about a guide at the tourism assistance kiosk in Hoskyn. Some resorts rent out mountain bikes for around P300/day and *Vallee Verde Mountain Spring Resort* has motorbikes for rent (P600/day). For better bikes and a guided ride contact Panay Adventure Travel & Tours, based in Iloilo (see p.331). Tours cost US$55/person and include round-trip transfers, bike hire, guide and lunch.

ACCOMMODATION

Guimaras is small enough that it doesn't matter too much where you base yourself. Even if you choose the solitude of a resort on one of the smaller islands nearby, it's easy to hop on a bangka back to Guimaras itself if you want to explore.

MAINLAND

Baras Beach Resort 10km from San Miguel on the island's west coast ☏ 0927 480 1027. A pretty little hideaway on a sheltered inlet, with fan cottages on stilts just a few steps away from the ocean and overlooking the bay. The food, almost all of it grown or caught by the staff, is good; there's not much of an à la carte menu, but there are ample buffet lunches and dinners for around P200. To get there either call ahead to arrange a pick-up or take a bangka (about P300) from Puyo wharf in Nueva Valencia. **P1000**

Raymen Resort Alubihod, Nueva Valencia ☏ 033 396 0383, ⓦ raymenresort.com. On the island's southwest coast, *Raymen Resort* has clean a/c rooms with TV (from P1350) and hot showers in a building set back from the beach, as well as cheaper fan rooms. For meals there's a simple canteen (set meals P85). The resort is 40min by road south from Jordan (P400 by tricycle), or P3000 if you charter a bangka from Iloilo. Avoid weekends if you don't like karaoke. **P700**

Valle Verde Mountain Spring Resort Off the San Miguel–Nueva Valencia road ☏ 0918 730 3446,

ⓦ valleverdemtnresort.com. For those who can bear to be away from the beach, friendly *Valle Verde* offers simple rooms set in a lush valley looking down towards pretty Lawi Bay. There are only seven rooms and they range from very basic fan huts to (slightly) more comfortable a/c cottages. As well as a natural spring at the bottom of the hill, there's also a large and inviting spring-water pool in the middle of the resort (P65 for non-residents). Motorbike hire P600/day. P800

OFFSHORE

Costa Aguada Island Resort Inampulugan Island, around 20min off the east coast of Guimaras by boat ☎ 02 896 5422, ⓦ costaaguadaislandresort.com. Swish

complex with spacious duplex as well as detached bamboo cottages, each with bathroom, telephone and balcony, plus a swimming pool, beachside bamboo restaurant, poolside bar, riding stables and tennis courts. P1500

Isla Naburot Resort Naburot Island, off the west coast of Guimaras ☎ 0918 909 8500. Beautiful and romantic, *Isla Naburot* has six private cottages built partly from flotsam and jetsam, with driftwood for window frames and shells for walls. There's no electricity; after dark you'll have to read by paraffin lamp and eat by candlelight. Top-class meals from local produce are included in the room rate. Activities include fishing, swimming, island-hopping, snorkelling and scuba diving. P4500 per person

DIRECTORY

Banks San Miguel has the island's only ATM, at the Land Bank.

Internet access Outside of the resorts, the easiest place to make phone calls and use the internet is the Gaitan Internet Café in San Miguel.

Hospitals Medical care is better than you might expect, with a provincial hospital in San Miguel and others at Buenavista and Nueva Valencia.

Police The Philippine National Police station is in the barangay of Alaguisoc in Jordan.

Panay

The substantial, vaguely triangular-shaped island of **PANAY** has been largely bypassed by tourism, perhaps because everyone seems to get sucked towards **Boracay** off its northern tip instead. There's room enough on Panay, though, for plenty of discovery and adventure: the island has a huge coastline and a mountainous, jungled interior that has yet to be fully mapped.

Panay comprises four provinces, **Antique** ("ant-ee-kay") on the west coast, **Aklan** in the north, **Capiz** in the northeast and **Iloilo** ("ee-lo-ee-lo") running along the east coast to the capital of the province, **Iloilo City** in the south. The province that most interests tourists is Aklan, whose capital **Kalibo** is the site of the big and brash **Ati-Atihan festival**, held in the second week of January (see box, p.336). This doesn't mean you should give the rest of Panay the brushoff. The northeast coast was badly affected by Typhoon Yolanda, but still offers bangka access to a number of unspoilt islands, while on the west side Antique is a raw, bucolic province of picturesque beaches and scrubby mountains.

ARRIVAL AND DEPARTURE   PANAY

By plane There are four major airports on Panay, all served by daily flights from Manila. Panay's principal airport is in Iloilo and has flights from Manila, Cebu, Davao and Puerto Princesa. On the north coast there are airports at Roxas (see p.334), Kalibo (see p.336) and Caticlan (see p.340). Roxas only has a few flights per day, while Kalibo, and particularly Caticlan, are mainly used by visitors on their way to Boracay. Kalibo is also served by international flights from around Asia with Air Asia, and so is an alternative port of entry into the Philippines. Caticlan is tiny but very popular, receiving upwards of thirty flights per day; the bulk are from Manila, although there are also services from Cebu.

By boat Passenger ferries operated by Cokaliong Lines

(ⓦ cokaliongshipping.com) and Trans-Asia Shipping Lines (ⓦ transasiashipping.com) leave from Cebu for Iloilo, while 2Go (ⓦ travel.2go.com.ph), Oceanjet (ⓦ oceanjet.net) and Weesam (ⓦ weesam.ph) run fast boats for the short trip between Bacolod and Iloilo (see p.309). In the north, Caticlan is served by boats from Roxas on Mindoro Oriental, part of the popular bus–ferry–bus–ferry route from Manila to Boracay (see p.340). Twice-weekly ferries also make the long haul up to Manila (22hr). Coming from Romblon (see p.348) there are bangkas to Roxas from Sibuyan Island, to Caticlan and Boracay from Looc on Tablas Island, or you can take a bangka to Carabao Island, north of Boracay, and from there to Boracay itself.

6

Iloilo City and around

ILOILO CITY is a useful transit point for Guimaras (see p.324) and has good ferry connections to many other Visayan islands, but there's nothing to keep you here for more than a day or two. The **city centre** occupies a thin strip of land on the southern bank of the Iloilo River, with views across to Guimaras. **General Luna Street** runs for nearly 3km along the northern boundary of the centre, and is one of the city's major arteries, lined by banks, hotels and restaurants. It's worth heading across the river to the **Smallville Commercial Complex** for dining and nightlife, while for more of a sense of history, the old areas of **Molo**, 3km west of town, and **Jaro**, 3km north, both make pleasant distractions. There are also more adventurous pursuits to be enjoyed around Iloilo, including trekking and caving in **Bulabog Puti-An National Park**, and trips to local Ati villages.

If you're visiting in January, the **Dinagyang** festival, loosely based on Kalibo's Ati-Atihan, adds some extra frenzy to the city during the fourth weekend. The **Paraw Regatta** falls in the third week of February and includes a race across to Guimaras.

Plaza Libertad and J.M. Basa Street

In the southeastern quadrant of the city is **Plaza Libertad**, where the first flag of the Philippine Republic was raised in triumph after Spain surrendered the city on December 25, 1898. There's little to remind you of the history though – the square today is a concrete affair with fast-food restaurants and busy roads on all sides.

The few old residential and commercial buildings that survive date back to Spanish and American colonial periods and are mostly to be found in **J.M. Basa Street**, which runs past the square linking Ledesma Street to the port area.

Museo Iloilo

Bonifacio Drive, just before the river • Mon–Fri 9.30am–5pm • P25 • A 15min walk north of town, or hop on a Jaro-bound jeepney.

An engaging and clearly presented repository of Iloilo's cultural heritage, the **Museo Iloilo** has a diverse range of exhibits including fossils, shells and rocks indicating the age of Panay Island. There are also ornamental teeth, jewellery excavated from pre-Spanish burial sites, pottery from China and Siam, coffins, war relics and some modern art.

Molo

Molo can be reached on foot from the city centre in 20min (10min by tricycle or jeepney; P8)

On the western edge of the city, the district of **Molo** makes for an interesting wander. In the sixteenth and seventeenth centuries Molo was a Chinese quarter like Parian in Manila. The main sight is **Molo Church** (St Anne's), a splendid nineteenth-century Gothic Renaissance edifice made of coral, with rows of female saints lining both sides of the aisle.

Asilo de Molo

Visits possible daily 10am–noon & 1–4pm; donation expected • ☎ 033 338 0252, ⊛ asilodemolo.com

About 1km west along the road from Molo Church is the **Asilo de Molo**, formerly an orphanage where vestments were hand-embroidered by orphan girls under the tutelage of nuns. The orphans have since been transferred to Manila, and the Asilo, still run by the Sisters of the Daughters of Charity, is now home to Iloilo's elderly poor, who also manage to turn out local handicrafts.

Jaro

Taxi, or jeepneys marked Jaro or Tiko (P8)

Three kilometres north of the centre across the Forbes Bridge, the historical enclave of **Jaro** is worth exploring. You can also wander among the old colonial homes of sugar barons and mooch through a number of dusty old antique shops, where prices are lower than in Manila. Jaro's **plaza** is an inspiring little piece of old Asia, dominated by Jaro Cathedral (see p.330) and its dignified but crumbling old belfry that was partially destroyed by an earthquake in 1984.

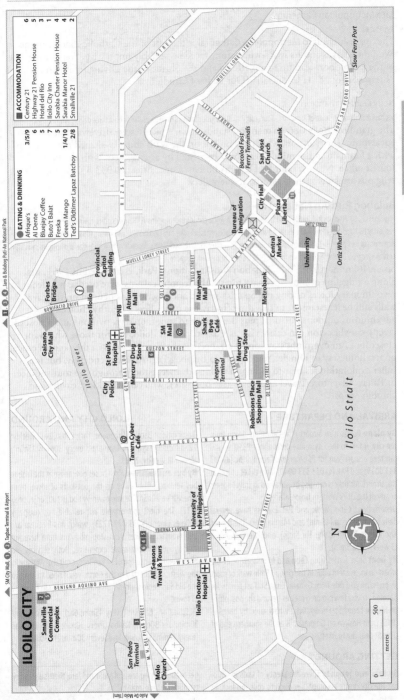

ILOILO CITY

■ ACCOMMODATION	
Century 21	6
Highway 21 Pension House	5
Hotel del Rio	3
Iloilo City Inn	1
Sarabia Charter Pension House	4
Sarabia Manor Hotel	4
Smallville 21	2

● EATING & DRINKING	
Afrique's	3/5/9
Al Dente	6
Bluejay Coffee	6
Buto't Balat	7
Freska	5
Green Mango	1/4/10
Ted's Oldtimer Lapaz Batchoy	2/8

6

Jaro Metropolitan Cathedral
Jaro Plaza

The Spanish-era **Jaro Metropolitan Cathedral** is the seat of the Catholic diocese in the Western Visayas and its ivory-white stone facade is suitably impressive. Steps either side of the main doors lead up to a platform and the Shrine to the Divine Infant and Nuestra Señora de la Candelaria (Our Lady of Candles).

Nelly Garden mansion
Set back from Luna St, south of Jaro Plaza • Tours cost P1000 per group; visitors need to reserve at least three days in advance

The grandiose **Nelly Garden mansion** stands down a picturesque driveway lined with eucalyptus. The mansion, which has murals on the walls and a U-shaped dining room with a fountain in the middle, can only be visited by arrangement with the Iloilo tourist office. Nearby, Lourdes Dellota's on East Lopez Street (☎033 337 4095) sells religious artefacts such as **santos**, and jewellery.

Bulabog Puti-An National Park
Foreigners P100, Filipinos P10, guide P150 (recommended if you're coming independently) • Ranger's office cabins P200/person, Dingle homestay P500/person • Panay Adventure Travel and Tours (see opposite) offer climbing (US$75) and caving (US$55) trips, with a minimum of four people • To reach the park independently, charter a taxi (P2000–3000, depending on vehicle size and how long you stay) or take a jeepney to Dingle (1hr), then tricycle (P15/person) to the park entrance

Some 40km north of Iloilo, **Bulabog Puti-An National Park**, established in 1961, sits along a ridgeline of intact primary forest. The region's caverns were used as a hideout by revolutionary forces during the Spanish period and inscriptions penned on the cave walls still bear testament to this time. Today the park offers a healthy choice of adventurous outdoor pursuits, plus the chance to spot monkeys, pythons and a host of creepy-crawlies. You can easily visit as a day-trip from Iloilo, but for those who want a closer look, an **overnight stay** can be arranged at the simple cabins in the ranger's office, or at a homestay in Dingle. You can get to Bulabog Puti-An independently, but for fuller exploration it's best to arrange a trip in advance, either through the tourist office, or Panay Adventure Travel and Tours (see opposite), who offer trekking, caving and climbing trips.

ARRIVAL AND DEPARTURE

ILOILO CITY AND AROUND

By plane Iloilo's new airport is at Cabutuan, 15km from the city. A taxi to the city centre costs about P350, or you can take a share-van for P50/person. Cebu Pacific (☎033 333 0015) and PAL (☎033 333 0040) have ticket offices at the airport. Air tickets can also be obtained at travel agents or any of the city's Western Union offices.

Destinations Cebu Pacific and PAL Express have several daily flights to Cebu (45min) and Manila (1hr). The former also flies to Davao (daily; 1hr 5min), and Puerto Princesa (3 weekly; 1hr 5min).

By boat Slow ferries from Cebu and Manila arrive at the wharf on the eastern edge of the city, a 15min walk or short jeepney/tricycle ride from General Luna St. Fast ferries for Bacolod arrive a few hundred metres beyond the post office on Muelle Loney St. Finally, Ortiz wharf, used by bangkas (P15) from Hoskyn on Guimaras, is at the southern end of Ortiz St near the market.

Destinations Bacolod (frequent; 1hr); Cebu City (7 weekly; 12–14hr); Hoskyn (on Guimaras; every 30min; 15min); Manila (1 weekly; 20hr).

By bus and minivan Most buses now arrive at the Tagbac bus terminal, 9km away on the outskirts of town, from where it's a 20min ride into town by taxi (P100) or jeepney (P12). The most comfortable and reliable bus company is Ceres Liner (☎033 329 1223), which has frequent a/c and ordinary services. Non-stop minivans from here are slightly quicker, but more expensive. Both services are most frequent until 1pm. For San José, capital of Antique in the west, and Libertad to the north, you'll need to head to the old San Pedro terminal on M.H. Del Pilar St in the west of town.

Destinations Caticlan (every 45min; 6hr); Estancia (every 20min; 3hr 30min); Kalibo (every 30min; 4–5hr); Roxas (every 30min; 3hr); San José (every 30min; 2hr 30min).

GETTING AROUND

By taxi and jeepney There are plenty of taxis in Iloilo, but the city centre is compact enough to cover on foot. To get to the outlying areas of Molo and Jaro, there's a jeepney terminal on Ledesma St.

INFORMATION AND TOURS

Tourist information The helpful tourist office (Mon–Fri 8am–5pm; ☎ 033 337 541) is in the grounds of the Capitol Building on Bonifacio Drive, one block north of J.M. Basa St and next to the Museo Iloilo.

Tours The tourist office has a list of accredited travel agencies, guides and drivers and can help you arrange trips in the surrounding region including to Guimaras, Bulabog Puti-An National Park and the churches of the south coast. More adventurous day-trips can be most easily arranged through Panay Adventures Travel & Tours (☎ 033 856 0558). They offer excursions in Bulabog Puti-An National Park (see opposite), biking trips to Guimaras (US$55/person), and tribal tours (US$65/person), which afford the opportunity to see the Ati weave, farm and hunt. All Seasons Travel & Tours, at the *Sarabia Manor Hotel* (see below; daily 8am–5pm; ☎ 033 336 7182), offer tours as well as ticketing, city tours and vehicle rental.

ACCOMMODATION

Century 21 Quezon St ☎ 033 335 8821, ⊕ ann2.net /hotels. Mid-sized, glass-fronted building offering basic, affordable rooms with a/c and cable TV. Singles are among the cheapest in town for this sort of quality, and family rooms for four are good value at P1825. Free wi-fi in the lobby. P1225

Highway 21 Pension House General Luna St ☎ 033 335 1220, ⊕ ann2.net/hotels. Excellent budget choice close to the *Sarabia Manor Hotel* with modern rooms and staff who are on the ball. All rooms have a/c, cable TV and hot water, but some are windowless. Good location with lots of restaurants on the doorstep. Free wi-fi. P1500

★ **Hotel del Rio** M.H. Del Pilar St, Molo ☎ 033 335 1171, ⊕ hoteldelrio.com.ph. Stylish and very professional hotel in a pleasant location on the river. Standard rooms have a/c, fridge, cable TV, king-size bed and river views. Superior (P3400) and deluxe rooms (P4200) are newer and more tastefully styled, but don't overlook the river. There's also a popular coffee shop, a good pool and free wi-fi. P2800

Iloilo City Inn 113 Seminario St, Jaro ☎ 033 320 2186. This friendly place enjoys a quiet location close to the sights in Jaro and has clean, comfortable a/c rooms at affordable prices. Downstairs, *Bavaria* serves good German food and beer and has wi-fi. The roof deck has views of the nearby cathedral. P850

Sarabia Charter Pension House General Luna St ☎ 033 508 1853. Arguably the best budget option in town, the *Sarabia Charter* is in the same quiet complex as the *Sarabia Manor Hotel*. The small, simple rooms are set around a small garden, and guests are entitled to use the swimming pool at *Sarabia Manor*. P720

Sarabia Manor Hotel General Luna St ☎ 033 335 1021, ⊕ sarabiamanorhotel.com. Iloilo's biggest hotel has seen better days, but is still worth considering for its vast array of rooms, pool and other facilities. The cheapest "Budget" rooms are small and very dated, but the "Economy" (P1100) and "Travellers'" rooms (P1485) are good value. The "Corporate" rooms (P1999–2999) are a considerable upgrade and also include breakfast. All rooms come with a/c and have cable TV. There's free wi-fi in the lobby or you can pay to use it in the room. The above prices are promo rates usually available in all room categories. P825

Smallville 21 Smallville Commercial Complex, Diversion Rd ☎ 033 501 6821, ⊕ ann2.net/hotels. This new addition to the homegrown *21* chain is perfect for those who want to have some of the city's best nightlife and restaurants on their doorstep, but otherwise a bit of a ride from the heart of town. Rooms are well kept, modern and fitted with dark wood furnishings. P1800

EATING AND DRINKING

Smallville Commercial Complex, across the river from the city centre, has everything from coffee shops and restaurants to bars featuring live bands, and full-blown clubs like *Aura*, *Ice* and *MO2*. *Coffeebreak* is a citywide chain which does good coffee and cakes.

Afrique's 100 Castilla St, Jaro ☎ 033 320 0554; 3 Valeria St ☎ 033 509 6092; Red Square Building, Smallville ☎ 033 509 4900; ⊕ afriquespizza.com. Atmospheric restaurant in a lovely old colonial house right behind Jaro cathedral. The menu is largely Italian and includes a huge range of pizzas along with specialities such as osso bucco pasta (P289). They also have more modern branches on Valeria St and at Smallville. Daily 10am–10pm.

ILOILO SPECIALITIES

Iloilo City is one of the best places in the country to try **seafood** and it's also known for a number of unique regional Illonggo delicacies, including **pancit Molo soup**, a garlicky noodle soup containing pork dumplings, which is named after the Molo area of the city and sold at numerous street stalls. **Batchoy**, an artery-hardening combination of liver, pork and beef with thin noodles, is also widely available.

6

Al Dente Sarabia Manor Hotel, General Luna St ☎033 336 7183, ⊛sarabiamanorhotel.com. Stylish, reasonably priced Italian restaurant serving tasty herb-roasted chicken (P155) and a range of delicious pasta dishes (P145–175). Daily 11am–10pm.

Bluejay Coffee Smallville Commercial Complex, Diversion Rd ☎033 333 3961, ⊛bluejaycoffee.com. *Bluejay* has moved from its central location to Smallville, but it still offers the same relaxed blend of comfy chairs and tasty food. The chunky apple and tuna salad sandwich (P120) is excellent, as is the coffee (P50–130). Mon–Sat 6am–midnight, Sun 8am–midnight.

★**Buto't Balat** Solis St ☎033 509 6770. A haven of tropical tranquillity and greenery in the midst of the downtown mayhem, this popular restaurant offers candlelit dining under thatched cabanas surrounding a small pond. Dishes to try include chilli shrimps (P245), pork Bicol Express (P175), beef *kare-kare* (P285), or there's fish by weight. Daily noon–midnight.

★**Freska** Smallville Boardwalk, Diversion Rd ☎0922 845 5260. *Freska* continues to make Illonggo dining easy

with its mouthwateringly good-value daily lunch and dinner buffets. Over forty dishes are on offer, including green mango salad, chicken *Inasal* (marinated and grilled – an Iloilo speciality), BBQ pork and a delicious dessert line-up. Your thirst can be quenched by the huge selection of imported beers and staff are upbeat to the point that they dance while they mop. Daily 11.30am–2.30pm & 5.30–10.30pm.

Green Mango Plaza Libertad; E. Lopez St, Jaro; SM City Mall, Diversion Rd; ☎0920 945 9406, ⊛greenmango .ph. Trendy Ilonggo fast-food chain with several branches around the city, including one in Jaro Plaza and another in SM City Mall. The extensive menu covers everything from chicken or *bangus* barbecue (P69) to noodles (P60), *pandesal* (P39) and *halo-halo* (P55–75). Daily 8am–8pm.

Ted's Oldtimer Lapaz Batchoy Valeria St & SM City Mall ☎033 337 9817. Though the precise origins of this famed Illongo dish are something of a mystery, *Ted's*, open since 1945, is without question *the* place to get an authentic helping of Ilonggo *batchoy* (P70). There's another branch on the ground floor of SM City Mall. Daily 8am–8pm.

DIRECTORY

Banks There are countless banks with ATMs. BPI and PNB both have branches on Plaza Libertad and General Luna St, there's a Metrobank on Iznart St and there are also ATMs in the malls.

Hospital St Paul's Hospital is at the eastern end of General Luna St (☎033 337 2741), towards the junction with Bonifacio. Dr Iloilo Doctors' Hospital is a 5min drive to the west of the city centre in Timawa Ave (☎033 337 7702).

Immigration The Bureau of Immigration (☎033 509 9651) is at the Old Customs House on Aduana St.

Internet access All of the big malls have internet cafés, including Netopia on the second floor of SM City, or you could try Tavern Cyber Café at the *Riverside Inn* on General Luna St, or Shark Byte Café on Yulo St (9am–7pm; P15/hr).

Pharmacies There are pharmacies in every mall. There's also a large branch of Mercury Drug opposite St Paul's Hospital on General Luna St.

Police The main city police department is in General Luna St (☎033 337 5511).

Post Iloilo's main post office is in Muelle Loney St, close to the junction with Guanco St.

The south coast

Heading southwest from Iloilo City along the coastal road – the only road – takes you through the atmospheric Spanish-era towns of **Oton**, **Tigbauan**, **Guimbal**, **Miag-ao** and **San Joaquin**. Each has an historic **church**, notably the Tigbauan's Baroque example (22km from Iloilo City) and, 13km further on, Guimbal's Catholic church, which stands close to a number of ruined seventeenth-century watchtowers.

Miag-ao Church

Pride of place along the southwest coast goes to **Miag-ao Church** (also known as the Church of Santo Tomas de Villanueva), 40km from Iloilo and built by the Augustinians between 1786 and 1797 as a fortress against Moro invasions. Declared a national landmark and a UNESCO World Heritage Site, the church is built of a local yellow-orange sandstone in Baroque-Romanesque style, a unique example of Filipino Rococo.

ARRIVAL AND DEPARTURE   THE SOUTH COAST

By car The easiest way to visit the church towns of the southwest is to hire a vehicle and driver in Iloilo for a day-trip, which should cost around P2500.

By bus and jeepney If you have time, it's also simple enough to travel between the towns by public transport. All buses from Iloilo City bound for San Joaquin (1hr) pass through Oton (10min), Tigbauan (15min), Guimbal (25min) and Miag-ao (50min), and plenty of jeepneys also ply the west coast route.

ACCOMMODATION

Anhawan Beach Resort Oton ☏033 336 2246, ⓦanhawanbeach.com. Overpriced resort not too far from the town with several different room types, all of which have a/c. There's also a nice pool and spa, plus an extensive activity line-up including jet-skiing, kayaking and horseriding. **P3600**

Bantayan Beach Resort Guimbal ☏033 315 5009. Named after the squat, Spanish-era watchtower on the property, this place has ordinary a/c cottages, some of which have recently been renovated (P1750). There's a pool table and free wi-fi in the restaurant. **P1400**

The west coast

Most of the west coast of Panay, made up largely of the province of **Antique**, is untouched by tourism. This is one of the poorest areas of the Philippines, with a solitary coastal road connecting a series of isolated villages and towns. It's an attractive coastline with a savage backdrop of jungled mountains that are only just beginning to be explored and climbed. The journey along the province's coast, from **San José** in the south to **Libertad** in the north, provides an excellent opportunity to experience a simple provincial life, shielded from the rest of the Philippines by mountains on one side and sea on the other.

San José

SAN JOSÉ is a busy little port town whose major claim to fame – apart from being capital of Antique – seems to be that its cathedral has the tallest bell tower in Panay. There are no tourist sights here, just a chaotic wharf, a cracked plaza and a main street, the National Highway, lined with pawnshops, canteens and rice dealers. The town's annual **Binirayan festival**, held from April 30 to May 2, commemorates the thirteenth-century landing of ten Malay chieftains who established the first Malayan settlement in the Philippines.

Tibiao

About halfway along Panay's west coast, **TIBIAO** is best used as a base for **whitewater kayaking**, **rafting** and **trekking** on the Tibiao River, at the head of which the town stands. Tibiao also stands in the shadow of Panay's highest peak, **Mount Madja-as** (2090m) – it's possible to climb this daunting mountain, but a permit and guide are essential.

Tibiao Eco Adventure Park

Entry P50, zip-line P300, whitewater kayaking P200 • Visits can also be arranged as part of a tour with Katahum Tours (see below)

A few kilometres inland, the **Tibiao Eco Adventure Park** (aka TEA Park) opened in 2012 and offers a host of outdoors activities from gentle introductory kayaking lessons through to whitewater rides, canyoning and rapelling. For many the highlight is the 1km long zip-line through the lush jungle.

ARRIVAL AND DEPARTURE   THE WEST COAST

By bus San José's bus station is in Isabel St, 1km west of the centre and the pier is on the western edge of the town. Buses running between San José and Caticlan pass through Tibiao.

ACTIVITIES

Katahum Tours Tibiao ☏0919 813 9893, ⓦkatahum .com. Fish spa and tour operator who can arrange everything from gentle day tours to rafting and trekking.

Tribal Adventures See box, p.339. Professional adventure operator running whitewater kayaking trips from their base in Boracay (see p.337).

ACCOMMODATION

SAN JOSÉ

Centillion House 2000 Brgy Bantayan ☏036 540 9403, ⓦcentillionhouse.com. Set above a small shopping mall this place has clean, well-maintained rooms with a/c and cable TV, and also serves the best meals in town. **P1400**

TIBIAO

Hometel University of Antique Campus, Main Rd. Twelve simple rooms mostly with shared bathrooms, set in the peaceful university campus. **P500** per person

Kayak Inn Beyond TEA Park, in the foothills outside

Tibiao ☎ 0905 906 2380. Simple lodge by the river with basic bamboo *bahay kubo* huts each with a *kawa*, a large wok-like bath heated by fire (originally used for cooking muscovado sugar; P200). **P500**

The east coast

Panay's **east coast** – from Iloilo City north to **Estancia** – is an undeveloped area of wilderness and sun-drenched barangays rarely seen by tourists. There are some wonderfully pristine islands off the coast, many of them unfamiliar even to locals, but to explore them you'll need time on your hands, patience and a willingness to spend nights camped on beaches. This region was badly hit by Typhoon Yolanda with heavy loss of life. In time tourism can have its role here, but for now the region is best left to get back on its feet.

Roxas

ROXAS, the capital of Capiz province, is renowned for its seafood, and also has a reputation among Filipinos as being a hotbed of witches and shamans. The city is connected by air, ferry and land, but aside from taking a trip out to the pleasant if unremarkable stretch of golden sand at **Baybay Beach**, 4km north of town, and trying the seafood, there is little to keep visitors in Roxas for long.

In late 2013 Roxas became the headquarters for the Yolanda relief operation in devastated northern Panay. While Roxas proper escaped without too much serious damage, many of the famous seafood shacks (and resorts) at Baybay were damaged or destroyed, but were already being rebuilt at the time of writing.

ARRIVAL AND INFORMATION   ROXAS

By plane The airport, 10min north of the city by jeepney or tricycle (P15) in Arnaldo Blvd, is served daily from Manila by PAL and Cebu Pacific flights, both of which have offices there.

By boat Ferries dock at the Calusi pier, 2km west of Baybay Beach. Tricycles run out to the pier for P20. Providing the weather is agreeable, bangkas leave every morning for Sibuyan Island in the Romblon group (4–5hr).

By bus, minivan and jeepney Services for Iloilo, Kalibo and Estancia use the Alba terminus south of the Panay River, reachable by tricycle. Direct services stop early, so another alternative is to catch one of the frequent buses to Sigma (until 6.45pm), and then change there for Kalibo or Caticlan.

Services To get online, head for Oracle Internet Café, Rizal St at Gomez St.

ACCOMMODATION AND EATING

ROXAS

Halaran Plaza Hotel Opposite City Hall, Rizal St ☎ 036 621 0649. In a central location, Halaran has a choice of spacious and comfortable fan and a/c rooms with solid wooden floors and high ceilings, although they can be noisy. **P850**

Roxas President's Inn Rizal Ave at Lopez Jaena St ☎ 036 621 0208, ⓦ roxaspresidentsinn.com. This hotel

is strewn with antiques and rooms are cosy and clean, with a/c, cable TV and hot showers. There's also a convivial café with wi-fi in the lobby. **P1400**

BAYBAY BEACH

Alma's Grill ☎ 036 521 3384. Quickly rebuilt after Yolanda destroyed the original shack, *Alma's* still serves the same standout *gambas* (P300 good for six people) and

---

TINDOG CAPIZ!

Visitors to Roxas can help with the Yolanda relief and recovery effort by taking one of the provincial tourist office's "Tindog Capiz!" (Arise Capiz!) tours (☎ 033 337 5411, ⓔ capiz.tourism @yahoo.com). **Voluntourism** trips were already in place prior to Yolanda, but now have more focus and purpose than ever. Projects include house and school building, mangrove replanting, food production and livelihood training programmes.

grilled fish from a bright yellow building on the seashore. Daily 7am–9pm.

Coco Veranda ⓣ036 621 6185. Pretty beachside restaurant with friendly service and a huge seafood menu. As well as excellent crab, scallops, oysters, mussels and prawns, there's also pink salmon sashimi (P160/100g), plus cocktails and desserts. Free wi-fi. Daily 10am–10pm.

Grand Gazebo ⓣ036 522 7726. Attractive, locally owned place just over the road from the beach, with bright, spacious a/c rooms with flat-screen TVs, set around a pleasant lawn. Free wi-fi access and breakfast included. **P1800**

San Antonio Resort ⓣ036 621 6638, ⓦthesanantonioresort.com. A range of rooms from tiny "econo-rooms" to luxurious suites overlooking an attractive lagoon just back from the beach. There's also a nice pool (with poolside wi-fi), and kayaking on the lagoon. **P980**

6

Kalibo

KALIBO, the capital of Aklan province, is the biggest – in fact the only – attraction of Panay's **north coast**, which from Roxas in the east to Caticlan in the west (see p.340) is mostly industrial and has no notable beaches. Served by flights from around Asia, Kalibo lies on the well-trodden path to Boracay and for most visitors is simply the place they get off the plane and onto the bus.

The town's major thoroughfare is **Roxas Avenue**, which runs into town from the airport in the southeast, with most streets leading off it on a southwest–northeast axis. It's really just another small town, full of tricycles and fast-food outlets, but it does have an interesting **museum**, and every second week of January it hosts what is probably the biggest street party in the country, the **Ati-Atihan** (see box, p.336), an exuberant festival that celebrates the original inhabitants of the area and the later arrival of Catholicism.

Museo It Akean

San Martelino St at Burgos St • Mon–Sat 8am–noon & 1–5pm • P15 • ⓣ036 268 9260

Kalibo is home to one of Panay's best museums, the **Museo It Akean**. Though modest, it's the only museum to document the cultural heritage of the Aklaňons (Aklan people), and contains exhibits of the area's old *piña* textiles, pottery, religious relics, literature and Spanish-era artefacts, many on loan from affluent local families. Among the most interesting exhibits are rare costumes that were worn by Aklan tribespeople during festivals. Despite serious earthquake damage in the 1980s, the museum building retains some of the original features; since its construction by the Spanish in 1882, it has also been used as a school, a courtroom and a garrison.

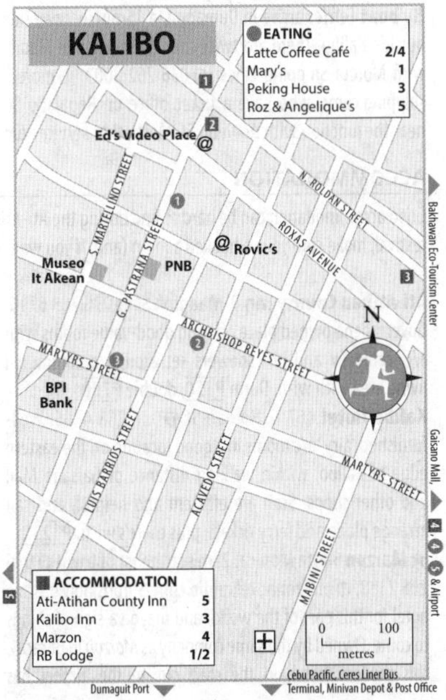
KALIBO
EATING
Latte Coffee Café 2/4
Mary's 1
Peking House 3
Roz & Angelique's 5
Ed's Video Place
N. Roldan Street
Roxas Avenue
S. Martellino Street
G. Pastrana Street
Rovic's
Museo It Akean
PNB
Archbishop Reyes Street
Martyrs Street
BPI Bank
Luis Barrios Street
Acavedo Street
Mabini Street
N
ACCOMMODATION
Ati-Atihan County Inn 5
Kalibo Inn 3
Marzon 4
RB Lodge 1/2
0 100
metres
Bakhawan Eco-Tourism Center
Gaisano Mall, & Airport
Cebu Pacific, Ceres Liner Bus Terminal, Minivan Depot & Post Office
Dumaguit Port

Bakhawan Eco-tourism Centre and Mangrove Park

Bakhawan • Daily 8am–5pm • P20

A short tricycle ride from town, the **Bakhawan Eco-tourism Centre and Mangrove Park** is the site of a mangrove replanting project. The project was principally initiated to prevent flood and storm surges, but also benefits local wildlife and affords visitors the chance to experience this little seen habitat up close. Once here you can walk along a pretty 1km-long boardwalk through the tangled mangrove thickets to the beach.

6

ATI-ATIHAN: KEEP ON GOING, NO TIRING

Ati-Atihan is a quasi-religious mardi gras held every January in Kalibo. The culmination of the two-week event is a procession through the streets on the third Sunday of the month, a sustained three-day, three-night frenzy of carousing and dancing. Transvestites bring out their best frocks and schoolgirls with hats made of coconuts join aborigines, celebrities and priests in fancy dress. Throw in the unending beat of massed drums and the average Filipino's predisposition for a good party, and the result is a flamboyant alfresco rave that claims to be the biggest and most prolonged in the country. The Ati-Atihan mantra *Hala Bira, Puera Pasma* translates as "Keep on going, no tiring."

The festival's **origins** can be traced to 1210, when refugees from Borneo fled north to Panay. Panay's Negrito natives, known as Atis, sold them land and both parties celebrated the deal with a feast, which was then repeated year on year. The fancy-dress element derives from the lighter-skinned Borneans blacking up their faces in affectionate imitation of the Atis. Later, Spanish friars co-opted the festival in honour of the **Santo Niño**, spreading the word among islanders that the baby Jesus had appeared to help drive off a pirate attack. It was a move calculated to hasten the propagation of Catholicism throughout the Philippines, and it worked. Ati-Atihan has since become so popular that similar festivals have cropped up all over the Visayas. Historians generally agree, however, that the Kalibo Ati-Atihan is the real thing.

ARRIVAL AND DEPARTURE
KALIBO

By plane The 10min tricycle ride into town from the airport, a distance of about 6km, costs P30. Air Asia, PAL (☎036 262 3260) and Cebu Pacific (☎036 262 5407) all have ticket offices at the airport; Cebu Pacific also has an office on Toting Reyes St, near the junction with Quezon Ave.
Destinations Busan, South Korea (2 weekly; 4hr 55min); Cebu (2 daily; 55min); Kuala Lumpur, Malaysia (4 weekly; 3hr 35min); Manila (15 daily; 1hr); Seoul, South Korea (2 daily; 5hr 15min); Taipei, Taiwan (1 daily; 2hr 30min).
By boat Ferries arrive in Dumaguit, a 15min jeepney ride outside Kalibo. There are twice-weekly services to Manila with Moreta Shipping Lines (☎036 262 3003, ⓦmoreta shipping.com), who have a ticket office on Regalado St, near the junction with Acavedo St. Most other services run

from Caticlan, with buses shuttling passengers from Kalibo's Ceres Liner terminal to the port (see p.340).
By bus and van Regular buses and vans serving Caticlan (the jumping-off point for Boracay) arrive and depart directly from the airport (P200; 2hr). Cheaper buses and vans (P100) to Caticlan leave from the Ceres Liner terminal on Osmeña Ave, from where there are also regular buses and vans to all other destinations listed. Roll-on-roll-off services also run from Kalibo bus terminal to Manila (via Caticlan, ferry to Roxas on Mindoro, bus to Calapan, ferry to Batangas and bus to Manila) costing P1100 for the journey (12hr).
Destinations Caticlan (frequent; 2hr); Iloilo (every 30min; 4–5hr); Roxas (hourly; 2hr); San José (hourly; 4hr).

ACCOMMODATION

Good accommodation can be hard to find during the Ati-Atihan, when rates double or triple, so if you're visiting during the festival, make sure you've booked a room (and, if you want to fly in, your plane ticket) in advance.

Ati-Atihan County Inn D. Maagma St ☎036 268 6116. Government-owned place offering good-value rooms with a/c, cable TV and hot showers set around a communal living area with wi-fi. Dorm P150, double P700
Kalibo Hotel 467 N. Roldan St ☎036 268 4765. Well-furnished, airy, a/c rooms in a good location on the eastern edge of Kalibo, within walking distance of Gaisano Mall and other shops. Staff are efficient and helpful, and can arrange plane and ferry tickets, plus there's wi-fi. P1232
★**Marzon** Santa Monica, 2km southeast of town ☎036 268 2188, ⓦmarzonhotelkalibo.com. Surprisingly upscale hotel for this part of the world, and maybe a sign of things to come. Owned by the same company as *Marzon* in Boracay, this modern hotel on the road out to the airport has

comfortable, stylish rooms and a huge swimming pool. *Latte Coffee Café* and *Roz & Angelique's* are also right next door (see opposite). P1600
RB Lodge G. Pastrana St & N.Roldan St ☎036 268 5200. Good-value and surprisingly chic little hotel which has recently opened a second branch just around the corner from the original. In the original building, the cheapest fan rooms are small and dark, but the better a/c rooms (P1150) on the second floor are quiet, nicely furnished and look over banana palms in the neighbouring backyard. There's also an internet café and a coffee shop. The new building on N. Roldan St has equally attractive a/c rooms with local accents and furnishings at the same price. Free wi-fi and breakfast. P800

EATING

Kalibo's dining options have improved in recent years, particularly out in Santa Monica on the way to the airport. In town there are a few independent places, but otherwise it's a choice of hole-in-the wall carinderias or fast-food chains which include *Chowking*, *Jollibee* and *Andok's*.

Latte Coffee Café Branches at Archbishop Reyes St and at Santa Monica ☎ 036 268 9026. There are two branches of this pleasant coffee shop in Kalibo, both of which sell great coffee, sandwiches and light meals (P140–350), alongside Havaiana flip-flops. Free wi-fi. Daily 9am–7pm.

Mary's G. Pastrana St ☎ 036 268 8204. Clean, bustling canteen-style place serving huge bowls of noodles (P130), sandwiches, desserts and coffee. Daily 8am–6pm.

Peking House Martyrs St ☎ 036 268 4752. Kalibo's most popular Chinese restaurant is often full of folk taking advantage of the delicious but inexpensive (Filipino) Chinese food. Mains P100–200. Daily 11am–8pm.

Roz & Angelique's Santa Monica ☎ 036 268 3512. A popular dining spot for Kalibo's well-to-do, this formal restaurant has an extensive menu featuring everything from crispy *pata* (P360, good for three) to crêpes (P120), burgers, sandwiches, crème brûlée and shakes. No MSG is used in the cooking and there's free wi-fi. Daily 10.30am–9pm.

DIRECTORY

Banks There are a number of banks with ATMs, including a BPI on Martyrs St and a PNB on G. Pastrana St.

Hospital The Kalibo provincial hospital (☎ 036 268 4917), an immense, modern, rose-pink building, is on Mabini St.

Internet access There are many small internet cafés, including Ed's Video Place on G. Pastrana St (daily 8am–9pm; P15/hr), and Rovic's on Luis Barrios St.

Post The post office is in the Provincial Capitol Building, off Osmena Ave in the south of town.

Boracay

Some 350km south of Manila, and just off the northeastern tip of Panay, the island of **BORACAY** is famed for picture-perfect 4km **White Beach**, its quality dining and wild nightlife scene, plus activities from scuba diving to kitesurfing. It may be only 7km long and 1km wide at its narrowest point, but Boracay has over thirty beaches and coves, and enough accommodation options to suit all budgets. Watching the graceful *paraws* (sailboats) setting sail at sunset is worth the journey in its own right.

For all its beauty, though, Boracay is of course the most developed resort in the Visayas, a situation which has its downsides – it can be hard to relax with the constant blare of music on the beach and the hum of tricycles on the island's main road. Many resort owners are aware of how fragile the island is and organize beach clean-ups and recycling seminars. The authorities are also finally waking up to some of the island's problems and threats to demolish resorts that have been built without permission have actually come into effect, plus a beach **smoking ban** has also been enforced. Unlike the rest of the country, **topless sunbathing** is common at Boracay but the authorities are keen to keep the island a family destination – in 2011 a "sex on the beach" ban was mooted after some Western couples were filmed being over amorous on New Year's Eve.

WET SEASON ON BORACAY

The two distinct **climatic seasons** in the Philippines have a marked effect on Boracay. Because of the island's north–south orientation, White Beach takes the brunt of onshore winds during the wet season (June–Oct), so don't expect it to look at its well-barbered best at that time. The waves can be big, washing up old coconuts, seaweed and dead branches. Many beachfront resorts and restaurants are forced to erect unsightly tarpaulins to keep out the wind and sand and some even close during July and August, the wettest months. The onshore wind makes for some thrilling windsurfing and kiteboarding, but other ocean activities move to calmer waters on the island's east side.

6

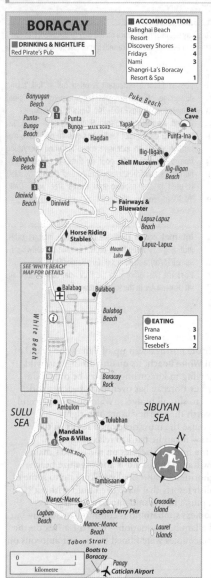

BORACAY

■ ACCOMMODATION
Balinghai Beach Resort	2
Discovery Shores	5
Fridays	4
Nami	3
Shangri-La's Boracay Resort & Spa	1

■ DRINKING & NIGHTLIFE
Red Pirate's Pub	1

● EATING
Prana	3
Sirena	1
Tesebel's	2

Banyugan Beach

Puka Beach

Bat Cave

Punta-Bunga Beach

Punta Bunga MAIN ROAD

Yapak

Hagdan

Punta-Ina

Balinghai Beach

Ilig-Iligan

Shell Museum

Ilig-Iligan Beach

Diniwid Beach

Diniwid

Fairways & Bluewater

Lapuz-Lapuz Beach

Horse Riding Stables

Mount Luho

Lapuz-Lapuz

SEE 'WHITE BEACH' MAP FOR DETAILS

Balabag

Bulabog

White Beach

Bulabog Beach

Boracay Rock

SULU SEA

Ambulon

Tulubhan

SIBUYAN SEA

Mandala Spa & Villas

MAIN ROAD

Malabunot

N

Tambisaan

Manoc-Manoc

Cagban Ferry Pier

Crocodile Island

Cagban Beach

Manoc-Manoc Beach

Laurel Islands

Tabon Strait

Boats to Boracay

Panay

Catlclan Airport

0   1
kilometre

White Beach

To many visitors the 4km talcum-powdery sand strip of **White Beach** is Boracay, but while the carnival of activities, touts and tourists is hardly an accurate representation of Philippines beach life, it is certainly fun. A short walk along the beach takes you past restaurants serving a veritable United Nations of cuisines, including Greek, Indian, Caribbean, French, Thai and more. The beach is also dotted with interesting little bars and bistros, some of them no more than a few chairs and tables on the beach, others where you can now sit in air-conditioned luxury eating Chateaubriand and smoking Cuban cigars.

Not so long ago bangkas from Caticlan would pull up directly to White Beach, at one of three **boat stations**. Though the stations themselves have disappeared, their names continue to be used to describe the three respective segments of the beach. The smartest places to stay are mostly towards the quieter far north section of the beach beyond Boat Station 1. To the south in Boat Station 2 the lively heart of the beach focuses on **D'Mall**, a warren of outdoor lanes and one main street, packed with cafés and shops. Things gradually quieten down as you move south towards Boat Station 3, where there's a clutch of budget accommodation set back from the beach, plus a *Marriott* development currently under construction.

Around the island

Most visitors fall in love with White Beach, but don't miss **Puka Beach** on the north coast, which is famous for shiny white seashells called *puka*. A pleasant way to get there is to hire a bangka on White Beach (P700 one way), and then take a tricycle back (P150). To the north of White Beach sits the little village of **Diniwid** with its 200m beach, accessible from White Beach on a path carved out of the cliffs. At the end of a steep path over the next hill is the tiny **Balinghai Beach**, enclosed by walls of rock. Meanwhile, on the other side of the island, **Bulabog Beach** has developed from a small fishing village into a popular kitesurfing destination.

In the northeast side of the island **Ilig-Iligan Beach** has coves and caves, as well as jungle full of fruit bats. **Mount Luho**, also in the north, is an easy ascent (P60 entry fee), and the reward is terrific 360-degree views of the island and neighbouring Romblon.

BORACAY'S ACTIVITY BONANZA

Boracay has the biggest range of **activities** to be found anywhere in the Philippines. In addition to the sports below, there are numerous dive sites and operators (see box, p.342).

KITEBOARDING AND WINDSURFING

Windsurfing has been popular in Boracay for some time, and in recent years the **kiteboarding** boom has seen the island emerge as one of the world's premier locations for this exciting new sport. Boarders gather on Bulabog Beach to take advantage of the constant wind during the peak season, while in the off-season the focus shifts to White Beach. There are a number of schools offering both windsurfing and kiteboarding equipment rental and lessons covering everything from basic introductory classes (P2750) to full-blown courses (P19,000).

OTHER WATERSPORTS

Other watersports on offer include **jet-skiing** (P2000/30min), **waterskiing** (P2500), **banana boat rides** (P250/person), **boat hire** (sailing boats P2500/hr; speedboats P3500/hr), **glass-bottom boat rides** (P750/person), **fly-fishing** (P600 for 15min), **ocean kayaking** (P500/hr or P1000 for 30min in a completely translucent "Crystal" kayak – immediately north of *Red Pirates Pub*; call ☎036 288 2818), **parasailing** (P2000) and even **mermaid swimming** (yes you read that correctly; P1500 for 3hr; call ☎036 288 3766).

For a true adrenaline experience, **flyboarding** (P7900 for 30min including return transport to Carabao Island, lunch and drinks; call ☎0910 230 0000) involves a jet propulsion tube sending riders several meters above the water. More natural highs can be achieved by **cliff diving** at Ariel's Point, a thirty-minute boat ride away from White Beach; trips can be arranged through *Boracay Beach Club* at Boat Station 1 (☎036 288 6770; P2000 for a full day out including transport, lunch and unlimited beers).

LAND SPORTS

On land the choices are equally extensive and you can take your pick from **quad biking** (P2500/hr), **golf** at Fairways & Bluewater, Newcoast (from P2000; ☎036 288 5587, ⓦfairwaysandbluewater.com.ph), **horseriding** in Balabag (P645/hr; ☎036 288 3311), **zip-lining** at Mount Luho (P700), **zorbing** (P580) or **mountain biking** (P150/hr). One of the nicest rides is to cycle from Punta Bunga to Tambisaan Beach, where the shoreline is dotted with installation art, including the famous Boracay Sandcastle. Up in the air you can get great views from even a ten-minute **helicopter ride** (P3500/person).

Further afield at **Tibiao** (see p.333) on the mainland of Panay there are a host of adrenaline-inducing options including whitewater kayaking, canyoning and further zip-lining opportunities: excursions here can be arranged through Tribal Adventures, or Katahum Tours in Tibiao itself (see p.333).

OPERATORS

You'll find **touts** offering almost all of the activities above along the beach, but for specialist activities it's best to head direct to the operators.

Allan B. Fun Tours Near Boat Station 2, White Beach ☎036 288 5577, ⓔallan_b68@yahoo.com. The go-to guy for many of the touts on White Beach, Allan B.'s is one of the most reliable places to arrange activities.

Filipino Travel Centre Boracay Tourist Center (see p.340). ☎036 288 6499, ⓦfilipinotravel.com.ph. Offers the usual activities, plus flights and tours in other parts of the Philippines. There's also a useful notice board here advertising new boat services, adventure tours, activities, nightlife and accommodation.

Funboard Centre Northern end of Bulabog Beach ☎0927 343 4071, ⓦwindsurfasia.com. Windsurf specialists who also offer kiteboarding from beginner to pro.

Hangin Kiteboarding Boracay Beach Resort, White Beach ☎036 288 3663; Greenyard, Bulabog Beach (Oct–May only) ☎036 288 3208, ⓦkiteboardingboracay.com. One of the best-established kiteboarding schools offering rental, storage, lessons and more. Beginner lessons cost P2750 (90min) or P6250 (3hr), with IKO Certification.

Tribal Adventures Boracay Sandcastles, Boat Station 1 ☎036 288 3207, ⓦtribaladventures.com. Professional operator running a host of adventurous trips around the Philippines. Their three-day Tibiao trip takes in hiking and whitewater kayaking and costs from P15,000/person with a minimum of four (all inclusive).

ARRIVAL AND DEPARTURE

BORACAY

Travelling to and from Boracay has never been easier and long-distance **ferries** have largely been superseded by countless **flights**. Unless you're coming from Carabao Island in the Romblon group, all visitors must pass through the hectic little town of **Caticlan**, from where frequent bangkas shuttle visitors across to **Cagban pier** in the south of Boracay. Boats cost P25 during the day and P30 at night, plus P75 environmental fee and a P100 boat terminal fee. From Cagban it's just a short tricycle journey to White Beach (P100). If you're flying in and have booked to stay at a resort, you might be met at the airstrip by their representative.

By plane Cebu Pacific and PAL flights connect Caticlan with Manila and Cebu. The same destinations are also served from Kalibo, which also has a handful of flights to other Asian countries (see p.336). Caticlan airstrip is a three-minute tricycle ride (P25/person) from the ferry terminal. As well as at the airport ticket offices, flights can be booked through Filipino Travel Centre inside the Boracay Tourist Centre.
Destinations Cebu (3 daily; 1hr), Manila (30 plus daily; 1hr).
By boat From Mindoro there are regular Montenegro Shipping Lines (☎ 036 288 7373, ⍵ montenegrolines.com .ph) and Starlite (☎ 036 288 7495) ferries from Roxas to Caticlan (around 4hr; from P300). For Romblon there are bangkas from Caticlan to Looc on Tablas, plus a weekly

car ferry to Odiongan (Sun; 3hr). Alternatively you can negotiate with a boat captain on White Beach to take you to Carabao, and then travel onwards to the main island group by bangka or pumpboat.
Destinations Carabao (2 daily; 1hr); Looc (on Tablas; 2 daily; 3hr); Roxas (on Mindoro; 6 daily; 4hr).
By bus and van Buses drop you on the main road through Caticlan, about 1km from the pier and airport, from where there are tricycles to take you the rest of the way. Many vans from Kalibo (particularly from the airport) will take you all the way to the ferry pier.
Destinations Iloilo (hourly until 4pm; 6hr); Kalibo (frequent; 2hr); San José (6 daily; 3hr).

GETTING AROUND

By tricycle Fares should be no more than P150 for a trip along the length of the island's main road – make sure you agree a fare before you climb on board as some drivers have a habit of adding "extras" at the end of the journey. Electronic tricycles ("e-trikes"), which charge similar rates, have recently been introduced to the island, with the ambitious plan of

gradually phasing out their petrol-driven predecessors.
By bangka You can hire 4–6-person bangkas or *paraw* for around P700/hr.
By bike Mountain bikes can be rented from several places along the beach. Try Arvin (☎ 0920 384 3430), next to *A Rock* apartments at Boat Station 3.

INFORMATION

Tourist information The Department of Tourism has a small, ineffectual tourist office (☎ 036 288 3689) in D'Mall, on the right-hand side as you enter. A few minutes' walk to the south, the Boracay Tourist Center (daily 9am–10pm, shop open until 11.30pm; ☎ 036 288 3704, ⍵ touristcenter .com.ph) is far more useful; as well as sending mail,

exchanging cash and selling maps, it also holds a branch of Filipino Travel Center (daily 9am–6pm; see box, p.339).
Listings The *Boracay Sun* (⍵ boracaysun.com) and expat newspapers, plus *My Boracay* mini-guide are all distributed free and have the latest details of what's new and happening in Boracay.

ACCOMMODATION

There are about three hundred **resorts** on Boracay which means that except at peak times (Christmas, Easter and Chinese New Year, when prices can rise by as much as fifty percent) you should be able to find a place to stay simply by taking a stroll down White Beach. Prices have risen sharply in recent years, with the best rooms in high-end places going for upwards of US$500 a night, but there are still cheapies out there. Broadly speaking, the beach is divided into three sections: **Boat Station 1 and north** is high end, **Boat Station 2 and around** is generally mid-range, while the lanes behind the beach **south of Boat Station 3** hold a selection of budget backpacker options, plus a smattering of mid-range and high-end places. Generally speaking the further back from the beach you're prepared to stay the cheaper the rooms you can find. It's always worth negotiating for a discount, especially if you plan to stay a while.

WHITE BEACH

BOAT STATION 1 AND POINTS NORTH

Discovery Shores At the northern end of White Beach, beyond Boat Station 1 ☎ 036 288 4500, ⍵ discovery shoresboracay.com; map p.338. At the upper end of

Boracay's price spectrum, *Discovery Shores* features bright, spacious and ultramodern rooms stretching back up the hill behind the beach. As you'd expect there's a pool and a decent restaurant, and all rooms are comfortable and contain an impressive array of amenities, which include

FROM TOP MASSKARA FESTIVAL, BACOLOD (P.307), WHITE BEACH, BORACAY (P.338) >

6

DIVING AROUND BORACAY

Boracay's diving isn't as varied or extreme as diving in Palawan or Puerto Galera, but there's still enough to keep everyone happy. The dive sites around the island, all easily accessible by bangka, include gentle drift dives, coral gardens and some deeper dives with a good chance of encounters with sharks. At **Crocodile Island**, 15min southeast of Boracay, there's a shallow reef that drops off to 25m and a number of small canyons where sea snakes gather. **Big and Small Laurel** are neighbouring islets with some of the best soft coral in the Visayas and shoals of snappers, sweetlips, eels, sea snakes, morays, puffers and boxfish. Probably the star attraction for divers here is **Yapak**, where you freefall into the big blue, eventually finding at 30m the top of a marine wall where there are batfish, wahoo, tuna, barracuda and cruising grey reef sharks. **Lapu Wall** is a day-trip from Boracay to the northern coast of Panay, but the diving is some of the most challenging in the area, with overhangs and caverns. Another good day-trip is north to Carabao Island (see p.351), in the province of Romblon, where there are splendid reefs, some peaceful, powdery beaches and a resort if you want to stay overnight.

DIVE OPERATORS

There are dozens of licensed dive operators along White Beach. A **Discover Scuba** introductory session with a dive master costs around P3000, while a full PADI **Open Water Course** (3–4 days) costs around P20,000. You can even try **helmet diving** (P3000/30min), whereby air is supplied underwater through a helmet. Of the countless dive operators on the island, the following are well established and PADI 5-star rated:

Blue Mango Blue Mango Inn (see opposite).
Calypso Diving Boat Station 2 & at Pinjalo Resort (see opposite).
DiveGurus Boat Station 3 ☏ 036 288 5486, ⓦ divegurus.com.

Fisheye Divers Boat Station 1 ☏ 036 288 6090, ⓦ fisheyedivers.com.
Victory Divers Boat Station 2 ☏ 036 288 3209, ⓦ victorydivers.com.

---

iPod dock, flatscreen TV, DVD player and free wi-fi. The premier rooms have an expansive outdoor living area with a large jacuzzi and views down to the sea. **P15,300**

Frendz Resort 100m off Main Rd, near Elementary School ☏ 036 288 3803, ⓦ frendzresortboracay.com; map opposite. Tucked halfway between the beach and main road, the simple cottages at *Frendz* present no-frills laidback beach living. The native huts have double beds, hot and cold showers and nice verandas. There are also separate male and female dorms and a café with wi-fi internet access. Bring a padlock for your locker. Two-night minimum stay for online bookings. Dorm **P600**, double **P2000**

★ **Fridays** Right at the northern end beyond Boat Station 1 ☏ 036 288 6200, ⓦ fridaysboracay.com; map p.338. One of Boracay's first resorts, and still one of the best, *Fridays* occupies a prime spot at the northern end of the beach and offers comfortable deluxe and premier rooms, and top-notch premier suites which enjoy great ocean views. All rooms are decked out in native style but with modern facilities. Although it's only a three-star property, the service and amenities run close to five star and include a decent pool and wi-fi throughout. **P18,050**

BOAT STATION 2 AND AROUND

★ **Bamboo Bungalows** Just north of D'Mall ☏ 036 288 6324, ⓦ bbboracay.com; map opposite. Great choice in the heart of the action, a stone's throw from

D'Mall. There's a range of cottages and apartments set around the lush garden, and some rooms at the front of the main building with beach views. **P4200**

Fat Jimmy's 300m inland, next to D'Mall ☏ 0922 875 3088, ⓦ fatjimmysresort.com; map opposite. One of a number of budget resorts along a path next to D'Mall. Relaxed, quiet and friendly, *Fat Jimmy's* has sixteen simple but charming fan-cooled or a/c rooms, five of which have their own small patio garden (P3000). Family rooms sleep four with a bunk bed for the kids and rates include a choice of Filipino or American breakfast. Free wi-fi and all-round good value. **P1500**

Mango-Ray Resort On the beach, 100m south of D'Mall ☏ 036 288 6129, ⓦ mangoray-boracay.com; map opposite. Nine tastefully furnished a/c rooms with fridge, cable TV, telephone and spacious porch, plus one suite at the front of the property looking out over the ocean. Floors are tiled, the whitewashed walls are decorated with tasteful Filipino art and the surrounding gardens are lush and peaceful. Breakfast and wi-fi included. **P5500**

Nigi Nigi Nu Noos 'e' Nu Nu Noos A 5min walk north of the Boracay Tourist Center ☏ 036 288 3101, ⓦ niginigi.com; map opposite. Long-standing and enduringly popular resident of White Beach featuring Indonesian-style cottages set in tranquil tropical gardens. All of the spacious cottages have thatched pagoda roofs and shady verandas. Free wi-fi and a decent restaurant and bar. **P5900**

Pinjalo Resort Down the footpath beside the Tourist Center, on the left ☎036 288 3206, ⓦcalypso-boracay .com/pinjalo; map below. Owned and operated by Calypso Diving, this place is worth the effort to find if you're looking for good-value, comfortable accommodation close to the beach but away from the noise of the bars and clubs. Standard rooms are on the small side making it worth paying the extra for the deluxe options (P6800). All rooms are tastefully furnished and look onto peaceful gardens, and there's poolside wi-fi. In addition, Calypso Diving also have some chic rooms (P5650) and suites (P8065) next to their dive shop. **P5400**

Seabird International Resort Set back from the beach a short walk north of D'Mall ☎036 288 3047, ⓦseabirdboracay.com; map below. An oldie but a goodie, *Seabird* continues to renovate to keep up with the new crowd and offers a range of rooms set in pleasant and quiet gardens just a minute's walk back from the beach. Good coffee, pancakes, breakfasts and fish in the restaurant. Free wi-fi. **P3300**

BOAT STATION 3 AND POINTS SOUTH

★**Angol Point Beach Resort** At the south end of the beach ☎036 288 3107, ⓦangolpointbeach.com; map below. *Angol Point*'s a little more pricey than many resorts of its ilk because the conservationist owner, Francis, has built only one cottage where most developers would have put three or four – which means you get expansive rooms, huge verandas and the benefit of acres of space in the peaceful coconut grove where the resort stands. It's a short walk from bars and restaurants and very quiet. Good choice for families. **P3000**

★**Blue Mango Inn** Southern end of the beach ☎036 288 5107, ⓦbluemangoinn.com; map below. This is a great-value choice with a wide range of rooms, either facing the beach or set around the wonderfully jungle-like garden. All rooms are attractively decorated and have a/c, cable TV, fridge and hot and cold shower. There's also a decent café with wi-fi on site and sunbeds on the beach for the use of guests. The resort also has a well-rated dive centre. **P3000**

■ ACCOMMODATION	
Angol Point Beach Resort	8
Bamboo Bungalows	11
Blue Mango Inn	9
Dave's Straw Hat Inn	7
Fat Jimmy's	13
Frendz Resort	1
Mango-Ray Resort	14
Marzon Beach Resort	4
Moreno's Cottages	5
Nigi Nigi Nu Noos 'e' Nu Nu Noos	2
Orchids Resort	6
Pinjalo Resort	3
Seabird International Resort	12
Tree House Beach Resort	10

● EATING	
Aria	6
Cyma	7
English Bakery and Tea Rooms	1
Lemon i Café	5
Manana	2
Pizzeria da Mario	4
Real Coffee and Tea Café	9
Steakhouse Boracay	3
True Food Restaurant	8

■ DRINKING & NIGHTLIFE	
Bom Bom Bar	5
Club Paraw	2
Cocomangas Shooters Bar	1
Epic	6
Red Coconut Bar	4
Sand Bar	3
Summer Place	8
Wave	7

● SHOPPING	
Boracay Tourist Center	2
Budget Mart	3
D'Mall	4
D'Talipapa Market	1

6

Dave's Straw Hat Inn Down the path next to Angol Point Beach Resort ☎036 288 5465, ⓦdavesstraw hatinn.com; map p.343. *Dave's* is a charming, homely little resort with comfortable a/c and fan rooms and good food. Fan-cooled rooms are one of the best deals on the island, while even deluxe doubles (P1800) have extra roll-out beds so a family of four can fit in at no extra charge. `P1500`

Marzon Beach Resort At the southern end of the beach ☎036 288 5064, ⓦmarzonboracay.com; map p.343. One of the cheapest right-on-the-beach options, *Marzon* has dated standard rooms and plusher deluxe rooms (P3800) set around a sandy courtyard, with the glistening blue of the ocean just beyond. All rooms have a/c and cable TV, plus there's free wi-fi. `P2772`

Moreno's Cottages At the southern end of the beach opposite Dave's Straw Hat Inn ☎036 288 2031 or ☎0939 118 9616, ⓔboracayjojo29@yahoo.com; map p.343. This friendly, locally run option has small and simple fan and a/c rooms set around a pleasant garden, just a 2min walk from a lovely section of White Beach. Free wi-fi. `P1500`

Orchids Resort A short walk inland from Moreno's Cottages ☎036 288 3313, ⓦorchidsboracay.com; map p.343. Owned by an affable American, *Orchids* offers great-value rooms and nipa huts a few minutes' walk from White Beach. Standard fan rooms are clean and have hot and cold showers, while the fan cottages offer more space and have cosy verandas with hammocks. A/c rooms also have cable TV, and there's wi-fi connection (P50/day) throughout. A few minutes' walk up the hillside, *Orchids* also has newer, thatch-roofed concrete villas with two beds in the a/c downstairs and a living room with cable TV, kitchen and balcony upstairs (P2500). `P915`

Tree House Beach Resort At the southern end of the beach ☎036 288 4386; map p.343. Rooms may be slightly dated, but they're comfortable, quiet and nicely furnished. The owner Mario also cooks a mean pizza and there's free wi-fi. The dorm rooms are cheap, but cramped and very simple. Dorm `P300`, double `P2000`

ELSEWHERE ON BORACAY

Balinghai Beach Resort Balinghai Beach ☎036 288 3646, ⓦbalinghai.com; map p.338. If you're looking for desert-island solitude and don't mind being a tricycle ride from the buzz of White Beach, *Balinghai* fits the bill. On a small, secluded cove surrounded by cliffs on the northern part of Boracay, it's set into a steep slope with lots of steps, and boasts a handful of private bungalows and houses built from local materials, with consideration for the environment. Each house is different and prices vary accordingly. One has a tree in the kitchen and another is carved from the rock face, with a balcony facing the sunset. There is also a small restaurant with wi-fi. `P4500`

Nami On the cliffside 20m above Diniwid Beach ☎036 288 6753, ⓦnamiresorts.com; map p.338. Reached by steep steps or a rickety lift, the spacious and stylish villas at this upmarket place, on the next cove along from White Beach, offer 180-degree ocean views, jacuzzi, butler service and DVD players. Service, however, doesn't quite hit the mark. `P10,675`

Shangri-La's Boracay Resort & Spa Brgy Vapak ☎036 288 4988, ⓦshangri-la.com/boracay/boracayresort; map p.338. Perched above its own private beach, the *Shangri-La* presents a range of attractively styled rooms and villas which blend comfortably into the lush hills. Service is top-notch and all of the usual *Shangri-La* facilities are on offer, along with nature trails and a dive centre. `P19,300`

EATING

Boracay has a more diverse dining scene than most cities in the Philippines and even in a two-week stay you need never eat in the same **restaurant** twice (although some are so good that you'll want to). Many restaurants are listed in the local info booklet *My Boracay*, which also has meal discount vouchers. As well as the listings below there are also plenty of **local vendors** who set up barbecues on the beach at sundown to cook everything from fresh lapu-lapu and squid to tasty local bananas sprinkled with muscovado sugar. The chains have also slowly moved in, and White Beach now has a *McDonald's*, *Starbucks*, *Subway*, *Shakey's* and *Yellow Cab Pizza* and more are sure to follow. A **cautionary note** is to be wary of the big seafood buffet places on the seafront, as sometimes the fish isn't quite as fresh as you might think and can be a fast track to stomach problems.

CAFÉS

English Bakery and Tea Rooms Balabag, halfway between White Beach and Bulabog Beach ☎036 288 3158; map p.343. The only remaining branch of the *English Bakery* in Boracay serves up great breakfasts (P130–175), yoghurts (P75), meals, cakes and shakes (P95). Shaded tables looking out over a small lagoon make a great spot to escape the heat and partake in a cup of Lyons English tea and some banana bread. Daily 6am–6pm.

★**Lemon i Café** D'Mall ☎036 288 6781, ⓦlemon icafeboracay.com; map p.343. Terrific bright and airy little café. Breakfast items include eggs Benedict (P260) and delicious coconut pancakes (P195). For lunch or dinner there's outstanding pan-fried mahi-mahi with warm potato salad and lemon butter garlic sauce (P390), lemon and thyme roast chicken with sautéed potatoes (P450) and a range of lemon desserts. Drinks range from refreshing calamansi juice, or a lemonijito (P210) if you feel like something stronger. Daily 8am–11pm.

★ **Real Coffee and Tea Café** Boat Station 2 ☎ 036 288 5340; map p.343. *Real Coffee* has moved back to the heart of the action, a stone's throw from D'Mall, yet its second floor location overlooking the beach is somehow removed from the hubbub. The bamboo interior harks back to a simpler time when this was the first "real" coffee (P80–160) on the beach. Good breakfasts (P175–350), as well as a great selection of teas (punchy ginger tea, P90) and cookies (P25). Daily 7am–7pm.

RESTAURANTS

Aria Beach entrance to D'Mall ☎ 036 288 5573, ☏ aria .com.ph; map p.343. This popular Italian place offers attractive alfresco dining under the palms. Pizzas (P390–590) and pastas (P345–450) are reliably good, and coffee and desserts are available from neighbouring *Café del Sol*. Daily 11am–11pm.

Cyma D'Mall ☎ 036 288 4283, ☏ cymarestaurants.com; map p.343. The owners may not be Greek, but *Cyma* serves the best tzatziki (P150) in Boracay in a tiny but boldly decorated restaurant. Delicious *horiatiki* (Greek salad; P265), chicken souvlaki (P365) and baklava (P200) are also on the menu, and it's worth checking the specials board. Daily 10am–11pm.

Manana Next to Starbucks between boat stations 1 and 2 ☎ 036 288 5405; map p.343. This lively Mexican restaurant serves tasty fajitas (P363), enchiladas and chimichangas (P352–418), which can be enjoyed in the brightly decorated interior or on tables out on the beach to the backbeat of Latino tunes. A giant frozen mango daiquiri (P148) rounds the meal off perfectly. Daily 10am–10pm.

★ **Pizzeria da Mario** At the southern end of White Beach ☎ 036 288 3601; map p.343. Thin-crust pizza (P200), pasta and risotto, all cooked to perfection by the Italian owner and served in simple surrounds with gorgeous views over the beach. Daily 7am–11pm.

Prana Mandala Spa & Villas, at the southern end of the main road ☎ 036 288 5858; map p.338. This classy vegetarian restaurant at the upmarket *Mandala Spa &*

Villas offers super-healthy dining in a wooden dining room looking out onto dense tropical foliage. The menu, created by a Swedish chef especially for the restaurant, includes interesting starters such as wasabi salad (P170), main courses like penne pasta with roasted vegetables (P260) and pan-fried tofu with asparagus, Baguio beans and peanut sauce (P260). Daily 7am–10pm.

★ **Sirena** Shangri-La's Boracay Resort & Spa, Brgy Vapak ☎ 036 288 4988, ☏ shangri-la.com/boracay /boracayresort; map p.338. The place to come for a splurge, with sophisticated seafood dining from a lofty perch overlooking two bays. Arrive for sunset drinks and see if you can snag one of the wonderful outdoor cliff perches before indulging in succulent wahoo, crispy fried prawns and *ube* crème brûlée, along with good wines. Expect to pay upwards of P2000 per person for a three-course meal. Daily 11am–2pm & 5–9pm.

Steakhouse Boracay Boat Station 1 ☎ 036 288 6102; map p.343. Excellent steak and salad restaurant which enjoys a great location looking out over the beach. Imported steaks (P610–650) are the mainstay, but the raclette (order one day in advance; P840) is also worth a try. Daily 10am–11pm.

Tesebel's On the main road, just off Puka Beach; map p.338. This long-standing restaurant is nothing fancy to look at, but people go back for the delicious fresh seafood, which includes garlic prawns with buttered honey (P175) and tangy *sinigang* with the catch of the day. Head here for a lazy lunch if you're in the Puka Beach area. Daily 6am–11pm.

★ **True Food Restaurant** Next door to Mango-Ray Resort, a short walk south of D'Mall ☎ 036 288 3142; map p.343. Tastefully styled restaurant where delicious Indian meals can be enjoyed sitting on cushions around a low table. There are dishes from all over the subcontinent including *aloo jeera*, biriani, pakora (P230) and *masala dosa* (P370), and the menu also extends to North Africa with its couscous offerings. Meals are nicely rounded off with a good old-fashioned cup of Indian chai. Daily noon–10.30pm.

DRINKING AND NIGHTLIFE

Nightlife in Boracay starts with drinks at sunset and continues all night. Hardcore partiers don't even warm up until midnight, with many dancing and drinking until sunrise. As well as the listings below there are countless other options which range from upscale resort bars to beach shacks.

BARS

Bom Bom Bar Right on the beach, 100m north of D'Mall; map p.343. An atmospheric little chilled-out beach hut, with seats on the sand where you can listen to local musicians come together for jam sessions on native instruments. Daily 8am–1am.

Red Coconut Bar Boat Station 2 ☏ redcoconut.com .ph; map p.343. Part of a popular resort, this loud and lively bar serves cocktails (P150–190) and offers itself as a

"husband daycare centre". Daily 6am–11.30pm.

Red Pirates Pub South end of White Beach beyond Boat Station 3 ☎ 036 288 5767; map p.338. Bare feet and sarongs are the order of the evening at this chilled-out little beach club far from the madding crowd. The music ranges from reggae to chill-out to tribal, ethnic and acoustic sounds. The owner, Captain Joey, has a sailing boat and offers sunset cruises, adventure tours and snorkelling trips around the island. Daily 10am–4am.

6

Sand Bar Boat Station 1 ☎ 036 288 3161, ⓦ thesandbar beachclub.com; map p.343. Trendy (but pricey) bar with sofas on the sand under a huge canopy. The nightly fire *poi* dancers are the best on the island (from 9.45pm), with flavoured hookahs available while you watch the show. Daily 5pm–midnight.

Summer Place 200m south of D'Mall ☎ 036 288 3144, ⓦ summerplaceboracay.com; map p.343. U-shaped bar facing the beach, with a dancefloor and music until the sun comes up, or until the last customer leaves. Daily 10am–4am.

CLUBS

Club Paraw Boat Station 1 ☎ 036 288 6151; map p.343. Spilling out onto the sand this popular club plays everything from techno to r'n'b. There's a P150 cover in peak season, but this includes a drink. Daily 10am–3am.

Cocomangas Shooters Bar On the main road inland from Boat Station 1 ☎ 036 288 6384, ⓦ cocomangas .com; map p.343. (In)famous for drinking games involving potent cocktails, this place stays raucous until the wee hours. Cover charge (P100) on Sat. Daily 10am–3am.

Epic On the edge of D'Mall ☎ 036 288 1417, ⓦ epic boracay.com; map p.343. In the daytime *Epic's* kitchen turns out tasty dishes from its international menu, and in the evening it transforms into one of the most popular clubs on the strip. Resident DJs serve up dance music from 10pm and guest DJs for party nights. Daily 11am–2am.

Wave Boracay Regency Beach Resort, near Boat Station 2 ☎ 036 288 6111, ⓦ boracayregency.com/savor/wave -bar-lounge; map p.343. Part of the upmarket *Boracay Regency Resort*, this trendy, modern beach lounge bar hosts DJs whose tunes are piped out to the dancefloor via state of the art Swiss "plane wave" speakers. Daily 5pm–3am.

SHOPPING

Boracay Tourist Center Halfway between Boat Stations 2 and 3 ☎ 036 288 3704, ⓦ touristcenter .com.ph; map p.343. Has everything from beachwear to foodstuffs, a travel agency, internet café and postal service, plus they can deliver groceries. Daily 8am–11.30pm.

Budget Mart Where D'Mall meets the main road ⓦ budgetmart.com.ph; map p.343. The most accessible decent-sized supermarket. Daily 7am–11.30pm.

D'Mall Behind the beachfront restaurants; map p.343. D'Mall has a warren of alleys packed with stalls and boutiques where you can pick up everything from clothes to dive gear and imported foods. Most shops 9/10am–9/10pm.

D'Talipapa Market map p.343. Sprawling market with the best and cheapest selection of beachwear in Boracay, plus a fruit, veg and wet market, with simple restaurants that will cook your freshly bought produce. Daily 8am–11pm.

DIRECTORY

Banks and exchange There are several banks with ATMs on Boracay, but during peak season they often run out of cash by the afternoon, so it's best to go in the mornings, and before the weekend. All banks offer exchange. There's an Allied Bank on the beach path at Boat Station 3, and another on the main road inland from the Boracay Tourist Center, which also changes cash.

Hospitals and clinics The main hospital is the 24hr Don Ciriaco Senares Tirol Senior Memorial Hospital (☎ 036 288 3041) on the main road a little south of D'Mall. The Metropolitan Doctors Medical Clinic, towards the southern end of the main road (☎ 116 or ☎ 036 288 6638, ⓦ boracaymd.com), can also provide first aid or deal with emergencies and will send a doctor to your hotel.

Immigration Visa extensions are available at the small Department of Immigration office in the *Nirvana Beach Resort* on Main Rd (Mon & Tues 7.30am–5.30pm; ☎ 036 288 5267). To extend your visa you'll need to take along a photocopy of your passport (front cover and arrival stamp), and fill in an application form.

Internet access Getting online in Boracay is a little more expensive than many parts of the country; reckon on anything between P60 and P150/hr. The internet café at the Boracay Tourist Center is convenient and has fast connection for

P70/hour. Other options are the business centre at *Nigi Nigi Nu's* (P70/hr), Station 168 (P70/hr) at the entrance to D'Mall and the Sheridan Internet Café (P60/hr) at Boat Station 3.

Laundry The place you're staying will probably arrange laundry for you, but for a cheaper service there are several launderettes on the island which charge around P40/Kg: Laundry Wascherei Is a little south of Boat Station 3, Lavandera Ko is next to *Cocomangas*, and Speedwash is on the main road inland from Boat Station 3.

Pharmacies There are pharmacies selling most necessities in D'Mall, Boracay Tourist Center and D'Talipapa.

Phones For cheaper rates than the resorts head to the Boracay Tourist Center.

Police The police station (☎ 036 288 3066) is a short walk inland between Boat Stations 2 and 3, immediately behind the Boracay Tourist Center. If you have lost something you can ask the friendly staff at the local radio station, YFS FM 91.1 (☎ 036 288 6107, ⓦ yesfm911boracay.blogspot .co.uk), to broadcast an appeal for help. They claim to have a good record of finding lost property, from wallets and passports to Labrador puppies. The station office is on Main Rd close to Boat Station 1.

Post The post office in Balabag, the small community halfway along White Beach, is open Mon–Fri 9am–5pm.

Romblon

Off the northern coast of Panay, between Mindoro and Bicol, the province of **ROMBLON** consists of three main islands – **Tablas**, **Romblon** and **Sibuyan**, plus a dozen or so more smaller islands. The province is largely overlooked by visitors because it's difficult to reach, and once you're here, to put it simply, there's not that much to do. However, as Boracay becomes increasingly crowded, Romblon makes an ever more appealing option, and little by little is making its way onto travellers' radars, aided by the opening of new resorts and activities, particularly on the southernmost island of **Carabao**. For now, though, most of Romblon remains wild and untouched and is home to some beautiful and rarely visited **beaches** and coral reefs, making it an excellent off-the-beaten-track destination for **scuba diving**, snorkelling or just exploring and getting a sense of provincial life in the archipelago.

ARRIVAL AND DEPARTURE   ROMBLON

BY PLANE

Tugdan Airport There's a small airport at Tugdan on Tablas Island, which is served by four weekly flights from Manila with Fil-Asian Airways (W filasianair.com). Jeepneys meet flights and run to Looc (P50; 40min) and San Agustin (P80; 1hr). There are also quicker vans for hire to Odiongan (P1200) or San Agustin (P1500), or

if you don't have too much luggage, motorbike taxis charge P50 to Looc and can also be chartered for destinations further afield. Many resorts across the island group can arrange airport pick-up, inclusive of boats and vans; as a guide, heading to Lonos on Romblon a private van pick-up (for up to four people) will cost around P3500.

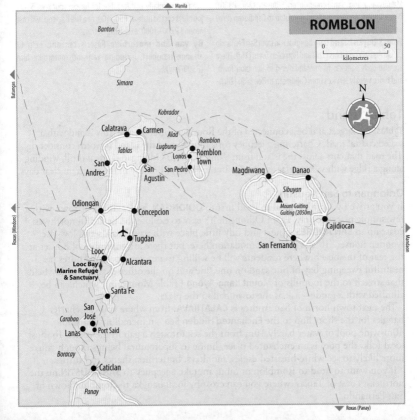

6

BY BOAT

From Manila Romblon Shipping Lines (☎ 02 243 5886, ⓦ romblonshippinglines.com) has a weekly departure from Manila to Romblon Town (Wed 5pm; 12hr). After an hour's break the ferry continues on to Cajidiocan on Sibuyan (1hr).

From Batangas There are far more ferry services from Batangas to Odiongan, on Tablas Island, including 2Go (ⓦ travel.2go.com.ph) which has twice-weekly services (Tues & Fri 9pm; 6hr), and Montenegro Shipping Lines (☎ 043 740 3201, ⓦ montenegrolines.com) which has a slower service (Mon, Thurs & Sat 5pm) for Odiongan (9hr) and Romblon (13hr).

From Mindoro There are three weekly bangkas from Roxas on Mindoro to both Odiongan and Looc (both 3–4hr).

From Panay and Boracay 2Go (ⓦ travel.2go.com.ph) run four weekly services from Caticlan to Odiongan (2hr). Alternatively there are also daily big bangkas (P300) from Caticlan to Looc, or you can also charter bangkas in Boracay itself for Carabao Island. Weather permitting, there are also daily bangkas every morning from Roxas to Sibuyan Island (4–5hr).

From Masbate Cajidiocan on Sibuyan's east coast is linked by occasional bangkas with Mandaon on Masbate.

GETTING AROUND

BY BOAT

From Tablas Island There are local bangkas from San Agustin on Tablas to Romblon Town (1hr; P150), and San Fernando on Sibuyan (2hr). There are also bangkas from Santa Fe to Carabao. Direct Odiongan–Romblon ferries run three times per week.

From Romblon Island There are daily bangkas from Romblon Town to San Agustin (1hr; P150) on Tablas, and Magdiwang and San Fernando on Sibuyan (2hr; P300). Twice a week, services go from Romblon to Cajidiocan (2hr) on Sibuyan.

From Sibuyan Island Daily bangkas run from San Fernando to San Agustin on Tablas (2hr) and Romblon Town (1hr). There are also daily bangkas from Magdawing to Romblon Town, and twice weekly services from Cajidiocan to Romblon (2hr).

BY ROAD

Once you've made it to the islands, the main modes of transport are jeepneys, tricycles and motorbikes.

By jeepney Jeepneys run set routes and tend to be most frequent in the mornings. Odiongan to Looc (45min), by way of example, costs P50.

By tricycle and motorbike taxi Motorbike taxis are one of the speediest ways to get around, although they aren't particularly comfortable for longer journeys. Short journeys cost as little as P50–100, or a full day-trip will cost around P700–1000, excluding petrol.

By van and motorbike Resorts can also help to arrange transport, including van and motorbike hire (P500/day).

Tablas Island

Tablas, the largest and best connected of the Romblon group, is a narrow island with a sealed coastal road. Chartering a jeepney for a tour around the island is worth considering. The road that cuts across the island from Concepcion to Odiongan is a real thrill, winding along a ridge with views as far as Sibuyan in the east and Boracay in the south on clear days.

Odiongan to San Agustin

If you arrive by air, it's typical to head first to **ODIONGAN**, a pleasant little town with a few simple places to stay. From Odiongan it's easy to explore the beautiful northwest coast up to **SAN ANDRES**, a neat and tidy little place with paved roads and low-rise wooden houses. There's no accommodation here, but there are a number of houses at the rear of the beach where residents will be willing to put you up. San Andres has a beautiful sweeping bay of fine sand on one side and on the other dazzling paddy fields that stretch to the foothills of **Mount Kang-Ayong** (Table Mountain), which can be climbed with a guide – ask at the town hall in the plaza.

The next town north of San Andres is **CALATRAVA**, from where you can charter a bangka for the short hop to the **Enchanted Hidden Sea**, an incredibly beautiful 40m-wide pool of water barely 10m from the sea through a gap in the rocks. To most local folks the pool is an enchanted place, home to supernatural beings though you're more likely to see white-breasted eagles, monkeys, butterflies, sharks and turtles.

If you want to head to Romblon or Sibuyan, take a jeepney to **SAN AGUSTIN** on the northeast coast of Tablas, where you can cross by local bangka to Romblon Town or San Fernando.

Looc and Santa Fe

The main town on Tablas is **LOOC**, a scenic place huddled among palm trees against a curtain of jungled hills and facing a wide natural harbour. It's worth hiring a bangka from the pier, at the southern edge of town near the *Morales Lodging Inn*, to explore the pretty bay and coves around Looc. Of principal interest is the **Looc Bay Marine Refuge and Sanctuary**, an area of the bay guarded 24 hours a day to allow corals damaged by dynamite fishing to regenerate. The guards, all volunteers, are stationed on a bamboo platform and are happy to welcome tourists aboard and let them snorkel in the area. Donations in the form of soft drinks and snacks are appreciated.

Further south there are good beaches in the district of **Santa Fe**, although the town itself is little more than the jumping off point for boats to Carabao.

INFORMATION

Tourist information The tourist office is in the Capitol Building on Looc's town plaza (8am–noon & 1–5pm; ☎ 0998 318 5890; ⌨ romblonprov.gov.ph).

Services In Looc, the Brainstorm Internet Café, near

the tourist office, has reasonably fast web access. In Odiongan, there's a small internet café and BPI bank with ATM on the plaza, plus a PNB bank with ATM on Formilleza St.

ACCOMMODATION AND EATING

ODIONGAN

Islands Gourmet Deli Quezon St ☎ 0919 483 8531. The best food in Tablas served up in this cosy little restaurant decked out in native materials. Organic ingredients are sourced locally to make tasty dishes ranging from stone-baked pizzas to BBQ chicken and pork, plus delicious smoothies. Daily 7am–9pm.

Lyn's Snacks Rizal St. Directly below the *Odiongan Plaza Lodge*, this place has outdoor seating where you can fill up on cheap local dishes (from P80). Daily 7am–7pm.

Odiongan Plaza Lodge Rizal St ☎ 042 567 5760. The best place in town for a short stay enjoys a central location opposite the town hall on the plaza and has well-kept a/c rooms with tiled floors and hot showers. P1000

SAN AGUSTIN

August Inn Town plaza ☎ 0919 592 2495. An adequate little lodging house with a/c rooms. Most rooms share communal bathrooms, although some of the doubles are en suite (P800). P400

Kamella Lodge Town plaza ☎ 0919 610 7104. Next door to *August Inn*, this place has small, ordinary a/c rooms that are okay for a short stay. P400

LOOC

Marduke Hotel Grimares St, near the town plaza ☎ 042 509 4078. Each of the eight rooms at this small,

friendly place has a/c and private bathrooms, and there's a simple restaurant. P800

Morales Lodging Inn Looc Pier. This place is a little run-down but still comfortable, and the friendly owner is something of an oracle on ferry schedules. P500

Pacific Garden Restaurant Town plaza. Chinese place serving noodle soup, piping-hot fried rice and deliciously peppery adobo, which comes with a lump of freshly steamed rice. Mains P80–150. Daily 7am–9pm.

SANTA FE

By the Sea Resort Campong Beach ☎ 0999 664 3917, ⌨ bythesearesort-tablas.com. Lovely little Italian-owned resort with huts nestled into the hillside above a pretty stretch of white sand, where there's also a pool. Rates sound expensive, but include include three top-notch meals a day, plus snacks, drinks and even Italian wine with dinner. P3600 per person

Morel's Private Island Resort Guinbiyaran Bay ☎ 0926 688 7564, ⌨ morelisland.com. Sitting on its own tiny island, this charming resort has a budget beach cottage with kitchen sleeping six (P1800), and small, attractive rooms, mostly with shared bathrooms. The resort can arrange pick-up from Santa Fe, from where it's a 20–30min drive to the pier at Guinbiyaran and then a short bangka ride. Alternatively they can arrange a boat direct from Boracay (P5000). P1000

Romblon Island

Romblon Island has been extensively quarried for decades to get at the beautiful Romblon marble, a favourite with the rich and famous in Manila. It's a picturesque island, with a pretty harbourside capital, an interior buzzing with wildlife and a coastal road, partly cemented, that you can whip around in half a day past some enticing beaches with a number of simple resorts. **Romblon Town** itself is a pretty place, with

Spanish forts, a cathedral built in 1726 and breathtaking views across the Romblon Strait from Sabang lighthouse

Romblon Town

One of the most attractive towns in the Philippines, low-rise **ROMBLON TOWN**, the provincial capital, sits at the back of a deep, tortuous bay, with red-roofed houses lining the water's edge and thickly jungled hills behind. Happily dozing in the balm of a more sedentary age, the town feels a few centuries behind the rest of the Philippines. In the mornings all you can hear is cockerels and in the afternoons almost everything stops for a siesta, stirring again at 3pm when the worst of the heat has gone from the sun and children can play along the shore.

The town has a few sights, all reachable on foot. Slap in the middle, overlooking the quaint little Spanish plaza, is **St Joseph's Cathedral**, a richly atmospheric seventeenth-century church where almost everyone in town turns out for Mass on Sunday at 8am and on weekdays in the early evening. On the seafront are the remains of **Fort San Andres** and **Fort San Pedro**, reminders of the risk Romblon Town once faced from pirates.

Beaches and resorts

There are good beaches with very simple hut accommodation on the coast near **Lonos**, 3km south of Romblon. Around 500m long, **Bonbon Beach** is accessed from the road between Romblon and Lonos, and has a gently sloping ocean floor that makes it safe for swimming. A little south of here, **Tiamban Beach** is a short stretch of white sand flanked by palm trees and wooden shacks. Further still, a number of resorts have sprung up along the stretch of coast from Tiamban south to **Ginablan** and the nearby barangay of **San Pedro**.

INFORMATION   ROMBLON ISLAND

Tourist information There's a helpful tourist office (Mon–Fri 8am–noon & 1–4pm; ☎042 507 2202, w romblonprov.gov.ph) in the Provincial Capitol Building in Romblon Town, a short tricycle ride from the pier.

ACCOMMODATION AND EATING

ROMBLON TOWN

Blue Ridge Hotel Gov Fetalvero Ave ☎0919 991 8132. A few minutes' north of sister hotel *Romblon Plaza*, this small place near the market has clean, comfortable rooms with stylish furnishings and TVs. **P1200**

Republika Bar & Restaurant Near the ferry pier. Cosy place to sample surprisingly good Western favourites, including pizzas and fresh fruit shakes. Daily specials including chicken and mushroom pie with mash, vegetables and gravy (P250). Daily 7am–9pm.

Romblon Deli Near the ferry pier. Almost next door to *Republika*, this welcoming place has great food and reliable travel information. British owner Dave and his wife Tess offer a taste of Blighty for homesick Brits in the form of bangers and mash (P210), fish and chips (P195) and some good old-fashioned northern hospitality. Daily 7am–9pm.

Romblon Plaza Roxas St ☎042 507 2269. Set one block back from the pier, this four-storey building has several categories of room, from en-suite doubles to superior suites, also with private bathroom (P1400). The hotel has its own very pleasant rooftop restaurant with daily specials, including some delicious fresh seafood. **P1000**

TIAMBAN BEACH

Tiamban Aqua Club ☎0939 509 1901, w emc.com .ph/tiambanp. Well-run place with native-style cottages right on lovely Tiamban Beach, many with shady verandas and sunset views. **P800**

SAN PEDRO

San Pedro Beach Resort Brgy San Pedro ☎0928 273 0515. A few minutes' drive south of Ginablan, this charming, relaxing hideaway has cottages nestled along a hillside overlooking sandy Talipasak Beach. There's home cooking in the restaurant and staff can arrange island-hopping and trekking. **P700**

ELSEWHERE ON THE ISLAND

Cabanbanan Dive Resort On the north coast ☎0910 283 7612, w romblon-isl.com. Only accessible by a 30min boat ride from Romblon (free for pre-booked guests or P300), this place offers pretty little huts nestled into the undergrowth set back from the beach. It's quite remote but there's a restaurant, dive shop and a free daily transfer to Romblon Town. **P800**

Sibuyan Island

The easternmost of the Romblon group, verdant **Sibuyan Island** has everything the adventurous traveller could dream of: a sparkling coastline; a thickly forested interior; and a couple of daunting mountain peaks, most notably the ragged, saw-like bulk of **Mount Guiting Guiting**. Dubbed "The Galapagos of Asia", the island moreover boasts an extraordinarily rich range of **wildlife**, including 700 plant species and 131 species of bird. Five mammal species (one fruit bat and four rodents) are unique to the island.

Much of Sibuyan was declared a nature reserve in 1996. However, this has not prevented the island from being targeted as a potential mineral mining site, and – much to the dismay of environmentalists and local communities – a Canadian mining company was granted exploratory mining rights in 2009. A moratorium on mining operations in 2011 marked a small victory for environmentalists, though corporations continue to conduct research.

Sibuyan's 47,000 residents, mostly subsistence farmers and hunters who rely on the forest and the ocean to supplement their meagre incomes, rarely see tourists but some know every cove, trail and cave on the island and are happy to act as guides. Most Sibuyan residents live in three towns, **San Fernando**, **Cajidiocan** and **Magdiwang**; most ferries dock at the latter.

Mount Guiting Guiting

Permits (P300), guides (P800–1000/day) and porters (P400–600/day) can be organized at Mount Guiting Guiting Natural Park headquarters (☎ 0928 490 1038) • The park is accessed by an 8km tricycle ride from Magdiwang (P100)

Rising directly from the coastal plain to a height of 2050m, the extinct volcano **Mount Guiting Guiting** is an unforgettable sight. This is not a climb to be undertaken lightly and if you plan on doing any serious trekking or climbing, you'll have to bring all your equipment with you. The trail to the top of the mountain (affectionately known as G2 by climbers) starts from the **Mount Guiting Guiting Natural Park** headquarters. It starts gently enough, winding through pleasant lowlands, but soon becomes very steep and culminates in a precarious traverse across "the knife edge" to the summit. Even experienced mountaineers regularly fail to summit, and you'll need to allow three days for the round trip including ten hours for the ascent.

Next to Guiting Guiting is **Mayo's Peak** (1530m), a secondary summit that, like its neighbour, is cloaked in mossy forests, ferns and rare orchids. The trek to the top is more straightforward, requiring only 24 hours.

ACCOMMODATION

SIBUYAN ISLAND

Sanctuary Garden Resort By the start of the trail up Mt Guiting Guiting ☎ 0920 217 4127, ✆ sanctuary gardenresort.com. This well-located place provides a great alternative to a beach stay, and offers everything from camping and dorm beds to a/c rooms with fridges, TVs and DVD players (P1800). They also rent out bicycles for P200/day – great for exploring the surrounding country-side. Dorm P250, double P1100

Vicky's Place M.H. Del Pilar St, Magdiwang ☎ 0920 530 8533. Next to the elementary school, this family home features bright, airy upstairs guest rooms with a shared bath-room. There's also a good restaurant in the garden. P600

Carabao Island

Only 6km wide from the capital of **San José** on the east coast to **Lanas** on the west, beautiful little **Carabao Island** is an idyllic place where fishing is the main industry and tourism has only just begun to have an impact. **Divers** arrive on day-trips to explore the dozen well-known dive sites in the reefs around the island, or, if you want to stay longer, there are a few decent resorts at **Inobahan Beach**, the island's best – a 1km stretch of powdery white sand a couple of minutes' walk from **Port Said**, where bangkas arrive. It's easy to hire a motorbike in San José to get around; an enjoyable ride takes you to **Tagaytay Point**, the highest point on the island from where there are magnificent views across to Boracay and beyond.

6

ACCOMMODATION AND EATING

CARABAO ISLAND

INOBAHAN BEACH

Ging Grill and Restaurant Next to Republic of Inobahan Beach Resort. Cheap, straightforward snacks and meals, including hot dog sandwiches, noodles and burgers for a bargain basement P40. Daily 11am–8pm.

Republic of Inobahan Beach Resort ☎ 0918 330 3718. Four thatched cottages, each spacious enough for three. There's also a small restaurant – intriguingly

named the *Sir Polyon Lounge* – serving breakfast, soup, hamburgers and grilled meat and fish. **P750**

White Beach Dive & Kite Resort ☎ 0998 181 6237, ⓦ carabao.whitebeachdivers.com. Formerly the friendly and popular *Ivy's Vine*, this place is under new management as of early 2014 and has improved the rooms and facilities. There's a selection of simple beach fan and smarter a/c rooms (P2600), plus a dive and kitesurfing centre. **P1500**

Samar

The island of **SAMAR**, between Bicol and Leyte and 320km from top to toe, has yet to take off as a major tourist destination, which is both a shame and a blessing. Administratively divided into three parts, **Northern, Western and Eastern Samar**, large parts of each remain unspoilt, wild and beautiful. Homonhon Island in Eastern Samar is where **Ferdinand Magellan** is reputed to have set foot for the first time on Philippine soil in 1521, but these days the island is better known as the arrival point for many of the Philippines' worst storms. **Typhoon Yolanda** made landfall in southeastern Samar in November 2013, and devastated numerous cities, towns and villages in its path. As well as the terrible human costs, the typhoon has had serious economic implications, and the fact that many of the island's key tourist destinations are out of action removes another source of income for locals. The east coast surfing mecca of Guiuan was almost completely destroyed and has been removed from this edition of the guide, while **Sohoton Natural Bridge National Park**, a prehistoric wilderness in Western Samar, remained inaccessible to visitors at the time of writing. Further north, the towns of **Calbayog** and **Catbalogan** escaped the worst of the damage and offer plenty of adventurous activities in their hinterlands, including the chance to explore some of Southeast Asia's biggest cave systems. Further north, there are dozens of wonderfully untouched islands off the coast near **Allen**.

ARRIVAL AND DEPARTURE

SAMAR

By plane There are airports at Calbayog and Catarman, both served by PAL.

By boat Coming from Cebu there are numerous slow ferry connections to various ports along Samar's west coast, including Calbayog and Catbalogan. Ferries from Matnog on Bicol in Luzon arrive in Allen, in the northwest of the island.

By bus and minivan Tacloban on neighbouring Leyte is linked to Samar by regular buses and minivans, crossing the 2km San Juanico Bridge, which spans the San Juanico Strait. From Manila, Eagle Star (ⓦ eaglestar.com.ph) buses cross on the Matnog–Allen ferry and run down the coastal road to Calbayog (12hr).

Northern Samar

Served by flights from Manila and boat from Luzon, **Northern Samar** is primarily used as an access point to the island, but there are also some beautiful islands offshore. The **Balicuatro** and **Biri-Las Rosas** island groups are slowly being developed for tourism, but most remain wonderfully pristine and untouched.

WHEN TO VISIT SAMAR

Samar has a different **climate** from the rest of the country, with rainfall possible throughout the year and a dry period only in May and June. Most of the rain falls from the beginning of November until February, when there can also be fierce typhoons. The **best time to visit** is from May to September, although the growing number of surfers who come here to take advantage of the swells that rip in from the Pacific might argue that the typhoon season is best.

Allen

Arriving from Luzon by bus or ferry, your first taste of Samar is the small port town of **ALLEN**, in northwestern Samar, which has basic services and amenities but little else of interest to travellers. Most people head straight from the boat onto a bus or van, or out to the nearby Balicuatro or Biri-Las Rosas island groups.

ARRIVAL AND DEPARTURE | ALLEN

By boat Ferries from Matnog on the southernmost tip of Bicol make the trip to the Balwharteco terminal in Allen, several times each morning (1hr).
By bus and jeepney From Allen there are dozens of buses and jeepneys a day east to Catarman (1hr) and

beyond, and south to Calbayog (2hr) and Catbalogan (4hr), where you can catch an onward bus to the southern half of the island. Buses heading south and east from Allen all pick up passengers at the port itself.

ACCOMMODATION

Wayang Wayang Beach Resort 5km south of town ☎0920 924 8070. There's no real beach here, but this quiet resort, a short tricycle ride from town, is the best

place to stay if you get stuck in Allen. Simple nipa cottages are set back from the beach, whilst plusher oceanfront rooms are bigger and come with cable TV. **P800**

The Balicuatro Islands

The remote **Balicuatro Islands** off Samar's northwest coast afford the chance to find your own slice of paradise for the day, although currently only a couple of them have anywhere to stay. The capital of **Dalupuri Island**, where most bangkas arrive, is **San Antonio**, a sleepy barangay with dozens of little bangkas that can take you on day-trips to other islands.

The rest of the islands, also largely unexplored by tourists, are mostly home to farmers and fishermen. **Capul**, for example, is a picturesque little island about one hour from San Isidro, with a majestic seventeenth-century fortified stone church built by the Spanish, and an almost derelict coastal road that takes you past some incredible coves and beaches.

ARRIVAL AND DEPARTURE | THE BALICUATRO ISLANDS

By boat Scheduled morning bangkas leave from Victoria, 8km south of Allen, to San Antonio on Dalupiri (30min). Private bangka trips can also be arranged direct to resorts on Dalupiri from San Isidro (P400), 7km south of Victoria. There is one morning bangka from Looc ferry terminal in

Allen to Capul (1hr) or you can arrange a private trip for around P500.
Services San Antonio in Dalupuri has a post office and a small hospital.

ACCOMMODATION

Capul Island Beach Resort Capul ☎0780 461 0095. Laidback resort on a lovely stretch of white sand with simple fan and a/c (P1000) cottages. They also have a two-bedroom house which can be rented out for as little as P1600 per night. **P500**
Octopussy Bungalow Resort Dalupuri ☎0916 399

4297, ⌨octopussy.ch. Pretty concrete-and-thatch cottages in quiet gardens close to some marvellous beaches. There aren't many places to eat in the area, but the resort also offers half- (P800 per person) and full board (P1100 per person). **P1400**

Catarman

The ramshackle north coast port city of **CATARMAN** is served by flights from Manila and – though it has never been a tourist destination – makes a good point of entry to Northern Samar if you want to save yourself a long bus or ferry journey. It's also only a short hop from the Biri-Las Rosas Islands.

ARRIVAL AND INFORMATION | CATARMAN

By plane PAL operates a daily flight from Manila and have offices at the airport, and also on J.P. Rizal St in town.

Tricycles (P60 or P10/person if you share) wait at the airport to take arriving passengers the 5km into town.

By bus and van To move on from Catarman, hourly buses from the terminal behind the market leave for Allen (1hr), Calbayog (1hr 30min), Catbalogan (3hr) and Tacloban (7hr). There are also Eagle Star services for Manila via Allen and Matnog (12hr; P600/1100 for ordinary/a/c). A quicker way for destinations south is to take a Grand Tours or D'Turbanada van, which both leave hourly.

Services There are a few banks with ATMs in Catarman, including a Metrobank on Garcia St and a PNB on Jacinto St. To get online, try Asphire Computer Works on Jacinta St.

ACCOMMODATION

GV Hotel Marcos St ☎055 500 6373, ⓦgvhotels.com .ph. Part of a small nationwide budget chain, this is a decent cheapie close to the market. Small, clean, brightly painted rooms have windows, cable TV and cold showers and a choice of fan or a/c (P595). **P375**

Pink City Pension House Roxas St ☎055 251 8695. True to its name, this place has bright pink rooms set around a central water feature. Standard rooms have a/c and cable TV but for hot water you'll need to fork out for an executive (P950) or family room (P1500–1800). There's free wi-fi in the lobby. **P750**

Sasa Pension House Jacinto St ☎055 251 8515. ⓔsasa pensionhouse@yahoo.com. The clean, comfortable fan and a/c rooms (P775) at this four-storey pension offer great value and it's often fully booked as a result. The cheapest rooms have shared bathrooms, but all rooms have wi-fi. **P375**

EATING AND DRINKING

Gilda's Coffee Shop Annunciacion St. *Gilda's* offers a decent cup of coffee plus free wi-fi and a small selection of local handicrafts for sale, the profits of which go to help local children and the elderly. Daily 8am–7pm.

Michz Western end of Jacinta St ☎055 500 9451.

Popular café serving sandwiches (P35–70), budget meals and drinks. Daily 8am–8pm.

The Nest Garcia St. Pizza (P200–300) and pasta dishes during the day and serves as a bar in the evenings with live music on Wed, Thurs and Fri. Daily 8am–11pm.

The Biri-Las Rosas Islands

Somewhere among the tantalizingly undeveloped cluster of idyllic outcrops called **Biri-Las Rosas**, you'll be able to find one to call your own for the day. Most of the islands are only inhabited by poor fisherfolk and the infrastructure is non-existent, but there are now a few places to stay offering idyllic beach living – many of the islands have fine beaches – and diving.

ARRIVAL AND DEPARTURE   THE BIRI-LAS ROSAS ISLANDS

By boat Bangkas from Lavezares, just east of Allen, head for Biri (P60; 1hr), or you can charter a boat from San José (where all buses stop) for around P1500 for a day-trip (you will have to provide food for the boatman).

ACCOMMODATION

Biri Resort Just south of Biri Town ☎0915 509 0604, ⓦbiri-resort.com. Well-kept resort just across the road from the sea, with simple fan and a/c rooms with TV and fridge (P1250). There's also a decent café on site, *The Reef Bar & Grill*. **P700**

Western Samar

Western Samar is dominated by its limestone topography, and has **caves**, gorges and waterfalls galore. Aside from the famous **Sohoton Natural Bridge National Park**, most natural attractions are still relatively undiscovered, and there is little tourist infrastructure. The provincial towns of **Calbayog** and **Catbalogan** are the best bases for exploring the region. Of the two, Calbayog is the more attractive and has better hotels and restaurants, but to really get up close and personal with the caves, a stop at Trexplore in Catbalogan is recommended.

Calbayog and around

Sitting pretty with the Calbayog River on one side and the Samar Sea on the other, **CALBAYOG**, on the west coast, makes a pleasant enough place for a stop on your way through Samar. **Bangon and Tarangban Falls** are within easy reach of the city, as is Guinogo-an Cave. To get to the falls take a jeepney to Tinaplacan, and then walk

(45min), or take a habal-habal direct. Once there you can swim in the plunge pool or hike up to Tarangban Falls.

Guinogo-an Cave

Free • Take a jeepney to Lungsod, from where you can hire a boat (P300 return), then you'll have to walk the last 15min to the cave

The entrance to **Guinogo-an Cave** quickly leads to a wade through chest deep water to emerge in a series of vaulted caverns, home to *kabyaw* (fruit bats). It's best to take a guide (and torch or lantern) with you, which can be organized through the tourist office. The vast Calbiga cave system is also accessible from Calbayog, but it is best to organize trips here through Trexplore (see box, p.356).

6

ARRIVAL AND DEPARTURE

By plane The airport is 8km out of town and a tricycle into the centre costs P100. PAL have three weekly flights from Manila (1hr 15min).

By boat Calbayog has six weekly ferries for Cebu (12hr), operated by Cokaliong (☎ 055 533 89590, ⓦ cokaliong shipping.com) and F.J. Palacio Lines (☎ 055 209 1946), both of which have ticket offices at the port, which lies on reclaimed land 2km from town. Tricycles into town charge P20.

By bus, van and jeepney Buses and jeepneys arrive at the Capoocan transport terminal north of the river, 10min

CALBAYOG AND AROUND

by tricycle from the town centre. There are buses every 30min for Catbalogan (2hr) and Tacloban (4hr). For Catarman there are four services a day (2hr), while Allen (2hr) is served by jeepneys which also leave from the bus station. A quicker alternative to the buses is to take a Grand Tours or Van-Vans van. Both companies have hourly services for Catarman, Catbalogan and Tacloban, which leave from their private terminals: Grand Tours is on Bugalion St, and Van-Vans is at the bus station. Finally, there are also Eagle Star bus–ferry–bus services for Manila.

INFORMATION

Tourist information Calbayog's friendly tourist office (Mon–Fri 8am–noon & 1–5pm; ☎ 055 209 4041, ⓦ calbayog tourism.byethost7.com) has a few brochures about local attractions and can offer transport advice as well as helping to arrange guides.

Services Opposite the Legislative Hall there's a park and

a post office, plus a daily market in Orquin St, on the northern edge of town near the river. There are several banks with ATMs, including a UCPB on Gomez St and a Metrobank on Rosales Blvd. Internet cafés around town include Chatwave on Nijaga St.

ACCOMMODATION

Almira Garden Hotel Gelera St ☎ 055 209 3240. Many of the rooms are windowless, but nonetheless they are clean, nicely painted and have comfy beds, hot and cold water, cable TV and free wi-fi, and the deluxe rooms have fridges (P1100). **P750**

Ciriaco Hotel South of town on the National Hwy ☎ 055 209 6521, ⓦ ciriacohotel-calbayog.com. By far Calbayog's best hotel, with excellent rooms with all mod cons, the more expensive of which look straight out to sea. There's also a trendy lobby café, with free wi-fi and a pool. **P4800**

EATING

Carlos n' Carmelos Nijaga St ☎ 055 209 1259. Fast-food favourites including burgers (P37) and fries, as well as more interesting choices such as fried mozzarella (P69). Daily 9am–8.30pm.

SO Coffee Nijaga St ☎ 055 209 6038. Next door to *Carlos n' Carmelos*, this smart little coffee shop has cakes, smoothies (P60) and free wi-fi. Daily 9am–10pm.

Catbalogan and around

Seventy kilometres south of Calbayog, the bustling port town of **CATBALOGAN** is the ramshackle capital of Western Samar. It is, however, mainly of interest to travellers as a base from which to explore the wilds of Western Samar, particularly the huge **cave systems** to be found within a couple of hours of the city (see box, p.356).

ARRIVAL AND INFORMATION

By ferry Roble Shipping has a weekly ferry to Cebu (Fri 8pm; 12hr), which leaves from the pier at the end of Allen Ave.

CATBALOGAN AND AROUND

By bus There are buses every 30min for Calbayog (2hr) and Tacloban (3hr), and less frequent services for Catarman (4hr) and Borongan (5hr). Eagle Star

SAMAR UNDERGROUND

Of the many caves in Samar, **Jiabong**, just 12km from Catbalogan, is the easiest to visit, and has plenty of weird and wonderful features including a ceiling carpeted with miniature stalactites. A little further away, **Langun Gobingob**, in Calbiga, stretches 7km through twelve different chambers, and is one of the largest cave systems in Southeast Asia. This utterly dark environment is home to blind crabs and fish, and of course bats. Both caves offer extreme caving –plenty of wading, swimming and squeezing through narrow spaces, with only your guide's lantern (or your torch) to guide you. **Permits** are required.

CAVING TRIPS

Trexplore Allen Ave, Catbalogan ☎ 055 251 2301, ⓦ trexplore.weebly.com. The best way to get underground is to arrange a guided trip through Joni Bonifacio at the Trexplore outdoor shop. He can arrange day- (P3000) or overnight (P6000–7000) trips to the caves including meals, permits, equipment and transport (minimum of two people).

bus–ferry–bus services run to Manila (18hr): the first (ordinary) service (P1090) is at 9am, and the second (a/c) bus is at 10.30am.
By van A quicker alternative to the buses around the island is to take a Duptours, Grand Tours or Van-Vans van. All three companies have regular services for Calbayog, Catarman and Tacloban, which leave from their private terminals – Grand Tours and Van-Vans on San Bartoleme St, and Duptours just around the corner on Allen Ave.
Services Practically speaking, Catbalogan has most things a traveller should need: there are branches of RCBC, BDO and Allied Bank, all with ATMs, on Del Rosario St, and plenty of internet cafés scattered around the city – try Movies n' Magic or Cyber Surf, both on San Roque St.

ACCOMMODATION

Casa Cristina San Roque St ☎ 0921 660 6665, ⓦ casa cristinahotel.com.ph. A cheap-and-cheerful option with clean, brightly painted rooms which share communal bathrooms, or for P80 more you can get an en suite with cold shower. A/c rooms (P700) are more comfortable, but none of the rooms have windows. P300
New Maqueda Bay Hotel Del Rosario St ☎ 055 251 2386, ⓦ newmaquedabayhotel.com. On the edge of town, the refurbished *New Maqueda Bay* enjoys a quiet location and looks straight out to sea. There are twin-bedded deluxe rooms, or bigger double suites (P1050), both of which have a/c, cable TV and hot showers. P950

Rolet Hotel Mabini Ave ☎ 055 251 5512. The best option in town, with a/c rooms, cable TV and good bathrooms. The friendly proprietors, Odie and Lolit Letaba, can answer most travel-related questions on the area, and there's free wi-fi in the canteen. P950
Rose Scent Pensionne House Curry Ave ☎ 055 251 5785. It's hard to resist the name, and once inside, this friendly family pension has clean and functional fan and a/c (P650) rooms with powerful cold showers, although many don't have windows. Meals are available if ordered in advance. P400

EATING

Pizza Factory San Roque St ☎ 055 251 5512. Modern café-restaurant which turns out half-decent pizzas (P135–160) and also does delivery. Daily 9am–10pm.
Tony's Kitchen Next to Pizza Factory on San Roque St. Friendly and deservedly popular place which does a good line in fried dishes – the whole chicken (P260) is particularly tasty. Other specialities include crab omelette (P125). Daily 7am–10pm.

Sohoton Natural Bridge National Park

Best known for a natural rock formation that forms a bridge across a gorge, the **Sohoton Natural Bridge National Park** includes some remarkable limestone caves and gorges, and lowland rainforest where you can see, even around the park's picnic areas, monitor lizards, macaques and wild boar. The national park lay directly in the path of Typhoon Yolanda, however, and while the natural bridge escaped damage, almost all of the boats used to ferry visitors into the park were destroyed, meaning that access at the time of writing was very limited. We have included practical details in the hope that the park will be fully operational again soon.

Much of the area can be toured by boat, although to reach the **natural bridge** itself you'll have to get out and walk; and as there are few marked trails, you'll need to hire a **guide** to find your way around. The boat trip into the park is spectacular, heading up the **Cadacan River**'s estuary which is lined with mangroves and nipa palms. As you approach the park the river begins to twist and is then funnelled into a gorge of limestone cliffs and caves.

The most accessible of the park's many impressive caves is **Panhuughan I**, which has extensive stalactite and stalagmite formations in every passage and chamber, many that sparkle when the light from your flashlight falls on them. If you're lucky you might come across a number of specialized spiders and millipedes that live their lives here in total darkness. There have been many significant archeological finds in the caves, including burial jars, decorated human teeth and Chinese ceramics. During World War II Filipino guerrillas used the caves as hideouts in their campaign against the occupying Japanese forces.

6

ARRIVAL AND INFORMATION   SOHOTON NATURAL BRIDGE NATIONAL PARK

Access The park is in the southern part of Samar, the only approach being through Basey, on Samar's southwest coast, where you can arrange a bangka for the 10km river trip to Sohoton. The quickest way to get to Basey is via Tacloban on Leyte, from where you can catch an early minivan or jeepney (45min); a tricycle will then take you to the Department of Environment and Natural Resources, near Basey's plaza.

Fees, guides and information At the Department of Environment and Natural Resources in Basey (☎055 276 1025, ⌨denr.gov.ph) you pay the P150 entrance fee, and can arrange a guide (P300), head torch (P300) and a bangka (P1200 for a seven-seater) to take you to and from the park. You can also get information about visiting the park at the tourist office in Tacloban (see p.361).

Marabut Islands

A hundred kilometres southeast of Catbalogan, the small settlement of Marabut is the jumping-off point for exploring the **Marabut Islands**, a striking collection of toothy limestone outcrops rising out of the sea only a few hundred metres offshore. In Marabut you can hire a bangka and there are also places in town where you can hire a kayak for the day. There's no **accommodation** on any of the islands, but there are some good options on the mainland.

ACCOMMODATION   MARABUT ISLANDS

Caluwayan Palm Island Resort Brgy Caluwayan, 17km northwest along the coast from Marabut ☎055 276 5206, ⌨caluwayanresort.com. *Caluwayan* offers luxurious accommodation with a/c, TV and DVD players in lovely native-style cottages on a pretty stretch of beach. They also offer kayak hire (P250/hr) and rock climbing. **P2500**

Marabut Extreme Adventure Marabut Marine Park, 15km north of Marabut ☎053 520 0414. Owned by the Leyte Park over in Tacloban, this quiet little resort has comfortable a/c wooden cottages with TVs and a restaurant serving fresh seafood. Free use of kayaks for guests. **P2600**

Eastern Samar

The eastern part of Samar is surf country, particularly around **Borongan**, and further south on beautiful Calicoan Island, accessed from the small and sleepy town of Guiuan. Calicoan has terrific beaches, caves and lagoons and was only just starting to see touristic development when Yolanda devastated the island, and almost entirely destroyed Guiuan; neither have been included in this edition of the guide.

The bus trip from Catbalogan across to the east coast is one of the great little road journeys in the Philippines, taking you up through the rugged, jungle-clad interior past isolated barangays and along terrifying cliff roads. After four hours the bus emerges from the wilderness onto the typhoon-battered east coast at Taft and turns south towards Borongan.

Borongan and around

BORONGAN has good surf at most times of year. The city was hit by Yolanda and although there were no fatalities in Borongan itself, electricity wasn't restored for nearly a month. If the surf's not up, you could always hire a bangka at the wharf in Borongan and take a trip along the coast or out to the pretty island of **Divinubo**. Divinubo's *Karawisan Eco-Tour Park Resort* was destroyed by Yolanda, meaning there's nowhere to stay on the island, but it remains an idyllic day-trip destination for exploring and snorkelling; make sure you take something to eat and drink.

ARRIVAL AND INFORMATION
BORONGAN AND AROUND

By bus and jeepney There are a few buses that ply the mountain route between Borongan and Catbalogan (5hr), as well as jeepneys and vans for Guiuan. The Duptours terminal is on Real St and Van-Vans is on E. Cinco St. If you like long road trips, Eagle Star runs once a day to Manila at 5.30am (21hr).
Tourist information The small tourist office (Mon–Sat

8am–4pm; ☎055 330 1139) is in the Provincial Capitol Building facing Borongan plaza.
Services There's a Metrobank opposite the church, and a PNB across from the Uptown Mall by *Hotel Dona Vicenta*, both of which have ATMs. For internet head for Jah's Internet Games near the *Domsowir Hotel* on Real St.

ACCOMMODATION AND EATING

GV Pension Real St ☎055 261 2580, ⓦgvhotels.com .ph. A short walk north of the centre of town, *GV* has clean, simple fan and a/c (P550) rooms with cable TV. **P350**
Hotel Dona Vicenta Real St ☎055 261 3585. The most luxurious accommodation in the town itself is to be found at this grand-looking hotel. Comfortable a/c rooms have cable TV, although many suffer from being too close to the noisy bar, which stays open until 2am. **P980**
Kandaga Resto Grill Real St ☎055 560 9154. Aside from the hotels, Borongan's dining options are limited,

but this place serves burger meals (P80), pizzas (P100–120) and Filipino dishes including *lumpia* with rice (P69). Daily 9am–midnight.
Pirate's Cove Beach & Surf Resort Brgy Bato, on a peninsula 1km east of town ☎0919 880 9157, ⓦpiratescovesurf.weebly.com. An eclectic place right on the ocean, run by amiable surfer Pete and his wife. As well as having interesting rooms that range from a treehouse to family cottages, all of which have kitchens, the resort also has a pool, jacuzzi, wi-fi and one of the most impressive Scalextric setups you'll ever see. **P1500**

Leyte

The east Visayan island of **LEYTE** ("LAY-tay"), separated from Samar to the north by a mere slither of ocean, the San Juanico Strait, is another sizeable chunk of the Philippines that has a great deal to offer visitors but is often overlooked. You could spend months on Leyte and still only scratch the surface: the coastline is immense, the interior rugged and there are lakes and mountains that are well off the tourist map, known only to farmers who have tilled their shores and foothills for generations.

In the sixteenth century, Magellan passed through Leyte on his way to Cebu, making a blood compact with the local chieftain as he did so. But to many Filipinos and war historians, the island will always be associated with **World War II**, when its jungled hinterlands became the base for a formidable force of guerrillas who fought a number of bloody encounters with the Japanese. It was because of this loyalty among the inhabitants that General Douglas MacArthur landed at Leyte on October 20, 1944, fulfilling the famous promise he had made to Filipinos, "I shall return".

Around the provincial capital of **Tacloban**, the usual arrival point, there are a number of sights associated with the war, notably the **Leyte Landing Memorial**, marking the spot where MacArthur waded ashore to liberate the archipelago. Tacloban is also now remembered as the site of the worst of Typhoon Yolanda's devastation – as well as the powerful winds and rain, a huge storm surge decimated large chunks of the city (see box opposite). To the north of Tacloban is the beautiful island of **Biliran** and, a short bangka ride away from Biliran, the islands of **Maripipi** and **Higatangan**, which both have terrific beaches, rock formations and caves. To the south of the clean and

TYPHOON YOLANDA

On November 8, 2013, **Typhoon Yolanda** (known internationally as Haiyan) hit the southeastern tip of Samar with wind speeds of up to 315 kph. The superstorm left a broad band of destruction through northern Leyte, northern Cebu, northeastern Panay and finally Busuanga, in Palawan, before leaving the archipelago. Yolanda made landfall near Guiuan, which was almost completely destroyed, and 2m-plus storm surges wreaked havoc in Tacloban. In spite of a huge **international relief effort**, many of the worst affected areas remained without power, clean water and supplies for weeks. Looting became a major problem, while in unaffected regions local businesses and individuals rallied to raise funds and support.

Economically the recovery period will be counted in years, but for the families of the six thousand dead the losses are clearly irreparable. Aid groups were camped out in Tacloban until at least mid-2014, but sustained support is needed to help rebuild. **Tourism** can have a role here, and in popular areas (Malapascua for example; see p.285), tourist dollars have catalysed recovery. However, the worst hit areas in Samar and Leyte were still – at the time of writing – reeling from the effects of Yolanda and principal tourist sights including Sohoton National Park remained inaccessible. Though there would be an argument to encourage tourism to the hardest hit areas in Samar or Leyte, as per the Department of Tourism's nationwide "**Bangon Tours**" programme, whereby at least five percent is donated to recovery projects (see ⓦtpb .gov.ph/bangon-tours), six months on infrastructure is still sketchy, many buildings are roofless, storm debris lines the streets and, unfortunately, the best advice for now is to avoid further straining limited resource in the worst affected areas, particularly Guiuan and Calicoan.

attractive town of **Ormoc**, the coastal road takes you through the ferry ports of **Baybay** and **Maasin** before reaching **Padre Burgos**, renowned for its scuba diving. Off the southern tip of Leyte is **Limasawa Island**, an isolated outcrop where some believe Magellan conducted the first Catholic Mass in the Philippines.

ARRIVAL AND DEPARTURE   LEYTE

By plane Leyte's only major airport is at Tacloban, served by several daily flights from Manila with Cebu Pacific, Philippine Airlines and Air Asia. Cebu Pacific also has two daily flights to Cebu.

By boat Fast ferry connections link the port of Ormoc with Cebu, and there are also slower boats from Cebu to Bato, Baybay, Hilongos and Maasin on Leyte's west coast. There are also sailings between Cebu City and Naval on the island of Biliran.

By bus Buses to Leyte operate from Manila (a long haul through Bicol and Samar) and there are also regular daily services to Tacloban from Biliran, and from Samar via the San Juanico Bridge.

Tacloban and around

On the northeast coast, **TACLOBAN** is associated by most Filipinos with that tireless collector of shoes, Imelda Marcos, who was born a little south of here in the small coastal town of Tolosa to the prominent Romualdez family. Numerous streets and buildings bear the Romualdez name, including the airport. In her youth, Imelda was a local beauty queen, and referred to herself in later life as "the rose of Tacloban". The famed **San Juanico Bridge**, presented by Ferdinand to Imelda as testimony to his love, is another legacy of the Marcos connection.

Several months after **Typhoon Yolanda**, recovery efforts were still in full swing at the time of writing, and although most hotels and restaurants were starting to get back on their feet, there were still huge encampments on the outskirts of town to house those who lost their homes in the storm. In many ways, though, it's business as usual in the city itself and Tacloban remains a typically busy, dirty city, with most activity centred around the port and the market. There are few tourist attractions, though if you are here for a day or two you'll find the city has everything you need: some good accommodation, numerous ticket outlets for onward journeys and banks and restaurants huddled in the compact centre to the south of **Magsaysay Boulevard**.

The city's major fiesta is the **Tacloban Festival** in the last week of June, which kicks off with the Subiran Regatta, a boat race held at the eastern entrance of the San Juanico Strait.

Santo Niño Shrine and Heritage Museum

Real St, 2km south of town • Mon–Sat 8–11.30am & 1–4.30pm • Guide P200 (obligatory) • ☎ 053 321 977

One of your first stops on any tour of Tacloban must be to gawp at the **Santo Niño Shrine and Heritage Museum**. A grand folly of a house that Imelda Marcos ordered built but never slept in, it was sequestered by the government after the Marcos regime was overthrown. Inside, there is evidence aplenty that nothing was too opulent or tasteless for the Iron Butterfly. Her personal chapel has sparkling diamond chandeliers,

6

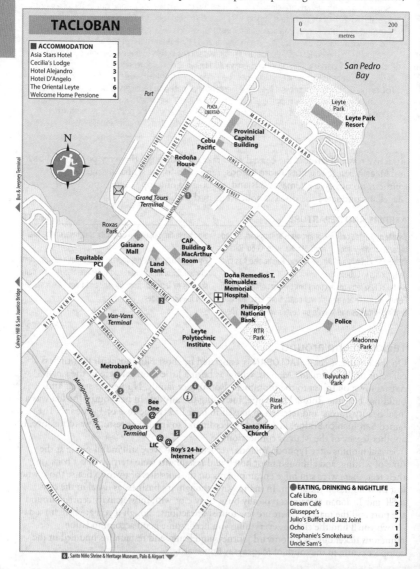

TACLOBAN

0 — 200 metres

■ ACCOMMODATION
Asia Stars Hotel	2
Cecilia's Lodge	5
Hotel Alejandro	3
Hotel D'Angelo	1
The Oriental Leyte	6
Welcome Home Pensione	4

San Pedro Bay

Leyte Park

Leyte Park Resort

Port

PLAZA LIBERTAD

MAGSAYSAY BOULEVARD

Provinicial Capitol Building

Cebu Pacific

Redoña House

JONES STREET

LOPEZ JAENA STREET

Grand Tours Terminal

Roxas Park

Gaisano Mall

Equitable PCI

Land Bank

CAP Building & MacArthur Room

Doña Remedios T. Romualdez Memorial Hospital

Philippine National Bank

RTR Park

Police

Madonna Park

Van-Vans Terminal

Leyte Polytechnic Institute

Metrobank

Bee One @

Duptours Terminal

LIC

Roy's 24-hr Internet

Santo Niño Church

Rizal Park

Balyuhan Park

◄ Bus & Jeepney Terminal

◄ Calvary Hill & San Juanico Bridge

RIZAL AVENUE

AVENIDA VETERANOS

Mangonbangon River

STA. CRUZ

ATHLETIC ROAD

BONIFACIO STREET

TRECE MARTIRES STREET

SENADOR ENAGE STREET

M.H. DEL PILAR STREET

SANTO NIÑO STREET

ZAMORA STREET

T. GOMEZ STREET

SALAZAR STREET

P. BURGOS STREET

M.H. DEL PILAR STREET

J. ROMUALDEZ STREET

P. PATERNO STREET

JUAN LUNA STREET

REAL STREET

● EATING, DRINKING & NIGHTLIFE
Café Libro	4
Dream Café	2
Giuseppe's	5
Julio's Buffet and Jazz Joint	7
Ocho	1
Stephanie's Smokehaus	6
Uncle Sam's	3

6 ▸ Santo Niño Shrine & Heritage Museum, Palo & Airport ▼

gold-framed mirrors and an expensive replica of the miraculous Santo Niño de Leyte (the original resides in the Santo Niño Church opposite Rizal Park in Real Street). There is also a dazzling collection of gifts that she acquired on her many overseas shopping trips.

CAP Building and around
J. Romualdez St • MacArthur Room Mon–Fri 9am–5.30pm, Sat 8.30am–noon • P25

One of Tacloban's most remarkable legacies of World War II is the extraordinarily flamboyant **CAP Building**. Formerly known as Price Mansion, this became General Douglas MacArthur's HQ after he landed in Leyte to set in motion the liberation of the Philippines; memorabilia of his stay are on display here in the **MacArthur Room**.

A five-minute walk north, in Senator Enage Street, is another war curiosity, **Redoña House** (no admission), the residence of Sergio Osmeña, the first President of the Commonwealth, and his staff during the liberation.

Calvary Hill
Ave Veteranos, on the western edge of the city, 1km from the centre

It's worth the sweat of a walk up to the top of **Calvary Hill**. This is a place of pilgrimage during Holy Week (before Easter) and the ascent is marked by the fourteen Stations of the Cross, with a five-metre statue of the Sacred Heart of Jesus at the summit. A good time to start the climb is late afternoon so you reach the top in time to watch the sun set. The views across Tacloban and San Pedro Bay are especially pretty after dark when the lights come on.

Palo and around
A taxi to Palo will cost P200–300, tricycle P100 and jeepney P20

About 5km south of Tacloban is the small town of **PALO**, known for its associations with MacArthur and the liberation. It was at Palo's **Red Beach**, about 1km from the town centre, that MacArthur waded ashore on October 20, 1944, fulfilling his famous vow to return. The spot is marked by the dramatic **Leyte Landing Memorial**, an oversized sculpture of the general and his associates, among them Sergio Osmeña walking purposefully through the shallows to the beach.

Just outside Palo, on **Hill 522**, there's an old Spanish church that was turned into a hospital during the war, and the remnants of a number of Japanese foxholes and bunkers. It's worth chartering a tricycle for the day when you reach Palo to take you from sight to sight.

ARRIVAL AND DEPARTURE | TACLOBAN AND AROUND

By plane Daniel Z. Romualdez Airport is located on a spit of land southeast of Tacloban, 10km by road from downtown. A jeepney into town costs P12, a tricycle around P150. Air Asia, Cebu Pacific and PAL currently have makeshift ticket offices at the airport, and Cebu Pacific (☎053 321 9410) and Philippine Airlines (☎053 321 7771) also have offices on Senator Enage St.
Destinations Cebu (2 daily; 50min); Manila (10 daily; 1hr 10min).

By bus, jeepney and van Buses and jeepneys from all points arrive at the terminal in Abucay, 2km northwest of

the city. Services to destinations within Leyte and Samar run regularly but are most frequent in the mornings. Many of these routes are also operated by quicker Duptours, Grand Tours and Van-Vans minivans, each of which leaves from their designated terminal: Duptours opposite the *Welcome Home Pensione* on Santo Niño St; Grand Tours from Trece Martires St, near the post office; and Van-Vans terminal on P. Burgos St.
Destinations Borongan (5hr); Calbayog (hourly; 4hr); Catbalogan (hourly; 3hr); Catarman (hourly; 6hr); Maasin (hourly; 5hr); Manila (3 daily; 24hr); Naval (every 30min; 3hr); Ormoc (hourly; 3hr).

INFORMATION

Tourist information The tourist office, on Santo Niño St, was closed at the time of writing; when open, it's normally a well-organized place, and their *Do-it-Yourself Tour of*

Tacloban & Environs brochure outlines a number of interesting sights that you can cover on foot.

6

ACCOMMODATION

Accommodation ranges from simple budget accommodation to affordable mid-range places, plus there are also a couple of plush hotels to consider, one of them a little way out of town at Palo. All of the hotels listed below are now open for business, though most of the biggest and best hotels were block booked by aid agencies at the time of writing.

Asia Stars Hotel Zamora St ☏ 053 321 5388, ☲ asia starshotel.com. Unattractive from the outside, but the rooms are fine, the staff friendly and the location central. Quiet doubles with fan or a/c, all with private shower, plus some rooms which have cable TV and a fridge. Free in-room wi-fi. **P1000**

Cecilia's Lodge 178 P. Paterno St ☏ 053 523 1759. This modest but comfortable little pension is the one many backpackers head to. It offers simple, clean singles, doubles and family rooms, most with a private shower and toilet. There's also a women-only building and staff are friendly and helpful. **P500**

★**Hotel Alejandro** P. Paterno St ☏ 053 321 7510, ☲ alejandro.tacloban.biz. Popular and well-managed hotel in an attractive 1930s building that was used as a refuge for evacuee families in World War II. Rooms are tastefully styled and have a/c, cable TV and fridges, although not all have external windows. There's a fascinating display of historic photographs on the second and third floors, and downstairs the restaurant and coffee shop has free wi-fi. There are just two budget fan rooms (P1000). **P1500**

Hotel D'Angelo Rizal Ave ☏ 053 325 2341. Well-located and clean, mid-sized establishment with simple, modern rooms with tiled floors and good bathrooms. The rooms on the upper floors have pleasant views across the city and of the sea. Free wi-fi in the lobby. **P1125**

The Oriental Leyte Palo, 5km south of Tacloban ☏ 053 323 3881, ☲ leyte.theorientalhotels.com. In a terrific location close to the Leyte Landing Memorial, this formerly government-run establishment is now a high-end beach resort. Rooms are luxuriously comfortable and the resort has all of the amenities and facilities you'd expect, in spite of having been swamped up to its second floor by Yolanda. **P3500**

Welcome Home Pensione South end of Santo Niño St, opposite the Caltex petrol station ☏ 0919 341 5213, ☲ welcomehomepensione.com. Close to the Duptours terminal with good-value rooms, and often fully booked as a result. There's a choice of fan or a/c rooms, with or without en-suite bathroom, plus it has free wi-fi in the coffee shop downstairs. **P600**

EATING, DRINKING AND NIGHTLIFE

These days Tacloban has a pretty sophisticated **restaurant** scene, and in between meals there are plenty of local specialities to **snack** on – *binagul*, a hot sticky concoction made of coconut and nuts, and chocolate *meron* can be bought freshly made every morning from hawkers along Rizal Ave. Most of the places below were flooded during Yolanda, but aside from *Café Libro*, all were fully operational at the time of writing.

Café Libro P. Gomez St. Quirky little café with good cakes and a book exchange. Closed at the time of writing but should have reopened by the time you read this.

Dream Café 222 M.H. Del Pilar St ☏ 053 325 8222, ☲ dreamcafe.ph. Australian–Filipino-owned, this clean and friendly little diner serves burgers (P145–215), sandwiches (P70–120), soups (P95–275), Aussie lamb chops (P850), tasty carrot cake (P98) and even imported wines. Free wi-fi. Daily 6am–11pm.

★**Giuseppe's** 173 Ave Veteranos ☏ 053 321 4910. Genuine Italian food in sophisticated surroundings. The stone-baked pizzas (P350–600) are as good as you'll find in this part of the world, and there's also ravioli ragu, spaghetti marinara, tiramisu, good coffee and free wi-fi. Daily 11.30am–2pm & 5–10pm.

Julio's Buffet & Jazz Joint P. Paterno St. Cosy little venue

with live acoustic music on Wed, Fri and Sat nights from 9pm. Drinks are reasonably priced (San Mig P50) and they also serve simple meals (P185). Daily 11am–midnight.

Ocho Senator Enage St ☏ 053 823 0211, ☲ ocho.ph. Stylish restaurant where you choose from super-fresh salads, fish, fruit and desserts laid out at the back of the restaurant; your main course is cooked to your taste. Two can dine for around P500. Daily 10am–9pm.

Stephanie's Smokehaus Ave Veteranos ☏ 053 325 3797. Popular and cosy buffet restaurant, where P200 buys a great-value all-you-can-eat spread. Daily 7am–10pm.

Uncle Sam's P Gomez St ☏ 0917 820 9620. Philly steak sandwich (P165) and mac and three cheeses (P175) are some of the menu highlights at this American-themed diner painted bright red and decked out with classic movie posters. Daily 10am–9pm.

DIRECTORY

Banks Most banks in Tacloban have ATMs. Metrobank is on P. Burgos, St, and there's a BPI on Rizal St, close to the shell of the *McDonald's* building.

Hospital The grandly monikered Doña Remedios T. Romualdez Memorial Hospital and Puericulture Centre (named after Imelda's mum) is on J. Romualdez St.

Internet Roy's 24hr Internet and Lic Internet on P. Paterno St, and Bee One, opposite *Welcome Home Pensione* on Santo Niño St, are just a few of the countless small internet places.

Police Local police headquarters are located on the P. Paterno Extension near the RTR Park.

Post office There's a post office near the harbour on Bonifacio St.

Biliran

The beautiful and largely undiscovered island of **Biliran** lies off the north coast of Leyte, connected by a bridge. An autonomous province, Biliran is the Philippines in microcosm: there's a lengthy coastline of coves and beaches, a jungled, mountainous interior and even its own small version of Banaue's **rice terraces** at Iyusan in the island's western interior. **NAVAL** is the capital, on the west coast.

Among the many natural wonders are nearly a dozen thundering **waterfalls**, most with deep, clear pools that are perfect for swimming: Kasabanga Falls is in the barangay of Balaquid on the south coast; Casiawan Falls, a little further along the coast near Casiawan village; Tinago Waterfall, near Cabibihan in the island's southeast; and last but not least Bagongbong near Iyusan.

Two of the best **beaches** on Biliran are on opposite sides of the island, but even on a day-trip you'll have time to see them both. On the east coast, near Culaba, is the beautifully deserted Looc White Beach, while the Shifting Sand Bar, 45 minutes by bangka towards Higatangan from Naval, is a curving spit of sand surrounded by shallow water ideal for swimming, though note that there's no shade.

Maripipi and Higatangan islands

For Maripipi there are two boats daily from Naval (10am and 10.30am; 1hr; P60), which both return at 5am the following day; two boats run daily to Higatangan (noon and 1pm; 40min; P40), and return the following morning; unless you charter a bangka (P2000–4000), overnighting is a necessity at both islands (see p.364)

If you get to Biliran make sure you allow enough time to take a bangka to some of the surrounding islands. **Maripipi** is a picturesque place of friendly people dominated by a stunning 900m volcano, while Higatangan Rocks on **Higatangan Island**, forty minutes west of Naval by bangka, should also be on your itinerary. The beach here is beautiful and the rocks have been carved into extraordinary formations by time and tide. Ask your guide (see below) to take you to Cavintan Cave, said in local legend to extend all the way to Masbate and to contain deadly legions of venomous snakes – neither story appears to be true. Both islands have places to stay.

ARRIVAL AND DEPARTURE   BILIRAN

By bus and minivan There are buses and Duptours minivans to Naval from Tacloban and Ormoc (both every 30min; 3hr).

By boat Roble Shipping (☎053 500 7898) have two

ferries per week from Cebu City to Naval (Mon & Sat; 9hr), but if you want to save time it's far quicker to take a fast ferry to Ormoc, and then a minivan from there.

GETTING AROUND

By bus and jeepney From Naval there are buses and jeepneys north to Almeria (P20), Kawayan (P25) and east to Caibiran and Culaba (P60), but no further in either direction.

By habal-habal To explore the island at leisure it's simpler to hire a habal-habal to take you around for the day (P900–1200).

INFORMATION

Tourist information The small provincial tourist office (Mon–Fri 8am–5pm; ☎053 500 9627) and museum is in the Capitol Building in Naval. To explore the more remote areas of the islands and to find the waterfalls, it's best to employ the services of a local guide (P300/day), which you can enquire about at the tourist office. Online

it's worth checking out ⊛tourism.biliranisland.com and ⊛biliran.ph.

Services For internet in Naval, Roderick's Internet Café is next to *Chooks to Go* by the State University on Naval St. There are Metrobank and PNB banks, both with ATM, on Sabenorio St.

ACCOMMODATION AND EATING

NAVAL

D'Jan Dell's Cabin P. Inocentes St ☎ 053 500 9545. Near the main gates to Naval State University and the Prince Naval Supermarket, this place has clean, simple rooms. A/c rooms (P400–650) come with en-suite bathroom and cable TV while the cheapest fan rooms can be noisy and share communal facilities. **P150**

D'Mei Residence Inn 213 P. Inocentes St ☎ 053 500 9796. The newest addition to Naval's hotel line-up offers attractive, clean and brightly painted a/c rooms with flatscreen TVs. Service is friendly and there's wi-fi plus a minimart on the ground floor. **P900**

Marvin's Seaside Inn Brgy Atipolo, 2km north of town ☎ 053 500 9171, ⬥ marvinsseasideinn.com.ph. A far better bet than staying in town, *Marvin's* has a choice of seaside rooms with cable TV and hot showers (but without sea views) in the main bright yellow block, and bigger, nicer rooms (P1200) with the same facilities set around the pool in a building across the road. The restaurant has a decent range of Western and Filipino dishes, plus free wi-fi. **P1000**

ELSEWHERE ON BILIRAN

Estrella's Sunset View Brgy Masagongsong, Kawayan, 15km north of Naval ☎ 0921 542 2003. Quiet little resort with a/c and cable TV in the rooms, and a nice spring pool looking straight out to sea. **P800**

VRC Resort On the coast near Almeria, 12km north of Naval ☎ 0916 466 5809, ⬥ agtabeach.com. Small, clean, friendly, family-run resort on a quiet stretch of beach. Rooms are well-maintained and there's a pool. **P600**

MARIPIPI AND HIGANTANGAN ISLANDS

Higantangan Island Beach Resort Higatangan Island ☎ 0910 573 5963, ⬥ higatanganislandresort.com. A good range of rooms and cottages spread through manicured gardens on the seashore. The resort can also arrange local hikes, bike and kayak rental, and provides a free shuttle to a nearby sand bar, a romantic spot at full moon. **P800**

Napo Beach Resort Maripipi Island ☎ 0921 347 6620. Maripipi's only place to stay is an attractive resort with brightly painted fan and a/c (P1200–2200) huts set at the base of mountains and looking straight out to sea. They also have budget backpacker rooms (P500). The resort has its own jetty, and two small pools. **P800**

Ormoc and around

The small and relatively neat town of **ORMOC**, on Leyte's west coast, faces Ormoc Bay at the mouth of the Isla Verde River. Ormoc was largely rebuilt after floods in 1992 caused untold damage and resulted in the loss of eight thousand lives. In 2013 Ormoc once again felt the full force of nature when Yolanda tore through the city, destroying countless homes and damaging almost every roof. The city seems to be recovering well though, and its bayside park is still a great place to watch the sunset.

Lake Danao

The lake can be reached from Ormoc by jeepney (P50) or you can hire a van for the day (P3000)

Lake Danao, 19km away from Ormoc, had many of its facilities wiped out by Typhoon Yolanda, but still makes for a pleasant half-day out. Once there you can hike to a number of different waterfalls including Inawasan Falls (30min), Tigbawan Falls (2hr) and Maga-aso Falls (3–4hr).

ARRIVAL AND DEPARTURE — ORMOC

By ferry Oceanjet (☎ 032 255 7560 in Cebu, ⬥ oceanjet.net), SuperCat (☎ 053 561 9818) and Weesam (☎ 053 561 0080, ⬥ weesam.ph) all have fast ferry sailings between Cebu and Ormoc (11 daily; 2hr 30min). 2Go (☎ 053 561 9818, ⬥ travel .2qo.com.ph), Lite Shipping (☎ 053 561 6036, ⬥ liteferries .com) and Roble Shipping (☎ 053 255 7631) run slower services for Cebu (5–6hr). There are ticket offices for all ferries at the port, which is within walking distance of the town centre.

By bus, jeepney and van The main bus terminal and jeepney terminal are next to each other on Ebony St, near the pier. Jeepneys also operate some of these routes below but are far slower. The quickest way to move on is by Duptours van, which cost slightly more than the buses, and leave from their terminal on Bonifacio St.
Destinations Baybay (hourly; 1hr); Maasin (hourly; 3hr); Naval (every 30min; 3hr); Tacloban (hourly; 3hr).

ACCOMMODATION

Don Felipe Hotel Bonifacio St, opposite the port ☎ 053 255 2460, ⬥ hoteldonfelipeormoc.com. *Don Felipe* is an imposing-looking place with economy rooms at the back and better superior rooms (P1850) with balconies looking straight out to sea on the front. There's free wi-fi in the lobby. The roof was damaged by Yolanda and undergoing repair work at the time of writing. **P530**

Ormoc Villa Hotel Obrero St ☎053 561 9744, ⓦormocvillahotel.com. This is an attractive and upscale place with 49 smart a/c rooms (some of which were damaged by Yolanda), coffee shop, restaurant, swimming pool, spa and free wi-fi. **P2500**

Pongos Hotel Bonifacio St ☎053 255 2540. *Pongos* has a vast array of rooms, ranging from tatty doubles in the main building to better a/c rooms (P900–1300) in the new building. They also have a restaurant and free wi-fi in the lobby. **P350**

★**TRN Travelers Inn** Rizal St ☎053 255 7700, ⓦtrntravelersinn.com. Starting to show signs of age but still great value, this budget hotel has small but clean and quiet rooms attractively decorated in a white and beige colour scheme. All rooms are a/c and have cable TV and some have free wi-fi access. Single rooms start from P700. There's also a snack bar and music lounge. **P1300**

Zenaida's Chateau Tourist Inn Lopez Jaena St at J. Navarro St ☎053 255 2517. A friendly establishment

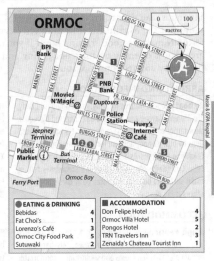

● EATING & DRINKING		■ ACCOMMODATION	
Bebidas	4	Don Felipe Hotel	4
Fat Choi's	1	Ormoc Villa Hotel	5
Lorenzo's Café	3	Pongos Hotel	2
Ormoc City Food Park	5	TRN Travelers Inn	3
Sutuwaki	2	Zenaida's Chateau Tourist Inn	1

with simple, brightly painted rooms. Singles have a fan and their own cold shower (P500), while many doubles have a/c and hot water. **P700**

EATING AND DRINKING

Bebidas Malacadios St ☎053 561 0040. *Bebidas* welcomes you with a billboard proclaiming "Coffee – do stupid things faster with more energy". Inside there's lively artwork on the walls, free wi-fi, and the menu includes spaghetti and sandwiches (P15–60), coffees, brownies and desserts. It's also a popular night-time drinking spot and serves San Miguel for P35 a bottle. Daily 9am–2am.

Fat Choi's San Pedro St ☎053 255 2765. Popular Chinese restaurant serving a range of dishes including beef with broccoli (P230) and Sichuan prawns (P260) which are designed to be shared, or rice bowl set meals (P90) for single travellers. Daily 9am–10pm.

Lorenzo's Café Larrazabal St. Pleasant café with comfy indoor seating and tables outside looking across to the ocean. The menu includes sandwiches, salads and burgers (P55–109). Daily 8am–10pm.

Ormoc City Food Park Imelda Blvd. At the bottom of San Pedro St, stalls at this night market sell cheap meals of barbecued fish and meat. Daily 8pm–midnight.

Sutuwaki Larrazabal St ☎0928 406 2583. Popular open-sided restaurant looking out to sea where you choose from the meat and fish at the counter and get it cooked to order. Daily 10am–midnight.

DIRECTORY

Banks There are plenty of banks with ATMs in Ormoc, including a BPI on Lopez Jaena St and a PNB on Bonifacio St.
Hospital The ciy's best hospital is OSPA (Ormoc Sugar Planter's Association; ☎053 561 1701), 1km east of town in Carlota Hills.

Internet access There are a number of cybercafés dotted around town including Huey's Internet Café on Malacadios St, and Movies n' Magic on Aviles St at Bonifacio St.
Police Ormoc's police station is on J. Navarro St at Aviles St.

The southwest coast

Heading south along the coast there are several towns which offer transport connections with Cebu and thus an alternative gateway to the diving to be found further south at Padre Burgos (see p.366). Fifty kilometres south of Ormoc, the frenetic port of **BAYBAY** is a functional town with a very busy wharf area and a main street lined with carinderias, convenience stores, pawnshops and a few banks. About halfway between Baybay and Maasin, clean, easy-going **HILONGOS** has a number of canteens huddled around a simple pier, but nowhere to stay. A little south of

6

Hilongos, the port town of **BATO** is a useful jump-off point for Padre Burgos. At the mouth of the Maasin River in southern Leyte, the otherwise dull, industrial port of **MAASIN** makes a good starting point if you're heading for the far south of Leyte, an area that is opening up for scuba diving and whale shark-watching. All four towns have ferry connections to Cebu.

ARRIVAL AND INFORMATION
THE SOUTHWEST COAST

By boat Hilongos (Kinswell 1 daily; Roble Shipping 1 daily; 3hr 15min), Baybay and Bato are all connected by regular slow ferries to Cebu and have onwards transport connections by bus, jeepney and van further south. From Maasin, Cokaliong and Trans-Asia Shipping Lines both run ferries to Cebu City (daily; 6hr). The boats are sometimes full, so make sure you book in advance; both these firms have offices at Maasin pier.

By bus If you're arriving by air in Tacloban you can catch an a/c minivan direct to Maasin (4hr; P180). Otherwise, buses from Tacloban take up to 6hr, an unpredictable and frustrating trip.

Tourist information You can get up-to-date information on diving and whale shark-watching from the Provincial Planning Development Office in Maasin's Provincial Capitol Building (☎ 053 570 9017).

ACCOMMODATION

Ampil Pensione Tomas Upos St, Maasin ☎ 053 570 8084. Located in the middle of town, this bare-bones budget place has fan rooms and slightly more comfortable a/c rooms with TV. **P250**

Maasin Country Lodge Mambajao, Maasin ☎ 053 570 8858. A little inland in a quiet, leafy location on the banks of the Canturing River, with comfortable a/c rooms that are spacious and well maintained, some with a TV, and there's also free wi-fi. **P650**

Padre Burgos and around

The area around **PADRE BURGOS** on Leyte's southern tip is making a name for itself as an exciting **scuba-diving** destination, with more than twenty sites documented by local divers. The town has a half-decent beach at **Tankaan**, a couple of kilometres to the south, while whale sharks, dolphins and manta rays can be seen in **Sogod Bay** immediately to the east.

Limasawa Island

Bangkas leave Padre Burgos 2–3 times early in the morning for Magallanes Brgy on Limasawa (45min; P60); if you miss the boat back you shouldn't have much trouble finding a home to stay in for the night (enquire first with the mayor)

It was atop a prominent hill on tiny **Limasawa Island**, that Magellan is said to have conducted the first Catholic Mass in the Philippines on March 31, 1521. After an often choppy boat ride from Padre Burgos, visitors can walk up concrete steps to a monument at the top of the hill, from where there are commanding views over the whole island. Limasawa also has some marvellous beaches and coves for snorkelling.

ARRIVAL AND DEPARTURE
PADRE BURGOS AND AROUND

By ferry The closest major port to Padre Burgos is Maasin, which is served by ferries from Cebu City (see above), although it's quicker to take a fast ferry to Ormoc, then a minivan (4hr).

By jeepney Jeepneys head up the coast to Maasin (P30; 1hr) from where there are transport connections to the rest of Leyte.

ACCOMMODATION

Peter's Dive Resort Padre Burgos ☎ 0917 791 0993, ⬤ whaleofadive.com. Affordable accommodation in standard rooms or duplex cottages for two and breathtaking views of Sogod Bay. The main building's lower terrace has a games room, where you can enjoy a round or two of pool, or play ping-pong. There's also a pool and an excellent little restaurant where the owners serve home-cooked food. The resort provides a pick-up service from Maasin (P650), Hilongos (P1800) or Tacloban (P4000). **P1790**

Southern Leyte Divers San Roque, Macrohon ☎ 0921 663 1592, ⬤ leyte-divers.com. Some 15min northwest of Padre Burgos by jeepney is this small German-owned lodge with charming native-style cottages in an idyllic beachside location. The restaurant serves German food, fish dishes and curry; the owners can, of course, arrange diving trips. P1600

Sogod Bay Scuba Resort Lungsodaan, 1km north of town ☎0916 376 0064, ⓦsogodbayscubaresort.com.

Lovely Spanish-style concrete rooms on the beach, plus diving facilities and internet. The restaurant has some appetizing fare, including Ron's beef and beer meat pies; Alisha's steamed fish in banana leaves; and the "world-famous" Dopey burger. The owners can help you arrange everything from diving and trekking to motorbike hire and caving trips. P1100

6

Palawan

BACUIT ARCHIPELAGO

Palawan

Palawan is the Philippines' fifth-largest island, a largely unexplored and unexploited final frontier of wonderful scenery and idyllic tropical beauty. Its location southwest of Luzon on the very edge of the archipelago, as close to Borneo as it is to Manila, has seen Palawan influenced by a series of external cultures and religions, and it instantly has a different feel to the rest of the Philippines. Beyond the centres of Coron, El Nido, Sabang and Puerto Princesa, tourism has yet to penetrate much of this 450km-long, sword-shaped island, and travellers who make it here will find a marvellous Jurassic landscape of coves, beaches, lagoons and razor-sharp limestone cliffs that rise from crystal-clear waters. Offshore, meanwhile, despite some damage from dynamite fishing and coral bleaching, there always seems an untouched reef to discover.

The capital of Palawan, **Puerto Princesa**, is the main entry point and is close to the mangrove islands of **Honda Bay** and the immense flooded cave systems that make up the mind-boggling **Underground River**. Further north you'll find the pretty beach resort town of **Port Barton**, the old fortress town of **Taytay** and the incredibly beautiful islands and lagoons of **El Nido** and the **Bacuit archipelago**. Many areas are still relatively unaffected by tourism, such as the friendly little fishing village of **San Vicente** and nearby **Long Beach**, one of the finest stretches of sand anywhere. Undeveloped **Southern Palawan** contains some of the least visited areas in the whole country, from the remains of a Neolithic community in the **Tabon Caves** and the turtle and cockatoo sanctuaries at **Narra** to **Brooke's Point**, the access point for **Mount Matalingajan**.

The **Calamian group** of islands, scattered off the northern tip of the main island of Palawan, has a deserved reputation for some of the best **scuba diving** in Asia, mostly on sunken World War II wrecks. Even if you're not a diver, there's plenty to do here. The little town of **Coron** on Busuanga is the jumping-off point for trips to mesmerizing **Coron Island**, with its hidden lagoons and volcanic lake and, to the south, the former leper colony of **Culion**.

It's best to **bring cash** to cover your stay in Palawan: outside Puerto Princesa credit cards are only accepted by some of the more established resorts (who will charge you commission), banks are few and ATMs almost nonexistent.

Puerto Princesa

PUERTO PRINCESA is the only major urban sprawl in Palawan, and its population of just over 250,000 makes up a third of the island's total. Even so it manages to live up to its name as a "forest city" and a few minutes' wander up any side street will soon find you amid greenery. There are a few sights around Puerto Princesa, but hardly any in the city itself (it was founded by the Spanish only in 1872), and most visitors treat it as a one-night

PORT BARTON

Highlights

❶ Dining out in Puerto Princesa Palawan's best eating destination boasts tasty mangrove worms, top-notch seafood and authentic Vietnamese noodles. **See p.375**

❷ The Underground River Take a boat trip under limestone cliffs and through sepulchral chambers, along a subterranean river that's said to be the longest in the world. See p.380

❸ Port Barton Laidback and convivial beach town with simple accommodation, rustic nightlife and a pristine bay of reefs and untouched islands. **See p.381**

❹ Long Beach Enjoy one of the nation's most alluring stretches of bone-white sand – and get there before the developers arrive. **See p.384**

❺ Bacuit archipelago Explore the majestic limestone islands, beaches and lagoons that stud the bays around El Nido. **See p.386**

❻ Scuba diving around Coron Some of the wildest diving in Asia, on sunken Japanese World War II wrecks. **See box, p.395**

❼ Lake Kayangan Arrive by bangka at a hidden blue lagoon off Coron Island, from where you scramble uphill to this dazzling volcanic lake. **See p.395**

HIGHLIGHTS ARE MARKED ON THE MAP ON P.372

stop on the way to or from Palawan's beaches and islands. **Rizal Avenue**, the main drag, runs west from the airport 3km through the centre of the city to the ferry port.

Immaculate Concepcion Cathedral
Plaza Cuartel, Rizal Ave • Daily 6am–7pm • Free

At the west end of Rizal Avenue, on Plaza Cuartel, the **Immaculate Concepcion Cathedral** is a pretty white and blue Neo-Romanesque structure with twin towers, though the interior is fairly ordinary. The plaza has a memorial dedicated to the 143 American soldiers who were burnt alive by the retreating Japanese Army in 1944.

Palawan Museum
Mendoza Park, Rizal Ave • Mon, Tues, Thurs & Fri 8.30am–noon & 2–5pm • P20

The small **Palawan Museum** offers an overview of the history, art and culture of Palawan. Most of the exhibits are fossils and old tools but there are, at least, informative English captions.

TOURS FROM PUERTO PRINCESA

There are several attractions around Puerto Princesa that you can easily visit in a day or less, including **Honda Bay** (see p.376) and the **Underground River** (see p.380) – note that for the latter you need to sort out a permit at least a day in advance (see below). All the hotels and agents in the area sell essentially the same tours, taking in the nearest sights for around P600 per person in a minivan, or P500–700 for a tricycle.

Most "city" tours take in **Butterfly Garden** (daily 7am–5pm; P50), a tropical garden with hundreds of brightly hued butterflies, and **Baker's Hill**, a manicured park and snack stop with a couple of aviaries. The **Crocodile Farm & Nature Park** (Mon–Sat 9am–noon & 1–4pm, Sun 2–4pm; P50) breeds endangered crocodiles, while the **Iwahig Prison & Penal Farm** (daily 8am–7pm; free) is an intriguing "Prison Without Bars" established in 1904.

RECOMMENDED TOUR OPERATORS

El Mundo National Hwy, Brgy San Miguel ☏0921 756 6762.
Island Paradise Tours Rizal Ave ☏048 433 2245.

Topstar Rizal Ave ☏048 433 8247.
Trip Buddies Rizal Ave ☏048 723 0160.

7

ARRIVAL AND DEPARTURE

PUERTO PRINCESA

By plane Flights arrive at tiny Puerto Princesa Airport at the eastern edge of the city on Rizal Ave. A small tourist office (☏048 434 4211) opens to meet flights. Most hotels will arrange to pick you up for free; tricycles cost around P50. Most passengers book tickets online (where rates can be very cheap), but hotels will also book them (for a fee). Of the airline offices at the airport, Philippine Airlines is open daily (8am–4.30pm; ☏048 433 4565), while Cebu Pacific (☏048 433 554) and the other airlines open for flights only.
Destinations Cebu (Air Asia: 2 daily; 1hr 10min); Manila (Air Asia, Cebu Pacific & PAL Express: 11 daily; 1hr 20min).
By ferry The port is at the western end of Malvar St, a short walk north of Rizal Ave.
Destinations 2Go operates a Puerto Princesa–Coron–Manila service (Sat midnight; 14hr to Coron, 30hr to Manila).
By bus, jeepney and van Most services depart from the San José terminal (also known as "New Market" after the

market next door), 7km north of the centre. Tricycles charge P100–120 from the city centre to San José; you can also catch multicabs (a minivan version of a jeepney; P15) and jeepneys from the corner of Rizal Ave and the National Highway (junction 1). Departures to all points north are most frequent in the early mornings; the times quoted here are guidelines only. Vans are typically 25 percent faster than buses, but are correspondingly more expensive, and often less comfortable – Daytripper Palawan (☏0917 848 8755, ⓦdaytripperpalawan.com) is a notable exception, and is well worth the extra money. They have one daily service from Puerto Princesa to El Nido in each direction at 9am (P900).
Destinations Brooke's Point (4 daily; 5hr); El Nido (10 daily, mornings; 6–8hr); Port Barton (daily 9am; 3hr); Quezon (hourly, mornings; 4hr); Roxas (10 daily, mornings; 3hr); Sabang (8 daily, 6.30am–3pm; 2hr 30min); San Vicente (2 daily; 5hr); Taytay (10 daily, mornings; 5hr).

GETTING AROUND

Tricycles There are no taxis in Puerto Princesa, but it's not difficult to find a tricycle. The standard fare per person within the city – including the airport and port – is P10 (more after 9pm), while hiring a tricycle privately will cost P50 for a short hop.

Motorbike rental There are numerous motorbike rental shops near the airport on Rizal Ave, all charging around P500/day or P3850/week (P800–1000/day for the bigger Honda trail bikes). ATO Motorbike Rentals (☏0920 491 3069) on Manalo Extension is a reputable operator.

INFORMATION

Tourist office Provincial Capitol Building, Rizal Ave, 1km west of the airport at the junction with the National Highway (Mon–Sat 9am–5pm; ☏048 433 2968).
Maps The tourist office's city maps (P50) are not as useful as the map in this Guide or the *EZ Map* of Puerto Princesa and Palawan (P99), sold at many city hotels.

Underground River permits If you're planning to visit the Underground River independently (see p.380), take your passport along to the park office in the City Coliseum, San Pedro (daily 8am–5pm; ☏048 723 0904) to arrange a permit on the spot.

7

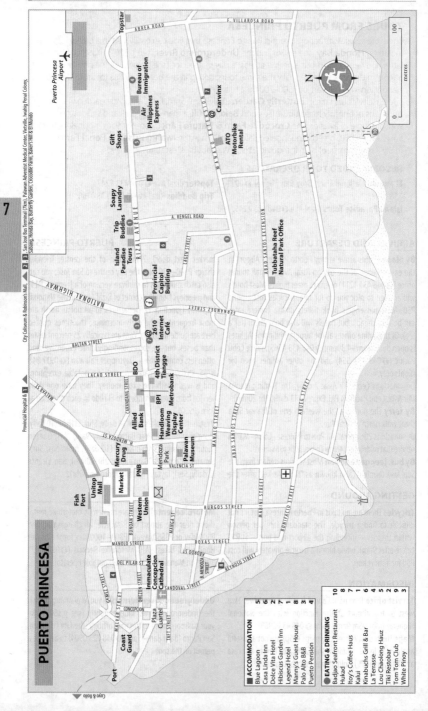

PUERTO PRINCESA

Puerto Princesa Airport

Cuyo & Iloilo

Port

Coast Guard

Provincial Hospital & ▲ 🚉

City Coliseum & Robinson's Mall, ▲ 🚉 🚉 🚉 San Jose Bus Terminal (7km), Palawan Adventist Medical Center, Vietville, Iwahig Penal Colony, Sabang, Honda Bay, Butterfly Garden, Crocodile Farm, Crocodile Farm, Baker's Hill & El Mundo

ABREA ROAD
F. VILLAROSA ROAD

Topstar

Bureau of Immigration

Air Philippines Express

Gift Shops

Soapy Laundry

Czarwinx

ATO Motorbike Rental

RIZAL AVENUE

A. RENGEL ROAD

Trip Buddies

Island Paradise Tours

Provincial Capitol Building

Tubbataha Reef Natural Park Office

LACEN STREET

ABAD SANTOS EXTENSION

ABAD SANTOS STREET

FERNANDEZ STREET

NATIONAL HIGHWAY

BALTAN STREET

2610 Internet Café

4th District Tiangge

BDO

LACAO STREET

CERANDING STREET

Allied Bank

BPI

Metrobank

Handloom Weaving Display Center

Mercury Drug

H. MENDOZA ST

Mendoza Park

Palawan Museum

MANALO STREET

Market

PNB

Western Union

Fish Port

Unitop Mall

BUNOAN STREET

VALENCIA ST.

BURGOS STREET

MANOLO STREET

DEL PILAR STREET

ROXAS STREET

MABINI STREET

BONIFACIO STREET

ARUEG STREET

MANGA ST

ABONDO ST.

REYNOSO STREET

Immaculate Concepcion Cathedral

Plaza Cuartel

MALVAR STREET

GOMEZ STREET

CONCEPCION

OBEZON STREET

TAFT STREET

SANDOVAL STREET

B. MENDOZA STREET

N

0   100
meters

■ ACCOMMODATION
Blue Lagoon 5
Casa Linda Inn 6
Dolce Vita Hotel 2
Hibiscus Garden Inn . 7
Legend Hotel 1
Manny's Guest House . 8
Palo Alto B&B 3
Puerto Pension 4

● EATING & DRINKING
Badjao Seafront Restaurant .. 10
Hukad 8
Itoy's Coffee Haus 7
Kalui 1
Kinabuchs Grill & Bar 6
La Terrasse 4
Lou Chaolong Hauz 5
Tiki Restobar 2
Tom Tom Club 9
White Pinoy 3

ACCOMMODATION

Puerto is overflowing with places to **stay**, many of which are to be found on or within a few minutes' walk of Rizal Ave. The most pleasant of these are towards the eastern end of the strip, and if you don't mind being a tricycle ride from the centre you could choose one of the good options in the leafy northern suburbs.

Blue Lagoon Purok Malaya ☎048 433 0118, ✪blue lagoon.com.ph. Clean, comfortable cottages with cable TV, fridge and wi-fi, set around a large swimming pool just a few minutes' walk from Rizal Ave. Staff are friendly and welcoming and there's a decent restaurant. **P2000**

Casa Linda Inn Trinidad Rd, off Rizal Ave ☎048 433 2606. Simple, friendly and convenient, with the bonus of good European and Asian food in the breezy café. The large rooms (ten a/c, three with fan) are arranged around a spacious courtyard garden. All are native style, with wooden floors and walls made of dried grass, and the place is always clean and orderly. Wi-fi P30/hr. **P1000**

★**Dolce Vita Hotel** 4 Victoria Romasanta St, San Pedro ☎048 434 5357, ✪hotels-palawan.com. This German-owned hotel is a real gem, with romantic canopy beds set in two-storey pavilions (cable TV, wi-fi, breakfast and a/c included). There's a decent pool and bar. A short tricycle ride from the centre of town. **P3400**

★**Hibiscus Garden Inn** Manalo Extension, near the airport ☎048 434 1273, ✪puertoprincesahotel.com. Great staff and friendly service, huge rooms with spotless tiled floors, a/c, cable TV and hot showers. There's also a leafy garden courtyard with hammocks and outdoor tables where breakfast is served. Free airport pick-up and wi-fi. **P1800**

Legend Hotel Northeastern end of Malvar St ☎048 434 4270, ✪legendpalawan.com.ph. The poshest

option, with luxurious a/c rooms and big, tiled bathrooms. Buffet breakfast included. Their boutique budget wing, *Pads by Legend*, offers smaller rooms (P2200) but the same amenities. **P3500**

Manny's Guest House 2 B. Mendoza St at Cuito St (aka Reynoso St), port end of Rizal Ave ☎048 725 1938, ✪intothespace.com/manny. The best-value backpacker or homestay accommodation in town, with three simple, clean and spacious fan rooms and one a/c room (P700) in an old Spanish-style wooden house, and lovely views over the bay and rooftops. Shared bathroom and kitchen; wi-fi P25/day. **P500**

★**Palo Alto B&B** Kawayanan St, Libis San Pedro ☎048 434 2159, ✪paloalto.ph. Some 4km north of town (a 15min tricycle ride), this warm, inviting family-run B&B is housed in impressive wooden buildings (sourced from sustainable forests in Palawan) around a central lawn. Cheaper rooms are on the small side but have a/c, flatscreen TVs and good bathrooms. There's a decent pool and the restaurant, *Salakot*, does a tasty adobo and has civet coffee. Free wi-fi in the lobby. **P3500**

Puerto Pension 35 Malvar St, near the port ☎048 433 2969, ✪puertopension.com. Cool, clean and quiet, with an alfresco top-floor restaurant that has views across the bay. Fan or a/c rooms, all with private bathrooms (with hot water) and cable TV; it's worth paying the extra for deluxe rooms. **P1170**

EATING AND DRINKING

There are plenty of enticing **restaurants** in Puerto Princesa, and several **bars**, most of them clustered between the airport and the city centre. Although most of the Vietnamese refugees who came to the city in the 1970s and 1980s have left, a few 24hr Vietnamese **noodle shops**, known as *chaolaongan*, remain.

★**Badjao Seafront Restaurant** Abueg Rd, Bagong Sikat ☎048 433 9912. Open-air, native-style restaurant with terrific views of the sea. It's reached on foot from Abueg Rd, at the end of Bonifacio St across a dainty bamboo bridge. Expect to pay about P500 a head for a meal of fresh, tasty grilled seafood such as salt-and-pepper squid or butter garlic shrimp. If you're here in the evening, getting transport back to the centre can be tricky, so you might want to pay a tricycle driver P150 to wait for the return trip. Daily 10am–10pm.

Hukad One Manalo Place hotel, Manalo Extension ☎0917 802 8222. This Cebuano institution has made its way to Palawan and efficiently serves up its standard menu of excellent Filipino cuisine including green mango salad (P65), blue marlin (P167) and pork Bicol (P129). Daily 11am–1.45pm & 5–9.45pm.

Itoy's Coffee Haus Rizal Ave ☎048 434 9918. Convivial

local café chain with a huge range of coffee-based drinks (P60–185). They also have decent desserts including cassava pudding (P60) and free wi-fi. Daily 6am–11pm.

KaLui 369 Rizal Ave ☎048 433 2580, ✪kaluirestaurant .com. Everyone who comes to Princesa seems to end up at this pretty bamboo restaurant. It's a bit overrated, but the beautifully crafted daily set meals (good for two; P435) are built around either seafood or meat, and most come with a salad and a small portion of fresh, raw seaweed. A la carte items include stingray in coco cream (P150), blue marlin (P185) and shrimps in garlic butter (P175). Reservations essential for dinner (call or ask at your hotel). Mon–Sat 11am–2pm & 6–10.30pm.

Kinabuchs Grill & Bar Rizal Ave ☎048 434 5194. The huge and enticing bar and garden at this Filipino restaurant is usually packed. The main attraction is the *tamilok* or "mangrove worms" (P135), believed to be an aphrodisiac rich in protein (actually a mollusc that tastes a bit like squid tentacle). Equally adventurous and more palatable dishes include Croc a la Bicol Express (P345), while the classic Filipino food is also excellent; try the sizzling seafood *sisig* (P230) or *singang na baboy* (P190). Daily 4pm–1am.

La Terrasse Rizal Ave ☎ 048 434 1787, ⓦ laterrasse palawan.com. Upscale but reasonably priced Filipino-European fusion restaurant – the airy interior is elegant and the food a delight. The trilogy of breads and dips (hummus, herbed cheese and eggplant dips with three breads; P210) whets the appetite for alluring mains, which include "adobo overload" (chicken and pork adobo fried twice and served with adobo fried rice) for P200. Daily 11am–11pm.

Lou Chaolong Hauz Rizal Ave. One of the city's few remaining Vietnamese diners, close to the airport. Though it is now Filipino-owned, it's still popular for its noodles – hand-pulled, and sourced from a local Vietnamese supplier (the beef stew is the most flavourful; P50) – and French

bread sandwiches (from P30). Daily 8am–4am.

Tiki Restobar Jct 1, Rizal Ave ☎ 048 434 1797. This big, busy open-sided bar on the city's main junction is getting to be a major venue for live bands (every night from 9.30pm) and events (when there's a P100 cover) such as the Kabilugan ng Buwan Fire Dancing Competition (Nov). Daily 6pm–2am.

Tom Tom Club Manalo Extension ☎ 048 433 3111. German-owned bar/restaurant – an expat favourite – offering a decent selection of steaks (pepper steak is the speciality; P320), paella (P540 serves two or three) and live music (Tues & Fri) to accompany late-night drinks. Fri–Wed 4pm–late.

White Pinoy Rizal Ave ☎ 0929 197 0445. New, simple little Slovenian-owned resto-bar serving decent European food, including home-made bread, pasta and pâté. Popular for evening drinks (San Miguel P60). Free wi-fi. Daily 11am–11pm.

DIRECTORY

Banks and exchange Banks in the centre include Allied Bank, Metrobank, BDO and BPI on the same stretch of Rizal Ave (all with ATMs), between Mendoza Park and the National Hwy. Make sure you get enough cash for the rest of your trip (there are hardly any ATMs between Puerto Princesa and Coron Town).

Hospitals and clinics There are two good hospitals, the Palawan Adventist Medical Center (☎ 048 433 4666, ⓦ palawanadventisthospital.org) on the National Hwy, 4km north of the city centre, and the Provincial Hospital, 1km north of the city centre on Malvar St.

Immigration Rizal Ave, near *La Terrasse* restaurant (Mon–Fri 8am–4.30pm; ☎ 048 433 2248). Can easily

extend visas on the spot.

Internet access There are lots of internet cafés near the *Hibiscus Garden Inn* on Manalo Extension, including Czarwinx (daily 9am–10pm; P13/hr). Nearer the centre, try 2610 Internet Café on Rizal Ave at Baltan St. Most hotels and resorts and some restaurants also have internet access.

Laundry Soapy Laundry, Rizal Ave (Mon–Sat 8am–noon & 1–8pm, Sun 1.30–8.30pm).

Pharmacies Mercury Drug (daily 6am–midnight; ☎ 048 433 3875) on Rizal Ave, opposite Mendoza Park. The branch at the Alicon Building, Malvar St (☎ 048 434 8618) is open 24hr.

Post The main post office is on Burgos St at Rizal Ave.

Honda Bay

Picturesque **Honda Bay**, 10km north of Puerto Princesa, is a shallow, lagoon-like expanse of water, backed by the spectacular range of mountains on the main island. The bay contains seven low-lying **islands**, most of them little more than sand bars fringed by mangrove swamp and small beds of coral – perfect for a day of island-hopping, lounging and snorkelling.

TUBBATAHA REEF NATURAL PARK

Located in the middle of the Sulu Sea, 181km southeast of Puerto Princesa, **Tubbataha Reef Natural Park** (☎ 048 434 5759, ⓦ tubbatahareef.org) has become a magnet for scuba divers, who reach it on liveaboard boats – most departing from Puerto Princesa between March and June. The reef is one of the finest in the world, with sightings of sharks, manta rays and turtles a daily occurrence. Dive operators in Manila, Puerto Princesa and Coron Town can arrange **packages** from around US$1600 for a one-week trip, including on-board accommodation and meals, the conservation fee of P3000 and up to four dives a day. For details of liveaboards, some of which visit the reef, see ⓦ expeditionfleet.com or ⓦ moonshadow.ch or visit the park office at 41 Abad Santos St, Puerto Princesa.

In addition to the major islands covered below you can also visit **Luli Island**, only accessible at low tide, and tranquil **Cowrie Island**. To snorkel at the lush **Pambato Reef**, the best place in Honda Bay for coral and giant clams, boats moor at a floating pier with a giant turtle-shaped roof. Some trips take in the swanky **Dos Palmas resort**, where you can use the resort facilities.

Snake Island

One of the most popular stops in Honda Bay is **Snake Island**, named after the curving sand bar that forms its main body. The central beach area here can be a bit of a carnival, with bangkas lined up offshore, large groups snorkelling, a row of trinket stalls, a bar and even some cooked food available. But if you walk a while you'll have the fine white sand to yourself, though the **snorkelling** opposite the stalls is best; there's an incredibly steep drop-off just beyond the beach, with great schools of tropical fish (in part encouraged by the dubious practice of feeding them).

Starfish Island

Starfish Island is a sand bar backed by mangroves named after the abundant horned sea star (starfish) that carpet much of the inner shallows around the island. The island also has some fine snorkelling towards the northern end, with delicate soft corals, butterfly fish and even moray eels further out.

Isla Pandan

Isla Pandan, managed by the *Legend Hotel* in Puerto Princesa (see p.375), offers expensive beach huts (P600), umbrellas, table and chair sets (P400) and massages – along with everything from paddleboards to buckets and spades. Simple seafood meals are also available from local vendors.

ARRIVAL AND INFORMATION   HONDA BAY

Tours Princesa hotels offer Honda Bay tours for P1500/person (P2500 with *Dos Palmas*), including transport to the San Lourdes pier, stops at three islands (usually Starfish, Snake and Pandan) and a picnic lunch. While this is convenient, you can save money (especially in a group) by arranging tours independently (see below).

By bangka Outrigger bangkas tour Honda Bay from the San Lourdes pier, 11km north of Princesa (see below). At the pier, the Honda Bay Boat Owners Association (daily 7am–5pm; ☎ 0929 864 9255 or ☎ 0908 635 3326) rents bangkas for P1300–1500 depending on the size of the vessel – there's also a P21/person terminal fee. Boats are rented by the day, and it's usual to make just three stops, plus Pambato Reef, but you can specify which islands you want to visit. You can rent masks, fins and booties (reef shoes) for P100 each. It's good to tip your boatmen if they've looked after you well. To get to the pier, the departure point for which is signposted around 1km off the National Highway, hotels can arrange minivans (P1500) or tricycles (P400–500), which comes with the convenience of return transport guaranteed. It's cheaper to grab a tricycle on the street (P100–150 one-way), though you might have to wait a while to get one heading back.

Island fees There are fees payable to visit Luli Island (P50), Cowrie Island (P75), Pambato Reef (P50), *Dos Palmas* resort (P500), Starfish Island (P50) and Isla Pandan (P150). Snake Island is free to visit.

Southern Palawan

A journey through southern Palawan represents one of the last great travel challenges in the Philippines. Much of the area is sparsely populated, with limited accommodation and nothing in the way of dependable transport, communications or electricity. The major attractions, south of **Quezon** village, are **Tabon Caves** – among the country's most significant archeological sites. On the east coast, around

Brooke's Point, there are hardly any buses and few jeepneys, but if you do make it here you'll find unspoilt countryside, quiet barangays and deserted, palm-fringed beaches backed by craggy mountains.

Narra and around

The small town of **NARRA**, about two hours by bus and 92km south of Puerto Princesa, makes a good introduction to southern Palawan, with several empty beaches in the area and **Rasa Island**, 3km offshore, the only place in the wild where you can see the endangered **Philippine cockatoo**. Around 250 of the estimated wild population of only one thousand reside here, although their habitat is threatened by plans for a 15MW coal-fired power plant less than 1km from the island. The island is a thirty-minute boat trip from the village of Panacan, a short tricycle ride from Narra. Further offshore, the **Isla Arena Marine Turtle Sanctuary** is a major nesting site for green turtles, where the tiny hatchlings are protected before being released into the wild.

Inland, the most rewarding excursion is to the **Estrella Waterfalls**, around 15km from Narra on the road back to Puerto Princesa. The water is wonderfully fresh and pure (you can swim here), and the falls are surrounded by lush jungle inhabited by monkeys.

ACCOMMODATION   NARRA AND AROUND

Crystal Paradise Resort Sea Road, Antipuluan ☎ 048 723 0952, ⊛ crystalparadiseresort.com. On the edge of Narra, this resort has good rooms and luxurious villas with their own pools (from P11,000). There's also a spa and staff can arrange trips to the nearby attractions. **P3500**

Tabon Caves and around

It was inside the **Tabon Caves** in 1962 that archeologists discovered a fragment of the skull dubbed "**Tabon Man**", dating back 22,000 years, which made it the oldest known human relic from the archipelago at the time. Crude tools and evidence of cooking fires going back some fifty thousand years have been unearthed in the caves, along with fossils and a large quantity of Chinese pottery dating back to the fifth century BC. Most of these artefacts have been transferred to the National Museum in Manila for preservation, though some are on display in the caves. It's still intriguing to wander through the damp caverns and tunnels, which may have been a kind of Neolithic workshop for making stone tools; researchers are still working here and are happy to show visitors the latest finds.

The caves are accessible from **QUEZON**, a fishing village consisting mainly of wooden houses on stilts, around 150km from Puerto Princesa. Before visiting the caves, stop first at the **National Museum** (Mon–Fri 9am–4pm; free) near Quezon wharf for orientation and information. There are actually more than two hundred **caves** in the area, but only 29 have been fully explored and of those only three are **open** to the public (Mon–Fri 9am–4pm).

ARRIVAL AND DEPARTURE   TABON CAVES AND AROUND

Tours Hotels and travel agents in Puerto Princesa organize day-trips to the Tabon Caves for around P1200/person.
By bus and bangka You can catch a bus from Puerto Princesa to Quezon (4hr). At Quezon wharf, bangkas can be chartered for P800 for the 30min ride to the caves and back.

ACCOMMODATION

Tabon Village Resort Tabon ☎ 0910 239 8381. The best place to stay near the caves, with simple cottage-style accommodation with fans and private bathrooms right on the water, plus a good restaurant. **P450**

Villa Esperanza Resort Tabon ☎ 0935 103 2820. Cheap resort with simple fan and a/c rooms set around a beachside garden. There's also a decent restaurant. **P250**

Brooke's Point and around

Deep in the southern half of Palawan, a four- to five-hour drive south of Puerto Princesa, the town of **BROOKE'S POINT** is flanked by the sea on one side and formidable mountains on the other. The town was named after the eccentric nineteenth-century British adventurer James Brooke, who became the Rajah of Sarawak (now Malaysia) after helping a local chieftain suppress a revolt. From Borneo he travelled north to Palawan, landing at what is now Brooke's Point and building an imposing **watchtower**, the remains of which stand next to a newer **lighthouse**.

Mount Mantalingajan

There's not much to do in Brooke's Point, but if you're looking for adventure you can hire a guide at the town hall to climb nearby **Mount Mantalingajan**, which at 2086m is the highest peak in Palawan. This is a seriously tough climb, which can take up to a week, so make sure you come well prepared; there's no equipment for rent locally. The usual route actually starts on the west coast from the barangay of Ransang near **RIZAL** (6hr from Princesa by Charing Bus Lines). Enquire at the town hall in Rizal, or call Fidel (☎0909 911 1600) who can help to arrange a guide and porter.

7

ACCOMMODATION	BROOKE'S POINT AND AROUND
Castelar Lodge Rizal ☎0921 504 4108. Ultrabasic lodging is as good as it gets in this remote spot. Dorms **P150**, doubles **P500** **Cristina Beach Resort** Tagusao shore, 7km northeast of Brooke's Point ☎048 433 4827. On a grey sand beach, this simple resort has fan and a/c rooms with or without	bath, or fan cottages with bathrooms. There's also a restaurant. **P300** **Silayan Lodge** Brooke's Point plaza, opposite the town hall ☎0928 347 0075. Functional rooms in the centre of town with a choice of fan or a/c and communal or private bathrooms. **P200**

Northern Palawan

Most visitors to Palawan focus their time in **Northern Palawan**, a wild mountainous land that crumbles into the mesmerizing islands of the Calamian chain. Two hours north of Puerto Princesa, the UNESCO World Heritage-listed **Underground River** meanders past a bewildering array of stalactites, stalagmites, caverns, chambers and pools. From here, **Port Barton** makes for a soothing stopover on the journey north to El Nido, with plenty of cheap accommodation and enticing snorkelling spots in the bay. **El Nido** itself is a wonderfully scenic resort town that remains relatively low-key, a gateway to the clear waters and jungle-smothered limestone islands of the **Bacuit archipelago**. If you have time, extend your trip to the islands around **Coron Town**, laced with crystal-clear lagoons, isolated beaches and dive and wreck sites.

Sabang

The jumping-off point for the Underground River is **SABANG**, a small village and laidback beach resort some 78km and two hours north of Puerto Princesa by road. The Underground River aside, Sabang's main appeal is its lovely white, palm-fringed sand **beach** facing St Paul's Bay. As well as sunbathing and swimming (pay attention to the flags, though, as currents can be strong), there's an 800m **zipline** at the far eastern end of the beach, **jungle trekking** and **kayaking**. You could also simply settle down in one of the numerous **massage shacks** (P350/hr) dotted along the beach.

ARRIVAL AND INFORMATION	SABANG
By bus, jeepney and van There are daily morning trips (2–3hr) from the San José terminal in Puerto Princesa to Sabang. The last departure from Sabang to Puerto is at	6pm (with Lexus vans), although the majority of services leave in the morning. For El Nido, catch a jeepney to the junction at Salvacion (7am, 10am, noon & 2pm) and

change there. You can buy a van seat in advance at *Green Verde's* travel centre.

By boat Unscheduled bangkas sometimes do the Sabang–Port Barton route (2hr 30min; P1200/person, P7200/boat), and might even continue on to El Nido (9hr) if there's demand – ask at *Green Verde's* travel centre.

Information and tours *Green Verde's* travel centre (📞 0926 230 9137) can assist with everything from bangkas and buses to motorbike rental and can help arrange a host of activities from ATV rides (P800/hr), jungle trekking (P500/person) and mangrove boat rides (P200 for 45min) to ziplining (P550).

ACCOMMODATION

Most of the growing number of places to stay on Sabang are aimed at backpackers. With the exception of the two upmarket resorts and *Green Verde*, all of the cheapies only have electricity from 6pm to 11pm and cold showers.

Blue Bamboo A 10min walk west from the wharf 📞 0910 797 0038. Owned by a friendly local, Lorena, this place has cottages set on the hillside and is perfect for anyone looking to escape it all (if you don't mind not being on the beach). The budget backpacker rooms are very simple, but great value, while the family rooms (P1000) are some of the most luxurious in Sabang (aside from the resorts) and have great views over the bay. **P350**

★ **Dab Dab** A 10min walk west from the wharf 📞 0949 469 9421 (no reservations). This budget option, facing a rocky shoreline, has seven spotless cottages scattered around a lush garden; the cheapest huts have shared bathrooms, but there are also en suites (P880) and family rooms (P1500). There's a gorgeous wooden restaurant, too. **P500**

Daluyon Beach Resort Eastern end of the beach 📞 048 433 6379, ⓦ daluyonresort.com. Tucked away, these attractive two-storey cottages have thatched roofs and luxurious rooms that open out to the sea. There's an attractive pool, 24hr power and wi-fi in public areas. **P5387**

★ **Green Verde** Towards the middle of the beach 📞 0910 978 4539. Small, clean and simple fan rooms with 24hr electricity and cold showers. The helpful travel service (see above), run by the owner's brother Miguel, can assist with everything from Underground River permits to Port Barton boats. **P800**

Mary's Beach Resort East end of the beach 📞 0910 384 1705. The cheapest accommodation in Sabang; no-frills, slightly shabby cottages with or without bathroom, right on the sand a 10min walk east of the pier. **P500**

Sheridan Beach Resort & Spa Middle of the beach 📞 048 434 1448, ⓦ sheridanbeachresort.com. Ultraposh (and expensive) hotel, right in the middle of the beach, with well-designed, modern rooms, a huge pool and a host of extras. Pick-ups from Princesa P3000. **P7000**

EATING AND DRINKING

Green Verde Green Verde hotel 📞 0910 978 4539. This wooden beachhouse restaurant is the best budget place to eat in Sabang, with a garden of individual *cabañas* facing the beach; expect fresh lapu-lapu, tuna and tasty barbecue pork for around P110; the crab curry (P130–150) or steamed crab in Sprite (P130–150) is definitely worth a try. Daily 7am–9pm.

Pawikan Restaurant and Coco Beach Bar Daluyon Beach Resort 📞 048 723 0889, ⓦ daluyonresort.com. This refined resort restaurant makes for a quiet evening, with frozen margaritas, pizza and pasta and excellent Filipino dishes on offer. Daily 6–10pm.

South Seas at the Sheridan Sheridan Beach Resort & Spa 📞 048 434 1448, ⓦ sheridanbeachresort.com. A decent range of local and international dishes served at tables looking over the beach. The native chicken *tinola* (with green papaya, chilli and pepper; P330) is good. This is also the best place in Sabang for a coffee (P130). Daily 6am–11pm.

The Underground River

Recognized as one of the "new Seven Wonders of Nature" in 2012, the **Underground River**, officially **Puerto Princesa Subterranean River National Park** ⓦ puerto-undergroundriver.com, protects a unique underwater river system that cuts through the limestone hills for 8.2km before emptying out into the South China Sea. The **caves** are completely natural and unlit, ranging from low-lying passages to vast, stadium-like caverns. It's a well-managed and untouched slice of Palawan, with numbers restricted by a daily quota.

Visiting the Underground River

After sorting out your permit (see opposite), from Sabang you'll take a twenty-minute bangka to the next bay along, followed by a short 150m walk through the forest to the river. Languid **monitor lizards** often congregate near the rangers' hut, while macaque monkeys hang out in the trees, looking to grab any loose snacks – don't feed them (or the lizards). Your boatman will point out the rock formations and wildlife inside (there are more than four hundred thousand bats) including the 62m high "**Cathedral**", a vast chamber that soars into the darkness and contains stalactites that resemble Mary, Jesus and friends.

Visitors get to see just 1.5km of the caves (45min); you can travel up to 4.3km into the system, but you'll need to arrange a special permit three days in advance. Afterwards, if you're feeling energetic, you can hike back from the mouth of the river to Sabang, a 5km trip through lush scenery, though this is steep and sometimes slippery, especially after rain.

ARRIVAL AND INFORMATION   THE UNDERGROUND RIVER

The Underground River is extremely popular, and the **daily quota** of nine hundred visitors is reached every day during peak season (Nov–May) – make sure you plan your visit ahead of time.

Permits Permits (P250) can be arranged at the park office in the City Coliseum in San Pedro, Puerto Princesa (☏ 048 723 0904), at least one day in advance. If you join an organized tour (see below) this will be done for you, but it's easy enough to arrange. It's best to secure a permit for 8am–9am (before the day-trippers arrive), but even if you're issued a different time you can just turn up at the wharf, show your permit and pay the P40 terminal fee – they'll probably put you on the next boat that has space. If you haven't pre-organized a permit in Puerto Princesa, local agents in Sabang (try *Green Verde*'s travel centre) can make the necessary arrangements up until 8pm the day

before you want to go.
By boat Your permit will specify the time you need to report to Sabang wharf for the 20min bangka ride (P700 for up to six) to the cave. Boat trips start daily at 8am and the last boat leaves at 3.30pm.
By van Renting a whole van for a day-trip to the Underground River will cost at least P3500.
Tours Day-tours from Puerto Princesa to the Underground River cost P1500/person, departing at around 7.30am, and including all fees, a basic lunch buffet on Sabang Beach and a short time for swimming. If you want to stay on in Sabang they'll drop you off after the tour.

Port Barton and around

On the northwest coast of Palawan, roughly halfway between Puerto Princesa and El Nido, **PORT BARTON** is far less developed than either of its busier rivals. The streets are all dirt tracks, there are no day-trippers and the rhythms of Filipino life go on largely undisturbed by the small groups of travellers lounging around in the handful of budget beach hotels. The hotels face crescent-shaped **Pagdanan Bay**, with its magical sunset views – **Port Barton Beach** itself, a gorgeous strip of sugary sand, is fine for a quick swim, but the water is often cloudy (especially after rain). Minutes away are fourteen pristine white sand islands, a number of top-notch dive and snorkelling sites and even a couple of waterfalls; **diving** trips can be arranged by Palawan Easy Dive (starting at around P2000; ⊕portbarton.info/padi) at the far southern end of the beach. Note that **electricity** is usually available between 6pm and midnight only in Port Barton and there are no banks.

Pagdanan Bay

You can rent a bangka from Port Barton for a day of island-hopping in **Pagdanan Bay**, aka Port Barton Marine Park. Popular targets include the spectacular coral reefs at **Twin Rocks** and **Aquarium Reef** (both a few minutes' ride from Port Barton); the former in particular offers vast banks of hard coral, including plenty of spiny staghorn, and hordes of tropical fish. The bay islands themselves are traditional desert island types where you can swim or just chill out. Most trips take in the beach at **Exotic Island**, which you'll usually have to yourself. The island is being developed as a cashew nut farm, but the beach is open to the public, and you can wade across the narrow sand bar to **Albaguen Island**, which has accommodation.

ARRIVAL AND DEPARTURE

By bus, jeepney and van From Puerto Princesa you can rent a minivan to Port Barton for around P5000 (3hr) or take the daily bus (9am; 3hr 30min) from the San José terminal (see p.373). The bus arrives in Port Barton on Rizal St, close to the beach and the town centre. Alternatively you can catch a bus, van or jeepney to Roxas, from where a daily jeepney runs to Port Barton (1hr) at around 9am, or to San José (at the Port Barton road junction) from where you can charter a motorbike or tricycle (P400–500) for the bumpy last 22km – this is not recommended during or after heavy rain, though. Some resorts can also arrange pick-ups from the San José turn-off (P1000/van). In the other direction jeepneys leave Port

PORT BARTON AND AROUND

Barton for Roxas at around 9am; from Roxas you can pick up services to El Nido, but be prepared to wait.

By boat By far the most appealing way to reach Port Barton is by boat. Unscheduled bangkas sometimes do the Sabang–Port Barton route (2hr 30min; P1200/person, P7200/boat), and there might also be services to El Nido (P1500/person, P9000/boat; 4hr 30min) if there's demand. Enquire at *Greenviews Resort* (see below). Local bangkas run to and from San Vicente in the mornings (45min–1hr; P100/person), or you can charter one for P1000. If San Vicente airport ever actually opens, the road to Port Barton (just 25km away) is also expected to be rebuilt.

ACCOMMODATION

Buses and boats arriving in Port Barton are met by staff from any number of **hotels**. If you don't have a reservation you're better off ignoring them; dump your gear at *Jambalaya* (see p.384) before making a choice. High season runs from mid-November to May – you'll get much cheaper deals outside this period.

PORT BARTON

Deep Gold Resort On the beach a short walk from Rizal St ☎0917 449 9212, ⌨deepgoldresorts.com. Big A-frame cottages, resembling Swiss chalets, all with balconies and private bathrooms, right on the sand. They also offer internet access and pick-up from San José (P1000). **P1200**

El Busero Inn ☎0999 486 3464. This is the best budget option, with basic rooms above the restaurant. There are also cottages for P1000. Discounts are available for extended stays. The big communal deck is a good place to meet fellow travellers. **P250**

Elsa's Beach Resort On the beach, towards the southern end of the strip ☎0906 308 0733, ✉elsasbeachresort @gmail.com. *Elsa's* enjoys a great location right on a pleasant stretch of beach, with an excellent restaurant and comfy cottages (some facing the garden). **P800**

★**Greenviews Resort** At the far northern end of the beach ☎0929 268 5333, ⌨palawandg.clara.net. Spotless nipa huts with fan and bathrooms (cold showers only) within a lush garden that attracts giant birdwing butterflies, sunbirds and the odd monitor lizard. Owners Dave and Tina Gooding also own the *Greenviews* near El Nido and can arrange onward transport and trips to the Underground River. Laundry service and wi-fi. **P1000**

Summer Homes ☎0906 215 1993, ⌨portbarton.info /summerhomes. One of the few places built of concrete and bricks rather than wood, but good value nevertheless. Rooms are simple but adequate (some have hot showers), and there are more comfortable beachfront cottages (P2000). They take credit cards and have wi-fi (free); non-guests can use it provided they spend a minimum of P150 in the restaurant (11am–3pm & 6–10pm). Also rent kayaks (P400/day) and motorbikes (P700/day). **P950**

PAGDANAN BAY

Blue Cove Island Resort Albaguen Island ☎0908 562 0879, ⌨bluecoveresort.com. An extremely tranquil collection of nipa huts (some with hot showers) over-looking the bay. The resort can arrange bangka pick-up from Port Barton for P800/couple. **P1200**

Coconut Garden Island Resort Cacnipa Island ☎0918 370 2395, ⌨coconutgarden.palawan.net. Wonderfully remote spot with attractive A-frame huts (P1250–1500) and cheaper rooms in a block at the back. It's a lovely place to while away the days, but there are also a host of activities on offer from volleyball to kayaking. The resort can arrange bangka pick-up from Port Barton or San Vicente for P250–300/person. **P970**

EATING AND DRINKING

Most of the **restaurants** in Port Barton are at the resorts; *Elsa's* has a good restaurant offering Filipino and European food for P200 or less per person, while *Greenviews* offers exceptionally high-quality meals. **Nightlife** is not part of Port Barton's appeal– there are a couple of local karaoke bars (try the *Owl's Nest Sunset Bar* next to *Greenviews*), but most people drink where they eat. Everything tends to shut down by 10pm.

Barton Bistro At the southern end of the beach. Serves an eclectic mix of comfort food from fish and chips (P250) to chilli con carne (P260); the little nursery with herbs and veggies provides the greens for the day. Popular for its happy hour sunset drinks. Daily 7am–midnight.

★**Jambalaya Cajun Café** On the beach next to the main pier. A great place to eat, sip coffee and get the latest information. They serve excellent jambalaya and play real Cajun music. You can leave luggage here too (free), and there's free internet. Daily 7am–8pm.

San Vicente

About 15km north of Port Barton is the sleepy fishing village of **SAN VICENTE**, accessible by bangka or bone-shaking jeepney ride from Princesa. It has a small market, a petrol station and a couple of snacks stalls but little else; it does offer an alternative to taking longer bangka rides between Port Barton and El Nido however, as it has road links to the north coast and Taytay.

The only reason to linger around here is **Long Beach**, a so-far undeveloped 14km stretch of sand south of town that ranks as one of the most extraordinary beaches in the country – you can see both ends only on a brilliantly clear day. Enjoy it while you can, as a planned new airport has already prompted the construction of large resorts and it is only a matter of time before the beach is "discovered" by package tours.

ARRIVAL AND DEPARTURE
SAN VICENTE

By plane There are plans to open an airport, though no one knows quite when that will be.

By bus, van and jeepney From Princesa there are buses (4–5hr) and Saviour vans (4 daily). Moving on you can either wait for a bus or van, or locals should be able to rustle up a driver; count on P2000 for the rough, bumpy 2hr 30min ride to Taytay, with only the main highway

between Roxas and Taytay surfaced.

By boat A bangka leaves for Port Barton at 8am (P100), otherwise you can charter a boat for the 45min journey (P1000).

By motorcycle To get to Long Beach, you will need to catch a lift on a motorcycle from San Vicente's market, near the pier, for around P50.

ACCOMMODATION

Picardal Lodge A short walk from the pier ☎ 0919 239 2224. This simple, friendly place has half-decent rooms and cottages set amid greenery. There's wi-fi and they can assist with island-hopping. **P800**

Taytay

On the northeast coast of Palawan, about 140km north of Port Barton by road and 50km south of El Nido, the quaint and friendly town of **TAYTAY** ("tie-tie") was capital of Palawan from the earliest days of Spanish conquest in the seventeenth century until Princesa assumed the role in 1903. Today little remains to show off this history save the half-ruined **Puerto de Santa Isabel** (P20), the smallish, squat stone fortress built by the Spanish between 1667 and 1738. As with many places in Palawan, the main attractions lie **offshore** – you can tour the wonderfully untouched islands in the bay by chartering a bangka for the day from the harbour (P2000–3000). **Elephant Island** is best known for its hidden lagoon, with a natural skylight in the roof that makes it a wonderful place to swim.

ARRIVAL AND INFORMATION
TAYTAY

By bus, van and jeepney All transport from Puerto Princesa and El Nido will drop you at the bus terminal on the edge of town; tricycles should shuttle you to the harbour (for tours of the bay) for P60.

Services There are a couple of banks in Taytay but neither have ATMs – you may be able to get a cash advance with your credit card at Palawan Bank in an emergency. Electricity is available from 5pm until 5am.

ACCOMMODATION

TAYTAY TOWN

Casa Rosa On a low hill behind the town hall ☎ 0920 895 0092. Pleasant little resort with simple, good-value rooms plus cottages (P1190) set in attractive gardens with ocean views. The café has delicious home-cooked spaghetti, pizza, fish and grilled chicken, plus wi-fi. **P500**

Pem's Pension House and Restaurant Rizal St (near the fort) ☎0916 461 0334 or ☎048 723 0463. Offers single rooms with a shared bathroom, plus smallish cottages with private bathrooms, either with fan (P500) or a/c (P1000). P400

TAYTAY BAY

Apulit Island Resort Apulit Island ☎02 894 5644, ⓦelnidoresorts.com. Run by *El Nido Resorts*, this swish hideaway is the closest to Taytay and offers accommodation in luxury cottages built on stilts over the water; you can spot baby sharks from your balcony. The resort has various

bars and restaurants, including a lovely little bar high on a rocky cliff at the back of the beach, reached by 109 steps. P22,000

★**Flower Island Resort** Flower Island ☎0917 504 5567, ⓦflowerisland-resort.com. This idyllic, eco-friendly, all-inclusive resort features 24 simple but romantic and attractively furnished nipa huts scattered along the shore, equipped with bathrooms (cold showers only except for the Deluxe Champagne rooms, which have solar-heated showers), fans (some have a/c) and verandas with hammocks. The restaurant serves buffet meals. Per person from P5000

El Nido and around

With its scruffy beach, narrow, tricycle-choked streets and unplanned rows of concrete hotels, the small but booming resort town of **EL NIDO**, in the far northwest of Palawan, makes a poor first impression, but the **surroundings** are jaw-dropping – the town is hemmed in between spectacular cliffs of jagged karst and an iridescent bay littered with jungle smothered outcrops of limestone. For now, El Nido remains refreshingly low-key, provincial and relatively cheap, with sari-sari stores selling San Miguel and snacks along the two main streets, Calle Hama and Calle Real – but it is changing fast.

The town is the departure point for trips to the mesmerizing **Bacuit archipelago**, the largest marine sanctuary in the Philippines. The archipelago's striking beauty has not gone unnoticed by developers, who have established a number of **exclusive resorts** on some of the islands. If a rate of more than $250 a night (per person) for a taste of paradise is too much for you, stay in El Nido itself – where **electricity** runs from 2pm to 6am only – and island-hop by day.

Don't miss the climb to the top of the marble cliffs of **Mount Taraw**, the ridge that backs El Nido; it's a strenuous haul, but the views are magnificent. Guided hikes take around three hours and cost P500 per person – ask at the *El Nido Boutique and Artcafé* (see p.389).

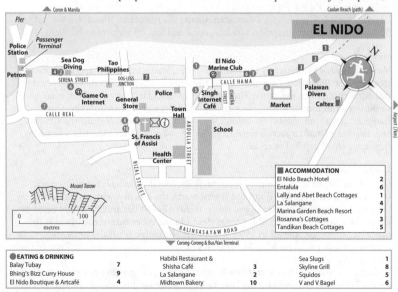

◼ ACCOMMODATION	
El Nido Beach Hotel	2
Entalula	6
Lally and Abet Beach Cottages	1
La Salangane	4
Marina Garden Beach Resort	7
Rosanna's Cottages	3
Tandikan Beach Cottages	5

● EATING & DRINKING					
Balay Tubay	7	Habibi Restaurant &		Sea Slugs	1
Bhing's Bizz Curry House	9	Shisha Café	3	Skyline Grill	8
El Nido Boutique & Artcafé	4	La Salangane	2	Squidos	5
		Midtown Bakery	10	V and V Bagel	6

7

DIVING AND SNORKELLING AROUND EL NIDO

The waters off El Nido are popular with **divers**, especially those looking to do a PADI course. **Snorkelling** is good, too, though much of the reef system has been killed off over the years due to crown of thorns starfish, bleaching and dynamite fishing. There are a few reliable **dive operators** in El Nido, who can also advise about trips to the Tubbataha Reef (p.376) and Apo Reef (p.258):

El Nido Marine Club Middle of the beach ☎0916 668 2748, ⓦelnidomarinediving.com. Dives from P2800; PADI from P19,000.

Palawan Divers Calle Hama ☎0939 958 1076, ⓦpalawan-divers.org. Two dives from P3100; PADI

from P21,900.

Sea Dog Diving Serena St ☎0916 777 6917, ⓦsea dogdivingpalawan.com. Similar rates and services to the other operators in town.

El Nido beaches

The El Nido bayfront has ravishing views, but the **beach** itself is average and not especially attractive for swimming because of the number of bangkas coming and going. **Caalan** or **Corong-Corong**, just a short walk north and south of town respectively, are much better. An even better option is **Nacpan Beach**, a vast swathe of usually empty white sand a 35–40-minute tricycle ride north of El Nido; take insect repellent, though, because the sandflies can be voracious.

The Bacuit archipelago

The main reason most people visit El Nido is to go **island-hopping** around the enchanting **Bacuit archipelago**, 45 limestone outcrops riddled with karst cliffs, sinkholes and idyllic lagoons.

Cadlao Island and Helicopter Island

The dramatic tower of rock just off El Nido is **Cadlao Island** (640m). The star here is **Ubugon Cove** at the back of the island, hemmed in by jagged rock, where you can snorkel, but this is also one of the few islands you can also explore on land. One-hour trekking tours (P2300 for three people) take in the unusual saltwater Makaamo Lagoon. Near Cadlao Island, **Dilumacad Island** (aka **Helicopter Island**) has a gorgeous 300m-long beach smothered in rare blue coral and lots of multicoloured shells.

Miniloc Island

Miniloc Island, 45 minutes by boat from El Nido, boasts one of the area's greatest treasures, the **Big Lagoon**, surrounded by towering limestone cliffs that look like a cathedral rising from the water. The lagoon is spectacular at any time, but even more so during a full moon, when light pours in from the top illuminating the water. Bangkas take a spin around the lagoon, but usually don't stop. Nearby, the similarly awe-inspiring **Small Lagoon** is only accessible by swimming (or sometimes kayaking) through a small gap in the rocks.

Matinloc Island

One of the largest islands in the group, **Matinloc Island** takes a bit longer to reach (around an hour from El Nido), but is well worth the journey, with several intriguing targets tucked away along its jagged shore. **Hidden Beach** lies around a tight bend in the rocks, a gorgeous cove hidden from view. On the other side of the island is the **Matinloc Shrine**, completed in 1993 – this Catholic shrine is usually quiet and windswept other than on May 31, when it's mobbed by believers for the Feast of the Lady of Matinloc.

Matinloc's main draw is **Secret Beach**, reached by a tiny gap you can swim through; on the other side is a spellbinding cove facing a white sand beach surrounded by steep rock walls. Tours also usually stop in the Tapitan Strait off Matinloc for the chance to see **turtles**, but it depends on weather conditions.

Southern islands

The main attractions in the southern archipelago include **Snake Island**, a serpentine sand bar lapped by crystal-clear waters, making it a great spot for sunbathing and a dip at low tide, and **Pangalusian Island** with its long, palm-fringed, white sand beach, perfect for swimming and snorkelling at any time.

ARRIVAL AND DEPARTURE

EL NIDO AND AROUND

By plane El Nido town is a 6km tricycle ride (P200) from the airport. Island Transvoyager (☎ 02 851 5664, ⓦ itiair.com) flies from and to Manila (3 daily; 1hr 15min); tickets can be booked well in advance through Manila booking agents or the *El Nido Boutique and Artcafé* (see p.389). There's a strict 10kg luggage allowance (including hand luggage); excess baggage is available at P100/Kg.

By boat Daily morning bangkas to Coron leave at 8am (P1800 including lunch; 7–8 hr). Arrange your ticket at *El Nido Boutique and Artcafé* (see p.389). An adventurous, if pricey, alternative is to join an El Nido–Coron boat trip

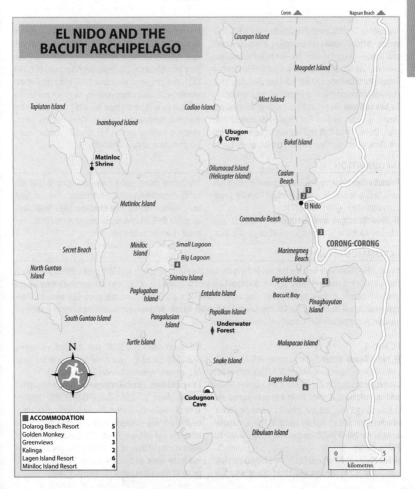

EL NIDO AND THE BACUIT ARCHIPELAGO

Coron
Napsan Beach

Cauayan Island

Maapdet Island

Mint Island

Tapiutan Island

Cadlao Island

Inambuyod Island

Ubugon Cove

Bukal Island

Matinloc Shrine

Dilumacad Island (Helicopter Island)

Caalan Beach

1
2
El Nido

Matinloc Island

Commando Beach

3

CORONG-CORONG

Secret Beach

Miniloc Island

Small Lagoon

Big Lagoon

Marimegmeg Beach

North Guntao Island

4

Shimizu Island

Depeldet Island

5

Paglugaban Island

Entaluta Island

Bacuit Bay

Pinagbuyutan Island

South Guntao Island

Pangalusian Island

Popolkan Island

Underwater Forest

Turtle Island

Malapacao Island

N

Snake Island

Lagen Island

6

Cudugnon Cave

Dibuluan Island

■ ACCOMMODATION	
Dolarog Beach Resort	5
Golden Monkey	1
Greenviews	3
Kalinga	2
Lagen Island Resort	6
Miniloc Island Resort	4

0   5
kilometres

7

ISLAND-HOPPING IN THE BACUIT ARCHIPELAGO

Bacuit archipelago **tours** (generally 9am–4pm) have been standardized into packages, and prices are set by the local government. They cost P1200–1400 per person (including lunch) depending on the islands visited, plus a P200 ecotourism development fee valid for ten days. Numerous places offer trips; one of the best options is the *El Nido Boutique and Artcafé*. **Tour A** takes in the attractions of Miniloc and Shimizu islands; **B** goes to Snake Island, Cathedral Cave and points south and **C and D** usually take in Matinloc and Tapiutan islands. The highlights are, naturally enough, scattered throughout each itinerary, designed to encourage several days of touring.

If time is short you can **charter your own boat**, taking in all the best locations; reckon on P4000–5000 per bangka. Another option is a **kayak tour**: Cadlao and Miniloc tours both cost around P1900 – you can book at *El Nido Boutique & Artcafé* or through El Gordo's Adventure Tours (☎0926 685 9798, ⊛elgordoadventures.com) in Sitio Tandul, west of the town centre. If you simply want to stay put on a **beach** for a few hours and do some snorkelling, you can charter a boat for P1200 to 7 Commando Beach (which has a small bar behind a lovely strip of sand), P1300 to Helicopter Island or P1600 to Shimizu Island.

organized by Tao Philippines (five days/four nights P23,000/ person; ⊛taophilippines.com), stopping at remote islands and villages along the way. For other destinations you generally have to charter your own bangka: it's P9000 to Port Barton (4hr 30min) and P12,500 to Sabang (7hr). Enquire at *El Nido Boutique and Artcafé* or *Greenviews* (see opposite).

By bus and van The bus and van "terminal" is in Corong-Corong, a 10min walk or P20 tricycle ride from El Nido town. There's a local fruit and wet market here where you can stock up on supplies. Regular and a/c buses run to Puerto Princesa (via Taytay and Roxas) with Roro and (more comfortable) Cherry; they take around 8hr. Faster and more expensive but often more cramped vans (6hr; P700) also leave throughout the day. Daytripper Palawan (☎0917 848 8755, ⊛daytripperpalawan.com; P900) is the comfortable alternative, although they currently only have one service a day, at 9am. There are more bus and van services in the mornings; the last trips leave at 10pm. For Port Barton change in Roxas (or the San José turn-off), and for Sabang jump off at the Salvacion turn-off.

INFORMATION

Tourist office Inside the DENR building near the town hall on Calle Real in El Nido, one block inland from the beach (daily 8am–8pm; ☎0917 841 7771).
El Nido Boutique and Artcafé On Serena St, this café (see opposite) is a good source of up-to-date local information (travel centre daily 7am–8pm; ☎0920 906 6317, ⊛elnidoboutiqueandartcafe.com). You can book tours, change money, rent mountain bikes (P500/day), go online (P90/hr) or make international calls (P30/min), and they accept credit cards.

ACCOMMODATION

It's just a 10–15min walk from the bus, van and jeepney terminal in Corong-Corong to El Nido proper, although it's worth taking a tricycle if you have heavy luggage. **Backpackers** tend to congregate in the heart of town where there are still plenty of cheaper accommodation options, but anyone looking for a bit more peace and quiet, plus more attractive surroundings, will be better off in **Corong-Corong** or **Caalan Beach**. Advance reservations are essential if you're on a budget, and especially at Christmas and Chinese New Year.

EL NIDO

El Nido Beach Hotel Calle Hama ☎048 723 0887, ⊛elnidobeachhotel.com; map p.385. Slick Korean-run hotel at the southern end of the beach; it's a big two-storey modern building that some might feel goes against the El Nido budget vibe, but the spacious rooms are stylish, with hot water and a/c, and the best ones have sensational views of the bay (P3600). Free wi-fi or computer use for P60/hr. P3000

★**Entalula** Calle Hama ☎0920 906 6550, ⊛entalula .com; map p.385. Elegant beachfront option with four fan-cooled *cabañas* (P3000) plus standard a/c rooms, beautifully crafted from wood and nipa, all with hot water and sea-view verandas. Laundry P70/Kg. P2800

Lally and Abet Beach Cottages Northern end of town on the shore, off Calle Hama ☎0917 850 2948 or ☎02 455 5656, ⊛lallyandabet.com; map p.385. Long-established, well-run resort with more than thirty fan or a/c rooms and cottages (P2400–4500), many with terrific views across the bay and balconies where you can sit and watch the world go by. Some rooms are a bit past their prime, so take a look before checking in. P1800

La Salangane 33 Serena St ☎0916 648 6994, ⓦlasalangane.com; map p.385. Enticing French restaurant and hotel combo with a choice of accommodation ranging from a beachfront suite (P4300) to premium (P2300) and budget doubles (P1500), all of which have hot water and wi-fi. They also have four apartments with kitchen (P1500) on Caalan Beach next to *Golden Monkey*. **P1500**

Marina Garden Beach Resort Calle Hama ☎0917 519 7722, ⓔmgelnido@gmail.com; map p.385. Very popular resort (booking essential) in the middle of the strip, with a few "family cottages" with shared bathrooms, a couple of slightly better fan rooms (P1070) and modern beachside (P2290–2690) or streetside (P1750) rooms. **P780**

Rosanna's Cottages Calle Hama ☎0920 605 4631; map p.385. Formerly a top budget choice, *Rosanna's* has moved a little upmarket, but still offers friendly service and beachfront rooms, these days with a/c, wi-fi and solar-powered hot water. **P2500**

Tandikan Beach Cottages Calle Hama ☎0919 944 6312; map p.385. Rustic resort in a fine location with sea and mountain views. The nine cottages are simple, but the service is friendly; you'll wake in the morning to find a flask of hot water on your balcony for coffee. **P1200**

CAALAN BEACH

Golden Monkey ☎0929 206 4352, ⓦgoldenmonkey elnido.com; map p.387. Peaceful little British-Filipino owned resort with well-constructed garden and beachfront (P4500) huts and smart rooms with views in the main block. They also have kayaks for rent (P500) and free wi-fi. **P2000**

Kalinga ☎0921 570 0021; map p.387. One of the few affordable options on pretty Caalan Beach. There are a variety of attractive rooms and huts set in a garden just back from the beach, all of which have cable TV and hot water. If you want a/c you just add P500 to the room price. Free wi-fi in the restaurant. **P1700**

CORONG-CORONG

Dolarog Beach Resort South of Corong-Corong ☎0927 420 7083, ⓦdolarog.com; map p.387. Peaceful beachside accommodation with thatched cottages and rooms in a grassy coconut grove on a quiet and rather isolated stretch of private beach. The resort is well run, serves excellent meals and is easy enough to reach from town by tricycle (P20/person) or bangka (about P200/boat). You can also arrange for staff to meet you at the airport. **P4000**

Greenviews 3km south of town ☎0921 586 1442, ⓦpalawandg.clara.net; map p.387. Popular resort (P20 via tricycle or a 25min walk from town) with a range of room types, free wi-fi and gorgeous sunset views all year (El Nido gets them May/June only). Owners Dave and Tina Gooding lay on handy free buses from town (9pm–midnight) – a nice touch. Kayaks are P700/day or P350/half-day. **P1000**

BACUIT ARCHIPELAGO

★**Lagen Island Resort** ☎02 894 5644, ⓦelnidoresorts .com; map p.387. Operated by *El Nido Resorts*, this private island paradise has superb beaches and diving, with stylish tropical accommodation in fan-cooled or a/c cottages. Package rates include meals and watersports. **P22,000**

★**Miniloc Island Resort** ☎02 894 5644, ⓦelnido resorts.com; map p.387. The other *El Nido* resort, very similar to *Lagen Island Resort* (see above), with equally stylish, high-quality accommodation and facilities. **P22,000**

EATING AND DRINKING

Dining and nightlife in El Nido are generally very relaxed affairs, with a handful of laidback **beach bars** offering simple food and cold beer, a few more sophisticated places that have opened in recent years, and cheap local places on Calle Real and Rizal St behind the beach.

★**Balay Tubay** Calle Real ☎0916 730 7266; map p.385. Historic wooden house and restaurant that hosts regular jam sessions on native instruments, reggae and other live music, as well as offering well-prepared Filipino food; choose fresh fish or squid and they'll grill it outside (mains P100–150). There's a smaller branch on Calle Hama. Daily 5pm–midnight.

Bhing's Bizz Curry House Calle Real ☎0915 624 4590; map p.385. One of El Nido's best-kept secrets, at least for those craving Indian food – the chicken curry (P350) serves two and is as authentic as you'll get in this part of the world. *Bhing's* is a great place to eat or just chill out with a book when it rains; it doubles as a spa and handicraft store. Daily 8am–9pm.

★**El Nido Boutique and Artcafé** Serena St ☎0920 902 6317, ⓦelnidoboutiqueandartcafe.com; map p.385. The heart of El Nido's traveller scene, thanks to its excellent travel centre (see opposite), the café itself offers friendly service, superb breakfasts, home-made bread, yoghurts and brewed coffee. Lunch and dinner features well-prepared salads, seafood, pizza (P260–300) and pasta. Vegetables are sourced from the café's own organic farm, 7km away. The bar also has live music every night except Tues. Daily 6.30am–11pm.

Habibi Restaurant & Shisha Café Calle Hama ☎0905 484 1764, ⓦhabibicafe.npage.de; map p.385. This German-owned place is justly lauded for its delicious food, an eclectic mix of fresh fish, some of the best coffee in town and that retro backpacker staple, banana pancakes. As the name suggests shisha pipes (P350) are on offer, too – try the mint or Red Bull (P400). Daily 7am–midnight.

La Salangane 33 Serena St ☎0916 648 6994, ⓦlasalangane.com; map p.385. Stylish place overlooking the beach, with a cool bar and great Filipino/French cuisine. The best deals are for Pinoy-style fresh fish (from P95), but it's worth shelling out for the steak tartare (P350) and trying the *île flottante* (P150) for dessert. They also offer good, flavoured, home-made rum. Daily 7am–10.30pm.

Midtown Bakery Rizal St; map p.385. The best bakery in town, with the usual buttery buns, white bread and *pandesal* (bread rolls) and a tempting array of cakes such as the sumptuous *pan de coco* and chocolate cookies, all for a few pesos – plenty of budget travellers load up here. Mon–Sat 7am–7pm.

Sea Slugs Calle Hama (on the beach); map p.385. El Nido's favourite beach bar, with candlelit tables spilling onto the beach and a loyal crowd who come to see their favourite local band play nightly. Seafood dishes are the speciality; try the chilli crab in coconut milk (P350). Free wi-fi. Daily 6am–midnight.

Skyline Grill Rizal St ☎0917 257 6978; map p.385. Cheapest diner in town, with tasty meals for less than P150. The burgers are pretty good (P100) and the foot-long sandwiches are a bargain at P65. Upstairs becomes a popular karaoke bar most nights. Daily 6am–11pm.

Squidos Calle Hama ☎0919 227 5537; map p.385. It's not on the beach, but this is one of the most popular backpacker hangouts in town, with cosy tables, free wi-fi and decent seafood (P150–200). Daily 24hr.

V and V Bagel Calle Hama ☎0926 706 0161; map p.385. Freshly baked bagels with a host of appetizing fillings, from the classic New York pastrami to the "Delicatessen" (cream cheese, smoked salmon, red onions and capers) – both P265. Daily 7.30am–8.30pm.

DIRECTORY

Banks and exchange There are no banks or ATMs in El Nido; the nearest is in Roxas (if it's working), so you should bring enough cash to last your stay. You can change money at many of the resorts and may be able to get a cash advance at the Petron petrol station (daily 7am–7pm) at the southern end of the beach near the pier (for which they will charge 7 percent commission).

Internet access You'll find numerous internet cafés in El Nido, though the connection only works when there's electricity (from 2pm). Singh Internet Café is on Calle Hama; on Serena St there's Game On Internet (most places 2pm–midnight; P50/hr). Numerous cafés and resorts also have free wi-fi.

The Calamian Islands

The island-hopping, kayaking, diving and trekking in the **Calamian Islands**, north of mainland Palawan, in many ways trumps the parent island, especially when it comes to its world-famous **wreck diving**. From the main settlement of **Coron Town** on the largest island, **Busuanga**, you can explore the awe-inspiring islands and reefs of Coron Bay, beginning with the lagoons and coves hidden among the staggering limestone cliffs of **Coron Island**. Here you can climb up to volcanic **Lake Lak**, not only a bewitching place to swim but also one of the Philippines' most unusual dive sites. Further south is **Culion Island**, an intriguing former leper colony, while **Calauit**, separated from the northern tip of Busuanga by the mangrove-lined Ditapic River, is the home of a curious **wildlife sanctuary**. The waters around the Calamians are also feeding grounds for the endangered **dugong** – the best tours to see them are arranged by *Club Paradise* on Dimakya Island (see p.393).

The Calamian group were badly affected by **Typhoon Yolanda**, and though the landscapes and diving remain largely intact many houses and buildings (including resorts) were damaged and electricity supply remains sketchy. All of the accommodation options listed in this Guide were at least partially open at the time of writing, and it is certainly still worth the long journey here.

Busuanga Island

Busuanga is the largest island in the group, but is mostly wild and undeveloped, with little to see beyond the lively fishing community of **Coron Town** on the south coast and its hinterlands. Coron Town is the main base for exploring the **shipwrecks** in adjacent

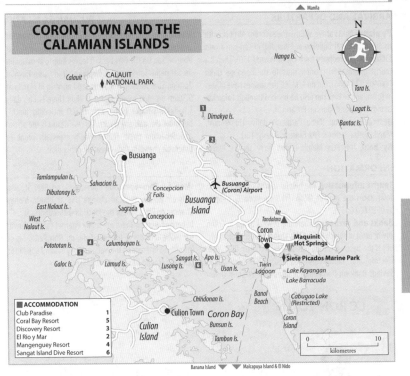

Coron Bay, but nondivers will find the pristine snorkelling, swimming and hiking trails nearby just as enticing.

Coron Town and around

With narrow streets shaded by trees, a thriving waterside market and a ramshackle wharf, **CORON TOWN** retains an old-fashioned provincial charm – for now. The town is a major resort-in-the-making, with regular flights from Manila helping to ramp up development, ambitious reclamation projects, ever-growing numbers of tricycles in the streets and even posh condos. The phenomenal views across the bay from the town to Coron Island never get old; these are best appreciated from the top of **Mount Tapyas**, a steep 30 to 45-minute hike along the trail at the end of San Augustin Street.

Maquinit Hot Springs

7km east of Coron Town • Daily 8am–8pm • P150 • Tricycles should charge P300 return from Coron Town for up to four people (they usually wait for 2hr); private minivan rental is P1200–1500, and some boat tours of Coron Bay include the springs

Facing Coron Bay, the **Maquinit Hot Springs** were damaged by Typhoon Yolanda but are now open again. They comprise a series of enticing open pools of spring water that feed each other before cascading into the sea; the springs are 36°C, making it best to visit during rain or the cool of the evening.

Mount Tandalara

Hikers can tackle the five-hour return trip to **Mount Tandalara** (936m), the highest point in northern Palawan, though the trail is not marked and it's best to hire a guide (P300) – *Sea Dive* (see p.393) can help. The trail starts from behind *KokosNuss Resort*, where you can also enquire about a guide.

ARRIVAL AND DEPARTURE

By plane Flights arrive at Busuanga (Coron) Airport, with its small terminal building and handful of sari-sari stores (30min by van/jeepney from Coron Town; P150). There's a tourist information counter next to the baggage claim (☏ 0918 725 4665), but no ATM. All the airlines have offices in town, and tickets can also be booked through Calamian Islands Travel and Tours on Rosario St.

Destinations Cebu (Cebu Pacific: 1 daily; 1hr 40min); Manila (Cebu Pacific & PAL Express: 3 daily; 1hr).

By boat The 2Go Manila–Coron ferry service leaves

Manila at 4pm on Fri, arriving in Coron Town at 6am on Sat morning; it departs 1hr later for Puerto Princesa, arriving at 9pm on Sat. On the way back, it leaves Puerto at midnight on Sat night/Sun morning, stopping off in Coron Town at 2pm on Sun, leaving at 3.30pm, and arriving in Manila at 5.30am on Mon morning. For El Nido there is one daily scheduled bangka (9am; 8hr; P1800 including lunch), bookable through any resort. Sea Dive Resort is the arrival and departure point. This service is especially prone to timetable changes, and is weather dependent.

INFORMATION

Tourist information The helpful tourist centre in Coron Town faces the market (Mon–Fri 9am–noon & 1–5pm; ☏ 0920 662 0057).

Banks and exchange There are several banks in Coron Town, most of which have ATMs that accept foreign cards. BPI is the best, up on the National Hwy (Cirrus, Plus, Visa, Electron and MasterCard accepted; P200 fee); Allied Savings Bank on Don Pedro St takes Visa. Western Union

(Mon–Sat 8am–6pm, Sun 8am–5pm), on Real St, also sells air tickets. You can change US$ at Bonito Money Changer on Rizal St near the junction with Valencia St.

Internet access There are many internet cafés in town: try Globe Telecom & Internet Café, on Don Pedro St, or Interspeed Internet on the National Hwy at San Augustin St (all daily around 11am–10pm; P30/hr).

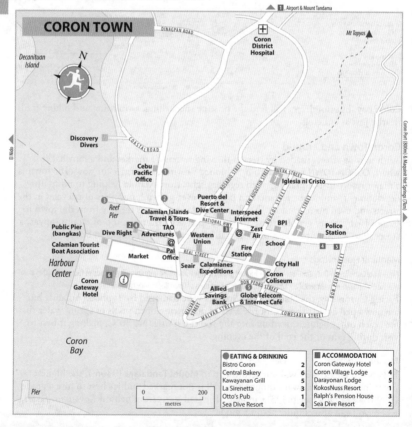

CORON TOWN

●EATING & DRINKING		■ACCOMMODATION	
Bistro Coron	2	Coron Gateway Hotel	6
Central Bakery	6	Coron Village Lodge	4
Kawayanan Grill	5	Darayonan Lodge	5
La Sirenetta	3	KokosNuss Resort	1
Otto's Pub	1	Ralph's Pension House	3
Sea Dive Resort	4	Sea Dive Resort	2

CORON TOWN TOUR OPERATORS

Most hotels can arrange various tours of the islands and attractions near Coron Town, but it's worth shopping around as itineraries and prices do vary. The following are recommended:

Calamian Tourist Boat Association At the town pier behind the market. This outfit has its own fixed prices for island-hopping.

Calamianes Expeditions 11 San Augustin St ☎ 0919 305 4363, ⓦ corongaleri.com.ph. An excellent budget choice. They need a minimum of five people to run tours, but will pair you with other groups to make up the numbers. Coron Island tours, for example, start at just P650/person including all admission charges and lunch.

Sea Dive Resort See below. In addition to their recommended dive trips (see box, p.395) this is a good place to check out when it comes to tours.

ACCOMMODATION

There are plenty of budget **places to stay** in Coron Town, as well as a growing number of mid-range options. While convenient, note that hotels around the market and harbour can be noisy. Some of the most luxurious and serene resorts in the Calamian chain lie off the **north coast of Busuanga**, a bus and boat ride from the airport and a 1hr drive from Coron Town. In spite of damage from Yolanda and ongoing repairs, all of the options below were at least partially open at the time of writing.

CORON TOWN

Coron Gateway Hotel Near the Coron Market ☎ 02 887 7107, ⓦ corongateway.com; map opposite. This plush hotel is right on the reclaimed waterfront next to the market, which could be seen as a plus or a minus. The huge rooms are stylishly decorated, with bathrooms with giant tubs, Japanese-style raised bed areas, cable TV and shared balconies, but the restaurant is mediocre, the wi-fi is not dependable and the staff are a bit disorganized (book tours elsewhere). P3000

Coron Village Lodge 134 National Hwy ☎ 0998 167 1968 or ☎ 0928 202 0819, ⓦ coronvillagelodge.com; map opposite. Ex-family home, now a friendly hotel with 25 rooms, a five-room apartment (with kitchen) and a lush garden. Rooms are bare-bones but spotless, with a/c, bathroom and TV. It also has some of the best tour packages in town. P950

Darayonan Lodge 132 National Hwy ☎ 0917 894 4593, ⓦ darayonan-coron.weebly.com; map opposite. Rambling bamboo hotel with decent deluxe rooms in the newer wing (P2300); the older rooms are a bit shabby. The pool is a nice extra, and the free wi-fi (in common areas) is pretty reliable. The alfresco restaurant, *Raphaella's*, serves breakfast, lunch and dinner. P1400

KokosNuss Resort 1km north of town ☎ 0919 776 9544 or ☎ 0919 448 7879, ⓦ kokosnuss.info; map opposite. The first accommodation as you approach Coron Town from the airport, set around a lovely garden area with hammocks and a small pool. Rooms range from basic with shared bath to private with a/c, hot showers, mosquito nets and flatscreen TVs. Free wi-fi. Renovations were underway at the time of writing and plans are for a concrete dorm room (P600) in place of the old nipa huts. P1680

Ralph's Pension House 172 National Hwy ☎ 0921 631 5449, ⓦ ralphspensionhouse.webs.com; map opposite. Cosy little guesthouse with ten bright, modern a/c rooms with bathroom, flatscreen TVs and verandas; you also get wi-fi, roof-deck bar, free coffee and mineral water, but service is sketchy. P1300

★ Sea Dive Resort 3 Don Pedro St ☎ 0918 400 0448, ⓦ seadiveresort.com; map opposite. Popular divers' resort offering simple, comfortable options including en-suite fan and a/c rooms (P1400) and budget rooms with shared bathrooms (P450). There's a decent restaurant, bar and internet access, and the dive facilities are first rate. Visa and MasterCard accepted (5 percent surcharge). It is also a well-equipped dive operation (see box, p.395), popular with beginners and advanced divers. P900

THE NORTH COAST

Club Paradise Dimakya Island ☎ 02 719 6971, ⓦ clubparadisepalawan.com; map p.391. Slick, German-owned place with cosy, modern a/c cottages a stone's throw from the beach and a fabulous house reef – turtles and dugongs have been sighted here. Rates include airport pick-up and full board. Per person P5500

El Rio y Mar Port Caltom, San José ☎ 02 838 4964 or ☎ 02 668 3929, ⓦ elrioymar.com or ⓦ dugongdivecenter.com; map p.391. Set on a 500m-stretch of beach facing a lagoon (it's on a promontory, not an island), with an infinity pool. The 24 spotless, beautifully maintained native or cedar *cabañas* all have hot water, TV and video, and there's basic wi-fi at the restaurant. The many activities, diving and tours on offer cost extra; kayaks are P750/day, a north coast island tour is P2500/person and a Coron Island trip is P3900. Per person P8000

7

EATING, DRINKING AND NIGHTLIFE

Coron Town's **eating** options have improved dramatically in recent years, with plenty of restaurants ranging from backpacker standards to a variety of places serving Filipino cuisine; dishes tend to be simple, however, with fresh fish often in short supply. The **Coron market** (most stalls daily 6am–7pm) by the piers in the centre of town has a number of cheap snack stalls and open-air grills. **Nightlife** is limited to a handful of Western-oriented bars, though the town does have a seemingly inexhaustible appetite for videoke.

CORON TOWN

Bistro Coron National Hwy at Don Pedro St ☎0918 305 0750; map p.392. Convenient and solid choice, serving mostly European cuisine; dishes such as chicken *cordon bleu*, coq au vin, pizzas, pastas and the odd Filipino choice. Grilled fish usually has to be ordered in advance (mains P150–250). Breakfasts are great value (P250). Daily 8am–10pm.

Central Bakery Don Pedro St; map p.392. The most convenient place to stock up on fresh buns, cakes, *hopia* (sweet bean-filled pastries) and *pandesal* (bread rolls) from P30. Daily 6am–7pm.

★**Kawayanan Grill** Don Pedro St ☎0905 320 2376; map p.392. Rustic Filipino restaurant with thatched candlelit *cabañas* and a lush garden, handicraft store and videoke. Great place for drinks, with so-so live bands and decent food; the *kare-kare* (P250) is an excellent peanut-packed delight, and the fresh coconut (P75), *halo-halo* (P120) and barbecued meats (P100) are good, too. Daily 11am–11pm.

La Sirenetta Reef pier (accessible via the alleyway beside Coron Divers and Coron Reef Pension House) ☎0918 903 7063; map p.392. Best location in town, if not the best food, stuck out on a pier opposite *Sea Dive Resort* with romantic views across the bay and tasty margaritas. The seafood isn't bad; mangrove crabs, mahi-mahi, Culion tiger prawns and local lobster usually grace the menu (mains around P250). Daily 11am–10pm.

Otto's Pub National Hwy; map p.392. Popular foreign hangout owned by local celebrity and Austrian expat Otto Putz, serving cold beers with Austro-German food (think *bratwurst*, beef goulash and meat loaf). Open most days till late.

Sea Dive Resort 3 Don Pedro St ☎0918 400 0448; ⓦseadiveresort.com; map p.392. This popular resort (see p.393) is traveller central, offering a good range of breakfasts (P140), pancakes (P90), burritos (P160), pizzas (P240), sandwiches and burgers (P150), pastas (P130–240), basic veggie dishes including *pinakbet* (P160) and lots of fresh seafood. Wi-fi is free and there's one terminal in the corner. Daily 7am–11pm.

Coron Bay Islands

The primary reason to stay in Coron Town is to explore the spellbinding islands and coves scattered around **Coron Bay** – also a fantastic destination for **wreck-diving** (see box opposite). Bangka trips are easy to arrange, but it's worth comparing the various packages on offer (see box, p.393). **Coron Island** is the most popular destination, but you should also try to spend some time on the smaller, less visited islands.

Coron Island

Sea Dive Resort (see p.393) offers day-trips (usually 8am–4pm) for around P1500 for a bangka of up to four people; the boat association (see box, p.393) charges P2000 – these prices do not include the various admission fees, and lunch is usually an extra P250/person

Most hotels and tour operators in Coron Town offer day-trips to **Coron Island**, an enchanting cluster of jagged limestone cliffs and peaks just fifteen minutes across the bay. The island offers truly spectacular landscapes and some rich snorkelling sites, though visitors are confined to the northern coast; Coron is the traditional home of the **Tagbanua** people and the rest of the island is strictly off-limits to outsiders. The Tagbanua in the two main east coast communities of Banuangdaan (Old Coron Town) and Acabugao now make most of their income from charging admission fees to the island's various attractions; this supplements their traditional sources of livelihood, fishing and bird's nest collecting.

Tours involve plenty of snorkelling and swimming. In between Coron Island and Coron Town you'll typically stop at the **Siete Picados Marine Park** (P100), which offers a relatively rich spread of coral and marine life (sea snakes, sea fans, clownfish and whale sharks are sometimes spotted on the deeper side of the reef).

WRECK-DIVING IN CORON BAY

Most divers come to the Coron area for the World War II **Japanese shipwrecks**. There are 24 wrecks in all, all sunk in one massive attack by US aircraft on September 24, 1944. Among the most interesting are:

Akitsushima A big ship lying on her side with a crane once used for hoisting a seaplane. Between Culion and Busuanga islands, near Manglet Island, the wreck attracts huge schools of giant batfish and barracuda.

Irako The best of the wrecks and still almost intact; it's home to turtles and enormous groupers, who hang in mid-water and eyeball you as you float past. A swim through the engine room reveals a network of pipes and valves inhabited by moray eels and lionfish, which have spines that deliver a hefty dose of poison.

Morazan Maru Japanese freighter sitting upright at 28m. Large shoals of banana fish, giant batfish and pufferfish the size of footballs can be seen, especially around the mast, bow and stern. It's easy to get into the cargo holds, making this a good wreck dive for beginners.

Taiei Maru Japanese tanker covered with beautiful corals and a large variety of marine life. The deck is relatively shallow at between 10m and 16m deep, and is well suited to wreck-dive beginners.

DIVE OPERATORS

There are a dozen or so dive operators in Coron Town. The following are reliable:

Discovery Divers A short walk out of town towards the airport ⓦ ddivers.com.
Dive Right Near L&M Pe Lodge ⓦ diveright
-coron.com.
Sea Dive Resort ☎ 0918 400 0448, ⓦ seadiveresort .com; see p.393.

7

Lake Kayangan
Daily 8am–4pm • P200

To visit volcanic **Lake Kayangan** boats dock at a gorgeous lagoon rimmed with coral and turquoise waters – here the Tagbanua have a small hut with basic information about the island and the tribe, with staff on hand to answer any questions. The lake itself is reached by climbing up a steep flight of steps – at the top, turn left along a narrow path to tiny **Kayangan Cave** for awe-inspiring views of the lagoon below. The main path continues down to the lake, where you can snorkel in the warm waters and spy schools of odd-looking needlefish.

The rest of the island
Lake Barracuda (P100) is encircled by jagged limestone outcrops that give way to lush jungle, but is only really worth the additional entrance fee if you are on a **dive trip**; on the surface the water is the usual temperature, but 18m down it heats up so much that you can drift along on hot thermals. To the west are the **Twin Lagoons** (P100), hemmed in by jagged pillars of limestone towering over the water like abstract sculptures. Boats dock at the end of the first lagoon, where you can swim through a low-lying water tunnel into the second one, a tranquil and very deep inlet (the other end opens to the sea). Odd coral formations cling to the sides of the lagoon, looking like a sunken city under the surface. A little further along the coast is **Skeleton Wreck** (P100), a sunken Japanese fishing vessel easily viewed by snorkellers, and a series of narrow **beaches** backed by sheer cliffs. Tours usually stop for lunch on one of these (Banol Beach is the most popular), but each one charges a P100 fee.

The southern islands
The boat association (see box, p.393) runs tours for P3500/boat; Calamianes Expeditions (see box, p.393) charges P950/person

One hour south of Coron Town lies the enticing trio of **Malcapuya Island** (P200), **Banana Island** (P100) and **Bolog Island** (P100), classic desert islands where the main activity is lounging on the beach. Malcapuya has monkeys inland, while Bolog features alluring **Malaroyroy Beach**, a curving bar of silky white sand.

Sangat Island

Sea Dive (see p.393) charges P3500/boat, while the boat association (see box, p.393) rate is P2500 and Calamianes Expeditions (see box, p.393) charges P950/person

Sangat Island, west of Coron Town (1hr 30min by boat), is yet another craggy, picture-perfect tropical island. As well as plenty of coral gardens laced with tropical fish, the island is close to eleven World War II shipwrecks, some of which can be explored by snorkellers at low tide.

ACCOMMODATION

CORON BAY ISLANDS

★**Coral Bay Resort** Pototot Island ☎0916 544 1843, ⓦ coralbay.ph; map p.391. Comfy, rustic accommodation in fan-cooled wooden huts on a 900m white sand beach about 1hr 30min from Coron Town by bangka (free transfer from Coron office if you stay two nights or more). This is a peaceful place to chill out, and you can trek around the island or snorkel just offshore on a beautiful reef teeming with tropical fish. **P3000**

Discovery Resort Decanituan Island ☎0918 398 7125, ⓦ discoverydiversresorts.com; map p.391. Popular dive-oriented resort, a 10min bangka ride from Coron Town, with a 24hr shuttle service back and forth. The bungalows all have private bathrooms and terraces with fine views of the bay. Staff are friendly and reasonably efficient, and there's a good restaurant. The beach here is nothing special, but horseriding and kayaking are available. **P1500**

★**Mangenguey Resort** Mangenguey Island ☎0908 896 8488, ⓦ mangenguey.com; map p.391. The top choice for splendid isolation, this luxury resort is a 1hr 30min boat ride from Coron Town – the island is private (with plenty of snorkelling and trekking), the suites are beautifully designed and furnished with art, and there's wi-fi, a/c and cable TV. Verandas provide views of the ocean and the food is exquisite. Minimum two nights except during peak season. **P11000**

★**Sangat Island Dive Resort** Sangat Island ☎0919 617 5187, ⓦ sangat.com.ph; map p.391. Established by a British expat in 1994 on a gorgeous island – 30min from Coron Town – with a giddy interior of cliffs and jungle and a shore of coves and coral reefs. Accommodation is in thirteen native-style beachfront and hillside cottages (with fans), and they specialize in diving courses. Free wi-fi or P100/hr for internet. Full board. Per person **P4500**

Culion Island

Few travellers make it to the curious island of **Culion**, around two hours south of Coron Town by boat. In 1904 the Americans decided to create an isolated but self-sufficient leper colony here – it became the world's largest **leprosarium**, a place that inspired fear and often revulsion. Today the leper colony has all but been erased, but haunting monuments of the island's past remain, as well as some untouched, empty beaches. Like Busuanga, Culion is quite large and undeveloped, but the main attractions lie in the pretty little capital, **Culion Town**. The approach to town is dominated by the striking coral-walled **La Inmaculada Concepción Church**, which was rebuilt in 1933 on the site of an older fortified Spanish chapel, completed in 1740. Beside it is the old lighthouse, with tremendous views north to Coron Town. Note that electricity only runs from noon to midnight in Culion, which can make for a hot night when there's no breeze.

Culion Museum

Culion Sanatorium and General Hospital compound • Mon–Fri 9am–noon & 1–4pm • P200

The intriguing **Culion Museum**, housed in the island's former leprosy research lab (built in 1930), details the history of the colony. Featuring medical relics and photographs from the turn of the last century, with a vast archive of patient records that you can browse, it also maintains the rooms where doctors worked, complete with original, rather frightening-looking equipment.

ARRIVAL AND INFORMATION

CULION ISLAND

By boat Culion can only be reached by bangka from Coron Town; the M/V *Santa Barbara* (P200) leaves daily at around noon from Coron Port (1hr 30min). It overnights in Culion – returning at 9am – so you'll have to stay unless you rent a private bangka from the boat association (see box, p.393) for a return trip (2hr one-way; P2500–3500), or join the tour (P1150/person) with Calamianes Expeditions (see box, p.393).

Tourist information Inside the town hall (Mon–Fri 9am–5pm; ☎ 0917 552 2277).

Services There are no banks or ATMs and credit cards are rarely accepted, so bring enough cash for your stay.

ACCOMMODATION AND EATING

Hotel Maya Next to the church ☎ 0939 254 2744. Culion's best hotel is actually a teaching hotel operated by the Jesuit-run Loyola College of Culion. Rooms are spacious and comfortable and service is friendly. Single rooms are available (P550). **P1100**

Tabing Dagat Lodging House A 5min walk from the port, opposite the local government offices ☎ 0921 653 1470. Comfy option offering doubles with shared bathrooms or larger a/c en suites with balconies (P750). There's also a decent Filipino restaurant. Credit cards accepted. **P550**

Calauit

P350, additional 2hr motorized tour P1000 for a group of six • From Coron bangkas cost P9000 (up to eight people; 4hr one-way), or more conveniently you can charter a van to Quezon and back (2hr 30min; P6500 for up to six people), where you can take a bangka (10min; P500) to Calauit – however, if you are alone you can save money by joining an organized tour (P2600/person) with Calamianes Expeditions (see box, p.393)

In 1977 President Marcos created a game reserve on **Calauit**, an island separated from the north coast of Busuanga by a narrow mangrove channel. All the original giraffes, zebras, elands, impalas and gazelles from Kenya have since died, but their offspring have multiplied to number more than five hundred. Also doing well are more than one thousand native **Calamian deer**. Other rare indigenous species here include the Palawan peacock, mouse deer, bearcats, pythons and porcupines. The draw for most visitors is the chance to **feed** the giraffes by hand, though this merely emphasizes how tame the animals have become.

Mindanao

KADAYAWAN FESTIVAL, DAVAO

Mindanao

Mindanao, the massive island at the foot of the Philippine archipelago, is in many ways the cultural heart of the country, a place where indigenous tribes still farm their ancient homelands and Christians live alongside Muslims who first settled here in the fourteenth century. Spanish rule came late to much of the island, and was tenuous at best throughout the nineteenth century; when the Americans occupied the islands, it was here that they met their most bitter resistance. Today the island remains a conflict zone, with countless bomb attacks and a full-scale coup in 2013, and in spite of a peace pact between the MILF rebels and the government early in 2014, caution is advised for travel anywhere on the island, and certain parts should be avoided altogether. All of this said, most visits to Mindanao are trouble-free, and much of the island is peaceful, friendly and stunningly beautiful.

North Mindanao, which sees the most tourist activity, is comparatively safe, although the lively gateway city of **Cagayan de Oro** (CDO) in the centre was the site of a bomb attack in 2013. Highlights include **Siargao Island**, famous for surfing, and **Camiguin**, a ravishing volcanic island off the north coast. The untouched **Agusan Marsh Wildlife Sanctuary** is inhabited by the Manobo tribe, while to the east are the hypnotic azure waters of the **Enchanted River**. Also worth exploring are the western cities of **Iligan** and **Dapitan** (where national hero José Rizal was sent into exile), and **Mount Malindang National Park**, a little-known area of dense rainforest near Ozamiz.

In the south, **Davao**, the island's de facto capital, is a friendly provincial metropolis with excellent restaurants and nightlife. Nearby are the beaches of **Samal Island** and majestic **Mount Apo**. West of the frenetic city of **General Santos**, around the shores of **Lake Sebu**, the friendly and artistic **T'boli** people still live in traditional wooden houses and wear hand-woven tribal garments and adornments.

Much of western Mindanao is part of the **Autonomous Region in Muslim Mindanao**, or ARMM, an area of huge tourism potential but with the security situation in a state of flux. Highlights include the traditional Muslim city of **Marawi**, which stands on the northern shore of serene **Lake Lanao**, and the hundreds of islands that make up the spectacular **Sulu archipelago**, especially Tawi-Tawi. You'll need to check the current **security** situation before considering a visit.

Northern Mindanao

Some of the most accessible (and safest) parts of Mindanao lie along the **north coast**, starting with the inviting city of **Cagayan de Oro**. The northwest coast stretching from **Iligan** to **Dipolog** is mostly rural and undeveloped, but peppered with alluring port towns and national parks, while the pint-sized island of **Camiguin** to the northeast is

LAKE SEBU

Highlights

❶ Whitewater rafting on the Cagayan de Oro River Shoot the rapids near Cagayan de Oro, with the full 15km course offering four hours of thrills. **See box, p.406**

❷ Dolphin Island One of the cheapest places in the world to swim with wild dolphins. See p.410

❸ Lanzones festival, Camiguin Visit this dazzling little island in October, when the colourful Lanzones festival is held. See p.412

❹ Enchanted River This magical but remote lagoon is a deep cove of crystalline water crammed with tropical fish. See p.416

❺ Siargao Island Tranquil resorts, powdery beaches, top-notch surfing and laidback nightlife. **See p.418**

❻ Samal Island Explore this rustic island of sandy beaches, bat caves and affordable resorts, just a few hours from Davao. **See p.428**

❼ Mount Apo The trek to the summit of the Philippines' highest peak takes you through thick jungle and past waterfalls to a steaming blue lake. See p.430

❽ Lake Sebu The best place to experience life among one of Mindanao's most creative tribes, the T'boli, and home to an exhilarating zipline. See p.432

HIGHLIGHTS ARE MARKED ON THE MAP ON P.402

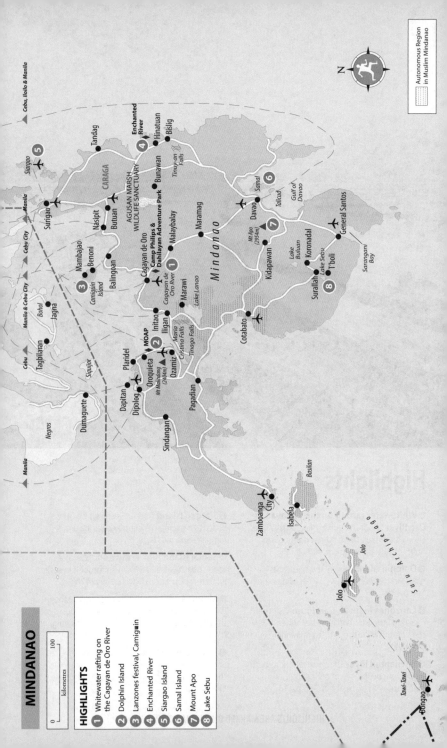

MINDANAO

0 — kilometres — 100

HIGHLIGHTS

1. Whitewater rafting on the Cagayan de Oro River
2. Dolphin Island
3. Lanzones festival, Camiguin
4. Enchanted River
5. Siargao Island
6. Samal Island
7. Mount Apo
8. Lake Sebu

N

Autonomous Region in Muslim Mindanao

THE MINDANAO PROBLEM

Despite its volatile political situation and advice from Western governments to avoid travelling to all of Mindanao, much of the island is relatively safe for foreign travellers. However, you should always check the **current situation** before travelling and read our advice on trouble spots (see box, p.433). Politically the situation is fluid and confusing, with a number of factions and splinter groups calling for varying degrees of autonomy from Manila.

The thorniest issue involves Mindanao's Muslims (known as Moros), who are seeking self-determination. The **Moro National Liberation Front** (MNLF) started a war for independence in the 1970s that lasted until 1987, when it signed an agreement accepting the government's offer of autonomy. As a result, the **Autonomous Region in Muslim Mindanao**, or ARMM, was created in 1990, covering the provinces of Basilan, Lanao del Sur, Maguindanao, Sulu and Tawi-Tawi, plus Marawi City. The **Moro Islamic Liberation Front** (MILF) splintered from the MNLF in 1981 and refused to accept the accord. It has since continued fighting and making uneasy truces (see p.445). At the height of the fighting, more than 750,000 people were displaced and about four hundred people killed. One of President Benigno Aquino's election pledges was to bring lasting peace to this troubled region, but the situation escalated in 2013 with an island-wide spate of bombings including previously "safe" cities such as Cagayan de Oro and Davao, plus a three-week-long full-scale occupation of Zamboanga by MNLF separatists. In spite (or perhaps because) of this, early in 2014 President Aquino witnessed the signing of the historic **Bangsamoro Agreement** between the government and the MILF, which proposes a wider Muslim autonomous ancestral homeland in Mindanao.

Hopefully this deal will bring the long-awaited peace that the island so desperately needs, but unfortunately Mindanao's problems don't end with the MILF. In the early 1990s another disaffected group of fighters founded **Abu Sayyaf**, whose name means "Bearer of the Sword". Based on **Basilan Island**, off Mindanao's south coast Abu Sayyaf is said to have ties to a number of Islamic fundamentalist organizations including al-Qaeda. The group finances its operations through robbery, piracy and **kidnappings** and is believed to have been responsible for the bombing of Superferry 14 in February 2004, which sank off the coast of Manila with the loss of 116 lives. In 2006 the group's leader, Khadaffy Janjalani, was shot dead in an encounter with government troops. However, Abu Sayyaf is not party to the Bangsamoro Agreement and still remains a threat. Likewise **communist rebels** (aka the New People's Army), who have been fighting for the establishment of a communist state in Mindanao since 1969, remain active in remote parts of the island.

Finally, much of the ARMM remains dangerous territory thanks to private armies aligned to corrupt local politicians. In 2009, 57 people (including 34 journalists) were tortured and murdered in what was dubbed the **Maguindanao Massacre**, apparently for attempting to register a rival candidate for the upcoming elections; the perpetrators were a private militia controlled by the powerful Ampatuan clan (who were arrested and tried in 2010).

one of the country's most appealing tourist spots. Northeastern Mindanao is known as **Caraga** (aka Region XIII), an area generally overlooked by foreign tourists though rich in ecotourism potential. Highlights include the ancient wooden boat discovered at **Butuan**, the spellbinding **Enchanted River** and the surfing hot spot of **Surigao**.

Cagayan de Oro and around

Sprawled along the north coast of Mindanao, the city of **CAGAYAN DE ORO** (CDO) makes an ideal introduction to the island, with a smattering of sights and fine restaurants in the city, and a handful of enticing attractions in the mountains beyond, with **whitewater rafting** on the Cagayan de Oro River. Sitting on the eastern bank of the river, the city stretches from **Vicente de Lara Park** in the north, with its age-old mahogany trees, to circular **Gaston Park** in the south, once the site of city executions, bull-fights and parades. Southwest of the park you'll find the **San Augustine Cathedral**, a dour off-white stone edifice, with immense stained-glass windows, rebuilt in the 1950s.

There's another park, a narrow strip of open space called **Plaza Divisoria**, running east–west between T. Neri Street and Abejuela Street, a good area for convenience stores and fast food. The park ends at Corrales Avenue and **Xavier University**. A couple of kilometres northeast of the university, the hip, modern heart of the city revolves around the **Limketkai Center**, an upscale mall, and the adjacent **Rosario Strip**, which was the site of the bombing in 2013 (see box, p.403).

Museum of Three Cultures

Capitol University, Corrales Ave, 2km north of Plaza Divisoria • Mon–Fri 9am–noon & 2–6pm, Sat 9am–noon, Sun 10am–noon & 3–5pm • P100 • ☎ 088 2272 3349

The **Museum of Three Cultures** is devoted to the Christians, Muslims and seven indigenous traditions (or "Lumad") of northern Mindanao. The first gallery is dedicated to history, with exhibits on the Huluga Caves, early trade with China and the Butuan boats (see p.415). The most interesting section is dedicated to the M'ranao of Marawi, an area at the heart of the Moro dispute. Exhibits cover Islamic brass work, giant ceremonial swords owned by the sultans and traditional *torogan*-style houses.

Gardens of Malasag Eco-Tourism Village

Cugman, Malasag Rd, 7km southeast of the city • Daily 24hr; tribal singing concerts daily 4.30pm • P30 day entry, P50 night entry; swimming pool additional P50 • ☎ 088 855 6183 • Taxis from the centre of Cagayan de Oro P250

The **Gardens of Malasag Eco-Tourism Village** is located in a reforested area in hills southeast of Cagayan de Oro. The "village" contains faithful replicas of various tribal houses in the region, hosts tribal singing concerts and has panoramic views of Macajalar Bay. On a clear day you can see as far as Camiguin Island.

Camp Philips

40km southeast on the highway to Davao • Minivans to Camp Philips from Cagayan de Oro's eastbound bus terminal (see p.406) P50

The small settlement of **Camp Philips** makes for an intriguing day-trip. The former US base is now at the centre of the massive Del Monte Philippines **pineapple plantation**, the largest in Southeast Asia, and stumpy, prickly pineapple plants smother the landscape in every direction. Today the camp houses Del Monte staff in pretty wooden houses that blend US and Filipino styles, but there's not much to do other than admire the fruit.

Dahilayan Adventure Park

40km southeast on the highway to Davao • Daily 8am–5pm • 320m zipline & 150m zipline P250 for both; 840m zipline P500; all three ziplines P600; package including zipline or whitewater rafting (see box, p.406), minibus transport from Cagayan de Oro, meal and snacks P1200, or P1999 for both rafting and zipline • ☎ 0922 880 1319, ⓦ dahilayanadventurepark.com • Habal-habals from next door to Camp Philips bus station charge P150 to the park; or a van and driver from CDO should cost P2500–3000/day, or take the 8am Sun a/c minibus from Coffeeworks, a café on Corrales St near Plaza Divisoria

Accessed by a dirt road from Camp Philips, the **Dahilayan Adventure Park** makes for another entertaining day out, primarily for its 840m **zipline** and refreshingly cool alpine location – the park nestles in the hills some 1370m above sea level. The main attraction, the **Dahilayan Zip Zone**, comprises three ziplines: an exhilarating 320m section and a tamer 150m segment; and the 840m finale, where you are chained into a full body harness before hurtling down the mountain at 90km per hour.

ULTRALIGHT FLIGHTS

Just outside Camp Philips, thrilling ultralight flights operated by **Carlito Freias** (☎ 0916 593 7034) allow you to soar high above the surrounding pineapple plantations, crisscross a couple of lush canyons and see a magnificent waterfall, with hazy mountains in the distance. Rides are P1500 per fifteen minutes, and he's prepared to fly any day, but you must book in advance.

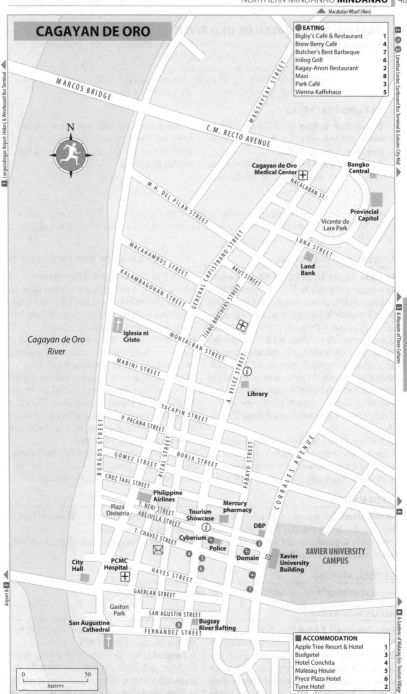

Macabalan Wharf (4km)

CAGAYAN DE ORO

8

● EATING	
Bigby's Café & Restaurant	1
Brew Berry Café	4
Butcher's Best Barbeque	7
Inilog Grill	6
Kagay-Anon Restaurant	2
Maxi	8
Park Café	3
Vienna Kaffehaus	5

MARCOS BRIDGE

C.M. RECTO AVENUE

MAGSAYSAY STREET

M.H. DEL PILAR STREET

Cagayan de Oro Medical Center

NACALABAN ST.

Bangko Central

Provincial Capitol

Vicente de Lara Park

MACAHAMBUS STREET

GENERAL CAPISTRANO STREET

AKUT STREET

LUNA STREET

Land Bank

KALAMBAGOHAN STREET

TIANO BROTHERS STREET

Iglesia ni Cristo

MONTALBAN STREET

MABINI STREET

A. VELEZ STREET

Library

Cagayan de Oro River

YACAPIN STREET

P. PACANA STREET

BURGOS STREET

GOMEZ STREET

RIZAL STREET

BORJA STREET

PABAYO STREET

CORRALES AVENUE

CRUZ TAAL STREET

Philippine Airlines

Plaza Divisoria

T. NERI STREET

ABEJUELA STREET

Tourism Showcase

Mercury pharmacy

DBP

T. CHAVEZ STREET

Cyberium @

Police

@

Domain

3

Xavier University Building

XAVIER UNIVERSITY CAMPUS

City Hall

PCMC Hospital

4

5

6

HAYES STREET

@

GAERLAN STREET

7

Gaston Park

SAN AGUSTIN STREET

San Augustine Cathedral

FERNANDEZ STREET

8

Bugsay River Rafting

■ ACCOMMODATION	
Apple Tree Resort & Hotel	1
Budgetel	3
Hotel Conchita	4
Malasay House	5
Pryce Plaza Hotel	6
Tune Hotel	2

0   50
metres

8

RAFTING THE CAGAYAN DE ORO RIVER

Whitewater rafting along the fourteen major rapids of the Cagayan de Oro River gained popularity after former President Gloria Macapagal-Arroyo took a ride here in 2002. The jump-off point is at the barangay of Mambuaya, a thirty- to forty-minute ride from the city proper. The wet months (Sept and Oct) are best for intermediate and professional levels (when the rapids range from class 3 to 4), while the rest of the year is OK for beginners.

RAFTING OPERATORS

Bugsay River Rafting ☎088 309 1991. Trips for anyone from beginners (12km, 3hr; P700) to extreme thrillseekers (15km, 4hr; P2000).

Great White Water Tours ☎088 851 7856, ⓦriver raftingcdo.com. Half- (P1200) or full-day tours, inclusive of snacks and meals. Rates include transport from *P. Joe's Diner* at the Limketkai Center, or there's a combo package with Dahilayan Zip Zone (see p.404) including hotel pick-up.

There's also whitewater rafting – either come with a group or call in advance and they should be able to place you in a boat (minimum six) – and overnight lodging in the *Pine Grove Lodge*.

ARRIVAL AND DEPARTURE

By plane The new Laguindingan International Airport, 46km southwest of the city, finally opened in June 2013, but has been plagued by problems with many cancellations. The airport is accessible by jeepney (P40 to Laguindingan turn-off, then P20 shuttle to the airport), shuttle vans (Magnum Express leave from Magnum Radio on CM Recto hourly from 4am to 3pm; P199) or taxi (P1200). Philippine Airlines has ticket offices at the airport (Mon–Fri 8.15am–4.30pm; ☎088 858 8864) and at 21 T. Neri St (same hours; ☎088 851 2295). Cebu Pacific (☎088 858 3936) is at the airport.

Destinations Air Asia, Cebu Pacific and PAL serve Cebu City (5 daily; 50min), Davao (daily; 1hr) and Manila (15 daily; 1hr 30min).

By bus The Eastbound bus terminal is near the Limketkai Center, 3km east of the centre (off Recto Ave), while the Westbound Bus and Jeepney Station lies 6km west of the centre on the Illigan road. From either you can take a

CAGAYAN DE ORO AND AROUND

jeepney (P10–12) or a taxi (around P50) into town.

Destinations from the Eastbound terminal Balingoan (for Camiguin; every 45min until 5pm; 1hr 30min); Butuan (every 45min until 5pm; 4hr); Camp Philips (frequent; 1hr); Davao (every 30min; 8hr); Surigao (2 daily; 6hr).

Destinations from the Westbound terminal Dipolog (2 daily; 6–7hr); Iligan (hourly; 1hr 30min); Marawi (hourly; 3hr); Ozamiz (hourly; 4hr); Zamboanga (hourly; 12hr).

By boat Ferries arrive at Macabalan, 4km north of the centre, from where jeepneys and taxis (P60) run into the city. 2Go runs the majority of services from CDO, with a few routes also served by Transa Asia. The main 2Go ticket office is at the pier at Macabalan, but a number of more convenient agents are located in town.

Destinations Bacolod (weekly; 21hr); Cebu City (3 weekly; 8hr); Dumaguete (weekly; 7hr); Iloilo (3 weekly; 14hr); Manila (weekly; 32hr); Tagbilaran (3 weekly; 8hr).

INFORMATION

Tourist offices The regional tourist office (Mon–Sat 8am–noon & 1–5pm; ☎08822 727 275), A. Velez St, offers maps, details of guided tours and accommodation lists. Further south, in the middle of Plaza Divisoria, the Tourism Showcase (Mon–Thurs 9am–5pm, Fri & Sat 9am–11pm) is stocked with basic information.

Website The detailed website ⓦcdoguide.com is helpful.

GETTING AROUND

Most locals use **tricycles** (6am–10pm P6–10 for city trips); **jeepneys** charge P6.50.

ACCOMMODATION

Apple Tree Resort & Hotel Taboc Beach, Opol ☎088 555 0003, ⓦappletreeresortcdo.com. A 10min taxi ride west of the city, this is the best seaside option near Cagayan. The beach gets swamped with locals at the weekends, but the location, with views of Camiguin Island, is fabulous. Rooms overlook the large pool and smaller jacuzzi pools, while suites (P4500) have ocean views. Free airport or bus station pick-up. P2800

★**Budgetel** Corrales Extension, north of Recto ☎088 856 4200, ⓔthebudgetel@gmail.com. Handy for the Eastbound bus terminal, this bargain hotel offers 34 en-suite a/c singles and doubles with free wi-fi and breakfast, and dorm beds with shared bathroom. There's a laundry, too. Dorms P250, doubles P900

Hotel Conchita Guillermo St and Yacapin Extension ☎088 856 3857, ⓦhotelconchita.com. Comfortable business hotel out towards the Limketkai Center. The cheaper standard rooms are perfectly adequate and come with a/c, cable TV and free wi-fi. P1120

★**Malasag House** Gardens of Malasag Eco-Tourism Village, Cugman ☎0917 596 1453, ⓦthemalasaghouse .com. For a real treat, stay in this lovely curio-filled B&B high above the city with scintillating views and a 1950s feel. The spacious rooms occupy a two-storey wooden lodge, with wonderful hosts and food making it tempting to simply hang out and read on the veranda – make sure you catch the sunset. P1500

Pryce Plaza Hotel Carmen Hill ☎088 858 4536, ⓦpryceplaza-cagayandeoro.com. One of the city's best hotels, *Pryce Plaza* has attractive, comfortable rooms set in pleasant grounds on a hill west of the city, across the river. P2600

Tune Hotel C.M. Recto Ave ☎02 519 0888, ⓦtune hotels.com. The CDO branch of Air Asia's hotel chain enjoys a good location close to the Limketkai Center, and its add-on price structure means you pay only for the facilities you need. Deals are available from as little as P788 if you book early, but will cost more if you don't book online. Rooms are bright, white and clean; add-ons include a/c, cable TV, wi-fi, early check-in and luggage storage. All-inclusive walk-in rate P2000

EATING AND DRINKING

Cagayan de Oro is the best place to eat in northern Mindanao, with a range of affordable **restaurants** and bars. The **Limketkai Center** and the Rosario Strip are crammed with Western-style restaurants and coffee shops, while the old centre contains plenty of cheaper Filipino joints.

Bigby's Café & Restaurant Rosario Arcade, Limketkai Center ☎088 857 5511, ⓦbigbyscafe.net. Local chain offering a fusion of Western and Filipino dishes; from "Rack a Bye Baby" (P399) and *katsu* dinner chops (P159) to sandwiches from P175. Don't miss the Midnight Dream Cake (P99/slice). Sun–Thurs 11am–10pm, Fri & Sat 11am–midnight.

Brew Berry Café A. Velez St at T. Chavez St ☎08822 725 291. Good coffee anytime, but worth a visit for the excellent-value buffets; breakfast (Western and Filipino dishes) is P139, while dinner (mainly Filipino dishes) is P199 and includes some of the best pork adobo in Mindanao. Mon–Sat 7am–10pm, Sun noon–8pm.

★**Butcher's Best Barbeque** (Xavier branch) Corrales St at Hayes St ☎088 857 7333. Popular budget barbecue restaurant with a/c and open terrace areas. Chargrilled sticks of pork, chicken and fish run from P12–15, but the Kenny Rogers Ribs (P75) and sizzling *sisig* (P75) are real treats. Mon–Sat 11am–2pm & 5–11pm, Sun 11am–2pm & 5–10pm.

Inilog Grill A. Velez St (second branch on Tiano St). Local favourite serving interesting dishes with unlimited rice: sizzling ostrich (P220) and goat adobo from P170.

San Miguel is P40, and there's usually live music at night. The Velez branch is like a dimly lit bar (with a/c) while the Tiano branch is open air. Daily 5pm–2am.

★**Kagay-Anon Restaurant** Rosario Arcade, Limketkai Center ☎08822 729 003. Best Filipino restaurant in the city, famous for local ostrich meat, raised down here since the early 1990s; the ostrich *salpicao* (P430) is delicious. Other dishes to try include steamed lapu lapu (P280–370), chicken pork adobo (P180), *pinakbet* (vegetable stew) and tuna *kinilaw*. Daily 10am–2pm & 5–10pm.

Park Café Plaza Divisoria at Corrales Ave ☎088 856 4444. Classic open-air bar and café in the heart of the city; sip San Miguel, coffee (from P40) or fruit shakes (P45), munch sandwiches (P110), or take breakfast (from P70) as city life flows past. Daily 24hr.

Vienna Kaffehaus 54 A. Velez St at T. Chavez St (in front of Grand City Hotel) ☎08822 712 700. Great coffee and snacks and a great story; the rival store in Limketkai Center, with almost the same name (*Vienna Coffeebar*), was established by the former girlfriend of the owner after an acrimonious split. Western breakfasts and mains from P200. Daily 7.30am–11pm.

DIRECTORY

Banks and exchange All the major Philippine banks have branches in Cagayan de Oro and most have ATMs. Land Bank is on the south side of Vicente de Lara Park while Citibank (☎088 856 2547) has a branch in Limketkai Center.

Hospitals and clinics Cagayan de Oro Medical Center, Nacalaban and Tiano Brothers streets (☎08822 722 256).

Internet access There are numerous places for internet

access near Xavier University: Cyberium and Domain on Plaza Divisoria, and Cyber Club on Corrales, all charge P20/hr. There is free wi-fi at the SM Mall, south of the city.

Laundry Labanderos, 135 Hayes St at Pabayo St (Mon–Sat 8am–8pm, Sun 8am–5pm; P23/Kg; ☎0918 309 4333).

Pharmacies Mercury Drug has a 24hr store on T. Neri St (☎08822 722 770).

Post The post office is on T. Chavez St.

Iligan and around

Some 90km west of Cagayan de Oro, the port city of **ILIGAN** is served by regular ferries from Manila and Cebu, making it an alternative gateway to Mindanao if you're travelling on a budget. Little more than a village in the early 1900s, it boomed as an industrial centre after the creation of a hydroelectric power scheme in the 1950s, but was almost completely rebuilt after a devastating fire in 1957. Famed for its **waterfalls**, it's a friendly, laidback place with a population of around 300,000. The best cluster of cascades lies on the west side on the highway towards Ozamiz and Zamboanga.

NPC Nature Park and the Maria Cristina Falls

8.5km southwest of Iligan on the highway to Ozamiz and Zamboanga • Daily 9am–4pm, zipline closed Tues • P30, zipline P200 • ☎ 63 221 9032 • It's 150m to the park entrance from the main road jeepney stop; walking to the falls from the entrance takes 20min (800m), or there's a park shuttle (P10)

The most impressive cascade in the region, within the **NPC Nature Park**, is the **Maria Cristina Falls**, which serves as the main source of power for much of Mindanao. The twin falls (named after two heartbroken girls that are supposed to have jumped from the top), plunge 100m into the torrential Agus River, and are at their best Saturday and Sunday at 11am, when the Agus VI Hydroelectric Plant upstream releases the most water. They can only be viewed from a deck inside the power station building – you can't get up close. The park itself also contains some shabby **animal exhibits** and a **zipline** across the river.

Timoga Springs and Macaraeg-Macapagal House

9.5km west of Iligan on the highway to Ozamiz and Zamboanga • **Timoga Springs** Daily 9am–6pm • Most resorts charge P50 for use of the pools • **Macaraeg-Macapagal House** Mon–Fri 8am–noon & 1–5pm, Sat & Sun 9am–noon & 1–4pm • Free

Just 1km beyond the Maria Cristina Falls, the ice-cold, crystal-clear and non-chlorinated **Timoga Springs** flow freely to a collection of privately owned swimming pools and resorts that can all get very crowded in summer.

Next door to the springs, right on the highway, is the **Macaraeg-Macapagal House**, sometime home to both Diosdado Macapagal, the ninth president of the Philippines and Gloria Macapagal-Arroyo, the fourteenth. As a child, Gloria spent many happy days in this house, built in 1950 by her maternal grandfather, and the handsome property has been well maintained, preserved as it would have looked in the 1950s. There's not much inside other than family portraits, including a sultry study of the ex-president from 1983, and a statue of Gloria as a child outside, playing on a swing.

Tinago Falls

15km southwest of Iligan, off the Zamboanga road • Free • Jeepneys will drop you off on the highway where you can hike or take a habal-habal to the start of the 365 steps down to the falls (P40/bike; arrange a return pick-up)

The **Tinago Falls**, a beautiful ribbon of water cascading 73m into a deep-blue pool, get their name from their location, nestled in a dramatic ravine (*tinago* means hidden). They became locally famous when they featured in the 2011 Pinoy movie *Forever and a Day*. From the top it's 365 steps down, so the falls are best avoided if it's raining.

ARRIVAL AND INFORMATION

ILIGAN AND AROUND

By bus The northbound bus terminal, off Bonifacio Ave, 3km north of the centre, serves Cagayan de Oro (hourly; 1hr 30min). The southbound terminal off Roxas Ave, just south of the centre, serves Dapitan (several daily; 4hr) and Ozamiz (hourly; 2hr) to the west, and Marawi (hourly; 2hr) and Zamboanga (8 hourly; 10hr) to the south. Jeepneys and taxis are usually easy to find near both terminals.

By boat Ferries from Cebu (7 weekly; 13hr) and Manila (3 weekly; 34hr) dock on the edge of the downtown area;

walk towards the first traffic circle and you'll find plenty of taxis and jeepneys.

Tourist information The tourist office (Mon–Fri 8am–5pm; ☎ 063 221 3426, ✉ iligancitytourism.yolasite.com) is at Bahay Salakot on leafy Buhanginan Hill, next to City Hall at the far eastern end of Quezon Ave; take a taxi or jeepney up here from downtown. The enthusiastic staff have maps and can help with transport and guides – ask here also about trips to Lake Lanao and Marawi (see p.433).

GETTING AROUND

By jeepney Most jeepney rides around town cost P6.50; **By taxi** A/c taxis charge P40 then P2.50/300m, while non-a/c "PU" taxis run fixed routes for a set rate of P30. Taxis should charge around P100/hr for tours of the waterfalls.

ACCOMMODATION

Celadon Pension House Ubaldo Laya Ave Circle ☎ 063 221 0711. Just north of Quezon Extension, this bright pink place is a decent budget choice with clean, basic singles and doubles, most of which have cable TV and internet access. "Deluxe" rooms (P600) have hot water. P500

Cheradel Suites Off Raymund Jeffrey Rd (north of Quezon Extension) ☎ 063 223 8118, ☻ cheradelsuites @yahoo.com. Attractive collection of rooms and suites within a pleasant whitewashed building around a small pool. Rooms are modern and comfortable and have a/c and cable TV; the biggest Residential Suite (P9500) has three bedrooms plus a kitchen. P1590

EATING AND DRINKING

Iligan is home to several celebrated food products: try the spicy coconut vinegar known as **pinakurat**, produced by *Suka Pinakurat* at 5 Sparrow Rd, near the end of Quezon Extension, or grab a bag of addictive toasted peanuts at *Cheding's Peanuts*, Sabayale St, downtown near the port.

★**Gloria's Ihaw-Ihaw** Zamboanga Hwy, opposite Timoga Springs and Macapagal House. Just one of numerous simple canteens that line the shoreline here, selling *lechon* (P350/kilo) or whole roast chicken (P190). *Gloria's* has a garden overlooking the sea where you can enjoy the famed stewed tuna jaw. Daily 11am–3pm.

Iliganon Restobar Quezon Ave Extension at Seminary Drive ☎ 063 225 4577. Serves decent coffee and excellent pizzas (medium from P130), morphing into a popular bar at night when local bands play live. Free wi-fi. Daily 10am–midnight.

Sunburst Fried Chicken House Tino Badelles St at Lumboy St ☎ 063 221 3401. The first branch of the now nationally famous fried chicken chain – aficionados claim that the chicken at this store tastes different (and much better) than at the others. It's not health food, but the fried chicken skin (P90) is certainly a mouthwatering treat. Daily 10am–10pm.

Zoey Café Aguinaldo St at Echiverri St ☎ 063 221 2876. Free wi-fi, roasted coffee and a selection of delectable treats (try the carrot walnut cake) make this the best coffee shop in town. Mon–Thurs 9am–8.30pm, Fri & Sat 9am–9pm.

8

Ozamiz

Sitting on the western side of Panguil Bay, the tumbledown port city of **OZAMIZ** was renamed in honour of World War II hero Senator José Ozamiz in 1948. There's not much to keep you in the city itself, but it's a decent base from which to explore Dolphin Island (see p.410) and Mount Malindang (see p.410).

Fort Santiago

Daily 8am–6pm • P5

The only real sight in Ozamiz is old **Fort Santiago**, or "Cotta", on the seafront, built by the Spanish in 1756. It was badly damaged by an earthquake in 1955, but there are panoramic views across Panguil Bay from its crumbling walls. Part of the outer walls house a venerated image of Mary (said to be miraculously growing), centrepiece of the open-air **Shrine of Nuestra Señora del Triunfo de la Cruz** (or *Birhen sa Cotta*).

ARRIVAL AND DEPARTURE
OZAMIZ

By plane Tiny Ozamiz Airport has two daily flight connections with Cebu City (1hr) and Manila (1hr 25min). Taxis into town cost P60.

By bus Coming from Iligan (hourly; 2hr) buses save a huge detour by taking the frequent car ferries (passengers P25; you get off the bus to pay) across Panguil Bay. Buses continue from the port (in the centre of town), to the main bus terminal on the outskirts and on to Dapitan (hourly; 2hr) and Zamboanga (2 daily; 7hr), but there are plenty of tricycles near the wharf to whisk you around the city should you wish to stay.

By boat There are ferry links with Cebu (2Go: 2 weekly; 7hr; Cokaliong: 5 weekly; 10hr). Tickets are available at the port.

ACCOMMODATION

Naomi's Botanical Garden and Tourist Inn Bañadero Hwy ☎ 088 521 2441. A little west of the city and easy to reach by tricycle (P20), this gem of a place has pretty rooms, in various shapes and sizes, looking out onto a beautiful garden. All have a/c and cable TV. P800

Royal Garden Hotel Burgos St at Zamora St ☎ 088 521 2888, ⓦ royalgardenozamiz.com. Newly renovated

rooms and good rates make this a solid downtown option. Rooms are decorated in muted tones and have 32" flat-screen TVs, wi-fi and rain-showers. The hotel also houses some of the city's best dining options. P1195

Sky Lodge Rizal Ave ☎ 088 521 1425. On the main street, this is a homely, spick-and-span option with pleasant a/c rooms with clean showers and toilet. P350

EATING

Dewberry Coffee Don Anselmo Bernad Ave. Near City Hall, this is the place to get your coffee fix, plus a range of sandwiches, beers and spirits. Daily 10am–10pm.

Hukad Royal Garden Hotel, Burgos St at Zamora St ☎ 088 521 2888. This Cebuano institution has made its way to Mindanao and dishes up excellent Filipino cuisine

including green mango salad (P65), blue marlin (P167) and pork Bicol (P129). Daily 10am–9pm.

Mooon Café Rizal Ave ☎ 088 564 2622. This popular Mexican chain restaurant offers *gambas a la luna* (P159), *chimichangas* (P79) and the odd Filipino dish. Daily 11am–9pm.

Mount Malindang National Park

Little known and little explored, **Mount Malindang National Park** is a densely forested region that offers some tough trekking and the opportunity to see rare species such as the tarsier and flying lemur.

Of the four main peaks in the park, Mount Malindang itself is the tallest, at 2404m. The area was extensively logged before being declared a national park in 1971, so most of the forest growth today is relatively new. There's a long-established tribal group living here, the **Subanon**, whom you may well encounter at their Lake Duminagat settlement. They consider Mount Malindang their tribal homeland and source of strength. The best time to visit is between January and April when the trails are dry.

INFORMATION   MOUNT MALINDANG NATIONAL PARK

Permits Permits (P200) to enter the park are available from the Protected Area Office (Mon–Fri 8am–4pm; ☎ 088 531 2184) at the back of the Provincial Capitol Building in

Orquieta, a 1hr bus ride north of Ozamiz.

Guides A guide is essential; arrange at the Protected Area Office (P1500/day).

Misamis Occidental Aquamarine Park (MOAP) and Dolphin Island

Fifteen kilometres north of Ozamiz, in the village of Sinacaban, the **Misamis Occidental Aquamarine Park** (MOAP) is an ambitious ecotourism project that features dolphins, fish ponds and mangrove restoration and offers chalet-style accommodation.

The real attraction is **Dolphin Island**, a series of man-made stilt huts over a sand bar 2km offshore. It's principally a dolphin rescue centre, with fenced-in seawater pens providing a safe haven for animals trapped or injured by fishermen – after rehabilitation they are released into nearby dolphin communities. At the time of writing the island was home to three spotted dolphins and one green turtle. You can **swim with the dolphins** here for just P250 – an incredible bargain – and you can rent snorkelling gear (P50/hr) and kayaks (P100/hr) or organize dive trips (P2300).

ARRIVAL AND INFORMATION   MOAP AND DOLPHIN ISLAND

By tricycle and boat Tricycles to MOAP from the Ozamiz ferry charge around P200 (30min). The 15min boat ride to

the island plus entry fee (P10) costs P300/person return (daily: hourly 8am–4pm; last boat back 5.30pm).

ACCOMMODATION AND EATING

In addition to the restaurant at the *Dolphin Island Resort*, there's one basic restaurant on Dolphin Island that serves fried chicken, pork and rice.

Dolphin Island Resort ☎ 088 586 0292. Rooms range from deluxe suites (P3000) to smaller cottages, all on stilts overlooking the shallow bay, with hot showers and TV. On-site restaurant. Dorm P250, doubles P500

Dapitan

The scenic north coast city of **DAPITAN**, with its red-roofed houses and sweeping ocean bay, is best known for its connection to national hero **José Rizal** (see box below), who was exiled here in the 1890s. Rizal designed a huge grass **Relief Map of Mindanao** that still exists today on F. Saguin Street. The main drag is **Sunset Boulevard**, a romantic seafront promenade where you'll find banks, shops and a number of hotels.

Rizal Shrine and Museum

Talisay • Tues–Sun 9am–4pm • Free • Take a tricycle from the city centre or walk – it's only 10min via Bagting Bridge with Dapitan Bay on your left

The **Rizal Shrine**, on the northern edge of the city, is a pleasant parkland area encompassing the grounds where José Rizal spent his exile. The park contains faithful reproductions of the simple cottage he lived in, the octagonal schoolroom where he taught, his chicken house and two clinics where he worked. The **Rizal Museum** contains memorabilia such as his books, notebooks and medical equipment.

ARRIVAL AND INFORMATION   DAPITAN

By plane Dipolog Airport is just 12km away; regular buses and minivans journey to Dapitan. Dipolog has daily connections with Manila (1hr 25min) and Cebu (daily; 55min) and a few flights to Davao (2 weekly; 1hr 15min).
By bus Dapitan sees buses from Cagayan de Oro (2 daily; 6–7hr), Dipolog (hourly; 45min) and Ozamiz (hourly; 2hr).

By boat Ferries arrive at Palauan wharf, halfway between Dapitan and Dipolog. Jeepneys (P10) and minibuses (P20) run into Dapitan.
Destinations Cebu (Cokaliong: 4 weekly; George & Peter Lines: 3 weekly; 9hr),

ACCOMMODATION AND EATING

Corazan de Dapitan City Plaza ☎ 065 213 6639. Aptly named, venerable bistro in the heart of town. Filipino dishes P50–200. Daily 10am–9pm.
Dakak Park & Beach Resort Brgy Taguilon ☎ 065 213 6813, ⓦ dakakresort.com. A few kilometres north of the city on a wide stretch of white sand, *Dakak* has a good choice of accommodation including comfortable bungalows and dorm-like family pavilion rooms with double beds and bunks. There's a decent restaurant and pool, plus lots of activities ranging from tennis to paint-balling, ATV rides and watersports. Good-value packages for groups. P7000
Dapitan City Resort Hotel Sunset Blvd ☎ 065 213 6316. Plain, comfortable rooms with a/c, hot showers, TVs and fridges. The hotel restaurant specializes in (very reasonably priced) seafood. P1680

JOSÉ RIZAL IN DAPITAN

Arrested for his association with the nascent revolutionary movement, **José Rizal** was exiled to Dapitan in 1892 in order that he should "publicly retract his errors concerning religion, and make statements that were clearly pro-Spanish and against revolution". During his four-year exile Rizal was famously productive: he practised medicine and pursued scientific studies, continued his artistic and literary works, widened his knowledge of languages and established a boys' school. It was in Dapitan that he met Josephine Bracken, the Irish woman whom he married in a private ceremony in his cell two hours before his execution in Manila in 1896. Tragically their son was stillborn, and is buried in an unmarked grave somewhere in Dapitan.

8

Camiguin Island

Around 20km off the north coast of mainland Mindanao, the little island of **Camiguin** ("cam-ee-*gin*") is one of the country's most appealing tourist spots, offering ivory beaches, iridescent lagoons and jagged mountain scenery. There's no shortage of adventure here, with reasonable scuba diving and tremendous trekking and climbing in the rugged interior, especially on volcanic **Mount Hibok-Hibok**. Another major tourist draw is the annual **Lanzones festival**, held in the fourth week of October. Revellers dressed only in lanzones leaves stomp and dance in the streets as a tribute to the humble fruit, one of the island's major sources of income.

The beauty of Camiguin is that it doesn't really matter where you stay because you can visit all the sights easily from anywhere. The **coastal road** is almost 70km long, making it feasible to circle the island in a day. If you don't want to depend on public transport, consider renting a motorbike or hiring your own private jeepney or tricycle for day-trips.

Mambajao and around

There's no reason to hang around in **MAMBAJAO** ("mah-bow-ha") the island's capital, other than to sort out the practicalities of your stay.

Of the nearby beaches, **Cabu-An Beach**, to the east, near the barangay of Balbagon, is marginally the closest, with some nice coral close to the shore and half a dozen decent resorts. **Agoho Beach**, 7km west of Mambajao, is wider and sandier, with many

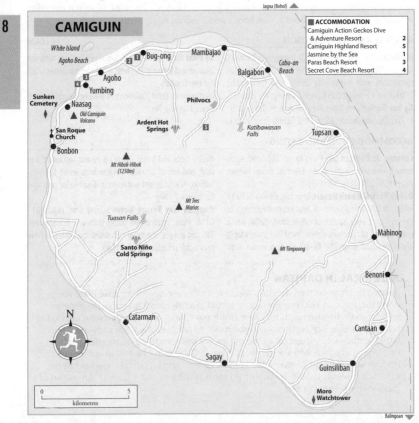

CAMIGUIN

■ ACCOMMODATION	
Camiguin Action Geckos Dive & Adventure Resort	2
Camiguin Highland Resort	5
Jasmine by the Sea	1
Paras Beach Resort	3
Secret Cove Beach Resort	4

Jagna (Bohol)

White Island
Agoho Beach
Bug-ong
Mambajao
Cabu-an Beach
Balgabon
Agoho
Yumbing
Philvocs
Sunken Cemetery
Naasag
Old Camiguin Volcano
San Roque Church
Ardent Hot Springs
Katibawasan Falls
Tupsan
Bonbon
Mt Hibok-Hibok (1250m)
Mt Tres Marias
Tuasan Falls
Santo Niño Cold Springs
Mt Timpoong
Mahinog
Benoni
N
Catarman
Cantaan
Sagay
Guinsiliban
Moro Watchtower
Balingoan

0   5
kilometres

resorts – an ideal place to base yourself for all sorts of activities, including scuba diving, bangka-hopping and walks into the island's interior.

Katibawasan Falls

P20 • Tricycle or minivan to the falls from Mambajao P300–400

Easily accessible by a dirt road – or you can trek along a marked trail from Balbagon (2hr) – the impressive **Katibawasan Falls** is a narrow, 70m-high cascade with a crystal-clear plunge pool at the bottom – perfect for a chilly swim.

Ardent Hot Springs

Daily 9am–10pm • P30

Some 3km inland from the barangay of Tagdo, **Ardent Hot Springs** can be reached in about an hour on foot from either Mambajao or Agoho Beach. The water in these pools, which lie in a verdant valley surrounded by jungle, is warmed by the volcanic interior of Mount Hibok-Hibok and can reach 40°C. The best time to visit is from late afternoon or after dark, when you can sit in a pool with a cold drink and gaze at the stars. There's a good little restaurant, a coffee shop and accommodation in a number of simple cottages. Unsurprisingly it gets busy, especially on weekends and holidays.

Mount Hibok-Hibok

In the northwest of the island, Camiguin's only active volcano, **Mount Hibok-Hibok**, had its last major eruption in 1951, with tremors and landslides that killed five hundred people. At a relatively modest 1250m it can be climbed in a day, but the strenuous trail crosses some very steep slopes and treacherous rocks and shouldn't be attempted alone. Many resorts have lists of local **guides** who can be hired for around P1500. Along the way you'll see steam vents and hot pools, while at the top there's a crater lake. Views from the summit are unforgettable, with the coast of Mindanao to the south and the islands of the Visayas to the north.

At **Philvocs** (Mon–Fri 9am–4pm), an easy 3km trip inland from Mambajao by tricycle, vulcanologists who monitor Mount Hibok-Hibok are happy to talk to visitors about their work, and have a number of spectacular photographs of past eruptions.

White Island

Return bangka trips around P500

About halfway between Mambajao and Bonbon off the island's northwest coast is one of Camiguin's most popular attractions, **White Island**, a dazzling serpentine ribbon of sand only visible at low tide and easily reached in a short bangka hop from nearby resorts. The views and the water are gorgeous, but there's no shade, so make sure you take a wide-brimmed hat and lots of sunblock.

Bonbon

The small fishing town of **BONBON** on Camiguin's west coast has an attractive little plaza and a pretty, whitewashed church; it also lies a few kilometres south of the slopes of the **Old Camiguin Volcano**, which you can climb easily in an hour. The path to the summit, from where the views are stunning, is marked by life-size alabaster statues representing the **Stations of the Cross**.

A little southwest of the old volcano you'll see a striking, enormous **white cross** floating on a pontoon in the bay. This marks the site of the **Sunken Cemetery**, which slipped into the sea during a volcanic eruption in 1871 – you can observe reef fish massing around the decaying tombs on a diving or snorkelling trip. The same eruption destroyed the seventeenth-century Spanish **San Roque Church** in Gui-ob on the northern fringes of modern Bonbon; its brooding ruins still stand, with a memorial altar inside.

Catarman and around

There are some quiet stretches of sandy beach near the ramshackle little town of **CATARMAN**, 24km south of Mambajao, plus springs and falls, but there's no accommodation in the area. On the southern coast near Guinsiliban Elementary School, fifteen minutes east by jeepney from Catarman, is a three-hundred-year-old **Moro Watchtower**; climb to the top for panoramic views across to mainland Mindanao.

Santo Niño Cold Springs and Tuasan Falls

Santo Niño Cold Springs P20; day-use huts at both sites P100 • It's a 30min walk (2.5km) along the dirt track from the main road to the springs, and then another 30min (2km) to the falls , or you can take a habal-habal

Some 6km north of Catarman, **Santo Niño Cold Springs** can be reached either on foot or by motorbike from the coastal road. Continuing 2km further up the track will bring you to **Tuasan Falls**. Both have deep pools that are good for swimming and the surroundings are pleasant, with rich vegetation and a few simple huts where you can change and take a nap.

ARRIVAL AND INFORMATION

By plane The airport, on the coast 1km west of Mambajao, sees daily Cebu Pacific flights to and from Cebu (50min).

By boat Ferries (roughly hourly 5am–6pm; 1hr) leave Balingoan on Mindanao for Benoni on Camiguin's southeast coast. From here, jeepneys run frequently to and from Mambajao.

Island transport Transport rates to everywhere on the island are fixed by the tourist office and displayed on a board at the pier in Benoni.

CAMIGUIN ISLAND

Tourist information The tourist office (Mon–Fri 8am–5pm; ☎ 088 387 1097, ✉ camiguin.tourism@gmail.com) is in the Provincial Capitol building a short tricycle ride from the centre of Mambajao. As well as accommodation suggestions they can also advise on activities, including climbing Hibok-Hibok.

Services In Mambajao there's a branch of PNB, an ATM, a couple of internet cafés and a cluster of cheap places to eat around the market area.

ACCOMMODATION AND EATING

Most of the seaside **accommodation** in Camiguin is west of Mambajao on the beaches between the small towns of **Bug-ong** and **Naasag**. The resorts in this area have lots of information about diving and trekking; resorts near the town of Agoho, a little west of Bug-ong, are popular because of their good access to White Island. East of Mambajao around the village of **Balgabon** you'll find more resorts, although the beach here isn't as good as at Agoho, Yumbing or Naasag. **Eating** on Camiguin is mostly limited to the resorts or the few nipa-style restaurants dotting the beaches. In Mambajao there are some local restaurants clustered around the Capitol Compound.

RESORTS

★ **Camiguin Action Geckos Dive & Adventure Resort** Agoho ☎ 088 387 9146, ⊕ camiguin.ph. Though the real standouts at this friendly resort are the budget "traveller" rooms (shared bathroom), the lovely wooden cottages on the beach – a/c and en suite, with verandas, hammocks and rocking chairs – are also great value (P2900). Dives from P1250 and PADI courses from P13,000. **P900**

Camiguin Highland Resort Lakas, Soro-soro ☎ 088 387 0515, ⊕ camiguinhighlandresort.com. Unusually, this tranquil resort is nowhere near the beach; instead you get awe-inspiring views of the coast, beautiful mountains and a top-notch restaurant, service and luxurious accommodation, with a few economy rooms. There's also a soothing pool and jacuzzi. **P1500**

Jasmine by the Sea Bug-ong ☎ 088 387 9015, ✉ melindawidmer@yahoo.com. One of the closest resorts to Mambajao, *Jasmine* is excellent value, with spacious fan cottages on the shore and a restaurant that serves some organic dishes. Motorbike rental P300/day. **P800**

Paras Beach Resort 4km beyond Bug-ong in Yumbing ☎ 088 387 9008, ⊕ parasbeachresort.com. In a spectacular position on the shore, this was a private beach house belonging to the Paras family until they decided to add compact a/c rooms (with hot showers and cable TV) and open it to the public. It's a good place to organize tours. **P2250**

★ **Secret Cove Beach Resort** Yumbing ☎ 088 387 9084, ⊕ secretcovecamiguin.net. This Canadian/Filipino-owned resort is a hidden gem with seven spacious and clean a/c rooms, a restaurant, a bar and internet access. On-site Johnny's Dive & Fun organizes dive trips. **P1400**

Butuan

The bustling capital of Agusan del Norte province, **BUTUAN** lies around 200km east of Cagayan de Oro. Butuan is thought to have been the first coastal trading settlement in the Philippines; in 1976 a carefully crafted and ornate oceangoing outrigger (*balangay*) was unearthed on the banks of the Agusan River and carbon-dated, astonishingly, to 320 AD. Of nine boats since discovered in the mud, two more have been excavated, dating from 1215 and 1250 and adding to the growing wealth of evidence that the Philippines was actively trading with Asia long before the Spanish arrived. The original "Butuan boat" is now in the small **Balangay Shrine** (Mon–Fri 9am–4pm; free) around 5km west of the city, along with the remains of a number of other ancient boats and various archeological and ethnological treasures such as ceramics and coffins.

Butuan National Museum

City Hall compound, 1km north of the city centre • Mon–Sat 9am–noon & 1–4.30pm • P20 • ☎ 085 527 4192

The **Butuan National Museum** is home to a small but intriguing collection including cooking implements and jewellery from pre-Hispanic Butuan. There are two galleries: the Archaeological Hall, which exhibits stone crafts, metal objects, pots, gold and burial coffins; and the Ethnological Hall, which focuses on the culture of the Manobo, Mamanua, Higaonon and lowland Butuanons.

ARRIVAL AND INFORMATION

BUTUAN

By plane The airport, served by Philippine Airlines from Manila (5 daily; 1hr 25min) and Cebu Pacific from Cebu City (3 daily; 45min), is 10km west of the city. Taxis (P200) and tricycles (P150) are on hand to take you into town.

By bus Frequent buses connect with Cagayan de Oro (hourly; 4hr), Davao (5–6 hr) and Surigao (hourly; 2hr). The terminal is on the northern outskirts of Butuan off Montilla Blvd; there are plenty of tricycles to take you into the centre.

By boat Ferries dock at the port town of Nasipit, 24km west of Butuan, from where it's a 30min jeepney ride into the city. 2Go has one weekly service on Sun to Manila (34hr) via Cebu (9hr).

Tourist information The provincial Department of Tourism office is at the Grateful Realty Corp Building, on Pili Drive (Mon–Fri 8am–5pm; ☎ 085 341 8413).

ACCOMMODATION

Almont City Hotel San José St, Rizal Park ☎ 085 342 05263, ⓦ almont.com.ph. Spacious, airy rooms, all with a/c, private bathroom and cable TV; those at the front have city views. The coffee shop, with its tinkling indoor waterfalls, offers light meals and pastries. **P1500**

Hotel Karaga Montilla Blvd ☎ 085 225 3888, ⓦ hotel karaga.com. Well located but a bit past its prime, the *Karaga* has bargain a/c rooms with cable TV and free internet (though signal is sketchy). Things are a little better if you opt for one of the rooms with balconies (P1300). **P900**

EATING

Caraga Square J.C. Aquino Ave. Your best bet for nightlife is this open-air place in the centre of town, which features local live bands most nights. Daily 10am–1am.

Red Apple Restaurant A.D. Curato St. The cakes and pastries are hard to resist, but this cafeteria-style place is also good for Filipino food and breakfasts. Daily 7am–10pm.

Rosario's J.C. Aquino Ave. Butuan's top restaurant is best known for its tasty Chinese dishes. There's a fine dining section (mains from P200) and cheaper fast-food area. Daily 10am–2pm & 5–10pm.

Agusan Marsh Wildlife Sanctuary

About 70km south of Butuan on the road to Davao, the **Agusan Marsh Wildlife Sanctuary** is a giant maze of interconnecting rivers, channels and lakes, with dramatic areas of **swamp forest** consisting largely of sago trees and inhabited by parrots, purple herons, serpent eagles and a good number of saltwater and Philippine **crocodiles**. The biggest-ever recorded crocodile, over 6m long, was captured here in 2011, having allegedly killed and eaten several carabao and two people.

Despite the crocodiles, and its isolation, the marsh is inhabited by about 2600 people, mainly the **Manobo**, an animist group that live across much of eastern Mindanao. Their houses are floating wooden structures with thatched roofs and rest on a platform lashed to enormous logs. Whole communities exist like this, their houses tethered to one another in one place, but moveable at any time. You can visit the marsh from the town of Bunawan from where you can rent a boat and guide for the three-hour ride along the river to the marsh area itself – be prepared for a full day out and take lots of water and sunblock.

ARRIVAL AND INFORMATION

By bus and tricycle The marsh is around 2hr 30min (100km) from Butuan and 3hr (200km) from Davao; whichever direction you're coming from, you need to get off the bus in the town of Bunawan (note that only slow non-a/c buses stop here), and then take a tricycle west to the Bunawan Tourism Center (☎0910 984 0285) to register and receive a briefing from the Department of the Environment and Natural Resources Office regarding

AGUSAN MARSH WILDLIFE SANCTUARY

sanctuary policies.

Tours The tourist office, and hotels in Butuan, can help arrange trips, while a locally arranged day tour in Bunawan costs around P2000 for the boat plus P1000 for the guide.

Accommodation There is some very basic accommodation in Bunawan, and some of the floating Manobo villages also offer lodgings – ask at the Bunawan Tourism Center.

The Enchanted River

12km from Talisay • P30; lifejackets can be rented for P15, as currents can be strong • The turning to the river and Talisay is signposted 2km north of Hinatuan on the main coast road, 150km south of Butuan; the main road is served by frequent buses between Butuan and Mangagoy; without your own transport it's a very long walk or habal-habal ride from Hinatuan

Swimming in the **Enchanted River** is one of the highlights of a trip to Mindanao. The accessible part of the river is more like a narrow saltwater lagoon that ends at an underwater cave and ravine crammed with all sorts of tropical fish that get fed every day at noon. The colours are mesmerizing; the water glows like liquid sapphire, surrounded by dense jungle and karst outcrops.

The site is managed as a small park (you can wander to a small beach from here), but it's well off the beaten path and few foreign tourists make it this far (although crowds of locals descend at weekends). The park lies at the end of a 12km dirt road, just beyond the pretty fishing village of **Talisay**.

Tinuy-An Falls

15km west of Bislig • P50; bamboo raft P200 • Most people hire a minivan and driver in Butuan (from P3000), but you can take a bus to Bislig or Mangagoy and then local transport to the falls (habal-habal P400 return)

Around 160km south of Butuan, near the port town of **Bislig**, a dirt road leads some 15km to the astounding **Tinuy-An Falls**, a thunderous, multitiered 95m cascade. Get here early and it's a magical place, with lush jungle, durian trees and giant ferns drooping over the river – you can lounge on the bank and enjoy the views or clamber up to the higher levels and paddle or swim in the pools, where a bamboo raft takes you closer in to get thoroughly soaked.

Surigao

The bustling, ramshackle capital of the province of Surigao del Norte, **SURIGAO**, some 120km north of Butuan, is essentially just a place to pass through on the way to the picture-postcard island of Siargao. It's a compact place and easy to get around on foot, but there's just not that much to do here: if you find yourself with time on your hands it's worth a trip up to the pretty pebble beach at **Mabua**, 12km north.

SURIGAO, SIARGAO ISLAND AND DINAGAT

0   25
kilometres

N

Manila

Tubajan Bay
Tubajon

Dinagat

Libjo Bay
Albor

Surigao Strait

Cebu

Hagakhak
Unib
San José
Sibanag Island
Dinagat
Magsaysay Islands
Hikdop Island
Awasan Island
Hanigad Island
Nonoc Island
Mabua Beach
Bayagnan Island
Surigao
Hinituan Island
Masapelid Island
Bucas Grande Island
Sohoton Cove

Hinituan Passage

Dinagat Sound

Alegria
Santa Monica
Burgos
San Benito
Siargao
Magpu-pungko Beach
Del Carmen
Siargao Airport
Pilar
Cloud 9
Tuason Point
Dapa
General Luna
Naked Island
Dako Island
East Bucas Island
Guyam Island
La Janoza
Mamon

Butuan

8

ARRIVAL AND DEPARTURE   SURIGAO

By plane The airport, 5km outside the city on the road to Butuan, sees daily flights to and from Cebu (Cebu Pacific: 2 daily; 55min) and Manila (PAL Express: 1 daily; 1hr 40min). Tricycles charge P50 into the centre of town.

By bus, jeepney and multicab Buses arrive at the terminal 4km west of the city centre. Jeepneys and multi-cabs head into town for P10/person (or P30 for a tricycle). Heading to Cagayan de Oro or Balingoan (for Camiguin) you'll need to change in Butuan.

Destinations Butuan (hourly; 2hr); Davao (hourly; 8hr).

By boat The Eva M. Macapagal Passenger Terminal is on the harbourfront; you can walk or take a tricycle from here to the city centre. The terminal fee is P20 for all departures. Coming from the Visayas, Cokaliong Shipping Lines serves Cebu (4 weekly; 9hr 30min). Heading to Siargao there are a variety of options from fast, cramped outriggers (2–3hr) to slower, more spacious and safer roll-on-roll-off boats (3–4hr). Montenegro (w montenegrolines.com.ph) runs a daily roll-on-roll-off service (3hr 30min), as does MV Lines' ferry *Fortune Angel* (3hr). Of the bangkas, MV Lines' daily *LOP* service is the biggest and safest. All of these boats leave Surigao for Dapa on Siargao in the morning, so it's best to arrive in town early or accept you'll spend a night in the city. For Dinagat there are several morning bangkas to San José (4hr).

INFORMATION

Tourist information At the southern end of Rizal St near the grandstand, the helpful Department of Tourism (☎ 086 231 9271) offers information about accommodation and ferries to Siargao and Dinagat islands.

Services The best place to look for internet cafés is around the central plaza and Magallanes St.

ACCOMMODATION

Almont Beach Resort Lipata ☎ 086 826 7544, w almont .com.ph. For a bit of luxury, 15min drive from the port, the *Almont* offers good rooms with sensational views of the bay. There's also a decent pool and on-site *Café Maharlika* (daily 6am–10pm; free wi-fi). P2500

Leomondee Hotel Borromeo St ☎086 232 7334. A block inland from the sea, this is a good budget place to try if you get stuck, with small but clean and comfortable a/c rooms and free wi-fi. P650

Tavern Hotel Borromeo St ☎086 231 7300, ⊛hotel tavern.com. Not far from the ferry terminal, this place has smart modern rooms in the newer west wing (P2200) and slightly cheaper rooms in the older east building. Sea views and balconies are also available for a little more. Breakfast and free pick-up included. P1900

EATING AND DRINKING

4As Barbecue Navarro St at Borromeo St ☎086 231 8898. No-frills canteen offering tasty barbecue chicken and pork. Daily 9.30am–11.30pm.

City Garden Restaurant Tavern Hotel, Borromeo St ☎086 231 7300, ⊛hoteltavern.com. The city's best restaurant has a huge menu offering everything from local seafood (P160–250) to imported steaks (P125–400/100g) and a host of Asian dishes. Also on site, *Dominic's Sport Tavern* (daily 5pm–1am) is a decent spot for a drink, with a large screen showing live sports. Daily 6am–midnight.

Siargao Island

Off the northeastern tip of Mindanao lies the teardrop-shaped island of **SIARGAO**, a largely undeveloped backwater with languid beaches, dramatic coves and lagoons battered by the Pacific Ocean and a verdant hinterland of rustic little barangays and coconut groves. Some of the first tourists here were **surfers**, who discovered a break at Tuason Point that was so good they called it **Cloud 9**. The annual **Surfing Cup**, held in late September or early October, has risen in profile over the past few years and attracts competitors from Australia, the US and Europe, as well as from around the Philippines.

Cloud 9

Most visitors arrive by ferry at **Dapa**, 16km from the modest but comfortable resorts around the island's friendly little capital of General Luna, known as **GL**, on the east coast. Resorts line the coast north of GL, and though there isn't really a beach, it's a lush, laidback strip, with swathes of coconut palms linked by a sand road. The whole area is generally referred to as **Cloud 9**, though the world-renowned break is actually at Tuason Point, 2km north of GL, towards the end of the hotel strip.

The peak **surf season** is September and October, while things tend to slow down at the end of the year; beginners will find the weaker surf in June and July more manageable. Even if you don't surf, wander out to the viewpoint at the end of the Cloud 9 **boardwalk**, a rickety wooden pier that cuts across the lagoon to the edge of the biggest waves.

SIARGAO ISLAND-HOPPING

The seas around Siargao are littered with unspoiled and rarely visited **islands**. The easiest to visit are the three islands just off the coast of GL (around 30min by bangka): half-day trips to all three cost from P2500 depending on the size of the boat. Most resorts can fix you up with local bangka operators.

Naked Island is little more than a giant sand bar and perfect for lounging in the sun. **Dako Island** is the largest of the three, smothered in coconut palms and home to a small fishing community. The villagers will happily serve you fresh coconut (P20) or barbecue chicken (P150) and you can even rent out the basic beach cottages overnight (P700). Tiny **Guyam Island** comes closest to the stereotype of a classic desert island, a circular clump of sand and palm trees ideal for picnics, swimming or sunbathing. The island caretaker usually charges a fee of P10 per person. **Snorkelling** isn't much good from any of these islands – the best reefs lie in between them, so ask your boat to make an extra stop.

Magpupungko Beach

P50, but this isn't always enforced; Fri night beach parties P20 • Minivans from GL should cost P1500–2500 (1hr); it's a long and bumpy ride by motorcycle (P700 for two passengers)

Travelling 35km north of GL, mostly via dirt road, brings you to **PILAR**, a village of traditional wooden stilt houses on the edge of the mangroves. It's best known for **Magpupungko Beach**, 2km further north, the site of regular Friday night beach parties. The sandy beach is one of the island's best, but the highlight is the giant natural swimming pool (basically a huge rockpool) that forms to the far left of the beach at low tide. The water is beautifully clear and inviting – assuming the weather cooperates.

Sohoton Cove

Bucas Grande • P100, plus P1000 boat fee/group • Bangkas from Siargao charge around P10,000 for an all-day trip (up to ten passengers), or you can join a group trip for around P2500/person

The enticing island of **Bucas Grande** lies between Siargao and Mindanao proper, with mushroom-shaped limestone rocks sprouting from its shimmering waters. **Sohoton Cove**, an entrancing inland lagoon on the east side of the island, is the top excursion from Siargao – you'll need the best part of a day to do it justice. The best time to visit is between March and July, when the weather and waves are calmest.

Once at the cove you'll have to sign in and get a short briefing about the site; you then transfer into another boat that will take you through the cave entrance into the lagoon, a cavernous space hemmed in by soaring vine-smothered cliffs and home to giant non-stinging jellyfish. It's a phenomenal sight and worth the expense, assuming the weather is good. There are several other caves here that your *banquero* should be able to guide you to with no extra charge: if you can hold your breath for long enough (unless it's low tide when there is a small gap), you can swim through a short tunnel into **Hagukan Cave** where there are bats, strange fish, stalactites, rock oysters and wild orchids.

ARRIVAL AND INFORMATION

SIARGAO ISLAND

By plane Cebu Pacific has one daily flight from Cebu to Siargao (1hr). The tiny airport is in the barangay of Sayak on the west coast; minivans will run to GL and Cloud 9 for P300–400/person or P1500–1800/vehicle – check with your accommodation in advance about pick-ups. Habal-habals (motorbikes) charge P500.

By bus Surigao is connected to Butuan (see p.415) by regular buses (2hr), where there are onward connections to Cagayan de Oro and Davao.

By boat The only other way to reach Siargao is by ferry from Surigao (where you must also pay a P20 terminal fee to board the boats). From here you have a choice of slower ferries (3hr–3hr 30min) or faster outriggers (2hr 30min); the latter can be bumpy in rough weather. Montenegro car

ferries (montenegrolines.com.ph) depart daily from the Eva M. Macapagal Passenger Terminal on the harbourfront in Surigao. MV Lines' *Fortune Angel* ferry also has one service daily in either direction. Of the bangkas, MV Lines daily *LOP* service is the biggest and safest. All boats leave Surigao for Dapa on Siargao in the morning so it's best to arrive in town early or accept you'll spend a night in the city.

Services There is an ATM in Dapa (although it doesn't accept all foreign cards), and several places accept credit cards; *Patrick's* (see opposite) will advance cash. There's internet access in Dapa, GL and Cloud 9 (P30/hr); wi-fi is also increasingly common.

GETTING AROUND

By habal-habal Your choices for getting around the island are fairly limited. Most locals use the habal-habal drivers, good for up to two people and light luggage. Rates are fixed: Dapa to Cloud 9 is P200, while Dapa to GL is P150. Rides between GL and Cloud 9 should be P15. Drivers will take you to Magpupungko for P700 return or the Tak-Tak Falls near Burgos for P1000 return.

Motorbike rental If you intend to do a lot of roaming

around, ask your accommodation about renting a motorcycle (P500/day).

Tricycles and minivans Tricycles will charge at least P30/person (P150/vehicle) between Dapa and GL, but sometimes ask for a lot more (it depends on how much commission they are expecting from your hotel). Minivans charge P300/person or P1500–1800 to the airport – other trips will be charged according to time and distance.

ACCOMMODATION

Siargao **accommodation** ranges from modest lodges aimed at backpackers and low-budget surfers to upmarket tropical resorts. Most accommodation is a short distance from GL, and can help arrange motorbike rentals, bangka trips and other forms of transportation.

Cherinicole Beach Resort Less than 1km from GL ☎0928 609 8963 or ☎0918 244 4407, ⓦcherinicole beachresort.com. Mid-range, well-run place with seventeen spacious and substantial wooden a/c cottages on the beach or in a pleasant garden. Fan cottages with twin beds and cold showers are good value, while a/c rooms (P1500–2900) and suites (P3500) offer more comfort. There's a swimming pool, café and beach bar. P1000

Island Dream Midway between GL and Cloud 9 ⓦislanddreamsiargao.com. Opened in 2010, with plush, new cottages near the seafront and a small pool in the garden. The "Lifestyles Cloud Nine" rooms are good value, while cottages (P2000–2400) and multiroom villas (P4400–6500) have spacious bathrooms and verandas. P1500

Kalinaw Resort Midway between GL and Cloud 9 ⓦkalinawresort.com. The most luxurious (and expensive) option on the island, next door to *Island Dream* and facing a pristine beach. The immaculate wooden villas have gorgeous minimalist interiors, free wi-fi, balconies and satellite TV. The pool villas (P16,600) have their own private infinity splash pool. There's also a top-notch French restaurant on site. P9900

Ocean 101 Cloud 9 ☎0910 848 0893, ⓦocean101 cloud9.com. Popular with surfers and offering a range of accommodation from spartan singles with shared bathroom to a/c doubles (P2000) with enough space for an extra bed. There's also a cosy restaurant and bar, free internet and credit cards are accepted. P750

Patrick's on the Beach Resort A 10min walk east of GL ☎0918 481 6483, ⓦpatrickonthebeach.com. Basic, local-style beach hut accommodation, with spacious beachfront cottages, garden cottages and economy cottages – check before agreeing to a room as some are better than others. Helpful staff can arrange everything from boats, air tickets and babysitting to laundry, massage and manicures. They have kayaks and wi-fi, and you can rent tents for just P400. P1500

★**Sagana Resort** Cloud 9 ☎0919 809 5769, ⓦcloud9 surf.com. The best choice at Cloud 9, *Sagana* has six Laotian-inspired cottages – two a/c and four with fan – in a landscaped garden with coconut trees and large, leafy plants. Rates are inclusive of three meals, and the restaurant is one of the island's best, with seafood such as tuna, marlin, and Spanish mackerel, as well as mud crabs and prawns from local fish farms. Free wi-fi. Per person P3300

EATING AND DRINKING

Most of the best places to eat and drink are in the **resorts**, but there are a few good independent places in GL and out at Cloud 9. Everywhere is lively during peak season, particularly during the Surfing Cup, when various places on Cloud 9 put on live music.

Bones Sports Pub On the seafront, Cloud 9. A surfer favourite, run by an Australian expat and serving curries and ice-cold beer (P35 during happy hour). Daily 5pm–late.

Jungle Disco Bar (aka Tattoo) GL. The only place resembling a club on Siargao plays anything and everything. P10 cover charge. Thurs–Sat 7pm–4am.

★**Maridyl's** Main Rd, GL. Dishes knocked out by the amiable Maridyl range from local squid and adobo to grilled tuna and (a rarity in these parts) fresh vegetables (P50–75/dish). Daily 7am–9pm.

Nine Bar Outside GL on the beach road ☎0912 691 7832. Just beyond *Patrick's* and *Cherinicole*, this Swedish-owned place cooks up a host of international dishes including huge burritos, and gets livelier as the night progresses. Daily noon–midnight.

Dinagat Island

There are several morning bangkas from Surigao to San José (4hr), from where bangkas (about P1000 for half a day) can take you virtually anywhere along the coast of Dinagat

Just a short bangka hop from Surigao, wild and undeveloped **Dinagat Island**, around 60km from tip to toe, is an adventure paradise-in-waiting. Its rugged coastline has tantalizing **islets**, beautiful sugary-sand **beaches** and sheer cliffs that are attracting an increasing number of **rock climbers**. The main drawback is the lack of **accommodation**: there are basic beach huts on the southwest coast around the town of Dinagat, but not much else. Only a handful of travellers make it this far.

The best way to get an overview of what Dinagat has to offer is to rent a bangka in San José, where ferries arrive from Surigao. On the west-coast islet of **Unib** you'll find unspoiled Bitaug Beach and several immense, largely unexplored caves. The waters of this area are fringed by good coral and deep sea walls, but there's no equipment for rent so you'll have to bring whatever you need, including snorkelling gear. In the same area, the uninhabited islet of **Hagakhak** is another beauty, with scintillating above-water and underwater rock formations.

The southeast

The **southeast** is home to Mindanao's largest city, **Davao**, a diverse and friendly place best known for its fresh fruit. Davao itself is not a city of legendary sights, but the nearby countryside and coast harbour plenty of attractions, from idyllic **Samal Island** to crocodile parks, ziplines and the **Philippine Eagle Center**. Davao is also the gateway to **Mount Apo**, the nation's highest peak and a magnet for trekkers and climbers. Further south, the tuna port of **General Santos** is the closest city to enigmatic **Lake Sebu**.

Davao

Known as the **durian** capital of the Philippines, **DAVAO** is a relaxed city that also has a reputation for delicious seafood. There are a couple of things to see in the city itself – and

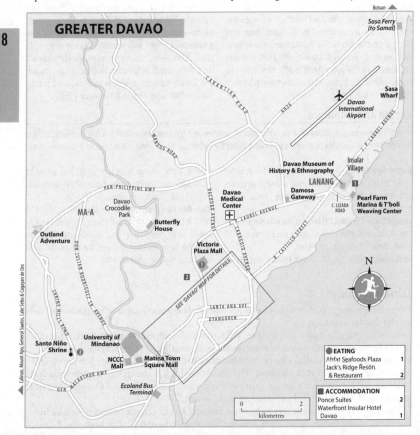

GREATER DAVAO

Butuan

Sasa Ferry
(to Samal)

Sasa Wharf

Davao International Airport

J. P. LAUREL AVENUE

CABANTIAN ROAD

AMJE

MANDUG ROAD

Insular Village

Davao Museum of History & Ethnography

LANANG

PAN-PHILIPPINE HWY

DACUDAO AVENUE

Davao Medical Center

Damosa Gateway

C. LIZADA ROAD

Pearl Farm Marina & T'boli Weaving Center

MA-A

Davao Crocodile Park

Butterfly House

R. CASTILLO STREET

F. TORRES AVENUE

CABAGUIO AVENUE

Victoria Plaza Mall

①

②

SEE DAVAO MAP FOR DETAILS

N

Outland Adventure

DON JULIAN RODRIGUEZ JR. AVENUE

SHRINE HILLS BLVD

SANTA ANA AVE.

UYANGUREN

University of Mindanao

Santo Niño Shrine ② ②

NCCC Mall

Matina Town Square Mall

GEN. MACARTHUR HWY

Ecoland Bus Terminal

Cavite, Mount Apo, General Santos, Lake Sebu & Cagayan de Oro

EATING	
Ahfat Seafoods Plaza	1
Jack's Ridge Resort & Restaurant	2

ACCOMMODATION	
Ponce Suites	2
Waterfront Insular Hotel Davao	1

0 2
kilometres

8

FAMILY FUN AT MA-A

Some 5km northwest of the city centre, the suburb of **Ma-a** contains several activity-based attractions, which can be a lot of fun, especially for kids. You can get there by taxi (P200) or on any of the jeepneys travelling via the NCCC Mall, west of the centre on the MacArthur Highway; jeepneys chug up to Ma-a and the Diversion Highway, where habal-habal motorcycles can take you to a specific attraction.

MA-A ATTRACTIONS

Davao Crocodile Park Riverfront, Corporate City, Diversion Hwy ☎ 082 286 8883, ⓦ psdgroupph.com. Ma-a's flagship attraction, with huge crocodiles and touristy croc-feeding shows (Fri–Sun 4.45pm); most of the crocs are fed at a distance, with only the babies close up. P200. Daily 8am–7pm.

Davao Wildwater Adventure ☎ 082 221 7823, ⓦ waterrafting.psdgroupph.com. Whitewater rafting on the Davao River (daily 8.30am–4.30pm; P2000/ person, trips only set off with a minimum of five people). Rates include transportation from the Crocodile Park and lunch.

Outland Adventure Diversion Hwy, across from the GAP Farm ☎ 082 224 5855, ⓦ outlandadventure .org. One of the fastest and tallest ziplines in Asia, taking you soaring over the river and forest. It's accessed after a short hike and raft ride across a lake. P300. Mon–Sat 8am–5pm, Sun 1–5pm.

in the barangay of **Lanang**, 6km north along the coast – but mostly Davao makes a good base for the surrounding area. Its formidable line-up of **annual festivals** are certainly worth attending, especially **Kadayawan**, a harvest festival held during the third week of August, which focuses on flamboyant tribal dance parades and a beauty pageant.

The city experienced terrorism of sorts in 2013 when two small **bombs** simultaneously exploded in separate cinemas, but it is still widely considered safe to visit, in spite of foreign government advisories to the contrary.

San Pedro Cathedral

San Pedro St at C.M. Recto St • Open during mass only • Free

The bizarre giant concrete bowl that is **San Pedro Cathedral** began life as a simple nipa chapel in 1848. A more solid structure went up in 1886, but the whole thing was rebuilt in the current Modernist style in the 1970s.

People's Park

J. Camus St • Daily 5.30–8am (for joggers) & 1–10pm (11pm Fri & Sat) • Free • ☎ 082 227 2273

A welcome slice of green in the heart of the city, liberally sprinkled with sculptures representing southern Mindanao's indigenous groups, **People's Park** is especially lively at weekends when there's a fountain show at 7pm (1hr).

Museo Dabawenyo

Pichon St • Mon–Fri 9am–6pm • Free • ☎ 082 222 6011

For an overview of Davao's turbulent and complex history and ethnic make-up, visit the **Museo Dabawenyo**, housed in the restored court building opposite Osmeña Park. It's small but well presented, and though there are fewer objects on display than at the Davao Museum (see p.425), it is easier to reach (and free). Indigenous tribes are described in detail, as is the fateful struggle between Datu Bago and conquistador Don José Uyanguren in the 1840s. Panels also throw light on the American occupation boom years in the early twentieth century, the massive migrations that took place from the Visayas thereafter and the arrival of Japanese settlers in the 1930s – hard to believe this was once "Little Tokyo".

Magsaysay Park

Daily 5am–9pm • Free

The eastern seaward side of downtown is framed by **Magsaysay Park**, where you'll find the tourist information centre, a couple of outdoor cafés and rows of **durian**

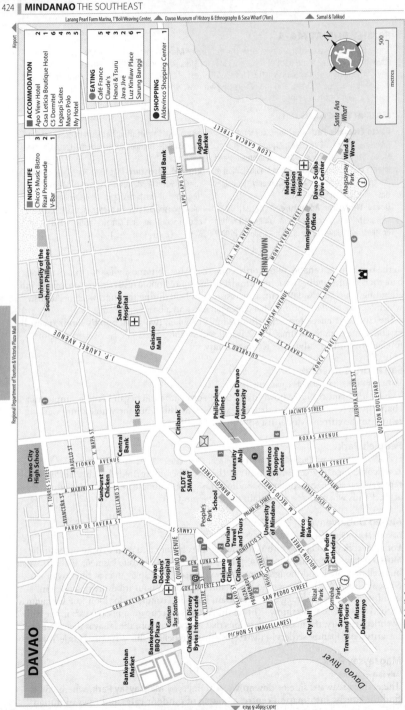

Lanang Pearl Farm Marina, T'Boli Weaving Center, Davao Museum of History & Ethnography & Sasa Wharf (7km) — Samal & Talikud

DAVAO

ACCOMMODATION
Apo View Hotel 2
Casa Leticia Boutique Hotel 1
CS Dormitel 6
Legaspi Suites 4
Marco Polo 3
My Hotel 5

EATING
Café France 5
Claude's 4
Hanoi & Tsuru 3
Java Jive 2
Luz Kinilaw Place 6
Sarung Banggi 1

SHOPPING
Aldevinco Shopping Center 1

NIGHTLIFE
Chico's Music Bistro 3
Rizal Promenade 2
V-Bar 1

Airport

Regional Department of Tourism & Victoria Plaza Mall

University of the Southern Philippines

Santa Ana Wharf

Agdao Market

Allied Bank

LEON GARCIA STREET

Medical Mission Hospital

Davao Scuba Dive Center

Magsaysay Park

Wind & Wave

LAPU-LAPU STREET

STA. ANA AVENUE

CHINATOWN

MONTEVERDE STREET

Immigration Office

SALES ST

R. MAGSAYSAY AVENUE

T. LUNA ST

San Pedro Hospital

D. SUAZO ST

Gaisano Mall

J.P. LAUREL AVENUE

GUERRERO ST

CHAVEZ ST

PONCE STREET

Davao City High School

E. TORRES STREET

A. MABINI ST

TIONKO AVENUE

V. MAPA ST

ARELLANO ST

HSBC

Central Bank

Sunburst Chicken

AVANCEÑA ST

PARDO DE TAVERA ST

Philippines Airlines

Ateneo de Davao University

E. JACINTO STREET

ROXAS AVENUE

AURORA QUEZON ST

QUEZON BOULEVARD

Citibank

People's Park

University Mall

Aldevinco Shopping Center

MABINI STREET

ARTIAGA ST

S. DE JESUS STREET

C. M. RECTO STREET

CM RECTO STREET

PALMA GIL STREET

BONIFACIO STREET

University of Mindanao

Merco Bakery

San Pedro Cathedral

BOLTON STREET

PLDT & SMART

C. BANGOY STREET

School

ILUSTRE ST

Durian Travel and Tours

Gaisano Citimall

Citibank

INIGO STREET

RIZAL STREET

RIZAL PROMENADE

PELAYO ST

MT. APO ST

Davao Doctors' Hospital

GEN. LUNA ST

E. QUIRINO AVENUE

Chikachat & Disney Bytes Internet café

@

GOV. DUTERTE ST

V. ILUSTRE ST

GEN MALVAR ST

Calinan Bus Station

Bankerohan BBQ Plaza

Bankerohan Plaza

Bankerohan Market

SAN PEDRO STREET

PICHON ST (MAGELLANES)

City Hall

Rizal Park

Osmeña Park

Surelite Travel and Tours

Museo Dabawenyo

DAVAO RIVER

Jack's Ridge & Maa

Ecoland Bus Terminal

8

N

0 500 metres

stalls just outside; this luscious (but smelly) treat costs around P60 per kilo, but most hotel won't allow durians inside – snack in the park or buy the durian jams or candy instead.

Pearl Farm Marina

Lanang • Weaving Centre Daily 8am–5pm • Free • Lanang is easily reached via jeepney (anything that is heading towards "Sasa") or taxi

At the **Pearl Farm Marina** in the barangay of Lanang, 4km north of Magsaysay Park, well-heeled travellers are whisked across the bay to the **Pearl Farm Resort** (see p.429) – well worth seeing if you have cash to spare. Day-trips (daily 8am; return 4pm; P1950 Mon–Thurs, P2500 Fri & Sat; ☎082 221 9970) include returns on the boat, lunch and use of the facilities.

Just inside the marina grounds, at the tiny **T'boli Weaving Center**, you can see weavers from Lake Sebu (see p.432) on traditional looms, crafting bold geometrical patterns that symbolize tribal beliefs on *tinalak* cloth. Colourful bags, belts, shoes, wallets, rugs and wall hangings are on sale.

Davao Museum of History & Ethnography

Insular Village 1, J.P Laurel Ave, Lanang • Mon–Sat 9am–noon & 1–5pm • P100 • Lanang is reached via jeepney (marked "Sasa") or taxi; sign in at the gate and then turn right, from where it's a 5min walk

You'll find the small but enlightening **Davao Museum of History & Ethnography** tucked away at the back of a gated community. On the ground floor a detailed timeline describes the city's key events, with temporary exhibits such as rare santos sculptures on display. Upstairs there's a decent introduction to Davao's fifteen indigenous tribes, including the Bagobos, with displays of ancient weaponry, betel nut boxes, jewellery (including a wildcat tooth necklace) and fancy brass work.

ARRIVAL AND DEPARTURE

DAVAO

BY PLANE

Davao International Airport The modern and spacious airport lies 11km north of the city centre. Ignore taxi touts quoting P300–500 for a ride into the city and head for the rank where metered fares cost P100–200.

Airline offices Air Asia, 4/F Gaisano Mall, J.P. Laurel Ave (☎02 742 2742); Cebu Pacific, Summit World, 2/F Victoria Plaza Mall, J.P. Laurel Ave (☎082 224 0960); Philippine Airlines, Ateneo de Davao University Building, C.M. Recto St (☎082 221 5513); Silk Air, Suite 056, 5/F Pryce Tower, J.P. Laurel Ave (☎082 227 5301).

Routes Davao airport has handy air links with a host of destinations in the Philippines, including Manila and Cebu, most of which are provided by Cebu Pacific. For all domestic flights, you'll have to pay a P200 terminal fee before departure. The only international destination is Singapore (3hr 35min), served by Silk Air.

Destinations Bacolod (3 weekly; 1hr 10min); Cagayan de Oro (2 weekly; 1hr); Cebu (5 daily; 1hr 5min); Dipolog (2 weekly; 1hr 15min); Iloilo (daily; 1hr 10min); Manila (15+ daily; 1hr 45min); Puerto Princesa (2 weekly; 1hr 30min); Zamboanga (2 daily; 1hr).

BY BUS

Terminal Calinan is served by frequent bus and jeepneys from the Annil transport terminal on San Pedro, just

north of Quirino Ave. All other buses depart the Ecoland terminal on Quimpo Blvd, across the Davao River from the centre of the city.

Operators and routes Bus operators, all based at the Ecoland terminal, include Bachelor Express (☎082 244 0654), Rural Trans (☎082 244 0637) and Weena Express (☎082 244 0033). All the information given below refers to express a/c buses.

Destinations Butuan (Bachelor Express: daily 1am–5pm, every 20min; 5–6hr); Cagayan de Oro (Rural Trans: daily 4am–10.30pm, every 30min; 7hr 30min); Cotabato (Weena Express: daily 4.30am–1.30pm, every 25min; 6hr); General Santos (Weena Express: every 30min; 3hr 15min); Kidapawan, for Mt Apo (Weena Express: daily 4.30am–1.30pm, every 25min; 2hr 30min); Korondal, for Lake Sebu (Weena Express: every 30min; 4hr 30min); Mangagoy (Bachelor Express: 2.30am & 2.30pm; 5hr); Surigao (Bachelor Express: direct, 8am; 9hr).

BY BOAT

Ferries Ferries arrive at and leave from Sasa wharf, 7km east along the coast, although aside from bus-ferry connections on the roll-on roll-off ferry across to Samal, there aren't any destinations of use from here.

Motorboats Outrigger motorboats ply the route from Santa Ana wharf near Magsaysay Park to Kaputian at the southern end of Samal (45min; P60) and Talicud.

8

8

DIVING AND SNORKELLING AROUND DAVAO

Most of Davao's **dive shops** are clustered at the end of Monteverde Street next to Magsaysay Park and the Santa Ana wharf; favoured destinations are the sparkling waters around **Samal** and especially **Talicud** (just 45min by boat), where there are some decent coral reefs and plenty of fish.

DIVE SHOPS

Davao Scuba Dive Center ☎082 226 2588, ⓦdavaoscubadive.net. Danish expat Frank Rasmussen offers two-tank dives from P1800 and PADI courses (3–4 days) from P18,000. He can also help locate the area's dwindling dugong population (less than twenty by some accounts); you can snorkel near these gentle creatures, but not dive.

Wind & Wave ☎082 300 7914, ⓦwindandwavedavao .com. Day dives and PADI courses at similar rates to the Davao Scuba Dive Center, plus kayaking and parasailing.

INFORMATION AND TOURS

Tourist information office South side of Magsaysay Park (Mon–Fri 8am–noon & 1–5pm; ☎082 222 1956, ⓦdavaotourism.com). Offers basic maps and leaflets and advice.

Regional Department of Tourism Fifth floor of the Landco Pacific Building, J.P. Laurel Ave, near Victoria Plaza (Mon–Fri 8am–5pm; ☎082 221 6955, ⓦdiscoverdavao .com). Come here for help with trips outside the city, including hikes up Mt Apo.

Tours Many hotels have tour desks and a host of tour operators vie for day-trip business. Durian Travel and Tours (☎082 221 6430, ⓦduriantravelandtours.com) is in the *Apo View Hotel*, while Surelite Travel and Tours (☎082 221 7601, ⓔsurelitetraveltours@gmail.com) is on Pichon St.

GETTING AROUND

By taxi It's cheap and easy to get around Davao by taxi; you can hail them in the street, meters start at P40 and after that it's P2.50/300m. They can also be hired out for day-trips from around P2000, but make sure you take a ride in the cab first, and clearly establish the price and what it entails.

By jeepney Jeepneys (P8 initial fare for up to 4km; P1/1km thereafter) run back and forth along all major thoroughfares with destinations pasted on the side – it's just a question of flagging one down and hopping on.

By tricycle Tricycles charge P7/person for trips within the city – this includes Santa Ana wharf, Ecoland bus terminal and north as far as Victoria Plaza.

Car rental Avis (daily 6am–7pm; ☎082 225 3337) is inside the *Apo View Hotel*; Europcar (ⓦeuropcar.com.ph) will deliver to your hotel and has desks at the airport (☎082 304 2438) and in the lobbies of the *Marco Polo* (☎082 221 0888) and *Pearl Farm* (Mindanao side; ☎082 304 4958). Rates start at around P3000/day including insurance.

ACCOMMODATION

Apo View Hotel 150 J. Camus St ☎082 221 6430, ⓦapoview.com; map p.424. The oldest upmarket hotel in Davao, with big, comfortable a/c rooms – it can't compete with the *Marco Polo* for luxury but it has a certain old-fashioned charm. You don't always get a view of Mt Apo, although on a clear day you can see it from the top-floor restaurant. P2500

Casa Leticia Boutique Hotel J. Camus St ☎082 224 0501, ⓦcasaleticia.com; map p.424. Attractive mid-range option with a/c, en-suite rooms ranging from studios and doubles to a smart presidential suite. All have free wi-fi and LCD TV. The hotel also has a reasonable restaurant and a lively music bar, *Toto's*. P2800

★**C5 Dormitel** Roxas Ave ☎082 228 6186, ⓦc5dormitel .com; map p.424. In a decent location in the new part of town, this budget boutique hotel sports artsy decor. Rates are reasonable, and there are two-bed dorms for P4500/month.

The a/c doubles are clean and comfy, though starting to show their age. Free wi-fi. P1200

★**Legaspi Suites** 115 P. Pelayo St ☎082 227 8613, ⓦlegaspisuites.com; map p.424. In a great location near nightlife and restaurants, this hotel offers high standards for a very reasonable price – rooms, elegantly furnished in dark wood and decorated in pastel shades, have a/c, LCD TVs and decent bathrooms, and the larger premier superior rooms (P1900) also have fridges. Breakfast included. P1700

Marco Polo C.M. Recto St at Roxas Ave ☎082 221 0888, ⓦmarcopolohotels.com; map p.424. The city's most luxurious hotel, with spacious rooms, large bathrooms, flatscreen cable TV and fine views of either the sea or, on a clear day, Mt Apo. The pool is a great place to hang out, with a bar and terrace restaurant facing Apo, and the breakfast buffets (usually included) are excellent. On the

downside they add "tax", VAT, 10 percent service charges, and VAT on the service charges, to everything. **P9800**
My Hotel San Pedro St ☎082 222 2021, ⊚myhotel davao.com; map p.424. The tiny, clean fan rooms with communal bathrooms are among the best bargains in the city, while the a/c rooms are more spacious and have cable TV (P995). Friendly staff and a great value all-you-can-eat buffet (P138) downstairs. **P250**
Ponce Suites Rd 3 at Rd 4, Doña Vicenta Village, Bajada ☎082 227 9070, ⊚poncesuites.net; map p.422. You're unlikely to have stayed in a budget hotel like this before

– every bit of public wall space is smothered in the exuberant artwork of Kublai Millan (whose sculptures also decorate the city). The rooms are more modest, but all are en suite with basic cable TV and free wi-fi. **P975**
Waterfront Insular Hotel Davao Km 7, Lanang ☎082 233 2881, ⊚waterfronthotels.net; map p.422. This plush resort-style hotel on the shore, 5km out of town, has pretty a/c rooms, a large outdoor pool and small beach area. It's the pick of the bunch if you've got the budget and are looking for relaxation and fresh sea breezes. **P4000**

EATING

Seafood (especially tuna) and fresh fruits such as **durian** (see p.423) take centre stage on Davao's enjoyable **eating** scene. You can buy freshly chopped durian and all sorts of derivative products at the stalls run by the Magsaysay Fruit Vendors Association on Magsaysay Park. Davao's best **restaurants** are scattered all over the city, but the safest bet for a cheap meal are the **food courts** located in or around the shopping malls. The food is hygienic, variety is reasonable and most dishes cost less than P70. The large car parking area outside Victoria Plaza Mall is good for Chinese and Korean restaurants; the Bankerohan BBQ Plaza offers cheap *lechon* and barbecue meats from P17/plate; and Market Basket (daily 9am–8pm) at Damosa Gateway is a great food court, with plenty of choices.

Ahfat Seafoods Plaza Victoria Plaza Mall, J.P. Laurel Ave (facing the car park behind the mall) ☎082 226 2688; map p.422. Cheap Chinese food in three buildings, all excellent quality; the original place is more like a canteen, while *Ahfat III* offers dim sum from 7am to 4.30pm. Try the steamed shrimp, spicy spare ribs and crab (dishes in each place average P160–200). Daily 10am–11pm.
Café France Rizal St ☎082 300 7322; map p.424. Take a break from the heat of the streets in the a/c wooden interior of this decent sandwich and coffee chain. The farmer's ham, brie and raspberry baguette (P245) is excellent. There are two other branches in Gaisano Mall. Daily 7am–9pm.
★**Claude's** 143 Rizal St ☎082 222 4287, ⊚claudes cafedavao.com; map p.424. Superb French and Mediterranean restaurant in an elegant 1920s house that was formerly the Mayor's residence and apparently once played host to Manuel Roxas. Now owned and operated by a French native, Claude Le Neindre, and his family, the restaurant serves food that's as exquisite as the architecture. The grilled blue marlin is outstanding (P285), and there are a host of speciality dishes including foie gras, mussels *marinière* (P395) and duck a la orange. Staff are courteous and efficient and there's live music on weekends. Daily 11am–2.30pm & 6pm–late.
Hanoi & Tsuru Camus St ☎082 284 1137; map p.424. Sleek modern restaurant divided into two and serving two different cuisines. *Hanoi* turns out authentic Vietnamese food including *pho tai* (P250), while *Tsuru*, the city's best Japanese restaurant, offers sushi, *ramen* (P285–350) and *sukiyaki* (from P295). Daily 11am–2pm & 5–10pm.

★**Jack's Ridge Resort & Restaurant** Shrine Hills, Matina ☎082 297 8831, ⊚jacksridgedavao.com; map p.422. Just across from the Santo Niño shrine, this complex is all about the views and cool breezes, and the Filipino food in the main *Taklobo Restaurant* is delicious: the *sinigang*, *lechon*, grilled tuna and barbecue chicken are all superb. It often has live bands at night and is also a great place for a beer or coffee. Take a taxi (P100). Daily 11.30am–1.30pm & 4.30pm–midnight.
Java Jive Quirino Ave ☎082 224 0272; map p.424. This new, locally owned café is already very popular for its excellent coffees (including famous civet coffee, P310), tasty sandwiches (P115–135) and yummy cakes. There's free wi-fi and weekly live music (Fri–Mon 9pm–midnight). Daily 24hr.
★**Luz Kinilaw Place** Quezon Blvd near Magsaysay Park ☎082 226 4612; map p.424. Classic, no-frills local favourite, with tuna, chicken and assorted seafood flame-grilled on the street just outside and sumptuous plates of squid and tuna served upstairs. Have a gut-busting breakfast or get there early for lunch or dinner to avoid a wait. Two can eat well here for P300. Daily 6am–10pm.
Sarung Banggi F. Torres St ☎082 221 5615; map p.424. Fun native-style dining, with waiting staff decked out in tribal-style outfits. The imaginative menu offers much more choice than most of the local grill restaurants. Notable dishes include seafood soup with sour mango and rice, Bicol Express with pork ribs and chilli and simple grilled tuna or swordfish with lime. Sun–Thurs 11am–2pm & 5–10pm, Fri & Sat 11am–2pm & 5–11pm.

8

NIGHTLIFE

It may not be as avant-garde as Manila, but there's some entertaining **nightlife** in Davao, with cosy live music venues, karaoke bars and discos. Apart from the odd spot downtown, most places tend to be clustered around newish malls or specially built compounds such as the large car parking area outside Victoria Plaza Mall, Damosa Gateway and in various places along **F. Torres St**, the busiest of the lot.

Chico's Music Bistro 29 Rizal St ☎082 255 5675; map p.424. A rare old wooden house and a fun place to eat or drink, with decent live acts every night and a happy hour (7–9pm). Daily 5pm–midnight.

Rizal Promenade Off Rizal St; map p.424. Entertainment arcade with loud (but not always lively) bars serving

San Mig for P40–50. If the noise gets too much for you, head for the central chill-out zone between the bars. Daily 7pm–midnight.

V-Bar Illustre St at General Luna St; map p.424. Popular place with an upstairs open-air bar looking out over the street. P30 cover. Daily 7pm–midnight.

SHOPPING

Aldevinco Shopping Center Opposite the Marco Polo hotel, between C.M. Recto Ave and Roxas Ave; map p.424. For souvenirs and handicrafts, head to this maze of

small shops selling tribal artefacts and cheap batik clothes. With a little bargaining, you can grab a sarong for P100 or statues and masks from P400. Daily 10am–6pm.

DIRECTORY

Banks and exchange There are plenty of banks in Davao, including Citibank at 547 J.P. Laurel Ave and an HSBC on Jacinto Extension, and there are ATMs in the malls.

Hospitals The city's major hospital is the Davao Doctors' Hospital (☎082 224 0616) on E. Quirino Ave, southwest of the city centre. San Pedro Hospital (☎082 224 0616) is on Guerrero St.

Internet access There are dozens of internet cafés on the main road outside Victoria Plaza; in the centre there's Chikachat & Disney Bytes on Illustre St (daily 9am–2am; P15/hr). Many hotels and cafés also have wi-fi.

Post The main post office is on Roxas Ave, close to the junction with C.M. Recto St and Magsaysay Ave.

Samal Island

Just across the narrow Pakiputan Strait from Davao, **Samal Island** is graced with lovely coves, beaches, excellent scuba diving and huge bat caves – there are also plenty of resorts to choose from. You can arrange **diving** trips at many resorts on Samal and also in Davao (see box, p.426). Most tourists visit Samal on organized tours but it's also easy to arrange a trip independently. You can spend time at one of the resorts (most of which allow day guests for a fee), or jump on a habal-habal and tour the island by motorbike. Samal is bigger than it seems, with an area of more than 300 square kilometres and nearly 100,000 permanent residents. Of the many beaches, it's worth taking the bumpy, hour-long ride across the island to **Canibad Beach Cove**, a pristine, untouched swathe of sand with little more than a sari-sari store selling soft drinks. Elsewhere on Samal you can visit bubbling waterfalls (modest but pretty **Hagimit Falls** is P40), numerous caves or even make the relatively quick hike up Samal's highest point, **Mount Puting Bato** (410m), for fine views of Davao and Mount Apo.

Monfort Bat Cave

Daily 8am–5pm • P100

Don't miss the **Monfort Bat Cave** in the northern part of the island, a vast cavern jam-packed with around 1.8 million fruit bats – it's a bit like staring at a giant black carpet. The bats usually hang in the cave during the day, but come sundown they flood out like a dark cloud – it's a chilling experience.

ARRIVAL AND DEPARTURE   SAMAL ISLAND

Getting to Samal from Davao is relatively straightforward. Most resorts on the island have **private boats** that zip guests across the Pakiputan Strait direct to the hotel grounds, and some of these – notably *Pearl Farm Resort* – also take day-trippers, for a fee (see opposite). Most hotels in Davao will also arrange **day tours** to the island for around P1000/person.

If you want to explore on your own you have three main ferry choices. Most of the resorts lie close to the Babak/Caliclic ferries; *Pearl Farm* is closer to Kaputian.

Santa Ana wharf to Kaputian Closest to Davao are the outrigger motorboats that ply between Santa Ana Wharf near Magsaysay Park and Kaputian at the southern end of Samal (45min; P60). Boats leave from the second pier, left of the entrance, but some go straight to Talicud, so check before jumping on board.

Sasa to Kinawitnon wharf Around 8km north of Davao along J.P. Laurel Ave in Sasa, a car ferry (24hr; 15min; P13/person) runs to Kinawitnon wharf in the barangay of Caliclic, Babak District; you must board the Island City Express bus to cross here (or catch the bus at its terminal at Magsaysay Park; P40 including ferry), as walk-on passengers are not allowed.

Sasa to Babak A short walk north of the car ferry are the public bangkas (daily 6am–10pm; P13) that sail every 15min or so from Sasa to Babak at the northern end of Samal; you must walk through the market to reach the pier (the entrance, on J.P. Laurel Ave, km 11, is next to a footbridge). Jeepneys marked "Sasa" will take you from Davao city centre to the market entrance; taxis should cost around P100.

GETTING AROUND

By habal-habal No matter which port you arrive at, if you want to get beyond the resorts you can choose from the many habal-habal riders offering personalized tours – it's a good idea to hire one for the whole day rather than try and get separate lifts. Rates vary, but expect to pay around P300 for a half-day; riders will suggest visiting all sorts of wondrous attractions, but the most popular are covered here.

Tricycles and minivans Tricycles and minivans are also available, but unless you have a group, these are much more expensive.

ACCOMMODATION

Most reasonably priced **resorts** on Samal are on the northwest coast, south of the barangay of Caliclic. From the wharf at Babak you can walk to many of these resorts, or hop on a tricycle. All the major resorts have private boats for guests – these depart from piers off R. Castillo St north of the city (some allow day guests to use them for a fee; see below).

Bluewaters Beach Resort Caliclic ☎084 301 4075, ⓦebluwaters.com. Fairly simple garden houses and bigger cottages, just a 4min boat ride from Davao; it's not luxury, but it's good value, and day guests can use the pool, watersports (rentals extra) and the resort beach for P100/day (P10 for the boat; 7am–5pm). P1200

Paradise Island Park & Beach Resort Caliclic ☎082 233 0251, ⓦparadiseislanddavao.com. This huge (eighty-room), popular resort can get busy at weekends with day-trippers escaping the city, but has attractive a/c cottages under shady trees in landscaped gardens, a convivial native-style restaurant and scuba diving. Day guests P200. P3500

★**Pearl Farm Resort** ☎082 235 1234, ⓦpearlfarmresort.com. South along the west coast is the island's classiest and most expensive resort, which has more than seventy native-style cottages either on a hillside overlooking the bay or perched on stilts in the sea. There are also seven luxurious and secluded villas on beautiful little Malipano Island, a short hop from the main resort. P6900

Talicud

Talicud Island, off the southwest coast of Samal, is even more torpid than its big brother, making it a perfect place to escape Davao's crowds. On the west coast there's good, easy diving and snorkelling in an area known as Coral Gardens, and there are a couple of more demanding drop-off dives off the north coast.

ARRIVAL AND DEPARTURE TALICUD

By boat Outrigger ferries regularly chug between Santa Ana wharf near Magsaysay Park in Davao and Santa Cruz on Talicud (6am–6pm, at least hourly; 1hr–1hr 30min; P60). Boats leave from the second pier, left of the wharf entrance; just jump on and pay. You can also hire a bangka from Kaputian on Samal Island (P300).

ACCOMMODATION

Leticia by the Sea ☎082 286 6086, ⓦleticiabythesearesort.com. Elegant but simple, this is a great escape – and you can visit for the day (P300). As well as a decent restaurant they also have kayaks for rent and an on-call masseuse. Rates include full board and boat transfers. Per person P5000

Calinan

The small but lively town of **CALINAN**, 45km northwest of Davao on the main highway to Cagayan de Oro, became a major Japanese farming community in the 1930s. Though there's little evidence of this today, the period is commemorated at the **Philippine Japanese Museum**, and there are a few attractions nearby. It's worth coming out here during the week to avoid the crowds, but if you find yourself in Calinan on a Sunday you could head for the *Malagos Garden Resort* (see below) bird show at 10.30am (P125).

Philippine Japanese Museum

De Lara St, in the Durian Village section of Calinan • Mon–Sat 8am–5.30pm • P20 • Take a habal-habal – it's hard to find

Calinan's curious and largely forgotten Japanese history is remembered through a collection of old photos and the fascinating written testimonies of Japanese settlers in the **Philippine Japanese Museum**. You'll also see pictures of the many memorials to Japanese people killed during World War II in the area.

Philippine Eagle Center

Malagos • Daily 8am–5pm • P50, Philippines Water Authority Grounds P5 • ☏ 082 224 2337, ⊛ philippineeagle.org • Many hotels and travel agents in Davao offer day-trips; alternatively, take a tricycle (P50) or habal-habal (P20–30) from Calinan

The **Philippine Eagle Center**, 5km west of Calinan, is known for its excellent work breeding the Philippine eagle, a majestic creature with a fearsome beak, distinctive frilly head feathers and a 2m wingspan. Sadly, the eagle is now officially on the endangered species list, with only a maximum of four hundred believed to be living in the wilds of Mindanao, Samar and Leyte. The centre's captive breeding programme focuses on developing a viable gene pool, the goal being to reintroduce the birds into their natural habitat. The first captive-bred bird, Pag-aso (meaning "Hope"), was born here in 1992 and the centre is now home to 34 Philippine eagles.

To get to the centre you first walk through the Philippines Water Authority Grounds before reaching the entrance proper and a pleasant café overlooking a lily pond. In addition to the large aviaries containing the big eagles, there are plenty of other birds of prey on display, from grass owls and kites to screeching fish eagles, and there are compounds for the Philippine brown deer, warty pig, long-tailed macaques and even a giant crocodile. In truth the centre is a bit like an old-fashioned zoo – some of the birdcages are very small. It can be uncomfortably busy at weekends, so try to schedule your visit for a weekday. Overall it's certainly educational and the eagles are awe-inspiring – it helps to bear in mind that eventually they will be released.

ARRIVAL AND DEPARTURE

CALINAN

By jeepney or bus Take one of the frequent a/c jeepneys (P40) or buses to Calinan (45min) from the Annil transport terminal on San Pedro, just north of Quirino Ave near the Bankerohan Market.

By car You can rent a vehicle from your hotel for the trip, or negotiate directly with a taxi driver – expect to pay P2000 for a day-trip including waiting time.

ACCOMMODATION

Malagos Garden Resort ☏ 082 221 1545, ⊛ malagos .com. A slightly faded garden resort with comfortable, worn, wood cabins set deep in extensive grounds. Family cottages can sleep four to six and have verandas. Camping (P350/person) is technically only possible if you come with a group of fifteen or more, but it's worth asking. Also on site there's a past-it pool, and an aviary and butterfly enclosure. Activities on offer include horse rides and cycling. Day entry P100 (excluding activities). **P2400**

Mount Apo National Park

Looming over all Davao, **Mount Apo** (2954m) is the highest mountain in the country: the name Apo means "grandfather of all mountains". Apo is actually a volcano, but is certified inactive and has no recorded eruptions. What it does have is enough flora and fauna to make your head spin – thundering waterfalls, rapids, lakes, geysers, sulphur pillars, primeval trees, endangered plant and animal species and a steaming blue lake. Then there are exotic ferns, carnivorous pitcher plants and the queen of Philippine orchids, the *waling-waling*. The local tribes, the Bagobos, believe the gods Apo and Mandaragan inhabit Apo's upper slopes; they revere it as a sacred mountain, calling it Sandawa or "Mountain of Sulphur".

   Climbing Mount Apo is not as hard as it sounds. It's a tough trek, but well worth it: the trail is lined with flowers and the views are mesmerizing, with the whole of Mindanao spread out before you.

Climbing Mount Apo

The Mount Apo summit can be approached via two main routes: the **Kidapawan Trail** on the Cotabato side features hot springs, river crossings and a steep forested trail that leads to the peak via swampy Lake Venado, while the tougher **Kapatagan Trail** on the Davao side cuts through more stereotypically volcanic terrain, culminating in a boulder-strewn slope up to the crater. The local tourist offices will recommend a three- to four-day expedition, but experienced tropical climbers will be able to summit faster. **Climbing** is generally permitted from November to May only (dry season), but even so, you'll need rainproof clothes and a small tent as rain is possible anytime and it gets cold at night.

Kidapawan Trail

Bus to Kidapawan (2hr), then habal-habal to Agko Springs (P100/person; 45min)

The **Kidapawan Trail** starts from Agko Springs near **Kidapawan**, 106km from Davao. The trailhead is around 20km from Kidapawan, where you must organize your permit and guide (see below): jeepneys will take you there in about 45 minutes. From the bubblingly hot Lake Agko you'll cross the Marbel River several times before reaching the first campsite at **Mainit Hot Springs**, where you can take a refreshing dip in a small pool. Around five hours from here (via a couple of rope and ladder-assisted scrambles) is dramatic **Lake Venado**, which looks like a scene from the Jurassic age, with giant trees, vines and a fine fog floating above the lake itself. From here allow three hours for the summit itself – most climbers plan to arrive for sunrise, which means camping near the lake.

Kapatagan Trail

Take a bus from Davao to Digos, a local jeepney to Kapatagan, then a habal-habal to Baruring

To hike this **trail** you can head directly to the **Kapatagan** registration office (see below) from where you'll need to take a habal-habal to the Baruring trailhead. The route takes two days to reach the summit via the spectacular "boulder trail".

INFORMATION   MOUNT APO NATIONAL PARK

Permits and guides Whichever trail you take, you'll need to buy a permit (P750) and to hire a guide (from P500/day) from one of the local tourist offices in charge of each route. The offices can also organize porters (P400/day), if necessary and will do a required equipment check and orientation, laying out all the usual rules.

Tourist offices The Kidapawan Tourist Center (☎064 278 3344) is next to city hall, while the Kapatagan registration office (no phone) is in the small settlement of Kapatagan.

Tours Climb Mt Apo (ⓦclimbmtapo.com) is a small-scale trekking organization that can arrange all elements of the climb for P5000 to P10,000. Their regular route hikes in through Kapatagan and exits via Lake Agko.

ACCOMMODATION

Agko Mahomanoy Mountain Resort Lake Agko ☎0927 383 8853. Right next to the trailhead, this place is perfect for making an early start up Mt Apo the following day. It has pleasant hot springs, a decent pool and simple overnight cottages (from P150), as well as rooms with (P500) and without (P300) bathrooms. P̲1̲5̲0̲

8

Old Barracks Suites Kidapawan ☎064 288 1299. Surprisingly comfortable lodgings with a choice of clean singles (P700), doubles, triples (P900) and family rooms (P1000). There's also a decent restaurant and free wi-fi. **P800**

General Santos

Around 140km southwest of Davao on Sarangani Bay, **GENERAL SANTOS** – or "Jen-san" – is the Philippines' southernmost city, a dense, noisy metropolis of more than half a million that isn't a significant tourist destination; it's something of a frontier town, founded by General Paulino Santos and 62 pioneers from Luzon in 1939. Its recent history has included a series of terrorist bombings, and it remains in the British foreign office's red zone (advising against all travel), though there haven't been any attacks in the city itself for several years. Today General Santos is best known as the centre of the tuna industry, and the hometown of boxing legend Manny Pacquiao – it's also a gateway to beautiful **Lake Sebu**.

ARRIVAL AND DEPARTURE
GENERAL SANTOS

By plane General Santos International Airport is about 20min and 12km west of the city, an easy trip by taxi (P300–350), or habal-habal (P100) if you don't have much luggage. Despite the name there are only domestic flights connecting the city with Cebu (2 daily; 1hr 10min) and Manila (4 daily; 1hr 45min).

By boat Ferries arrive at Makar wharf, 10min and 2km west of the centre on P. Acharon Blvd.

By bus Buses from Cotabato (several daily; 5hr), Davao (every 30min; 3hr 15min) and Koronodal (hourly; 3hr) arrive at the City Terminal near Bulaong Ave on the western edge of the centre, near the river.

By tricycle In the city, tricycles are the best way to get around.

ACCOMMODATION AND EATING

JMIX Bar JMP Building 2, Aparente St ☎083 554 2368. Owned by boxing legend Manny "Pacman" Pacquiao, who grew up in Gensan and still lives here as the congressman for Sarangani, this is a good place for a drink and a game of pool. You might even get to meet the great man, a mean pool player himself. Daily 11am–midnight.

Ranchero's Grill National Hwy ☎083 563 9298. Sumptuous grilled seafood, steak, ribs and grilled tuna jaw, and a good line in shakes, including some unusual flavours – try the dragonfruit. Daily 11am–10pm.

Tierra Montana Hotel National Hwy ☎083 554 7733, ⓦtierramontanahotel.com. Good-value, modern, stylish hotel offering well-designed a/c rooms with wi-fi and flatscreen TVs. There's also a pleasant pool and jacuzzi area. Breakfast included. **P1650**

T'boli and Lake Sebu

Fifty kilometres west of General Santos, the small town of **T'BOLI** sits on the shores of enchanting **Lake Sebu**, in a natural bowl surrounded by wooded hills and rolling plantations. This is the ancestral homeland of the T'boli tribe, whose members often wear traditional woven clothes and eye-catching handmade jewellery. It's a great place to see T'boli culture first hand; you can also rent a boat and take a **trip on the lake** itself (45min; P400) and shop in the weekly **Saturday market** for brassware, beads and fabric. The main sights around the lake are the **Seven Falls**, a series of plunging cascades you can hike up to or fly over on what is probably the most thrilling **zipline** in the Philippines (P300). The annual Lem-Lunay T'boli **festival**, held here every year on the second Friday of November, concludes with traditional horse fights.

ARRIVAL AND INFORMATION
T'BOLI AND LAKE SEBU

By bus To reach T'boli, take a bus from General Santos to Koronadal (1hr 30min), from where buses, jeepneys and a/c minivans head south to Surallah (45min). From Surallah it's another 30min or so to T'boli and Lake Sebu by minivan or habal-habal.

Tourist information and tours On arrival make for the Lake Sebu Tourism Office (☎0906 389 0328), which can help with accommodation and tours. Alternatively contact a travel agent in General Santos, such as Go Sarangani Travel (☎083 304 4398, ⓦgosarangani.com).

GETTING AROUND

By motorbike Habal-habal are the main form of transport in T'boli; short trips cost P10 but it's best to hire a rider for half a day to travel around the lake (P250).

ACCOMMODATION AND EATING

Punta Isla Lake Resort A short ride out of town along the lakeshore ☎ 0919 515 015, ⓦ puntaislalakeresort .com. Rudimentary but adequate fan cottages or dorm beds. There's also a breezy restaurant serving a decent selection, including tasty tilapia burgers. Dorm P100, cottages P950

Autonomous Region in Muslim Mindanao

While it is potentially one of the most beguiling areas of the Philippines, the **Autonomous Region in Muslim Mindanao (ARMM)**, a patchwork of several predominantly Muslim provinces in the western part of the island, is not entirely safe to visit. Created in 1989, the regional government (based in Cotabato) has the power to levy taxes and apply Shariah law to Muslims. Despite this autonomy, the region remains extremely poor and the epicentre for anti-government protest.

Marawi and Lake Lanao

Nestled on the shores of Lake Lanao just 25km south of Iligan (see p.408), **MARAWI** is the centre of the Islamic religion in the Philippines: 92 percent of the population is Muslim. During the Marcos years, the area around Marawi was where kidnappers were said to hide their victims, but these days the city is generally peaceful, with incidents related to the fight for Muslim autonomy rare. If you do visit, it is still highly recommended that you do so with a driver and a guide. Contact the Iligan tourist office (see p.408).

Marawi's greatest natural attraction is placid **Lake Lanao**, which sits in a green bowl circled by distant mountains. It's the second-largest lake in the Philippines and easy to explore via a circumferential road; there are said to be some 350 mosques ringing the lake and it's the best place to see striking *torogans*, the traditional wooden homes of Marawi's upper class.

At the **palitan**, a two-storey market in the heart of the city, you can find virtually any type of clothing from jeans to traditional tribal garments, colourful raw cloth

---

ARMM TRAVEL ADVICE

The US, UK and Australian governments (and most Filipinos) usually advise foreigners to **avoid ARMM** entirely, but the situation on the ground is less clear-cut. Most of these places feel pretty friendly most of the time, but while actual **incidents** are rare, those that do occur often end in tragedy – a car bomb killed eight people and injured forty others in Cotobato City in August 2013, while Zamboanga City was occupied by separatists for nearly a month in September the same year. **Kidnapping** is still a lucrative business, likewise piracy, particularly on Basilan, an Abu Sayyef stronghold on the northernmost island in the Sulu chain, and if any unequivocal recommendation can be given it is that you definitely shouldn't go there.

Hopefully the 2014 **Bangsamoro Agreement** (see p.448) will finally bring peace to the region, but in the meantime it's worth considering if you really need to make that trip to Marawi, Lake Lanao or even Zamboanga, when there are several thousand more, extremely beautiful, islands to explore in the Philippines …. If you do decide to go, seek the advice of the local tourism office before visiting any of the following locations, and where possible arrange a local guide when travelling. Avoid travelling at night altogether.

8

⌐ batik products, gold jewellery, exquisite wooden chests and **brassware**
⌐nufactured in the nearby barangay of Tugaya. The city's annual festival, the
Kalilang (April 10–15), is dominated by Koran-reading competitions and traditional
singing and dancing.

Aga Khan Museum
Mon–Fri 9–11.30am & 2–4.30pm • Free

The best views of the lake can be had from the **Mindanao State University** campus. On
campus you'll also find the **Aga Khan Museum**, which has an interesting collection of
Moro art from Mindanao, Sulu and Palawan. The campus was also the site of a grisly
encounter between unidentified **gunmen** and the military in 2012, which ended with
three dead soldiers and several others injured (including civilians).

Zamboanga City

On the southernmost tip of the Zamboanga peninsula, **ZAMBOANGA CITY** is closer
to both Malaysia and Indonesia than it is to the capital of the Philippines: it feels
like another country, where different dialects are spoken (the native language of
Zamboanga City is **Chavacano**, a Spanish Creole) and Manila is well off the radar.
While the economy has grown considerably in recent years, Zamboanga has seen its
share of Mindanao's armed struggle: a suicide bomber killed himself and a bystander
at the airport in 2010 and much of the city was occupied by **separatist rebels** in
September 2013. The proximity to Basilan and the **Sulu archipelago**, stronghold of
Abu Sayyef and out of bounds to foreign visitors, further enhances Zamboanga's
reputation as a no-go area for tourists.

Fort Pilar
Valderosa St • Mon–Fri 9am-4pm • Free • ☎ 062 527 4192 • A 10min taxi ride east of the city centre

The city's major attraction is **Fort Pilar**, ruined fortress, outdoor Catholic shrine
and a branch of the **National Museum**. The squat stone structure was built by the
Spanish in 1635 and is today dedicated to Nuestra Señora del Pilar, patroness of
Zamboanga. The museum highlights local marine life and the history and culture
of local tribes.

Rio Hondo
Though the dome of its mosque is clearly visible from some way off, you will need a
guide to penetrate the maze of bamboo walkways and open-fronted homes that is **Rio
Hondo**, a stilted Muslim village. Enquire at the tourist office and dress conservatively.

ARRIVAL AND DEPARTURE   **ZAMBOANGA CITY**

By plane From the airport on the northern outskirts of
the city it takes about 20min to get to the city centre by
taxi (P150–200); you can take a tricycle for P40 or a
jeepney marked for "Canelar" for P7.
Destinations Cebu City (1 daily; 1hr 15min); Davao
(2 daily; 1hr); Manila (7 daily; 1hr 40min); Tawi-Tawi
(1 daily; 1hr).

By bus Buses from Cagayan de Oro (hourly; 10–12hr),
Dipolog (2 daily; 7–8hr), Iligan (8 daily; 8–10hr) and
Ozamiz (2 daily; 6–7hr) arrive at one of two terminals right
next to each other at the northern end of Veterans' Ave.
By boat The ferry wharf, at the southern end of Lorenzo St,
is easy to reach by taxi, jeepney and tricycle. George & Peter
Lines have a weekly connection to Cebu (16hr).

INFORMATION

Tourist information The best tourist assistance is to be
found at the DoT's regional office (Mon–Sat 8am–noon &
1–5pm; ☎ 062 991 0218) in the *Lantaka Hotel* (see opposite).

Travel agent There's a travel agent in the *Lantaka Hotel*
Services There are a number of banks with ATMs and
internet cafés in the centre of town.

ACCOMMODATION

Lantaka Hotel On the waterfront, Valderosa St ☎062 991 2033. An ageing concrete establishment with old-fashioned but spacious rooms, some with balconies, plus a restaurant, a pool and free wi-fi in the lobby. **P1200**

Marcian Business Hotel Mayor Cesar C. Climaco Ave ☎062 991 0005, ⓦmarcianhotels.com. Newish hotel in a good, central location with a/c, cable TV and wi-fi in the rooms. There's also a pool and restaurant. **P1300**

EATING

Alavar Seafood House Don Alfaro St, Brgy Tetuan ☎062 981 2483. Just 10min northeast of the city by tricycle (P40), *Alavar* is best known for its delicious crab dishes (from P200). Daily 11am–10pm.

Mano Mano Na Greenfield Restaurant Gov Ramos St, Brgy Santa Maria ☎062 992 4717. A cheap option with native-style barbecued meals served on bamboo trays (P80). Daily 9am–9pm.

8

MAP OF MANILA BAY, C.1902

Contexts

History

Philippine history is frequently dismissed as "beginning with the Spanish and ending with the Americans", yet the modern country is a result of many diverse influences – Malay, Chinese, Spanish and American – that have collided in the archipelago down the centuries. While the influence of Spain and the US is significant, recent scholarship has thrown light on the native and Islamic civilizations that flourished here before Magellan's arrival in 1521, and – thanks to new archeological discoveries – their highly developed trade links with the rest of Asia. Today one issue looms over all others: in 1960 the population of the Philippines was just 27 million; in 2014 it was estimated to have topped 100 million. Such explosive growth has meant that real economic gains made in the last fifty years have had a negligible effect on poverty and it remains, along with corruption, one of the country's biggest problems.

Prehistory

Human fossil remains found in Palawan suggest that humans first migrated to the Philippines across land bridges from Borneo during the Ice Age, some fifty thousand years ago. Carbon dating of fossilized human remains discovered at the Tabon Caves in Palawan showed so-called "**Tabon Man**" was living in the cave about 22,000 years ago. Deeper excavations of the caves indicated humans were in the area from 45,000 to 50,000 years ago.

The **Aeta** or Negritos, the country's indigenous people, are said to be descended from these first migrants. Successive migrations populated the islands through the centuries. **Malays** from Indonesia and the Malay peninsula streamed into the archipelago more than two thousand years ago, sailing across the Sulu Sea and settling first in the Visayas and southwestern Luzon. Their outrigger boats, equipped with lateen sails, each carried a family or clans led by a chief. Once ashore, they remained together in villages – known as barangays, after the name for their boats (*balangays*). The bulk of Filipinos today, at least in the Visayas and Mindanao, are descended from these Malay settlers.

Hindu kingdoms and Islamic sultanates

The early Malay communities gradually developed into a complex patchwork of kingdoms such as the Rajahnates of Butuan and Cebu, influenced by the powerful **Hindu empires** in Java and Sumatra. Several archeological finds hint at the sophistication and wealth of these early civilizations: the Laguna Copperplate Inscription, the earliest writing found in the Philippines, dates from around 900 AD and concerns a debt of gold in the Hindu-Malay state of Tondo, around today's Manila

900–1535	1380	1475
So-called "Classical States" period; the archipelago ruled by Hindu-influenced kingdoms	Karim ul' Makdum establishes the Islamic Sultanate of Sulu	Shariff Mohammed Kabungsuwan establishes the Islamic Sultanate of Maguindanao

. Equally enlightening is the Surigao Treasure, a trove of sensational gold objects up by accident in Mindanao in 1981 and dating from the tenth to thirteenth centuries. Also decorated with gold, the *Boxer Codex* manuscript, created in around 1595, includes fifteen drawings of Filipino natives of the sixteenth century. Finally, recently excavated Chinese shipwrecks loaded with porcelain prove that trade ties with China and the rest of Asia were extensive by the tenth century.

Contact with Arab traders, which reached its peak in the twelfth century, drew Sufis and missionaries who began the propagation of **Islam** in the Philippines. In 1380, the Arab scholar Karim ul' Makdum arrived in Jolo and established the Sultanate of Sulu. In 1475 Shariff Mohammed Kabungsuwan of Johor (Malaysia), married a native princess and established the Sultanate of Maguindanao, ruling large parts of Mindanao. During the reign of Sultan Bolkiah (1485–1521), the Sultanate of Brunei absorbed Tondo; by the time the Spanish arrived, Islam was established as far north as Luzon, where a great Muslim chief, Rajah Sulaiman II, ruled Manila.

Spanish rule

The archipelago's turbulent relationship with Spain began on April 24, 1521 when **Ferdinand Magellan** arrived in Cebu after sailing for four months across the vast ocean he named the Pacific. Magellan planted a wooden cross to claim the islands for Spain, baptizing a local king, Raja Humabon. **Lapu-Lapu** (1491–1542), a chief on the nearby island of Mactan, and Humabon's traditional enemy, resisted; in a subsequent skirmish known as the Battle of Mactan (see box, p.281), Magellan was killed and Spain's conquest of the Philippines was put on hold. Lapu-Lapu is now regarded as a Filipino hero.

Spanish conquistador Ruy López de Villalobos tried once again to claim the islands for Spain in 1543, but was driven out by the natives a year later – though not before naming the islands the Philippines, in honour of the future King Philip II. In 1564 **Miguel López de Legazpi** (1502–72), a minor Basque aristocrat, was chosen to lead a hazardous expedition to establish a permanent base in the Philippines, which the Spanish hoped would act as a wedge between Portugal and China. Legazpi sailed to the Philippines on board the *Capitana*, established a colony in Bohol in 1565 and then moved on to Cebu where he erected the first Spanish fort in the Philippines. But a series of misunderstandings – one involving the gift of a concubine that Legazpi piously refused – made the situation in Cebu perilous, and Legazpi looked for a more solid base.

In 1570 a Spanish expedition defeated Rajah Sulaiman III, and a year later Legazpi occupied his former base; a new Spanish capital – **Manila** – was established on the site of Sulaiman's old Islamic kingdom. Spanish conquistadors and friars zealously set about propagating **Catholicism**, building churches and bringing rural folk *debajo de las compañas* ("under the bells") into organized Spanish *pueblos*, establishing many of the country's towns and cities. They imposed a **feudal system**, concentrating populations under their control into new towns and estates, and resulting in numerous small revolts. Most of the Philippines, however, remained beyond the pale of the colonial authorities.

The Friarocracy

The islands were administered from the Spanish colony of **Mexico**, and its Spanish residents, especially those in Manila, grew prosperous and corrupt on the strength of

1485–1521	1521	1565
The Sultanate of Brunei extends Islamic rule as far as modern-day Manila	Ferdinand Magellan arrives in Cebu; killed fighting local chief Lapu-Lapu	Miguel López de Legazpi founds permanent Spanish settlement on Bohol

the galleon trade, a venture that involved re-exporting goods from China through Manila to Mexico. The Catholic Church, dreading change, did nothing to improve the subsistence economy, while in the capital, according to an early diarist, "the rich spend ten months of the year with nothing to do".

In theory, the Philippines was ruled by civil and military representatives of the King of Spain, but in practice it was the Catholic **friars** who ran the show. They derived their power from the enormous influence of the monastic orders – Augustinian, Dominican and Franciscan – which spanned the world like global corporations. Secular officials came and went, but the clergy stayed. Many friars ignored their vows of celibacy and sired children with local women. They exercised their power through a number of administrative functions, including setting budgets, conducting the parish census, screening recruits for the military and presiding over the police. There were cosmetic local administrations, but they could not act without the friars' consent.

It wasn't until the late eighteenth century that the ossification brought about by the colonial regime began to ease, the result of a series of external shocks. Attempts by the Dutch, Portuguese and Chinese to establish a presence in the archipelago were repelled, but the **British** managed to occupy Manila in 1762, raiding it in a sideshow to the **Seven Years' War**. They handed it back to Spain under the conditions of the Treaty of Paris, signed in 1763, but their easy victory served notice that the Philippines was vulnerable. In 1821 Mexico became independent, the galleon trade ended and the Philippines were administered directly from Madrid thereafter, ushering in a period of relatively enlightened colonial rule and prosperity.

The independence movement

The Spanish began to establish a free public school system in the Philippines in 1863, increasing the number of educated and Spanish-speaking Filipinos. The opening of the Suez Canal in 1869 (combined with the increasing use of steam power) cut travel times between Spain and the Philippines to weeks rather than months, and many of this new generation were able to continue their studies in Europe. They frequently returned with liberal ideas and talk of freedom.

A small **revolt** in Cavite in 1872 was quickly put down, but the anger and frustration Filipinos felt about colonial rule would not go away. Intellectuals such as Marcelo H. Del Pilar and Juan Luna were the spiritual founders of the independence movement, but it was the writings of a diminutive young doctor from Laguna province, **José Rizal** (1861–96), that provided the spark for the flame. His novel *Noli Me Tángere* was written while he was studying in Spain in the 1880s, and portrayed colonial rule as a cancer and the Spanish friars as fat, pompous fools. It was promptly banned by the Spanish, but distributed underground along with other inflammatory essays by Rizal and, later, his second novel, *El Filibusterismo*.

In 1892, Rizal returned to Manila and founded the movement La Liga Filipina, which espoused moderate reform, though never revolution. Its members swore oaths and took part in blood rites, and, innocuous as the movement was, the friars smelled sedition. Rizal was arrested and exiled to Dapitan on Mindanao. **Andrés Bonifacio** (1863–97) took over the reins by establishing the secret society known as the Katipunan or KKK (its full name was Kataastaasan, Kagalanggalang na Katipunan nang mga Anak ng Bayan, which means "Honorable, respectable sons and daughters of

1571	1570–1890s	1762
Legazpi founds Manila; formal Spanish control over the islands begins	The "Friarocracy" controls the Philippines during the colonial Spanish period; the Manila galleon trade links Asia with Spanish Mexico	British occupy Manila during the Seven Years' War.

nation"). In August 1896, an armed struggle for independence broke out, and Rizal ; accused of masterminding it. Rizal had, in fact, called the revolution "absurd and savage" and had earlier turned down an invitation from Bonifacio to participate. His trial lasted a day, one of the seven military judges concluding that Rizal's being a native must be considered "an aggravating factor". Rizal's Spanish military lawyer did little for him so he finally rose to defend himself. "I have sought political liberty," he said, "but never the freedom to rebel." He was duly found guilty and executed by firing squad in Manila in what is now known as Rizal Park on December 30, 1896. The night before he died he wrote *Mi Ultimo Adios*, a farewell poem to the country he loved (see p.65).

The Philippine Revolution

News of Rizal's martyrdom inflamed the uprising ignited by Bonifacio. Spanish officials deluded themselves, blaming it on a few troublemakers, but by now Bonifacio had decided violence was the only option and, with his young firebrand general, **Emilio Aguinaldo** (1869–1964), he called openly for a government "like that of the United States". Aguinaldo, a local government official from Cavite, had joined the Katipunan in 1894 and once the fighting started swiftly became the rebels' most successful commander. At the **Tejeros Convention** in 1897 Aguinaldo was elected president of the new Republic of the Philippines by his fellow *katipuneros* – when Bonifacio was offered a far lower position, he declared the election void in a fit of rage. Soon after, Aguinaldo had Bonifacio and his brothers arrested, sentenced in a mock trial and executed. At the end of 1897, the Spanish finalized a truce with Aguinaldo, the **Pact of Biak-na-Bato**: the Spanish would pay the rebels 800,000 pesos, half immediately, a quarter when they laid down their arms and the rest after a Te Deum to mark the armistice was chanted in Manila Cathedral. In exchange Aguinaldo agreed to go abroad. A cheque in his pocket, he sailed for Hong Kong, disavowing his rebellion.

However, in 1898, as a result of a dispute over Cuba, war broke out between the **United States** and Spain, and as an extension of it the US decided to expel Spain from the Philippines. The Spanish fleet was soundly beaten in Manila Bay by ships under the command of George Dewey, who on the morning of April 30, 1898, gave the famous order to his captain, "You may fire when you are ready, Gridley." The Filipinos fought on the side of the US, and when the battle was over General Aguinaldo, now back from Hong Kong having disavowed his disavowal of the rebellion, declared the Philippines independent; the First **Philippine Republic** was formally established by the **Malolos Constitution** in January 1899, with Aguinaldo as first president. The US, however, had other ideas and paid Spain US$20 million for its former possession. Having got rid of one colonizing power, Filipinos were now answerable to another.

American rule

After the Spanish left the country, the Filipinos continued to fight for independence in what's known as the **Philippine–American War**, a savage conflict that is virtually forgotten in the US today. Fighting began in early 1899 and lasted for three years, although skirmishes continued for another seven years, especially in Mindanao. US troops used tactics to pacify locals that they would later employ in Vietnam, such as strategic hamleting and scorched-earth, and by the end of February, Manila was ablaze

1821	1872	1887	1892
Mexico becomes independent; the Manila galleon trade ends.	Cavite Revolt	José Rizal's novel *Noli Me Tángere* published in Berlin	Andrés Bonifacio founds the Katipunan to fight for independence from Spain

as American troops took charge of the city. But crushing the Filipinos was not easy. The US forces, for all their superior firepower, were nagged by relentless heat, torrential rain and pervasive disease. Aguinaldo still commanded Filipino forces, though the intensity of the Manila assault had shocked him. Malolos, to the north of Manila, the seat of his revolutionary government, was overrun, but by June 1899 the Americans had become bogged down and controlled territory no more than 40km from Manila. The war degenerated into a **manhunt** for Aguinaldo, and when he was finally captured in March 1902 in Palanan on Luzon's east coast, the war ended officially three months later. After a brief internment, the wily general took an oath of allegiance to the US, was granted a pension from the US government and retired from public life until 1935 (see below). The war had resulted in the death of at least 600,000 Filipinos and 4234 Americans; exact records were not kept of Filipino casualties.

From the beginning, Washington was divided over how much independence its erstwhile charge should be given, what measures would be in place to ensure the protection of US interests there and who would be president.

Benevolent assimilation

When the Philippine–American War ended, American teachers fanned out across the country to begin President McKinley's policy of **"benevolent assimilation"**, and soon became known as Thomasites, after the ship on which they had arrived. The spread of schools has been applauded by historians as America's single greatest achievement in the Philippines. The Thomasites took to their task with apostolic fervour and Filipinos quickly achieved the highest literacy rate in Southeast Asia.

The American administration in the Philippines, guided by Washington, sought to inculcate Filipinos with American ethics, to turn the Philippines into a stable, prosperous, self-confident model of democracy in a developing country. Filipinos learned to behave, dress and eat like Americans, sing American songs and speak Americanized English. American educators decided that teaching Filipinos in their many own languages would require too many textbooks, so American English became the lingua franca of the Philippines. Meanwhile, the debate was still raging over what form of government the Philippines should have. It wasn't until 1935 that a bill was passed in Washington allowing President Roosevelt to recognize a new Philippine constitution and the ten-year transition status of **"Commonwealth of the Philippines"** – autonomous but not completely independent. Presidential elections were held in September of that year and won by **Manuel Quezon** (1878–1944), leading light among a new breed of postwar politicians, who soundly beat Aguinaldo who had come out of retirement. (Aguinaldo was to cooperate with the Japanese in World War II, but after briefly being jailed by the Americans a second time, lived to see Philippine independence.)

World War II

One of the questions about the new Commonwealth was a military one: could it defend itself? Quezon realized how vulnerable the archipelago was and invited the US commander of the country, **General Douglas MacArthur**, to become military adviser to the autonomous regime. MacArthur accepted, demanding US$33,000 a year and an air-conditioned suite in the *Manila Hotel*.

1896	1897	1898
José Rizal executed by the Spanish in Manila; the Philippine Revolution breaks out	Bonifacio is executed by rival rebel leader Emilio Aguinaldo	Spanish–American War; the US navy destroys the Spanish fleet in Manila Bay

ostilities broke out in the Philippines within minutes of the attack on **Pearl Harbor** December 1941, as waves of Japanese bombers targeted military bases in Cavite and at Clark. MacArthur appealed for help from Washington, but it never came. He declared Manila an open city to save its population and prepared for a tactical retreat to Corregidor, the island citadel at the mouth of Manila Bay, from where he would supervise the defence of the strategic Bataan peninsula. Quezon, now increasingly frail from tuberculosis, went with him.

The Philippines, especially Manila, underwent heavy **bombardment** during World War II and casualties were high. Japanese troops landed on Luzon and occupied Manila on January 2, 1942. MacArthur and Quezon abandoned Corregidor when it became clear the situation was hopeless, but after arriving in Darwin, Australia, MacArthur promised Filipinos, "I have come through and I shall return."

When he fled, MacArthur left behind soldiers engaged in a protracted and bloody struggle for **Bataan**. When the peninsula inevitably fell to Japanese forces, Corregidor was next. The Japanese launched an all-out assault on May 5, 1942, and the island, defended by starving and demoralized troops huddled in damp tunnels, capitulated within days. During the notorious Bataan Death March that followed, as many as ten thousand Americans and Filipinos died from disease, malnutrition and wanton brutality. The exact figure is unknown even today.

Two years of **Japanese military rule** followed. Frustrated in their efforts to quell popular opposition and a nascent guerrilla movement, the Japanese turned increasingly to brutality, beheading innocent victims and displaying their bodies as an example. The guerrillas multiplied, however, until their various movements comprised two hundred thousand men. The strongest force was the People's Anti-Japanese Army, in Tagalog the Hukbalahap or the **Huks** for short, most of them poor sharecroppers and farm workers looking for any opportunity to improve their abysmal lot. MacArthur, meanwhile, kept his promise to return. On October 19, 1944, with Quezon at his side, he waded ashore at Leyte, forcing a showdown with the Japanese and driving across the island to the port of Ormoc. The Huks later helped the US liberate Luzon, acting as guides in the push towards Manila and freeing Americans from Japanese prison camps. No guerrilla exploited his wartime adventures more than an ambitious young lawyer from Ilocos who now had his sights set on entering the political arena in Manila: **Ferdinand Marcos**.

The Marcos years

The Philippines received full **independence** from the US on July 4, 1946, when Manuel Roxas, an experienced politician from Panay, was sworn in as the first President of the Republic. His government marred by corruption and conflict with the now outlawed Huks, Roxas died of a heart attack in 1948 and was replaced by his Ilocano vice-president Elpidio Quirino. The 1950s were something of a golden age for the Philippines, with the presidency of Ramón Magsaysay (1953–57) considered a high point: politics was largely corruption-free, trade and industry boomed and the country was ranked Asia's second cleanest and best governed after Japan. In the early 1960s, however, the Liberal government of Diosdado Macapagal was crippled by Nacionalista Party opposition in Congress. It was in these years that **Ferdinand Marcos** came to power, promoting himself as a force for unification and reform.

1899	1899–1902	1935
Philippine Republic proclaimed with Emilio Aguinaldo president, but Spain cedes the Philippines to the US	Philippine–American War; US introduces "benevolent assimilation"	The Commonwealth of the Philippines is established: Manuel Quezon is the first president

THE IRON BUTTERFLY

Imelda Remedios Visitación was born on July 2, 1929, in the little town of Tolosa in Leyte. Her youth was troubled, her parents always quarrelling, separating and reconciling, her feckless father unable to hold down a job. Aged 23 she left Leyte for Manila with just five pesos in her purse, seeking her fortune. Her break came in 1953, when a magazine editor featured her face on his cover; she then entered a beauty contest and won the title of **Miss Manila**. Ferdinand Marcos later recounted that he saw the magazine picture and told friends, "I'm getting married." He arranged an introduction and, after an eleven-day courtship, proposed.

Following his 1965 election victory, Marcos said of Imelda, "She was worth a million votes." In fact, Imelda had cleverly inveigled tycoon Fernando Lopez into standing as Marcos's vice president, bringing with him his family's immeasurable fortune. Once the election was won, Imelda announced she would be "more than a mere decorative figure" and in 1966 made her international debut when she sang to Lyndon Johnson at a White House dinner. "A blessing not only to her country, but also to the world", gushed a US newspaper columnist.

Imelda believed that nothing succeeds like excess and laid on lavish fiestas for every visiting dignitary. She also posed as a patron of the arts flying in international stars such as Margot Fonteyn. Her husband later made her **governor of Manila** with a brief to turn the city into a showpiece. She set about the task with gusto, spending P37 million on the Coconut Palace (see p.70) and at least P100 million on the Manila Film Center (see box, p.70). As well as a patron of the arts, the First Lady also appointed herself the country's roving envoy, relentlessly roaming the world on jumbo jets "borrowed" from Philippine Airlines to meet the likes of Fidel Castro, Emperor Hirohito and Chairman Mao. A prodigious social climber, she pursued Rockefellers and Fords, and dreamed of betrothing her daughter Imee to Prince Charles.

Throughout much of the 1980s Imelda went on notoriously profligate **shopping binges** to New York and Los Angeles, spending millions of dollars on grotesque art, jewellery and the occasional apartment. In Geneva, another favourite haunt, she spent US$12 million in jewellery in a single day. After her husband's downfall in 1986, Imelda became deeply upset at reports that three thousand pairs of **shoes** had been found inside the Malacañang Palace, claiming she had only accumulated them to promote the Philippine shoe industry in her trips abroad. The shoes became the most potent symbol of her mad spending.

Imelda returned to Manila in 1991, and in a shocking confirmation of her continued popularity in some quarters, she was elected Congresswoman of Leyte (her home province), four years later; in 2010 she was elected to represent the second district of Ilocos Norte, replacing her son Ferdinand Marcos, Jr. (who was elected to the Senate), and was re-elected to the same post three years later. Various corruption cases against Imelda have dragged on painfully through the courts over the years, but her nickname – the **Iron Butterfly**, for her thick-skinned bravura – is surely well deserved.

Marcos (1917–89) was born in Sarrat, Ilocos Norte. A brilliant young lawyer who had successfully defended himself against a murder charge, he was elected to the Philippine House of Representatives in 1949, to the Senate in 1959 and became president in 1965 on the Nacionalista Party ticket, defeating incumbent Macapagal. Marcos's first term as president was innovative and inspirational. He invigorated both populace and bureaucracy, embarking on a huge **infrastructure** programme and unifying scattered islands with a network of roads, bridges, railways and ports.

1942	1944	1946
Japan defeats US forces in the Philippines in World War II.	US forces retake the Philippines	Republic of the Philippines becomes fully independent; Manuel Roxas first president

ring these early years of the Marcos presidency, before the madness of martial law,
st Lady Imelda (see box, p.443) busied herself with social welfare and cultural
projects that complemented Marcos's work in economics and foreign affairs.

Martial law

In 1969 Marcos became the first Filipino president to be re-elected for a **second term**.
The country's problems, however, were grave. Poverty, social inequality and rural
stagnation were rife. Marcos was trapped between the entrenched oligarchy, which
controlled Congress, and a rising communist insurgency that traced its roots back to
the Huks (see p.442), fuelled mostly by landless, frustrated peasants led by the
articulate and patriarchal José Marie Sison (b.1939), who lives today in exile in the
Netherlands. The country was roiled by student, labour and peasant unrest, much of it
stoked by communists and their fledgling military wing, the **New People's Army**.
Marcos used the protests, and the spurious excuse of several attempts to liquidate him,
to perpetuate his hold on power. On September 21, 1972, he declared **martial law**,
arresting **Benigno "Ninoy" Aquino** (1932–83) and other opposition leaders. A curfew
was imposed and Congress was suspended. Marcos announced he was pioneering a
Third World approach to democracy through his "New Society" and his new political
party the New Society Movement. His regime became a byword for profligacy,
corruption and repression.

The **Mindanao** problem also festered. After the Jabidah Massacre in 1968, when
Filipino troops executed 28 Muslim recruits who refused to take part in a hopelessly
misconceived invasion of Sabah, Muslims took up arms against the government,
forming the **Moro National Liberation Front** (MNLF; see box, p.403). Marcos made few
real efforts to quell the insurgency in the south, knowing it would give him another
unassailable excuse for martial law. The US became worried that the longer Marcos's
excesses continued the faster the communist insurgency would spread, threatening
their military bases in the islands, which had long been of mutual benefit to both the
US and the Philippines.

The People Power Revolution (EDSA)

By the 1980s it looked as if Marcos would never relinquish power or martial law – with
his American allies seemingly unwilling or unable to influence the dictator, it took a
real ground-roots movement to oust him.

The revolution was sparked by the martyrdom of **Ninoy Aquino**, who by the spring of
1980 had been languishing in jail for seven years. Aquino was released from jail on
condition he went into exile in the US. In 1983 he decided to return and when he
emerged from his plane at Manila airport on August 21, 1983, he was assassinated. The
country was outraged. In a snap election called in panic by Marcos on February 7,
1986, the opposition united behind Aquino's widow, **Corazón Aquino** (1933–2009),
and her running mate Salvador Laurel. On February 25, both Marcos and Aquino
claimed victory and were sworn in at separate ceremonies. Aquino, known by the
people as Cory became a rallying point for change and was backed by the Catholic
Church in the form of **Archbishop Cardinal Jaime Sin** (1928–2005), who urged people
to take to the streets; the **People Power Revolution** (also known as the EDSA
Revolution) had begun.

1965	**1969**	**1972**	**1981**
Ferdinand Marcos becomes president	Marcos is re-elected amidst allegations of electoral fraud	Marcos declares martial law	Martial law is lifted; Marcos wins presidential elections again

When Marcos's key allies saw which way the wind was blowing and deserted him, the game was up. Defence Minister Juan Ponce Enrile and Deputy Chief of Staff of the Armed Forces, General **Fidel Ramos** (b.1928) later to become president, announced a coup d'état. The US prevaricated, but eventually told Marcos to "cut and cut cleanly". Ferdinand and Imelda fled from the Malacañang Palace to Clark in helicopters provided by the CIA, and from there into exile in Hawaii, where Ferdinand died in 1989. Conservative estimates of their plunder put the figure at US$10 billion, US$600 million of it spirited into Swiss bank accounts – rumours persist that Marcos had also appropriated a hoard of Japanese war loot dubbed "Yamashita's Gold", though this has never been proven. Back in Manila, the people stormed through the gates of the Malacañang Palace.

The return of democracy

Having ousted Marcos, hopes were high for the presidency of **Cory Aquino**, but she never managed to bring the powerful feudal families or the armed forces under her control. **Land reform** was eagerly awaited by the country's landless masses, but when Aquino realized reform would also involve her own family's haciendas in Tarlac, she quietly shelved the idea: most of the country's farmers remain beholden to landlords today. Aquino survived seven coup attempts and made little headway in improving life for the majority of Filipinos who were – and still are – living below the poverty line. The communist New People's Army (NPA) emerged once again as a threat, and human rights abuses continued.

Aquino also had to deal with another thorny issue: the presence of **US military bases** in the country; Clark Air Base and Subic Naval Base. Public opinion had been turning against the bases for some time, with many seeing them as a colonial imposition. In 1987 Congress voted not to renew the bases treaty and the US withdrawal, set for 1991, was hastened by the portentous eruption of **Mount Pinatubo** (see box, p.123), which scattered ash over both Clark and Subic, causing millions of dollars of damage to US aircraft and ships. The pullout made jobless six hundred thousand Filipinos who had depended on the bases for employment either directly or indirectly.

In **Mindanao**, the Aquino administration had mixed success. The **Moro National Liberation Front** started a war for independence in the 1970s that dragged on until 1987, when it accepted the offer of autonomy instead – the Autonomous Region in Muslim Mindanao, or ARMM, was created in 1990 (see box, p.403). However, the more radical **Moro Islamic Liberation Front** (MILF) refused to accept the 1987 accord and continued fighting.

Ultimately, Aquino's only legacy was that she maintained some semblance of a democracy, which was something for her successor, **Fidel Ramos**, to build on. President Ramos took office on July 1, 1992 and announced plans to create jobs, revitalize the economy and reduce the burdensome foreign debt of US$32 billion. But the first thing he had to do was establish a reliable electricity supply. The country was being paralysed for hours every day by **power cuts**, and no multinational companies wanted to invest their hard-earned money under such difficult conditions. Ramos's success in breathing new life into the ailing energy sector – at least in Manila and many cities – laid the foundations for a moderate influx of foreign investment, for industrial parks and new

1983	1986	1989
Benigno Aquino returns to the Philippines, but is assassinated as he leaves his plane	People Power Revolution (aka EDSA Revolution) sees Marcos flee the country; Corazon Aquino becomes president	Ferdinand Marcos dies in exile in Hawaii

manufacturing facilities. The economy picked up, but foreign debt was crippling and tax collection was so lax that the government had nothing in the coffers to fall back on. Infrastructure improved marginally and new roads and transit systems began to take shape. Ramos also liberalized the banking sector and travelled extensively to promote the Philippines abroad. Most Filipinos view his years in office as a success, although when he stepped down at the end of his six-year term, poverty and crime were still rife.

Erap: scandal and EDSA II

Ramos's successor, former vice president **Joseph Estrada** (b.1937) was a former tough-guy film actor with pomaded hair and a cowboy swagger who is known universally in the islands as **Erap**, a play on the slang word *pare*, which means friend or buddy. Estrada had a folksy, macho charm that appealed to the masses and was elected to the presidency in 1998 against politicians of greater stature on a **pro-poor** platform. His rallying cry was *Erap para sa mahirap*, or "Erap for the poor". He promised food security, jobs, mass housing, education and health for all, but got off to a troubled start in the Malacañang Palace, plagued by a series of tawdry scandals that he swept aside. More seriously, accusations surfaced in the media of a lack of direction and a return to the **cronyism** of the Marcos years. Erap bumbled his way from one mismanaged disaster to the next. The **economy** was floundering and every day there was some new allegation, always denied by Erap with a combative flourish, of mismanagement, favours for friends or plain incompetence.

The Philippine Center for Investigative Journalism (PCIJ) began its research into Estrada's wealth in the first quarter of 2000. Its report listed seventeen pieces of **real estate** worth P2 billion that had been acquired by Estrada and his various family members since 1998. Some, it was alleged, were for his favourite mistress, former actress Laarni Enriquez. Later in 2000 Luis Singson, governor of Ilocos Sur, alleged that Estrada had received P500 million in **gambling payoffs** from an illegal numbers game known as *jueteng* (pronounced "wet-eng"). On November 13, 2000, Joseph Estrada became the first president of the Philippines to be **impeached**, setting the stage for a trial in the Senate that would hold the nation in its grip for weeks. When the Senate let him off, people began gathering on the streets to demand the president's resignation. The church and its leader, Cardinal Jaime Sin again became involved and urged Estrada to step down. Half a million people gathered at the EDSA shrine in Ortigas in scenes reminiscent of those before the downfall of Marcos – the four-day demonstrations were later dubbed **EDSA II**. Fifty thousand militants massed near Malacañang Palace, preparing to kick out the president by force if necessary. On the evening of Friday January 19, 2001, cabinet members saw the cause was lost and began to defect.

The decisive blow came when the **military** announced it had withdrawn its support for Estrada. The next morning he was ushered ignominiously from the Malacañang Palace and vice president Gloria Macapagal-Arroyo was promptly sworn in as the fourteenth President of the Republic of the Philippines. Anti-Erap forces hailed what they deemed a noble moral victory. But a nagging question remained. Estrada had been voted into office by a landslide of 10.7 million people and removed by a predominantly middle-class movement of five hundred thousand who took to the streets. His impeachment trial had been aborted and he had been found guilty of nothing.

1991	1992	1996	1998
The US abandons Clark Air Base after the Mount Pinatubo eruption smothers it with ash; Imelda Marcos returns to the Philippines	Fidel Ramos becomes president; US naval base at Subic Bay closed	Peace agreement reached with Muslim separatist group, the Moro National Liberation Front	Joseph Estrada elected president

THE GREATEST AND THE PACMAN

Boxing has been a Filipino passion for over one hundred years. Ferdinand Marcos capitalized on the nation's love of the sport by using government money to finance the "**Thrilla in Manila**" in 1975, a notoriously brutal encounter between Muhammad Ali and Joe Frazier often ranked as one of the greatest fights of twentieth-century boxing. Fought at the Araneta Coliseum in Quezon City, Ali won in the 15th and final round. The beneficent Marcos even stumped up the cash for the fight's multimillion-dollar purse.

Filipinos have never made it in the high-profile heavyweight game, but in the lighter divisions they've excelled. In recent years, one name stands out in particular: **Manny "the Pacman" Pacquiao** (b.1978), the poor boy from Mindanao who became world super featherweight champion, made a movie, made millions and was the first boxer in history to win ten world titles in eight different weight divisions (he's current super welterweight champ). In probably his most famous bout, he defeated Oscar De La Hoya in Las Vegas in 2008, in what was dubbed the "Dream Match". In 2010 Pacquiao was elected to the House of Representatives, representing the province of Sarangani, fuelling rumours about his **political ambition**; it's conceivable he could stand for higher office once he retires from boxing.

Macapagal-Arroyo: the politics of the elite

The presidency of **Gloria Macapagal-Arroyo** (b.1947) proved slightly less dramatic than her predecessors, but just as divisive. During her two terms in office, Macapagal-Arroyo made great play of her economic prowess and the fact that she was an assiduous administrator, not a flamboyant but empty figurehead. The first years of her presidency were solid if unspectacular, her main priority simply to survive and bring some level of stability. The House of Representatives and Senate were bitterly divided along pro- and anti-Estrada lines, with the two main parties unable to agree on anything. It was not until 2007 that Estrada was finally found guilty of plunder, but was promptly pardoned by the president.

After winning her second term in 2004, things started to unravel for Macapagal-Arroyo; she was accused of vote-rigging, though two attempts to impeach her failed. In 2006 an army plot led to a state of emergency being implemented across the country. On the economy – her strong suit – the president could claim some success, with GDP growth rates over five percent a year the strongest in decades, though critics claimed the figures were inaccurate, and in any case, had failed to improve the lives of poorer citizens.

In Mindanao, things looked even worse. A new terrorist organization, **Abu Sayyaf**, emerged on Basilan Island, thought to be responsible for the bombing of *Superferry 14* in February 2004, which sank with 116 dead. In 2008 the Moro Islamic Liberation Front launched new attacks on government troops after the Supreme Court ruled that a deal offering them large areas of the south went against the constitution. Finally, 57 people (including 34 journalists) were murdered in 2009 in what was dubbed the **Maguindinao Massacre**, part of a local "clan" war at election time.

Macapagal-Arroyo's term finished in 2010, marred by claims of cronyism, extrajudicial killings, torture and illegal arrests; corruption still ran unchecked, and the gap between the impoverished and a thin layer of super-wealthy had grown ever wider, with the dirt-poor growing in numbers and wretchedness, accounting

2001	2005	2009	2010
EDSA II: Estrada is replaced by his vice-president, Gloria Macapagal-Arroyo	The influential cardinal Jaime Sin dies	Maguindanao massacre; 57 people killed in Mindanao	Benigno "Noynoy" Aquino becomes president; Imelda Marcos is elected to Congress

probably for sixty percent of the population of nearly one hundred million. After standing down as president, Macapagal-Arroyo defied convention and remained in politics. She currently serves as member of the House of Representatives for the second district of Pampanga.

The return of the Aquinos

The presidential election of 2010 was typically dramatic. In 2009, Cory Aquino died from colon cancer, aged 76, sending the country into a five-day period of deep mourning – the former president was genuinely loved. Following her funeral many voters appealed to Cory's son, senator **Benigno Aquino III** ("Noynoy Aquino" or just "PNoy"; b.1960), to stand for president; the "Noynoy Phenomenon" posed a special dilemma because Aquino's Liberal Party had already chosen a candidate for the presidency, Manuel "Mar" Roxas (grandson of the first president), and the former leader's son had until then not been expected to run. Driven by nostalgia as much as politics, support for Benigno Aquino grew so fierce that Roxas withdrew from the race. Aquino's rival in the election was none other than Joseph Estrada, the convicted and now-pardoned ex-president, who seemed as feisty as ever. After a keenly fought campaign Aquino became president after winning 42.08 percent of the vote; Estrada came second with 26.25 percent.

Benigno Aquino is a fascinating character, respected for his family connections, obsessed over in the tabloids for his love life (the president is the first to be a bachelor), a teetotaller, and self-styled fighter of corruption; one of his first acts was to establish a truth commission to investigate corruption allegations against Macapagal-Arroyo. He's also made some progress in Mindanao: the island has been generally peaceful since 2010 and Aquino signed a **peace deal** with the MILF in 2014. In return for finally withdrawing their demands for independence, a new Muslim autonomous entity called **Bangsamoro** is to be created by 2016 (replacing the Autonomous Region of Muslim Mindanao).

More controversially, Aquino supports the promotion of contraceptive use enshrined in the **Reproductive Health Bill**, which in various forms was debated in Congress for years and finally passed in 2012: however, in 2013 the Supreme Court voted to delay implementation of the law until various petitions calling for its repeal can be heard. In a sign of what he's up against, the vice chairman of the Catholic Bishops' Conference of the Philippines said that Aquino's support for the bill was a declaration of "open war"– this despite a huge body of research linking a fast-growing population and poverty.

The vulnerable state of much of the population was highlighted in November 2013 when Typhoon Haiyan (known as **Yolanda** in the Philippines) devastated the Visayas, killing at least 6268 people – bodies were still being found three months later (see box, p.359). Full recovery will take many years, with places like Tacloban City virtually destroyed and infrastructure shattered throughout the region. Aquino's administration was heavily criticized for its slow reaction and in the following weeks over four million people were displaced. Damages are estimated to be around P40 billion.

2012	2012	2013
Peace plan signed with the Muslim rebel Moro Islamic Liberation Front	Congress votes for state-funded contraception	Typhoon Yolanda devastates the central part of the country, killing over six thousand

Religious beliefs

Religious belief – among Muslims as well as Christians – is genuine and deeply held all over the Philippines. Though the nation remains predominantly Roman Catholic, parts of Mindanao are one hundred percent Islamic, and even traditional Catholic communities have been shaken up by new Catholic movements such as El Shaddai. Perhaps most surprising has been the success of Protestant churches such as Iglesia ni Cristo, which has branches all over the archipelago.

Catholicism

The Philippines is one of only two **predominantly Catholic** nations in Asia (the other being East Timor) – more than eighty percent of the population is Roman Catholic, with around ten percent Protestant. In addition to the Christian majority, there is a Muslim minority of between five and ten percent, concentrated on the southern islands of Mindanao and Sulu.

Yet to describe the Philippines as a Roman Catholic country is an over-simplification. Elements of tribal belief absorbed into Catholicism have resulted in a form of "**folk Catholicism**" that manifests itself in various homespun observances – a folk healer might use Catholic liturgy mixed with native rituals, or suited entrepreneurs might be seen scattering rice around their premises to ensure their ventures are profitable. And the infamous **re-enactments of the Crucifixion** held near San Fernando, Pampanga, every year (see box, p.121) are frowned upon by the official church. Even the **Chinese** minority has been influential in colouring Filipino Catholicism with the beliefs and practices of Buddhism, Confucianism and Taoism; many Catholic Filipinos believe in the balance of *yin* and *yang*, and that time is cyclical in nature.

The new Catholic movements

Today, the supremacy of the Catholic Church in the Philippines is being challenged by a variety of Christian sects. The largest of these is **El Shaddai**, established by lay preacher Mike Velarde on his weekly Bible-quoting radio show in the 1980s. Known to his followers as Brother Mike, Velarde has captured the imagination of poor Catholics, many of whom feel isolated from the mainstream Church. Velarde started preaching in colloquial and heavily accented Tagalog at huge open-air gatherings every weekend on Roxas Boulevard – the movement moved into a purpose-built P1 billion "House of Prayer" in Paranaque, Metro Manila, in 2009. Velarde tends to wear screamingly loud, made-to-measure suits and outrageous bow ties, but his message is straightforward: give to the Lord and He will return it to you tenfold. He now has over eight million followers, most of whom suffer from *sakit sa bulsa*, or "ailment of the pocket", but are nevertheless happy to pay ten percent of their income to become card-carrying members of the flock. Brother Mike's relationship with the mainstream Catholic Church is uneasy. His relationship with politicians is not. With so many followers hanging on his every word, Brother Mike is a potent political ally and few candidates for high office are willing to upset him. In the 1998 elections, Brother Mike backed Joseph Estrada, which was a significant factor in the former movie actor's initial success. The **Neocatechumenal Way**, a Catholic movement that started in Spain in the 1960s, also has a very large and expanding presence in the Philippines.

THE ASWANG WHO CAME TO DINNER

Heard the one about the pretty young housewife in a remote Visayan village who was possessed by the spirit of a jealous witch? Or the poor woman from a Manila shantytown who had taken to flying through the barangay, terrorizing her neighbours? These are stories from the pages of Manila's daily tabloid newspapers, reported as if they actually happened. Foreign visitors greet news of the latest barangay haunting with healthy cynicism, but when you are lying in your creaking nipa hut in the pitch dark of a moonless evening, it's not hard to see why so many Filipinos grow up embracing strange stories about creatures that inhabit the night. Even urbane professionals, when returning to the barangay of their childhood on holiday, can be heard muttering the incantation *tabi tabi lang-po* as they walk through paddy field or forest. Meaning "please let us pass safely", it's a request to the spirits and dwarves that might be lying in wait.

Most Filipino **spirits** are not the abstract souls of Western folklore who live in a netherworld; they are corporeal entities who live in trees or hang around the jeepney station, waiting to inflict unspeakable horrors on those who offend them. The most feared and widely talked about creature of Philippine folklore is the **aswang**; hundreds of cheesy films have been made about the havoc they wreak and hundreds of *aswang* sightings have been carried by the tabloid press. By day the *aswang* is a beautiful woman. The only way to identify her is by looking into her eyes at night, when they turn red. The *aswang* kills her victims as they sleep; threading her long tongue through the gaps in the floor or walls and inserting it into one of the body's orifices to suck out the internal organs.

Other creatures on the bogeyman list include the arboreal *tikbalang*, which has the head of a nag and the body of a man, and specializes in the abduction of virgins. Then there's the *duwende*, an elderly, grizzled dwarf who lurks in the forest and can predict the future, and the *engkanto*, who hides in trees and throws dust in the faces of passers-by, giving them permanently twisted lips.

Protestantism and the new religious movements

Some of the fastest growing religious movements in the Philippines are actually Protestant. One of the candidates in the 2004 and 2010 presidential elections (he came last both times), Eddie Villanueva established the charismatic **Jesus is Lord Church** in 1978, which he claims has some six million members, with branches in Asia, Europe and North America.

You'll see the distinctive fairy-tale spires of **Iglesia ni Cristo** churches throughout the Philippines, an independent, purely Filipino movement founded by Felix Manalo in 1914 (the movement is currently run by his grandson, Eduardo V. Manalo). Iglesia ni Cristo is explicitly anti-Catholic in its beliefs (the doctrine of the Trinity is rejected, for example) and is very influential during elections. Membership is estimated to be over three million but is probably much higher.

One of the churches most successful at expanding overseas is the **Pentecostal Missionary Church of Christ**, founded in 1973 and based in Marikina City. **The United Methodist Church** in the Philippines is an umbrella group for around one million Methodists in the country, while there are about twenty different **Baptist** groups in the islands, at least half a million **Mormons** and half a million **Seventh-Day Adventists**.

Another well-known loose affiliation of groups, the **Rizalistas**, have only a tenuous connection with standard Christian doctrine. All regard José Rizal (see p.439) as the second son of God and a reincarnation of Christ, and some hold Mount Banahaw (see p.198) in Quezon province to be sacred, regularly attending pilgrimages to the mountain.

Islam

Islam spread north to the Philippines from Indonesia and Malaysia in the fourteenth century, and by the time the Spanish arrived it was firmly established on Mindanao and Sulu, with outposts on Cebu and Luzon.

Islam remains a very dominant influence in the southern Philippines (25 percent of Mindanao's population is Muslim), and Muslims have added cultural character to the nation, with Filipino Christians expressing admiration over their warlike defiance of colonization. However, many Muslims feel they have become strangers in their own country, ignored by the Manila-centric government and marginalized by people resettled in Mindanao from Luzon; the **Autonomous Region in Muslim Mindanao** was established in 1990, the only region that has its own government (see box, p.403).

While all Filipino Muslims follow the basic tenets of Islam, their religion has absorbed a number of indigenous elements, such as making offerings to spirits which are known as **diwatas**. A spirit known as **Bal-Bal** is believed in among many Muslim tribes; with the body of a man and the wings of a bird, Bal-Bal is credited with the habit of eating out the livers of unburied bodies. In Jolo and Tawi-Tawi, Muslims use mediums to contact the dead, while many Muslim groups trade amulets, wearing them as necklaces to ward off ill fortune.

Muslim **women** are freer in the Philippines than in many Islamic countries, and have traditionally played a prominent role in everything from war to ceremonies. "The women of Jolo", wrote a Spanish infantryman in the eighteenth century, "prepare for combat in the same manner as their husbands and brothers and are more desperate and determined than the men. With her child suspended to her breast or slung across her back, the Moro woman enters the fight with the ferocity of a panther."

Filipino culture

In *El Filibusterismo*, José Rizal worried that Filipinos would become "a people without a soul". It's a theme that has been much developed by travel writers ever since, from Pico Iyer's description of "lush sentimentality" and Filipina "obsession" with high-school romance and pageants in *Video Night in Kathmandu*, to Michael Palin observing that American interest in the country is "unashamedly obvious" in *Full Circle*. Yet there is a lot more to Philippine culture than cover bands, girlie bars and endless beauty pageants. Over the years Filipino writers, rappers, film-makers and artists have developed distinctive styles that incorporate elements of all the nation's disparate cultural elements.

Fine arts

Classical painting in the Philippines goes back to the Spanish period, but there are two acknowledged Filipino masters: **Juan Luna** (1859–99) and **Félix Hidalgo** (1855–1913). Both artists helped shine attention on the Philippines after submitting paintings to the 1884 Exposición General de Bellas Artes in Madrid. Luna's huge and drama-laced *Spolarium* (1884) is perhaps the most famous painting in the Philippines (on display at the National Art Gallery; see p.66), while his equally admired *The Blood Compact* graces the Malacañang Palace. Luna spent most of his career in Europe and died in Hong Kong, and he's best known today for painting literary and historical scenes. Hidalgo also spent much of his career in Europe and died in Spain, creating haunting works such *Las Virgenes Cristianas Expuestas al Populacho* ("The Christian Virgins Exposed to the Populace") and *Laguna Estigia* ("The Styx").

With the end of Spanish rule and a growing sense of independence in the twentieth century, Filipino painters were more content to develop their craft at home. **Fernando Amorsolo** (1892–1972) studied at the University of the Philippines' School of Fine Arts and gained prominence during the 1920s and 1930s for popularizing images of Philippine landscapes and demure rural Filipinas; his *Rice Planting* (1922) became one of the most popular images of the American period, and he became the first "National Artist" in 1972. Meanwhile, **Victorio Edades** (1895–1985) introduced Modernism to the Philippines with *The Builders* (1928), a style he'd developed in the US in direct contrast to Amorsolo. He went on to establish the UST College of Fine Arts in the 1930s, a bastion of avant-garde art.

World War II changed the way artists saw the world: Amorsolo's pastoral scenes gave way to the grimmer, urban images of **Vicente Manansala** (1910–1982), as portrayed in works like *Jeepneys* (1951). Other notable late twentieth-century painters include **José T. Joya** (1931–95), the Filipino abstract artist, and **Fernando Zóbel de Ayala y Montojo** (1924–84), a Modernist painter who also developed his craft in the US.

The **contemporary art scene** in the Philippines is dynamic and eclectic, fed in part by exceptionally good art schools in the capital, with popular current forms and styles covering everything from installation art and video to realism and street art. One of the most highly acclaimed contemporary artists is **Ronald Ventura**, whose *Grayground Painting* fetched almost P47 million at auction in 2011, making it the most expensive Philippine painting ever sold. Pilipinas Street Plan (ⓦpilipinastreetplan.blogspot.com) and the Juju Bag (ⓦthejujubag.wordpress.com) are **art communities** that showcase street art, graffiti, posters, stickers and installations, while **Rocking Society through Alternative Education** (Rock Ed; ⓦrockedphilippines.org) has produced some cutting-edge art through its work with schools and prisons. One of the hottest visual artists today is **Maya Muñoz**, whose work is often displayed in Manila's galleries.

Film

Although film-making has a distinguished history in the Philippines, and locally made movies (and their stars) remain popular, they remain a long way behind their Hollywood counterparts in terms of audience and income.

Early movies arrived in the Philippines in the late 1890s, but the first genuinely Filipino film is credited to **Jose Nepumuceno**, the "Father of Philippine Movies", who made a version of a popular play *Dalagang Bukid* ("Country Maiden") in 1919. The domestic film industry didn't really get going until the 1950s, when four big studios (Sampaguita, LVN, Premiere and Lebran) churned out hundreds of movies such as Gerardo de Leon's *Ifugao* (1954) and Manuel Conde's *Genghis Khan* (1952). Despite Gerardo de Leon's lauded adaptations of the Rizal novels *Noli Me Tángere* (1961) and *El Filibusterismo* (1962), the following decade was much poorer creatively and all four studios eventually closed.

Despite censorship during the Marcos years, **avant-garde** movie-making flourished in the 1970s, with Lino Brocka's *The Claws of Light* (1975) considered by many critics to be the greatest Philippine film ever made, and Kidlat Tahimik's *Mababangong Bangungot* ("Perfumed Nightmare") winning the International Critic's Prize at the Berlin Film Festival of 1977. Brocka's *This Is My Country*, which tackles the issue of labour union control under Marcos, was entered into the 1984 Cannes Film Festival.

The late 1980s and 1990s is regarded as a weaker period, but since the turn of the century **independent Filipino movies** have been undergoing something of a renaissance, in part thanks to digital technology. In 2003 Mark Meily scored a big hit with the comedy *Crying Ladies*, about three Filipinas working as professional mourners in Manila's Chinatown, while *Ang Pagdadalaga ni Maximo Oliveros* ("The Blossoming of Maximo Oliveros"; 2005) by Auraeus Solito and *Kubrador* ("The Bet Collector"; 2006) by Jeffrey Jeturian were internationally acclaimed. Filipinos have also excelled in other formats: Carlo Ledesma won best short film at the Cannes Film Festival in 2007 for *The Haircut*. In 2008, Brillante Mendoza's *Serbis* ("Service") became the first full-length Filipino film to compete at Cannes since 1984; the account of a day in the life of a family running a porno film theatre in Angeles City is bawdy and brutally realistic. Mendoza's *Kinatay* ("Butchered") competed at Cannes the following year.

Lavish historical drama *El Presidente* (2012), another film directed by Mark Meily, is the nation's most expensive movie to date, starring several acting heavyweights and exploring the life of Emilio Aguinaldo. The **Metro Manila Film Festival** showcases the latest Filipino films over the Christmas period every year, not all of them arthouse material. To get a feel for what Filipinos like to watch today – from kitsch and campy romantic comedies to fantasy romps – see *Enteng Ng Ina Mo* (2011), a fantasy parody; *Sisterakas* (2012), a contemporary slapstick comedy starring vet Vice Ganda (the name is a play on "Sister Act"); and blockbuster *The Unkabogable: Praybeyt Benjamin* ("Private Benjamin"; 2011), an action comedy also starring Ganda as a reluctant soldier – the name is a loose reference to the 1980 Goldie Hawn movie, but the slapstick and sexual themes are very different.

Music

Any Friday night in Manila (and all over Asia), countless Filipino **showbands** can be seen in countless hotel lobbies performing accomplished cover versions of Western classics. While there's no doubt that when Filipinos mimic they do it exceedingly well, **indigenous music** does survive. Tagalog pop and rap artists and to a lesser extent rock groups have all been making a comeback in recent years, part of a slow but discernible trend away from the adulation of solely American pop stars and celebrities. A useful website for general information about Filipino music is ⊕philmusic.com.

Traditional tribal music

Folk songs and stories, handed down orally, are still sung at tribal gatherings and ceremonies among indigenous peoples. Among the ethnic and tribal groups of Mindanao and the Sulu archipelago there's a sophisticated musical genre called **kulintang**, in which the main instruments are bossed gongs similar to the Indonesian gamelan. *Kulintang* is commonly performed by small ensembles playing instruments that include the *kulintang* itself (a series of small gongs for the melody), the *agung* (large gongs for the lower tones) and the *gandingan* (four large vertical gongs used as a secondary melodic instrument). *Kulintang* music serves as a means of entertainment and a demonstration of hospitality; it's used at weddings, festivals, coronations, to entertain visiting dignitaries and to honour those heading off on or coming back from a pilgrimage. It is also used to accompany healing ceremonies and, up to the beginning of the twentieth century, was a form of communication, using goatskin drums to beat messages across the valleys.

The Manila Sound

The "**Manila Sound**" was the sound of the 1970s in the Philippines. Against a backdrop of student riots and martial law, some audiences found comfort with bell-bottom-wearing bands, like **The Hotdogs** and **The Boyfriends**, who set romantic novelty lyrics to catchy melodic hooks. Some sneered at the frivolity of it all, but the Manila Sound was as big as disco. Today it's effectively extinct, but it gave rise to a number of major stars who evolved and are still going strong. The most well known is indefatigable diva **Sharon Cuneta**, who is known throughout the country by the modest moniker "The Megastar". She first appeared in the Philippine pop charts at the age of 12 singing the disco tune *Mr. D.J.* and has since released numerous albums including one of duets with other apparently ageless Filipina singers such as Pops Fernandez (the "Concert Queen") and Sunshine Cruz.

The folkies

In the 1970s the only truly original artists performing in Manila were folksy beatniks such as singer-songwriters **Joey Ayala** and **Freddie Aguilar**. In the 1980s, Aguilar wrote a popular ballad called "**Anak**" and found himself a fan in First Lady Imelda Marcos who, ever eager to bathe herself in the reflected glory of Manila's celebs, invited him to Malacañang Palace so they could sing the song together at banquets. Aguilar was appalled by the excesses he saw inside the palace and never went back.

As the anti-Marcos movement grew, so did the popularity of "*Anak*". Aguilar, by now something of a talisman for left-wing groups opposing martial law, took the opportunity to become even more political, recording a heartfelt version of "*Bayan Ko*" ("My Country"), a patriotic anthem that now took on extraordinary political significance.

One of the most well-known groups of the new generation was **APO Hiking Society**, a foursome from Ateneo University whose anthem "*Handog ng Pilipino sa Mundo*" ("A New And Better Way") has been covered by numerous Filipino artists. Its lyrics are carved on the wall of Manila's Our Lady of EDSA Shrine, traditionally a focal point of protests and revolutions.

Tribal-pop and OPM (Original Pilipino Music)

In the 1990s – largely as a reaction to the decline of the protest movement and the creeping Americanization of Filipino music – a roots movement emerged that took the traditional rhythms and chants of tribal music such as *kulintang* and merged them with contemporary instruments and production techniques. One of the chief exponents of so-called tribal-pop (the term **Original Pilipino Music** or Original Pinoy Music was coined in the late 1980s) was **Grace Nono**. She never quite cracked the big time, but cleared the path for others, including **Pinikpikan**, the most successful tribal-pop band in the country (the band reformed as **Kalayo** in 2007). Over the last few years the term

OPM has become diluted, and now encompasses the young stars of the twenty-first century, most of whom have modelled themselves on Celine Dion and Michael Bublé, not the revolutionary Manila singers of the Marcos years. This new generation includes **Kyla**, **Erik Santos**, **Sarah Geronimo** and **Christian Bautista**.

The mainstream: Filipino pop, rock and alternative music
Any consideration of mainstream popular **rock music** in the Philippines won't get off the ground without reference to the irreverent **Eraserheads**. After more than a decade at the top they disbanded in 2003 but remain the most popular Filipino band ever. Many current popular groups have been inspired by their infectious blend of irony and irresistibly melodic pop, including **Rivermaya**, still producing platinum-selling albums at a rate of knots, and **Parokya ni Edgar**, one of the few bands that have come close to equalling the Eraserheads; their 1996 debut album, *Khangkhungkherrnitz*, features a tribute to the nation's favourite food: instant noodles. Today Filipino pop, rock and alternative music is flourishing, with bands such as **6cyclemind**, **Kamikazee**, **Chicosci**, **Sponge Cola** and **Sandwich**.

But despite the proliferation of progressive acts, the popular Philippine music scene has become dominated in recent years by comely solo performers singing plaintive **ballads** in the style of Whitney Houston or Mariah Carey. In the hierarchy of balladeers, Regine Velasquez and Martin Nievera are at the top. **Regine Velasquez**'s story is the quintessential Tagalog movie script: a beautiful girl from the sticks – she grew up in Leyte in the 1970s – wins a singing contest in 1989 (with a performance of "*You'll Never Walk Alone*" in Hong Kong) and heads off to Manila. Her repertoire is typical of the Filipina diva canon, comprising misty-eyed love songs such as "*Could It Be?*" "*What You Are to Me*" and "*Long For Him*". Velasquez follows in the tradition of Sharon Cuneta, Pops Fernandez and Kuh Ledesma, who at one time or another have all been dubbed the country's "concert queen" by the media. **Martin Nievera** puts his success – he's been recording since 1982 – down to the fact that Filipinos love a good drama. His songs are indeed melodramatic, his album *Forever, Forever* being an open book about his high-profile marital breakup with singer-actress Pops Fernandez.

Filipino hip-hop
Filipino hip-hop or **Pinoy rap** emerged in the 1980s, with tracks by **Dyords Javier** and **Vincent Dafalong**. The genre hit the mainstream with **Francis Magalona**'s debut album, *Yo!* in 1990, which included the nationalistic hit "*Mga Kababayan*" ("My Countrymen"), a call to political arms that bore the hallmarks of Freddie Aguilar. In 1994, Death Threat released the first Filipino gangsta rap album *Gusto Kong Bumaet* ("I Want to be Good"). Since 2004 the **Philippine Hip-Hop Music Awards** has been held annually in Metro Manila and the genre remains incredibly popular throughout the country; current stars include **Gloc-9** (former member of Death Threat), **Abra** and **Pikaso**. The most successful Filipino-American rapper is the Black Eyed Peas' **apl.de.ap**, who was born in Angeles City in 1974 and moved to Los Angeles at the age of 14.

DISCOGRAPHY

FOLK

Freddie Aguilar *Collection* (1985). A mixture of studio and live recordings featuring most of the folk hero's greatest songs, including "*Trabaho*" and a cover version of Joey Ayala's "*Mindanao*". "*Pinoy*" is a dark, but melodic exposition of the average Filipino's lot, while the lyrical "*Magdalena*" was based on conversations Aguilar had with Manila prostitutes, all of whom desperately wanted to escape the life. There's no "*Anak*", but there are plenty of other Freddie Aguilar collections that feature it.

TRIBAL-POP

Cynthia Alexander *Insomnia and Other Lullabyes* (1996). Introspective but affecting collection of progressive/tribal ballads from Joey Ayala's talented little sister. The navel-gazing becomes wearisome at times, but there are also some memorable moments, including "*No Umbrella*", a pleading love song with sonorous strings and plaintive fretless bass.

Barbie's Cradle *Music from the Buffet Table* (1999). Their semi-acoustic sound dominated by the frail but evocative voice of Barbie Almalbis, Barbie's Cradle injected a new note of realism into OPM songwriting, with lyrics – in both English and Tagalog – that spoke not of love and happiness, but of vulnerability and dysfunction. Highlights include *"Money for Food"*, a musical poem about poverty, and *"It's Dark and I Am Lonely"*, a personal and frank assessment of modern life for young people.

Grace Nono *Isang Buhay* (1997). Quintessential Nono, this is an album of sometimes strident but hypnotic tribal rhythms and original tribal songs blended with additional lyrics drawing attention to the plight of the tribes, the environment and the avarice of the country's rulers. *Isang Buhay* means one house; the title track is Nono's plea for unity.

Pinikpikan *Kaamulan* (2003). Psychedelia meets tribal tradition on this, Pinikpikan's third album, released in 2003. The band's influences are eclectic and worn on the sleeve, from the Hindu overtones on *"Child"* to the flute solos – inspired by the wooden-flute music of the Manobo tribe of Mindanao – on *"Butanding"*, a haunting stream-of-consciousness piece about the endangered whale shark.

ROCK, POP AND HIP-HOP

6cyclemind *Project 6 Cyclemind* (2009). The last album by the popular alt-rockers before the controversial departure of lead singer Ney Dimaculangan is primarily a collection of thoughtful tunes and ballads, though the band still gets to rock out on tracks such as *"Mahiwagang Pag-ibig"*.

Abra *Abra* (2012). First solo album from the gifted rapper of Pinoy hip-hop group, Lyrically Deranged Poets, his trademark lyrical style and humorous raps in full effect – the smooth R&B-inspired hit *"Gayuma"* (featuring the son of Freddie Aguilar) has over 27 million hits on YouTube, a record in the Philippines.

Bamboo *Tomorrow Becomes Yesterday* (2008). Bamboo's fourth, final and best album: intelligent and thoughtful indie rock in Tagalog and English, with everything from acoustic ballads to hard rock anthems.

Eraserheads *Ultraelectromagneticpop* (1993). Thoroughly enjoyable debut album featuring spirited Beatles-inspired pop, novelty pieces that poke fun at everyone and everything, and the brilliant *"Pare Ko"* ("My Friend"), which had the establishment in a spin because it contained a couple of swearwords and gay references. The band matured after this and even got better – their second album, *Circus*, includes the track *"Butterscotch"* which takes a not so gentle dig at the Catholic Church ("Father Markus

said to me/Just confess and you'll be free/Sit yer down upon me lap/And tell me all yer sins") – but *Ultraelectromagneticpop* will always be special because it blazed a trail.

Gloc-9 *Liham at Lihim* (2013). The seventh album ("Letter and Secret") from current godfather of Tagalog rap sees speed-rapper Gloc-9 collaborating with Rico Blanco and even veteran chanteuse Regine Velasquez.

Kamikazee *Romantico* (2012). If you want to get a taste of current Tagalog indie rock this is for you, with the catchy riffs and jangling guitars on the Manila punk band's fourth album reminiscent of Green Day.

Kitchie Nadal *Kitchie Nadal* (2004). The debut album of the soulful Filipino singer-songwriter Nadal, featuring the award-winning *"Wag na Wag Mong Sasabihin"*, an indie anthem worthy of Coldplay.

Martin Nievera *Live with the Philippine Philharmonic Orchestra* (2000). Two-disc set recorded in Manila that captures some of the energy of Nievera live, when he's a much greater force than on many of his overly sentimental studio recordings. A master of patter and performance, Nievera sings in English, in Tagalog, on his own, and with guests including the popular Filipina singing sisters Dessa and Cris Villonco – and his dad, Bert. The highlight is a mammoth montage of Broadway hits from *Carousel*, *West Side Story* and *Evita*, the nadir a self-indulgent spoken preamble to one of his signature songs, *"Before You Say Goodbye"*.

Rivermaya *It's Not Easy Being Green* (1999). Rivermaya's audience is unashamedly middle of the road and so is their music, an amiable blend of guitar-driven pop and laidback love songs for twenty-somethings. This album is typical, suffused with British influences ranging from the Beatles to Belle and Sebastian. The highpoint, however, is pure pinoy, the ironic ballad *"Grounded ang Girlfriend Ko"* ("My Girlfriend's Grounded Me"), which owes more to Eraserheads than Britpop.

Sponge Cola *Ultrablessed* (2014). Fifth studio album of the award-winning Pinoy rock band and the much-awaited follow up to 2011's bestselling *Araw Oras Tagpuan*. It includes the single *"Anting-Anting"*, featuring Gloc-9, and plenty of the band's trademark smooth pop-rock.

Regine Velasquez *Unsolo* (2000). This was the album that marked the beginning of Velasquez's attempts to become an international star, or at least a pan-Asian one, raising her profile with duets featuring the likes of David Hasselhoff – for a syrupy rendition of *"More Than Words Can Say"* – and Jacky Cheung. There's only one song in Tagalog.

Books

The Philippines hasn't been as well documented in fiction or non-fiction as many of its Asian neighbours. There are, however, a number of good investigative accounts of two subjects – American involvement in the Philippines and the excesses of the Marcoses. Some of the books reviewed below are published in the Philippines, and are unlikely to be on sale in bookshops outside the country; you should have more luck online.

HISTORY AND POLITICS

Alan Berlow *Dead Season: A Story of Murder and Revenge*. This brilliantly atmospheric work is the story of three murders that took place in the 1970s on Negros, against the backdrop of communist guerrilla activity and appeals for land reform. It's impossible to read without feeling intense despair for a country where humble, peaceful people have often become pawns in a game of power and money played out around them. Cory Aquino comes out of it badly – the Church asked her to investigate the murders but she refused, fearful that this might entail treading on too many toes.

Raymond Bonner *Waltzing with a Dictator*. Former *New York Times* correspondent Bonner reports on the complex twenty-year US relationship with the Marcos regime and how Washington kept Marcos in power long after his sell-by date: US bases in the country needed a patron and Marcos was the right man. Marcos cleverly played up the threat of a communist insurgency in the Philippines, making it seem to Washington that he was their only hope of stability.

Luis Francia *History of the Philippines: From Indios Bravos to Filipinos*. A welcome history of the archipelago offering the perfect introduction to the country and plenty of new insights about the Spanish and American periods in particular.

★**James Hamilton-Paterson** *America's Boy: The Rise and Fall of Ferdinand Marcos and Other Misadventures of US Colonialism in the Philippines*. A controversial narrative history of the US-supported dictatorship that came to define the Philippines. The author makes the very plausible claim that the Marcoses were merely the latest in a long line of corrupt Filipino leaders in a country which had historically been ruled by oligarchies, and gathers first-hand information from senators, cronies, rivals and Marcos family members, including Imelda.

★**James D. Hornfischer** *The Last Stand of the Tin Can Sailors*. Gripping and in parts harrowing narrative of the battle between the Americans and Japanese off Samar in October 1944, and the larger battle of Leyte Gulf that followed, the beginning of the American liberation of the Philippines. Hornfischer also intelligently provides a Japanese perspective to the battle. Well written and easy to read.

★**Stanley Karnow** *In Our Image: America's Empire in the Philippines*. This Pulitzer Prize-winning effort is really a book about America, not about the Philippines. The Philippines is the landscape, but the story is of America going abroad for the first time in its history at the turn of the last century. The book examines how the US sought to remake the Philippines as a clone of itself, an experiment marked from the outset by blundering, ignorance and mutual misunderstanding.

Eric Morris *Corregidor*. Intimate account of the defence of the island fortress, based on interviews with more than forty Filipinos and Americans who battled hunger, dysentery and malaria in the run-up to the critical battle with Japanese forces. As the book explains, the poorly equipped Allied troops, abandoned by General MacArthur and almost forgotten by military strategists in Washington, had little chance of winning, though against all the odds Corregidor held out for six months.

Ambeth Ocampo *Rizal without the Overcoat* (Anvil). This collection of essays and musings (originally a column in the *Philippine Daily Globe*) offers entertaining and easily digested insights into the great Filipino hero. It's become almost as common in schools as Rizal's *Noli* (see p.459).

Beth Day Romulo *Inside the Palace: The Rise and Fall of Ferdinand and Imelda Marcos*. Beth Day Romulo, wife of Ferdinand Marcos's foreign minister Carlos Romulo, was among those who enjoyed the privileges of being a Malacañang insider, something she feels the need to excuse and justify on almost every page. Her book borders on being a Marcos hagiography – she clearly didn't want to upset her old friend Imelda too much – and is gossip more than investigative, but does nevertheless offer some insight into Imelda's lavish and frivolous lifestyle, and the disintegration of the regime.

William Henry Scott *Barangay: Sixteenth-Century Philippine Culture and Society*. This lucid account of life in the Philippines during the century the Spanish arrived is the best there is of the period. The author's love for the Philippines and his deep knowledge of its customs are reflected in this scholarly but accessible investigation into Hispanic-era society, the country's elite, its tribes and their customs – everything from that most quotidian of rituals, taking a bath, to the once common practice of penis piercing.

Hampton Sides *Ghost Soldiers: The Epic Account of World War II's Greatest Rescue Mission*. Recounts the astonishing and mostly forgotten story of the combined US Ranger and Filipino guerrilla force that managed to free hundreds of POWs from behind Japanese lines in 1944.

CULTURE AND SOCIETY

Sheila Coronel (ed) *Pork and Other Perks*. Comprising nine case studies by some of the country's foremost investigative journalists, this pioneering work uncovers the many forms corruption takes in the Philippines and points fingers at those responsible. The book is concerned mainly with what happens to "pork", the budget allocated annually to every senator and congressman. It's thought that much of the money goes towards hiring corrupt contractors who use below-par materials on infrastructure projects, with the politicians themselves benefiting from the discrepancy between the official and actual cost of the projects concerned.

★**James Hamilton-Paterson** *Playing With Water: Passion and Solitude on a Philippine Island*. "No money, no honey," says one of the characters in Hamilton-Paterson's lyrical account of several seasons spent among the impoverished fishermen of Marinduque. This is a rich and original book, which by turns warms you and disturbs you. The author's love of the Philippine landscape and the people – many of whom think he must be related to US actor George Hamilton – is stunningly rendered. The diving accounts will stay with you forever, as will the episode in which H-P discovers he has worms.

★**F. Sionil José** *We Filipinos: Our Moral Malaise, Our Heroic Heritage*. By turns deeply cynical and incredibly patriotic in equal measure, this collection of essays from the nation's pre-eminent writer is required reading for anyone wanting to get under the skin of Philippine culture.

★**Manny Pacquiao** *Pacman: My Story of Hope, Resilience, and Never-Say-Never Determination*. Ghost-written? Certainly. Full of corny sentiment? Perhaps. But Pacquiao's story is so remarkable it's hard to put this "autobiography" down, charting the tenacious fighter's rise from the back-streets of Mindanao to boxing champion of the world and multi-millionaire. Inspirational stuff.

Earl K. Wilkinson *The Philippines: Damaged Culture?* Written by a longtime expat, this book explores the underlying reasons for the many maladies affecting the country. *Damaged Culture* is never pontificating or presumptuous, but it is sometimes shocking in its revelations of corruption in high places, highlighting a number of travesties of justice which the author campaigned to put right. He also offers solutions, arguing that the nation's entrenched elite could start the recovery ball rolling by abandoning its traditional antipathy towards free-market competition.

ARCHITECTURE

Pedro Galende *San Agustin*. An evocative tribute to the first Spanish stone church to be built in the Philippines, San Agustin in Intramuros. The first part of the book is a detailed account of the church's history, while the second is a walking tour, illustrated with photographs, through the church and the neighbouring monastery.

Pedro Galende & Rene Javelana *Great Churches of the Philippines*. Coffee-table book full of beautiful colour photographs of most of the country's notable Spanish-era churches. The accompanying text explains the evolution of the unique "earthquake Baroque" style developed to protect stone structures against earthquakes. The style typifies Philippine churches and provides a reminder that many of these stunning buildings are in a perilous state, with little money available to guarantee their upkeep and survival.

THE ENVIRONMENT

Robin Broad et al. *Plundering Paradise: The Struggle for the Environment in the Philippines*. Disturbing but often inspiring account of how livelihoods and habitats are disappearing throughout the Philippines as big business harvests everything from fish to trees, turned into packaging for multinational companies and chopsticks for restaurants. The authors travelled through the Philippines, recording the experiences of people who are fighting back by working alongside NGOs and environmental groups to police the environment and report illegal logging, poaching and fishing, much of which is allowed to take place through the bribing of local officials.

Gutsy Tuason and Eduardo Cu *Anilao* (Bookmark). Winner of the Palme d'Or at the World Festival of Underwater Images in Antibes, France, this hard-to-get but stunning coffee-table collection of colour photographs were all taken around Anilao, Batangas, one of the country's most popular diving areas. What's remarkable about the book is the way it makes you take notice of the small marine life many divers ignore; the images of bobbit worms, ghost pipefish and sea fans are terrific.

FOOD

Reynaldo Alejandro et al. *The Food of the Philippines*. Proof that there's so much more to Filipino cuisine than adobo and rice. The recipes range from classics such as chilli crab simmered in coconut milk to a fail-safe method for that trickiest of desserts, leche flan. Every recipe details how to find the right ingredients and what to use as a substitute if you can't. There's also a revealing history of Filipino food.

Glenda Rosales-Barretto *Flavors of the Philippines*. Rosales-Barretto is chief executive officer of the popular *Via Mare* restaurant chain in Manila, and what she doesn't know about Filipino food isn't worth knowing. This lavishly illustrated hardback highlights recipes region by region. There's a classic Bicol Express, with lots of spices and fish paste, but many of the recipes here are far from standard – instead, modern variations feature, such as fresh vegetarian pancake rolls with peanut sauce and roast chicken with passionfruit.

FICTION

Cecilia Manguerra Brainard *When the Rainbow Goddess Wept*. The moving story of Yvonne Macaraig, a young Filipina during the Japanese invasion of the Philippines in World War II; the myths and legends of Philippine folklore sustain her despite the carnage all around. Though some of Brainard's character development and language is uneven, it's this connection with the rural, pre-Hispanic Philippines that makes the book so memorable. Brainard was born in Cebu but emigrated to the US in 1968.

Jessica Hagedorn (ed) *Manila Noir*. Hagedorn's latest project forms part of New York-based Akashic Books' *Noir* series, a collection of compelling short stories with Manila as a focus for Gothic, supernatural and crime genres. The plots might be fictional but up-and-coming writers such as Gina Apostol and Budjette Tan portray the city with uncanny realism.

F. Sionil José *Dusk*. This is the fifth book in the author's acclaimed saga of the landowning Rosales family at the end of the nineteenth century. It wouldn't be a quintessential Filipino novel if it didn't touch on the themes of poverty, corruption, tyranny and love; all are on display here, presented through the tale of one man, a common peasant, and his search for contentment. *Dusk* has been published in the US in paperback, though you can always buy it from José's bookshop, Solidaridad in Manila (see p.98).

★ **F. Sionil José** *Ermita*. Eminently readable novella that atmospherically evokes the Philippines from World War II until the 1960s and stands as a potent allegory of the nation's ills. The Ermita of the title, apart from being the *mise en scène*, is also a girl, the unwanted child of a rich Filipina raped in her own home by a drunken Japanese soldier. The story follows young Ermita, abandoned in an orphanage, as she tries to trace her mother and then sets about exacting revenge on those she feels have wronged her.

★ **José Rizal** *Noli Me Tángere*. Published in 1886 (and banned by the Spanish), this is a passionate exposure of the double standards and the rank injustice of colonial rule; it's still required reading for every Filipino schoolchild. It tells the story of Crisostomo Ibarra's love for the beautiful Maria Clara, infusing it with tragedy and significance of almost Shakespearean proportions. Rizal's second novel *El Filibusterismo* takes up Ibarra's story thirteen years later, but the conclusion is just as bitter.

Miguel Syjuco *Ilustrado*. Winner of the 2008 Man Asian Literary Prize, this gripping saga takes over 150 years of Philippine history, as well as offering a scathing indictment of corruption and inequity among the Filipino ruling classes. Syjuco is a Filipino writer now based in Montreal.

THE PHILIPPINES IN FOREIGN LITERATURE

William Boyd *The Blue Afternoon*. Boyd has never been to the Philippines, but spent hours researching the country from England. In flashbacks, the novel moves from 1930s Hollywood to the exotic, violent world of the Philippines in 1902, recounting a tale of medicine, the murder of American soldiers and the creation of a magical flying machine.

Alex Garland *The Tesseract*. Alex Garland loves the Philippines, so it's hardly surprising that the follow-up to *The Beach* is set there. Garland may get most of his Tagalog wrong, but his prose captures perfectly the marginal existence of his characters. The story involves a foreigner abroad, a villainous tycoon called Don Pepe, some urchins and a beautiful girl. The characters may be clichéd, but Garland's plot is so intriguing that it's impossible not to be swept along by the baleful atmosphere the book creates.

Jessica Hagedorn *Dogeaters*. Filipino-American Jessica Hagedorn assembles a cast of diverse and dubious characters that comes as close to encapsulating the mania of life in Manila as any writer has ever come. Urchins, pimps, seedy tycoons and corpulent politicos are brought together in a brutal but beautiful narrative that serves as a jolting reminder of all the country's frailties and woes.

★ **James Hamilton-Paterson** *Ghosts of Manila*. Hamilton-Paterson's excoriating novel is haunting, powerful and for the most part alarmingly accurate. Much of it is taken from real life: the extra-judicial "salvagings" (a local word for liquidation) of suspected criminals, the corruption and the abhorrent saga of Imelda Marcos's infamous film centre. From the despair and detritus, the author conjures up a lucid story that is thriller, morality play and documentary in one.

Timothy Mo *Brownout on Breadfruit Boulevard*. Mo wrote this blunt satire of cultural and imperial domination in 1995 when he'd fallen out with his publisher (the book is still self-published), and his career subsequently fell off a cliff; the novel starts with a now infamous sex scene involving excrement. This story is much better than its sales (and the first page) suggested, though, set in the fictional town of Gobernador de Leon and following a motley bunch of locals and foreigners attending a conference.

Language

English is widely spoken in the Philippines, a legacy of the country's time under US rule. Most everyday transactions – checking into a hotel, ordering a meal, buying a ferry ticket – can be carried out in English, and most people working in tourism speak it reasonably well. Even off the beaten track, many Filipinos understand enough to help with basics such as accommodation and directions. However, it's worth learning a few words of Tagalog, the official language of the islands. You will be a source of amusement if you try, even though the response will most likely come in English. Tagalog has assimilated many Spanish words, such as *mesa* (table) and *cuarto* (bedroom, written *kuwarto* in Tagalog), though few Filipinos can speak Spanish today. Cebuano (or "Visayan") spoken in the south of the archipelago uses even more Spanish – including all the numbers. This section focuses on Tagalog; Cebuano is covered in the Visayas chapter (see box, p.266).

Tagalog

Tagalog, also known as Filipino or Pilipino, is spoken as a first language by seventeen million people mostly on Luzon and was made the official language in 1947. The structure of Tagalog is simple, though the **word order** is different from English; as an example, take "*kumain ng mangga ang bata*", which literally translates as "ate a mango the child". Another key difference between the two languages is the lack of the verb "to be" in Tagalog, which means a simple sentence such as "the woman is kind" is rendered *mabait ang babae*, literally "kind the woman". For **plurals**, the word *mga* is used – hence *bahay/mga bahay* for house/houses – although in many cases Filipinos simply state the actual number of objects or use *marami* (several) before the noun.

Consonants and vowels

Tagalog sounds staccato to the foreign ear, with clipped vowels and **consonants**. The **p**, **t** and **k** sounds are never aspirated and sound a little gentler than in English. The **g** is always hard, as in **g**et. The letter **c** seldom crops up in Tagalog and where it does – in names such as Boracay and Bulacan, for example – it's pronounced like *k*. The hardest sound to master for most beginners is the **ng** sound as in the English word "si**ng**ing" (with the *g* gently nasalized, not hard); in Tagalog this sound can occur at the

---

TAGLISH: FILIPINO ENGLISH

Educated Filipinos move seamlessly between English and Tagalog, often in the space of the same sentence, and many English words have been adopted by Filipinos, giving rise to a small canon of patois known affectionately as **Taglish**. Many of these peculiarities stem from the habit of translating something literally from Tagalog, resulting in Filipinos "closing" or "opening" the light, or "getting down" from a taxi. Among those who don't speak English so well, an inability to pronounce the f-sound is common, simply because it doesn't exist in any Philippine tongue. Filipinos are well aware of this trait and often make self-deprecating jokes about it, referring to forks as porks and vice versa. Other ear-catching Taglish phrases include "I'll be the one to" – as in "I'll be the one to buy lunch" instead of "I'll buy lunch" – and "for a while", meaning "wait a moment" or "hang on".

beginning of a word, eg in **ng**_ayon_ (now). The **mg** combination in words such as _mga_ looks tricky but is in fact straightforward to pronounce, as _mang_.

As for **vowels and diphthongs** (vowel combinations):

a is pronounced as in apple	iw is a sound that simply doesn't exist in English; it's close to the _ieu_ sound in "lieu", but with greater
e as in mess	
i as in ditto, though a little more elongated than	separation between the vowels (almost as in "lee-you")
in English	oy as in noise
o as in bore	uw as in quarter
u as in put	uy produced making the sound oo and continuing it
ay as in buy	to the i sound in "ditto".
aw in mount	

Vowels that fall consecutively in a word are always pronounced individually, as is every syllable, adding to the choppy nature of the language; for example, _tao_ meaning person or people is pronounced "ta-o", while _oo_ for yes is pronounced "o-o" (with each vowel closer to the _o_ in "show" than in "bore").

Stress

Most words are spoken as they are written, though working out which syllable to **stress** is tricky. In words of two syllables the first syllable tends to be stressed, while in words of three or more syllables the stress is almost always on the final or penultimate syllable. In the vocabulary lists that follow, stressed syllables are indicated in **bold** text except where the term in question is obviously an English loan word. Note that English loan words may be rendered a little differently in Tagalog, in line with the rules mentioned above; thus "bus" for instance has the vowel sound of the English word "put".

USEFUL WORDS AND PHRASES

GREETINGS AND CIVILITIES

hello/how are you?	kamusta	sorry	sorry
Fine, thanks	mabuti, salamat (_formal_) okay lang (_informal_)	what's your name?	anong pangalan mo?
		my name is …	ang pangalan ko ay …
		do you speak English?	marunong ka bang mag-**Ing**les?
goodbye	bye	I (don't) understand	(hindi) ko naiintindi**han**
good morning	magan**dang** umaga	could you repeat that?	paki-ulit?
good afternoon	magan**dang** hapon	where are you from?	taga saan ka?
good evening/good night	magan**dang** gabi	I am from … (most countries are rendered as in English)	taga … ako
please … (before a request)	paki …		
thank you	salamat	I don't know (used to avoid confrontation)	ewan
excuse me (to say sorry)	ipagpau**man**hin mo **ak**	okay?/is that okay?	puwede?/puwe**de ba**? (_informal_)
excuse me (to get past)	makikira**an** lang po/ pasensiya ka na	mate, buddy	pare

---

FORMAL LANGUAGE: THE USE OF "PO"

Tagalog has formal and informal **forms of address**, the formal usually reserved for people who are significantly older. The "po" suffix indicates respect and can be added to almost any word or phrase: _o-po_ is a respectful "yes" and it's common to hear Filipinos say _sorry-po_ for "sorry". Even the lowliest beggar is given esteem by language: the standard reply to beggars is _patawarin-po_, literally, "forgive me, sir". First names are fine for people of your own generation; for your elders, use Mr or Mrs (if you know a woman is married) before the surname. It's common to use _manong/manang_ (uncle/aunt) and _kuya_ (brother/sister) to address superiors informally, even if they are not blood relatives (eg _manong_ Jun, _kuya_ Beth).

COMMON TERMS

yes	oo
no	hindi
maybe	siguro
good/bad	magaling/masama
big/small	malaki/maliit
easy/difficult	madali/mahirap
open/closed	bukas/sarado
hot/cold	mainit/malamig
cheap/expensive	mura/mahal
a lot/a little	madami/konti
one more/another...	isa pa ...
beautiful	maganda
hungry	gutom
thirsty	nauuhaw
very ... (followed by adjective)	tunay ...
with/without ...	meron/wala ...
watch out!	ingat!
who?	sino?
what?	ano?
why?	bakit?
when?	kailan?
how?	paano?

GETTING AROUND

airport	airport
bus/train station	istasyon ng bus/tren
pier	pier
aeroplane	eroplano
ferry	barco (for large vessels – "ferry" will also do)
boat (outrigger)	bangka
taxi	taxi
bicycle	bisikleta
car	kotse
where do I/we catch the ...to ... ?	saan puwedeng kumuha ng ... papuntang ...?
when does the ... for ... leave?	kailan aalis ang ... papuntang ...?
when does the next ... leave?	anong oras ho aalis ang ...?
ticket	tiket
can I/we book a seat	puwedeng bumili kaagad ng ticket para i-reserba ang upuan
I'd/we'd like to go to the ... please	gusto naming pumunta sa ...
[I'd like to] pay (to a jeepney or tricycle driver)	bayad po
how long does it take?	gaano katagal?
how many kilometres is it to ...?	ilang kilometro papunta sa ...?

please stop here	paki-tigil ditto or para
I'm in a hurry	nagmamadali ako

DIRECTIONS

where is the ...?	saan ang ...?
bank	banko
beach	beach
church	simbahan
cinema	sinehan
filling station	gasolinahan
hotel	hotel
market	palengke
moneychanger	taga-palit ng pera (or just "money-changer")
pharmacy	botika
post office	koreo or post office
town hall	town hall
left	kaliwa
right	kanan
straight on	derecho/diretso
opposite	katapat ng
in front of	sa harap ng
behind	sa likod ng
near/far	malapit/malayo
north	hilaga
south	timog
east	silangan
west	kanluran

ACCOMMODATION

do you have any rooms?	meron pa kayong kuwarto?
could I have the bill please?	puwedeng kunin ang check?
bathroom	CR (comfort room) or banyo
room with a private bathroom	kuwarto na may sariling banyo
single room	kuwarto para sa isa
double room	kuwarto para sa dalawang tao
clean/dirty	malinis/marumi

EMERGENCIES

fire!	sunog!
help!	saklolo!
there's been an accident	may aksidente
please call a doctor	paki-tawag ng duktor
ill	may sakit
hospital	ospital
police station	istasyon ng pulis

air-conditioner	aircon	60	animnapu	sesenta
fan	elektrik fan	70	pitumpu	setenta
key	susi	80	walampu	otsenta
telephone	telepono	90	siyamnapu	nobenta
mobile phone/	cellphone or cell	100	sandaan	syen
cellphone		1000	isang libo	mil
laundry	labahan	1,000,000	isang milyun	un miyon
passport	pasaporte	a half	kalahati	medio/a

SHOPPING

do you have …?	meron kang …?
[we have] none	wala
money	pera
how much?	magkano?
it's too expensive	masyadong mahal or sobra (too much)
I'll take this one	kukunin ko ito
cigarettes	sigarilyo
matches	posporo
soap	sabon
toilet paper	tisyu

NUMBERS

Filipinos often resort to Spanish numbers, spelt as they are pronounced, especially when telling the time.

	Tagalog	Filipino Spanish
0	zero	sero
1	isa	uno
2	dalawa	dos
3	tatlo	tres
4	apat	kuwatro
5	lima	singko
6	anim	seis
7	pito	siyete
8	walo	otso
9	siyam	nuwebe
10	sampu	dyis
11	labing isa	onse
12	labing dalawa	dose
13	labing tatlo	trese
20	dalawampu	bente
21	dalawampu't isa	benteuno
22	dalawampu't dalawa	bentedos
30	tatlumpu	trenta
40	apatnapu	kwarenta
50	limampu	singkwenta

TIMES AND DATES

Days of the week and months of the year are mostly derived from Spanish.

what's the time?	anong oras na?
9 o'clock	alas nuwebe
10.30	alas diyes y media
morning	umaga
noon	tanghali
afternoon	hapon
evening/night	gabi
midnight	hating-gabi
minute	minuto
hour	oras
day	araw
week	linggo
month	buwan
year	taon
today/now	ngayon
tomorrow	bukas
yesterday	kahapon
Monday	Lunes
Tuesday	Martes
Wednesday	Miyerkoles
Thursday	Huwebes
Friday	Biyernes
Saturday	Sabado
Sunday	Linggo
January	Enero
February	Pebrero
March	Marso
April	Abril
May	Mayo
June	Hunyo
July	Hulyo
August	Agosto
September	Setyembre
October	Oktubre
November	Nobyembre
December	Disyembre

FOOD AND DRINK TERMS

Most menus in the Philippines are in English, although in places that specialize in Filipino cuisine you'll see Tagalog on the menu, usually with an explanation in English below. For foods that arrived in the Philippines comparatively recently there often isn't an equivalent Filipino word, so to have cake, for example, you ask for cake. Even in the provinces waiters and waitresses tend to speak enough English to understand what you're after.

GENERAL TERMS

can I see the menu?	patingin ng menu?
I would like ...	gusto ko ...
delicious	sarap
hot (spicy)	maanghang
can I have the bill please?	puwede kunin ang check
I'm vegetarian	vegetarian ako or gulay lang ang kinakain ko (literally "I only eat vegetables")
breakfast	almusal
lunch	tanghalian
dinner	hapunan (rare) or dinner
fork	tinidor
knife	kutsilyo
plate	plato
spoon	kutsara
glass	baso

STAPLES AND COMMON INGREDIENTS

bread	tinapay
bread rolls	pan de sal
butter	mantikilya
cheese	keso
chillies	sili
coconut milk	gata
egg	itlog
fermented fish/ shrimp paste	bagoong
fish sauce	patis
garlic	bawang
ginger	luya
noodles	pancit
onion	sibuyas
pepper	paminta
rice	bigas (the uncooked grain) or kanin (cooked rice)
salt	asin
soy sauce	toyo
sugar	asukal
tomato	kamatis
vegetables	gulay

MEAT (*KARNE*) AND POULTRY

baboy	pork
baka	beef
crispy pata	deep-fried pig's knuckle
kambing	goat
kordero/karnero	lamb
lengua	tongue
manok	chicken
pato	duck
pugo	quail
tenga ng baboy	pig's ears

COMMON MEAT DISHES

adobo	chicken and/or pork simmered in soy sauce and vinegar with pepper and garlic
beef tapa	beef marinated in vinegar, sugar and garlic, then dried in the sun and fried
Bicol Express	fiery dish of pork ribs cooked in coconut milk, soy sauce, vinegar, *bagoong* and hot chillies
bistek tagalog	beef tenderloin with lime and onion
bulalo	beef shank in onion broth
dinuguan	pork cubes simmered in pig's blood with garlic, onion and laurel leaves
ginisang monggo	any combination of pork, vegetables or shrimp sautéed with mung beans
kaldereta	spicy mutton stew
kare-kare	rich oxtail stew with eggplant, peanut and *puso ng saging* (banana hearts)
lechon (de leche)	roast whole (suckling) pig, dipped in a liver paste sauce
longganisa/longganiza	small beef or pork sausages, with a lot of garlic
longsilog	longganisa with garlic rice and fried egg
mechado	braised beef
pochero	boiled beef and vegetables
sinigang	Sour fish, pork, beef, shrimp or chicken soup or stew flavoured with tamarind
sisig	fried chopped pork (usually including pig's head), liver and onions
tapsilog	beef tapa with garlic rice and fried egg
tinola	tangy soup with chicken, papaya and ginger

tocino	marinated fried pork
tosilog	marinated fried pork with garlic rice and fried egg

> A glossary of **Filipino fruits** is given in Basics (see box, p.32).

FISH (*ISDA*) AND SEAFOOD

alimango	crab
bangus	milkfish
hipon	shrimps
hito	catfish
lapu-lapu	grouper
panga ng tuna	tuna jaw
pusit	squid
sugpo	prawns
tahong	mussels
talaba	oysters
tanguingue	popular and affordable sea fish, not unlike tuna in flavour

COMMON SEAFOOD DISHES

daing na bangus	*bangus* marinated in vinegar and spices, then fried
gambas	shrimps sautéed in chilli and garlic sauce
pinaksiw na lapu-lapu	lapu-lapu marinated in vinegar and spices, served cold
rellenong bangus	stuffed bangus

SNACKS (MERIENDA) AND STREET FOOD

adidas	chicken's feet served on a stick with a choice of sauces for dipping
arroz caldo	rice porridge with chicken
balut	raw, half-formed duck embryo
camote	sweet potato fried with brown sugar, or boiled and served with a pat of butter
chicharon	fried pork skin, served with a vinegar dip
dilis	dried anchovies, eaten whole and dipped in vinegar as a bar snack or added to vegetable stews
ensaimada	sweet cheese rolls
fishballs, squidballs	mashed fish or squid blended with wheat flour and deep fried; served on a stick with a sweet sauce

goto	rice porridge often containing pork and garlic
isaw	grilled chicken or pig's intestines served with a cup of vinegar for dipping
lugaw	plain rice porridge
lumpia	fried spring rolls (from Hokkien)
mami	noodle soup
mais	steamed corn-on-the-cob
pugo	hard-boiled quail's eggs, sold in packets of fifteen to twenty
pulutan	general term for snacks or finger food
puto	rice muffins
sinangag	garlic fried rice
siopao	Chinese buns filled with spicy pork
sorbetes	ice cream

DESSERTS

bibingka	cake made of ground rice, sugar and coconut milk, baked in a clay stove and served hot with fresh, salted duck's eggs on top
bilo-bilo	glutinous rice and small pieces of tapioca in coconut milk
brazos	meringues, often with cashew-nut filling
cassava cake	dark, sticky cake with a fudge-like consistency
champorado	chocolate rice pudding
guinatan	chocolate pudding served with lashings of coconut cream
halo-halo	sweet concoction made from ice cream, shaved ice, jelly, beans and tinned milk; the name literally means "mix-mix"
kutsinta	brown rice cake with coconut shavings

leche flan	caramel custard	beer	beer
maja blanca	blancmange of corn and coconut cream	buko juice	coconut water
polvoron	sweets made from butter, sugar and toasted flour, pale in colour with a crumbly texture	calamansi juice/soda	calamansi juice (see box, p.32), made into a cold drink by adding soda or a hot one with boiled water and a touch of honey
puto bumbong	glutinous rice steamed in a bamboo tube, infusing it with a delicate, woody taste	chocolate-eh	thick hot chocolate
		gatas	milk
		ginebra	gin
sago at nata de coco	blend of sago and coconut served cold in a glass	juice	juice
		kape	coffee
		lambanog	alcoholic drink made from fermented fruit and available in a range of flavours
suman	sweet and sticky rice cake served inside a banana leaf		
turon	banana and jackfruit in a fried spring roll	mineral	mineral water
		rum	rum (the popular Tanduay brand has become almost synonymous with rum)

DRINKS (*INUMIN*)

(merong/walang) yelo	(with/without) ice		
(merong/walang) asukal	(with/without) sugar	tapuy	rice wine
alak	wine (in practice, everyone just says "wine")	tsa	tea
		tubig	water
		tubo juice	sugar-cane juice

Glossary

amihan the northwest monsoon from November to April (dry season)

bahay house

bahay kubo wooden house

bahay na bato house built of stone

bangka boat carved from wood, with stabilizing outriggers made from bamboo; the so-called "big bangkas" are used as ferries and often feature cabins

barangay the smallest political voting unit, whose residents elect "barangay captains" to represent their views to the mayor; barangays take different forms, ranging from part of a village through a whole village to a district of a town or city. In the Guide barangay is used more generally to mean "village".

barong or **barong tagalog** formal shirt worn by men, woven from fine fabric such as *piña* and worn hanging outside the pants

barrio village

bulol rice god carved from wood, used by many northern hill tribes in religious rituals

buri type of palm used to make mats and rugs

butanding whale shark

capiz a white seashell that's almost translucent when flattened and is used to make windows and screens

carabao water buffalo

carinderia canteen where food is presented in pots on a counter-top

chinito a Filipino/Filipina who looks Chinese

chinoy slang for Filipino/Filipina Chinese

cogon/kogon wild grass that is often used as thatch on provincial homes and beach cottages

CR toilet (= "comfort room")

DoT Department of Tourism

earthquake Baroque style of church architecture typical of Spanish churches in the Philippines, which were built with thick buttresses to protect them from earthquakes and a separate bell tower that wouldn't hit the main church if the tower collapsed

GRO guest relations officer; waitress or hostess in a bar who receives a cut of the payment for the drinks a customer buys her; often a euphemism for sex worker

habagat southwest monsoon from May to October (wet season)

ilustrado the wealthy elite

isla island

kalesa or **calesa** horse-drawn carriage, still seen in some areas including Chinatown in Manila and Vigan

kalye street

kuweba cave

mabuhay literally, "long live". Used most often at toasts, at rallies, or to welcome guests (and in tourism campaigns).

malong tube-like woven garment worn by many Muslims in Mindanao, similar to a sarong

Moro Muslim

narra the national tree, whose wood is considered best for furniture

nipa short, sturdy palm that is dried and used for building houses

nito native vine woven into hats, mats and decorative items such as lampshades

Pasalubong The (almost mandatory) Filipino tradition of bringing back gifts, usually food items, for friends and family from abroad – one which serves tourist shops well

Pilipino Filipino; also means Tagalog

piña fibre taken from the outside of the pineapple and woven into fine, shiny cloth

pinoy/pinay slang for Filipino/Filipina

poblacion town centre

rugby boys street children, named after the "Rugby" brand of glue they are often addicted to sniffing

sabong cockfighting

sala living room

santo saint; also small statues of the saints found in churches and sold in antique shops

Santo Niño the Christ Child; patron of many communities, revered by Christian Filipinos

sari-sari store small store, often no more than a hut, selling essentials such as matches, snacks, shampoo and toothpaste

sikat native grass woven into various items, especially rugs

sitio small village or outpost, often consisting of no more than a few houses

tamaraw dwarf water buffalo, an endangered species found only on Mindoro

terno classic Filipino formal gown popularized by Imelda Marcos, with high butterfly sleeves and low, square-cut neckline

tinikling folk dance in which participants hop adeptly between heavy bamboo poles as they are struck together at shin height, at increasing speed

tsinoy slang for Filipino/Filipina Chinese

Small print and index

A ROUGH GUIDE TO ROUGH GUIDES

Published in 1982, the first Rough Guide – to Greece – was a student scheme that became a publishing phenomenon. Mark Ellingham, a recent graduate in English from Bristol University, had been travelling in Greece the previous summer and couldn't find the right guidebook. With a small group of friends he wrote his own guide, combining a highly contemporary, journalistic style with a thoroughly practical approach to travellers' needs.

The immediate success of the book spawned a series that rapidly covered dozens of destinations. And, in addition to impecunious backpackers, Rough Guides soon acquired a much broader readership that relished the guides' wit and inquisitiveness as much as their enthusiastic, critical approach and value-for-money ethos.

These days, Rough Guides include recommendations from budget to luxury and cover more than 120 destinations around the globe, as well as producing an ever-growing range of ebooks.

Visit **roughguides.com** to find all our latest books, read articles, get inspired and share travel tips with the Rough Guides community.

Rough Guide credits

Editor: Edward Aves, Sam Cook
Layout: Nikhil Agarwal
Cartography: Animesh Pathak
Picture editor: Rhiannon Furbear-Williams
Proofreader: Anita Sach
Managing editor: Keith Drew
Assistant editor: Prema Dutta
Production: Charlotte Cade

Cover design: Nicole Newman, Rhiannon Furbear-Williams, Nikhil Agarwal
Photographer: Simon Bracken
Editorial assistant: Rebecca Hallett
Senior pre-press designer: Dan May
Programme manager: Helen Blount
Publisher: Joanna Kirby
Publishing director: Georgina Dee

Publishing information

This fourth edition published October 2014 by
Rough Guides Ltd,
80 Strand, London WC2R 0RL
11, Community Centre, Panchsheel Park,
New Delhi 110017, India
Distributed by Penguin Random House
Penguin Books Ltd,
80 Strand, London WC2R 0RL
Penguin Group (USA)
345 Hudson Street, NY 10014, USA
Penguin Group (Australia)
250 Camberwell Road, Camberwell,
Victoria 3124, Australia
Penguin Group (NZ)
67 Apollo Drive, Mairangi Bay, Auckland 1310,
New Zealand
Penguin Group (South Africa)
Block D, Rosebank Office Park, 181 Jan Smuts Avenue,
Parktown North, Gauteng, South Africa 2193
Rough Guides is represented in Canada by Tourmaline
Editions Inc. 662 King Street West, Suite 304, Toronto,
Ontario M5V 1M7
Printed in Singapore by Toppan Security Printing Pte. Ltd.

480pp includes index
A catalogue record for this book is available from the
British Library
ISBN: 978-1-40935-134-4
The publishers and authors have done their best to
ensure the accuracy and currency of all the information
in **The Rough Guide to the Philippines**, however,
they can accept no responsibility for any loss, injury, or
inconvenience sustained by any traveller as a result of
information or advice contained in the guide.
1 3 5 7 9 8 6 4 2

MIX
Paper from
responsible sources
FSC www.fsc.org   FSC™ C018179

Help us update

We've gone to a lot of effort to ensure that the fourth
edition of **The Rough Guide to the Philippines** is
accurate and up-to-date. However, things change – places
get "discovered", opening hours are notoriously fickle,
restaurants and rooms raise prices or lower standards. If
you feel we've got it wrong or left something out, we'd like
to know, and if you can remember the address, the price,
the hours, the phone number, so much the better.

Please send your comments with the subject line
"Rough Guide the Philippines Update" to @ mail@uk
.roughguides.com. We'll credit all contributions and send a
copy of the next edition (or any other Rough Guide if you
prefer) for the very best emails.

Find more travel information, connect with fellow
travellers and plan your trip on ⓦ roughguides.com.

ABOUT THE AUTHORS

Kiki Deere is a travel writer who has worked on over a dozen travel titles worldwide. She first visited the Philippines in 2003 and has returned a number of times since to explore more of the country's 7000-plus islands. Her favourite spots are the UNESCO rice terraces of the Cordilleras and the remote little islands of Batanes off the coast of Northern Luzon.

Simon Foster has been contributing to a variety of international guidebooks and magazines since 1999, and completed his first solo work in 2008. Simon and his wife founded their own travel company, Bamboo Trails (ⓦbambootrails.com) in 2009 and now lead and operate adventure tours all over Asia (including the Philippines). They live in sunny southern Taiwan with their two daughters and dog.

Stephen Keeling spent seven years as a financial journalist and editor in Hong Kong, Singapore and Shanghai before writing his first Rough Guide in 2005. Since then he's written numerous travel books and articles. He first visited the Philippines in 1996 and returns frequently to visit his in-laws and eat as much *halo-halo* as possible. He lives in New York City.

Acknowledgements

Kiki Deere would like to thank all those who helped out during her travels, in particular: Jaimee Cruz-Descaliar of the PTB for her help and assistance; Ferdinand de Guzman for all his patience, support and wonderful driving skills; Roger at *Rama Beach Resort* for his assistance; Ian McFeat Smith and his wife Eileen for their warm hospitality and superb beach BBQ; Graham Taylor in Banaue and Elvis for the fun rice terraces trek and for his excellent knowledge of the region; Purificacion Molintas, Erlinda Fines and the rest of the wonderful CAR office staff, with special thanks to Jaime Munar and Paul for the fun company on the road; Tom Santos and DOT staff in Tuguegarao for their assistance; Trevor at Jotay Resort in Santa Ana for his willingness to help out; special thanks to Milo Oropeza for all his help with my Southern Luzon itinerary; Butsoy for guiding me around Masbate; Carmel Garcia and her little son in Catanduanes; Juliet Dela Cruz for shaking up those potent margaritas in Donsol; Alec Francis Santos in Naga; Myline Cordial in Caramoan for showing me around; Gillian Abadilla and Gladys Quesea for coordinating my Marinduque trip; and all the jovial DOT staff in Lucban for showing me the town's best spots. Special thanks to Ed Aves and Samantha Cook in London for their editing skills and patience with those pesky bus journey details.

Simon Foster Thanks to Jinky & Jochen in Moalboal; Vangie, Elsie, Joel and crew for helping us through the hard times in Dumaguete; in Dauin, thanks to Gabby and Matt at *Atmosphere*, Tim & Zoe at *Liquid* and Mike; and in Bacolod, thanks to Angelo Bibar. Over in Palawan a big thank you to Aaron and Pauline in Puerto Princesa. Thanks also to Andrew & Jadranka, Ken & Angie, and Christine, Tot, Molly and Sasha for their help and support. And to all of the staff at Rough Guides, but especially Ed Aves and Sam Cook for their patience and painstaking attention to detail. And finally, to everyone in the Philippines for their help, support and continued optimism in the face of the devastation caused by Typhoon Yolanda.

Stephen Keeling Thanks to Emilio and Aning Go for their kindness, advice and hospitality in Manila, Connie Wu and Helen Tan for being such fearless travel companions, Basilio and Mary Ngo for the day-trips and dinners, and Manuel Gaw for all his help in Subic Bay and Taal; thanks also to my fellow authors Kiki Deere and Simon Foster, editor Edward Aves, who did a great job in London, and as always, Tiffany Wu, without whose love and support none of this would have been possible.

Readers' updates

Thanks to all the readers who have taken the time to write in with comments and suggestions (and apologies if we've inadvertently omitted or misspelt anyone's name):

Heini Bachmann; Brian R. Bate; Solange Berchemin; Dom Beverley; Lizeth Boonstra; Eveline van Dooren & Daan de Rooij; Katharina and Theresa Rossboth; Juraj Stripaj; Cristina Tabora; David Todd; Luca Weskott

Photo credits

All photos © Rough Guides except the following:
(Key: t-top; c-centre; b-bottom; l-left; r-right)

p.1 Corbis/Jacob Maentz
p.2 AWL Images/Christian Kober
p.4 AWL Images/Michele Falzone
p.7 Christian Kober (t); AWL Images/Danita Delimont/Keren Su (bl); Robert Harding Picture Library/José Fuste Raga (br)
p.8 Alamy Images/Thomas Cockrem
p.9 Alamy Images/Julio Etchart
p.10 Alamy Images/WaterFrame
p.11 Lety's Buko Pie (t); AWL Images/Michele Falzone (c); Ayala Museum/Neal M. Oshima (b)
p.12 Corbis/John Harper
p.13 LOOK Die Bildagentur der Fotografen GmbH (t); Robert Harding Picture Library/Andre Seale (c); Alamy Images/Michele Falzone (b)
p.14 Getty Images/Laurie Noble (tl); Steve Bloom Images (tr); Alamy Images/John Warburton-Lee Photography (bl); Robert Harding Picture Library/Dave Stamboulis (br)
p.15 Corbis/Mike Theiss/National Geographic Society (t); Alamy Images/Maximilian Weinzierl (c); Alamy Images/Charly Lataste (b)
p.16 Alamy Images/imagebroker (t); Getty Images/AFP/Noel Celis (c); AWL Images/Michele Falzone (b)
p.17 Corbis/Bruno Morandi (tl); Alamy Images/nobleimages (tr, br); Alamy Images/ZUMA Press, Inc. (bl)
p.18 Alamy Images/imagegallery2 (t)
p.21 Corbis/Deddeda/deddeda.com/Design Pics
pp.54–55 Robert Harding Picture Library/José Fuste Raga
p.57 Alamy Images/Hemis
p.71 Alamy Images/Prisma Bildagentur AG (t); AWL Images/Danita Delimont/Keren Su (br)
p.85 AWL Images/Travel Pix Collection (tl); Alamy Images/Marc F. Henning (tr); Alamy Images/Victor Paul Borg (bl); Robert Harding Picture Library/José Fuste Raga (br)
pp.102–103 Alamy Images/LOOK Die Bildagentur der Fotografen GmbH
p.105 Alamy Images/David Fleetham
p.115 Alamy Images/imagebroker (t); Robert Harding Picture Library/Oriental Touch/Hugo D. Yonzon III (bl); Alamy Images/John Warburton-Lee Photography (br)

pp.130–131 Alamy Images/imagebroker
p.133 Getty Images/AFP/Ted Aljibe
p.153 Alamy Images/Hemis (t); Getty Images/Laurie Noble (b)
p.173 Kiki Deere (tl); nobleimages (tr); Alamy Images/Design Pics Inc. (b)
pp.190–191 AWL Images/Christian Kober
p.193 Robert Harding Picture Library/Alain Evrard
p.211 Robert Harding Picture Library/Jean-Pierre De Mann (t); AWL Images/Christian Kober (b)
p.227 Robert Harding Picture Library/Oriental Touch/Ivan Sarenas (t); Alamy Images/Romero Blanco (bl); Alamy Images/Quincy (br)
pp.236–237 Alamy Images/Prisma Bildagentur AG
p.239 Alamy Images/WaterFrame
p.251 Robert Harding Picture Library/Christoffer Askman (t); Alamy Images/Thomas Cockrem (b)
pp.260–261 AWL Images/Michele Falzone
p.263 Robert Harding Picture Library/LOOK/Per-Andre Hoffmann
p.303 Alamy Images/Design Pics Inc.
p.323 Robert Harding Picture Library/Andre Seale (tl); Luca Tettoni (tr); Corbis/Luca Tettoni (b)
p.341 Alamy Images/imagegallery2 (t)
p.371 Corbis/AWL Images/Michele Falzone
p.383 Alamy Images/John Warburton-Lee Photography (tl); Alamy Images/Emmanuel Lattes (tr)
pp.398–399 Corbis/Eli Ritchie Tongo/NurPhoto
p.401 Getty Images/Allan Barredo/Flickr Open
p.419 Alamy Images/age fotostock (t); Corbis/Hironobu Takeuch (b)
p.436 Alamy Images/Universal Images Group Limited

Front cover Green sea turtle © Getty Images/Narchuk.com
Back cover Beach near El Nido, Palawan © AWL Images/Michele Falzone (t); jeepney © Hemis/Alamy (bl); Banaue rice terraces © AWL/Alex Robinson (br)

Index

Maps are marked in grey

Map symbols

The symbols below are used on maps throughout the book

✈	Airport	E	Embassy/consulate
★	Bus stop	⊠	Gate
Ⓛ	LRT	⬧	Point of interest
Ⓜ	MRT	∴	Ruin
Ⓒ	Telephone office	⛳	Golf course
@	Internet café/access	⊙	Statue
ⓘ	Tourist office	⚑	Church (regional)
⊞	Hospital/clinic	☪	Mosque
⊠	Post office	卍	Chinese temple
Ⓟ	Parking	⛩	Monastery

ᴹᴹ	Spring/spa		Beach
⊤	Gardens		Lighthouse
🏛	Waterfall		Museum
ᴹᴹ	Swamp		Market
⌣	Bridge		Building
▲	Mountain peak		Church (town maps)
⋀⋀	Mountain range		Stadium
⌒	Cave		Beach
🐢	Turtle nesting site		Park
⚓	Shipwreck		Cemetery

Listings key

- ■ Accommodation
- ● Eating
- ■ Drinking/nightlife
- ● Shopping

Cozee Monkey Backpackers
10 Galayia St. Extension
Multinational Village
paranaque city, Metro manila